This book is thorough, and it helps fill the doctr
today in our churches. It can be a valuable resou
the church well.

— **Bob Russell**, retired Senior Minister of Southeast Christian Church

This body of work is a great overarching explanation of good biblical theology
with an extra emphasis on making disciples. The authors present a very balanced
overview of theology that any Christian can easily digest, learn from, and then
use to live out a stronger faith while also leading others into a relationship
with God.

— **Corey Trimble**, Lead Pastor of The Experience Community

Real Life Theology is an exceptional tool to help all believers both personally
and in their daily ministry to reach out and disciple more people. This series is
a toolbox for reaching more people for Christ! It is rooted in the Word of God
and reminds believers and leaders to stay there. Bobby Harrington and Daniel
McCoy put together an all-star list of writers. They brought together people
I have come to know and respect during my years of traveling to Restoration
Movement churches.

— **Doug Crozier**, CEO of The Solomon Foundation

While no book on theology may ever achieve 100 percent agreement among
its readers, the *Real Life Theology Collection* provides a practical, poignant, and
purpose-driven place for all believers who hold fast to the Scriptures to find
grounded, thorough, biblical perspective.

— **Rick Rusaw**, President of Spire Network

Whether we realize it or not, we're all theologians. And if you think theology
is too hard, too boring, or irrelevant for your daily life, the *Real Life Theology
Collection* is for you. The authors of each chapter will help you love God better
with your mind so you can also love him with all your heart, soul, and strength.
As a former director of a homeschool tutorial and a homeschooling mom for

twelve years, I consider this book essential curriculum for any family wanting to equip their kids with a Christian worldview.

— **Renée Webb Sproles**, Founder and Co-Director of Discipleship Tutorial, Murfreesboro, TN

This is a true masterpiece and marvelous Collection for anyone interested in learning what faithful and effective disciple making is and how to live it out. Each chapter is filled with a profound depth of insight into the theology that should shape and fuel faithful disciple making. This is a must-read for any believer and church interested in being faithful to the Great Commission. The pages in this book will teach you how to become a disciple of Jesus who truly loves people, and it will create a passion within you to make disciples who make disciples.

— **Andrew Jit**, Founder of MiT Global

Biblical discipleship is a major challenge in churches today for a host of reasons. Teaching timeless truths from a diverse group of authors is a refreshing way to accomplish the mission.

— **Darren R. Key**, CEO of Christian Financial Resources (CFR)

Believers soon realize that hearing sermons is not enough to transform broken humans into redemptive image bearers for Jesus. We require usable, effective, faithful resources to facilitate the essential process of developing disciple making disciples. Renew.org's *Real Life Theology Collection* is just such a resource.

— **Chuck Sackett**, Professor of Preaching, Lincoln Christian University

Solid, well-constructed foundations are important! This primer on theology by Bobby Harrington and his team of writers is an excellent work, offering biblically accurate and clear information on critical doctrines taught in Scripture. Every disciple maker should read this volume and see it as a critical tool in building their foundation for making disciples who are making disciples. I highly recommend it to disciple makers everywhere.

— **David Roadcup**, Professor, TCM International Institute

Loved the series. Practical, straightforward, like having a conversation with the authors. I believe the church is well-served by having this series in circulation.

— **Randy Garris**, Co-Director of Life and Ministry Preparation Center, Ozark Christian College

"The most important thing about us," said A. W. Tozer, "is what comes into our minds when we think about God." Since our beliefs about God and his kingdom have an almost endless number of real-world consequences, it's imperative that we do theology wisely and well, and this book is a fantastic help! The writing itself is careful, biblical, and accessible, but more importantly, the writers' lives bear good fruit because of "what comes into [their] minds when [they] think about God." This book truly represents "real life theology," and I can't wait to see more lives changed by God's truth in these pages.

— **Matt Proctor**, President of Ozark Christian College

As a church, we're focused on unleashing the full force of our lay leaders to love people one at a time. We want them to be intentional, relational, and sacrificial followers of Jesus who are rooted in God's Word, prayer, and mission. We're excited to integrate *Real Life Theology* into our leadership development resources at Southeast Christian Church.

— **Matt Reagan**, Associate Pastor of Southeast Christian Church

I am so grateful for the work Bobby Harrington and the Renew.org Network have done to create *Real Life Theology*. I love that they not only create clear and concise theology for every believer, but they also are disciple makers who seek to live out what they teach. This series will help churches in their training of pastoral staff as well as the everyday disciple maker in their church or ministry.

— **Jim Putman**, author of *Real-Life Discipleship*

As our churches become more diverse and our culture less biblically literate, we increasingly need *Real Life Theology*. Our people don't need more dogmatism but more application. That's why this series of short books is so helpful for groups in the local church. The series is for Christians in the trenches, and it focuses on enacting our doctrine more than asserting it.

— **Mark Moore**, author of *Core 52*

This book offers a comprehensive and biblical theology for those wanting to be faithful Christ-followers in the twenty-first century. Each author is committed to the truth and beauty of the Scriptures, has a deep grasp on what the Scriptures say, and is committed to making disciples by using the Scriptures. This book is a one-of-a-kind for our generation. I highly recommend it!

— **David Young**, author of *King Jesus and the Beauty of Obedience-Based Discipleship*

REAL
LIFE
THEOLOGY

**FUEL FOR EFFECTIVE
AND FAITHFUL
DISCIPLE MAKING**

*A COLLECTION
OF 13 THEOLOGY
BOOKS*

GENERAL EDITORS,
BOBBY HARRINGTON
& DANIEL MCCOY

RENƎW.org

Real Life Theology: Fuel for Effective and Faithful Disciple Making
Copyright © 2021 by Renew.org

CONTENTS

INTRODUCTION: *Why This Book and How to Use It*
  Bobby Harrington and Daniel McCoy 13

BOOK 1: *Grand Metanarrative: God's Story as an Invitation to Theology*
  Tony Twist and Mihai Malancea 19

BOOK 2: *God's Word: The Inspiration and Authority of Scripture*
  Orpheus J. Heyward 63

BOOK 3: *Christian Convictions: Discerning the Essential, Important, and Personal Elements*
  Chad Ragsdale 133

BOOK 4: *The Gospel Precisely: Surprisingly Good News About Jesus Christ the King*
  Matthew W. Bates 177

BOOK 5: *Faithful Faith: Reclaiming Faith from Culture and Tradition*
  Mark E. Moore 231

BOOK 6: *New Birth: Conversion and Baptism*
  Michael Strickland and Anessa Westbrook 277

BOOK 7: *Holy Spirit: Filled, Empowered, and Led*
  David Young 333

BOOK 8: *Disciple Making: The Core Mission of the Church*
Bobby Harrington and W. Scott Sager 389

BOOK 9: *Kingdom Life: Experiencing God's Reign Through
Love and Holiness*
Kelvin Teamer 447

BOOK 10: *Countercultural Living: What Jesus Has to Say
About Life, Marriage, Race, Gender, and Materialism*
Carol M. Swain 495

BOOK 11: *The End: The Return of King Jesus and the
Renewal of All Things*
Gary L. Johnson 555

BOOK 12: *Truth About God: What Can We Know and How Can
We Know It?*
Richard A. Knopp 603

BOOK 13: *Eternal Security: Walking in Faithfulness*
Bobby Harrington 687

CONCLUSION: *What You Can Do Right Now*
Bobby Harrington and Daniel McCoy 735

*APPENDIX A: Renew.org Network Leaders' Values and
Faith Statements* 747

APPENDIX B: Glossary of 100 Theology Words 755

BOOK 1: *Grand Metanarrative: God's Story as an Invitation to Theology*

TONY TWIST (PhD, Indiana University) grew up in Texas and Australia. He served churches in Virginia, Tennessee, and Indiana, focusing on disciple making. He currently serves as President and CEO for TCM International Institute, a global graduate school for disciple makers.

MIHAI MALANCEA (DTh, University of Bucharest) grew up in the USSR and now lives in Moldova. He has served churches in Moldova and in post-Soviet countries in Central Asia. He serves as President of DGU (Divitia Gratiae University) in Moldova and teaches for TCM International Institute.

BOOK 2: *God's Word: The Inspiration and Authority of Scripture*

ORPHEUS J. HEYWARD (DMin, Knox Theological Seminary) is the Senior Minister of the Renaissance Church of Christ. Having received his Master of Arts in Theology (Tennessee Temple University), Master of Arts in Biblical Studies (Baptist Bible College and Seminary), and Doctor of Ministry in Theological Exegesis, he is a constant student of the Bible.

BOOK 3: *Christian Convictions: Discerning the Essential, Important, and Personal Elements*

CHAD RAGSDALE (DMin, Talbot School of Theology) is Academic Dean of Ozark Christian College and has served on its faculty since 2005. He teaches Christian apologetics, philosophy, and biblical interpretation. He has a Bachelor of Arts in Preaching and a Master of Divinity in Contemporary Theology, both from Lincoln Christian University. His Doctor of Ministry is in Engaging Mind and Culture.

BOOK 4: *The Gospel Precisely: Surprisingly Good News About Jesus Christ the King*

MATTHEW W. BATES (PhD, Notre Dame University) is an award-winning author and Associate Professor of Theology at Quincy University in Quincy, Illinois. His popular books include *Gospel Allegiance* (Brazos, 2019), *Salvation by Allegiance Alone* (Baker Academic, 2017), and *The Birth of the Trinity* (Oxford University Press, 2015). He cofounded and cohosts the *OnScript* podcast.

BOOK 5: *Faithful Faith: Reclaiming Faith from Culture and Tradition*

MARK E. MOORE (PhD, University of Wales) is Teaching Pastor at Christ's Church of the Valley (CCV) in Peoria, Arizona, and author of *Core 52*. Prior to joining the CCV team, Mark was a New Testament Professor at Ozark Christian College (1990–2012). He continues as an adjunct professor for Ozark, Hope International University, and Haus Edelweiss in Vienna, Austria.

BOOK 6: *New Birth: Conversion and Baptism*

MICHAEL STRICKLAND (PhD, University of Birmingham) is Director of Instruction and Associate Professor of Theology and Mathematics at Amridge University. He also holds a Bachelor and Master of Science in Mathematics from Auburn University and Master of Arts in Biblical Studies from Lipscomb University.

ANESSA WESTBROOK (DMin, Fuller Theological Seminary) is Assistant Professor of Bible and Ministry at Harding University. She also holds a Master of Arts in Church Growth and a Master of Divinity from Harding School of Theology. Her doctoral research focused on the spiritual development of women.

BOOK 7: *Holy Spirit: Filled, Empowered, and Led*

DAVID YOUNG (PhD, Vanderbilt University) is the Lead Minister for the North Boulevard Church of Christ in Murfreesboro, Tennessee. He has taught New Testament at several universities and traveled widely teaching and preaching. He is the author of several books, including *A New Day*, *A Grand Illusion*, and *King Jesus and the Beauty of Obedience-Based Discipleship*.

BOOK 8: *Disciple Making: The Core Mission of the Church*

BOBBY HARRINGTON (DMin, Southern Baptist Theological Seminary) is CEO of Renew.org and Discipleship.org, both national disciple making networks. Bobby is the founding and Lead Pastor of Harpeth Christian Church. He is author or coauthor of more than a dozen books on disciple making.

W. SCOTT SAGER (DMin, Southern Methodist University) is Lead Minister at the Green Hills Church in Nashville and Vice President for Church Services at

Lipscomb University, where he teaches in the College of Bible and Ministry. Scott is the author of *Jesus in Isolation*. He founded Christ's Family Ministries and serves with several charities.

BOOK 9: *Kingdom Life: Experiencing God's Reign Through Love and Holiness*

KELVIN TEAMER (DMin, Amridge University) serves as the evangelist of the Church of Christ at Bouldercrest in Atlanta, GA. In addition to his DMin, Kelvin has earned degrees from Southern Illinois University, Georgia School of Preaching and Biblical Studies, and Amridge University (MDiv). He also serves as an Adjunct Professor of Theology at Amridge University.

BOOK 10: *Countercultural Living: What Jesus Has to Say About Life, Marriage, Race, Gender, and Materialism*

CAROL M. SWAIN (PhD, University of North Carolina at Chapel Hill) is an award-winning political scientist and former professor at Princeton University and Vanderbilt University. She has authored or edited nine books, one of which (*Black Faces: Black Interests*) has won three national awards. She has appeared on Fox News, ABC Headline News, CNN, BBC Radio, and NPR, among other outlets.

BOOK 11: *The End: The Return of King Jesus and the Renewal of All Things*

GARY L. JOHNSON (DMin, Grace Theological Seminary) is Executive Director of e2: Effective Elders and author of *LeaderShift*. He has served in pastoral ministry for four decades. In addition to his Doctor of Ministry, he holds a Master of Arts in Church History (Lincoln Christian Seminary) and a Master of Ministry and a Master of Divinity (Cincinnati Bible Seminary).

BOOK 12: *Truth About God: What Can We Know and How Can We Know It?*

RICHARD A. KNOPP (PhD, University of Illinois) is a Professor of Philosophy and Christian Apologetics at Lincoln Christian University. He is the Program Director of Room for Doubt (www. roomfordoubt.com) and WorldView Eyes.

Prior to full-time teaching, he served in two youth ministries and in a five-year preaching ministry.

BOOK 13: *Eternal Security: Walking in Faithfulness*

BOBBY HARRINGTON (DMin, Southern Baptist Theological Seminary) is CEO of Renew.org and Discipleship.org, both national disciple making networks. Bobby is the founding and Lead Pastor of Harpeth Christian Church. He is author or coauthor of more than a dozen books on disciple making.

INTRODUCTION

WHY THIS BOOK AND HOW TO USE IT

For a four-syllable word, "theology" is fairly short. Yet depending on whom you ask, it might be the most massive "ology" word ever invented. After all, theology is "to reason about God" or "the study of God." And if God is *God*, then we can employ "theology" as an umbrella term over all sorts of influential sub-studies. For example, theology encompasses the study of what's wrong within humans and how God saves us. Theology delves into where history is headed in the end. These are all different "ologies" that come under "theology."

But what happens to theology if you stop believing in the centrality of God? In a post-Christian culture, people have a strong tendency to relegate theology to sub-status under some human-centered topic. For example, some might view the study of God as a curious sub-study under human psychology. Or perhaps they see theology as a spiritualized branch of philosophy.

A glance through the contents page of *Real Life Theology* should make it clear that we at Renew.org see "theology" as the umbrella word, not a subdiscipline. In this book, our authors tackle life's most consequential topics all under the category of theology. *How should we view human life? What is our core mission? What is love?* We find true answers to such questions by studying God.

WHO DOES THEOLOGY?

THE TRUTH IS "THEOLOGY" can be *so* broad that the word becomes frustratingly versatile. As we use the word in *Real Life Theology*, we mean an orderly, coherent set of beliefs that we put into practice in real life. "Coherent" is a helpful word in describing our theology, because not only should our beliefs be coherent with each other, but they should also be coherent with how we live. We study God and his Word to be able to put this truth into practical, everyday use.

At the same time, more specialized branches of theology are possible. For example, one can study the various theologies of Christians throughout history ("historical theology"). Theology can also refer to someone's distinctive way of theologizing; for example, biblical scholars might speak of "the apostle Paul's theology of justification" or "Johannine theology" (the theology of the apostle John). The word can refer to various views of God, both orthodox (e.g., Calvinist theology, Arminian theology) and less-than-orthodox theologies, such as process theology (the belief that God's essence changes throughout history) and liberation theology (a way of interpreting the Bible in order to effect political activism).

The versatility of the word "theology" suggests that a theologian is not a one-size-fits-all job title. Indeed, if we return to the core concept of theology as reasoning about God, then doesn't basically *everybody* do that at one time or another? The term "theologian" is still useful to describe scholars who devote their careers to studying theology. Yet in a sense, aren't we all theologians? Everyone—from the child who wonders what heaven will be like to the atheist who reasons that the idea of an all-powerful, all-good God doesn't exist—does theology at some level.

AREN'T WE ALL THEOLOGIANS?

"Everyone's a theologian," sounds like an inspirational sentiment. Maybe so, but it's also a true statement. And because it's true, the statement is actually a bit frightening. Since billions of people are on the planet, then that means billions of people do theology. Just as it is inescapable for us to do theology, the inescapable conclusion also is that many people do it wrong. Some do theology flippantly with more thought about what they will wear on a given day than on where they will spend eternity. Others do theology sneakily with too much thought regarding how they can tweak their church's theology to bring about a desired result.

Bad theology exists. Hence, we need to do it well.

TWO POOR WAYS TO DO THEOLOGY

Before exploring how people *should* do theology, let's look at two broad ways of doing theology poorly. We will call them "brainiac theology" and "brainwashed theology."

Brainiac Theology. Please don't misunderstand us here. God gave us brains, and we should use them well in doing theology. Brain*less* theology is no way of honoring God. What we're calling *brainiac* theology isn't a matter of using your brain to do theology (that's important to do); rather, it's making your brain the ultimate *point* of theology. Brainiac theology is doing theology for the end goal of learning information and getting smarter. Such a stagnant end goal produces spiritual inertia and intellectual arrogance, both of which are galaxies apart from the church's core mission of making disciples (Matthew 28:18–20). As Paul explained in 1 Corinthians 8:1, "Knowledge puffs up while love builds up." Theologians puffed up on their own intelligence can become unproductively sectarian as they lose the disciple making focus of what they're supposed to be doing. Doing theology well means doing more than just theology.

Brainwashed Theology. While some people treat theology as an intellectual end in itself, others come to theology with an opposite error: they use theology merely as a means of accomplishing a predetermined agenda. They have a goal in mind and then rework their faith until it serves the goal's purpose. Agenda-driven theologizing can be an especially effective means of arriving at more culturally popular views on biblically inconvenient teachings. If you think about it, manipulating God's truth in this way is quite arrogant, yet it can ironically be made to sound humble. For example, one might say, "In light of new understandings, I found myself needing to deconstruct my old theology, listen to other voices, and creatively reconstruct a new theology that is fresh and life-giving."

> AGENDA-DRIVEN THEOLOGIZING CAN BE AN ESPECIALLY EFFECTIVE MEANS OF ARRIVING AT MORE CULTURALLY POPULAR VIEWS ON BIBLICALLY INCONVENIENT TEACHINGS.

I (Daniel) saw this during my doctoral studies in which I studied the work of Buddhist and Christian interfaith scholars. Here was a group of theologians determined to play matchmaker with Buddhism and Christianity. They felt that if they could bring together in interfaith matrimony the most influential religions of the East and the West, then they could accomplish the perfect synthesis for a better, more united world. In many ways, however, Christianity and Buddhism are as different from each other as a starfish and a starship.

So the interfaith scholars got to work on altering the religions (especially Christianity) to make the marriage work. To make Christian theology compatible with Buddhist thought, the scholars proposed a number of drastic changes. Scriptural truth would be redefined as one's own faith community's experience.

According to Buddhism everything is dependent upon everything else for its existence (a concept known as "dependent co-arising"); therefore, God would need to be redefined as living only in interdependence with creation (as in process theology). A new type of conversion would need to replace the traditional kind: Instead of converting Buddhists to Christianity, Christians should convert their faith to become more like Buddhism.

If you are familiar with the Bible, then reading a brainwashed theology prompts you to say, "But that's not what the Bible says," at practically every mile marker. Such a problem isn't problematic, however, to the people who are concerned, not with what the Bible says, but with what they can make it say. For them, the agenda determines their theology. The predetermined cause is the true north to which they make theology align.

A BETTER AGENDA

YET THE BOOK YOU are reading also comes to theology with an agenda. Agenda is not always a bad thing. In fact, an agenda can simply mean a goal or purpose. The subtitle of this book, then, makes our agenda plain: *Fuel for Effective and Faithful Disciple Making.* This theology is to take you down a predetermined road. What road? One that *fuels disciple making.* We take our cue from Jesus' final command to "make disciples of all nations, baptizing them in the name of the Father and of the Son and of the Holy Spirit, and teaching them to obey everything I have commanded you" (Matthew 28:19b–20a).

So we admit as early as the book's front cover: we want this theology to *fuel disciple making.* Yet we feel justified in this agenda because it's not our agenda. It's the agenda of Jesus. Theology shouldn't be "me-ology" with the individual at the center. At the center of our theology is a God who dwelt among us and called us to the core mission of disciple making. Any theology worthy of its name ought to fuel this final command of Jesus, and we hope ours accomplishes that goal.

What kind of disciple making? We are aiming for disciple making that is both *effective* and *faithful.*

Why *effective*? Because brainiac theology misses the point. As Tony Twist and Mihai Malancea point out in Book 1 of this Collection, theology is to be a "full-body engagement involving our head, heart, hands, and feet" (see pg. 56 of *Grand Metanarrative).* Jesus did not print off handouts for his disciples to study.

Rather, he led them and called them to follow. Our theologizing ought to fuel effectiveness as we live out what we learn.

Why *faithful*? Because brainwashed theology co-opts the point. Christian theology begins not with our ingenuity but with God's revelation. We ought to *treasure* what God has revealed to us, not transfigure it. Who are we to use this precious treasure God has entrusted to us as some kind of power tool for renovating God's will to conform to our plans? God has proved his faithfulness more times than we can count, and he deserves faithfulness from us more times than we can hope to offer in a single lifetime. Yet one thing we can surely offer in our lifetime is to do theology in a way that is faithful to what he has revealed.

> WE OUGHT TO *TREASURE* WHAT GOD HAS REVEALED TO US, NOT TRANSFIGURE IT.

For the cause of effective and faithful disciple making, we offer this theology Collection and pray it helps fuel disciple making in you and in your church.

HOW TO USE THIS BOOK

REAL LIFE THEOLOGY is built around the Faith Statements of the Renew.org Network (see Appendix A). It is a Collection of twelve short books that flesh out the Faith Statements, plus an additional book, *Eternal Security: Walking in Faithfulness.* The twelve core books are also published as a series of twelve individual books for individual, family, ministry, and church usage. Each of these individual books includes three pages following each chapter with questions for reflection and/or group discussion (not included in the Collection). These core books are also organized according to fifty-two total questions and answers, along with fifty-two Scriptures. These twelve core books therefore provide up to fifty-two individual sessions or weeks of curriculum.

There's an additional important usage for the fifty-two questions, answers, and Scriptures. These elements will be formatted to create forthcoming devotional and discipleship tools, which will be especially useful for family discipleship and training new believers in the basics of the Christian faith. The question-and-answer format can serve well as a catechism. Families, youth ministries, Christian schools, and others who disciple new believers will find these tools helpful for summarizing and supplementing the core books in the *Real Life Theology* series.

By design, the authors are all personally aligned with the Renew.org Network's Faith Statements, and they all possess a Doctor of Ministry degree or a Doctor of Philosophy degree.

We also sought diversity among the contributors because the Renew.org Network's vision includes reflecting among our leaders and audience the diversity of the US, then the world. The ultimate vision is the picture of God's people in eternity found in Revelation 7:9, which describes people from every nation, language, tribe, and people group. We only have a modest start in this book, but we are optimistic God will bless us to reflect better the diversity he desires with future Renew.org growth in the US and then around the world.

The writers of this book also reflect a theological heritage that is broader than just one stream, with everyone being convinced of the foundational beliefs of Renew.org. At the same time, a majority of the authors have roots in the best of the Restoration Movement's theological tradition. Everyone also gravitates back to the best of the Protestant Reformation, including Anabaptist thought, and then continues back through the church fathers of the second, third, and fourth centuries. But most importantly, we all rely on the only sure foundation, which is Jesus Christ and the sixty-six books of the Bible, which are inspired by God and authoritative for the church.

Scripture, and Scripture alone, is our final and ultimate authority.

In sum, we believe the greatest mission on planet earth is making disciples, and through this Collection of books, among other efforts, we seek to excel at that mission in God's power. Why does theology matter? Because we believe:

> *The Jesus you preach and the gospel you uphold and the faith*
> *you coach will determine the disciple you produce.*

For King Jesus,
Bobby Harrington and Daniel McCoy
General Editors, *Real Life Theology* Series

GRAND META NARRATIVE

GOD'S STORY
AS AN INVITATION
TO THEOLOGY

TONY TWIST
& MIHAI MALANCEA

To my wife, prayer partner, and best friend, Suzanne.
— Tony

To my wife, Lidia, and family, children, and grandchildren.
— Mihai

CONTENTS

General Editors' Note 25

Introduction 27

CHAPTER 1: The Power of Stories 29

CHAPTER 2: Answering Questions with Stories 33

CHAPTER 3: A Metanarrative of Renewal 45

CHAPTER 4: Theology Starts Here 53

Appendix: Book Recommendations for Further Study 59

Notes 61

GENERAL EDITORS' NOTE

We all need to see the big picture before we can understand the parts—the forest before the trees. This book helps us do that with the Bible, setting the stage and helping us see where we come from and where we are headed. Tony Twist and Mihai Malancea discuss this metanarrative, our overarching story, as uniquely gifted thinkers who serve globally together with the Training Christians for Ministry International Institute (TCMII).

Tony Twist currently serves as President and Professor of Leadership and Spiritual Formation for TCMII. He and his wife, Suzanne, have served churches in Virginia, Tennessee, and Indiana, with the focus of disciple making. His passions are disciple making, spending time with Suzanne, working out, and making new friends around the world. Tony earned a Doctor of Philosophy in Communication Studies at Indiana University and a Doctor of Ministry with a focus on discipleship at Southern Baptist Theological Seminary.

Mihai Malancea serves as Academic Dean of Divitia Gratiae University in Chisinau, Moldova, and Professor of Intercultural Studies at TCMII. He earned his Doctor of Philosophy in Theology at the University of Bucharest. He has served churches in Moldova and post-Soviet countries in Central Asia. He enjoys discipling people who belong to different ethnic groups. Mihai and his wife have five children, all of them involved in ministry, as well as five grandchildren.

This book expounds on the introduction to the Renew.org Leaders' Faith Statements:

> We believe that Jesus Christ is Lord. We are a group of church leaders inviting others to join the theological and disciple-making journey described below. We want to trust and follow Jesus Christ to the glory of God the Father in the power of the Holy Spirit. We are committed to *restoring* the kingdom vision of Jesus and the apostles, especially the *message* of Jesus'

gospel, the *method* of disciple making he showed us, and the *model* of what a community of his disciples, at their best, can become.

We live in a time when cultural pressures are forcing us to face numerous difficulties and complexities in following God. Many are losing their resolve. We trust that God is gracious and forgives the errors of those with genuine faith in his Son, but our desire is to be faithful in all things.

Our focus is disciple making, which is both reaching lost people (evangelism) and bringing people to maturity (sanctification). We seek to be a movement of disciple making leaders who make disciples and other disciple makers. We want to renew existing churches and help plant multiplying churches.

*See the full Network Faith Statements at the end of this book.

You can find three to seven-minute video teachings that summarize the book, as well as each chapter, at Renew.org. These short videos can function as standalone teachings. But for groups or group leaders using the book, they can also be used to launch discussion of the reading.

May God use this book to fuel faithful and effective disciple making in your life and church.

For King Jesus,
Bobby Harrington and Daniel McCoy
General Editors, *Real Life Theology* Series

INTRODUCTION

God is very, very smart.

"Theology" comes from two words meaning "God" (*theo*) and "word" or "reason" (*logos*). So theology means "the word about God" or "to reason about God." God's smartness ought to be the beginning of theology. Unfortunately, a lot of people come to theology with the assumption that it is *the theologians* who are very, very smart. In fact, the word "theologian" often evokes images of an academic who says and writes in a way that might impress but whose teachings are inaccessible and impractical for everyday life. Or worse: the word might bring to mind holy professionals like the Pharisees who debated nuanced, theological questions for hours yet did not understand or receive the Messiah. Not smart.

Smart theology calls us to clear and solid thinking. Yet theology should not be seen as merely a mental exercise. God created us to use our minds to their fullest capabilities for the goal of *love*—namely, loving God and others. In addition to the command to love God with "all your mind," a very, very smart Jesus says also to use "all your heart . . . all your soul . . . all your strength" too (Mark 12:30). When disciples of Jesus reason about him, we ought to make it a matter of head, heart, hands, and feet. Theology engages all of us. It's holistic. It involves asking not just, *How should I think (head)?* but also, *How should this change my inner self (heart)?* not to mention, *What should I do with this truth (hands)?* and, *To whom should I go tell (feet)?* If theology doesn't transform all of us, then it's an activity foreign to the expectations of us laid out in Scripture.

If we view theology as an academic discipline only for smart people, we might come away amazed at our own brilliance. But when we engage theology with all of us, we'll come away amazed at the brilliance of someone else: Jesus.

If we pursue theology hoping for exhaustive answers for all our questions, Jesus may at times disappoint us. However, if we pursue theology to transform heads, hearts, hands, and feet, then Jesus will *amaze* us.

This is because Jesus gave us something far more transformative than an answer

book filled with explanations; he gave us a family album filled with stories. A metanarrative is a story of stories. What is this "grand metanarrative" then? It is *our story of stories*.

In this book on God's grand metanarrative, we will first explore why God chose to communicate to us in stories. Second, we will walk through significant family stories along the grand metanarrative and observe how they answer some of life's biggest questions. Third, we will trace the grand metanarrative to its conclusion and see how God renews what was lost. Finally, we will ask how God's grand metanarrative can help us do theology well.

Our desire is that this book encourages you to exclaim, along with the apostle Paul, "Oh, the depth of the riches of the wisdom and knowledge of God!" (Romans 11:33a).

1

THE POWER OF STORIES

What makes you *you*? You might say your name, your job title, or your family members. But if a person really wants to know who we are, we give them stories. We tell them how our parents decided on our name. When we learned we were interested in our chosen career. How we met our spouse. The list goes on.

Where are you from? This is another identity question. We might tell them the name of our state or hometown. But if we really want to communicate where we come from, we tell a story or two. About the ice storm and weeklong power outage. About the local music "talent" at the annual festival. Or about the childhood prank that went terribly wrong.

Stories dynamically shape and communicate our identity.

Jared Ellis, a storyteller, pastor, and Renew.org contributor, explains the "weight" of stories, which he learned early on in life:

> I grew up in a very hospitable home. There were always people at my house. When company would come over, all the furniture was moved out into a massive circle in the living room and there, my father would entertain dozens with his stories. I remember sneaking into the living room, leaving my friends and crawling in under his dining room chair and lying down just to listen. The effect that his stories had on me and those who were listening was powerful: shock, surprise, anticipation, empathy, sadness, laughter. But these were not mere emotions to me; they were tactile, not vague, feelings that eventually dissipate into the ethereal.

They were substance. They were something like glory, weight.

He wielded that gift with such power, force, and precision that he could hold the entire room in his hand, using only words.[1]

Sometimes stories tell false narratives, and sadly that doesn't prevent them from being powerful. Stories in the hands of arrogant storytellers have fueled empire-making nationalisms. Some stories have animated guillotines and incited genocides. Others have nourished nihilism and despair.

Yet the God of the Bible was not content to leave us to answer big questions by using false stories. God, the grand storyteller, inspired a book so full of stories that readers would think stories are his preferred method of truth-telling.

STORIES ARE GOD'S PREFERRED METHOD OF TRUTH-TELLING.

Another Renew.org contributor, James Bard, has made it his life's work to understand unreached "oral cultures" in order to bring the gospel to them (cultures that prefer to learn orally rather than through the written word). As he's learned how oral cultures communicate, and thus receive truth, James was delighted to discover how we as Christians already have the tools necessary to reach oral cultures. James writes:

> During my journey to understand "oral cultures," I've had the privilege of studying under the most amazing Middle Eastern man I've ever met. I've never met anyone that knows the Word of God more than he does. There's something about this man that people are just drawn to, and that I'm drawn to. For one thing, it is clear that he is full of the Holy Spirit. For another, it doesn't matter what question we ask him, he always answers with a story or a brilliant illustration. It's actually sometimes frustrating how indirect he can be in his answers! I've sat there and wanted him to just come out and say it! But when he gets going telling stories, people can't resist! I've seen rooms packed out to hear his stories.[2]

The Middle Eastern man James refers to is, of course, Jesus. Mark 4:33–34 says, "With many similar parables Jesus spoke the word to them, as much as they could understand. He did not say anything to them without using a parable." It is true that Jesus would speak plainly to his disciples when they needed extra clarity (Mark 4:34b). Yet just as in the Old Testament, the New Testament that his disciples wrote was full of stories. Apparently, stories are one of God's favorite ways to give us truth.

When we read the stories of the Bible together, we easily see how they are interconnected. They are all parts of the grand metanarrative spanning from the original creation to the new heavens and new earth. As the people of this God, we find in the grand metanarrative of God answers to life's most important questions.

OVERVIEW OF THE GRAND METANARRATIVE

IN THE BEGINNING WAS a family: the Father, Son, and Holy Spirit. This family from all eternity overflowed with love, light, and life. Such love desires to share their life with children.

So they took eons of time to prepare everything. Angelic servants. A universe. An improbable planet. A beautiful garden with a tree of life. Then beloved children from the first couple, birthed in their own image. They were children destined to rule and reign, in keeping with their royal family resemblance, children blessed and commanded to be fruitful and multiply (Genesis 1:28).

Unfortunately, about a third of the angels did not share their joy. *Why*, these angels reasoned, *should gloriously bright and powerful spirits like us help raise up dusty and weak creatures like them to rule and reign over us?* So they rebelled. And horrifically, when we had the opportunity, *we* joined their rebellion when we ate the forbidden fruit.

Our family album, the Bible, details our family story, our grand metanarrative—our heritage, origin, fall, redemption, calling, mission, and destiny. This family album tells us that joining the rebellion was not the end. We have a Redeemer through whom we are chosen and adopted back into our eternal family (Ephesians 1:5). It assures us that we are now sons and daughters of Abraham, called out of Egypt, given the Law and the Prophets, the Incarnate Word, the Written Word, and the martyrs, trailblazers, guides, friends, and all the intercessors though the ages.

OUR FAMILY ALBUM, THE BIBLE, DETAILS OUR FAMILY STORY, OUR GRAND METANARRATIVE.

But that's not all. The love between the Father, Son, and Holy Spirit now transforms us (2 Corinthians 3:18). We are being recreated to live in our heart's true home: this eternal relationship of love waiting to welcome us back to our prepared place at the family table. As our relationship with our Father grows, our deepening love for him and others reveals its health (Matthew 22:34–40). Life becomes a "process of being conformed to the image of Christ for the sake of others."[3]

We do this by journeying toward the Ancient of Days, the One who brought Adam into existence; who led Abraham out of Ur in search of our heart's true home;[4] who spoke to Moses face to face; who sent his Son to reveal himself (John 14:8–9); who gives us his Word to light our path; who gives his Spirit to make us whole; and who provides a home where we will be loved by our forever Father and family (John 14:1–4).

This is what we were made for and who we are. Our Great Commission (to make disciples) based on his Great Commandment (to love God and people) means nothing less than creating a new heaven and new earth. The restoration of all creation to God our Father, through his Son, in the power of his Holy Spirit.

It is the story of our forever family: *the grand metanarrative of the Bible*. As we begin combing through our family album in the next chapter, we will find true and transformative answers to life's most important questions.

2

ANSWERING QUESTIONS WITH STORIES

When we share stories with one another, we internalize the values of those stories. In a sense, stories answer questions for us. What are some questions that get answered by internalizing the stories in the Bible, our family story album? We want to offer one such list of questions, the answers to which we'll seek to answer in this chapter.

- What is our purpose?
- What is our problem?
- What is God's heart?
- How does God rescue?
- How should we live?
- What is God's role in our lives?
- What is God's goal for us?
- Where is God when we suffer?

Is this an exhaustive list of all the major questions of life? Far from it. Curiosity can be a gift, and God has given us the ability to seek out answers to these and a host of other questions. Yet these questions are an excellent sampling of the curiosities that arise from the heart's most persistent pursuit, which boils down to wondering "Who is God?" and "Can I trust him?" The idols that people of the world trust and follow lead them to disillusionment. Scripture's response to this disillusionment is that we pursue God, who is here with us, who has spoken, and who has acted in history. He exists, and we learn who he is not by philosophizing our way to him but by loving him as he has revealed himself—through the stories of Scripture. And through these true stories we learn, yes, that we can trust God and follow him on the journey to our heart's true home.

WHAT IS OUR PURPOSE?
THE STORY OF THE TREE OF LIFE

WHY DID GOD CREATE humans? To answer this, let's look at story one, the story of creation. In the beginning, God created our world. After creating water and sky, he created fish and birds to fill them. After creating dry land, God created land animals to fill it. But his final act, which crowned creation, was humans. God said:

> "Let us make mankind in our image, in our likeness, so that they may rule over the fish in the sea and the birds in the sky, over the livestock and all the wild animals, and over all the creatures that move along the ground." So God created mankind in his own image, in the image of God he created them; male and female he created them. God blessed them and said to them, "Be fruitful and increase in number; fill the earth and subdue it. Rule over the fish in the sea and the birds in the sky and over every living creature that moves on the ground." (Genesis 1:26–28)

He put the first humans in a garden to tend it and to enjoy his creation. After surveying all he had made, God looked at his works and saw "it was very good" (v. 31). In the middle of the garden, God placed the "tree of life," giving humans access to immortality. It was designed to be a place to enjoy forever.

What do we learn about humanity's purpose from this story? While other ancient creation stories taught that mythological gods created humans to be their slaves, the God of the Bible created humans to rule and reign with him over his creation. This royal stamp on humanity helps explain God's ongoing intention throughout history to create "a chosen people, a royal priesthood" (1 Peter 2:9), a "kingdom and priests to serve our God, and they will reign on the earth" (Revelation 5:10; see also Revelation 22:5).

God formed the first man "from the dust of the ground and breathed into his nostrils the breath of life, and the man became a living being" (Genesis 2:7). He became a conscious and responsible being, gifted with reason and free will. The obvious care and weighty purpose with which God created humans is a subject of wonder to the psalmist:

> When I consider your heavens, the work of your fingers, the moon and the stars, which you have set in place, what is mankind that you are mindful of them, human beings that you care for them? You have made them a little lower than the angels and crowned them with glory and honor. You made them rulers over the works of your hands; you put everything under their feet. (Psalm 8:3–6)

This royal purpose that God had in mind when he created us makes the next scene all the more shocking.

WHAT IS OUR PROBLEM?
THE STORY OF THE SERPENT

HUMANS ARE DEEPLY FLAWED. How can this be the case for a people whose origin was so grand and promising? The answer is found in the next story in our family album. God created the first two humans, Adam and Eve, placed them in a garden, and gave them food and freedom. Although God had given them "trees that were pleasing to the eye and good for food" (Genesis 2:9), he gave them one restriction: "You are free to eat from any tree in the garden, but you must not eat from the tree of the knowledge of good and evil, for when you eat from it you will certainly die" (v. 17). Then along came a tempter with a question: "Did God really say, 'You must not eat from any tree in the garden'?" (Genesis 3:1). Eve replied to the serpent that eating from the tree in the middle of the garden would certainly result in death.

> "You will not certainly die," the serpent said to the woman. "For God knows that when you eat from it your eyes will be opened, and you will be like God, knowing good and evil." When the woman saw that the fruit of the tree was good for food and pleasing to the eye, and also desirable for gaining wisdom, she took some and ate it. She also gave some to her husband, who was with her, and he ate it. (vv. 4–6)

The immediate aftermath of this defiance by Adam and Eve's decision shows us the genesis of our problems in seed form. When they realized they were naked, they felt shame instead of innocence (v. 7). When they heard God coming, they felt dread instead of delight (v. 8). When God questioned them about their decision, they pointed fingers and shifted blame instead of taking responsibility (vv. 11–13). They experienced the dreadful separation from God that disobedience brings. Their relationship with their environment turned colder, with field work yielding thorns. Childbirth brought pain (vv. 16–19). And just as Adam had been formed from dust, so he would "return to the ground" and become dust once again (v. 19).

In the midst of the chaos, however, comes a fascinating and merciful promise that shows us the grand metanarrative of God is far from over. God said to the serpent, "I will put enmity between you and the woman, and between your offspring and hers; he will crush your head, and you will strike his heel" (v. 15). In the moment of despair, God deployed his missionary plan to one day crush the tempter under the feet of the woman's offspring. Our next stop will be in the land of Ur. With a few steps in between.

WHAT IS GOD'S HEART?
THE STORY OF THE CALL

THE UPSIDE OF LEARNING who God is from stories is that we receive a multifaceted picture more than a dictionary definition. And a morally perfect God interacts differently toward injustice and violence than he does toward repentance and kindness. Our family album shows God offering surprising mercy, for example, toward Adam and Eve and toward their firstborn, Cain, when Cain murdered his brother, Abel.

Yet a few chapters later in Genesis, the violence and evil intentions had grown so much that God issued a warning. Since only Noah and his family remained faithful, God flooded the earth and "restarted" humanity with Noah's family. In light of this mixture of mercy and wrath, what can we make of God's heart? The next major story in the grand metanarrative answers this for us.

God chose a childless couple of Chaldean descent (which would be like someone from modern-day Iraq) named Abram and Sarai. Chose them for what? Listen to the beginning of the story:

The LORD had said to Abram, "Go from your country, your people and your father's household to the land I will show you. I will make you into a great nation, and I will bless you; I will make your name great, and you will be a blessing. I will bless those who bless you, and whoever curses you I will curse; and all peoples on earth will be blessed through you." So Abram went, as the LORD had told him. (Genesis 12:1–4a)

Did you catch the end result of this promise to Abram? "All peoples on earth will be blessed" (v. 3). God would bless Abram in order to eventually *bless everybody.* From this story, we learn that Abram and his family were blessed to be a blessing. We learn that faith trusts and follows God, even when not every detail is made clear (e.g., "Go from your country . . . to the land I will show you," v. 1). From God's ability to build a nation from a childless couple, we learn that God can do miracles. From God's continued faithfulness to Abram's son Isaac (a child born in their old age) and Isaac's son Jacob (whose name God changed to "Israel," and whose sons became the twelve tribes of Israel), we learn that our failures do not change the purpose of God.

But perhaps the most important lesson we learn from the story of God's call to Abram is that God is a missionary. His heart beats with passion for reaching all peoples

> OUR FAILURES DO NOT CHANGE THE PURPOSE OF GOD.

in every nation and bringing them back into his family. This plan is like a bright golden thread throughout all the books of Scripture.

HOW DOES GOD RESCUE?
THE STORY OF THE LAMB

THE NATION THROUGH WHICH God would eventually bless "all peoples on earth" was the nation of Israel. The infant nation was not without sins, however. One of Jacob's sons, Joseph, was sold by his jealous brothers into slavery in Egypt. God used this travesty for good, however, for Joseph grew in wisdom and miraculously rose through the ranks of Egypt to become overseer of its food distribution during a far-reaching famine.

Then, when his estranged family came down to Egypt to buy food to survive the famine, Joseph was able to give them not only food but a place to live. When the Jewish family stayed in Egypt, prospering and expanding for generations, the Egyptian government felt threatened and enslaved them. Not only that, but the pharaoh made it law that any new baby boy who was born to the Jews (called "Hebrews" at the time) would be immediately drowned in the Nile. But God did not forget his promise to Abram to give him a promised land, and he put into action a plan to rescue his chosen people from their slavery.

How does God rescue exactly? For one thing, he enlists less-than-perfect people. He picked a Jewish fugitive named Moses who had run away after killing an Egyptian who was beating a fellow Israelite. God sent the reluctant Moses to tell the pharaoh to "Let my people go" (Exodus 5:1). When the pharaoh kept refusing, God sent plagues to show the Egyptians how serious he was. The pharaoh's final refusal was met with a tenth and final plague: the death of every firstborn son in Egypt. Only the firstborn sons in Israel were saved by the blood of a lamb sprinkled over their doorposts.

At this point in the story, we learn another key to understanding how God rescues: through sacrifice. Although God would send fierce wrath upon the nation of Egypt for how it had treated his chosen people, we also see how God provided escape from wrath by means of a sacrifice. Each Jewish family was instructed to kill a lamb and paint its blood on the beams of the door to their house. That way, when God came through the nation to extinguish the life of each firstborn son, he would see the lamb's blood on doors and would "pass over" that house (Exodus 12:12–13). Hence, the annual day to remember this event was called the Passover.

Animal sacrifices would become a regular feature of Israelite dealings with God, as the priests would make offerings to atone for Israel's sins. Notably, it was during a Passover feast many centuries later that a Jew named Jesus would take a cup of wine and say, "This is my blood of the covenant, which is poured out for many for the forgiveness of sins" (Matthew 26:28). The next day, Jesus would be killed in a once-for-all final sacrifice (Hebrews 7:27).

HOW SHOULD WE LIVE?
THE STORY OF THE COMMUNITY

After God rescued the Israelites out of slavery, he led them toward the land he had promised Abram centuries before. Yet the people had much to learn before they were ready to enter that land. They stopped at Mount Sinai for God to give them his commands for how they would live. Although there were hundreds of laws in all, ten in particular formed the foundation. Here is the story:

Moses led the people out of the camp to meet with God, and they stood at the foot of the mountain. Mount Sinai was covered with smoke, because the LORD descended on it in fire. The smoke billowed up from it like smoke from a furnace, and the whole mountain trembled violently. . . . The LORD descended to the top of Mount Sinai and called Moses to the top of the mountain. So Moses went up. . . . And God spoke all these words: "I am the LORD your God, who brought you out of Egypt, out of the land of slavery." (Exodus 19:17–18, 20; 20:1–2)

Then God spoke the following ten commandments that would set his people apart as his holy and distinct family. These commandments from Exodus 20:2–17 came from a Father who wanted the best for his children:

1. You shall have no other gods before me.
2. You shall not make for yourself an idol.
3. You shall not misuse the name of the Lord.
4. Remember the Sabbath day by keeping it holy.
5. Honor your father and mother.
6. You shall not murder.
7. You shall not commit adultery.
8. You shall not steal.
9. You shall not give false testimony against your neighbor.
10. You shall not covet.

Some of God's laws would have struck the surrounding peoples as odd: *Only one God? Don't bow down to an idol?* Indeed, God's family was always meant to live counterculturally in this fallen world.

WHAT IS GOD'S ROLE IN OUR LIVES?
THE STORY OF THE KINGDOM

THE STORY OF THE Exodus from Egypt displays how God rescues. Yet once God rescues us, what role does he play in our lives? Does he give us moral rules, and then largely retreat from our lives until we need his intervention again? Or does he desire something more for us?

Although their stubbornness prolonged their journey to the promised land, God's chosen people were finally ready to enter. They drove out many of the inhabitants and settled by tribes throughout the land. In the early conquest of the promised land, full control of the land eluded them. And persistent threats came from other conquering nations. During these times, God enlisted "judges" such as Samson, Gideon, and Deborah to drive out invaders and to rule over the people.

A final godly judge, Samuel, enjoyed a close relationship with God and sought to lead well the people of God. Yet the Israelites envied how other nations had kings to lead them. They wanted a change in leadership. When Samuel brought the matter before God, God responded in a way that reveals a major role he desires to play in our lives.

> Listen to all that the people are saying to you; it is not you they have rejected, but they have rejected me as their king. As they have done from the day I brought them up out of Egypt until this day, forsaking me and serving other gods, so they are doing to you. (1 Samuel 8:6b–8)

This reveals how one of the major roles God wants to play in our lives is that of king. Israel would become a kingdom with its own kings, but even before the nation officially became a monarchy under its first king, Saul, God already thought of his people as a kingdom, with himself as the king.

With God's blessing, Samuel anointed Saul, who seemed like a strong person to be king. Yet Saul's reign turned out to be a bitter experience because of a character trait that drove him mad: Saul's jealousy became paranoia. We see this when a loyal, younger warrior named David kept stealing the spotlight. This cast a dark shadow over his kingship. In the end, Saul's reign sputtered, spiraled, and ended in his death on the battlefield.

David, whom Saul had driven out of the kingdom, was brought back and made Israel's second king. Not without his own significant character defects, David was nonetheless a "man after God's own heart," who regularly humbled himself before God and even wrote many of the worship songs (psalms) in the Bible.

With a reign that stabilized and expanded the kingdom, David became the first of a long line of hereditary kings. Moreover, God promised that through David's lineage a kingdom would be set up that would endure forever (2 Samuel 7:16). Later prophecies echoed this and promised the coming of a Messiah who would be divine ("Wonderful Counselor, Mighty God," Isaiah 9:6) and who would "reign on David's throne and over his kingdom" (Isaiah 9:7). It should be no surprise, therefore, that when the Messiah came, he announced *the kingdom of God* had come near (Mark 1:15).

WHAT IS GOD'S GOAL FOR OUR LIVES?
THE STORY OF THE TEMPLE

EVEN THOUGH GOD SINGLED out a particular nation to be his chosen people, God never wanted them to lose sight of his intention to bless "all peoples on earth" through them (Genesis 12:3). Throughout one of David's psalms, we catch a vision of all nations worshiping God and enjoying his blessings:

> May God be gracious to us and bless us and make his face shine on us—so that your ways may be known on earth, your salvation among all nations. May the peoples praise you, God; may all the peoples praise you. May the nations be glad and sing for joy, for you rule the peoples with equity and guide the nations of the earth. (Psalm 67:1–4)

Living in relationship with God and under his kingship is living the blessed life. But what is the ultimate goal of this blessedness? To answer, we look at the story of the temple's dedication under David's son King Solomon.

Under Solomon, a temple to God was built to be a central location of worship for the entire nation. Yet even as we will see from Solomon's words as he dedicated the temple, the ultimate goal went far beyond the nation itself. Standing before the assembly, Solomon offered a prayer dedicating the temple of God, and then prayed,

> As for the foreigner who does not belong to your people Israel but has come from a distant land because of your name—for they will hear of your great name and your mighty hand and your outstretched arm—when they come and pray toward this temple, then hear from heaven, your dwelling place. Do whatever the foreigner asks of you, so that all the peoples of the earth may know your name and fear you, as do your own people Israel, and may know that this house I have built bears your Name. (1 Kings 8:41–43)

Just as God's ultimate plan went far beyond Israel, so his ultimate blessings on us are meant to ripple outward to far more than just ourselves. Like his temple was for Israel, God's goal for our lives goes beyond us. God wants to make a global significance through us by leading us to "make disciples of all nations" (Matthew 28:19).

WHERE IS GOD WHEN WE SUFFER?
THE STORY OF THE BROKEN COVENANT

ISRAEL LARGELY PROSPERED DURING the reigns of King David and King Solomon. That was when the nation was still unified. However, after Solomon's son Rehoboam revealed himself to be an arrogant, unbending ruler, the northern tribes split off from the Davidic southern tribes. The northern kings immediately led the new nation into idolatry, and after centuries of disregarding God, they were defeated by the Assyrians in the eighth century BC. The southern kings alternated between following neighboring idols and renewing their commitment to God.

HIS ULTIMATE BLESSINGS ARE MEANT TO RIPPLE OUTWARD TO FAR MORE THAN JUST OURSELVES.

After a string of faithless rulers and unwise decisions, the Southern Kingdom was defeated by the Babylonians in the sixth century. The Babylonians put their capital city, Jerusalem, under siege, starving the people until breaking through the city walls. Once inside, the Babylonians set fire to the houses, the palace, and most tragically of all—the temple. Much of the population was carried into exile. Though tragic, none of this would have been surprising to a student of the Old Testament law, for in Deuteronomy 28 God had promised eventual siege, famine, and exile if the nation broke its covenant with God. Unfortunately, this story just seems to continue again and again!

Every era of human history has seen its share of suffering—whether physical, mental, emotional, or spiritual. Believers in God have a special reassurance that God watches over them and will make things right in the end. Yet they also deal with a unique confusion: If God is so good, then where is he during all the suffering? The story of Israel's broken covenant helps us find answers.

Arriving at a lower point than this devastating episode in Israel's history is hard to imagine. Starving mothers and fathers were reduced to cooking and eating their own children. The nation's religious and political centers became piles of ashes. Enchained processions of people were marched to foreign captivity. Where was God in all this?

If we advance a few pages forward in their history, we discover that the destruction of their homeland was not the end of the story. One of the eyewitnesses of the destruction was the prophet Jeremiah, whose book of Lamentations mourned the city's destruction even as he reaffirmed that God's "compassions never fail" (Lamentations 3:22). In captivity, Israelites such as the prophet Daniel served the Babylonian empire honorably and became a blessing to multiple nations. God used Daniel and his friends' faithfulness to God to teach pagans about God's power and goodness (Daniel 1–6). Within decades of Jerusalem's destruction, the Medo-Persian Empire came to power in Babylon and released the Jewish people to return home and rebuild, as described in the books of Ezra and Nehemiah.

The Babylonian exile itself yielded positive results for the people of God at home and abroad. When they returned home, they were less inclined toward idols. As for the Jewish people still scattered over the Babylonian Empire, now pockets of people were throughout the known world ready and waiting for the Messiah to come. When the Messiah came and sent his disciples throughout the world to make disciples, some among the diaspora were ready to hear the good news. As the story of Israel shows, even amid unspeakable suffering, God has a marvelous way of inverting the tragedy and turning it out for good for those who love and trust in him (Genesis 50:20; Romans 8:28). But more of that in Chapter 3!

3

A METANARRATIVE OF RENEWAL

Often, when we read the Bible, we come across a story or symbol that can give us a feeling of *déjà vu*. Take Abraham's almost-sacrifice of Isaac (Genesis 22). When God commanded Abraham to sacrifice his beloved son, Isaac, God halted the slaughter at the last moment, for it was a test. But it was more than a test; it was a picture of something to come: *God's sacrificing his beloved Son in the New Testament.* This chapter will feature many such moments, where God accomplishes something in the second half of the grand metanarrative that reminds us of something that happened in the first half. At each step, what was lost is renewed.

Déjà vu hits strongly in the first chapters of the Gospel of Matthew, which had Jesus go down into Egypt after his birth, come through the waters of the Jordan at his baptism, spend forty days in the desert, and then go up on a mountain to give his disciples new commandments. Where have we seen all that before? If we retrace the crucial steps along Israel's history, we see signposts of this narrative from the early years in Egypt, the people's miraculously spending forty years in the desert, and their trek across the dry Jordan riverbed. We hear in the new commandments spoken from the Mount of Beatitudes updates of the old commandments given at Mount Sinai.

Interestingly, some of the echoes of the Bible's ancient stories and symbols throughout the grand metanarrative seem to have a symmetrical arrangement. For example, the Bible begins and ends with a garden. When you line up some of the major events in God's grand storyline, parallels emerge—and in symmetry with each other. Taking the destruction of the temple under the Babylonians as the low point of Israel's history, the following framework might be a helpful visual for memorizing some of these major movements in the storyline:

Tree of Life *(Genesis 2:9)*
Serpent *(Genesis 3:1)*
Call *(Genesis 12:1–3)*
Lamb *(Exodus 12:13)*
Community *(Exodus 19:5–6)*
Kingdom *(2 Samuel 5:12)*
Temple *(1 Kings 5:18)*
Broken Covenant *(2 Chronicles 36:15–20)*
Temple *(Ezra 6:15)*
Kingdom *(Matthew 4:17)*
Community *(Matthew 5:13–16)*
Lamb *(Matthew 26:28)*
Call *(Matthew 28:18–20)*
Serpent *(Revelation 12:17)*
Tree of Life *(Revelation 22:2)*

In the following sections, we will explore the same themes we have already covered, but in a reverse pattern that brings us back to God's original intended paradise. Let's go through these in more detail.

THE TEMPLE REBUILT

As mentioned already, the Persian Empire that followed the Babylonian Empire allowed the Jewish people to go back home and rebuild. In addition to reconstructing Jerusalem, they rebuilt the temple (albeit in smaller form). This "second temple" figures prominently in the intertestamental story of the Maccabees, a Jewish family that reconquered their nation from the Seleucids and rededicated the temple after it was desecrated by the Seleucid rulers. This rededication of the temple is celebrated today in the festival of Hannukah. Moving on into New Testament times, it was Herod the Great who expanded this modest temple into one of the impressive structures of the ancient world.

THE KINGDOM REKINDLED

ALTHOUGH THE DAVIDIC KINGDOM had ended tragically—with its final king being forced to watch his sons be slaughtered before being blinded himself—God had promised that David's kingdom would last forever (2 Samuel 7:16). Moreover, there were rumors from the prophets that a Davidic king was on the way to restore the kingdom (Isaiah 9:7; 16:5; Jeremiah 23:5; 33:15).

When Jesus came onto the scene, his message was, "The time has come. . . . The kingdom of God has come near. Repent and believe the good news!" (Mark 1:15). His famous Sermon on the Mount promised the kingdom to people who were poor in spirit and persecuted for righteousness' sake and for following him (Matthew 5:3, 10–12). It wasn't just this sermon, though; his parables largely centered on the kingdom of God (e.g., Matthew 13). "Christ" was not his last name but rather his title, and it meant the "anointed one," which carried royal significance. The first verse of the New Testament drips with royal implications, calling him "Jesus the Messiah the son of David" (Matthew 1:1). He was officially crucified for claiming to be "king of the Jews" (Matthew 27:37), a charge he did not deny (Matthew 27:11). With Jesus, the kingdom was back.

Yet it was not to be the kind of kingdom many of the Jews of Jesus' day were looking for. Rather than conquering their enemies and driving out the occupiers, Jesus told his disciples to love their enemies (Matthew 5:44). Rather than strictly enforcing the Mosaic law by applauding dutiful law-keepers and shunning sinners, Jesus was so notorious for his unglamorous friendships that one of his nicknames became the "friend of sinners" (Luke 7:34). The kingdom Jesus inaugurated was very clearly from somewhere else, a truth that came into clear focus in this exchange Jesus had with the Roman governor Pilate:

> Jesus said, "My kingdom is not of this world. If it were, my servants would fight to prevent my arrest by the Jewish leaders. But now my kingdom is from another place." "You are a king, then!" said Pilate. Jesus answered, "You say that I am a king. In fact, the reason I was born and came into the world is to testify to the truth. Everyone on the side of truth listens to me." (John 18:35b–37)

It was to be a kingdom that emerged without swords and arrows. Yet somehow it would outlast the Roman Empire and truly be a kingdom "established forever"

(2 Samuel 7:16). Its durability can be traced to the years Jesus spent slowly, intentionally building a resilient community of disciples.

THE COMMUNITY RENEWED

JUST AS GOD HAD once chosen a people during the Old Testament era to live counterculturally, Jesus came and began forming a community to be holy and distinct—a group whom he called disciples ("students"). Jesus called these disciples to experience the fulfillment of the Law and the Prophets (i.e., the Old Testament) in himself and the life he offered them by pointing them to a greater type of righteousness that moves beyond simply not doing evil. This righteousness was basic and focused on doing what is right on the inside and out, surpassing the righteousness of the Pharisees: "So in everything, do to others what you would have them do to you, for this sums up the Law and the Prophets" (Matthew 7:12).

Whereas the religious elites of Jesus' day felt justified by their many ways of *not* working on the Sabbath (from Friday evening to Saturday evening), Jesus exploded expectations by intentionally healing people *on* that day. Jesus asked the religious leaders who were incensed by Jesus' merciful acts done on the Sabbath, "I ask you, which is lawful on the Sabbath: to do good or to do evil, to save life or to destroy it?" (Luke 6:9). By focusing on actively showing mercy and seeking justice, Jesus modeled a life that prioritized the "weightier" matters of the law: "Woe to you, scribes and Pharisees, hypocrites! For you tithe mint and dill and cumin, and have neglected the weightier provisions of the Law: justice and mercy and faithfulness" (Matthew 23:23, NASB).

THE MOST DISTINCTIVE CHARACTERISTIC OF ALL WAS TO BE LOVE.

The most distinctive characteristic of all was to be love: Jesus told them, "A new command I give you: Love one another. As I have loved you, so you must love one another. By this everyone will know that you are my disciples, if you love one another" (John 13:34–35). Jesus spent three years investing in twelve disciples in life-on-life training as well as investing in a larger group (i.e., the Seventy-Two in Luke 10). Far better than training students merely to get an A on a test, Jesus spent time discipling these men and women to replicate his values and beliefs in their entire lives.

THE LAMB REVEALED

ALTHOUGH JESUS PREPARED HIS disciples for what was coming, they were shocked when it actually happened. Jesus was arrested, put on trial, convicted on trumped-up charges, and sentenced to death by crucifixion. It was more than coincidence that he died during the week of the Passover celebration, commemorating the lamb's blood, which saved God's people from his wrath. It was all part of the plan.

John the Baptist had prophetically announced Jesus to his followers, "Look, the Lamb of God, who takes away the sin of the world!" (John 1:29). Centuries before, the prophet Isaiah had foreseen someone "pierced for our transgressions . . . crushed for our iniquities," who was "led like a lamb to the slaughter" (Isaiah 53:5, 7). The evening before his death, Jesus had told his disciples that he was about to pour out his blood "for many for the forgiveness of sins" (Matthew 26:28). The New Testament writers saw in Jesus "our Passover lamb" (1 Corinthians 5:7), a "lamb without blemish or defect" (1 Peter 1:19).

The death Jesus died was no accident; it was the heel strike of the serpent—and the blow that would crush the serpent's skull (Genesis 3:15). Jesus' death on the cross was the conclusive sacrifice to pay for humanity's sins and welcome them back into relationship with God: "While we were God's enemies, we were reconciled to him through the death of his Son" (Romans 5:10).

THE CALL REISSUED

THE ISAIAH PROPHECY, WHICH we mentioned of the man "pierced for our transgressions . . . crushed for our iniquities," follows up the man's death with a strange twist. First, Isaiah made it clear that the man was clearly dead. "He was cut off from the land of the living," Isaiah explained. "He was assigned a grave. . . . He poured out his life unto death" (Isaiah 53:8, 9, 12). And yet here's the twist: somehow God would see the man's sacrifice unto death and would "prolong his days" (v. 10).

Similarly, each of the Gospels—Matthew, Mark, Luke, and John—ends with a remarkable twist. Here's the backdrop: Jesus was dead. A soldier even made doubly sure by thrusting a spear into Jesus' side, "bringing a sudden flow of blood and water" (John 19:34). They placed his corpse in a tomb on Friday and sealed it with a stone. Yet on Sunday, when some of his women disciples approached the tomb to put spices on the body, the stone was rolled away. The tomb was empty. Jesus' body was gone. They rushed and told the other disciples, some of whom ran to the tomb and confirmed their story.

Yet the disciples' panic was met by Jesus' invitation to receive peace.

> Jesus himself stood among them and said to them, "Peace be with you." They were startled and frightened, thinking they saw a ghost. He said to them, "Why are you troubled, and why do doubts rise in your minds? Look at my hands and my feet. It is I myself! Touch me and see; a ghost does not have flesh and bones, as you see I have." (Luke 24:36–39)

Jesus appeared to his disciples on numerous occasions. He died, but he was now alive. The resurrected Jesus wasted no time in preparing his disciples for their task. Shortly, he would leave and return to his Father, but he would send the Holy Spirit to indwell them and propel them to carry on his mission. The Gospel of Matthew ends with Jesus giving his disciples a call similar in scope to the call God had given Abram millennia before:

> All authority in heaven and on earth has been given to me. Therefore go and make disciples of all nations, baptizing them in the name of the Father and of the Son and of the Holy Spirit, and teaching them to obey everything I have commanded you. And surely I am with you always, to the very end of the age. (Matthew 28:18b–20)

The Father, Son, and Spirit have never lost their desire to bring their image bearers back into the family fold. All three work together to rescue and renew us to our original intended purpose.

THE SERPENT RESURFACED

YET THIS RESTORATION OF God's wayward children does not go unchallenged. As the apostle John relates a vision he received from Jesus, in the apocalypse of Revelation, he describes violent persecution and cultural seduction of the church coming from villains such as a harlot drunk on the blood of God's people and a beast who demands worship or decapitation. Pulling the strings behind the scenes is a ferocious dragon (Revelation 13:2). We have seen him before.

John describes the dragon as "that ancient serpent called the devil, or Satan, who leads the whole world astray" (Revelation 12:9). And in a grand reversal, this ancient serpent is at long last seized, judged, and cast out forever, finally making way for the people of God to return from their exile from paradise.

THE TREE OF LIFE RESTORED

THEN JUST AS THE grand metanarrative began, it ends with access to a tree of life—this time in a garden-city paradise. In the new heavens and new earth, the people of God once again live in perfect peace and without fear of death. The eternal relationship of love welcomes us back to our prepared place at the family table. Whereas in the beginning, "God created the heavens and the earth" (Genesis 1:1), we are now invited into a "new heaven and a new earth" (Revelation 21:1). Here, "God's dwelling place is now among the people, and he will dwell with them" (v. 3). With God living among his people at last, he will bring into fullest reality the hints of heaven that Jesus had demonstrated while he walked on the old earth: No more tears. No more pain. Death is swallowed up in life. The old order of things is reversed (v. 4). John describes the scene:

> He who was seated on the throne said, "I am making everything new!" . . . Then the angel showed me the river of the water of life, as clear as crystal, flowing from the throne of God and of the Lamb. . . . On each side of the river stood the tree of life, bearing twelve crops of fruit, yielding its fruit every month. And the leaves of the tree are for the healing of the nations. No longer will there be any curse. (Revelation 21: 5; 22:1–3a)

Some of the scenes of the grand metanarrative were scary and scarring. Yet this final chapter is like a baby's birth after hours of labor. The gladness of the new heaven and new earth will put in purposeful perspective any pain that came before.

NOW WHAT?

INSPIRING AS ITS ENDING may be, the grand metanarrative of Scripture is not an escape from the real world like a favorite novel can be. Rather, this narrative calls us to join in and participate. This is *our* story. As such, we have a part to play in the particular pages into which God has written us. As the people of God

WE PARTICIPATE IN A REAL-LIFE STORY.

today, we live between the call to go make disciples and the final defeat of the serpent. This grand metanarrative is a matter of real life. In fact, the grand metanarrative of Scripture is precisely what gives our lives meaning and significance. For we are not mere dots on a timeline that will eventually taper off into extinction. Rather, we participate in a real-life story that will continue forever.

Stories can be powerful—especially ones that tell of restoration. Even more powerful are stories of restoration that are true. Imagine how much more power a story holds that promises restoration, is true, *and* invites you to be one of its characters. That is our story, and it's found in our family album.

4

THEOLOGY STARTS HERE

The stories we covered in the content of this book are more than just *stories*. They are movements in God's grand metanarrative. This metanarrative is the story of history from before the beginning to after the ending. It is all-encompassing. It is reality's story. What's beautiful about it is that it's also *our story*.

Real Life Theology is rooted in the recognition that we are part of God's grand metanarrative. This story tells us that we are and have always been loved by our Father in heaven. That who we are can be summed up in one word: "His." It forms our life's mission. And it gives our hopes shape and substance. Within it, we can live as children delighting to hear again and again our stories found in our family album.

The garden, the serpent, the call, the lamb, the community, the kingdom, the temple, and the covenant are more than timeline markers. They tell our stories; they anchor our identities. We were exiles from Eden who are now citizens of the coming paradise. We were snakebit sinners who are now the ones under whose feet God will soon crush Satan (Romans 16:20). We were the nations Abram was called to bless, and at the same time, we are called by Jesus to make disciples of the nations. We were the families huddled behind the door with lamb's blood while God's wrath passed over, just as we are now the heavenly congregation that worships the "Lamb, looking as if it had been slain, standing at the center of the throne" (Revelation 5:6). We are God's community, citizens of his kingdom, Spirit-dwelt temples, and heirs of his covenant promises.

REMAINING IN HIM

WE ARE GOD'S COMMUNITY, CITIZENS OF HIS KINGDOM, SPIRIT-DWELT TEMPLES, AND HEIRS OF HIS COVENANT PROMISES.

"Remain." . . . at first glance, this word can sound dull and stagnant. Instead of moving forward, you remain where you're at. Instead of going out and accomplishing something, you remain in place.

Yet there are also instances where "remaining" is the only way to accomplish something. For example, let's say a tree branch has its own free will and decides that it is tired of living in the same place all its life. Let's say it twists this way and that until it wriggles itself free from the trunk. Finally free from the rest of the tree, the branch is now in a free fall.

Will the disconnected branch continue to sprout leaves each spring? Will it bear fruit like the other branches who remain on the tree?

Jesus used the metaphor of branches to explain the importance of remaining *in him*: "I am the vine; you are the branches. If you remain in me and I in you, you will bear much fruit; apart from me you can do nothing. If you do not remain in me, you are like a branch that is thrown away and withers" (John 15:5–6a).

These words are meant for you and me as believers, but we can go a step further and apply this to theology. Real Life Theology remains in Christ and bears fruit. It is not meant to be an extra five hundred pounds of intellectual corpulence for us to lug around. Rather, it's meant to be a bulking up of spiritual power for the building up of the church in love. As the apostle Paul puts it, "Knowledge puffs up while love builds up" (1 Corinthians 8:1b).

Our character counts in theology. When we do theology within God's grand metanarrative, we are equipped with virtues crucial to the task. As children, we come humbly, knowing that we do theology not as clever innovators but as wide-eyed discoverers. We come wisely, ready to learn and put into practice. We come securely, knowing our Father's love and our identity as his beloved children. We come gently, ready to "help the weak [and] be patient with everyone" (1 Thessalonians 5:14). Most of all, we come as people who "love because he first loved us" (1 John 4:19). Like Jesus, we can love well because we know where we come from and where we are going:

"Jesus knew . . . that he had come from God and was returning to God; so he got up from the meal, . . . poured water into a basin and began to wash his disciples' feet." (John 13:3–5)

God's grand metanarrative invites us to live this way. When we know where we've come from, whose we are, where we're going—and the answers to other questions we've raised in this book—our Real Life Theology can accomplish much fruit in our lives and in those we influence.

AVOIDING DITCHES

WHEN WE TAKE OUR theology away from God's story, we keep it from remaining in Christ and bearing fruit. As a result, it tumbles off and goes in one of two main directions. Or to use the metaphor of a road, theology whose aim is not making disciples of Jesus will veer off into one of two ditches.

On one side of the ditch lies "ineffective traditionalism." This is an approach to theology that roots its conclusions not in the way of Jesus but in whatever way the person or community has traditionally thought and behaved. Because it's rooted in at least *something*, this theology can feel like faithfulness. But without dedicated pursuit of the way of Jesus, it ends up being mere traditionalism and lacking the power to transform. This is a theology that says, "This is the way we've always done things, so this is the way we'll always do things." No strategizing is made on how to reach the culture. It's a wagon-circling approach that feels validating to insiders all the while leaving outsiders out in the cold. Rather than disciple making, the goal of this theology is tradition keeping.

On the other side of the ditch lies what we can call "unfaithful progressivism." This is a rewriting of the script of Christianity in order to play well with cultural sensibilities. Rather than strategically reaching the culture, which the traditionalist has forgotten how to do, the progressives immerse themselves so deeply into culture that they allow the culture to rewrite their theology. Progressivism is often an overreaction to traditionalism. In the attempt to cut through obstacles between people and God, the progressive loses the ability to discern between disposable tradition and timeless truth. Progressive theology tends to treat obedience to God's Word as an unnecessary obstruction to faith, especially when God's ways are culturally unpopular.

Between these two ditches is a Real Life Theology rooted in God's grand metanarrative and committed to Jesus' Great Commission to "make disciples of all nations" (Matthew 28:19). As such, it avoids both unfaithfulness and ineffectiveness. Our family album is full of stories of how God is faithful to his people through the good times and the bad. It teaches us to remain faithful to him and to his Word—regardless of the cost. Likewise, our grand metanarrative tells of God clearing away obstacles between himself and us, whether they be personal, cultural, social, or anything else. He cares about effectiveness in reaching lost people. So when we live out Real Life Theology, we remain committed to cultural effectiveness. Our ministry can be biblically faithful and culturally effective. We are not disembodied minds contemplating ethereal ideas; rather, we do theology as in-the-flesh "ambassadors," with God making his appeal through us.

FUELING DISCIPLE MAKING

ALTHOUGH MY (TONY) ACADEMIC career included a Master of Divinity and two doctorates, I went to school as a part-time student. Even though this approach meant stretching the degrees out over multiple years, it was important for me to go to school part-time so I could serve in the local church. This on-the-job training enabled me to apply what I was learning to my disciple making. And taught me a lesson that is with me still.

As I studied theology, I would ask myself: *Okay, how can I teach this in children's church?* I loved those little disciples and wanted to use my theological studies somehow to serve them. It usually meant finding and telling the most appropriate biblical stories. The children taught me through this process that Real Life Theology is much more than a matter of the head; it's full-body engagement involving our head, heart, hands, and feet. It's a matter of asking, *How can what I'm learning help us love God and others better? How can this help fuel effective disciple making? Have I really learned this well enough to feed his lambs and take care of his little ones?*

Recently, I (Mihai) had students who were unable to return to their home countries because of COVID-19. They remained on campus and needed something to do during the summer. So we made regular trips into the villages in Moldova to implement what they had learned in the theology classes they took with me. As one example of putting our theology into practice, the students began doing what they could to serve a man who had fallen out of a building from multiple stories, had broken many bones, and was bedridden. God used their service to this man in a powerful way, and now the man is doing much better. In fact, he will walk soon, his mother came to know Jesus and was baptized, and while his father has not yet come to faith, he is visiting the church.

This may sound like a strange way to end a theology book, but the truth is, we were never called in the Bible merely to teach or to learn theology. Technically, our most fundamental job is not even to teach Scripture. I (Tony) often give my graduate students around the world an interesting test. I quote to them the Great Commission and afterward, I will ask if I've left anything out:

> Jesus came to them and said, "All authority in heaven and on earth has been given to me. Therefore go and make disciples of all nations, baptizing them in the name of the Father and of the Son and of the Holy Spirit, and teaching them everything I have commanded you. And surely I am with you always, to the very end of the age."

"Have I left anything out?"
Pause. No hands go up. No answers are given.
"Are you sure I didn't leave anything out?"
"No, I don't think so."
Then I will explain that I did, in fact, leave out two words—two very important words. Here's the first half of verse twenty with the words I had left out:

> And teaching them *to obey* everything I have commanded you.

We often don't realize how much we consume biblical knowledge but neglect obedience.

We study Scripture. We do theology. But our fundamental job is not to teach Scripture or theology. Rather, our fundamental job is to teach *obedience*. It's about trusting and following Jesus, whatever the cost. That's a mission that no amount of reasoning about abstract concepts convinces us to take.

But when we know and love our heavenly Father with our identity firmly in him and his family album, we feel his pleasure. Especially when we bring his lost children back home. He smiles with great joy every time we bring one of them to their waiting chair at his table.

OUR FUNDAMENTAL JOB IS TO TEACH OBEDIENCE.

APPENDIX

Andrew Murray, *The Believer's School of Prayer* (Minneapolis: Bethany House, 1982).

M. Robert Mulholland, Jr., *Invitation to a Journey: A Road Map for Spiritual Formation* (Downers Grove: InterVarsity Press, 1993).

Allan Coppedge, *Portraits of God: A Biblical Theology of Holiness* (Downers Grover: InterVarsity Press, 2001).

Dallas Willard, *Renovation of the Heart: Putting on the Character of Christ* (Colorado Springs: NavPress, 2002).

Dallas Willard, *The Spirit of the Disciplines: Understanding How God Changes Lives* (San Francisco: HarperSanFrancisco, 1988).

NOTES

1. Jared Ellis, "Sustained by a Story," Renew.org, accessed May 1, 2021, https://renew.org/sustained-by-a-story/.

2. James Bard, "Reaching the Unreached with Stories," Renew.org, accessed May 1, 2021, https://renew.org/reaching-the-unreached-with-stories/.

3. We like very much this definition of spiritual formation given by M. Robert Mulholland in *Invitation to a Journey: A Road Map for Spiritual Formation* (Downers Grove: InterVarsity Press, 1993), 12.

4. Kenneth Leech makes the point that the God of the Old Testament is the God of the wilderness, and it was in the process of wandering that Abraham and his children encountered the living God. See Kenneth Leech, *Experiencing God: Theology as Spirituality* (Eugene: Wipf and Stock Publishers, 2002).

GOD'S WORD

**THE INSPIRATION
AND AUTHORITY
OF SCRIPTURE**

ORPHEUS J. HEYWARD

To my family. I am appreciative of the friendship of my wife, Sony. I am also grateful to my two vibrant children, Nevaeh and Nehemiah. Thank you for your support during this most difficult time.

CONTENTS

General Editors' Note 69

Introduction 71

CHAPTER 1: What Is the Old Testament? 75

CHAPTER 2: What Is the New Testament? 85

CHAPTER 3: How Did We Get Our Bible? 95

CHAPTER 4: How Do We Interpret the Bible? 103

CHAPTER 5: How Is the Bible Our Final Authority? 115

Appendix A: Book Recommendations for Further Study 123

Appendix B: The Apocrypha 125

Notes 129

GENERAL EDITORS' NOTE

Theology for disciples of Jesus must come from Scripture. But studying Scripture leads to questions: What are the main themes of the Bible? What does it mean to say the Bible is "inspired"? And how did it come down to us in our day?

Orpheus J. Heyward is a helpful guide as we seek answers to these types of questions. He is the Senior Minister of the Renaissance Church of Christ. Having received his Master of Arts in Theology, Master of Arts in Biblical Studies, and Doctor of Ministry in Theological Exegesis, he is a constant student of the Bible.

This book expounds on the section from the Renew.org Leaders' Faith Statement called "God's Word":

> We believe God gave us the sixty-six books of the Bible to be received as the inspired, authoritative, and infallible Word of God for salvation and life. The documents of Scripture come to us as diverse literary and historical writings. Despite their complexities, they can be understood, trusted, and followed. We want to do the hard work of wrestling to understand Scripture in order to obey God. We want to avoid the errors of interpreting Scripture through the sentimental lens of our feelings and opinions or through a complex re-interpretation of plain meanings so that the Bible says what our culture says. Ours is a time for both clear thinking and courage. Because the Holy Spirit inspired all sixty-six books, we honor Jesus' Lordship by submitting our lives to all that God has for us in them.

> *See the full Network Faith Statements at the end of this book.

Support Scriptures: *Psalm 1; 119; Deuteronomy 4:1–6; Deuteronomy 6:1–9; 2 Chronicles 34; Nehemiah 8; Matthew 5:1–7:28; 15:6–9; John 12:44–50;*

Matthew 28:19; Acts 2:42; Acts 17:10–11; 2 Timothy 3:16–4:4; 1 Peter 1:20–21.

The following tips might help you use this book more effectively (and the other books in the *Real Life Theology* series):

1. *Five questions, answers, and Scriptures.* We framed this book around five key questions with five short answers and five notable Scriptures. This format provides clarity, making it easier to commit crucial information to memory. This format also enables the books in the *Real Life Theology* series to support our catechism. Our catechism is a series of fixed questions and answers for instruction in church or home. In all, the series has fifty-two questions, answers, and key Scriptures. This particular book focuses on the five that are most pertinent to God's Word.

2. *Summary videos.* You can find three to seven-minute video teachings that summarize the book, as well as each chapter, at Renew.org. These short videos can function as standalone teachings. But for groups or group leaders using the book, they can also be used to launch discussion of the reading.

May God use this book to fuel faithful and effective disciple making in your life and church.

For King Jesus,
Bobby Harrington and Daniel McCoy
General Editors, *Real Life Theology* Series

INTRODUCTION

God has spoken. The author of the book of Hebrews writes, "In the past God spoke to our ancestors." But how did he speak? The writer continues by describing how God spoke: "through the prophets at many times and in various ways." Yet God didn't stop there. He then gave us his culminating Word: Jesus Christ: "But in these last days he has spoken to us by his Son" (Hebrews 1:1–2).

God has not left his people without the benefit of his voice. His words have long functioned as a guide to the people of God. His message finds climax in what Jesus spoke in these last days through his apostles. In this passage, the author of the book of Hebrews covers the spectrum of both old and new covenant history, declaring that God has provided his words in "the prophets" of long ago and in the person of Jesus.

> **GOD HAS NOT LEFT HIS PEOPLE WITHOUT THE BENEFIT OF HIS VOICE.**

The God who spoke throughout biblical-era history ensured that the spoken revelation would be written down. God's written Word of the Old Testament is often referred to in the Bible as "the Writings" (often translated "Scripture" or "the Scriptures"). In 2 Timothy 3:16–17, the apostle Paul provides a description of Scripture that gives insight into its nature:

> All Scripture is God-breathed and is useful for teaching, rebuking, correcting and training in righteousness, so that the servant of God may be thoroughly equipped for every good work. (2 Timothy 3:16–17)

The word that Paul uses for "inspired" (*theopneustos*) is an adjective that carries the meaning of God's *breathing* or *blowing*. The point is that God is the source of Scripture; it is "breathed out" by him. A look at the context of these verses shows that Paul has in mind the Old Testament Scriptures (2 Timothy 3:15). Yet there is reason to think that Paul would also see this description as applying to the full corpus of Scripture, including the New Testament writings. We see this through Paul's use of a New Testament passage, as he places it next to an Old Testament passage and treats both as having equal authority. Notice in 1 Timothy 5:17–18 as Paul addresses the elders who labor in preaching and teaching:

> The elders who direct the affairs of the church well are worthy of double honor, especially those whose work is preaching and teaching. For Scripture says, "Do not muzzle an ox while it is treading out the grain," and "The worker deserves his wages." (1 Timothy 5:17–18)

In establishing the precedent that we should honor elders who labor in preaching and teaching, Paul provides two citations. The first reference is from Deuteronomy 25:4. The second reference is from Luke 10:7. This suggests that Paul believed that both Old and New Testament writings were "Scripture," thus treating both as authoritative.

The purpose of the book you're reading is to show how God's Word has been given by God, written by chosen writers under the guidance of the Holy Spirit, and that it teaches what we need to know for life and godliness. As Paul wrote in 2 Timothy 3:16–17, these inspired writings are beneficial for teaching, reproof, correction, and training in righteousness. Through the providential care of God, these Scriptures have been collected and preserved for perpetual use by God's people.

In the chapters that follow, I intend to lead you through a study of five questions that will focus on God's Word as sacred communication, which must be handled appropriately. These questions are:

1. What is the Old Testament?
2. What is the New Testament?
3. How did we get our Bible?
4. How do we interpret the Bible?
5. How is the Bible our final authority?

May the answers to these fundamental questions encourage you to engage with biblical texts and gain more insight into God's Word and character.

We will look at how the Bible teaches us God's commands and covenants throughout history. We will explore how the Bible came into existence, how it functions authoritatively for God's people, and how it should be responsibly interpreted so we can understand the meaning of God's communication. Although 2 Timothy 2:15 was written to a particular evangelist in a local church, the verse teaches us all how we should handle God's Word: "Be diligent to present yourself approved to God as a worker who does not need to be ashamed, accurately handling the word of truth" (NASB). To this worthy end, let's begin our exploration of God's Word.

1

WHAT IS THE OLD TESTAMENT?

Answer: The Old Testament is thirty-nine books containing God's promises, covenant laws, and guidance for ancient Israel throughout its history. It served as a tutor to lead Israel to recognize their need for a coming Messiah.

I will praise you with an upright heart as I learn your righteous laws.
— Psalm 119:7

Throughout the years, people use the term "Old Testament" in two main ways: The content of the Old Testament books, and the old covenant as a governing law for Israel. For instance, consider this statement: "God commanded Israel to build the tabernacle in the Old Testament." And consider another statement, which uses the term the same way: "I read in the Old Testament how God brought Israel out of Egyptian bondage." When used in this first way, "Old Testament" means the content of the Old Testament books ranging from Genesis to Malachi.

Let's consider the second way in which "Old Testament" is sometimes used: the old covenant as a governing law. For example, you may have heard a person say, "Keeping the Sabbath is a part of the Old Testament," or, "'You should not covet' is a command in the Old Testament." When used this way, "Old Testament" can be a term referring to the content of the law that God gave when Israel met God at Mount Sinai. In this way, "Old Testament" is a synonym of "old covenant," the sacred promise God made with the Hebrew people at Mount Sinai. Both usages are accurate and proper when used appropriately.

It should also be noted that the phrase "Old Testament" is not a phrase used by the authors of Scripture. Christians first used it as a designation for the Hebrew

Scriptures. The Hebrew Scriptures were traditionally divided by Jewish people into a twofold categorization of "Law and Prophets" (see Luke 24:27), or sometimes into a threefold categorization of "the Law, Prophets, and the Writings" (see a possible allusion to this in Luke 24:44, where "Psalms" is shorthand for "the Writings"). The Jewish Bible is still categorized according to law, prophets, and writings, while our Protestant Bible organizes the books more according to literary types: law, history, poetry, and prophecy (first Major Prophets, then Minor Prophets).[1]

Before describing particular books in the Old Testament, let's flesh out the threefold division (law, prophets, and writings) a little more. The first five books of the Bible, often referred to as the "law of Moses," are also referred to as the "Torah" or the "Pentateuch." "Torah" is a Hebrew word that means "instruction" or "law." So when it's used to refer to the first five books of the Bible, it emphasizes these books as God's law. The term "Pentateuch" (from Greek, *pentateukos*) starts with *"penta"* (Greek for "five") and highlights these books as a five-volume compilation: Genesis through Deuteronomy. After the law of Moses comes the prophets. These included many of the books from Joshua to Ezekiel, as well as the collection of twelve books commonly called the "Minor Prophets." The third and last division ("the Writings") included Psalms, Proverbs, Job, Song of Solomon, Ruth, Lamentations, Ecclesiastes, Esther, Daniel, Ezra, Nehemiah, and 1 and 2 Chronicles.

"THE WRITINGS"	PSALMS, PROVERBS, JOB, SOLOMON'S SONG, RUTH, LAMENTATIONS, ECCLESIASTES, ESTHER, DANIEL, EZRA, NEHEMIAH, 1 CHRONICLES, 2 CHRONICLES
"THE PROPHETS"	JOSHUA, JUDGES, 1 SAMUEL, 2 SAMUEL, 1 KINGS, 2 KINGS, ISAIAH, JEREMIAH, EZEKIEL, THE TWELVE MINOR PROPHETS
"THE LAW"	GENESIS, EXODUS, LEVITICUS, NUMBERS, DEUTERONOMY

Now, let's take a deeper dive into the content of the Old Testament books before moving on to the concept of "covenant," which is one of the central concepts in understanding the Old Testament.

THE CONTENT OF THE LAW

IT CAN BE A little confusing to set out to read the five books of the law and realize that, instead of lists of laws, it starts with stories. In fact, much of the content of the first five books of the Bible is narrative. Although these books do include the content of the laws God provided Israel, they are set in the unfolding of history as God shaped his chosen people. These first five books provide ancient Israel with a historical perspective of their development into a people beginning with the first man, Adam, and culminating with their preparation to receive the promised land of Canaan.

The order of the first five books—Genesis, Exodus, Leviticus, Numbers, and Deuteronomy—follows a chronological order of historical events. After narrating God's creation of the world, Genesis describes the apostasy of mankind (Genesis 3–11) and then the formation of a chosen people through Abraham (Genesis 12–50). Genesis gives ancient Israel a documented history of their founding in the twelve sons of Abraham's grandson Jacob/Israel (the "twelve tribes of Israel") and their subsequent move to Egypt to survive (through God's providentially working through Joseph) during the famine (Genesis 50:19–20). This ultimately sets up the reader to prepare to understand their dramatic exodus from Egypt (narrated in the book of Exodus).

After the Jewish people in Egypt were enslaved, God brought them out of Egyptian bondage through Moses (Exodus 3:7–11). The reader is invited into the experience of how God moved Israel from being slaves in a foreign nation to becoming his covenant people. After God delivered them from Egypt through a series of miracles, they received God's law at Mount Sinai (Exodus 19–24).

We read many more of God's laws in the book of Leviticus as well as in the book of Numbers. Leviticus is named after the Israelite tribe of Levi, which was set apart to serve in the temple; hence, Leviticus contains laws detailing such rituals as temple sacrifices. Numbers narrates how the Israelites were numbered according to tribe in order to prepare for their entrance into the promised land.

The people of God had lost their resolve to enter the promised land, so they wandered, even as God led them, in the wilderness. They wandered for decades before they were ready to finally enter the land. At the culmination of this wandering, Moses prepared Israel to take possession of the promised land prior to his death. Before entering, the new generation was reminded of God's law, which was told to them in the book of Deuteronomy (a word meaning "second law").

From a theological perspective, these first five books begin to unfold God's purpose to destroy the works of the serpent, who tempted the first humans to reject God's authority (Genesis 3). God created a good world that was cursed when Adam and Eve chose to obey the serpent's words over God's. In Genesis 3:15, God declared his purpose to eventually defeat evil through the "woman's offspring." This prophecy is commonly referred to as the "proto-evangelium" (Greek for "first gospel") in which God declared that the offspring of the woman would be victorious over the offspring of the serpent, resulting in the crushing of the serpent's head. This enmity between the people of God and the forces of evil was displayed throughout Old Testament history, beginning with the conflict of Cain and Abel (Genesis 4:1–8) and continuing on through the church's perpetual conflict with Satan as they follow Jesus in the face of persecution.

This promise of victory over the serpent was ultimately achieved by Jesus:

> The one who does what is sinful is of the devil, because the devil has been sinning from the beginning. The reason the Son of God appeared was to destroy the devil's work. (1 John 3:8)

Similarly, Paul declares victory for the church over Satan during the days of antagonism from the Roman Empire:

> Everyone has heard about your obedience, so I rejoice because of you; but I want you to be wise about what is good, and innocent about what is evil. The God of peace will soon crush Satan under your feet. The grace of our Lord Jesus be with you. (Romans 16:19–20)

To this end, clearly the events of the Pentateuch should be understood through its own announcement of the promise of God to destroy the works of the serpent, later revealed to be Satan himself (Revelation 20:2). Every subsequent move of the hand of God in the history of humanity, Israel, and the church is to fulfill this promise.

THE CONTENT OF THE PROPHETS

THE PROPHETS IS THE second division of the Hebrew Old Testament. These books include what's often categorized as the Former Prophets, the Later Prophets, and the Minor Prophets (the Minor Prophets is also known as the Book of the Twelve).

- The Former Prophets: Joshua, Judges, Samuel, Kings
- The Later Prophets: Isaiah, Jeremiah, Ezekiel
- The Minor Prophets (the Twelve): Hosea, Joel, Amos, Obadiah, Jonah, Micah, Nahum, Habakkuk, Zephaniah, Haggai, Zechariah, Malachi

The writings of the Former Prophets are actually part of what are known in the Protestant Bible as the books of history. These books describe Israel's conquest and settlement in the land of Canaan, where they were ruled, first by Israelite judges and then by Israelite kings. The book of Joshua is named after Moses's successor who led them into Canaan. The book of Judges describes a pattern of Israel's rebellion against God, followed by God's deliverance from foreign nations through raising up Israelite judges. The books of Samuel and the Kings cover Israel's ups and downs under the reign of a kingship system beginning with King Saul, eventually splitting into two kingdoms ("Israel" in the north, "Judah" in the south), which were both defeated and carried into exile by foreign empires (the north by Assyria, the south by Babylon).

The Later Prophets include three of the prophets known in the Protestant Bible as Major Prophets: Isaiah, Jeremiah, Ezekiel. The Minor Prophets are shorter books also known as the "Twelve" (e.g., in the Septuagint, an ancient Greek translation of the Old Testament). It is important to note that these Minor Prophets are called "minor" only on the basis of their length and not based on their significance. It is plausible that Stephen, the first Christian martyr, references these books in Acts 7:42 in his speech to the Jewish authorities when he mentions the "book of the prophets" and goes on to reference Amos 5:25–27.

These prophetic books continued to lead the Jews through the dissolution of their kingdoms—the northern and southern tribes—and throughout their captivity among foreign nations. Prophets reminded the people to follow God's laws and not to lose hope of future restoration, even through very difficult times. For example, Israel and Judah's experiences at

PROPHETS REMINDED THE PEOPLE TO FOLLOW GOD'S LAWS.

the hands of Assyria shed light on the books of Hosea, Amos, and Micah. The demise of Assyria and the rise of Babylon function as the background for Nahum, Habakkuk, and Zephaniah. The restoration of Judah under the Persian Empire provides context to the books of Haggai, Zechariah, and Malachi.

THE CONTENT OF THE WRITINGS

THE WRITINGS CONSIST OF:

- The Psalms: a book of 150 songs to be used in worship
- The Proverbs: a collection of wise sayings for ethical instruction
- Job: a book of poetry following the tragedies of a follower of God trying to determine the source of his sufferings
- The Song of Songs: a poetic celebration of romantic love
- Ruth: a story of a Moabite woman who accepts the Jewish God and joins the Jewish people
- Lamentations: reflections on the fall of Jerusalem to the Babylonians
- Ecclesiastes: reflections on the meaning of life in an often-senseless world
- Esther: the story of a Jewish woman who becomes a Persian queen
- Daniel: a book that records both history and prophecy through the lens of a trusted Jewish official in Babylon during the exile
- Ezra–Nehemiah: a narration of the rebuilding of the Jewish homeland after their return under the Persians
- Chronicles: a record of the events of Samuel and Kings

The Writings were used to explicate life under the law, facilitate worship, and function as a corpus of wisdom literature. Five of these—the Song of Songs, Ruth, Lamentations, Ecclesiastes, and Esther—form a category known as "the Five" or *Megilloth*, meant to be publicly read, one at each of the five major Jewish holidays.

The Hebrew Bible makes a total of twenty-four books. Why then does the Protestant Bible list thirty-nine books? It's the same content packaged differently. The books of Samuel, Kings, and Chronicles are each divided into two parts (e.g., 1 and 2 Samuel). Ezra–Nehemiah is treated as two books. The Minor Prophets are listed as twelve separate books.

As mentioned earlier, it is also common for the Protestant Bible to use a different categorization than the Hebrew Bible, so the books are listed in the basic progression of law (Genesis–Deuteronomy); history (Joshua–Esther); poetry (Job–Song of Solomon, sometimes referred to as wisdom literature); and prophecy (both Major and Minor Prophets).

LAW	Genesis, Exodus, Leviticus, Numbers, Deuteronomy
HISTORY	Joshua, Judges, Ruth, 1 Samuel, 2 Samuel, 1 Kings, 2 Kings, 1 Chronicles, 2 Chronicles, Ezra, Nehemiah, Esther
POETRY	Job, Psalms, Proverbs, Ecclesiastes, Song of Songs
MAJOR PROPHETS	Isaiah, Jeremiah, Lamentations, Ezekiel, Daniel
MINOR PROPHETS	Hosea, Joel, Amos, Obadiah, Jonah, Micah, Nahum, Habakkuk, Zephaniah, Haggai, Zechariah, Malachi

UNDERSTANDING THE OLD TESTAMENT AS COVENANT

As I mentioned, "Old Testament" can carry one of two different meanings. Let's focus now on the second, less common meaning, which refers to the old covenant law given by God through Moses. When biblical writers of both the Old and New Testaments speak of a "new covenant," this implies the existence of an old covenant. The author of the New Testament book of Hebrews contrasts the two covenants and draws the conclusion that the new covenant is superior, built on better promises and through an even better lawgiver than Moses. Such an argument was designed to dissuade the Jewish recipients of the letter from retreating back into Judaism. Hebrews 8:6 explains that Jesus "has obtained a more excellent ministry, to the extent that He is also the mediator of a better covenant, which has been enacted on better promises" (NASB). The writer of Hebrews goes on to contrast this covenant through Jesus with the "first covenant," which was broken by the people. With the first covenant broken, God sought to establish a "second" covenant, which was predicted by the Old Testament prophet Jeremiah (Jeremiah 31:31–34).

This old covenant was the law given to Israel at Mount Sinai, summarized in the Ten Commandments. Taken altogether, the law functioned as a national law to govern the people of God. Through their acceptance of the covenant stipulations, God would make Israel a people for his own possession, a holy nation, and a kingdom of priests (Exodus 19:5–6). This covenant would inaugurate the formal relationship between God and his chosen people. The content of the law would explain their relationship to the God who delivered them from bondage, and their interpersonal relationship with the community of Israel. It was Jesus who explained the vertical (between God and people) and horizontal nature (person to person) of God's covenant laws in Matthew 22:34–40:

> Hearing that Jesus had silenced the Sadducees, the Pharisees got together. One of them, an expert in the law, tested him with this question: "Teacher, which is the greatest commandment in the Law?" Jesus replied: "'Love the Lord your God with all your heart and with all your soul and with all your mind.' This is the first and greatest commandment. And the second is like it: 'Love your neighbor as yourself.' All the Law and the Prophets hang on these two commandments." (Matthew 22:34–40)

To accent that the law teaches relationship to God and people, Jesus quoted the two greatest commandments, originally given in Deuteronomy 6:4–5 and Leviticus 19:18. In essence, the law taught to love God and love people. This covenant law anticipated the coming of the Messiah and exposed the people's need for this person.

The anticipation of his coming is expressed in Galatians 3:24–5. Paul refers to the law as a guardian that leads to Jesus: "Therefore the Law has become our guardian to lead us to Christ, so that we may be justified by faith. But now that faith has come, we are no longer under a guardian" (Galatians 3:24–25, NASB). The context here is Paul's effort to correct the folly of trying to use our obedience to the old covenant law as our grounds of our righteousness. Instead, he argues the purpose of the law was to lead to the "Messiah" (a Hebrew word translated into Greek as the word "Christ"). Additionally, the law served as a legal system condemning the law breaker at the first infraction. In other words, to be guilty of breaking one law makes one guilty of the entire system.

THE LAW TAUGHT TO LOVE GOD AND LOVE PEOPLE.

And if the law's elaborate system of animal sacrifices teaches us anything, it is that God does not leave guilt unpunished. Paul states it this way:

For all who rely on the works of the law are under a curse, as it is written: "Cursed is everyone who does not continue to do everything written in the Book of the Law." Clearly no one who relies on the law is justified before God, because "the righteous will live by faith." The law is not based on faith; on the contrary, it says, "The person who does these things will live by them." (Galatians 3:10–12)

Do any of us obey "everything written in the Book of the Law"? According to Paul, one who does not practice maintaining the entire law remains under condemnation. That's not good news, but it sets us up to be ready to hear the *good news*—a phrase encapsulated in the New Testament word "gospel." So we see the Old Testament—as thirty-nine books of Israelite history, prophecy, *and* as a system of laws—cultivates a longing for the Messiah to come and make things right. The Old Testament narrates a broken covenant and promises a new one.

It is to this Messiah, Jesus, and his new covenant that we now turn.

2

WHAT IS THE NEW TESTAMENT?

Answer: The New Testament is the apostles' teachings in twenty-seven books that reveal a new covenant through Jesus the Messiah and how the covenant was lived out in the early church.

This is the covenant I will make with the people of Israel after that time," declares the LORD. "I will put my law in their minds and write it on their hearts. I will be their God, and they will be my people.
— Jeremiah 31:33

The Old Testament ends without a resolution. Although God had been faithful to bring his people back from exile to return and rebuild their homeland, the vast majority of Old Testament prophecies remained unfulfilled at the end of the Hebrew Bible. The final words of the final prophet (Malachi) promised the reappearance of Elijah, who would turn the "hearts of the children to their fathers." And if they rejected the Godsent message, God would "strike the land with complete destruction" (Malachi 4:5–6, NASB). Who was this "Elijah" who was going to come again? In a parallel prediction, Malachi had also promised, "Behold, I am sending My messenger, and he will clear a way before Me. And the Lord, whom you are seeking, will suddenly come to His temple" (Malachi 3:1, NASB).

Although the events of the New Testament take place some four hundred years after the Old Testament's final book, the New Testament begins where the Old Testament leaves off. For starters, John the Baptist served as the Elijah "to come." His birth to aged, previously infertile parents was followed soon by the birth of Jesus, the Messiah, to a virgin betrothed to be married. John the Baptist grew up and became the "voice of one calling in the wilderness, 'Prepare the way for the Lord'" (Matthew 3:3). John pointed his followers to Jesus as Messiah, and in turn Jesus confirmed that "John himself is Elijah who was to come" (Matthew 11:14, NASB). In step with Malachi's prediction, Jesus came to Jerusalem's temple, preached the gospel to a people who predominantly rejected him (John 1:11), and predicted destruction for the city and sacred site (Matthew 24:2; Luke 23:28–31). The rest is history from there.

OVERVIEW OF THE NEW TESTAMENT CONTENT

THE NEW TESTAMENT NARRATES the life, ministry, death, and resurrection of Jesus as well as the establishment of his kingdom. His kingdom expanded throughout the then-known world, beginning with the Jews and extending to the non-Jewish world (the Gentiles). Like the Old Testament, these books cover a variety of genres such as historical narratives, letters, and apocalyptic literature. The four Gospels—Matthew, Mark, Luke, and John—are historical narratives that describe the ministry of Jesus, which culminates with his resurrection and commission of his disciples to make disciples all over the world. The New Testament also includes a history of the early church called the book of Acts.

Additionally, we have letters (also known as "epistles") written to churches and individuals, which provide instructions with regard to faith and practice. These letters can be categorized into Pauline Letters (written by Paul to specific churches and individuals) and General Letters (written by various authors without a clearly designated audience in view). The General Letters, also called "Catholic Letters" ("catholic" simply means "universal"), include correspondences written by James, Peter, John, and Jude, as well as the anonymous letter of Hebrews. The Bible ends with a prophetic book called Revelation. Most present-day Bibles—whether Protestant, Catholic, or Eastern Orthodox—arrange the books of the New Testament according to the following basic order:[2]

GOSPELS	HISTORY	LETTERS OF PAUL	GENERAL LETTERS	APOCALYPSE
Matthew	Acts of the Apostles	Romans	Hebrews	Revelation
Mark		1 Corinthians	James	
Luke		2 Corinthians	1 Peter	
John		Galatians	2 Peter	
		Ephesians	1 John	
		Philippians	2 John	
		Colossians	3 John	
		1 Thessalonians	Jude	
		2 Thessalonians		
		1 Timothy		
		2 Timothy		
		Titus		
		Philemon		

THE CONTENT OF THE GOSPELS

THE GREEK WORD TRANSLATED "gospel" (*euangelion*) originally meant "good news." The word became an appropriate word for the long-awaited message Jesus came to bring because he came with a message of hope for the hopeless and freedom for the oppressed. The first words of Jesus recorded in the Gospel of Mark are: "The time is fulfilled, and the kingdom of God is at hand; repent and believe in the gospel" (Mark 1:15, NASB). Then, when four narrations of the life of Jesus were written by his apostles or by close friends of the apostles, it also made sense to call these four documents "Gospels." The Gospels were ancient biographies written to teach us about the life and ministry of Jesus.[3]

The four Gospels taught the life of Jesus from four vantage points to four unique audiences. Because of their similar narrative order, as well as some shared content, Matthew, Mark, and Luke are considered the "Synoptic Gospels" ("synoptic" meaning "to see together"). John's Gospel is not considered a Synoptic Gospel because of its significant number of unparalleled information from the other three Gospels. Even so, each Gospel has its own unique fingerprint.

Matthew. The Gospel According to Matthew was written with a Jewish audience in mind. This is evident because Matthew's Gospel quotes a good deal of Old Testament passages with the intent of showing their fulfillment with the coming of

Jesus as the predicted Messiah. A significant word found throughout the fabric of Matthew is "fulfill" or "fulfilled." After narrating an event in Jesus' life, Matthew often connects it to the Old Testament: for example, "This took place to fulfill what the Lord had said through the prophet" (Matthew 1:22), and, "This has all taken place that the writings of the prophets might be fulfilled" (Matthew 26:56). "Fulfill" or "fulfilled" is used sixteen times in the book of Matthew, and the majority of the references draw a connection between Jesus and an Old Testament foreshadowing.

Additionally, the theme of the "kingdom of heaven" runs throughout the Gospel of Matthew. In the days of Jesus, there was a clear expectation of the coming of the kingdom of God, which had been predicted by the Old Testament writers. Many of the Jewish people of Jesus' day had anticipated a militaristic kingdom, so there was often a mismatch between expectations and Jesus' message. Yet through his many parables in the Gospel of Matthew, Jesus painted an inviting, even if surprising, picture of a kingdom that would conquer far more than a physical army could ever do. This kingdom of righteousness—described so comprehensively in Matthew's Sermon on the Mount—was a limitless treasure (Matthew 13:44) that would outlast the powers of darkness. In it, "the righteous will shine like the sun in the kingdom of their Father" (Matthew 13:43).

Mark. The Gospel According to Mark was written to a predominantly Gentile audience. We see this in how Mark describes Jewish customs (Mark 7:1–5) and phrases (Mark 5:41; 7:34; 10:46; 15:22, 34) as though his audience was unfamiliar with these things. The Gospel of Mark invites the Christian to embrace humble service as exemplified in Jesus Christ, as he explains: "Whoever wants to become great among you must be your servant. . . . For even the Son of Man did not come to be served, but to serve, and to give his life as a ransom for many" (Mark 10:43, 45). Mark's Gospel also concerns itself with the coming of the kingdom of God. Mark uses the phrase the "kingdom of God" in parallel with the "kingdom of heaven" language in the Gospel of Matthew. Then, whereas Matthew's Gospel intersperses Jesus' miraculous deeds with sermons, Mark's Gospel tends to focus more on Jesus' miracles in a fast-paced narrative that spends the final third of the book on Jesus' final week in Jerusalem before his resurrection.

Luke. The Gospel According to Luke was written to the "most excellent Theophilus" (Luke 1:3). His title suggested he was a Roman official. This Gospel was an investigated account, in which Luke carefully and accurately researched the testimony of witnesses. Through a meticulous process of documenting historical detail, Luke provides a detailed sketch of the life, death, and resurrection of Christ. His stated purpose was that Theophilus would know the "certainty" of the gospel (Luke 1:4)

The Gospel of Luke uniquely emphasizes Jesus' mission to *all* of humanity, from hopeless sinners to historic outcasts. This is not surprising, given that Luke seems to be the only Gentile author in the New Testament (with the possible exception of Hebrews). Jesus' intention to reach outside of conventional molds for making disciples can be seen in some of the parables unique to Luke's Gospel, such as the parable of the prodigal son, the parable of the good Samaritan, and the parable of the pharisee and the tax collector. Luke, a close friend of the apostle Paul, wrote his Gospel as the first in a two-part series ending with the book of Acts.

John. The Gospel According to John is considered the last of the four Gospels to be written. Written by Jesus' disciple John in his old age, this document combines a simple style with theological reflections on the events that happened when John was a young man. While the Synoptic Gospels displayed Jesus' divine nature, for example, in instances such as being incarnated and born of a virgin (Luke 1:35), forgiving sins (Matthew 9:4–6), receiving worship (Matthew 14:33), and calling himself divine names (Matthew 27:43)—the Gospel of John makes Jesus' divinity a point of emphasis. John's opening prologue places an accent on the theological truth that God became flesh: "In the beginning was the Word, and the Word was with God, and the Word was God," and, "The Word became flesh and made his dwelling among us" (John 1:1, 14). The author strategically chooses a set of seven miracles as manifestations of Jesus' divine glory. The author explains that many signs were done among the disciples, yet the ones written were so the reader would believe that Jesus is the Son of God (John 20:31–31).

The Gospel of John also includes seven "I am" statements in which Jesus fleshes out his character in a manner that matches God's way of referring to himself. In Exodus 3:14, God told Moses, "I AM WHO I AM," when Moses asked his name. In the same way, Jesus uses language that accents his divinity so the reader can clearly see the uniqueness of his sonship. For example, "I am the bread of life" (John 6:35), "I am the light of the world" (John 8:12), and "I am the way and the truth and the life" (John 14:6). At one point, Jesus even told a shocked audience, "Before Abraham was born, I am!" (John 8:58). This Gospel was written during the rise of what became known as "Gnostic" teachings, which rejected the importance of physical substance; thus, John wrote in part to remind people of the truth that God indeed came in the flesh.

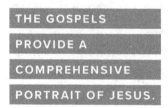

The Gospels provide a comprehensive portrait of Jesus, allowing the readers to see his central place in the scheme of redemption. The climactic death, burial, and resurrection is the destination of each Gospel while narrating different snapshots of his life and teachings to arrive at this target.

THE HISTORY OF THE CHURCH IN ACTS

THE BOOK OF ACTS plays a crucial part in the New Testament. As mentioned above, Acts is the second part of Luke's two-volume work meant to show the recipient, Theophilus, the truthfulness of Christianity. In this second volume, Luke highlights the spread of the gospel under the guidance of the Holy Spirit, who had been given to all who believed (Acts 2:17–21). Acts 1:8 is a central passage that provides a geographical outline of the book of Acts: Jesus promised, "You will receive power when the Holy Spirit has come upon you; and you shall be My witnesses both in Jerusalem and in all Judea, and Samaria, and as far as the remotest part of the earth" (NASB). Jesus' disciples went from Jerusalem (Acts 1–2) to Judea and Samaria (Acts 3–8), and the "remotest part of the earth" was a figurative way of expressing "Gentile territory" (Acts 9–28).

In Jerusalem during a celebration of the Jewish festival of Pentecost, the Holy Spirit came upon the apostles. As a result, they began to speak supernaturally in the native languages of the gathered celebrants. On that first day, three thousand people were baptized into Jesus, and the church began devoting themselves to "the apostles' teaching and to fellowship, to the breaking of bread and to prayer" (Acts 2:42).

As I mentioned, Acts explains how the gospel spread outward from Jerusalem, reaching people as diverse from each other as an Ethiopian government official (Acts 8), a Roman centurion (Acts 10), a Greek jailer (Acts 16), and—very notably—a Jewish Pharisee who had hated the new faith and tried to stamp it out by force (Acts 9). While the apostle Peter took a central role in the first chapters of the book, it was the former hater of the faith—Luke's mentor Paul—whose missionary travels take center stage for the latter half of the book. Acts ends with Paul's arrival as a prisoner at the seat of imperial power: Rome. Acts describes a church that faced persecution with resilience and theological disputes with grace, truth, and dependence on the Holy Spirit.

PAULINE LETTERS

PAUL WAS RESPONSIBLE FOR writing thirteen letters of the New Testament. Having accomplished three recorded missionary journeys, Paul had a tremendous influence over the churches throughout the known world at the time. These letters cover a variety of circumstances. Several of the letters express Paul's intimate relationship with the churches he planted. The different occasions birth a variety of thematic emphases.

Throughout the letters of Paul, we find efforts to bring clarity to the doctrine of the grace of God, explaining that the law was not a means to establishing right standing with God. While the law of Moses exposed sin, it was incapable of eradicating sin. This thematic emphasis is seen in letters such as Romans and Galatians. The heresy of binding the Jewish law upon Gentiles as a means for them to obtain righteousness before God was designated by Paul as a "different gospel" (Galatians 1:6–10).

In other letters like the Corinthians correspondences, Paul takes on a pastoral posture when troubleshooting malignant behaviors within the life of the congregation. We can see this in 1 and 2 Corinthians when Paul addressed a spirit of division that permeated the church at Corinth. Their divisions arose from a number of issues. For example, some of them separated into factions based on which preacher had delivered the gospel to them (1 Corinthians 1:10–13). They took each other before the law for trivial matters (1 Corinthians 6). They engaged in practices such as eating meat offered to idols, which was insensitive toward fellow Christians (1 Corinthians 8). They manifested arrogance over whose gift was superior in the church (1 Corinthians 12).

It is also common to witness Paul as an encourager promoting unity and faithfulness among believers. Take, for example, his letter to a Christian named Philemon to appeal that Philemon accept back his escaped slave, "no longer as a slave, but better than a slave, as a dear brother" (Philemon 1:16), or his letter to the Philippians, inviting a disposition of joy in the midst of their suffering as a church. There are letters with end times concerns, in which the letter is intended to clarify the nature of our hope in Christ. There are also the "Pastoral Epistles"—1 and 2 Timothy and Titus—by which Paul sought to explain "how people ought to conduct themselves in God's household, which is the church of the living God, the pillar and foundation of the truth" (1 Timothy 3:15). The Pauline epistles account for almost half of the New Testament and provide insight into the ethics of the church and early Christian worship (e.g., Christ-centered "hymns" recorded in Philippians 2:5–11 and Colossians 1:15–20).

GENERAL EPISTLES

THE GENERAL EPISTLES WERE written to more generic audiences of Christians, and not limited to Christians in one geographical location. They were wider in scope. These letters include James, 1 and 2 Peter, 1, 2, and 3 John, and Jude (and sometimes Hebrews). The letter of James was written by James—the half-brother to Jesus and early leader in the Jerusalem church. It focuses on practical living, and James articulates how the gospel can be lived out in everyday scenarios and how trials produce patience.

The letters of the apostle Peter (1 and 2 Peter) were written in a hostile climate under the rule of Emperor Nero and encouraged Christians to remain faithful as they endured suffering. Both James and Peter were eventually martyred, James in Jerusalem and Peter in Rome.[4] The apostle John, also considered to be the author of the Gospel and Revelation, wrote the letters of 1, 2, and 3 John to encourage orthodoxy in the face of the Gnostic-like teaching that I mentioned. Like James, Jude was also a son of both Joseph and Mary, and he wrote the letter of Jude, charging his audience to "contend for the faith that was once for all entrusted to God's holy people" (Jude 1:3).

An argument can be made that the book of Hebrews is a general epistle, although it does not as naturally fit into this category. It is arranged more like a sermon than a letter. The anonymous author writes to a Jewish-Christian audience who was tempted to reject Jesus and revert back into Judaism. The content is a comprehensive argument that Jesus is superior to whatever elements of Judaism—angels, Moses, Joshua, etc.—might attract the recipient back into Judaism.

REVELATION

REVELATION IS A PROPHETIC book written by the apostle John in the ancient genre of apocalypse. "Apocalypse" means "uncovering" or "revealing," and in the context of genre suggests the usage of rich literary symbolism. Thus, this book is appropriately called "Revelation" in English as it reveals King Jesus as being ultimately victorious in the cosmic war between good and evil. Numerous interpretive lenses offer themselves for reading Revelation, many of which are based on how to read the "thousand years" (a millennium) of Jesus' reign described in Revelation 20. Hence, the frameworks for understanding Revelation as a whole, which come from one's view of the millennium in Revelation 20, often have the word "millennium" in them (e.g., premillennialism, postmillennialism, amillennialism).

Regardless of one's interpretive framework, we can make clear observations about the book of Revelation: The original recipients of this letter were Christians in Asia Minor (modern-day Turkey), who were facing persecution for the faith. John directly addressed the churches in seven cities of Asia Minor with a message from Jesus written specifically to each church at the beginning of the book (Revelation 2–3). Another useful observation is that within the twenty-two chapters comprising the book, there are hundreds of allusions to events and other features of the Old Testament. So anyone who wants to be a serious student of Revelation needs to be a serious student of the Old Testament as well. Finally, Revelation reveals how God meets frightening persecutions from anti-Christian governments with decisive judgments, all culminating in the return of King Jesus to judge evil once and for all. In the end, God will restore creation to the Eden-like relationship that existed between God and humans in the beginning.[5]

THE NEW TESTAMENT AS GOD'S NEW COVENANT LAW

As with the Old Testament, the New Testament is the name of a collection of documents (or "books"), but the term itself suggests a sacred promise between God and humans. The Greek word *diatheke* is a legal term that can mean "last will and testament" or "covenant" or "contract." The word is used approximately thirty-three times in the New Testament, and a significant number of those times refers to the new covenant law ratified by the blood of Christ that provides us with the promise of salvation from our sins.

The first usage of the term is found during Jesus' observance of Passover the evening before being crucified. Pulling from the imagery of the slain lamb during the Exodus (Exodus 12:7), whose blood covered the houses of the Hebrews at the time death entered Egypt, Jesus announced his blood would be the basis of our forgiveness: "This is my blood of the covenant, which is poured out for many for the forgiveness of sins" (Matthew 26:28).

When the New Testament speaks of the "blood of the covenant," it suggests that death was necessary to enforce the covenant. This was true of the old covenant (for example, the animals that were sacrificed), and also true of the new covenant. This is well expressed in Hebrews 9:15–17, where the Hebrew writer speaks of the necessity of the death of the one who makes the covenant, in the manner of a last will and testament. The passage says:

> For a covenant is valid only when people are dead, for it is never in force while the one who made it lives. Therefore even the first covenant was not inaugurated without blood. (Hebrews 9:17–18, NASB)

A key passage in understanding the new covenant is the predictive prophecy of Jeremiah where he contrasts the old covenant and new covenant.

> "For this is the covenant which I will make with the house of Israel after those days," declares the LORD: "I will put My law within them and write it on their heart; and I will be their God, and they shall be My people. They will not teach again, each one his neighbor and each one his brother, saying, 'Know the LORD,' for they will all know Me, from the least of them to the greatest of them," declares the LORD, "for I will forgive their wrongdoing, and their sin I will no longer remember." (Jeremiah 31:33–34, NASB)

God announced through Jeremiah that he would establish a new covenant that would stand in contrast to the old. The contrast is then specified as placing his laws within their hearts and not on tablets of stone as with the old covenant (2 Corinthians 3:2–3). The righteousness of God would emanate from an inward change and not simply an outward conforming to law. He would be their God, and they would be his people in an eternal relationship of knowing and being known.

The New Testament, therefore, is a covenant provided by God that offers forgiveness of sins and results in eternal salvation. This covenant is made known to us through the books of the New Testament that unfold God's scheme of redemption and the Christian faith. Understanding the content and the designations of the Old and New Testament provokes the question: *How did we get the Bible?*

3

HOW DID WE GET OUR BIBLE?

Answer: Our Bible has come together through a process guided by God through his Holy Spirit, which includes revelation, inspiration, and canonization.

> For prophecy never had its origin in the human will, but prophets, though human, spoke from God as they were carried along by the Holy Spirit.
> — 2 Peter 1:21

The question of how we got our Bible requires a multifaceted answer. When the question is posed, some might refer to how we got the sixty-six books that are within our current Bible. Others might be asking about the process of how we went from God speaking to his people through spokespersons to having documented Scripture that is considered God's Word. Some might be curious how we got our current versions of the Bible into our own languages and preferred styles. While each one of these questions makes for great discussions, this chapter will handle only the general process of how the Bible went from being God's spoken word to the written Word we call Scripture, which we believe to be the Word of God.

We must take important steps to trace rightly the journey from God's spoken word to the written Scriptures. The three key words we will spend the most time unpacking are *revelation*, *inspiration*, and *canonization*:

- Revelation means the process of God disclosing his will.
- Inspiration means God is the source of Scripture, safeguarding the transmission of his message.

- Canonization means the process by which the church recognized which writings would be included in Scripture.

Let's go through these one by one.

REVELATION

THE APOSTLE PAUL PENNED the book of Ephesians, likely writing to a predominantly Gentile audience. His intent was to display the plan of salvation as it accomplishes the bringing together of Jews and Gentiles into one spiritual body. Paul's usage of the word "revelation" in the context of the letter as a whole aids us in understanding how we got the Bible:

> For this reason I, Paul, the prisoner of Christ Jesus for the sake of you Gentiles—if indeed you have heard of the administration of God's grace which was given to me for you; *that by revelation* there was made known to me the mystery, *as I wrote* before briefly. By referring to this, *when you read you can understand* my insight into the mystery of Christ. (Ephesians 3:1–4, NASB)

A careful examination of this passage will provide a helpful way of understanding how we got the Bible. As Paul describes the plan of salvation, which began with God before time started, he refers to it as a "mystery" (Ephesians 3:3–6). The word "mystery" as used by Paul describes something kept secret until made known. This mystery, according to Ephesians 3:6, was the inclusion of the Gentiles alongside Jews in the body of Christ.

How was this mystery made known? The answer is given in verse three: "by revelation." "Revelation" here means to unfold, disclose, or to make known. Revelation is the unveiling of the will of God to the mind of a human vessel, so that a person has the opportunity to understand. After this, Paul mentions the documentation of the revelation, saying, "As I wrote before briefly" (Ephesians 3:3, NASB). Paul received revelation from God, and then made it known through his writing.

Unlike a deist god, who creates the world and then leaves it behind, the God of the Bible is intent on revealing himself and his will to people. Romans 1:20 explains, "Since the creation of the world God's invisible qualities—his eternal power and divine nature—have been clearly seen." The psalmist sings, "The heavens declare the glory of God; the skies proclaim the work of his hands. Day after day they pour forth speech; night after night they reveal knowledge" (Psalm 19:1–2). In addition to revealing himself through creation, God revealed himself and his will throughout the Bible through such conduits as dreams (Numbers 12:6), laws (Deuteronomy 29:29), audible words (1 Samuel 3:21), predictions (2 Kings 8:10), visions (Daniel 2:19), and miracles (John 2:11). Through the Son, God revealed himself most fully (Hebrews 1:1–4). This desire to make himself known to people continues from the Bible's opening pages, where God called out after Adam sinned, "Where are you?" (Genesis 3:9) to its closing chapters in Revelation.

INSPIRATION

WHEN GOD'S REVELATION IS written down under the guidance of the Holy Spirit, it is then called inspired Scripture. It is the Word of God documented. As mentioned earlier, both the Old and the New Testaments are referred to in the Bible as Scripture. Consider a common passage that we used in the introduction of this book.

> GOD'S REVELATION WRITTEN DOWN IS CALLED INSPIRED SCRIPTURE.

> And that from childhood you have known the sacred writings which are able to give you the wisdom that leads to salvation through faith which is in Christ Jesus. All Scripture is inspired by God and beneficial for teaching, for rebuke, for correction, for training in righteousness; so that the man or woman of God may be fully capable, equipped for every good work. (2 Timothy 3:15–17, NASB)

This letter from Paul was written to encourage a timid Timothy for the work of ministry in the city of Ephesus. Paul indicates that Timothy was reared from childhood to know the Old Testament Scriptures, which were able to make him wise in regard to salvation. Paul goes on to describe the nature of Scripture as being "inspired" or "God-breathed." This speaks to the divine origin of Scripture. God should be understood as the source of Scripture.

Additionally, inspiration involves the supervision of the Holy Spirit to move the human vessel to speak or document what God has revealed. God discloses himself and his will in various ways (revelation), and the Holy Spirit inspires the writer to write it down (inspiration). In 2 Peter 1:20–21, Peter speaks to this truth:

But know this first of all, that no prophecy of Scripture becomes a matter of someone's own interpretation, for no prophecy was ever made by an act of human will, but men moved by the Holy Spirit spoke from God. (NASB)

A pivotal word in 2 Peter 1:21 in the context is the word "moved." This word is in the passive voice, which suggests that the human vessel is being acted upon. He is being guided by the Holy Spirit, who is the ultimate author of what is spoken. To this end, inspiration includes God safeguarding his message as it is spoken by human vessels led by the Holy Spirit.

This confidence in inspired Scripture is further undergirded in Acts 1:16, when the apostles were looking to choose someone to replace the traitorous disciple Judas. The same Peter announced the Scriptures must be fulfilled and a new apostle be chosen (Psalm 109:8). Notice what Peter's statement says about the origin and authoritativeness of Scripture:

Brothers, the Scripture had to be fulfilled, *which the Holy Spirit foretold by the mouth of David concerning Judas,* who became a guide to those who arrested Jesus. (Acts 1:16, NASB)

This passage implies David was not the original source of these words; rather, the Holy Spirit inspired David to speak these prophecies. Additionally, when David's spoken word became a written word, it was called "Scripture."

Over and over, we see the Old Testament writers believing themselves to be speaking words inspired by God, prefacing their statements by saying, "This is what the Lord says." Jesus shared this conviction, believing Scripture to be unbreakable (John 10:35) and forever (Matthew 5:17–18). Moreover, he believed the entirety of Old Testament Scripture pointed to him (Luke 24:25–27). In addition, Jesus promised the Holy Spirit would guide the apostles into all truth (John 16:13–16), in which they would be moved by the Holy Spirit as were the Old Testament prophets. Accordingly, even as the New Testament was in the process of being written, we find its authors reference New Testament passages as Scripture (1 Timothy 5:17–18; 2 Peter 3:15–16).

If the Bible is God's inspired Word, as Jesus and the biblical writers taught, then the next logical step is to affirm its truthfulness, a conviction I develop further in Chapter 5.

CANONIZATION

"CANONIZATION" REFERS TO THE process of recognizing which books were considered Scripture by the people of God at the time of compiling the Bible as we know it today. The term "canon" suggests a standard.[6] Ultimately, when discussing the idea of canon as it relates to the Bible, we are speaking about those books that are considered the standard of the Christian faith. At times, people have come to the erroneous conclusion that the books of the Bible were chosen by a select few people. However, canonization had more to do with recognition of the books that were already in circulation and accepted as authoritative within the context of God's covenant people.

The *Anchor Bible Dictionary* provides a synopsis of the term *canon* stating:

> The word "canon" comes from the Gk *kanōn*, "measuring stick." By extension it came to mean "rule" or "standard," a tool used for determining proper measurement. Consequently, the word has come to be used with reference to the corpus of scriptural writings that is considered authoritative and standard for defining and determining "orthodox" religious beliefs and practices.[7]

Jesus and his apostles assumed the canon of the Hebrew Old Testament. The New Testament either cites or alludes to the vast majority of Old Testament books, a fact which attests to the widespread acceptance of the Old Testament's canonicity and authority by Jesus, the New Testament authors, and the Jews in their time. In addition, the argument could be made that Jesus considers the entire spectrum of Old Testament canon when he mentions "the blood of righteous Abel to the blood of Zechariah" (Matthew 23:35). The mention of these two righteous men put to death by godless people spans the Old Testament from the Hebrew Bible's first book (Genesis) to its final book according to the Hebrew Bible listing (2 Chronicles).

The process of a canon of the New Testament was already set in place by the last words of Jesus to his apostles. In Matthew 28:18–20, Jesus told the apostles it was their duty to make other disciples using the teachings that he had given to them:

> Then Jesus came to them and said, "All authority in heaven and on earth has been given to me. Therefore go and make disciples of all nations, baptizing them in the name of the Father and of the Son and of the Holy Spirit, and

teaching them to obey everything I have commanded you. And surely I am with you always, to the very end of the age."

The teachings of Jesus, given through the apostles, formed the basis of the canon or standard of objective truth. This is why the earliest church devoted themselves to the apostles' teachings in Acts 2:42: "They devoted themselves to the apostles' teaching and to fellowship, to the breaking of bread and to prayer." So the teachings and writings of the apostles—sometimes written down by their associates—formed the core of teachings of the new covenant. The existence of recognized books of the New Testament is found within the New Testament books themselves.

For instance, as mentioned earlier, Peter recognized Paul's writings as Scripture (2 Peter 3:15–16). Paul cites from Luke's Gospel (1 Timothy 5:17–18). Paul commanded that his letters be read to other churches (1 Thessalonians 5:27; Colossians 4:16). These are all clear indications that there were accepted letters that functioned as authoritative to the church.

The books in the New Testament were all written before the end of the first century (that is, before AD 100).[8] New Testament scholar Michael Kruger, an expert in the formation of the canon of the New Testament, describes the attitude of the church's leaders following the first century:

> Early Christians had a high view of the apostolic office, viewing the apostles as the very mouthpiece of Christ himself. Thus any document containing apostolic teaching would have been received as an authoritative written text (and the beginning of the canon).[9]

However, after the first century, these writings were not the only ones in circulation that claimed authoritativeness. In order to protect Christians from false teaching after the death of all the apostles, the early leaders needed to delineate writings that were apostolic—and therefore the authoritative words of Jesus—from those which were not. Some books claimed authority but were, in reality, written in later centuries by people falsely claiming to be Jesus' apostles (for example, the Gospel of Thomas and the Gospel of Peter). All the while, there was a core of first-century books that were recognized early on as being part of the canon (the four Gospels, Acts, Paul's epistles, etc.), as well as early books that were not as quickly recognized by all regions of the church but came to be recognized as part of the canon (e.g., Hebrews and James). Kruger explains:

Not only was there a "core" canon of the New Testament books that were well established from early time, but disagreements over peripheral canonical books were less problematic than is often portrayed.[10]

After persecution subsided and the church as a whole was able to publicly gather in the fourth century, they were able to land on an authoritative list of inspired books that comprised the New Testament. The early Christians recognized as authoritative those books that met three key criteria:[11]

1. The authoritative book had to be written by apostolic authors (or authors who were closely associated with apostles).
2. They taught the orthodox faith of the apostles.
3. They had been widely accepted in earliest churches from the beginning.

In order for the church at large to recognize what books had already long been accepted as authoritative by the churches, it measured the books by these standards. Recall the literal meaning of the word "canon" as "measuring stick." We see lists containing core New Testament books. For example, the Muratorian Fragment of the late second century includes the core books, even though, as only a fragment of the original document, the list is incomplete. Other lists include the full twenty-seven books as early as AD 250 (by Origen) and AD 367 (by Athanasius).[12] In AD 367, when the official list as we know it today was recognized by the church, the church was not imposing something new upon Christian communities; rather, they were codifying the documents that contained the historical beliefs and practices of those communities. Kruger explains, "The canon was like a seedling sprouting from the soil of early Christianity—although it was not fully a tree until the fourth century, it was there from the beginning."[13]

In the process of clarifying the final list of authoritative books, these Christians affirmed the church itself had been established by the words and works of Jesus as communicated by the apostles (Ephesians 2:20). Thus, the written works associated with the apostles were the objective norm by which the church was to measure and evaluate itself.[14] What gave the New Testament canon its authority is that it contained the teachings of Jesus given to the world through his apostles or those associated with the apostles.

In recognizing the canon, the early believers held that Christians, leaders, and churches were subject to the objective record of the apostles' teachings. No church body could have an authority over the Bible or equal to the Bible, as Roman Catholic and Orthodox leaders sometimes claim to have. The apostolic teaching created the church; the church did not create the Bible.[15] Clark Pinnock sums up the authority of the Bible over any church or ancient or modern form of Christianity:

> THE APOSTOLIC TEACHING CREATED THE CHURCH; THE CHURCH DID NOT CREATE THE BIBLE.

> By accepting the norm of Scripture, the church declared that there was a standard outside herself to which she intended to be subject for all time. . . . The church can fall into error and needs the Bible to measure herself by. In turn, the church serves the canon by continuing in the truth and faithfully proclaiming the Word of God.[16]

The twenty-seven books of the New Testament were combined with the thirty-nine books of the Old Testament to form the canon of Scripture as the sixty-six books contained in the modern Protestant Bible.

What did we learn in this chapter? The three major steps in the process by which we received the Bible are revelation, inspiration, and canonization. We also learned the God of heaven disclosed himself and his will to the mind of human vessels who were moved by inspiration to communicate the message, and the authors wrote down the message. Finally, these messages were brought together through a canonization process of recognizing the authoritative books that circulated among God's covenant people.

4

HOW DO WE INTERPRET THE BIBLE?

Answer: The Bible must be read by seeking God and with an awareness of the world of the Bible and understood through observation, interpretation, and application to how we live today.

Do your best to present yourself to God as one approved, a worker who does not need to be ashamed and who correctly handles the word of truth.
— 2 Timothy 2:15

While we are grateful to have the Scriptures, it is necessary to have a process by which we can understand its meaning. Without question, the Bible requires interpretation. Like any other written communication, such as newspapers, emails, periodicals, novels, or poetry, the writings of Scripture necessitate a careful handling so the communicated message can be received. Moreover, it is not enough to have just any method of interpretation. Some people approach the Bible with little more than gut-level reactions and impulsive feelings as the lens through which they interpret Scripture. Others intentionally approach the Bible with prior commitments to a cultural bias. They deliberately read the Bible through this lens, which they know yields results favorable toward their chosen cause. As the Word of God, however, the Bible ought to be studied carefully—not

THE BIBLE OUGHT TO BE STUDIED CAREFULLY.

casually or crookedly—in order to bring about authentic understanding and faithful obedience.

The field of study that approaches the task of seeking to interpret and understand the Bible is called "hermeneutics." Hermeneutics is the art and science of interpretation. It is an art because language is a form of creative expression. However, it is also a science because interpretation possesses rules that aid the reader in understanding the intent of the author. Because of the many "diverse modes of thought and ambiguities of expression" in language, hermeneutics helps remove the obstacles and bridge the gap between the author and the reader so that the reader can understand the meaning of the author.[17]

The term *hermeneutics* comes from a Greek word *hermēneuō*, meaning to interpret or explain. The word is closely associated with the Greek god Hermes (known as the messenger of the gods). The word is used in the New Testament to describe the process of translation. There is a sense in which translation is in fact interpretation. This is witnessed in the three usages of the term *hermēneuō* in Scripture (in italics):

> Jesus looked at him and said, "You are Simon son of John. You will be called Cephas" (which, when *translated*, is Peter). (John 1:42)
>
> "Go," he told him, "wash in the Pool of Siloam" (this word *means* "Sent"). So the man went and washed, and came home seeing. (John 9:7)
>
> First, the name Melchizedek *means* "king of righteousness"; then also, "king of Salem" *means* "king of peace." (Hebrews 7:2)

The meticulous process of translating from one language to another requires a translator to do some level of interpretation because words and expressions have a range of meaning from which to choose. The task is to choose the right term or phrase in the language of translation that reflects the original meaning of the statement. Thus, the term "hermeneutics" became the general word used for the entire process of interpretation.

WHY THE NEED FOR A PROCESS OF INTERPRETATION?

INTERPRETATION IS A PART of our everyday lives. Each time we read a text message or a post on social media, we engage in the process of interpretation. Because we are familiar with how our culture communicates and the various linguistic devices we use to express thought, it is easy for us to interpret messages spoken and written in our own culture. However, interpretation can have a series of obstacles the further one is removed from the author's particular culture.

Perhaps you have gone to a foreign country and interfaced with their culture that spoke a different language and came with a different set of social norms. In order to operate and function within that culture, you had to overcome several barriers in order to communicate with the people of that society. Several obstacles had to be removed for there to be understanding and communication. The same is true of reading an ancient document that may not reflect the values, politics, language, or socioeconomic reality of your current culture.

Even more so, when we interface with ancient documents, it can be challenging to understand what the original author was communicating in writing them because these documents came into existence in such a different time frame and culture. With this in mind, we must understand the Bible is an ancient document that reflects, or at least interacts with, a variety of cultures, religions, philosophies, languages, socioeconomic status, and politics. In order to interface with the Bible in a fruitful way, we must become more knowledgeable about these various elements so we can read God's Word as intended.

Before we discuss some of the tools for understanding the author's intended meaning, it is helpful to make one point: Is it true that a text has only one intended meaning? Couldn't Peter or Paul have intended multiple meanings when they wrote what they wrote? After all, can't a Bible verse mean something different for me than it does for you, or can't I discover a new insight from a Bible verse that I never recognized when I read it ten years ago? This is where it is helpful to introduce the distinction between "meaning" and "significance."

Meaning is what an author intended to convey by his words. You and I cannot go back and change what an author intended to convey; that's already set. *Significance*, however, is a relational word.[18] Significance describes what effects and implications and relationship the text has in my life. That is, "What did the author mean to say?" is a different question from, "What is the significance of this Bible verse for my life?" Even as its significance expands throughout your life, a text of Scripture will still mean the same thing it has always meant. The meaning of a text is a matter of discovery, not innovation.

CLOSING THE DISTANCE

SINCE THE BIBLE IS an ancient document, there are distances we need to try to close in order to have a proper understanding of the original meaning. It is much like crossing a bridge to another world so as to understand its historical context.

Thankfully, many scholars have been diligent to build bridges across these divides so modern Christians are not without resources. What are the interpretive distances that students of Scripture continue to travel in order to arrive at the meaning of a text? Let me explain five.

Time Distance. Time distance simply indicates the time between our culture today and the era in which these events happened. A significant amount of time has elapsed between current believers and the original audience. We have no access to the author nor the recipients in order to have conversations about the meaning of what they wrote or how they intended it to be received. At the very least, acknowledging this distance should give us humility to avoid impulsive, gut-level interpretations as well as curiosity to learn as much about ancient biblical history as we can. Like other "distances" we will read about in this chapter, much of the time distance can be bridged using solid resources such as Bible encyclopedias and study Bibles, which provide relevant background information for understanding the text.

Linguistic Distance. Long before our translations, such as the New American Standard Bible or the English Standard Version, the Bible was written in three ancient languages: Hebrew, Aramaic, and Koine Greek. The Old Testament was predominantly written in the Hebrew language (with some Aramaic), and the New Testament was written in Koine Greek. In an ideal world, everyone would have the ability to read such languages so this distance would be removed, but even someone who reads or speaks modern Greek and Hebrew today is still worlds apart from biblical Koine Greek and the Hebrew of the Bible. While it is certainly true that we have a plethora of reliable English translations that allow us to gain a solid understanding of biblical texts, we can still face times when some meaning is lost in the process of professional translation. To this end, it is important for serious students of the Bible, when possible and especially for teachers of the Word, to gain a basic understanding of how to use proper linguistic tools to engage with the languages of the Bible. For example, it is helpful to become familiar with lexical books to interface with these ancient languages.

Geographical Distance. The geographical distance is significant because many believers today are unfamiliar with the geographical landscape in which the events of the Bible took place. Some of the geographical terms of the Bible may be difficult to locate inasmuch as we do not have a mental picture of the landscape. Learning them, though, can aid proper interpretation.

For instance, when Jesus told the parable of the good Samaritan, he mentioned a certain man went down from Jerusalem to Jericho. What was Jesus referring to when he spoke of going down to Jericho from Jerusalem? And why would this man get robbed during the journey? A look into the geography reveals that Jericho sat about 1,500 feet below sea level, which made it much lower in elevation than Jerusalem, which was around 2,500 feet above sea level. Additionally, a look at the history of the region shows that the road from Jericho to Jerusalem was often crawling with robbers who would wait to prey upon somebody in order to steal their possessions. When Jesus spoke this parable, it would have been very plausible for the audience to picture someone traveling "down" to Jericho and getting robbed. By understanding the geography, it informs a proper understanding of the passage.

Cultural Distance. In the days of the Bible, there were various norms, customs, and ways of living that can inform a proper interpretation of Scripture. Becoming culturally informed of the norms of the biblical world can help us answer questions such as: What was so surprising about Jesus washing the feet of his disciples in John 13? Why would the apostle Paul say we should salute one another with a holy kiss in Romans 16:16? Part of understanding the cultural context of their day requires understanding their occupational world. A great many of Jesus' parables were agricultural, while others highlighted the activity of fishing. Both of these were dominant occupations within the Palestinian world.

Spiritual Distance. We have just looked at some of the prominent distances that the interpreter seeks to cross in order to arrive at a proper interpretation and fuller understanding of the text. One that I have not mentioned, however, but is the most influential divide of all, is the spiritual distance people naturally have with the Bible and the God who inspired it. If we do not humble ourselves before God and approach his Word with a willing and obedient heart, we will miss its point, even if we score A's on all the hermeneutical tests. If the Bible is the Word of God, then to study it merely out of academic pursuit or pure intellectual curiosity would be akin to taking the Lord's Supper merely for its nutritional value.

Studying the Bible with no intention of letting it bridge the spiritual distance between you and God is to prove the proverb, "Knowledge puffs up while love builds up" (1 Corinthians 8:1). Whether spoken or written, the words of God are meant to be loved (Psalm 119:97), internalized (Psalm 119:11), and obeyed (John 14:15). For this reason, it is important to read the Bible *prayerfully*, acknowledging that our study of God's Word can give rise to legalism (Luke 18:11–12) or even sinful cravings (Romans 7:7–8) if not grounded in humility before God. And a delightful surprise we experience when we do trust God enough to obey his Word is that obedience leads to understanding in a richness that study alone can never yield.

BECOMING AWARE OF GENRE

ONE CONCEPT THAT CONTRIBUTES a lot of mileage for closing the interpretive distance is genre. "Genre" in the context of biblical hermeneutics means the kind of literature of a given book of the Bible. The Bible is rich with a variety of literary genres. Being familiar with the various genres helps us read the text more accurately. For example, one of the dominant literary types in the Bible is historical narrative, such as Genesis and Acts. The Bible also contains wisdom literature, such as Song of Solomon, Proverbs, and Ecclesiastes. There are letters written to particular church groups or individuals. Additionally, we have books containing apocalyptic literature, such as Revelation and Daniel. There are books of prophecy and law. There are sermons and parables. Moreover, poetry comprises as much as one third of the Bible.

As we each study the Bible, we must be sensitive with regard to literary genre and understand that each genre cannot be read in the exact same way. Historical narratives primarily report events, while letters address certain occasions. Wisdom literature is practical and encourages seeking virtue and divine favor, while apocalyptic contains vivid language and utilizes signs and symbols.

New Testament professor Dean Deppe provides insight to how genre affects how we read the text:

> The determination of genre is crucial to detecting the meaning of a literary text, since like an infrared lens it offers a photo that we do not always observe in normal light. . . . Genres trigger different expectations and thus demand divergent reading strategies.[19]

The goal of the interpreter is to ascertain what the author under the influence of the Holy Spirit is attempting to communicate. If we ignore the literary type, then we become vulnerable to misrepresenting the meaning. We need to read only a few words of the following description of Jesus to realize we are no longer reading a biography of Jesus in the Gospels:

> Among the lampstands was someone like a son of man, dressed in a robe reaching down to his feet and with a golden sash around his chest. The hair on his head was white like wool, as white as snow, and his eyes were like blazing fire. His feet were like bronze glowing in a furnace, and his voice was like the sound of rushing waters. (Revelation 1:13–15)

Apocalyptic literature such as we see here in Revelation 1 uses vivid imagery filled with signs and symbols.

As I mentioned, a shocking percentage of the language of Revelation comes to us from the Old Testament. Reading an unfamiliar genre (apocalypse) that borrows its imagery from the less familiar testament (the Old Testament) should invite us to tread humbly and cautiously, so as not to abuse the text. With all this in mind, how can we best understand this apocalyptic passage undergirded with symbolism? If we take it as a literal picture of the physical description of Jesus, our interpretations could yield rather odd results. Let's walk through the text.

IF WE IGNORE THE LITERARY TYPE, THEN WE BECOME VULNERABLE TO MISREPRESENTING THE MEANING.

John describes Jesus in this text as having a robe reaching to his feet with a golden sash around his chest; his hair is white like snow and white wool; his eyes are like fire and feet like burnished bronze; and his voice is like the sound of rushing water and a two-edged sword is coming out of his mouth. Perhaps it's no wonder why Jesus needed to say in verse seventeen, "Do not be afraid."

Where do these symbols come from? The picture of Jesus dressed with a robe and sash echoes how the priests were dressed under the Old Testament law (Leviticus 16:3–4). Even more vivid is the picture of Jesus as having hair like white wool. This language recalls Daniel 7:9, where the Ancient of Days (God) is described in the same way, having his holiness placed on display. Jesus having eyes like fire recalls the language of Daniel 10:6, which reveals the image of a celestial being. His feet like bronze recalls the language of Micah 4:13, where Israel is figuratively said to have been given feet like bronze to trample out the enemy. The two-edged sword coming out of his mouth is a symbol of judgment through his word (Isaiah 49:1–2; Hebrews 4:12). His voice as rushing water is imagery of God in Ezekiel 43:1–2.

If we take all this background information under consideration and put it together with the reality that the recipients of this book were under Roman persecution needing encouragement, we arrive at something far more understandable than the incomprehensible image of Christ we started with: Christ is presented as God who is a priest to serve his people, with a sword prepared to judge, and feet that can trample out the enemy. To accent that he is God, he cites the words of Isaiah 44:6 in which Yahweh said, "I am the first and I am the last."

As this example shows, knowing the genre will help the reader handle the text accurately, according to its literary form.

THREE STEPS INVOLVED WITH UNDERSTANDING A TEXT

CULTURAL CONTEXT, GEOGRAPHICAL DISTANCE, literary genre—all of these are important considerations for interpretation. But let's take a step back from these bridge-building principles and tools and look at three broad *steps* that have long been useful in handling the Bible. This plan for handling Scripture has helped scholars, pastors, and laypeople alike approach Scripture in an accurate and faithful way. The three steps are observation, interpretation, and application. Before delving into the steps, however, let's acknowledge a posture we need to take when approaching the text: prayer. We saturate the process in prayer because our most important goal is to hear from God.

Observation is seeing what is there. It is not putting into the text something that is not there but pulling from the text that which is there. With this step we begin to know the details and answer the interrogatory questions of who, what, where, when, why, and how. These are the types of report questions we can ask of Scripture:

Who: Who is speaking? To whom is he speaking?

What: What is the subject of the text? What is the situation of the text? What is the conflict in the text? What is the solution in the text?

Where: Where are the events of this text located? Where are the original recipients located? Where is the author located?

When: What is the specified era of the text?
When are these events taking place?

Why: What are the reasons for some of the actions in the text?
Why is the author making a particular statement? Why are the
recipients responding the way they are (negatively or positively)?

How: How are the recipients to accomplish the task at hand? How is the
author moving the recipients to action? How did the recipients overcome the
problem? How did the author overcome the problem?

Observation is the first interaction with the text. We are unlikely to arrive at a proper understanding of a text if we do not take the time to make thorough observations. The bridge-building principles we looked at earlier can help us at this stage as we try to observe everything we can about the text. However, these tools can also be helpful as we ask a more focused question: "What does this text *mean*?" This question takes us to our next step.

Interpretation moves beyond observation to getting at the meaning. This is especially where word studies and phrase studies are helpful. Words have meaning that can be determined by their context and relationships with other words. There are times when a lexicon (a foreign language dictionary) can shed light on a word's range of meaning, but it's the word's *context* that will determine the usage.

For a simple example, let's consider how the Bible defines "water." Here are two instances of the same word in the same chapter:

> When a Samaritan woman came to draw *water*, Jesus said to her, "Will you give me a drink?" . . . Jesus answered her, "If you knew the gift of God and who it is that asks you for a drink, you would have asked him and he would have given you living *water*." (John 4:7, 10)

How do we tell the difference in usage? We look at context. In John 4:7, we are meant to picture physical water. This is because the Samaritan woman was coming to a well to draw it. In John 4:10, Jesus again referred to water, but the word "living" impacts the word "water." Whatever Jesus was talking about, it's clear that it was no ordinary well water.

So how do we determine what this "living water" is referring to? For one thing, as we zoom out to the rest of the verse, we discover that it's a "gift of God." When we search the context surrounding verse ten, we discover that "living water" is connected with "eternal life" (4:14). Three chapters later, John came right out and gave the "living water" a name: "By [living water], he meant the Spirit" (7:39). What did Jesus mean by offering the woman "living water"? By seeing the context around the verse, we discover that Jesus offered her eternal life through the Holy Spirit.

In the same way, after making initial observations, we interpret what a text means by studying words and phrases in their context.

Application seeks to understand the significance of the biblical text to contemporary life. Application answers the question, "Now what?" Once the meaning of the text is understood based on the observation and interpretation, then the interpreter engages application. The interpreter should now ask questions like, "What does this passage challenge the believer to do?" and, "Is there a correlation between the circumstance of the text and the circumstance in my contemporary life?"

As we read the text, we should look to see whether each passage teaches a doctrine, exposes a false behavior, provides correction, or provides instruction in righteousness (see 2 Timothy 3:16). Perhaps your passage of choice contains a warning to heed. Take for example the warning in Hebrews 6:4–6 concerning turning away from the once-and-for-all sacrifice of Christ. Or perhaps it contains an encouragement to receive, such as that in 1 Thessalonians 4:17, when Paul wrote to reassure believers who were concerned about the Second Coming. Application itself is often a two-step process, as the reader asks, "What was this text designed to accomplish for the original hearers?" and, "How can I apply this to my present-day life?"

It is important to note that all three steps fall under the heading of "understanding a text." It is obvious that the steps of observation and interpretation are crucial in understanding a text. What may be less obvious is the role that faithfully applying the Bible to our lives plays in actually understanding it. We are missing the point—and we'll often skew the meaning—if we stop short of obeying what we read. As David Young points out, "Obedience is the best hermeneutic when it comes to the Bible."[20]

Understanding the Bible is a very important part of Christian faith. We do not display faithfulness as followers of Jesus when we flippantly read the Scriptures according to gut-level feelings or inadvertently reinterpret its texts to fit them comfortably within our cultural sensibilities. Our goal in reading Scripture is to understand what *God has revealed*. To avoid fanciful interpretations and convoluted meanings, we must prayerfully study each text in its context and utilize the bridge-building principles of observation, interpretation, and application.

5

HOW IS THE BIBLE OUR FINAL AUTHORITY?

Answer: As the Word of God, the Bible guides our convictions and character, and, when properly understood, it has authority over all other thoughts, practices, and claims to inspiration.

All Scripture is God-breathed and is useful for teaching, rebuking, correcting and training in righteousness.
— 2 Timothy 3:16

In our brief exploration of the Bible, we have dug up too many life-altering implications to keep the information at arm's length as an object of curiosity. If the Bible is God's inspired Word, then it is true, reliable, and authoritative. And it's meant to be *our* final authority.

At Renew.org, we describe the Bible as "infallible," which means that it cannot fail in what God sets out to accomplish.[21] That is, God's Word cannot fail to communicate the truth we need about God to be saved, trained in righteousness, and transformed into the image of Jesus. It is God's uniquely inspired message to humanity that infallibly reveals God's identity, character, and will—and the path to salvation. Its purpose stands regardless of cultural winds or human weakness. We find a description of this infallibility of God's purpose in Isaiah 55:10–11:

> **GOD'S WORD CANNOT FAIL TO COMMUNICATE THE TRUTH WE NEED ABOUT GOD TO BE SAVED.**

As the rain and the snow come down from heaven, and do not return to it without watering the earth and making it bud and flourish, so that it yields seed for the sower and bread for the eater, so is my word that goes out from my mouth: It will not return to me empty, but will accomplish what I desire and achieve the purpose for which I sent it.

So if the Bible is true, reliable, authoritative, and infallible, then each of us has a very sober question to consider: Will the Bible be *our* final authority? Of course, this doesn't mean the Bible pretends to teach everything there is to know about every subject matter. But the Bible is an authoritative set of documents that expresses God's will for our lives. Peter declares God has provided all things that pertain to "life and godliness":

His divine power has granted to us everything pertaining to life and godliness, through the true knowledge of Him who called us by His own glory and excellence. (2 Peter 1:3, NASB)

In the immediate context of this passage, Peter encourages godly living since God has granted everything that pertains to "life and godliness." How do we receive this? It is granted "through the true knowledge of [Christ]." The term "life" as used in this context is more than likely speaking of eternal life as an abundance of life that will be fully realized in the presence of God. The term "godliness" refers to holy living. The Greek word for this is *eusebeia*, which expresses the idea of piety. God grants us these precious promises of life and godliness through the "true knowledge of Him who called us" (NASB), and a major way we come to this knowledge of him is through God's revelation as given through the Old and New Testaments. The gospel of Jesus is not just about forgiveness from sin; it is also for the lifelong shaping of one's character to reflect God's holiness. The implications of the Bible's claims here are as personally relevant as a claim could get.

THE AUTHORITY OF THE NEW TESTAMENT

THE GOAL OF THE New Testament is to help form our lives around Jesus Christ, in the power of the Holy Spirit, to the glory of the Father—in short, to help us to be true disciples of Jesus. So throughout the letters of the New Testament to various churches, we see several times where the writers pointed their people directly to the example of Jesus Christ. Every church struggled with weaknesses, which carried the potential to malignantly affect their church as a whole. At times, there were divisions, selfish ambitions, doctrinal disputes, or a variety of other difficulties. The authors' strategies on such occasions was often to bring the church back into Christ-centered thinking and behavior.

The Philippian church struggled with a spirit of divisiveness. In Philippians 2:1–3, the apostle Paul encourages the church to relinquish the spirit of self-centeredness and learn to honor others before themselves. In order to accent this point, Paul points to the example of Jesus:

> Have this attitude in yourselves which was also in Christ Jesus, who, as He already existed in the form of God, did not consider equality with God something to be grasped, but emptied Himself by taking the form of a bond-servant and being born in the likeness of men. And being found in appearance as a man, He humbled Himself by becoming obedient to the point of death: death on a cross. (Philippians 2:5–8, NASB)

Jesus was humble enough to empty himself of divine advantages, take on our human nature, and die a cruel and humiliating death on a cross. From looking at Jesus and his sacrifice, we see ethical values we ought to implement in our lives as believers.

The apostle Peter, similarly, in a context where suffering was a Christian's reality, highlighted the suffering of Jesus as an example to be followed. While many suffered under Nero's reign at the time of the letter, Peter encouraged the church to suffer patiently, imitating the lifestyle of their Savior. In 1 Peter 2:21–24, Peter states,

> For you have been called for this purpose, because Christ also suffered for you, leaving you an example, so that you would follow in His steps, He who committed no sin, nor was any deceit found in His mouth; and while being abusively insulted, He did not insult in return; while suffering, He did not threaten, but kept entrusting Himself to Him who judges righteously; and He Himself brought our sins in His body up on the cross, so that we might die to sin and live for righteousness; by His wounds you were healed. (1 Peter 2:21–24, NASB)

The encouragement to suffer comes from the example of Jesus, which is an authoritative model to which Christians are to conform. So we can see the authority of the New Testament through its presentation of Jesus as a behavioral paradigm.

The Bible also presents the teaching of the apostles as authoritative for the church. Luke declares the church was devoted to the apostles' teachings (Acts 2:42). The convictions of the church are grounded in the teachings of the apostles (John 17:20). Apostleship was an authoritative position established by Jesus (Luke 6:13) in which the apostles taught truth under the direct influence of the Holy Spirit (John 14:26; 16:13). Notice how Peter views the words spoken by the apostles as the words of Jesus:

> Beloved, this is now the second letter I am writing to you in which I am stirring up your sincere mind by way of reminder, to remember the words spoken beforehand by the holy prophets and the *commandment of the Lord and Savior spoken by your apostles.* (2 Peter 3:1–2, NASB)

In the context of this passage, where Peter encourages the church to stand against those who mock Jesus' Second Coming, he declares the church should keep in mind the words of the prophets. In concert with this admonition, the church is to also remember the words of the Savior spoken through the apostles. The apostles' teachings are to be viewed as coming from Jesus, which is a clear indication of their authoritative nature.

To briefly summarize what we've seen thus far, Jesus chose and sent out the apostles. The Holy Spirit directed them and inspired their teachings. The church devoted itself to these teachings, and when these teachings were written down, they were treated by the early Christians—as well as by fellow apostles—as inspired Scripture (e.g., see 1 Timothy 5:18; Luke 10:7; 2 Peter 3:15).

THE AUTHORITY OF THE OLD TESTAMENT

THE OLD TESTAMENT WAS WRITTEN FOR OUR LEARNING.

Throughout the New Testament, the authors used the Old Testament as an authoritative document to substantiate their new covenant theology. Paul states the Old Testament was written for our learning (Romans 15:4). It is important to note that during the days of the New Testament era, the canon of the Old Testament was in existence. The Old Testament was the Bible of the New Testament church while the New Testament documents were in process of being written. An excellent example of the authoritative nature of the Old Testament is that the book of Hebrews was written to prove the superiority of Jesus while using the Old Testament as authoritative evidence. Although the old covenant has been fulfilled as a system and is no longer binding—for example, animal sacrifices, temple protocols, Israel's national regulations—the Old Testament is still an authoritative document that supports foundational Christian doctrine.

I already mentioned how Hebrews accentuates the supremacy of Jesus, but notice how the author uses arguments from the Old Testament to present Jesus' superiority:

> For to which of the angels did God ever say, "You are my Son; today I have become your Father"? Or again, "I will be his Father, and he will be my Son"? And again, when God brings his firstborn into the world, he says, "Let all God's angels worship him." In speaking of the angels he says, "He makes his angels spirits, and his servants flames of fire." But about the Son he says, "Your throne, O God, will last for ever and ever; a scepter of justice will be the scepter of your kingdom. You have loved righteousness and hated wickedness; therefore God, your God, has set you above your companions by anointing you with the oil of joy." He also says, "In the beginning, Lord, you laid the foundations of the earth, and the heavens are the work of your hands. They will perish, but you remain; they will all wear out like a garment. You will roll them up like a robe; like a garment they will be changed. But you remain the same, and your years will never end." To which of the angels did God ever say, "Sit at my right hand until I make your enemies a footstool for your feet"? Are not all angels ministering spirits sent to serve those who will inherit salvation? (Hebrews 1:5–14)

The Hebrew writer cites several passages to substantiate his position regarding Christ, such as Psalm 2:7, one of the royal psalms used for the inauguration of a king. This passage acknowledges Jesus as being not only the Son of God but also the *appointed Son*, who now reigns over his kingdom. Then, the author provides a loose quotation of Psalm 104:4 to contrast the angels to God's Son. To accent the superiority of Jesus, the author quotes Psalm 45:6–7, attributing divinity to Jesus Christ. While in the original context, the psalmists praised God for his greatness, the writer of Hebrews interprets the passage as an exclamation of God to his Son. In essence, God referred to his Son as God, proclaiming he would reign forever and ever. The author goes as far as to cite Psalm 102:25–26 to acknowledge Jesus was at work creating the world in Genesis 1.

Clearly, the Bible is an authoritative charter for the church as it presents Christ as the quintessential model for living and the object of Christian faith. That authority is also manifested through the authoritative word of the apostles and undergirded by Old Testament revelation. Its authority over the people of God means we subject our lifestyles to its norms (2 Timothy 3:16–17); we submit our thoughts to its truth (Mark 12:24); we surrender our practices to its commands (Mark 7:13); and we reject all other claims to inspiration that defy the once-for-all faith that has been entrusted to us (Jude 1:3; Galatians 1:7–9).

Thus, we return to the central question of this chapter: How is the Bible *our* final authority? After having explored ways in which the Bible exercises authority for the people of God, perhaps the best way to answer the question personally is with another question: How much do you truly trust Jesus? Part of trusting Jesus this side of heaven means to follow his teachings. For Jesus, how we treat the Bible is a relational question more than an intellectual or even ethical one. For Jesus told his disciples, "If you love me, keep my commands" (John 14:15).

Culture will often challenge the authority of the Word of God. Paul speaks to this:

> The time will come when people will not put up with sound doctrine. Instead, to suit their own desires, they will gather around them a great number of teachers to say what their itching ears want to hear. They will turn their ears away from the truth and turn aside to myths. (2 Timothy 4:3–4)

Whichever way worldly cultures might drift, the authority for a disciple of Jesus remains clear, as Paul tells Timothy a handful of verses earlier: "All Scripture is God-breathed and is useful for teaching, rebuking, correcting and training in righteousness" (2 Timothy 3:16).

There will be days when we don't feel like trusting Jesus by following his teachings. This will be a good time to remind ourselves that trees do not derive their health from their impressive branches or fancy foliage but from being connected to their source. As the psalmist writes:

> Blessed is the one . . . whose delight is in the law of the LORD, and who meditates on his law day and night. That person is like a tree planted by streams of water, which yields its fruit in season and whose leaf does not wither—whatever they do prospers. . . . For the LORD watches over the way of the righteous, but the way of the wicked leads to destruction. (Psalm 1:1–3, 6)

On dark and confusing days, you can know the direction to take because God's Word is a "lamp for [your] feet, a light on [your] path" (Psalm 119:105). Praise God that you have "the prophetic message as something completely reliable, and you will do well to pay attention to it, as to a light shining in a dark place, until the day dawns and the morning star rises in your hearts" (2 Peter 1:19).

God has spoken. May we be a faithful people who listen and trust and follow.

APPENDIX A

BOOK RECOMMENDATIONS
FOR FURTHER STUDY

Craig Blomberg, *Can We Still Believe the Bible? An Evangelical Engagement with Contemporary Questions* (Grand Rapids: Brazos Press, 2014).

F. F. Bruce, *The Canon of Scripture* (Downers Grove, IL: InterVarsity Press, 1988).

Kevin DeYoung, *Taking God at His Word* (Wheaton, IL: Crossway, 2014).

John Frame, *The Doctrine of the Word of God* (Phillipsburg, NJ: P&R, 2010).

Michael Kruger, *The Question of Canon: Challenging the Status Quo in the New Testament Debate* (Downers Grove, IL: InterVarsity Press, 2013).

Michael Kruger, *The Canon Revisited: Establishing the Origins and Authority of the New Testament Books* (Wheaton, IL: Crossway, 2012).

Anthony N. S. Lane, "Sola Scriptura? Making Sense of a Post-Reformation Slogan," in *A Pathway into the Holy Scripture*, ed. Philip Satterthwaite and David Wright (Grand Rapids: Eerdmans, 1994).

Bruce M. Metzger, *The Canon of the New Testament* (Oxford: Oxford University Press, 1987).

APPENDIX B

THE APOCRYPHA

Is it possible that there were meant to be more than sixty-six books in the Bible? There are additional books that are considered by Roman Catholic and Eastern Orthodox Churches to be part of the biblical canon. In this appendix, we will briefly explore the Apocrypha and ask whether these additional books were meant to belong in the Bible.

Although all Christians accept the sixty-six books of the Old and New Testaments as authoritative, Roman Catholic and Eastern Orthodox Churches include additional books sometimes called "deuterocanonical" or "apocryphal" books. These additional books were included in the Greek translation of the Hebrew Bible (the Septuagint) and subsequently adopted by some Christians as authoritative. They include the books of Tobit, Judith, 1 and 2 Maccabees, the Wisdom of Solomon, Ecclesiasticus, Baruch, and additional portions of Daniel and Esther.

Although these books are accepted within Catholic and Eastern Orthodox traditions as canonical, they are not seen as authoritative by Protestant traditions. A major reason Protestants reject the canonicity of the Apocrypha is that these books were not part of the Hebrew canon and were not part of the authoritative Hebrew and Aramaic text known as the Masoretic Text. Similarly, the Apocrypha was not included in first-century Jewish historian Josephus's description of the Hebrew canon.[22]

What was the Apocrypha's relationship with the New Testament? None of the apocryphal books were directly quoted in the writings of the New Testament as authoritative. This is in contrast to the many Old Testament quotations throughout the New Testament. However, the New Testament does include allusions to apocryphal writing.

While we do not consider these books to be canonical, they still hold value. For example, they can provide historical and reliable snapshots of faithfulness to God during difficult times. The stories of a Jewish family that helped restore the nation between the Seleucid and Roman takeovers are fascinating and provide valuable background information to understand the New Testament world. We can read these stories in the apocryphal books of 1 and 2 Maccabees. But while they are valuable, we must not put the apocryphal books on the same level as inspired Scripture. Fifth-century church father Jerome articulated a helpful perspective on the Apocrypha with a similar sentiment: "These are books that, though not esteemed like the Holy Scriptures, are still both useful and good to read."[23]

Throughout church history there had been voices, such as Augustine's, arguing for the full canonicity of the apocryphal books, but it was not until after the Protestant Reformation that this became official Roman Catholic doctrine. The Roman Catholic Church made acceptance of these books their official position at the Council of Trent in reaction to the Protestant Reformation. The question of the Apocrypha's canonicity is not insignificant for church doctrine because some of the apocryphal books have been used to substantiate doctrines that are not explicitly taught in either the Old Testament or New Testament. These include prayers for the dead, the worship of angels, the veneration of saints, purgatory—issues which Protestants and Catholics have historically disagreed over.

Here is a list of reasons why we recommend treating the Apocrypha as mere historical documents and not as Scripture:

1. They were written in the intertestamental times, after the Old Testament canon was closed.
2. The Jews rejected the Apocrypha as part of the Old Testament canon in the time of Jesus and afterward. It was part of the Greek translation of the Old Testament called the Septuagint, but not part of the Hebrew translation called the Masoretic Text.
3. Jesus Christ and the apostles never directly quoted from them or cited them as Scripture, even though there are some allusions to apocryphal writings.
4. They contain historical problems and contradictions regarding doctrinal teachings taught elsewhere in the Bible.

5. After centuries of debate, the Apocrypha was officially included as authoritative Scripture for the Roman Catholic Church in the 1500s, and it was in response to the rise of Protestantism.

NOTES

1. The alteration to this three-fold division was in part due to the Scriptures' being written in Greek (e.g., the Septuagint), which organized the books according to literary type of law, history, poetry, and prophecy. Julius Scott Jr. explains the shift from the traditional threefold division into a more topical organization: "The advent of Hellenism and the subsequent appearance of the Scriptures in Greek brought a challenge to the consensus. The books in the Septuagint, other than the five of Moses, were arranged according to literary types. This undermined the threefold division and its implications for interpretation." See Julius Scott Jr., *Jewish Backgrounds of the New Testament* (Grand Rapids: Baker Academic, 2000), 138.

2. Rachel Klippenstein and J. David Stark, ed. John D. Barry et al., *The Lexham Bible Dictionary* (Bellingham, WA: Lexham Press, 2016), s.v. "New Testament."

3. Craig S. Keener, *Christobiography: Memory, History, and Reliability of the Gospels* (Grand Rapids: Eerdmans, 2019), 1.

4. See Josephus, "Josephus on James" in *Antiquities,* book 20, chap. 9, https://pages.uncc.edu/james-tabor/ancient-judaism/josephus-james/, and Philip Schaff, *Nicene and Post-Nicene Fathers,* ser. 2, vol. 1, chap. 25, https://www.ccel.org/ccel/schaff/npnf201.iii.vii.xxvi.html.

5. For more on the end of history, see Gary L. Johnson, *The End: The Return of King Jesus and the Renewal of All Things* (Renew.org, 2021).

6. For more detailed information about what follows, consult the seminal works of F. F. Bruce, *The Canon of Scripture* (Downers Grove, IL: InterVarsity Press, 1988), and Bruce M. Metzger, *The Canon of the New Testament* (Oxford: Oxford University Press, 1987).

7. David Noel Freedman, ed., *The Anchor Bible Dictionary* (New York: Doubleday, 1992), s.v. "canon."

8. David A. deSilva, *An Introduction to the New Testament: Contexts, Methods & Ministry Formation,* 2nd ed. (Downers Grove, IL: IVP Academic, 2018).

9. Michael J. Kruger, *The Question of Canon: Challenging the Status Quo in the New Testament Debate* (Downers Grove, IL: InterVarsity Press, 2013), 206.

10. Michael J. Kruger, *Canon Revisited: Establishing the Origins and Authority of the New Testament Books* (Wheaton, IL: Crossway, 2012), 292.

11. See Bruce M. Metzger, *The Canon of the New Testament* (Oxford: Oxford University Press, 1987).

12. Michael J. Kruger, "10 Misconceptions About the NT Canon: #10: 'Athanasius' Festal Letter (367 A.D.) Is the First Complete List of New Testament Books,'" December 11, 2012, accessed January 19, 2021, https://www.michaeljkruger.com/10-misconceptions-about-the-nt-canon-10-athanasius-festal-letter-367-a-d-is-the-first-complete-list-of-new-testament-books/.

13. Michael Kruger, *The Question of Canon*, 210.

14. This is an important fact that is in contradistinction to the claims of the Roman Catholic Church as definitively stated by Oscar Cullman in the advanced debates leading up to Vatican II; see "The Tradition," in *The Early Church* (London: SCM Press, 1956).

15. Kruger, *The Question of Canon*, 91.

16. Clark H. Pinnock, *The Scripture Principle* (Vancouver: Regent College Publishing, 1984), 81–82.

17. Milton S. Terry, *Biblical Hermeneutics: A Treatise on the Interpretation of the Old and New Testaments,* ed. George R. Crooks and John F. Hurst, New Edition, Thoroughly Revised, vol. 2, Library of Biblical and Theological Literature (New York; Cincinnati: Eaton & Mains; Curts & Jennings, 1890), 17.

18. For the difference between meaning and significance, see E. D. Hirsch, *Validity in Interpretation* (New Haven: Yale University Press, 1967), 8.

19. Dean B. Deppe, *All Roads Lead to the Text: Eight Methods of Inquiry into the Bible* (Grand Rapids: Eerdmans, 2011), 7.

20. David Young, *A Grand Illusion: How Progressive Christianity Undermines Biblical Faith* (Renew.org, 2019), 72.

21. For more on Renew.org's understanding of infallibility, see I. Howard Marshall, *Biblical Inspiration* (Vancouver: Regent College Publications, 2004).

22. To read Josephus's description of the Hebrew canon as well as a helpful commentary on it, see "Josephus: Historical Evidence of the Old Testament Canon," *Blue Letter Bible,* May 29, 2012, accessed July 26, 2021, https://blogs.blueletterbible.org/blb/2012/05/29/josephus-historical-evidence-of-the-old-testament-canon/.

23. David E. Briones, "A Brief History of the Apocrypha," November 6, 2019, accessed January 19, 2021, https://faculty.wts.edu/posts/a-brief-history-of-the-apocrypha/.

CHRISTIAN CONVICTIONS

DISCERNING THE ESSENTIAL, IMPORTANT, AND PERSONAL ELEMENTS

CHAD RAGSDALE

To my mom and dad,
who were my first teachers of models
of the essentials of Christian belief

CONTENTS

General Editors' Note 139

Introduction 141

CHAPTER 1: Does What We Believe Really Matter? 143

CHAPTER 2: What Is the Difference Between Essential,
Important, and Personal Elements? 147

CHAPTER 3: What Are the Essentials of Biblical Christianity? 153

CHAPTER 4: How Should We Treat Elements of Our Faith
that Are Not Essential? 161

CHAPTER 5: How Should We Treat Those Who
Disagree with Us? 167

Appendix: Book Recommendations for Further Study 173

Notes 175

GENERAL EDITORS' NOTE

The Bible teaches us many truths. How do we understand the importance of these teachings? Are they all equally important? Some seem to be more important than others. In fact, some teachings appear to be core to the faith, while others seem to be comparatively peripheral.

Chad Ragsdale is uniquely qualified to help us sort out elements of the faith that are essential, important, and personal. Chad is the Academic Dean at Ozark Christian College, where he has served on the faculty since 2005. He teaches primarily in the areas of Christian apologetics, philosophy, and biblical interpretation. Chad has been married to his wife, Tara, since 2001 and has three kids, Logan, Adeline, and Ryane. He has a Bachelor of Arts in Preaching and a Masters of Divinity in Contemporary Theology—both from Lincoln Christian University. He has a Doctor of Ministry in Engaging Mind and Culture from Talbot School of Theology.

This book expounds on the section from the Renew.org Leaders' Faith Statement called "Christian Convictions":

> We believe the Scriptures reveal three distinct elements of the faith: essential
> elements which are necessary for salvation; important elements which are
> to be pursued so that we faithfully follow Christ; and personal elements
> or opinion. The gospel is essential. Every person who is indwelt and sealed
> by God's Holy Spirit because of their faith in the gospel is a brother or a
> sister in Christ. Important but secondary elements of the faith are vital.
> Our faithfulness to God requires us to seek and pursue them, even as we
> acknowledge that our salvation may not be dependent on getting them right.
> And third, there are personal matters of opinion, disputable areas where God
> gives us personal freedom. But we are never at liberty to express our freedom

in a way that causes others to stumble in sin. In all things, we want to show understanding, kindness, and love.

*See the full Network Faith Statements at the end of this book.

Support Scriptures: 1 Corinthians 15:1–8; Romans 1:15–17; Galatians 1:6–9; 2 Timothy 2:8; Ephesians 1:13–14; 4:4–6; Romans 8:9; 1 Corinthians 12:13; 1 Timothy 4:16; 2 Timothy 3:16–4:4; Matthew 15:6–9; Acts 20:32; 1 Corinthians 11:1–2; 1 John 2:3–4; 2 Peter 3:14–16; Romans 14:1–23.

The following tips might help you use this book more effectively (and the other books in the *Real Life Theology* series):

1. *Five questions, answers, and Scriptures.* We framed this book around five key questions with five short answers and five notable Scriptures. This format provides clarity, making it easier to commit crucial information to memory. This format also enables the books in the *Real Life Theology* series to support our catechism. Our catechism is a series of fixed questions and answers for instruction in church or home. In all, the series has fifty-two questions, answers, and key Scriptures. This particular book focuses on the five that are most pertinent to Christian convictions.
2. *Summary videos.* You can find three to seven-minute video teachings that summarize the book, as well as each chapter, at Renew.org. These short videos can function as standalone teachings. But for groups or group leaders using the book, they can also be used to launch discussion of the reading.

May God use this book to fuel faithful and effective disciple making in your life and church.

For King Jesus,
Bobby Harrington and Daniel McCoy
General Editors, *Real Life Theology* series

INTRODUCTION

I still remember approaching my dad at the campfire that night. It was the summer of my seventh-grade year, and we were at one of my favorite places on earth: summer camp at Lake Region Christian Assembly. My dad was the dean of the week, and I was a camper with a spiritual dilemma that had been stirring within me all week. I was baptized into Christ very young, at the age of seven. I remember being deeply troubled by how much more I knew about Jesus at the age of thirteen than I did when I was seven. This seems a little funny to say now that I am in my forties looking back at what I thought I knew when I was thirteen. It is now obvious to me that we naturally continue to grow and progress in all sorts of ways as we age, but as a middle school student, my spiritual growth was causing me anxiety. Attending camp that week had the twin effect of both spurring on my faith yet arousing the fear that perhaps my baptism was not sufficient. Had I really known enough at my baptism in order to be saved? So after our evening worship around the campfire, I went to my dad with a simple question: "Do I need to get baptized again?"

In some sense, this book is about my dad's answer to that question. His answer was twofold. First, he reminded me about one of the most important truths of discipleship: we are always in the process of growth. He assured me that if I did not know more about Jesus at thirteen than at seven, then there would be something terribly wrong with my development. He told me that he was still learning new and exciting things every day as he followed Jesus. He was also constantly reminded of his need for Jesus. In those moments, he told me, we need not fret about whether our baptism was enough. Instead, we celebrate the unending truth of our baptism. A line I have used with my own kids is, "God's grace does not need booster shots."

Second, he reminded me that the basic truths of my faith had not changed; I had simply come to understand them at a deeper level. We briefly walked through those essential things that Christians believe. With a father's pastoral care, he assured me that I had "known enough" to be baptized even at a young age. The essential beliefs that were "enough" are the focus of this brief book.

Following an earthquake in the ancient city of Philippi, a terrified jailer kneeled before Paul and Silas and asked a pressing question: "What must I do to be saved?" (Acts 16:30b). This is like the question my thirteen-year-old self asked and what many people continue to ask: "What must we believe to be saved?"

THE BASIC TRUTHS OF MY FAITH HAD NOT CHANGED; I HAD SIMPLY COME TO UNDERSTAND THEM AT A DEEPER LEVEL.

People approach this question in different ways. It has become fashionable for many today to wonder if it matters at all what a person believes. This will be the subject of the first chapter of this book. Others are confident that what a person believes matters, but they struggle to distinguish between beliefs that are essential for salvation, beliefs that are important in order to faithfully follow Christ, and beliefs that are personal preferences or opinions. Chapters 2 and 3 are dedicated to identifying these different kinds of Christian beliefs.

The final two chapters are dedicated to addressing practical concerns related to beliefs: How should we treat those elements of our faith that are not essential for salvation? How should we treat those who disagree with us on matters of belief? As in all things, we will take our cues principally from the pages of Scripture. We recognize that answering these questions is complex, but we can do no better than to seek the wisdom and truth found in God's Word. That is my primary aim, but as I answer, I also want to capture my father's pastoral care in the way I answer these questions. Seeking to understand Christian beliefs—and their level of importance—is not merely an intellectual exercise; identifying the truths of our faith cuts to the very core of life and salvation.

1

DOES WHAT WE BELIEVE REALLY MATTER?

Answer: Yes. To have faith is not simply a feeling or emotion. Faith begins with believing that certain things are true about God and his Son, Jesus.

For God so loved the world that he gave his one and only Son, that whoever believes in him shall not perish but have eternal life.
— John 3:16

Starting in the spring of 2020, much of society temporarily shut down because of the COVID-19 pandemic. These shutdowns, of course, dramatically affected local churches because they were forced, in many cases, to stop meeting in person for worship. Laura Kelly, the governor of Kansas, faced criticism for her decision to shut down churches in her state, and defended her stance:

> Religion is really not about the building. It's about the faith, it's about how it feels on the inside. The need to congregate is important but not during a pandemic. . . . I am not trying to suppress religion. I'm just trying to save Kansans' lives.[1]

There is a lot we could say about this statement, but for the purposes of this chapter, I want to focus on the second sentence, "It's about the faith, it's about how it feels on the inside." I agree that faith is more important than buildings, but is it true that faith is about "how it feels on the inside"?

To answer this question, let us turn first to the biblical Gospels. In the Gospel of John, the word "believe" appears ninety-eight times in its twenty-one chapters. In the overwhelming majority of those cases, belief is directed toward a person—Jesus. John 3:16 is the most famous example, but another good example is John 11:25: "I am the resurrection and the life. The one who believes in me will live, even though they die."[2] What is most important to Jesus is that people would believe in him and be saved. We observe a similar idea in Matthew's Gospel. For example, Jesus asked Peter a critical question: "Who do you say I am?" Peter responded by affirming, "You are the Messiah, the Son of the living God" (Matthew 16:15–16). It is Peter's true confession of Jesus' identity, not simply his feelings, which serves as the bedrock foundation for the church.

BELIEVING WITH THE WHOLE SELF

IN THE LETTERS OF Paul, we discover a consistent emphasis on believing rightly. One of the best and simplest examples is in Romans 10:9–10.

> If you declare with your mouth, "Jesus is Lord," and believe in your heart that God raised him from the dead, you will be saved. For it is with your heart that you believe and are justified, and it is with your mouth that you profess your faith and are saved.

The modern reader might read this and associate "heart" with "feelings," but this would be a mistake. To the ancients, a person's heart did not primarily represent their feelings. It represented the innermost being of a person. To believe with your heart means that you believe something beyond superficial faith. It means that you have believed with your whole self. To Paul here, much like to Jesus in the Gospels, salvation is tied to what the saved believe. The notion that faith is merely about feelings would have been foreign to Paul.

Now, it is important to know that biblical faith in Jesus is not *merely* about belief. The book of James reminds us that "faith by itself, if it is not accompanied by action, is dead" (James 2:17). Paul agrees with this in the Romans passage above! He reminds us in the passage above that believing in Jesus is more than just an intellectual exercise; we believe with our hearts and minds. Our beliefs bring about an effect in every part of us. This idea is also at the core of what Jesus called the Greatest Commandment. He told us to love God "with all your heart and with all your soul and with all your mind" (Matthew 22:37). Our belief really looks a lot like love in a marriage. It is comprehensive; it includes affection, trust, faithfulness, and loyalty.[3] The Greek word for "faith" in the New Testament is *pistis*. It encompasses everything you would find in a loyal relationship between a husband and wife that endures over the decades. So faith is more than belief, but we must add that believing is never *less* than affirming certain truths with our intellect. Loving God is difficult without any knowledge of who that God is. This leads me to my next point.

MANY PATHS UP THE SAME MOUNTAIN?

DESPITE WHAT SCRIPTURE SAYS, it is fashionable for some in our culture to insist that it does not really matter what you believe about God or religion. To these religious relativists, religious beliefs are different from other kinds of beliefs like beliefs about science, mathematics, or even history. The assumption is that specific beliefs about God are like opinions on music: everyone has their own preference and no one is any closer to the truth than the next person. They sometimes compare beliefs about God to taking different paths up a mountain. The paths might be different, but the destination is ultimately the same. So when it comes to God, distinct beliefs do not matter. Religious beliefs are merely about personal preferences and not about what is objectively true.

We should point out that there is a fundamental problem with this many-paths-up-the-same-mountain illustration. It assumes that God is simply a place. If God were a place, then the illustration would work because we can of course take multiple paths to get to the same place. But God is not a place; God is a person. Remembering how Jesus talks about faith in the Gospel of John, we know that God calls us not to believe in abstractions but in him as a person (John 11:25). He calls us to believe *in him*. This sort of faith in Jesus is personal and exclusive.

GOD CALLS US NOT TO BELIEVE IN ABSTRACTIONS BUT IN HIM AS A PERSON.

This kind of faith might be illustrated by a marriage relationship. What does it mean for me to "believe in" my wife? Well, my belief in this case would look a lot like trust, commitment, and even love. My belief in my wife is personal and exclusive to her. I do not believe in my wife and love her well by committing myself to other women. Such a belief would be adulterous. It is not by accident that the false worship of idolatry in the Bible is so often compared to adultery (e.g., Ezekiel 23:37; Jeremiah 3:8–9; Hosea 1:2). Believing in other gods creates a fracture in our relationship with the living God.

There are consequences to assuming that beliefs do not really matter. For example, according to Barna, almost half of practicing Christian millennials say it is wrong to try to evangelize people of other religions.[4] This statistic reveals how many who self-identify as Christians today do not think specific beliefs matter. Why else would they think it's wrong to evangelize? This shows that when people reduce religion to feelings and faith to opinions, the passion for spreading the life-saving truth of the gospel wanes. Tragically, we often find that a faith emptied of concrete beliefs soon becomes no faith at all. On the other hand, we know that believing in Jesus and following him is the only path to freedom (see John 8:31–32). The truth of Jesus sets us free from the power of sin and from the lies that masquerade as truth in this world. What we believe about God matters. It matters for true life and for salvation.

2

WHAT IS THE DIFFERENCE BETWEEN ESSENTIAL, IMPORTANT, AND PERSONAL ELEMENTS?

Answer: Essential elements are necessary for salvation. Important elements do not save us, but are necessary in order to follow Jesus faithfully. Personal elements are based on marginal convictions or preferences.

There is one body and one Spirit, just as you were called to one hope when you were called; one Lord, one faith, one baptism; one God and Father of all, who is over all and through all and in all.
— Ephesians 4:4–6

In the last chapter, we established that our beliefs about God matter, but not every belief matters in the same way. For instance, I believe that Mercury is the planet that orbits closest to the sun, but while that belief is true, it does not necessarily *matter* for how we live our lives. We have many beliefs just like that—beliefs that are true yet inconsequential. Likewise, we have other beliefs that may be proven incorrect at some point in time to relatively little consequence. If I believe that the Chicago Cubs will likely win today, for example, but they end up losing, my life will not have changed other than some mild frustration. In addition, we each have a host of personal preferences and personal opinions that may be true for us but not for others. Many of these preferences are also relatively inconsequential for others, even though they may be meaningful for me. My preference for Mexican food over

Italian food does not mean that Mexican food is better than Italian food for everyone, just me and others with that preference.

We also have beliefs we hold that are very consequential. I am not a good swimmer, for example, which has been confirmed by multiple negative experiences I've had trying to swim. If I were to believe that I am a good swimmer, that could actually put my life at risk. My beliefs about my swimming abilities matter differently than my preference for Mexican food. As another example of how beliefs can matter or not, my belief in the orbital position of Mercury does not matter, but my belief in the connection between smoking and cancer does.

SOME BELIEFS ARE ESSENTIAL FOR LIFE AND WELL-BEING. The point here is that when it comes to beliefs and how we live them out, they do not all matter in the same way. Some beliefs are essential for life and well-being. Some are not essential, but they are still very important. Other beliefs matter only as far as our personal preferences matter to us. Many of our beliefs fall somewhere on this spectrum of categories.

SPECTRUM OF THEOLOGICAL BELIEFS

OUR BELIEFS ABOUT GOD are similar: not all of our beliefs matter in the same way. There are some beliefs that we can call "essential for salvation." These beliefs are so important that not believing them keeps a person from being saved. Other beliefs we can call "essential for orthodoxy." Orthodoxy, in this case, simply means "proper belief." We ought to pursue these so that we can faithfully follow Christ. They are important enough that if we get them wrong, we will need correction and instruction. Our salvation, however, is not determined by our ability to get all of these beliefs exactly right. Finally, there are many beliefs, especially those about the practice of faith, that qualify as personal preferences in our relationship with God. They may be very important to an individual or to a group of like-minded people, but they are not essential for salvation or important for living a faithful life. These three categories are the essential, important, and personal elements of our faith.

In discussing these essential, important, and personal elements, we are not just talking about the truths we believe but also how we respond to these truths by faith. Faith is the language of our relationship with God; faith is a living, breathing thing. By faith we seek God, repent from sin, obey the teachings of Jesus, and live in step with the Spirit (Hebrews 11:6; Galatians 5:16–21). Faith is the essential human response to God and his grace (Ephesians 2:8–9).

It can be a challenge for us to properly distinguish between essential, important, and personal elements. What one person labels as merely "important," another person might call "essential." Another person might take a belief that should rightly be called essential and relegate it to the realm of personal preferences. I dedicate the next chapter to identifying what Scripture calls essential, but in this chapter, I describe two exercises I've used with college-age students that have helped them identify essential beliefs. May these exercises help you to begin thinking in these categories.

EXERCISE 1: WRITING A PARAGRAPH

First, get out a blank sheet of paper and write a short paragraph summarizing what you consider to be your most important beliefs about God. When I issue this exercise in class, I give my students only one minute to write a maximum of three sentences, and then they read them aloud or turn them in to me. It sounds daunting at first. How can a person—especially a Bible college student eager to impress their professor—possibly summarize their beliefs about God with such limitations? With libraries literally full of books reflecting on the depths of theology, it seems almost wrong even to have students attempt to summarize essential beliefs in this way. The benefit of the exercise, however, is that it functions sort of like a fire drill in the mind. If you had to exit the house quickly and could only take what you could carry, what would you take? The pressure surfaces what really matters to a person versus what is merely important.

After I have them write their paragraphs, I usually have a few students volunteer to read what they have written. This sparks a fun conversation and analysis among the students about what beliefs really matter. Using this exercise, I have gotten some extremely thoughtful and impressive paragraphs through the years. I encourage my students to do two things with their paragraphs: First, I encourage them to critically examine what they have written. Without giving them any time constraints, I have them go back to their paragraph in private and carefully ask themselves why they wrote what they did. *Would you change anything? If so, why?* Second, I encourage the students to repeat the exercise from time to time in order to continue clarifying their thinking.

EXERCISE 2: DRAWING A BULLSEYE

THE SECOND EXERCISE THAT I use to help students identify their core beliefs involves drawing a large target with three concentric circles on the board. The target represents all of their beliefs about God. I ask them, "What is at the bullseye of your target?" The bullseye is necessarily small, so not much can or should fit in the bullseye. "Bullseye beliefs" are our immovable and foundational beliefs about God that are so important that, if they were to change, everything else in our lives would have to change as a result. "Important beliefs" may come close to the bullseye of the target and still others are on the outer edges of the target.

I usually illustrate the usefulness of the target exercise with several examples. One of my favorite examples is dinosaurs. Teaching apologetics for many years, I have come to dislike some questions. I dislike them not because they are inappropriate, but because they miss what is essential and even what is important. "What does the Bible say about dinosaurs?" is one of those questions. I just do not really care because even if we were to find them in the Bible, it does not matter. I think dinosaurs are cool, mind you, but finding them in the Bible is not anywhere near the center of my target. My faith does not rise or fall based on what the Bible says about the Tyrannosaurus Rex.

Another example I use to show the importance of the target exercise is the story of Jonah: "Is the story of Jonah real history or is it meant as a sort of allegory?" I ask. There are different perspectives on this, even among Old Testament scholars. Without providing an answer to the question, I ask the class where the importance of answering such a question should be placed on the target. The students are often divided in their responses. Some students are inclined to place a particular interpretation of Jonah closer to the center of the target than others. Allowing for these differences, I point out that no one places the answer to this question near the bullseye. As a biblical text, the story of Jonah is surely important, but our particular interpretation of it is not a matter of salvation. I also ask students questions about where various practices of faith would appear on the target. For instance, "Where would you place your beliefs about Christians drinking alcohol?" How we answer questions like these is often a matter of personal preference or convictions. Again, they do not come anywhere close to the center of what we believe. They are not important for orthodoxy or essential for salvation but personal elements of our faith.

Other issues come closer to the center. They are not the bullseye, but they surround the bullseye as "important elements." For example: *What do you believe about the inspiration of Scripture? What do you believe about baptism? What do you believe about how the Second Coming of Jesus will occur?* These kinds of questions are very important. In class, we sometimes have spirited discussions about how close some of these questions should come to the center of the target. The students typically agree that, while they are closer to the center, it would be a mistake to place them on the bullseye.

TWO TAKEAWAYS FOR CHRISTIAN CONVICTION

THESE EXERCISES—ESPECIALLY THE target exercise—help my students to realize two important truths. First, they are a reminder that not every issue is worth fighting for in the same way. I typically talk about "fighting" for truth when I walk my students through this exercise in a class I teach on Christian apologetics. Apologetics is the discipline of defending the faith using sound reasons. In my experience, skeptics often try to undermine a person's faith by nibbling at issues that occupy the periphery of the target. I cannot count how many times I have been asked by an incredulous skeptic, "You really believe that a snake talked to a woman in some ancient garden?"

> NOT EVERY ISSUE IS WORTH FIGHTING FOR IN THE SAME WAY.

The target exercise reminds me that I do not have to defend everything. Some elements of my faith are much more important than my particular interpretation of the Genesis narrative about the serpent and Eve. I encourage my students to have conversations with skeptics only about the things that are absolutely essential rather than trying to defend every square inch of the target of faith.

Second, this exercise reminds my students and us today of the dangers of what I call "epistemic legalism." "Epistemic" is just a fancy word that means "knowledge." The New Testament tells us very clearly that we cannot be saved by our own good works (Ephesians 2:8–9), and attempts to earn salvation through good works is sometimes called "legalism." Yet many who rightly reject "good works" legalism still struggle with epistemic legalism. They worry that unless they believe absolutely everything in the right way, God will reject them. They imagine God to be a cruel, celestial teacher who will greet us with a multiple-choice exam when we die. If we answer any of the questions wrongly, then he will reject us. This is just another form of legalism, in which we try to earn salvation not with good works but with perfect belief. This is not an accurate picture of God or of the gospel. Plus, it does not paint a realistic picture of ourselves. Because we are human, not one of us is capable of perfect belief. Paul reminds us that now we see things only in part in this life (1 Corinthians 13:12). We need to understand and believe what is essential and humbly ask for grace in what we might get wrong the further we move away from the bullseye. This progression naturally leads to the need for us to identify what is essential, to which we now turn.

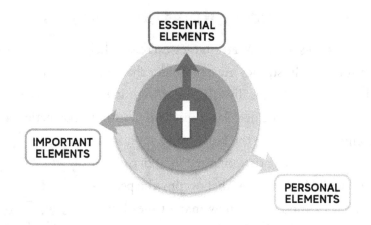

3

WHAT ARE THE ESSENTIALS OF BIBLICAL CHRISTIANITY?

Answer: The essential truths are that God exists, Jesus is Lord, Jesus is the risen Savior, and salvation is by grace and not by human effort. The essential markers of our salvation are the indwelling of the Holy Spirit and a faith that perseveres.

> And without faith it is impossible to please God, because anyone who comes to him must believe that he exists and that he rewards those who earnestly seek him.
> — Hebrews 11:6

Many elements are important to our Christian faith, and a few are actually essential (meaning that we cannot be saved without them). Some of these essential beliefs have been articulated and passed down to us in various creeds, such as the Apostles' Creed. These statements can be very helpful in identifying core Christian teachings. My goal with this chapter is not to create a new creed. Instead, I go to Scripture to identify the essential elements of the Christian faith. These elements include core doctrines we believe and an active faith by which we live. Because of this, we should expect that there are fewer of them than what we find in a traditional creed. This is a task I enter humbly and prayerfully, wanting to speak only where Scripture speaks. It is clear to me that Scripture identifies six essential elements.

1. IT IS ESSENTIAL FOR A CHRISTIAN TO BELIEVE THAT GOD EXISTS (AND TO EARNESTLY SEEK HIM).

IT MAY SEEM OBVIOUS that a person cannot be saved if they do not believe in God's existence, but we must not let what is obvious go unsaid. I remember watching a video on YouTube discussing Europe's new atheists. One particular interview was with a college student in Ireland who identified as a "Christian atheist." He had rejected the existence of God but still "respected Jesus" enough to call himself a Christian. This is absurd. Hebrews 11:6 says, "And without faith it is impossible to please God, because anyone who comes to him must believe that he exists and that he rewards those who earnestly seek him." A person cannot please God without faith, and faith begins with the acknowledgement that God exists. Similar to this is the conviction that everything else that exists was created by God (Hebrews 11:3; see also Genesis 1:1; John 1:1–3).

You will notice that Hebrews 11:6 does not stop at mere belief in God. The verse associates belief in God with earnestly seeking him. Seeking God takes us beyond vague ideas of a deity and brings us to the personal God of Scripture. An intellectual belief in God is not enough for salvation; we must also actively orient our lives toward him. This is the kind of faith that pleases God and is rewarded by God. By faith, we must be committed to seeking God and submitting to him. James makes a similar point in James 2:17, which I quoted in Chapter 1, with a subsequent jarring point about demons.

> In the same way, faith by itself, if it is not accompanied by action, is dead. But someone will say, "You have faith; I have deeds." Show me your faith without deeds, and I will show you my faith by my deeds. You believe that there is one God. Good! Even the demons believe that—and shudder. (James 2:17–19)

I would argue that believing in God without seeking him amounts to practical atheism. Believing without seeking is like a young married man who acknowledges his marriage yet lives every day as if he were single. Living faith is reflected in a lifestyle directed toward God (more on that below).

2. IT IS ESSENTIAL THAT A CHRISTIAN BELIEVES JESUS IS LORD.

PAUL SAYS IN ROMANS 10:9, "If you declare with your mouth, 'Jesus is Lord,' and believe in your heart that God raised him from the dead, you will be saved." The confession that Jesus is Lord was essential to Christian belief from the very beginning.[5] John 20:28 is an important passage that tells us the story of Thomas, who, upon seeing and touching the resurrected Jesus, cried out, "My Lord and my God" (John 20:28b). This simple yet shocking declaration becomes a cornerstone belief of any follower of Jesus. Biblical scholar Grant Osborne puts it this way: "At the heart of true Christian worship is the realization that Jesus is more than a mere Rabbi, more even than a Messiah. He is fully God and Lord of all."[6]

As Osborne points out, calling Jesus "Lord" is so much more than a title of respect. The Jews associated lordship with God himself. Around six thousand times in the Hebrew Scriptures (our Old Testament), God is referred to as "Lord." Even Gentiles (non-Jews) would have associated the title of Lord with the authority granted to a divine figure. This title was sometimes associated with the emperor who reigned in a "more-than-merely-human sense."[7] Therefore, when we confess Jesus is Lord, we are doing much more than merely saying that he is our "personal Lord." No, to confess that Jesus is Lord is to agree with Jesus' words to his disciples at the end of Matthew's Gospel: "All authority in heaven and on earth has been given to me" (Matthew 28:18b). Only God himself can hold all authority.

With this being said, it is also important to recognize that the belief in Jesus as Lord is deeply personal. Jesus has all authority in heaven and earth, which includes authority over our lives. This is the heart of discipleship. Paul says toward the end of his letter to the Romans, "If we live, we live for the Lord; and if we die, we die for the Lord. So, whether we live or die, we belong to the Lord" (Romans 14:8). To declare "Jesus is Lord" means that he is the center of our lives, or, as Paul puts it in another place, "I have been crucified with Christ and I no longer live, but Christ lives in me" (Galatians 2:20a). A Christian who says Jesus is Lord is not just describing something about the world; they are also describing something about their own heart. Jesus has given them—us—a new identity, a new hope, and a new purpose to live for his glory.

3. IT IS ESSENTIAL THAT A CHRISTIAN BELIEVES THAT JESUS IS THE RISEN SAVIOR.

In the verse from Romans 10 quoted above, it is not only the confession that Jesus is Lord that Paul associates with salvation. He adds the belief in the resurrection of Jesus from the dead as essential to salvation. Lordship and resurrection go hand in hand, not just here but also in places like Acts 2. In that passage, Peter preached the founding sermon of the church. He declared that, although Jesus had been crucified, "God has raised this Jesus to life, and we are all witnesses of it" (Acts 2:32). A few verses later, he said, "Therefore, let all Israel be assured of this: God has made this Jesus, whom you crucified, both Lord and Messiah" (Acts 2:36). It is common in the New Testament for Jesus to be called Lord. He is often called "Lord Jesus" (forty-three times) or "Lord Jesus Christ" (sixty times). Notably, these titles do not occur in the Gospels before the resurrection, but they are used extensively after it. The confession of Jesus' lordship and the belief in his resurrection are vitally connected.

A professor of mine in graduate school put it this way: "If Jesus has risen from the dead, then nothing else matters. If Jesus has not risen from the dead, then nothing at all matters." This echoes the thought of Paul in 1 Corinthians 15. At the beginning of the chapter, Paul says he wants to remind the Corinthians of the gospel. He writes, "By this gospel you are saved" (1 Corinthians 15:2a). Then, in verses 3–8, Paul briefly explains the gospel:[8]

> For what I received I passed on to you as of first importance: that Christ died for our sins according to the Scriptures, that he was buried, that he was raised on the third day according to the Scriptures, and that he appeared to Cephas, and then to the Twelve. After that, he appeared to more than five hundred of the brothers and sisters at the same time, most of whom are still living, though some have fallen asleep. Then he appeared to James, then to all the apostles, and last of all he appeared to me also, as to one abnormally born.

These verses show us how Jesus saves us. He died as a sacrifice for our sins, and that death was followed by a physical resurrection. Later in the chapter, Paul makes a blunt point: "If there is no resurrection of the dead, then not even Christ has been raised. And if Christ has not been raised, our preaching is useless and so is your faith" (1 Corinthians 15:13–14). Believing in Jesus' resurrection is essential for salvation because without the resurrection there is no salvation. Without the resurrection, Jesus' death on the cross was of no consequence, and we are still in our sins (1 Corinthians 15:17). The good news, however, is that Jesus is both our risen Savior and our Lord. The resurrection is the truth that revolutionized the world and continues to transform lives.

4. IT IS ESSENTIAL THAT A CHRISTIAN IS SAVED BY GRACE THROUGH FAITH AND NOT BY HUMAN EFFORT.

IN EPHESIANS 2:8–9, PAUL says, "For it is by grace you have been saved, through faith—and this is not from yourselves, it is the gift of God—not by works, so that no one can boast." Grace is the *means* of our salvation. We are not able to save ourselves. Even though we deserve death and separation from God because of sin, salvation is an unearned gift (see also Romans 6:23). Faith is the *agency* of our salvation. We are not saved *by* faith; we are saved *through* faith.

> GRACE IS THE MEANS OF OUR SALVATION. WE ARE NOT ABLE TO SAVE OURSELVES.

One way we can understand this is to think about how we are physically alive right now. We are living *by* oxygen. Without oxygen, we would suffocate and die, but we are also living *through* our lungs. All the oxygen in the world will do us no good without properly functioning lungs. So we are saved by God's grace and receive that grace through faith.

Paul makes it emphatically clear in the above verses that our good works do not save us. As he points out in the following verse (Ephesians 2:10), we are saved *to do good works*, but we cannot earn our salvation *by good works*. Attempting to be "good enough" to earn our salvation denies the sufficient work of Jesus on the cross. This is why Paul declares to the Galatian Christians that they have been bewitched into following a non-gospel that denies grace (Galatians 3:1). He summarizes, "I do not set aside the grace of God, for if righteousness could be gained through the law, Christ died for nothing!" (Galatians 2:21).

Denying grace seemed to get Paul incredibly angry. It got Jesus angry too. In the Gospels, Jesus regularly rebuked the Pharisees for their hypocrisy and public displays of righteousness. Ironically, it was the tax collectors, the prostitutes, and other sinners who were repenting and believing in Jesus (Matthew 21:32). The self-righteousness of the religious leaders was actually keeping them from believing and thus from being saved. In the same way, our salvation is dependent on our trust in the work of Jesus and not in our own works of righteousness. Paul reminds us of this: "You see, at just the right time, when we were still powerless, Christ died for the ungodly" (Romans 5:6). This is good news! It is only upon discovering our own powerlessness that we are truly ready to be saved.

5. IT IS ESSENTIAL THAT A CHRISTIAN BE BORN AGAIN BY THE HOLY SPIRIT.

ONE NIGHT, JESUS WAS approached by a religious leader named Nicodemus. Like many people today, Nicodemus was not only curious but also cautious about Jesus. Nicodemus asked Jesus a question about his identity, and in Jesus' typical style, he answered the question indirectly: "Very truly I tell you, no one can see the kingdom of God unless they are born again" (John 3:3). We can easily understand why Nicodemus was confused by the answer: *Born again? How does that work? How is a fully grown man born again?*

Jesus responded, "Very truly I tell you, no one can enter the kingdom of God unless they are born of water and the Spirit. Flesh gives birth to flesh, but the Spirit gives birth to spirit" (John 3:5–6). It is likely that Jesus was calling to mind the words we find in Ezekiel 36:25–28, in which God promised a time when he would renew his people and place his Spirit within them. Jesus was telling Nicodemus the amazing news that the time anticipated by Ezekiel had arrived in him! God has granted us a new life and a new place in his kingdom by being born again by the Holy Spirit.

I used to ask students in one of my freshman Bible classes at the beginning of the semester, "What really makes a person a Christian?" Sometimes, I put it another way: "How do we know if a person is a Christian?" I would get a variety of answers. Often, answers would gravitate toward behaviors typical of a Christian: a Christian goes to church, a Christian engages in disciplines like prayer or Bible reading, a Christian acts in ways that are distinct from the world. The expectation implicit to these responses is that being a Christian does change the way a person lives their life (e.g., Ephesians 4:1–2). Yet to Jesus what matters for salvation is new life in the Spirit. It's not just important but essential to salvation. The distinguishing mark of a Christian is that the Holy Spirit has taken up residence in their life to make them a new person.

We observe this in the book of Acts when the church was born through the power of the Holy Spirit working through the apostles (Acts 1:8). New believers were promised the gift of the Holy Spirit upon their repentance and baptism (Acts 2:38). Paul also emphasizes the new life we experience in the Spirit in Ephesians when he says that we are included in Christ when we believe the gospel, adding that believers are "marked in him with a seal, the promised Holy Spirit, who is a deposit guaranteeing our inheritance until the redemption of those who are God's possession—to the praise of his glory" (Ephesians 1:13b–14). Paul makes the same point in Romans, that "if anyone does not have the Spirit of Christ, they do not belong to Christ" (Romans 8:9b). He goes on to say that even though we are subject to death because of our sin, the Spirit gives us life (Romans 8:10–11), and we are now children of God by the Spirit (Romans 8:14–17). John expresses the point too: "This is how we know that we live in him and he in us: He has given us of his Spirit" (1 John 4:13).

As we said in the previous point, we are saved only by God's grace. It is also true that we experience new life only through the Holy Spirit's work within us. God does call us to pursue righteousness and godliness with our lives, but this pursuit is *in response* to being born again by the Spirit (see Ephesians 2:10; 4:1). A life that is lived independently of the power and influence of the Holy Spirit is not a Christian life. On the other hand, a life that has been reborn of the Spirit will produce righteous fruit (Galatians 5:22–25) and gifts to be used for building others up (1 Corinthians 12:7–30).

6. IT IS ESSENTIAL THAT A CHRISTIAN PERSEVERE IN A FAITHFUL FAITH.

THE BOOK OF HEBREWS was written to a group of Christians who were growing weary in their faith because they had encountered hardship and opposition as a result of their faith. Thomas Long summarizes their situation this way: "Tired of walking the walk, many of them are considering taking a walk, leaving the community and falling away from the faith."[9] Hebrews was written in order to encourage its recipients to persevere in their faith. The author warns them to "pay the most careful attention, therefore, to what we have heard, so that we do not drift away" (Hebrews 2:1). Then, in the next chapter, the author challenges them to encourage each other daily because "we have come to share in Christ, if indeed we hold our original conviction firmly to the very end" (Hebrews 3:14). Later, in Hebrews 6, the author exhorts them to not "become lazy, but to imitate those who through faith and patience inherit what has been promised" (Hebrews 6:12). Then he says to remember the example of Jesus, "who endured such opposition from sinners, so that [they would] not grow weary and lose heart" (Hebrews 12:3). The message of Hebrews is clear: believers must persevere in their faith, not giving up but being resolute in their commitment to Christ.

Perseverance is a common theme not just in Hebrews but also throughout the New Testament. Jesus tells us a parable comparing his kingdom to a farmer who went out to sow his seed. Some of the farmer's seed falls on rocky ground. The plant sprouts up quickly, but then it withers just as quickly. Jesus says this is the person who believes for a little while, but falls away during testing (Luke 8:13). The book of James puts it this way: "Blessed is the one who perseveres under trial because, having stood the test, that person will receive the crown of life that the Lord has promised to those who love him" (James 1:12). Paul also regularly talks about the need for perseverance and endurance. Perseverance in the midst of suffering is essential for a mature faith (Romans 5:3–5; see also 2 Corinthians 1:6; 1 Thessalonians 1:3–4).

A living faith perseveres. Believers express faith through a repentant lifestyle (Hebrews 10:26; Galatians 5:19–21). It is easy in this world to gradually "drift away" from our faith, sometimes because of hardships, pain, or suffering. Some of us know from experience that faith can become difficult to maintain in those moments. More often, though, we drift because we simply get distracted or sidetracked by all of the other issues of life and our commitment to Jesus just withers from inattention. Then, other times, our sin deceives us (Hebrews 3:13). For all these reasons, we must remain actively and intentionally engaged in the life of the church each and every day to encourage our brothers and sisters in the faith (see Hebrews 10:19–25).

A LIVING FAITH PERSEVERES.

4

HOW SHOULD WE TREAT ELEMENTS OF OUR FAITH THAT ARE NOT ESSENTIAL?

Answer: Important but secondary elements of the faith are vital. Our faithfulness to God requires us to seek and pursue them, even as we acknowledge that our salvation may not be dependent on getting them right.

He began to speak boldly in the synagogue. When Priscilla and Aquila heard him, they invited him to their home and explained to him the way of God more adequately.
— Acts 18:26

Two circumstances from my early days in ministry come to mind when I think about the question of this chapter. In one circumstance, I had just finished teaching a Bible study at the small church I was pastoring on the book of Revelation where the question of the rapture had come up. The issue of the rapture divides many believers. I do not personally believe that the Bible teaches the rapture. I explained to the class that belief in the rapture is a relatively new belief among Christians and those who use biblical passages to support the rapture misinterpret those passages. Perhaps you agree with me. Perhaps you disagree. Well, a woman in the class very strongly disagreed. In fact, she was alarmed! She just could not understand how a person could be a Christian, let alone a minister, and not believe in *the rapture*. To her, the issue was so important that she felt she could no longer worship with our church.

In another circumstance, I was meeting with a woman who was thinking about joining our church after visiting for many months. She had some questions about what we believed as a church, especially with regard to baptism. I explained to her what Scripture had to say about baptism and why our church was committed to believer's baptism for the remission of sins. She asked me whether or not she could be saved without being baptized. Personally, I really do not like this question: it turns baptism into a "have to" instead of a "get to." I told her that God's grace is what saves us. Baptism is our act of obedience in which we *get to* publicly commit ourselves to a covenant relationship with him. She was disappointed at my response, or should I say her interpretation of my answer disappointed her. To her, if baptism is not "essential," then there is really no point in getting baptized.

These two stories represent two common mistakes we sometimes make with non-essential beliefs. We tend to either make them essential to the point that we condemn anyone who does not hold our belief or we make our beliefs unimportant and not worthy of our concern. The Renew.org Network Leaders' Faith Statement about "Essential, Important, and Personal Elements" avoids both of these errors: *important* but secondary elements of the faith are vital but non-essential to salvation. That is, our faithfulness to God requires us to seek and pursue them, even as we acknowledge that our salvation may not be dependent on getting them right.

IMPORTANT BUT SECONDARY ELEMENTS OF THE FAITH ARE VITAL BUT NON-ESSENTIAL TO SALVATION.

Three New Testament stories in particular help us to know how we should treat non-essential elements of our faith.

STORY #1: THE WOMAN AT THE WELL

In John 4, Jesus had a remarkable conversation with a Samaritan woman while at a well in the middle of the day. This conversation was a violation of several social norms. In those days, a respected teacher would never have a private conversation with a woman, especially if the teacher was Jewish and the woman was a hated Samaritan. None of that mattered to Jesus. He simply saw a woman in desperate need of "living water." In the midst of their conversation, the woman asked Jesus what appears to be a peculiar question about the proper place to worship: Should people worship in Jerusalem or in Samaria? While this may seem a strange question to us, this was an important theological dispute in this woman's community. She was eager to have Jesus settle the argument. Jesus answered this way:

> "Woman," Jesus replied, "believe me, a time is coming when you will worship the Father neither on this mountain nor in Jerusalem. You Samaritans worship what you do not know; we worship what we do know, for salvation is from the Jews. Yet a time is coming and has now come when the true worshipers will worship the Father in the Spirit and in truth, for they are the kind of worshipers the Father seeks. God is spirit, and his worshipers must worship in the Spirit and in truth." (John 4:21–24)

Notice what Jesus did here. He answered her question by redirecting her to the heart of the issue. It is not *where* you worship that ultimately matters. It is *how* you worship.

Jesus' example instructs us on how to handle important but non-essential issues. He did not dismiss her question as unimportant, but he did direct her to a deeper issue and a more important truth than what she had considered to be of utmost importance. This is the case with many of our important beliefs. It is not that these beliefs are unimportant, but there is sometimes a deeper issue that we should consider has a higher priority. Revisiting one of the examples above, the woman in my ministry had asked a question about baptism. It was an important question, but her concerns about baptism revealed the deeper issue of obedience and submission to Jesus as Lord. When we understand the joys of following Jesus and the requirements of discipleship on our lives, we stop debating baptism. Instead, it becomes a gift in which we get to partake. The essential issue of Jesus' lordship takes precedence over the non-essential—yet important—role of baptism.

STORY #2: APOLLOS

WE CAN LEARN SOMETHING about how to treat nonessential elements of the faith from the story of Apollos as well. We first meet Apollos in Acts 18. Luke describes him as a Jew from Alexandria, who was "a learned man, with a thorough knowledge of the Scriptures" (Acts 18:24b). The text goes on to say that "he had been instructed in the way of the Lord, and he spoke with great fervor and taught about Jesus accurately, though he knew only the baptism of John" (Acts 18:25). Apollos seemed to know what was essential and what was nonessential but important. He taught about Jesus accurately and with passion, but he still needed further instruction on the important issue of baptism. The very next verse tells us that Priscilla and Aquila, leaders in the church at Ephesus, took him into their home and "explained to him the way of God more adequately" (Acts 18:26b). Priscilla and Aquila could have condemned Apollos for his incomplete knowledge. A well-educated and articulate person like Apollos could have responded with pride or hostility at his being corrected. Thankfully—because of Priscilla and Aquila's careful instruction and Apollos's willingness to be taught—he went on to become a very important leader in the church at Corinth.

This story teaches us about the importance of what Paul calls "growing in the knowledge of God" (Colossians 1:10). There is always more to learn, and we should be very careful not to rest content with incomplete or elementary knowledge with regard to our faith (see Hebrews 5:11–6:3). This is the way our faith becomes stunted and fruitless. When I teach high school students, I often tell them to care enough about their faith to be curious about it. Develop the regular discipline of studying Scripture; discover Christian authors who can help you to grow in your knowledge of God; and place yourself under the instruction of persons who are more mature in their faith. Apollos provides for us a model of a person who was humble enough to be taught and passionate enough to want to learn more. He knew the essentials, but he wanted to know more. He cared enough about Jesus that he wanted to follow him even more accurately. The important elements of our faith provide an invitation to continue learning and growing.

STORY #3: AN EARNEST FATHER

THE THIRD STORY IS found in Mark 9. In this chapter, we read about a father's anguish for his son who had been possessed by an evil spirit from childhood. The spirit regularly sent the boy into convulsions, putting his life in danger. Jesus' disciples could not drive out the demon, so the man came to Jesus and asked, "If you can do anything, take pity on us and help us" (Mark 9:22b). Jesus responded by telling him that "everything is possible for one who believes" (Mark 9:23b). The father did not have to think very long for his reply: "Immediately the boy's father exclaimed, 'I do believe; help me overcome my unbelief!'" (Mark 9:24).

I DO BELIEVE; HELP ME OVERCOME MY UNBELIEF!

I have always thought this was one of the most honest verses in the entire New Testament. The father believed, yet he recognized that his belief was not perfect. His belief was not without questions, not without some shadow of doubt, not without uncertainty. He was crying out not only for Jesus to heal his son but also for Jesus to heal his belief.

Many Christians (and non-Christians) labor under the assumption that all true beliefs require absolute certainty. I have personally witnessed this assumption turn toxic in a disciple's life. Because they cannot satisfactorily arrive at absolute certainty, their faith turns to despair. Sometimes this leads to nagging questions concerning whether or not God can accept them. At other times, this leads to the questioner's rejection of faith in God altogether. It is important for us to notice that Jesus does not rebuke the man for his lack of perfect belief. Instead, he dramatically heals his son. The lesson that we learn from this man is that we can honestly and prayerfully take our questions and our doubts to Jesus. We all struggle with clarity and understanding on all sorts of issues related to God and faith. As I mentioned in Chapter 2, many of us labor under the burden of epistemic legalism. This father gives us all hope. Learn this prayer from this unnamed yet earnest father: *I do believe; help me overcome my unbelief.*

5

HOW SHOULD WE TREAT THOSE WHO DISAGREE WITH US?

Answer: When we disagree about matters of personal preference, we are to respond to each other with grace and truth. We are never at liberty to express our freedom in a way that causes others to stumble in sin. In all things, we want to show understanding, kindness, and love.

> Accept the one whose faith is weak, without
> quarreling over disputable matters.
> — Romans 14:1

Up to this point, we have addressed beliefs that are essential for salvation, as well as how to approach beliefs that are important for our discipleship but are not core, essential issues. This chapter goes into detail on the third category of beliefs, which I introduced above. I call these beliefs "preferences" or "matters of personal opinion." Returning to the target illustration from Chapter 2, these beliefs are typically near the outer edge of the target. They are important enough to be on the target, but not critical enough to be near the center. It is my observation that, even though these preferences are not what we call "bullseye beliefs," they do often become the center of many of our arguments and lead to defensiveness. The further we get from the center of the target, the more likely we are to argue with those who disagree with us. These personal preferences become the beliefs that distinguish us and separate us from others. This can cause conflict.

This tendency should not really surprise us. For instance, the resurrection of Jesus, as part of the gospel, is a well-established and essential belief within the Christian community. If I met a person who did not believe in the resurrection but claimed to be a Christian, I would not only dispute their belief about the resurrection but I would also dispute their claim to be a Christian. By contrast, consider beliefs about methods of worship. These beliefs are on the target, but they exist as personal preferences on the outer edge of the target. Hopefully it would never occur to someone to question another person's salvation because they have a different preference in worship style. Unfortunately, however, I've observed that many more churches have split over worship preferences than over beliefs regarding inerrancy or the resurrection. My point is this: unless we are committed to hanging out only with people who agree with us on everything, we will have to figure out how to respond to people who disagree with us, especially with regard to our personal preferences. Fortunately, Scripture provides us some help.

THE EXAMPLE OF JESUS

FIRST, LET US CONSIDER the example of Jesus himself. John 1:14 says, "The Word became flesh and made his dwelling among us. We have seen his glory, the glory of the one and only Son, who came from the Father, full of grace and truth." This is a breathtaking verse about the identity of Jesus, but for our purposes, I want to focus only on the last phrase: Jesus came into the world "full of grace and truth."

Grace and truth serve as twin anchor points for Jesus' ministry. Initially we may think that grace and truth oppose each other. Truth, we assume, is unbending and rigid. Grace, on the other hand, is flexible and forgiving. Jesus demonstrates, however, that rather than opposing each other, grace and truth are necessary complements to one another. Grace without truth becomes flimsy and cheap; truth without grace becomes oppressive and cold. In Jesus, we observe that perfect balance. He came bringing truth and light into a dark world (John 1:4–5; 3:19; 8:12; 9:5). Jesus was passionate about truth. The word *truth* occurs twenty-eight times just in the book of John, but this truth was not oppressive. No, the truth Jesus introduced to the world brought us the opportunity for grace and forgiveness (John 3:16–21).

Jesus' lifestyle of grace and truth provides a lesson for us about how to engage with people who disagree with us. We must remain committed to truth and vigilant about accepting ideas that are false or harmful to our faith. This is the heart of Paul's encouragement to "take captive every thought"

(2 Corinthians 10:5b). Discipleship calls on us to question the conventional wisdom of the world (1 Corinthians 1:20–31), while watching our lives and doctrine closely (1 Timothy 4:16). We also recognize that the truth of the gospel is truth about the grace we have received in Christ.

Jesus had some very harsh words for people who expected to be forgiven yet were unwilling to show forgiveness to others (Matthew 6:14–15; 18:21–35). I once heard a Christian author repeat a proverb he heard growing up: "It is no use cutting off a man's nose and then asking that he smell a rose." He was making a point about the necessity of truth seasoned with grace. If we declare the truth about Jesus with hostility and without any grace or forgiveness, it will be impossible to convince a person that Jesus sacrificially loves them and wants to save them from their sin.[10]

Paul models the difficult balance between grace and truth in 2 Timothy 2:1–25: He begins the chapter by exhorting Timothy to "be strong in the grace that is in Christ Jesus" (2 Timothy 2:1). To Paul, being strong in grace requires strong teaching and commitment to truth. He tells Timothy to entrust this teaching to reliable people who can teach others (2 Timothy 2:2). Later, he tells Timothy to remember the essentials of the faith (2 Timothy 2:8) and to warn people about "quarreling about words" (2 Timothy 2:14) and "godless chatter" (2 Timothy 2:16). Godless chatter is so dangerous because it works like a disease that spreads through a community, and if left unchecked, it may even result in the destruction of faith (2 Timothy 2:16–18). The chapter closes with Paul warning Timothy to avoid "foolish and stupid arguments" (2 Timothy 2:23). Paul is warning Timothy about getting caught up in arguing about issues that are unimportant. Instead, Timothy should gently instruct his opponents "in the hope that God will grant them repentance leading them to a knowledge of the truth" (2 Timothy 2:25).

Do you see grace mixed with truth in these instructions? Commit yourself to the truth and to sound teaching. Do not give in to foolish arguments. Instead, gently instruct your opponents in the hopes that they will arrive at the truth. We should also add this note: We may not always identify with Timothy in this text. Often we are the ones who need correction and teaching. Grace and truth require that we have the humility to receive this instruction.

So the first way to answer the question of how to treat those with whom we disagree in the body of Christ, then, is this: The manner in which Jesus came into the world is also the way that we conduct ourselves in the world—full of grace and truth. The second answer to the question has to do with my kids and their shoes.

KIDS AND SHOES

ONE OF THE CONSTANT battles my wife and I fight in our house involves kids and shoes. We remind our kids to pick up their shoes and put them away after they have taken them off. Way too often, however, my kids will come in the door and leave their shoes wherever they happen to take them off. (I must confess that it is not just the kids who have this habit!)

The floor of our kitchen and living room quickly becomes a labyrinth of discarded flip-flops and tennis shoes. I explain to them that there are two problems with leaving their shoes out. First, it just looks messy, and second, it is a safety hazard. They—we—create an obstacle course of shoes this way, just inviting someone to trip over them, especially at night when it is hard to see. We remove the potential tripping hazard by putting our shoes where they belong, and this is a way of saying that we care about one another. This is true about shoes in the middle of the floor, but it is also true about beliefs that are a matter of personal preference. Let me explain.

Paul talks about the idea of personal preferences in faith in Romans 14 (see also 1 Corinthians 8). Paul's exhortation to the Romans begins, "Accept the one whose faith is weak, without quarreling over *disputable matters*" (Romans 14:1). Apparently, members of this Christian community had not yet grown into maturity in their faith. Paul instructs them to accept these people who were young in their faith rather than quarrel with them about disputable matters. John Stott, in his commentary on Romans, says that to accept someone means "to welcome [them] into one's fellowship and into one's heart. It implies the warmth and kindness of genuine love."[11] Instead of judging one another on these matters, Paul tells the Roman Christians, "Make up your mind not to put any stumbling block or obstacle in the way of a brother or sister" (Romans 14:13b). In other words, do not use your convictions on disputable matters to destroy the community or destroy your brother or sister's faith. Instead, "make every effort to do what leads to peace and to mutual edification" (Romans 14:19).

DO NOT USE YOUR CONVICTIONS ON DISPUTABLE MATTERS TO DESTROY THE COMMUNITY.

The principle is that we love each other enough to willingly remove hazardous obstacles to faith for those who might not share our personal convictions on disputable matters. This does not mean that we compromise on the essentials of our faith; neither does it mean that we stop caring about those important beliefs that are not essential. This principle of accepting those with weak faith means that in matters of personal preference we prioritize love for each other and the unity of our community over "being right."

Let me offer an example to illustrate the point further. The matter of drinking alcohol has long been a source of debate among Christians. Some Christians believe that drinking alcohol is permissible as long as a person avoids drunkenness. Other Christians believe that because drinking alcohol so consistently leads to abuse, it is not permissible for a Christian to drink any alcohol. I believe that this issue falls into the category of personal preference, what Paul calls "disputable matters." A person's position on drinking alcohol does not come anywhere close to a bullseye belief. So how does the Romans 14 principle help us to approach the issue?

First, we are committed to loving those who disagree with us and to protecting the unity of the body of Christ. Disagreements do not exempt us from the command to love one another (John 13:34–35; Romans 12:10; 13:8). It is possible and necessary to disagree without condemning one another on matters like these. Second, our love for each other means that we should be ready to forgo our personal preferences for the sake of *the weaker Christian*. I may believe that I have freedom to consume alcohol, but if my drinking alcohol is a potential stumbling block for someone in my community, love compels me to submit my freedom to their spiritual need (see 1 Corinthians 8:9). This does not mean that we cannot talk about the issue among those who disagree, but we should not allow disagreement on the issue to hinder anyone's faith. As the Renew.org Network Leaders' Faith Statement says, "We are never at liberty to express our freedom in a way that causes others to stumble in sin. In all things, we want to show understanding, kindness, and love."

> IN ALL THINGS, WE WANT TO SHOW UNDERSTANDING, KINDNESS, AND LOVE.

APPENDIX

BOOK RECOMMENDATIONS FOR FURTHER STUDY

Rebecca McLaughlin, *Confronting Christianity: 12 Hard Questions for the World's Largest Religion* (Wheaton: Crossway, 2019).

Mark Moore, *Core 52: A Fifteen-Minute Daily Guide to Build Your Bible IQ in a Year* (Colorado Springs: WaterBrook, 2019).

Ben Myers, *The Apostles' Creed: A Guide to the Ancient Catechism* (Bellingham: Lexham Press, 2018).

C. S. Lewis, *Mere Christianity* (New York: HarperOne, 2015).

N. T. Wright, *Simply Christian: Why Christianity Makes Sense* (New York: HarperCollins, 2006).

NOTES

1. Carol Kuruvilla, "Kansas Governor Sues GOP Leaders for Subverting Order Limiting Church Meetings," *Huffpost*, April 10, 2020, https://www.huffpost.com/entry/kansas-coronavirus-churches-religious-freedom_n_5e90ab2ec5b6d641a6be4d13.

2. See also John 3:36; 5:24; 6:29, 35, 47; 7:38.

3. For more on how faith is more than merely belief or even trust, see Mark Moore's book in the *Real Life Theology* series, *Faithful Faith: Reclaiming Faith from Culture and Tradition* (Renew.org, 2021).

4. "Almost Half of Practicing Christian Millennials Say Evangelism is Wrong," *Barna*, February 5, 2019, https://www.barna.com/research/millennials-oppose-evangelism/.

5. See Acts 2:36; 10:36; 1 Corinthians 8:6; 12:3; 16:22; 2 Corinthians 4:5; Philippians 2:11; Colossians 2:6.

6. Grant R. Osborne, *Romans*, The IVP New Testament Commentary Series (Downers Grove, IL: InterVarsity Press, 2004), 271.

7. Ben Witherington, "Lord," eds. Joel B. Green, I. Howard Marshall, and Scot McKnight, *Dictionary of Jesus and the Gospels* (Downers Grove, IL: InterVarsity Press, 1992), 484.

8. For more on the gospel, see a book in the *Real Life Theology* series by Matthew W. Bates called *The Gospel Precisely: Surprisingly Good News About Jesus Christ the King* (Renew.org, 2021).

9. Thomas Long, *Hebrews*, Interpretation: A Bible Commentary for Teaching and Preaching (Louisville: Westminster John Knox, 1997), 3.

10. For more on how we can hold convictions while cultivating healthy relationships with people we disagree with, see Bobby Harrington and Jason Henderson, *Conviction and Civility: Thinking and Communicating Clearly About What the Bible Teaches* (Renew.org, 2019).

11. John R. W. Stott, *The Message of Romans: God's Good News for the World*, The Bible Speaks Today (Downers Grove, IL: InterVarsity Press, 2001), 359.

THE GOSPEL PRECISELY

SURPRISINGLY GOOD NEWS

ABOUT JESUS CHRIST

THE KING

MATTHEW W. BATES

For Dr. Roger Mohrlang,
Professor Emeritus of Theology, Whitworth University

In gratitude for your teaching
and embodiment of the gospel.
It changed my life.

CONTENTS

General Editors' Note 183

Introduction 187

CHAPTER 1: What Is the Gospel? 189

CHAPTER 2: Why Do We Need Royal Good News? 197

CHAPTER 3: How Is Jesus' Kingship Beneficial? 205

CHAPTER 4: Who Is the God of the Gospel? 213

CHAPTER 5: How Do We Share the Gospel? 219

Appendix: Book Recommendations for Further Study 227

Notes 229

GENERAL EDITORS' NOTE

Jesus' rescuing kingship is the best imaginable news. The Bible teaches us that this gospel, or "good news," is the essential message for our salvation and lives. At Renew.org Network, we believe that "the Jesus you preach, the gospel you uphold, and the faith you coach will determine the disciple you will get."

Matthew W. Bates is the ideal author to teach us about the gospel. He is an award-winning author. His popular books include *Gospel Allegiance* (Brazos, 2019); *Salvation by Allegiance Alone* (Baker Academic, 2017); and *The Birth of the Trinity* (Oxford University Press, 2015). Bates has earned an advanced degree in biblical studies from a leading Protestant seminary (MCS, Regent College) and from a top Catholic university (PhD, University of Notre Dame). He is a Protestant by conviction, but serves as Associate Professor of Theology at a religiously diverse Catholic institution, Quincy University. He has practical experience teaching, sharing, and seeking to live out the gospel. Bates also co-founded and co-hosts the popular *OnScript* podcast (OnScript.study). He enjoys hiking, baseball, and chasing around his seven children. You can connect with him on Facebook or Twitter (@ MatthewWBates), or visit his author page at MatthewWBates.com.

This book expounds on the section from the Renew.org Leaders' Faith Statement called "The Gospel":

> We believe God created all things and made human beings in his image, so that we could enjoy a relationship with him and each other. But we lost our way, through Satan's influence. We are now spiritually dead, separated from God. Without his help, we gravitate toward sin and self-rule. The gospel is God's good news of reconciliation. It was promised to Abraham and David and revealed in Jesus' life, ministry, teaching, and sacrificial death on the cross. The gospel is the saving action of the triune God. The Father sent the Son into the world to take on human flesh and redeem us. Jesus came as the

promised Messiah of the Old Testament. He ushered in the kingdom of God, died for our sins according to Scripture, was buried, and was raised on the third day. He defeated sin and death and ascended to heaven. He is seated at the right hand of God as Lord and he is coming back for his disciples. Through the Spirit, we are transformed and sanctified. God will raise everyone for the final judgment. Those who trusted and followed Jesus by faith will not experience punishment for their sins and separation from God in hell. Instead, we will join together with God in the renewal of all things in the consummated kingdom. We will live together in the new heaven and new earth where we will glorify God and enjoy him forever.

*See the full Network Faith Statements at the end of this book.

Support Scriptures: Genesis 1–3; Romans 3:10–12, 7:8–25; Genesis 12:1–3 & Galatians 3:6–9; Isaiah 11:1–4; 2 Samuel 7:1–16; Micah 5:2–4; Daniel 2:44–45; Luke 1:33; John 1:1–3; Matthew 4:17; 1 Corinthians 15:1–8; Acts 1:11; 2:36; 3:19–21; Colossians 3:1; Matthew 25:31–32; Revelation 21:1ff; Romans 3:21–26.

The following tips might help you use this book more effectively (and the other books in the *Real Life Theology* series):

1. *Five questions, answers, and Scriptures.* We framed this book around five key questions with five short answers and five notable Scriptures. This format provides clarity, making it easier to commit crucial information to memory. This format also enables the books in the *Real Life Theology* series to support our catechism. Our catechism is a series of fixed questions and answers for instruction in church or home. In all, the series has fifty-two questions, answers, and key Scriptures. This particular book focuses on the five that are most pertinent to the gospel.

2. *Summary videos.* You can find three to seven-minute video teachings that summarize the book, as well as each chapter, at Renew.org. These short videos can function as standalone teachings. But for groups or group leaders using the book, they can also be used to launch discussion of the reading.

May God use this book to fuel faithful and effective disciple making in your life and church.

For King Jesus,
Bobby Harrington and Daniel McCoy
General Editors, *Real Life Theology* series

INTRODUCTION

don't intend to waste your time. You're busy. But when a message is urgent, we go to great lengths to catch attention—sparkles, flashing lights, loudspeakers, threats, extravagant promises. Then the message is delivered clearly and concisely.

Make no mistake about it. I have the privilege of relaying the most important announcement of all time: God's own good news for the world, the gospel as presented in Scripture. But sorry. I'm fresh out of glitter. You'll need to settle for the unadorned gospel. Since he is the God of the manger and of the cross, we can trust that God is content to reveal himself in non-flashy ways. Got ears? You'll hear.

"No bells and whistles" does not mean no surprises, though. For example, in our modern world of voting, consensus, and representative government, who would dream that *a king* is God's ultimate good news? Doesn't kingship inevitably lead to tyranny? And who would dare to imagine that the ideal king would turn out to be a man *crucified* by the government as a traitor? God's ways are shocking.

> WHO WOULD DREAM THAT *A KING* IS GOD'S ULTIMATE GOOD NEWS?

The surprises don't stop there. The contemporary church's insufficient grasp of the gospel's framework, as the Bible presents it, means that a basic presentation will offer fresh insights for most. Indeed, since I have led pastors and church leaders through numerous Scripture-based studies of the gospel, I can say with confidence: those who think they know the gospel best are frequently the most surprised by its true shape, content, boundaries, and purposes.

Given the gospel confusion prevalent today, how can we make sure our grip on it is firm? There are four ways. First, give pride of place to Scripture's own summaries. Second, discover how the gospel fits into God's wider story and purposes. Third, differentiate between the gospel itself and closely related ideas such as forgiveness, repentance, and faith. Finally, since we learn most fully when we disciple others, be prepared to share the good news. We'll take up these tasks in the chapters that follow.

Precision is needed. Bridges, such as the Tacoma Narrows, have collapsed due to inaccurate engineering calculations. How much more is at stake here? The gospel remains at the heart of the church, beating for the sake of the world. We dare not get it wrong. That means this study, drawing from the Bible, will be exacting. Those eager for more can consult lengthier books that I and others have written on the gospel and salvation (see the final section for recommended reading).

The result? Surprisingly good news worth sharing: *the gospel precisely.*

1

WHAT IS THE GOSPEL?

Answer: Jesus is the saving king. He preexisted with God the Father. In accordance with God's promises, Jesus became human in the line of David, died for our sins, was buried, was resurrected on the third day, was seen, was installed as king at God's right hand, sent the Spirit, and will return to rule.

For what I received I passed on to you as of first importance: that Christ died for our sins according to the Scriptures, that he was buried, that he was raised on the third day according to the Scriptures.
— 1 Corinthians 15:3–4

We need the real gospel. Urgently. There are many false gospels. These are cultural stories about how to achieve full human flourishing. They are not overtly called "gospels," but because they promise to result in a fulfilled life, people adopt them as their version of life's good news. But these false gospels don't deliver. They leave people hurt, broken, and lifeless. They are counterfeits.

Since these false gospels blend pop culture with a spiritual sensibility, you'll hear some of them proclaimed in churches. Hopefully not in yours. They will tell you that God wants you to be rich, healthy, attractive, and in control of your future. They'll proclaim that God desires you to be successful in your career, athletic, and smart. They might promise that you'll find your soulmate, or if not, at least trendy friends.

These pseudo-gospels will nearly always encourage you to undertake a journey of "self-discovery" (that is, selfish discovery) to find out who you truly are: *I've gotta be free to be me.* When someone questions your self-centered journey, you'll be encouraged to jettison your relationship with them by labeling "toxic" anyone who won't unconditionally affirm who you are becoming. Those who disagree with your vision for yourself are canceled.

But there is one thing false gospels will never ask you to do. This is how you can most easily spot the fraud. They will *never* consistently encourage you toward a cross-shaped allegiance to Jesus and his kingdom. The goal will never be the transformation of you (and those around you) into his suffering-for-others-yet-glorified image.

The more precise we are in our grasp of the gospel, the more readily we can avoid false gospels, embrace the true one, and share it effectively. If you want to know *the gospel precisely*, the best way to achieve this is to explore Bible passages that intentionally summarize it.[1]

JESUS IS THE CHRIST

HIDDEN IN PLAIN SIGHT. So obvious that it is usually missed. Scripture most frequently summarizes the gospel simply by identifying *Jesus as the Christ*. For example, "Every day in the temple and from house to house, they did not cease teaching and gospeling, 'The Christ is Jesus'" (Acts 5:42, AT). English doesn't have a verb for "gospel" activity. But in the original Greek of the New Testament, the noun *euangelion* ("gospel," "good news") has a corresponding verb, *euangelizō* ("to gospel"). To make it clear where gospel activity is in view, I've translated it "gospeling." The early church was continually gospeling, "The Christ is Jesus."

Numerous passages summarize the gospel or gospel-activity with the claim that Jesus is the Christ:

- "Now those who were scattered went about *gospeling* the word. Philip went down to the city of Samaria and *proclaimed to them the Christ*" (Acts 8:4–5, AT);
- "Yet Saul . . . baffled the Jews living in Damascus by *proving that Jesus is the Messiah*" (Acts 9:22);
- "Paul . . . reasoned with them from the Scriptures, explaining and proving that it was necessary for *the Christ* to suffer and to rise from the dead, and saying, '*This is the Christ, this Jesus, whom I am proclaiming to you*'" (Acts 17:2–3, AT);

- "Paul was occupied by preaching, testifying to the Jews that *Jesus is the Messiah*" (Acts 18:5, AT);
- "By the Scriptures Apollos showed *the Christ to be Jesus*" (Acts 18:28, AT).

According to Scripture's own testimony, "Jesus died for my sins" is *not* the basic gospel message. As we'll see, the full gospel involves forgiveness. But if we build on an incorrect foundation, we skew the whole building. "Jesus is the Christ" is the basic gospel message in the Bible.

WHAT "CHRIST" MEANS

FIRST THINGS FIRST. WHAT does it mean to say, "Jesus is the Christ"? The words "Messiah" (from Hebrew) and "Christ" (from Greek) pertain to oil. Prophets, priests, and kings were anointed with holy fluid—oil—in order to be devoted for special purposes in the Old Testament (Exodus 40:15; 1 Kings 19:16; Psalm 89:20). God sent prophets to declare that a king would come in the future to restore his people (Isaiah 9:1–7; 16:5; Jeremiah 33:14–16; Ezekiel 37; Hosea 3:5). The hope for this Messiah-king crystallized around God's promises to David regarding an eternal throne for one of his offspring (2 Samuel 7:12–16; Psalm 89:3–4, 20–49; 132:10, 17). "Christ" is the New Testament word for this long-awaited anointed king.

Surprise! The gospel is political. This future Christ-king would not only lead over spiritual affairs but also exercise real-world *political* power to restore the fortunes of his downtrodden people. And not only his own people, the Jews, but also the non-Jewish nations, the Gentiles, would experience the effects of the Messiah's sovereignty. In this way, the Christ would be a universal king.

THE KING PROCLAIMS HIS KINGDOM

THE FIRST VERSE OF the earliest Gospel, Mark, links the gospel to messianic kingship: "The beginning of the gospel of Jesus the Christ, the Son of God." The gospel is about Jesus, the universal king. Shockingly this king also turns out to be God's own Son (see Chapter 4).

Since the gospel is about a king, it relates intimately to *the kingdom of God*. When Jesus first heralds the gospel, he speaks of the nearness of the kingdom of God: "Jesus came into Galilee proclaiming *the gospel* of God and saying, 'The time has been fulfilled, and *the kingdom of God* has drawn near; repent and believe in *the gospel*'" (Mark 1:14–15, AT). We'll discuss repentance and belief later (see Chapter 5). For now, notice that these responses to the gospel of the kingdom's nearness are not merely private religious decisions. They are political responses— with social implications—to the public announcement of a new king.

"The kingdom of God" was the time when God would rule overtly through agents that he would appoint—above all, through his Messiah. Although God always reigns, sometimes his rule is subtle, at other times obvious. Jesus proclaimed that an era dominated by God's explicit reign was emerging. Jesus could herald the nearness of the kingdom with integrity because he knew that the Messiah-king had just been anointed—himself!—at his baptism.

Although the Son was already chosen as Messiah by God, at his baptism Jesus became Messiah *within history*. Jesus received a holy anointing from heaven, making him "Christ." He was christened by the Holy Spirit rather than with oil. The Father confirmed Jesus' identity: "You are my beloved Son; with you I am well pleased" (Mark 1:11, AT).

Once Jesus became the Christ within history at his baptism, he could publicly announce the gospel of his emerging kingship, drawing from Isaiah:

> The Spirit of the Lord is upon me, because he has christened me *to gospel* to the poor. He has sent me to proclaim liberty to the captives and recovery of sight to the blind, to set at liberty those who are oppressed, to proclaim the year of the Lord's favor. (Luke 4:18–19, AT, citing Isaiah 61:1–2 and 58:6)

Jesus' Spirit-anointing as king was gospel for the people—especially for the poor, the blind, the oppressed, and the captives. This new king would be radically for the down and out.

Jesus anticipated an earthly political rule during a future era of renewal. When Jesus said his kingdom was not "from [*ek*] this world" (John 18:36, AT), he was speaking of its divine source or origin, not the kingdom's final outworking. (This is indicated by *ek* in the original Greek.) Jesus announced that in the age of restoration, he will judge and rule over earthly leaders (Matthew 19:28; compare Matthew 16:27; 25:31–46; 26:64).

The gospel was proclaimed by Jesus *before* his death. This hints that the gospel is about more than responding to what happened at the cross. Jesus summarizes his life purpose as gospel proclamation: "I must preach the gospel of the kingdom of God to the other towns as well; for I was sent for this purpose" (Luke 4:43, AT).

Jesus proclaimed the good news that he was becoming the king. His anointing as king had set in motion a cross-and-resurrection-shaped process that would culminate in his complete, liberating, and cross-and-resurrection-shaped reign.

The church's main purpose today is to further this gospel announcement by declaring its fulfillment: *Jesus is the Christ.* Jesus has now been installed at God's right hand where he rules as the eternal king.

THE MISSING KING

But we've missed it. Although "Jesus is the Christ" repeatedly summarizes the gospel in Scripture, it is often absent from gospel presentations today. For to say that "Jesus is the Christ" or "Jesus is the Messiah" is to claim he is a royal *political* figure, *a human king.* (Albeit a divine king too.) We struggle to make kingship the most basic gospel category. It is not immediately obvious how a bare affirmation—Jesus is king—could be the essence of the good news. What about salvation? The cross? Forgiveness? The resurrection? We'll get to those in due course.

But first, we need to take the missing king seriously as a gospel problem. "Christ" has been reduced to a mere name, personal identifier, or alternative way of referring to Jesus. "In Christ alone," and the like, is the language we find in our songs and theology textbooks. To most Christians, "Christ" is equivalent to "Jesus."

Christ is a title. But to treat "Jesus" and "Christ" as equivalent terms is a huge mistake. On the one hand, it is true to say "Jesus saves" and "Christ saves." Likewise, one could truly say "Matt teaches" and "the professor teaches" because that accurately reflects my job title. But "Matt" does not mean the same thing as "professor." "Christ" is comparable to "His Majesty" if we're describing an English king. It is a special title designed to bring renown. "Christ" is the title for the universally significant Davidic king. Failure to treat "the Christ" as a title has contributed to a second reason why kingship has been missing from the gospel.

Forgiveness without kingship? Our haste to get what we so badly need causes us to misunderstand *how* forgiveness is available. What is foremost in our minds when we consider the gospel is a transaction at the cross: Jesus is savior, redeemer, atoning sacrifice, and lamb of God. Perhaps he has some vague authority too as Lord. We fail to see that forgiveness flows not just through a person, but through *a person in his official capacity as king*—crucified, raised, and reigning. While serving as king at God's

> FORGIVENESS FLOWS THROUGH A KING— CRUCIFIED, RAISED, AND REIGNING.

right hand, he is also the high priest and the sacrificial offering that covers our sins. As will become clear, *Jesus' forgiving power cannot be separated from his royal authority as head of a new creation.*

THE KING DEAD AND RAISED

ALTHOUGH THE FOUNDATIONAL SUMMARY of the gospel in Scripture is "Jesus is the Christ," the most famous is 1 Corinthians 15:3–5. "The gospel" (1 Corinthians 15:1–2) Paul received and passed along faithfully to the Corinthians is:

> That the Christ died for our sins in accordance with the Scriptures, and that he was buried, and that he has been raised on the third day in accordance with the Scriptures, and that he appeared to Cephas [Peter], then to the Twelve. (1 Corinthians 15:3–5, AT)

Notice that forgiveness flows through kingship. Paul says nothing here about "Jesus." Instead, he speaks about *the Christ's* death for our sins. By mentioning the Christ rather than Jesus, Paul stresses that kingship is the vessel through which forgiveness flows.

Second, the king helps a whole bunch of people. Just as we short-circuit kingship in our haste to find *personal* forgiveness, we can easily miss how *the king's actions are group-oriented.* Paul says nothing about how you, I, or any other individual becomes right with God in this gospel summary. Rather, the king died for "our" sins. It's about what the Messiah has done for his *entire people.* Don't misunderstand. Benefits, like forgiveness of sins, that attend Jesus' kingship can be yours personally. But they are group-first benefits. Forgiveness belongs to individuals— you and me—only when we become part of the king's people.

Third, resurrection is gospel too. The Christ was raised on the third day. The validity of the king's death and resurrection was made doubly certain by God. For his death and resurrection were attested not only by Scripture (anticipated in the Old Testament) but also by historical occurrences. As part of the gospel, the Christ's death was confirmed by his *burial* and his resurrection by post-resurrection *appearances* to witnesses. The gospel includes the king's death for our sins, burial, resurrection on the third day, and appearances as historical events.

THE DIVINE AND HUMAN KING

IN THE TWO FOLLOWING passages, Paul offers gospel summaries. What are some emphases?

> The gospel of God, which he promised beforehand through his prophets in the holy Scriptures. This gospel concerns his Son, who came into being by means of the seed of David as it pertains to the flesh, who was appointed Son-of-God-in-Power as it pertains to the Spirit of Holiness by means of the resurrection from among the dead ones, Jesus the Christ our Lord. (Romans 1:2–4, AT)

> Remember Jesus the Christ, raised from among the dead ones, of the seed of David, according to my gospel. (2 Timothy 2:8, AT)

Both gospel summaries focus on Jesus as the royal Christ (or Messiah), his Davidic lineage, and his resurrection.

Concerning resurrection, there is something curious in both passages. They emphasize the king's resurrection not from his personal state of death (although he was personally dead), but *from among those who were also dead.* In the original Greek, the phrase *ek nekrōn* ("from among the dead ones") indicates that the dead king was with other dead people. Here's the point: if God raised him, he will raise others who are like him too. The king's resurrection from the dead is the first fruit, but a full harvest of additional resurrections will happen for all the king's people (1 Corinthians 15:20–22). King Jesus' resurrection is good news because it anticipates the resurrection of all those united to him through his death.

Let me offer a few more words about Romans 1:2–4 as a gospel summary. Paul takes a cosmic perspective. The Son took on human flesh, fulfilling God's promises to David. But God had a grander scheme. After the Son's death, his resurrection triggered his elevation to a new ruling office. The Son became *the Son-of-God-in-Power.* He has always been the divine king. But the Son has not always been a human king. Now he is the divine *and human* king, ruling creation powerfully. Since Jesus' reign in power pertains to the Spirit of holiness, his kingship is especially operative wherever the Holy Spirit is present. The Son's incarnation and enthronement are gospel.

THE GOSPEL PRECISELY

WE HAVE NOW EXPLORED the main summaries of the gospel in Scripture. If we were to add more, the most important are Peter's and Paul's speeches in Acts. Notice how Peter's gospel proclamation at Pentecost doubles down on Jesus' attainment of sovereignty: "Therefore let all Israel be assured of this: God has made this Jesus, whom you crucified, both Lord and Messiah" (Acts 2:36). Just as elsewhere in the New Testament, the cross is essential, but the gospel reaches its climactic energy with Jesus' rule as the Christ.

> THE GOSPEL REACHES ITS CLIMACTIC ENERGY WITH JESUS' RULE AS THE CHRIST.

When we bring together what the New Testament teaches, the gospel is about the process by which Jesus came to rule on God's behalf, restoring his glory.

The gospel is that Jesus the king:

1. preexisted as God the Son,
2. was sent by the Father,
3. took on human flesh in fulfillment of God's promises to David,
4. died for our sins in accordance with the Scriptures,
5. was buried,
6. was raised on the third day in accordance with the Scriptures,
7. appeared to many witnesses,
8. *is enthroned at the right hand of God as the ruling Christ,*
9. has sent the Holy Spirit to his people to effect his rule, and
10. will come again as final judge to rule.

Each event is repeatedly identified as part of the gospel in the New Testament. Elsewhere I've called this "the gospel-allegiance model."[2] But it's simpler to say these ten events are *the gospel precisely*. Above all, the gospel is the true story about how Jesus became the victorious, saving king.

2

WHY DO WE NEED ROYAL GOOD NEWS?

Answer: God created humans in his image to rule. Sin distorts God's glory in our image-bearing. Only a king who flawlessly bears God's image can carry God's full glory to creation, vanquishing the personal, social, and cosmic effects of sin.

> For all have sinned and fall short of the glory of God.
> — Romans 3:23

Contemporary Christian culture encourages us to see the gospel as salvation instructions, but this is not an accurate view of the gospel. The instructions run like this: We need to acknowledge that because of Adam and Eve's sin, we all have a sin problem. As a result, you and I deserve death and punishment. God is by nature an impartial judge, so he is required to give us what we deserve. So death and punishment will be our fate sooner or later. But good news! God's fairness allows for substitution. Jesus was sinless yet carried your sins. Simply trust that Jesus died for your sins, paying the price for you. Then you can go to heaven.

These salvation instructions are not the gospel. We do have a sin problem. We are in a state of death. We do need to trust in Jesus as the sinless perfect substitute that provides atonement for our sins. And we can be united to his eternal life. As accurate as all of this is, in the Bible the gospel is about Jesus as the Christ. These salvation instructions only partially correspond to the gospel in Scripture because they do not feature Jesus' kingship. There is a disconnect.

The disconnect stems from an incomplete picture of God's purposes for humanity. The topic of sin helps us see why. What is so bad about sin?—after all, we are all sinners. Much is bad about it, in every way (Romans 6:1–2)! Yet when the gospel is incorrectly treated as personal salvation instructions, sin is one-dimensional. From this flat viewpoint, sin is only a problem because it *personally separates* you and me from God. This ignores the *social* and *cosmic* aspects of sin. To grasp why the gospel had—and must continue—to feature an actual *human* king, we need a bigger view of Scripture's story.

CREATED TO RULE

Sin does personally separate us from God. Adam and Eve, after transgressing, are removed from direct fellowship with God.

But how does sin affect God's goals? What if God created humans for a purpose within his wider creation project—a purpose that is no longer achievable because of sin? What if God's aim in seeking to save sinners is to rescue them *for* as much as to rescue *from*?

WHAT IF GOD'S AIM IN SEEKING TO SAVE SINNERS IS TO RESCUE THEM *FOR* AS MUCH AS TO RESCUE *FROM*?

Sin is not merely a guilt or debt problem that needs to be overcome to rescue us from separation from God or from death. Sin also prevents humans from fulfilling God's aims.

God's basic purpose for humans is announced in the first chapter of Genesis. God created the earth and universe as good. He created humans—male and female—and said they were very good (1:31). God made humans in his image, so that when humans rule over creation on God's behalf, God's own rule is made tangible and present to creation.

> Then God said, "Let us make mankind in our *image*, in our likeness, *so that they may rule* over the fish in the sea and the birds in the sky, over the livestock and all the wild animals, and over all the creatures that move along the ground." So God created mankind in his own *image*, in *the image of God* he created them; male and female he created them. God blessed them and said to them, "Be fruitful and increase in number; fill the earth and subdue it. *Rule* over the fish in the sea and the birds in the sky and over every living creature that moves on the ground." (Genesis 1:26–28)

Repetition makes it emphatic: three times in this short passage, humans are said to be made in the image—with it clear the *image of God* is intended. The purpose of carrying the image of God is *to rule* the various creatures, as well as the earth. We know ruling is the main human aim because God says it twice—first and last in this passage.

Scripture subsequently describes what this rule looks like. It is not coercive or enslaving. Adam is placed in order *to serve* (*'abad*) and *to safeguard* (*shamar*) the garden (2:15). After Adam's placement, Eve is given to Adam to be his helper (*'ezer*) in these tasks (2:18–22). If we miss that ruling in the Bible is about *serving* and *safeguarding*, we'll be endlessly confused about the royal gospel.

God's style of rule operates contrary to typical human expectations. We think a king should *be served* by his fellow creatures, that the ultimate king would place everyone and everything at his own disposal, his beck and call. If, on the other hand, God thinks kings should *serve* and *safeguard* creation, then the best king would . . . ?

Would what? If we are talking about the ultimate God-style king, *how far* would this king go to serve and safeguard? "For even the Son of Man did not come *to be served*, but *to serve*, and to give his life as a ransom for many" (Mark 10:45). Suddenly, the cross begins to make sense not just as a solution to the human sin problem. It is that!—but also more. The cross reveals who God is, and who we need to become.

BEARING GOD'S IMAGE

HUMANS ARE CREATED IN God's image to rule creation by making his glory present. In the ancient world of the Bible, an "image" (*tselem* in Hebrew) was primarily a statue. Images were believed to make a god present.

Within Israel and surrounding nations, for worshipers of idols, the image did not just represent but was also a real manifestation of the divinity. That is, worshipers believed each "image" or "idol" of a god to be permeated with that god's presence, so that the god could appear to his worshipers at many locations at once. This is why different images of one and the same god could be placed in various temples but the worshipers could still feel that they were in the presence of that god.

For the convinced worshiper, the image made it possible to experience the god directly. More specifically, they could genuinely encounter *the glory* (weightiness, splendor, reputation, honor) of the god via the image. The image is what made the god locally present, so that anyone or anything in the presence of the image would necessarily experience *the glory* of that god.

From a biblical standpoint, images also make the one true God present. The Old Testament unilaterally rejects non-human *physical* images and idols of God. It is dangerous and wrong to represent God that way. At the same time, it endorses the image of God as an accurate and unique way to describe humans. Why?

Idols cannot carry God's image. Humans are forbidden to craft images of God out of wood, clay, and stone because they cannot make God present. As Scripture attests, the problem with idols is that people can't experience the glory of the living God through a mute, deaf, dumb, dead image (Isaiah 42:8; 45:20–25). That is, things crafted by human hands can't serve as an authentic place of encounter with God (Zechariah 10:2). At least, they cannot apart from being dignified first by Jesus' incarnation.[3]

Yet humans do bear God's image. Unlike dead idols that have no spirit (Jeremiah 10:14), humans make present the glory of the living God. Each human is permeated with the spirit/breath that God gives (Genesis 2:7), so they can make the living God's *glory* present in a local place. This is why in the midst of his words about image and ruling, God also commanded humans to be fruitful and multiply. Reproduction of humans bearing the image spreads God's glory to more locations (Genesis 5:3).

God designed us so that when other creatures, animals, or things encounter a human, God's glory is available at that place and moment. Psalm 8 explains: Humans are "made a little lower than *God [Elohim]*" (8:5, AT). (The Hebrew text says "God," but this may also include heavenly beings such as angels—see Hebrews 2:7–9.) As those made a little lower than God, humans have a glory that derives from God's own glory. They are crowned with "*glory* and *honor*" and given dominion over creation, so they can make God's glory available by their rule over it (Psalm 8:5, AT). When anyone or anything is in the presence of a human, God's glory—his tangible weightiness and splendor—is radiating outward through that human. Or, at least, it should be.

Disciple making highlights this point. Its goal is to help everyone conform to Jesus' image, as we reflect God's glory through the Spirit. Paul describes the purpose of his disciple-making ministry in 2 Corinthians 3:2–3 as crafting "living letters" written by the Spirit. He then describes the end result for disciples:

transformation "into his image with ever-increasing glory, which comes from the Lord, who is the Spirit" (2 Corinthians 3:18).

SIN DISTILLED

ONCE WE UNDERSTAND WHY humans were made in God's image, we can see why Adam and Eve's disobedience is about more than personal separation from God. Humans are commanded to make God's glory present. Sin leaves creation bereft, so that it isn't experiencing God's glory. Sin results in a *systemic failure for all creation*. But what is sin's root? What is its essence?

God grants Adam and Eve access to all the trees in the garden but forbids one (Genesis 2:17). It is not an apple tree—it is the tree of *the knowledge of good and evil*. That is an odd tree. The strange specificity of this tree's description is of utmost importance for understanding sin.

In God's goodness, he tells us what is right and wrong. God defines human *moral behavior*, because he knows what will result in the ultimate good. But the serpent tempts: "God knows that when you eat from it your eyes will be opened, and you will be like God, knowing good and evil" (Genesis 3:5).

The fundamental human sin is to make our own moral choices apart from God's directives. This is sin distilled: God tells us how we should behave, but we do not trust that he has our best interests in mind, so we decide what is right and wrong for ourselves. Then we act on it.

Practically, the outworking looks like this: God gives a command, "Do not commit adultery." I think, for example: *Well, that sounds arbitrary. You see, there's this girl, and she needs me. And I need her. Plus, I know, God, that you say this relationship wouldn't be best. But I want this, and she does too. It's a messy world, so this choice is good enough given the circumstances.* So, based on this thought pattern, I act on my desire. I've just eaten the forbidden knowledge-of-good-and-evil fruit.

Adam is a model human. Each of us is born into his image and pattern of life (1 Corinthians 15:47–49; Romans 5:12). We do not fully trust God's directives with regard to right and wrong. We eat the fruit by creating and implementing our own ungodly moral standards. We do not deserve death because of Adam and Eve's sin; we deserve it for our own sins, because we freely make the same choice to violate God's commands. Again and again, each of us reenacts their fundamental sin in our own life story. The result?

THE MANGLED IMAGE

LIKE ADAM AND EVE, we have become like God, knowing good and evil. It sounds positive. But we are deceived. When we violate God's standard, we discover that God remains good but that we have joined *team evil*. Like God we possess moral knowledge. But ironically, this neither makes us like God in his goodness nor does it enable us to restore our own goodness. Quite to the contrary. We are naked, ashamed, and helpless in our sins. Our knowledge of good and evil exposes our moral ineptitude and embarrassing ongoing wickedness.

Meanwhile, God seeks us out, offering a path toward healing. God can ultimately turn our wrong choices to good (Romans 8:28). But unless we accept God's assistance, we remain separated from him, trapped in a vicious cycle of deluded disobedience. As the apostle Paul puts it, prior to and apart from the gospel, humanity as a whole is "dead" in "transgressions and sins" (Ephesians 2:1). The effects of sin are death-dealing, grievous, and far-reaching.

Sin is personal. Personal separation from God is one problem caused by sin. Salvation includes restoration of a personal relationship with a holy God through Jesus' sinless offering on the cross (1 Peter 2:22–24; 1 John 3:5). But much gospel confusion is caused by a failure to move beyond the personal.

Sin is social. My sin problem is not merely my separation from a holy God. My sin is *your* problem—*our problem*. With some sins, like murder and adultery, it is obvious that personal sin harms other people and society. But private sins like jealousy or pride hurt other people too. They limit our ability to serve God and others.

Sin is cosmic. In response to Adam's sin, God announces that *the very ground* has been impacted. The pleasures of the garden give way to thorns and thistles (Genesis 3:17–19). The apostle Paul explains that the whole "creation was subjected to frustration" (Romans 8:20). In fact, it's worse, because the fundamental cosmic elements can be controlled by sin (Galatians 4:3, 9; Colossians 2:8). Even God's good gifts, like the Law of Moses, are perverted by sin, leading not to rescue but to death when pursued apart from the Christ (Romans 7:7–13). Although God made the old creation good, due to sin, it remains in such severe disrepair that it can't sustain eternal life.

Since sin is personal, social, and cosmic, sin's effects are *systemic*. This means its consequences are *universal within every system*. Sin impacts beryllium, balloons, banks, bombs, businesses, banquets, boyfriends, and your Aunt Bonnie. Everything. We desperately need rescue.

SIN CAUSES LACK OF GLORY

DOES THE BIBLE EXPLAIN why the effects of sin are universal and devastating? Yes, consider Romans 1:18–32. The systemic effect is not arbitrary. *Sin disrupts image-bearing, so humans and all creation have a deficit of God's glory.* A *human* king is required to restore glory.

HOW GLORY IS LOST

ALTHOUGH WE KNOW TRUE things about God through creation, we suppress these truths, because we would rather worship idols of our own making. We may not craft physical statues, but our idols are as prevalent and real today as in antiquity. Our most popular idols are the big three: money, sex, and power. Humans continue to worship idols, because they allow us to pursue our selfish body-centered appetites (Romans 1:24–27).

Paul bluntly explains how idols harm us: humans have "exchanged *the glory* of the immortal God *for images* made to look like a mortal human being and birds and animals and reptiles" (Romans 1:23). This glory exchange refers to the loss of our image-bearing capacity, as we turn away from God toward false images.

When humans worship images (idols) rather than the living God, they are swapping an encounter with God's glory for a bankrupt experience. When we make this exchange—and we've all made it—humans no longer fully carry God's image to one another or to the rest of creation, but we become like the false idols we worship (Psalm 115:5–8). Idolatry leaves us empty (2 Kings 17:5; Jeremiah 2:5), bereft of the fullness of God's glory. When we worship idols, the result is decreased exposure to God's glory, so that our derivative glory is not mutually refreshed when we encounter one another. Instead, we experience the opposite: a downward spiral into gross moral depravity ensues (Romans 1:24–32). When we worship idols rather than God, other humans and the remainder of creation fail to receive God's glory *through* us. We dishonor God too.

Given this is a universal human problem (apart from our union with Jesus the king), the slide into moral bankruptcy is fast and steep. Paul concludes his remarks about the human problem in Romans 3:23 with his famous words: "All have sinned *and fall short of the glory of God.*" Notice that even though it is true that we are unrighteous, he does not say, "All have sinned and fall short of God's perfect standard of righteousness." Rather, Paul speaks about the lack of God's *glory*.

Paul wants to remind us that salvation is about more than a personal falling short of God's holy standard. We need the restoration of human image-bearing, *so*

that everyone and everything in creation will no longer lack God's glory. Then God will be glorified by his creatures. This focus helps us to remember that our goal in the local church is Spirit-empowered disciple making, which transforms everyone more and more into the image of King Jesus.

THE KING RESTORES IMAGE-BEARING

WE ALL NEED GOOD news about a king because creation needs the restoration of proper human rule. God intends humans to carry his image to creation, so it can experience his glory. But image-bearing has become distorted by sin. We need a flawless *human* king who can restore God's glory amid humanity's brokenness. Then creation can be ruled by humans properly again and God can receive the glory that is his due.

3

HOW IS JESUS' KINGSHIP BENEFICIAL?

Answer: King Jesus frees us from our misguided self-rule. Christians alone have the benefits of forgiveness of sins and everlasting life with God. But as the king's glory radiates outward, non-Christians and the rest of creation profit too.

> Salvation is found in no one else, for there is no other name under heaven given to mankind by which we must be saved.
> — Acts 4:12

The gospel is *Jesus is the Christ, the universal king*, because salvation was never about rescuing humans simply for their own sakes. Salvation is for humanity's sake, for creation's sake, and for God's own sake—that he might receive the honor that he deserves.

This chapter explores key benefits of the gospel. The most obvious benefit pertains to the failure of my self-rule. I am not a very good king of my own life. I need King Jesus to lead me. So do you—and so does our troubled world.

Under Jesus' kingship, we are finally free to cast off our misguided self-rule— our pathetic attempt at life apart from God. Jesus' servant kingship results in full human flourishing. From Jesus we learn to reject inappropriate desires, handle wealth and its trappings, forgive our enemies, pray for those who persecute us, turn the other cheek, practice open-handed generosity, care for the downcast, and more. Jesus' Sermon on

UNDER JESUS' KINGSHIP, WE ARE FINALLY FREE TO CAST OFF OUR MISGUIDED SELF-RULE.

the Mount (Matthew 5–7) is especially revealing. It shows us a picture of life under Jesus' kingship. The benefits are countless.

Yet there are different categories of benefit. That is, the gospel helps Christians, non-Christians, planets, penguins, plants, and pencils—but not all equally. A simple yet accurate way is to work from the narrowest to the most general. This suggests three categories of gospel benefits: exclusively Christian, human in general, and cosmic.

EXCLUSIVELY CHRISTIAN BENEFITS OF THE GOSPEL

The gospel has been badly misunderstood if we think it helps only those who become Christians. The gospel is bigger than that. But the most important benefits are *exclusively* for those who commit to King Jesus.

Ultimate salvation is exclusively Christian. Jesus alone. "Salvation is found in no one else, for there is no other name under heaven given to mankind by which we must be saved" (Acts 4:12). Regarding eternal salvation, Jesus is not one of many possible ways, one form of the truth among many, and one solid model for life amid other equal options. As Jesus himself put it, "I am *the* way and *the* truth and *the* life. *No one* comes to the Father except through me" (John 14:6). Apart from King Jesus, there is no path to the Father, no road to eternal life.

For final salvation, Jesus the Messiah is the only way. But Scripture provides numerous ways to picture the rewards of this singular salvation: reconciliation, peace, union, atonement, redemption, becoming holy, enrichment, victory, triumph, exaltation, glory, rule, return from exile, rest, feasting, marriage, and life in the New Jerusalem. There are many more. But let's focus on four additional, distinctive Christian benefits of the gospel: adoption, right-standing with God, fruit of the Holy Spirit, and eternal life. These are vital to grasp for a full understanding of salvation, but are sometimes misunderstood.

Adoption. It's helpful to begin with adoption into God's family, because it is imperative to see the gospel's benefits are *for us* as a group—the church—before they are *for me* as an individual. God is creating a people, a special family, by the gospel's effects. That family existed before you and I were born. It will exist after we die. We get the opportunity to join it.

God's purpose to adopt a people is both timeless and timebound. In a timeless fashion, God chose the church as a group in the Son for adoption before creation (Ephesians 1:5). But that needed to be worked out in history. By the promises God made to the patriarchs, Israel—as a whole people—came to possess "sonship" (Exodus 4:22; Romans 9:4). Yet, since God's saving promises run through the king as a matter of history and fulfillment, these promises are ratified for Israel today only when Jesus is publicly acknowledged as Messiah and Lord (Romans 9:30–10:4; 10:9–10). In the wake of the gospel, Israel is saved only by faith in Jesus as the Christ. Non-Jews (Gentiles), although a wild olive shoot, can be grafted into these family promises to Israel as these promises climax in Jesus the king (Romans 11:17–27).

When this engrafting happens, non-Jews are adopted. The Father sent the Son for this express purpose, "that we might receive adoption" (Galatians 4:5). The result is that Jesus is not ashamed to call us brothers and sisters (Hebrews 2:11). Through the Christ, everyone—Jew and non-Jew—can join God's family.

Right-standing with God. A key benefit of the gospel is right-standing with God. This imagery refers to a court of law. God is the judge. All humans stand guilty. Yet through Jesus the king, this verdict can be reversed. Sins can be atoned (that is, covered over) by Jesus' substitutionary sacrifice. When an accused person is declared "not guilty," they have joined the one and only family that has right-standing with God, the true church.

The process of gaining right-standing before God is called "being justified" in the Bible. The resulting status is "justification" or "righteousness." Paul announces righteousness as a core gospel benefit in Romans 1:16–17: "For I am not ashamed of the gospel, for it is the power of God for salvation. . . . For in the gospel the righteousness of God is revealed, righteousness that is by faith for faith, as it is written: 'The righteous [one] by faith will live'" (AT). The righteousness of God is a quality that God's people can possess or enjoy (Romans 3:21–22; Philippians 3:9). It is something God's people can become (2 Corinthians 5:21). The king makes "the righteousness of God" available "by faith." Here "faith" is best understood as going beyond *belief* or *trust* to include also *loyalty* or *allegiance*.[4] The king's people are forgiven and have right-standing with God.

Holy Spirit fruit. Not only do we gain right-standing with God, with the king's assistance, but we also make progress in becoming Christlike in our attitudes and activities. Part of the gospel is that the Father and Son have sent the Spirit to dwell within God's people permanently. The church is comparable to a temple of the Holy Spirit (1 Corinthians 3:16; Ephesians 2:22). Again, this gospel benefit is communal but personalized. At Pentecost when the Spirit was given to the community of disciples (Acts 2:1–4), it was experienced collectively (wind filled the whole house where they were sitting) and individually (separate tongues of fire came to rest on each). Likewise, the Spirit indwells God's people as a group (John 14:17; 2 Timothy 1:14), but each person who continues to confess, "Jesus is Lord," has a share in the Spirit (1 Corinthians 12:3).

The Holy Spirit guides the community into all truth, correcting, rebuking, and judging (John 16:8–11). The Spirit is the church's deposit, the down payment that guarantees its future salvation (2 Corinthians 1:22; 5:5; Ephesians 1:14). Those who remain attached to the vine—the king himself—produce fruit (John 15:1–5). Those detached from the king wither, die, and ultimately become fuel for the fire (John 15:6).

The fruit produced by the Spirit includes "love, joy, peace, forbearance, kindness, goodness, faithfulness, gentleness and self-control" (Galatians 5:22–23). In other words, the gospel benefits us because the Holy Spirit transforms us from fruitless to fruitful. The coming of the Holy Spirit is a foundational gospel benefit, since the Holy Spirit applies the communal benefits of the gospel to us personally. As disciples of Jesus, we are transformed so that we bear the image of Jesus in the fruit of the Holy Spirit.

Eternal life. This final gospel benefit is crucial but demands clarification. Scripture speaks frequently of "eternal life" (*zōē aiōnios*) as part of salvation (e.g., John 3:16; Acts 13:48; Romans 2:7). Yet this is not heaven. In fact, the Bible never explicitly says the gospel's purpose is to help a person get to heaven. On the contrary, as far as Scripture is concerned, the clearest statement of the gospel's purpose is found in Romans, stated the same way twice: "the obedience of faith" in all the nations (Romans 1:5; 16:26, AT). The gospel's final aim is not heaven but loyal obedience to Jesus the king in a new era—an era characterized by "everlasting life." Let me explain.

Heaven and eternal life are different. This phrase *zōē aiōnios* ("eternal life") is more precisely "era life" or "life characterized by the era." *Zōē aiōnios* intends life characterized by the kingdom-of-God era. This is the time period when Jesus reigns victoriously over sin, sickness, and death. It's an era humanity can enter right now (John 5:24–25)! Since in its fullness, this era includes the defeat of death and the presence of resurrection life, it is accurate to translate *zōē aiōnios* as "everlasting life." But unfortunately, this is easy to confuse with heaven. We are on steadier biblical ground if we say a key gospel aim is *everlasting resurrection-life* rather than heaven.

Scripture teaches about heaven and hell, but the topics are frequently misunderstood. They cannot be nuanced further here except to say heaven is best considered a holding stage in preparation for a renewal so dramatic that God says, "Behold, I am making all things new" (Revelation 21:5, AT). In the end, we won't go up to heaven; we are now waiting for the new heaven and new earth, which is when God's heaven comes down to us on earth. The heavenly city, the New Jerusalem, will descend like a bride prepared for her husband (21:2). It will be beautiful! The dwelling place of God will be with humans forever (21:3). Evildoers will be excluded. But all names written in the lamb's book of life will be included (21:8, 27). We will have everlasting resurrection-life as we reign over creation with the King of kings (Revelation 22:5; see also Matthew 19:28; 2 Timothy 2:12).

GENERAL HUMAN BENEFITS OF THE GOSPEL

WHILE THE BEST BENEFITS of the gospel are reserved for Jesus' disciples, those who reject him are aided during their earthly life too—although in the end, they are excluded from final salvation. Jesus announces that his gospel brings relief for the poor, oppressed, blind, and captives (Luke 4:16–21). Non-Christians are better off due to Jesus' kingship because they experience social and political good when they encounter authentic disciples. The hungry get fed. The poor are aided. The cold receive a blanket. When the church acknowledges Jesus' kingship—and it always does when the real church gathers—they create an alternative social and political order that benefits the marginalized.

Delivery of these benefits to the marginalized can be hindered by wolves in sheep's clothing. These wolves claim Jesus as Lord, but their wicked deeds prove otherwise. In the end, Jesus will tell such people plainly, "I never knew you. Depart from me you evildoers" (Matthew 7:23, AT). The world is far better because of genuine disciples. But more often than we'd like to admit, the problem is not just the wolves. Followers of Jesus, even the best, remain part of the problem. We do not merely stumble. We fall flat on our faces. At least, at times. How can the gospel benefit non-Christians, when even devoted Christians keep falling short?

COSMIC BENEFITS OF THE GOSPEL

INSTALLING JESUS AS KING, a human who perfectly images God, is key to God's rescue operation that benefits the whole universe. It jumpstarts a slow, lengthy salvation process for humanity and creation. *God's new-creation king initializes a restorative spiral upward of glory.* This is why Paul describes the good news as "the gospel of *the glory* of the Christ, who is the image of God" (2 Corinthians 4:4, AT).

The gospel's benefits are as wide as the universe because the problem is that wide too. We need deliverance not merely from the guilt that burdens us, but from the collapse of the old order. As Paul puts it, the Lord Jesus, the Christ, "gave himself for our sins *to rescue us from the present evil age*" (Galatians 1:4). We need to be brought into a new epoch.

In Scripture the old era ("this age") is under the sway of the evil one, "the god of this age" (2 Corinthians 4:4). God's first creation is reeling because the basic elements upon which it is founded have proven inadequate. *New creation* is the main cosmic benefit of the gospel.

Scripture's name for these old elements is the *stoicheia*. Paul speaks unfavorably of these elements, seeing them as enslaving: "When we were children, we were enslaved under the *elements of the world* [the *stoicheia*]" (Galatians 4:3, AT). Because the *stoicheia* can be controlled by sin to capture humanity, God had to do something dramatic: "But when the set time had fully come, God sent his Son, born of a woman, born under the law, to redeem those under the law, that we might receive adoption to sonship" (4:4–5). God had to free us from the old age by adopting us into his new-creation family.

Paul was distressed because some of the Galatians had turned back to childhood. They had re-enslaved themselves to the *stoicheia*, the foundational old elements, by performing the commands of Moses for right-standing with God. They falsely believed these works of the law showed that they were more right with God than others. But they'd compromised the gospel's result: one and only one justified family (Galatians 2:7–21). They were deeply misguided. As Paul states in the conclusion of his letter, God has established a "new creation," and this alone matters (6:15).

God's new creation ultimately can only be his work alone. But is this correct? On the one hand, it must be true. God alone is the creator of both old and new creation (Isaiah 45:18; 65:17–18; Revelation 21:1–5). Unlike God we cannot create from nothing. Humans can *rearrange* created matter and energy. But the matter and energy had to come from somewhere. So certain new-creation actions belong to God alone: God's establishment of fresh foundations for the universe, Jesus' resurrection from the dead, his enthronement at God's right hand, and the sending of the Holy Spirit to the church. These are all acts of new creation that God has already originated.

On the other hand, although God is the source, he uses humans to distribute his new-creation refreshment. God designed creation to be ruled by humans who bear his image locally within the world. Transformed disciples make God's new-creation glory present in the world.

The gospel provides benefits to Christians, non-Christians, and all creation. Through the process of Spirit-led image restoration, God transforms humans and then partners with them to bring his new-creation gospel benefits to all creation. What does this transformation look like?

IMAGE DEGRADATION AND RESTORATION

Broken mirrors—that's the result of image degradation. Shattered, fragmented, tarnished. If humans are no longer carrying God's image properly, then the whole created order lacks God's glory. You can't receive God's glory adequately through me, nor I through you, so it is never replenished. Failure in bearing God's glory is a vicious cycle, a spiral downward for humans and all creation.

"Image restoration" is the process by which the glory begins to spiral upward again. It starts with the incarnation. Jesus' incarnation is every bit as essential to the gospel as the cross. We cannot understand the gospel unless we see that the Son had to take on human flesh in order for God's glory to be restored. The restored glory of God in the lives of the people in the local church is the local church's goal in disciple making. Image restoration happens this way:

Step 1: Incarnate glory. God sends the prototype, his very Son, to become the human king. The Son is the pristine original image of God (Colossians 1:15; 2 Corinthians 4:4). When Jesus takes on human flesh, perfectly serving and safeguarding, humans are given the opportunity to gaze on the spotless image of God: "The Word became flesh and made his dwelling among us, and we have seen his *glory*" (John 1:14, AT).

Step 2: Transformed glory. As we willingly choose to gaze upon the Son as the perfect image of God, seeing his glory, we begin to be transformed. Again, Paul describes the process: "All of us who with unveiled faces are beholding as in a mirror *the glory* of the Lord are being *transformed* into *the same image* from *glory* into *glory*" (2 Corinthians 3:18, AT). As we turn away from the world and behold our king, we are being transformed by the Spirit into his image. Our minds are renewed (Romans 12:2). Our capacity to radiate God's glory is recharged.

Step 3: Conformed glory. We are increasingly *conformed* to the image of the royal Son (Romans 8:29; see also 1 Corinthians 15:49). The intensity of God's glory reflected through us to others increases. It's a group process. (This is one of many reasons why participating in church matters.) A cycle of recovery for humans and all creation ensues through mutual glory refreshment. As Paul says, in our present sufferings, we can scarcely begin to imagine "the glory that will be revealed in us"—a glory that renews creation in the midst of its present futile state (Romans 8:18)! Through renewed humanity, creation will finally be set free, "brought into the freedom of the *glory* of the children of God" (Romans 8:21, AT).

In sum, the degraded image of God within humanity had to be refreshed through an encounter with *the original image of God*, Jesus, in all his royal-servant splendor. It is our Christian destiny to be conformed to the image of the Son as part of our final salvation. This is the Spirit's new-creation work. As image restoration transpires, God's new-creation glory is breaking into the midst of the old creation, reinvigorating it.

THE DEGRADED IMAGE OF GOD WITHIN HUMANITY HAD TO BE REFRESHED.

Yet the completion of our conformity to the Son's image awaits his climactic appearance, as does the full restoration of God's glory for creation. "We know that when he appears we will be like him, because we will see him just as he is" (1 John 3:2, AT). When we see the returned king in his full splendor, the church's image-bearing will finally be perfected.

All the benefits of the gospel ultimately flow through the new-creation power of Jesus as he rules at the Father's right hand. Jesus' incarnation, death for sins, resurrection, enthronement, Spirit-sending, and final rule are all gospel. The glorious king has broken sin's tyranny, allowing us to be true disciples who bear God's glory to one another and creation.

4

WHO IS THE GOD OF THE GOSPEL?

Answer: God, who reveals himself through creation, showed himself specially to Abraham and his descendants. In the gospel, God revealed himself as three persons but one God: the Father sent his only Son, and they sent forth the Spirit.

The Word became flesh and made his dwelling among us.
We have seen his glory, the glory of the one and only Son,
who came from the Father, full of grace and truth.
— John 1:14

We usually think about the gospel simply as what saves us. We do not ordinarily think of it as God's definitive way of revealing who he is. But the gospel unveils the Trinity. If we think that the doctrine of the Trinity is merely a tacked-on idea from subsequent church history, we've not yet understood the gospel. The Bible does not use the word "Trinity," but describes it in various ways.

THE TRINITY

TRINITY MEANS THERE ARE three persons—Father, Son, and Holy Spirit—but only one God. We see multiple divine persons but their deep oneness in Scripture. For example, Jesus stated, "I am in the Father and the Father is in me" (John 14:11), and "I and the Father are one" (John 10:30). How the three persons of the Trinity are one was clarified at the early Christian Councils of Nicaea and Constantinople in the 300s by using Scripture.[5] The three persons are one because they are the same substance or essence ("consubstantial" or *homoousios*).

The three persons are eternal. Each has always existed. But the persons eternally exist in different ways. Despite the various descriptions of the Father, Son, and Spirit in the Bible, in the final analysis, the eternal persons are only truly distinct in terms of 1) origin or cause and 2) the Son's incarnation (at least, that is all we can safely say).

How is each eternal person distinct with regard to their origin? The Father is uncaused (or unoriginated). Since the Christ (further described as the Son) ascribes the source of his begetting to God the Father long before Jesus was born in the flesh, we can conclude the Son is eternally begotten of the Father (Psalm 2:7; see also Psalm 110:4; Acts 13:33; Hebrews 1:5; 5:5; John 1:14). This means that the Father always has produced the Son in a fatherly fashion, and always will. Meanwhile the Father and the Son eternally send (John 15:26) or breathe forth the Holy Spirit (John 20:22). So in a timeless fashion, the Father is uncaused, the Father eternally generates the Son, and the Father and Son together breathe forth the Spirit.

The reason Christians by and large agree about the Trinity is that to deny it is tantamount to denying the gospel. The activities of these three persons are variously described in the Bible. But the gospel showed us clearly for the first time that God is triune. After the giving of the gospel, however, we can see hints in the Old Testament that God has always been more than one person. Yet the historical events that constitute the gospel are God's definitive self-revelation in time: the Father sent the Son, and then they sent the Spirit.

> THE GOSPEL SHOWED US CLEARLY FOR THE FIRST TIME THAT GOD IS TRIUNE.

WHO IS THE FATHER AS REVEALED IN THE GOSPEL?

IN TERMS OF THE gospel, who is God the Father? The one true God revealed himself to Abraham, David, and many others. God entered into *covenants* (legally binding agreements) with his chosen people. The oneness of God is announced clearly in Israel's covenant law: "Hear O Israel: the LORD our God, the LORD *is one*" (Deuteronomy 6:4). Then, when the time was ripe, God sent his Son, initializing the gospel.

Although Israel knew that there was only one God, the gospel revealed God to be the Father of a unique Son. And if we suggest that God wasn't the Father until the virgin Mary became pregnant with Jesus, we err. Scripture announces the Son preexisted with God and was part of God's redemptive plan *before* Jesus appeared as a man (e.g., Galatians 4:4–5; Romans 8:3; 2 Corinthians 8:9; Philippians 2:5–7). Moreover, if God only recently became a Father, then he fundamentally changed. But God does not change in such basic ways (e.g., Malachi 3:6; James 1:17).

Therefore, the events of the gospel showed that God must be at least two persons—eternal Father and eternal Son. We see evidence for this in the opening of John's Gospel: "In the beginning was the Word, and the Word was with God, and the Word was God. He was with God in the beginning" (1:1–2). This eternal Word (*Logos*) that preexisted with God the Father became flesh in the person of Jesus of Nazareth (John 1:14). The Father raised Jesus from the dead and enthroned him. At Pentecost, the Father collaborated with the Son in the sending of the third person, the Holy Spirit (Acts 2:1–4).

It would be misguided to detail the Father's unique saving role in comparison with the Son or with the Spirit. Except for special circumstances pertaining to Jesus' humanity (see below), when any one person of the Trinity is involved in rescuing, the others are also. In general, it is problematic to assign unique activities to the persons of the Trinity.

Consider the resurrection as a test case for mutual involvement. It is true that Scripture prefers to say God (the Father) raised the Son, since we find this affirmation dozens of times (e.g., Acts 2:24; Romans 10:9; 1 Corinthians 6:14). Yet Jesus also claims that he will raise himself: "Destroy this temple, and I will raise it again in three days" (John 2:19). Jesus was referring to the resurrection of his own body (John 2:19–22). The Father raised Jesus, but Jesus also raised himself.

The Son always participates in the Father's work. As Jesus puts it, "Whatever the Father does, the Son also does" (John 5:19). The Spirit was active in God's resurrection of Jesus and is active in ours too: "If the Spirit of him who raised Jesus from amid the dead dwells in you, he who raised Christ from amid the dead will also give life to your mortal bodies through his Spirit who dwells in you" (Romans 8:11, AT). The Father, Son, and Spirit are involved in one another's actions—at least, when those actions are directed toward creation.

So we must use caution when saying "the Father sent the Son," and the like, lest we give the impression this is the Father's work alone. The preexistent Son willed it too. The author of Hebrews reminds us, "When Christ came into the world, he said: 'Sacrifice and offering you did not desire, but a body you prepared for me . . . . Then I said, "Here I am—it is written about me in the scroll—I have come to do your will, my God"'" (Hebrews 10:5–7). The Christ as the eternal Son told the Father that he was voluntarily taking on a human body as a form of sacrifice, according to his Father's will.[6] In short, when one person of the Trinity acts to save, we cannot neglect the involvement of the others.

WHO IS THE SPIRIT AS REVEALED IN THE GOSPEL?

BECAUSE THE PERSONS OF the Trinity are involved in each other's actions, it would be wrongheaded to absolutize the unique function of the Spirit in our salvation. But broadly considered, Scripture describes the Spirit's saving activity in this way: the Father and the Son sent the Holy Spirit at Pentecost to the king's people as an end-of-the-age promise (Acts 2:17–21). *As God's new-creation power, the Holy Spirit makes Jesus' reign functionally present by indwelling the church in order to apply the benefits of the king's gospel* (see "Holy Spirit fruit" in the previous chapter). When an individual hears the good news about the king and responds, they join the ranks of God's people. This individual is immersed in the Holy Spirit, so that they have a personal share in the rewards that the king's people as a whole possess.

WHO IS JESUS AS REVEALED IN THE GOSPEL?

GENERALLY, WE MUST SAY that all the persons of the Trinity are involved in every saving action. Except! The Son's incarnation gives him a special role. The Son eternally preexisted as the second person of the Trinity, but became fully human in the first century as Jesus. But when the eternal Son united with Jesus' humanity, he did not cease being God. The gospel reveals Jesus to be both human and divine. Classically this is explained by saying Jesus is *only one person with two natures*—a fully human nature and fully divine (the Chalcedonian definition). Jesus is God and man—one hundred percent of each—all the time. Jesus, while remaining fully God, did not opt to use all his divine privileges, but emptied himself, for our sake—even to the point of death (Philippians 2:6–8).

In this way, Jesus on the cross is God and is God's ultimate self-revelation. The Son did not cease to be fully God when dying for our sins, so he showed us that to be God means to be selflessly for others. God humbled himself to such a degree that he died an agonizing death *for us*. God displayed an incredible depth of love for us—even while we were sinners (Romans 5:8; 1 John 4:10). For God to be God, and for us to be conformed to God's image, is to take up the cross willingly to serve and safeguard the well-being of others.

The Son's uniqueness as the only person of the Trinity to become human means that some of the saving actions announced in the gospel can be carried out *only by the Son*. Although all three persons of the Trinity were invested in the sending of the Son, Jesus alone took on human flesh. Jesus alone suffered for our sins by dying.[7] Moreover, although the Father, Son, and Spirit all hold the new-creation power of resurrection, Jesus alone was raised from death. Only he appeared to his disciples in his same real and tangible body—although it had been transformed as befits the power and splendor of the new creation that God is unveiling. Jesus was then taken up into heaven *bodily* while two men in white and his disciples gazed at him (Acts 1:9–11).

The bodily ascension of Jesus is vital for our salvation, for Jesus' *body* is part of the new creation. Mysteriously, Jesus is embodied still today as he reigns at God's right hand. Apparently resurrected bodies are suitably transformed so that they can exist in such a capacity. We know this because upon his ascension, Jesus was seated *bodily* at the very right hand of God, where he now serves as the King of kings (Ephesians 1:20–21) and our great high priest (Romans 8:34; Hebrews 8:1). Christians are *bodily* seated at God's right hand too, since we are hidden within our embodied king, who is resurrected and reigning from this position (Colossians 3:1–3).

Although the resurrected Christ, as divine *and human*, rules at the invitation of the Father, the Spirit is also involved. The Spirit makes King Jesus' rule functionally present (Romans 1:4; 8:1–17; 2 Corinthians 3:17). But the office of ruling as the divine-human King of kings belongs to Jesus alone. The *bodily* reign of Jesus at God's right hand is essential, for creation needs to be ruled not just by God but also by a perfect human who can restore humans. For ultimately creation must be ruled by humans who make God's glory present with their bodies. That is how God designed creation.

This is why among the persons of the Trinity, being "the Christ" is Jesus' office alone. It is essential that a flawless, embodied, human king rule creation, so that flawed humans can gaze on him in order to be restored in their image-bearing.[8] Then, they can make God's glory fully present to creation once more by ruling under and alongside the King of kings. This is why Paul, while speaking about the necessity of perseverance in the process of salvation, reminds us, "If we have *died* with him, we will

> **IT IS ESSENTIAL THAT A FLAWLESS, EMBODIED, HUMAN KING RULE CREATION.**

also *live* with him; if we *endure*, we will also *reign* with him; if we disown him, he also will disown us" (2 Timothy 2:11–12, AT). Rather than disown our king, we must persist in confessing allegiance. Those who have *died* with the king will enjoy *resurrection-life*. Those who *endure* with the king will one day *reign* with him. Having been transformed into his glory-bearing image, Jesus' disciples will be fit to rule too.

For creation to reach the fullness of its glory, it must be ruled by humans: by King Jesus as he is assisted by his resurrected kings and queens. This is "the gospel of the glory of the Christ, who is the image of God" (2 Corinthians 4:4, AT).

5

HOW DO WE SHARE THE GOSPEL?

Answer: We share the gospel by testifying in word and deed that Jesus is the victorious, rescuing king. We encourage others to become loyal followers of the king through a faith response of trusting allegiance, repentance from sins, and baptism.

We are therefore Christ's ambassadors, as though God were making his appeal through us. We implore you on Christ's behalf: Be reconciled to God.
— 2 Corinthians 5:20

If only we could condense the shock, horror, beauty, and love of the gospel into an elixir. Then, we could bottle and pass it—astonishing!—to a neighbor, coworker, or friend. But God did not design creation's rescue, nor its rule, to work that way. For God's plan of salvation to reach non-Christians and the world, there is only one option: *disciples must function as image-bearers, testifying in word and deed that Jesus is the victorious king.* In response, hearers of the gospel are faced with a decision: Will they give allegiance?

HEARERS OF THE GOSPEL ARE FACED WITH A DECISION: WILL THEY GIVE ALLEGIANCE?

HUMAN TESTIMONY REQUIRED

For the gospel to be effective, God needs not just Jesus but us also. Without humans opting to testify, Jesus' significance as the divine-human king would be lost in the mists of time. Fortunately, the apostles and others did bear witness—and in durable ways. The New Testament is largely the result of early testimony. Apart from the faithfulness of disciples of Jesus past and present, the gospel would never have reached us.

Bearing witness is key to the church's gospel mission. That is what Jesus told us just prior to his ascension. He described for his disciples *the way* the kingdom would be restored to Israel—and in so doing reach the world: "But you will receive power when the Holy Spirit comes on you; and *you will be my witnesses* in Jerusalem, and in all Judea and Samaria, and to the ends of the earth" (Acts 1:8). The kingdom will be restored through Spirit-empowered testimony that Jesus is the Christ. The early church grew by witnessing in this way. Likewise, testimony to King Jesus can fuel the church's mission today.

HOW DO WE WITNESS IN WORD?

To share the gospel effectively, we must bear witness to Jesus as king in word, character, and deed. To many people, sharing *in word* can seem pushy or offensive today. Is it really wise? If so, how do we do it?

Words are necessary. We can't share through our actions alone. The beauty of Jesus' plan of restoration is that witnessing allows us to announce the objective truth clearly, but from a subjective vantage point that minimizes affront.

The objective side of proclamation. When I say that the gospel is objective truth, I mean its claims are not a matter of personal opinion—yours, mine, or anyone else's. Key gospel events are matters of history. As such they are part of the public record, open to scrutiny. We share the objective gospel with others when we tell them the ten events, what I've called *the gospel precisely.*

The gospel is that Jesus the king:

1. preexisted as God the Son,
2. was sent by the Father,
3. took on human flesh in fulfillment of God's promises to David,
4. died for our sins in accordance with the Scriptures,
5. was buried,
6. was raised on the third day in accordance with the Scriptures,
7. appeared to many witnesses,
8. *is enthroned at the right hand of God as the ruling Christ,*
9. has sent the Holy Spirit to his people to effect his rule, and
10. will come again as final judge to rule.

It is impossible to share the gospel without words because these ten events cannot be communicated by deeds or character alone.[9]

Since words are required, we should know these ten events intimately. So that you have a tool for sharing, I'd encourage you to memorize them. But then feel free to expand or contract, using your own words to share the gospel.

If you find memorization difficult, notice that the gospel has a story shape that makes it easy to remember: It begins with the Son in glory with the Father. The Son became human, died on the cross for our sins, and rose. The gospel climaxes with Jesus' enthronement as king. (This is why it is italicized.) The Spirit has been sent. The Son will return to rule creation. In short, the gospel is the complete story of the Son, viewed from the lens of how God is using Jesus to bring about holistic restoration.

We must know the gospel well enough that we can tell it to others. Practice! But if you lack confidence or are afraid you'll forget something, don't worry. It is about sharing the good news, not following a script slavishly. Keep the *cross, resurrection, and especially Jesus' enthronement as king* in view. Then, trust, and share the gospel as the Spirit leads regardless of your fears.

The subjective side of proclamation. The genius of bearing witness to the gospel is that although the gospel refers to real events, it is always attested from a subjective (personal) vantage point. In announcing these ten events, I'm asserting that I'm *personally* committed to their truthfulness. In light of the testimony of others, I made a decision to acclaim Jesus as the king and by faith to give him my allegiance as his disciple. Now that I've done that, I've begun to enjoy the rewards. I can share how I've personally benefitted.

When sharing the gospel, we should be quick to add our own testimony to the validity of Jesus' kingship. This is especially helpful today because non-Christians are frequently sensitive to pushiness. I can say, "Let me tell you about my life." I can testify to how I made the mistake of thinking that I knew better than God in some area of life—money, relationships, sexuality, ladder-climbing, dealing with resentment. I can tell how I let someone or something else rule as king, at least in a season or a reckless moment. I can share about how I'm still struggling. Vulnerability opens hearts. Then, I can speak about how I came to discover (or rediscover) that Jesus is the only true King of kings—and how I'm still trying to learn it today.

I can then share the full gospel, the ten events, expanding on them or compressing as the Spirit guides. We can testify to the forgiveness he offers at the cross and his new-creation power, as evidenced by his resurrection and sending of the Spirit.

We add our own personal witness: I know that I am forgiven, created afresh, and imperfect but empowered, because of my life change. **WE NEED TO TESTIFY TO HIS PRESENT RULE AS KING.** Above all, we need to testify to his present rule as king, and how allegiance to him has led to partial but true victory for ourselves and others. We can share what it means to live day by day as his disciple. We can invite others to give allegiance too.

HOW DO WE WITNESS WITH DEEDS?

WORDS ARE REQUIRED FOR sharing the full gospel, but deeds and character reinforce its truthfulness. If I assert that Jesus is my liberating king and that I have become a new creature through the power of the Holy Spirit, but there is little or no evidence of this in my bodily activities, the claim rings empty. Hearers of the gospel's words will likely reject Jesus' kingship.

We all know hypocrisy undermines the gospel. But since we are all sinners and imperfect, isn't some hypocrisy inevitable? How do we tell people we've been genuinely changed yet remain honest about our ongoing sinfulness?

To answer, let's step back: Why would God use broken, sinful humans to share the good news? (Suddenly the elixir idea sounds more reasonable.) Unless God were to abandon his design for creation, it *must* be this way. Remember, the gospel is not a you-are-forgiven-so-you-can-go-to-heaven transaction. Creation requires human rule. Paul calls the good news "the gospel of the glory of the Christ, who is the image of God" (2 Corinthians 4:4, AT). The gospel is about a divine-human king who begins to restore God's glory by fully bearing his image. Since we all begin as mangled image-bearers and image recovery is a group process, it takes time. It will not result in perfection until we fully see the king. It is a spiral upward of glory restoration (see Chapter 3).

We can answer authentically by telling others that we are broken mirrors, trying to reflect glory, *while in the process of restoration*. Cracks and tarnish still exist. When saying this, however, deeds and character matter. If non-Christians cannot see a shimmer of glory in the midst of our brokenness—a glimmer that shows that the transformation underway is due to God and not us (2 Corinthians 4:7–12)—then they will likely reject the gospel. This is why our Christian deeds and character are integral to our gospel witness.

In sum, the primary way a non-Christian sees God and Jesus is to see God in you, me, or another disciple. If a non-Christian is to be saved, they must encounter a disciple (past or present) in the process of image restoration, who shares the gospel in words while giving a partial glimpse of God's glory in deeds and character.

HOW SHOULD WE RESPOND TO THE GOSPEL?

SHOUT, SING, PRAISE, DANCE. We should respond to the gospel with astonished gratitude and heartfelt joy! The gospel is God's grace (Acts 20:24). Sinful humanity as a whole did not deserve the grace of the gospel, but it is a gift that has proven effective for transforming sinners into the image of King Jesus. God acts first—and he has done this within history by the events that constitute the gospel—but human action is required in response.

We respond to God's grace by accepting the gospel of Jesus' kingship through faith, repentance, and baptism. Faith, repentance, and baptism are best regarded not as part of the gospel in Scripture. Rather, they are *how we respond to the gospel* in order to accept God's grace. Each connects to the gospel of Jesus' rescuing kingship.

Faith (*pistis*) involves *believing* certain things (the truthfulness of the ten events of the gospel) and *trusting* that the gospel is God's provision for salvation. But it goes further. Faith is not just mental; it is expressed with your body through relationships (Galatians 2:20; James 2:14–26). As a response to the gospel, above all faith is allegiance to your new king (e.g., Romans 1:2–5; 1:8; 1:16–17; 3:21–26; 2 Thessalonians 1:4–8).

Repentance (*metanoia*) is not just feeling remorse over your past sins. It is an active change of mind, heart, and behavior. Jesus calls those who want to follow him to repent (Matthew 3:2; Mark 1:15). Repentance is a *turning away* from wrong activities and sin-inspired loyalties (Acts 8:22). At the same time, it is a *turning toward* obedience to God and his rule over you (Acts 26:20). Repentance is a rejection of your old non-God loyalties as you instead submit to Jesus' kingship.

Baptism (*baptisma*) is a deliberate identification with the death, resurrection, and enthronement, not merely of Jesus but *of Jesus in his royal capacity as the Christ* (Romans 6:1–11). Baptism is said to be saving in the New Testament (e.g., Acts 2:38; 1 Peter 3:21), probably because baptism includes faith (Galatians 3:25–27) and is the definitive way to embody faith decisively. Some of our earliest descriptions of

Christian baptism indicate that it included "calling upon the name" of the Lord Jesus (Acts 22:16, AT), which is best understood as undertaking an oath of loyalty to Jesus as sovereign.

After sharing the gospel, we need to summon hearers to choose. The center point of the decision is not whether to trust that Jesus died for your sins—for this distorts the *royal* gospel and misses the fullness of the required response. Rather, it is whether to give ultimate allegiance to the Christ-king. Once that decision is made, forgiveness of sins comes as a gospel benefit. The response is a call to salvation *and* discipleship into the ways of King Jesus.

Allegiance should be ratified through baptism. The best baptismal practices today will give ample space for the person being baptized to respond to the King Jesus gospel by repenting from past allegiances and declaring loyalty publicly. It should also be an opportunity for the gathered church as a whole to renew its allegiance.

TESTIFYING TO THE GOSPEL TODAY

A GLORY-BEARING DISCIPLE OF Jesus is shaped by the gospel pattern of life, especially the cross. A disciple should be prepared to testify about Jesus the king in word and deed. But doing this in our modern world is complex. Each age has opportunities and challenges. Four topics are especially pertinent to sharing the gospel today.

More than forgiveness. First, do not reduce the gospel to forgiveness at the cross. The cross is essential. But when we reduce the gospel only to what happened at the cross, we promote a self-serving parody of the gospel: personal rescue from a sin predicament so that the individual can enjoy the delights of heaven. The real gospel invites us to join the king's rescued people (the church), so that together, while being restored, we can serve others and creation in a cross-shaped fashion.

Responding to the king. Second, do not give kingship short shrift. If you haven't proclaimed to someone that Jesus is the Christ, the King of kings, then you haven't shared the full gospel yet. Moreover, if the king is missing, it is nearly impossible for the person hearing to respond accurately: Are you going to turn away from other loyalties and submit to his rule? The call to live as disciples of King Jesus rightfully realigns our entire lives. Disciples give allegiance to King Jesus and learn to align all we are and all we do under his authority and commands (Matthew 28:18–20).

Rewards and punishments. Third, do not be afraid to speak of judgment, rewards, and punishments. (On the benefits of the gospel, see Chapter 3.) Many are reluctant to bring up such things today—and let the Spirit lead—but generally reticence is unwise. Jesus and the apostles frequently taught about the punishments and rewards that surround this all-important decision (e.g., Matthew 13:41–43; 16:27; 22:11–13). Jesus is the pivot for individual and universal destiny. Everything is at stake. We should remind that the choice to follow or not follow King Jesus has tangible consequences—past, present, and future.

Yet I'd caution you when sharing the gospel against describing the punishment as hell and the reward as heaven, unless you can immediately explain further. Rather, speak of eternal separation versus resurrection-life with God. Heaven and hell are taught in Scripture, but these concepts have accrued cultural meanings that only partially align with Scripture's ultimate vision, so they need considerable unpacking. Talk about heaven and hell when appropriate. But even when opting for different language when sharing the gospel, it will usually be wise to emphasize the final judgment and the benefits/punishments—in this life and the next—that hang upon allegiance.

Incarnation matters. Fourth, make elements that have been neglected, such as the incarnation, a fresh opportunity. Consider how the incarnation is rarely featured when the gospel is shared but is integral to it. If you have a hurting friend, you can emphasize how God entered our hurt by becoming human through the incarnation. God knows and God himself has entered the full depths of our pain. Or share the gospel solution with a coworker who finds lack of respect for the environment detestable: God's placement of King Jesus as his fully divine *and human* image is the beginning of how God is restoring his *glory* over a renewed creation.

How can we share with a person who is convinced that they have already heard all this forgiveness gospel stuff before? When we explain why Jesus took on human flesh—not as a random fact but as an integral part of the saving gospel—perhaps we can get a fresh hearing.

Wanderers who find life purposeless may find their hearts stirred when they discover the gospel is not just rescue *from* sins but rescue *for* a fantastic purpose: they've been invited to join God's mission, to begin ruling under and with Jesus.

Good news! Let's tell others: Jesus is the rescuing king of glory, the King of kings.

APPENDIX

Matthew W. Bates, *Gospel Allegiance: What Faith in Jesus Misses for Salvation in Christ* (Grand Rapids: Brazos, 2019).

Michael J. Gorman, *Becoming the Gospel: Paul, Participation, and Mission* (Grand Rapids: Eerdmans, 2015).

Scot McKnight, *The King Jesus Gospel: The Original Good News Revisited* (Grand Rapids: Zondervan, 2011).

Paul A. Rainbow, *The Way of Salvation: The Role of Christian Obedience in Justification* (Milton Keynes: Paternoster, 2005).

N. T. Wright, *How God Became King: The Forgotten Story of the Gospels* (New York: HarperOne, 2011).

N. T. Wright, *Simply Good News: Why the Gospel Is News and What Makes It Good* (New York: HarperCollins, 2015).

NOTES

1. For a fuller development of the central ideas in this chapter, see Matthew W. Bates, *Gospel Allegiance* (Grand Rapids: Brazos, 2019), 40–54, 86–104.

2. This ten-event consolidation of the gospel is drawn verbatim from Matthew W. Bates, *Gospel Allegiance* (Grand Rapids: Brazos, 2019), 86–87. Point 8 is italicized because it is the climax of the gospel in the New Testament. The events are given expanded treatment on pages 87–104.

3. Today most Christians agree that through Jesus' incarnation, God dignified the whole created order so that physical materials can now be used to make icons of Jesus and other holy people as an aid. These icons can be reverenced but not worshiped. The story of how most Christians came to this agreement relates to the resolution of an eighth and ninth-century dispute called the iconoclast controversy.

4. The Greek word *pistis* (traditionally translated "faith") is better translated "faithfulness," "fidelity," "loyalty," or "allegiance" in Romans 1:17 (and also in 1:5; 1:8; 1:12; 3:3; 3:22; and other passages). In Romans 1:17, "by *pistis*" refers to Jesus the king's faithful loyalty to God and "for *pistis*" refers to our faithful loyalty to Jesus as the king. For discussion, see Bates, *Gospel Allegiance*, 73–82.

5. See Matthew W. Bates, *The Birth of the Trinity: Jesus, God, and Spirit in New Testament and Early Christian Interpretations of the Old Testament* (Oxford: Oxford University Press, 2015).

6. Since Hebrews 10:5–7 quotes Psalm 40:7–9, this is one of those intriguing Old Testament passages that, in light of the gospel, hints that God is more than one person. For discussion, see Bates, *The Birth of the Trinity*, 85–87.

7. In fact, to say that the Father suffered on the cross is a heresy the early church rejected called "Patripassianism."

8. For a more in-depth discussion of the essentials of the Christian faith, as well as of its important elements and personal elements, see Chad Ragsdale, *Christian*

Convictions: Discerning the Essential, Important, and Personal Elements (Renew.org, 2021).

9. This gospel definition is from Bates, *Gospel Allegiance*, 86–87. On sharing the gospel, see Bates, *Salvation by Allegiance Alone* (Grand Rapids: Baker Academic, 2017), 198–210.

FAITHFUL FAITH

RECLAIMING FAITH
FROM CULTURE
AND TRADITION

MARK E. MOORE

Dedicated to Reggie Rice and the Adult Ministries team at Christ's Church of the Valley. They are leading the charge for disciples to make disciples to impact the world.

CONTENTS

General Editors' Note 237

Introduction 239

CHAPTER 1: What Is Faith? 241

CHAPTER 2: Why Is Faith a Necessary Response to Grace?....... 247

CHAPTER 3: How Does Jesus Call Us to Both Salvation
and Discipleship? 253

CHAPTER 4: What Is Faith Without Works? 259

CHAPTER 5: How Does Faith Respond to the
Enthronement of King Jesus? 265

Appendix: Book Recommendations for Further Study 273

Notes 275

GENERAL EDITORS' NOTE

The Bible teaches that we live by "faith." It is central to our relationship with God. We are saved by grace "through faith" (Ephesians 2:8). The book of Hebrews says, "Without faith it is impossible to please God" (11:6).

But what is real faith? Is it just mental assent to biblical truths? Is it just trust in Jesus to save us?

Mark E. Moore is uniquely qualified to address the teaching of Scripture on this topic. He joined the staff at Christ's Church of the Valley (CCV) in Phoenix, Arizona, in July 2012, as a teaching pastor. CCV currently has eleven locations across the valley. Prior to joining the CCV team, Mark was a professor at Ozark Christian College in Joplin, Missouri (1990–2012). Currently, he is an online professor for Ozark, an adjunct professor at Hope International University in Fullerton, California, as well as at Haus Edelweiss, in Vienna, Austria. Mark is also the author and coauthor of many books, mostly on the life of Christ, book of Acts, and Revelation.

This book expounds on the section from the Renew.org Leaders' Faith Statement called "Faithful Faith":

> We believe that people are saved by grace through faith. The gospel of Jesus' kingdom calls people to both salvation and discipleship—no exceptions, no excuses. Faith is more than mere intellectual agreement or emotional warmth toward God. It is living and active; faith is surrendering our self-rule to the rule of God through Jesus in the power of the Spirit. We surrender by trusting and following Jesus as both Savior and Lord in all things. Faith includes allegiance, loyalty, and faithfulness to him.

> *See the full Network Faith Statements at the end of this book.

Support Scriptures: Ephesians 2:8–9; Mark 8:34–38; Luke 14:25–35; Romans 1:3, 5; 16:25–26; Galatians 2:20; James 2:14–26; Matthew 7:21–33; Galatians 4:19; Matthew 28:19–20; 2 Corinthians 3:3, 17–18; Colossians 1:28.

The following tips might help you use this book more effectively (and the other books in the *Real Life Theology* series):

1. *Five questions, answers, and Scriptures.* We framed this book around five key questions with five short answers and five notable Scriptures. This format provides clarity, making it easier to commit crucial information to memory. This format also enables the books in the *Real Life Theology* series to support our catechism. Our catechism is a series of fixed questions and answers for instruction in church or home. In all, the series has fifty-two questions, answers, and key Scriptures. This particular book focuses on the five that are most pertinent to faith.

2. *Summary videos.* You can find three to seven-minute video teachings that summarize the book, as well as each chapter, at Renew.org. These short videos can function as standalone teachings. But for groups or group leaders using the book, they can also be used to launch discussion of the reading.

May God use this book to fuel faithful and effective disciple making in your life and church.

For King Jesus,
Bobby Harrington and Daniel McCoy
General Editors, *Real Life Theology* Series

INTRODUCTION

I f I could capture what it means to have faith and be a disciple of Jesus with one story, I would point to Acts 14. Paul and Barnabas were preaching in Lystra after being run out of town in Antioch and Iconium. At first, they were wildly successful. They healed a crippled person, so the crowds took them to be gods. They even tried to offer a sacrifice to them. Paul and Barnabas were mortified, of course, and prevailed upon the crowd to cease and desist. They pointed the people to *Jesus* as Savior and Lord (Acts 14:8–18).

Soon after, however, the faith of the crowds at Lystra was completely reversed by a group of Jewish people who had arrived from Antioch and Iconium in order to oppose Paul and Barnabas. As quickly as the crowds acclaimed Paul and Barnabas, they were just as quickly convinced these men were satanic. What faith they had was fickle. Paul was stoned, dragged out of the city, and left for dead. There were, however, a group of disciples who had true faith. They gathered around Paul, who suddenly got up and went back into the city. After a day of rest, he started a sixty-mile journey to Derbe (Acts 14:19–20).

This story shows two kinds of faith. The first is fickle and easily swayed by the mood of the crowd or the intellectual argument of a scribe. The second type endures—even in the face of persecution or death. The second type of faith is obviously the genuine one. It displays fidelity.

Whether Paul and Barnabas were making a tent, preaching on the streets, debating in synagogues, performing miracles, or raising up Christian leaders, they pressed on. It was through trib-

REAL FAITH ENDURES.

ulation that they were able to expand the gospel, and it was hope that sustained them through it all. The radical devotion they displayed practically requires us to examine our own faith and ask some very hard questions. It is my hope that the following pages will deepen your understanding of biblical faith and help you take the next step on your discipleship journey.

1

WHAT IS FAITH?

Answer: Biblical faith is trust in and faithfulness to Jesus. It is fidelity or allegiance for the grace we have received.

> Now faith is confidence in what we hope for and
> assurance about what we do not see.
> — Hebrews 11:1

Faith has many faces. It is a father saying to his eight-year-old son, "I believe in you." It is a couple with trembling hands renewing their vows on their fiftieth anniversary. It is a defendant sitting before a judge pleading, "You gotta believe me." It is a marketing campaign for a vehicle declaring it to be trustworthy.

So before we can ever know what biblical faith is, we have to know where it begins. In the realm of religion, outsiders often see faith as blind belief. For insiders it can be a divine mystery that God somehow embeds in our innermost selves. For fundamentalists it can be a standard set of doctrines to which one adheres. Faith, from different perspectives, can migrate from our heads, to our hearts, to our hands.

With all these options on the table, perhaps it would be best to define faith from the Bible. After all, if God is the one calling us to faith, perhaps it would be responsible to ask, "What does he mean by faith?"

THE MEANING OF FAITH

THE GREEK WORD FOR faith is *pistis*. It is typically translated as "faith" or "belief" or "faithfulness." In the time of the New Testament, it was not a word primarily focused on the interior thoughts and feelings of an individual, but rather on relationships. It was used in relational circles to indicate trust, trustworthiness, faithfulness, and good faith.[1] The word has a range of meaning, including "belief," "trust," and "confidence," along with "allegiance," "fidelity," and "faithfulness." Take a look at a few passages that show the different connotations of this word in a few different contexts.

In the following passage, *pistis* means "confidence" and "assurance" in God and his promises: "Now *faith* is confidence in what we hope for and assurance about what we do not see" (Hebrews 11:1). In the next passage, *pistis* means "faithfulness" to God as a fruit of the Holy Spirit's work in a person's life: "But the fruit of the Spirit is love, joy, peace, forbearance, kindness, goodness, *faithfulness*" (Galatians 5:22). And in the next passage, *pistis* means the content of Christianity, as the Greek puts the word "the" in front of faith.

> Dear friends, although I was very eager to write to you about the salvation we share, I felt compelled to write and urge you to contend for the *faith* that was once for all entrusted to God's holy people. (Jude v. 3)

We will spend time in this short book exploring the various nuances of what it means for a person to have faith, with a special focus on what Jesus teaches us in the Gospels. We will see that the words "fidelity" and "allegiance" reflect a crucial way that *pistis* was used in the New Testament and first century. A disciple is someone who both trusts and follows Jesus and thereby gives their fidelity and allegiance to God through him.

IN OR OF?

To FURTHER ILLUSTRATE THE significance of how we understand "faith," let's look at an important debate within New Testament scholarship. There is a phrase used in the New Testament that could mean either our "faith in Christ" or the "faithfulness of Christ." That's a pretty big difference, isn't it? The debate focuses on the little Greek word *tou*. The phrase *pistis tou Christou* ("faith of/in Christ") is ambiguous, and it is the center of the conversation.

Let's take, for example, Galatians 2:16, which says, "Know that a person is not justified by the works of the law, but by *faith in Jesus Christ*." Some theologians translate it "faith in Christ" (along with the ESV and NASB), yet others go with "faithfulness of Christ" (along with the ISV and NET). Prior to Martin Luther's German translation, translators left the phrase ambiguous. Luther chose the interpretive translation of "faith in Christ" (the German equivalent of this phrase) because he believed that the Christian was responsible, in part, for their own salvation.

Translations have differed over time because a grammatical case can be made for either translation and because theologians differ in their beliefs about a human's responsibility in salvation. Does *our* faith in Christ save us, or is it *Christ's* fidelity to God that saves us? Is faith given or chosen? Is faith a condition or a response?

These monumental questions can set us up for a continental divide of sorts. A raindrop that lands one inch to the west of the divide ends up in the Pacific Ocean, while one that lands one inch to the east of the divide goes to the Atlantic. The same can be true concerning the interpretation of *pistis tou Christou*. This little word *tou* goes in very different directions depending on how we read it.

People favor the "faithfulness of Christ" interpretation for compelling reasons; for example, such a translation might help avoid some potential repetitiveness in the text (as we see in Galatians 2:16, which says, "We, too, have put our *faith* in Christ Jesus that we may be justified by *faith* in Christ"). "Faithfulness of Christ" is also attractive in that it places the emphasis less on our response and more on Christ himself. The logical result is for us to respond by living out the same type of faithfulness that Jesus demonstrated.

"Christ's faithfulness" is grammatically possible, and Christ indeed showed us the epitome of faithfulness (Hebrews 3:6). Yet I personally find "faith in Christ" to be the better translation. The translation "faithfulness of Christ" isn't found in the works of the earliest commentators, who would have been more familiar with Paul's Greek than we are today.[2] Faith in Galatians is illustrated by the story of Abraham, who "believed God, and it was credited to him as righteousness" (Galatians 3:6). If the focus were on "Christ's faithfulness," that might work against Paul's usage of Abraham as an example of faith in Galatians. Likewise, our faith in God makes us Abraham's descendants (Galatians 3:9) and allows us to receive the Holy Spirit (Galatians 3:14).

However we interpret the phrase, let's not miss the point: The word typically translated "faith" is a multifaceted word that can leave even trustworthy New Testament scholars debating among themselves. And while we're at it, let's remind ourselves of an even more important point: Regardless of how a particular phrase in Galatians, Romans, etc., is translated, the New Testament perpetually calls us deeper into faith in Jesus. The persistence and magnitude of this call to faith underscore the importance of putting in the work to understand what we are being called to. In our pursuit of faith, let's look in the next section at how the definition of faith has changed since New Testament times.

THE EVOLUTION OF "FAITH"

THE DEFINITION OF FAITH evolved, in part, to the rise of science and modernity. Consider some of the changes Europe underwent since the late Middle Ages. In the thirteenth century, the works of Plato, Aristotle, and Ptolemy were brought back to Europe by Crusaders. Cathedral schools began to be replaced by universities. The Holy Roman Empire was declining and would eventually be replaced by nation-states. Then came the French Revolution in the late 1700s. The result of this revolution was the emergence of a secular state governed by the will of its citizens and based on rationalism.[3] In this environment, religion lost its place in the public square. The rise of rationalism and science led to the questioning of everything, including the Bible.

One reaction by Christians to the increasing dominance of secular philosophy was to recast faith as something more emotional than rational. Søren Kierkegaard was a Danish philosopher considered to be the first existentialist. He was also a theologian and a poet. He couldn't ignore the march of science, but neither could he ignore his experiential faith. So to answer both, he tried to bridge science and religion. The result was that faith came to be characterized as a leap in the dark. As culture became increasingly secular, trust in the Bible continued down the path of being more emotive than intellectual.

To illustrate the consequence of this modern definition of faith, allow me to share a story. I once broached the topic of faith with my brother, who is proud to be called pagan. I was arguing for the historical veracity of the bodily resurrection of Jesus. He completely subverted the entire conversation, even though I explained why I believe what I believe. The apologetics, history, and documents didn't matter to him. He said, "It's good for you that you believe that; I just don't believe that." He treated faith simply as a feeling. His viewpoint was this: "You feel it, so it's totally real and legitimate for you. I don't feel it, so it's totally illegitimate for me."

Fundamentalist Christians, on the other hand, have moved the center of faith twelve inches north from the heart to the head. This sort of rationalistic thinking replaces biblical faith with nothing more than cognitive volition. Paul G. Heibert notes in his book *Transforming Worldviews* that our Western tendency to separate reality into spiritual and physical means that our spiritual beliefs are likely to remain disconnected from real life. This tendency, he says:

> Has left many Western Christians with a spiritual schizophrenia. They believe in God and the cosmic history of creation, fall, redemption, final judgment, and new creation. This provides them with ultimate meaning and purpose in life. Yet they live in an ordinary world that they explain in naturalistic terms—one in which there is little room for God. They drive cars, use electricity, and ingest medicines—all products of scientific understandings that reinforce a scientific way of thinking.[4]

But mere cognitive volition is not what Jesus is after. As James pointed out, even the demons believe and shudder (James 2:19).

In our current climate, we need to move out of the siloed realms of emotion alone and intellect alone in order to be able to view and practice faith biblically. Faith is found not only in our hearts and heads but also in our *hands*. James says this much: "Faith by itself, if it does not have works, is dead" (James 2:17, ESV). The only true way to know if someone believes is by the way they live.

BUT MERE COGNITIVE VOLITION IS NOT WHAT JESUS IS AFTER.

HEAD, HEART, AND HANDS

I ONCE KNEW A young Bible college student who was very proud of his faith in Jesus. Any time he entered a room, he would greet others enthusiastically by exclaiming, "Man of God! Man of God!" as he patted the shoulders of his friends and shook their hands. At face value, he appeared to be a great example of faith. Unfortunately, he was also known for cheating on his assignments, sexual immorality, frequent drunkenness, drug use, and hateful bigotry toward those who disagreed with him on social issues. Despite these serious character flaws, he was 100 percent confident that his "faith" in Jesus made him righteous.

This is a sad example of how faith has been hijacked in our culture. The young man lived this way because he assumed this kind of "faith" was acceptable. His "faith" was missing a key component of biblical faith. That component is *fidelity*.

Faith is a responsibility, and perhaps the most fitting metaphor to use when describing faith is a marriage relationship. A marriage relationship starts when you meet someone, fall in love with them, commit to them, and by *your actions* demonstrate the commitment that is in your heart. Even non-believers recognize authenticity by action. You can talk the talk, but if you don't walk the walk, you're a fraud. As the saying goes, "Actions speak louder than words."

James addresses this issue directly. In James 2:14–17, he references one who talks to a person in need, instead of actually helping them. This kind of behavior is evidence of a dead faith. An interesting parallel is found in 1 John. Speaking of love, John mirrors James's words about faith in action. We learn in 1 John 3:14 that those who do not love abide in death. What does it mean to love? According to John, to love means to act in deed and truth, not just word or talk (1 John 3:16–18). According to James, to have faith means to perform good deeds, not just bless people with our mouths.

Action is the authentic expression of love and faith. Our actions demonstrate

ACTION IS THE AUTHENTIC EXPRESSION OF LOVE AND FAITH.

that we actually do love others and that we actually do have faith. John asks an important question in 1 John 3:16–17: Does God's love even abide in someone who does not perform acts of love? The same question must be asked of faith: Does faith even abide in someone who does not perform good deeds?

Our understanding of faith must be deepened. It's not just a cognitive decision, even though our heads do play a part. It's not just an emotional leap in the dark, although sometimes it does feel that way. Fidelity to our core convictions and commitments—to God himself—comes from our hearts and heads, but it is expressed through our hands. Authentic fidelity to Christ calls for nothing less.

2

WHY IS FAITH A NECESSARY RESPONSE TO GRACE?

Answer: As gratitude is the response to a great gift, faith and faithfulness are the human response to God's grace in Jesus Christ.

For it is by grace you have been saved, through faith—and this is not from yourselves, it is the gift of God—not by works, so that no one can boast.
— Ephesians 2:8–9

The Gospel of John is unique. Other Gospels are packed full of miracles. Not so with John. Instead, he focuses on only seven miracles, which he calls "signs." Why was John's Gospel written this way? The author indicates the reason in John 20:31: these signs, he wrote, are written "that you may believe that Jesus is the Messiah, the Son of God."

The seven signs are turning water into wine (John 2:1–11), cleansing the temple (John 2:12–17), healing the nobleman's son (John 4:46–54), healing the lame man (John 5:1–15), feeding the multitude (John 6:1–15), healing the blind man (John 9), and raising Lazarus (John 11). Of these seven, two of them focus on faith. This is a significant portion of only seven.

John was chosen as one of Jesus' first disciples and was part of Jesus' inner circle. He witnessed the transfiguration, arrest, and crucifixion, and he heard Jesus' last words too. He was a witness of the failed faith of Judas Iscariot. Later, he was called a "pillar" of faith (Galatians 2:9). So when John emphasizes a lesson on faith, it would be wise of us to pay attention.

BIG FAITH HAS A RESPONSE

THE FIRST SIGN THAT focused on faith involves Jesus' encounter with a royal official in Cana in John 4:46–54. The royal official was determined to meet Jesus because his son was sick and nearing death. When the official found Jesus, he begged him to come to Capernaum and heal his son. Interestingly, Jesus responded by saying, "Unless you see signs and wonders you will not believe" (John 4:48, ESV). It is important to note that both instances of the word *you* in this phrase are plural. Jesus wasn't just addressing the official; he was addressing the crowd, who craved miracles.

Jesus was addressing the people's desire to get something *from* him without *following* him. The official had faith to get something out of Jesus, but did he have the faith to follow Jesus? It is a common theme that the crowds were often excited about Jesus without being willing to give him their allegiance. We better understand Jesus' rebuke of the royal official in this light.

DID HE HAVE THE FAITH TO FOLLOW JESUS?

The other issue is that the faith of the crowd and of the official was not big enough. The crowd thought Jesus needed to be present to perform a miracle. Not so. He is Lord of the universe, above space and time. Can you believe that? Can you follow Jesus to a more expansive faith? If your faith is not big enough, your behavior will not follow.

The royal official asked Jesus again to come and heal his son. Jesus challenged the official, telling him to go and that his son would live. In response, the royal official did two important things following Jesus' words: he believed what Jesus said and did what Jesus asked. Upon arriving home, the man discovered his son's fever had left at the exact time Jesus told him that his son would live.

Jesus' act of grace changed the lives of both the royal official and his son. John notes the behavioral effect: the royal official and all his household believed. Here we see what the positive response of a big faith looks like. The man and his entire household showed loyalty to Jesus by believing (John 4:53). Their faith followed Jesus' grace; it was a necessary response because of what Jesus had done for them. But faith gets bigger still.

After this event, Jesus would later perform another "distance healing" in Capernaum. This time, it was for a centurion (who likely interacted with the royal official of John 4). He too had a young man he wanted healed. He too asked Jesus to help. But unlike the nobleman, he actually *stopped* Jesus from coming to his home because he already believed Jesus could say the word and his servant would be healed (Luke 7:7). Jesus' response was, "I tell you, not even in Israel have I found such faith" (Luke 7:9, ESV).

A FAITH LIKE JUDAS ISCARIOT'S

IMMEDIATELY AFTER TELLING THE story of the miraculous healing of the official's servant, John moves to the fourth sign in his Gospel (John 5). This fourth sign is the second sign in the Gospel of John that is focused on faith. John has given an example of positive faith and is now going to give an example of negative faith. The key difference is found in the different responses to grace.

In this case, Jesus encountered a man, who had been lame for thirty-eight years, at the pool of Bethesda in Jerusalem near the Sheep's Gate. Tradition stated that an angel of the Lord would stir up the waters of the pool from time to time, and the first to touch the waters would be healed. Jesus asked the man if he wanted to be healed. The man's response indicated that he was devoid of any knowledge of who Jesus was. He said he couldn't get healed because he couldn't get to the water first (John 5:7). Jesus immediately commanded the man to pick up his pallet and walk, and the man was healed.

Again, we see a man perfectly happy to receive healing from Jesus. In this case, however, the grace he received *did not* result in allegiance to Jesus. Soon after, the man was confronted by Jewish religious leaders for carrying his pallet. He tried to shift blame to Jesus, but Jesus had already slipped away into the crowd. When Jesus found the man in the temple later, he warned him to stop sinning.

What is going on here? Why did Jesus tell him to stop sinning? That Jesus was referring to the man's carrying his pallet on the Sabbath is unlikely (after all, just a few verses later, Jesus told the religious leaders that he too was working on the Sabbath). Maybe this man was guilty of past sins of which the reader is unaware. But I think it is likely that Jesus' rebuke was more of a warning about the man's current response to Jesus. A faith that does not extend beyond what one can get from Jesus without actually following him is a sin. Jesus even warned the man that something else bad might happen if he continued his current path. Despite this, the man later betrayed Jesus by revealing his identity to the Jews (John 5:15). This betrayal led to increased persecution for Jesus. The paralytic had a faith like Judas Iscariot's.

THE PATRON-CLIENT SYSTEM

THE CLEAREST STATEMENT OF salvation by grace through faith comes from Paul's letter to the Ephesians. It's one of those banner statements of the Bible.

> By grace you have been saved through faith. And this is not your own doing; it is the gift of God, not a result of works, so that no one may boast. For we are his workmanship, created in Christ Jesus for good works, which God prepared beforehand, that we should walk in them. (Ephesians 2:8–10, ESV)

While this description of salvation is the clearest on record, it also introduces a paradox. We're saved by grace through faith, yet this passage tells us that we're created for good works. So the question is this: What's the relationship between grace, faith, and works? In other words, if we're saved by grace, why are we expected to perform good works? The simplest answer is that what we accomplish for Christ by faith is a by-product of our salvation, not the foundation of it.

WHAT WE ACCOMPLISH FOR CHRIST BY FAITH IS A BY-PRODUCT OF OUR SALVATION.

There's a social setting for this description of salvation that paints a picture of the relationship between grace, faith, and works. In the economy of the ancient world, about 2 percent of the population controlled virtually all the goods and services. These elites were called "patrons." The patrons hired employees or slaves in their homes who were doctors, lawyers, teachers, and artists. These servants were called "brokers," and they made up approximately 5 percent of the population. Meanwhile, those employed outside the home—day laborers, farmers, craftsmen, etc.—were called "clients." This group made up the majority of the population (about three quarters). This left the bottom 15 percent or so as "expendables," who served in the lowest occupations—such as miners, prostitutes, ditchdiggers—and had very short life spans. [5]

These patrons, brokers, and clients had clearly defined social roles and responsibilities. The patron's job was to provide the resources needed in order for his clients to survive, such as a job, home, land, medical care, and legal protection. These gifts the patron provided were called "grace."

The broker's task was to expand the patron's influence. In fact, brokers were evangelists responsible for acquiring more clients. But why would patrons want more clients if they constantly had to give them gifts? Wasn't it an economic liability to provide for clients? It certainly was. In the ancient world, however, wealth wasn't the most coveted commodity: *honor* was. The more clients a patron provided for, the more honored the patron was in the community.

The clients, on the other hand, had one primary purpose: to honor their patron. Their only job was to make him famous. If he was running for political office, they ran behind him, promoting his campaign. If he was harvesting a field, they would go work in the field. If he was addressing a crowd, they gathered to sing his praises. So while a patron would give gifts but never mention them again, the client was never to fail to mention every gift the patron gave as often as possible.

The Greeks used a word to describe this loyalty that the clients offered their patron. The word was "faith" (*pistis*), perhaps better translated as "fidelity" or "allegiance." So Paul's statement "by grace you have been saved, through faith [fidelity]" (Ephesians 2:8) was a description of Jesus as the patron and us as his clients. Simply put, our role as Christians is to do whatever we can to make Jesus famous.[6]

3

HOW DOES JESUS CALL US TO BOTH SALVATION AND DISCIPLESHIP?

Answer: For Jesus, salvation is not an event, but a lifelong relationship. Discipleship deepens that relationship by sustaining and expanding faith.

> Then he called the crowd to him along with his disciples
> and said: "Whoever wants to be my disciple must deny
> themselves and take up their cross and follow me."
> — Mark 8:34

The wellness industry is thriving. Those promoting these products know something: everyone wants to be a better and healthier version of themselves. Everywhere we look, we see advertisements promoting a product that will make us feel better, slimmer, younger, or healthier. There are plenty of distractions in our culture when it comes to wellness.

Our interest in health is hardly new. Remedies have been sought for thousands of years. For example, a 5000-year-old Sumerian clay slab from Nagpur was discovered that described 12 medicinal plant recipes with references to over 250 different plants. Around 2500 BC, Emperor Shen Nung wrote a book about medicinal plants called *Pen T'Sao*. The Jewish Talmud and the Old Testament indicate the use of aromatic plants during healing rituals.[7] People don't just want to be well; they've been seeking cures for disease throughout history.

Enter Jesus, who had the power to heal with a touch. It is no wonder that people thronged to be near him. But for Jesus, wellness wasn't just a physical state.

He offered a deeper and more significant wellness—one that not only addressed the body but also the soul. On several occasions, Jesus associated faith (*pistis*) with wellness (*sōzō*). We'll focus on two miracles to help us understand the wellness Jesus brings. The first is the healing of the woman with the flow of blood (Matthew 9:20–22; Mark 5:25–34; Luke 8:43–48). The second is the healing of the ten lepers (Luke 17:11–19).

A DEEPER HEALING

BOTH MATTHEW AND LUKE record the healing of the woman with the flow of blood, but Mark includes an additional important detail that helps us understand the distinction between being well and being healed. Both Matthew and Luke recall Jesus telling the woman, "Your faith has made you well" (ESV), but only Mark includes the second part of what Jesus said: "Go in peace, and be healed of your disease" (Mark 5:34, ESV). Here we see that Mark differentiates "well" (*sōzō*) and "healed" (*hygiēs*). What's the difference?

Sōzō can mean the full restoration of health, but it is also used to represent deliverance from spiritual death. *Hygiēs*, on the other hand, is used only for full restoration of physical health. Why would Jesus say, "Your faith has restored your health; go and your health will be restored"? It doesn't make sense in English, but Jesus wasn't being redundant according to the Greek. Mark is helping us understand that faith involves *sōzō*, not just *hygiēs*. The woman's faith resulted in spiritual healing, and Jesus kindly granted her physical healing as well. Indeed, every instance in which Jesus is quoted saying, "Your faith has made you well," the word *sōzō* is used.

In Luke 17:11–19, Jesus encountered ten lepers who cried out for his help. He told them to show themselves to the priest in accordance with the Torah (Luke 17:14). As they were going, they were cleansed. One of the lepers, a Samaritan, realized that he had been healed. The word for healed in verse fifteen is *iaomai*, which means a physical healing, but can also be used to mean a spiritual healing. The Samaritan turned back, praising God. When he got back to Jesus, he fell at Jesus' feet and gave him thanks. Jesus told the Samaritan, "Your faith has made you well [*sōzō*]" (Luke 17:19, ESV).

Three things happened in this parable that are important. First, the other lepers were aware only of the physical cleansing they had received from Jesus, but the Samaritan seemed to be aware that he was healed physically *and* spiritually.

Second, the Samaritan turned back; he realized that the grace he had received deserved a faithful response, which is also evidence of his spiritual health. Third, the Samaritan was the one who received *sōzō* on account of his *pistis*.

There is a type of belief that only wants to get something from Jesus. This type of belief takes advantage of the love of Jesus and may even receive some benefit like the nine lepers did. Then there is *pistis*, a holistic and loyal faith. It is this type of faith that leads to *sōzō*: spiritual healing and rescue. This is the salvation to which Jesus calls us.

But is salvation where our transformation stops? Certainly not. *Sōzō* is not the beginning or the end, but the middle of the journey. The beginning of this journey occurs when we are drawn toward Christ. A journey has many steps, encounters, and tasks to complete along the way.

HEARING THE CALL

In Mark 3:13–15, Jesus went up into the mountains. Once there, he picked his team—twelve men he desired to have around him—and appointed them as apostles. He called them with purpose. First, Jesus wanted these men to be around him and with him. Second, he wanted to send them out to preach and to have authority to cast out demons. So did Jesus want the apostles *with* him, or did he want to send them *out* from him? The conundrum actually tells us a lot about what it means to be called.

The simplest analogy to explain this involves something we carry around and use every day: a cell phone. When people want to reach someone, they use their cell phone to dial a number and wait for the other person to answer. On the other end, the person hears the call and answers. Until the act of conversation starts, however, the phone call is meaningless. By definition, a phone call involves answering a call and having a conversation, not just possessing a phone. In the same way, a calling from Jesus involves response and action, not just hanging out in a holy huddle.

For example, in Matthew 4:18–19, Jesus said to Andrew and Peter, "Follow me, *and* I will make you fishers of men" (ESV). They immediately answered the call, left their nets, and followed him. Soon after, they came across James and John. Again, Jesus called them, and they too immediately left their nets and followed him.

Latter events show that the disciples didn't just respond with their eyes and ears. No, Jesus wasn't just asking them to come and see; he was calling them to go and do. However, Jesus knew that they needed to come and see in order to be able to go and do. In short, the disciples weren't just called for their benefit; they were called to benefit others. This pattern is repeated throughout Scripture. A calling involves a specific task to be completed.

HE WAS CALLING THEM TO GO AND DO.

When God called Abraham in Genesis 12:2–3, God told him that he would be blessed, and also that Abraham would be a blessing to the entire world. Key here is the understanding that God expected Abraham *to live and act* in a way that blessed the world. That was his task. Noah's calling involved the task of *building a boat and preserving life*. Moses' calling involved *leading Israel* out of bondage and into freedom.

In Luke 9:1, Jesus gathered his disciples and gave them authority to cast out impure spirits and to heal. Like Moses, they would free others from the bondage of sickness or oppression, or both. This resulted in multiplication. In Luke 10:1, Jesus sent the Seventy-Two ahead to heal people in the towns he planned to visit.

The Great Commission given by Jesus in Matthew 28:19–20 is another example: "Go therefore and make disciples of all nations, baptizing them in the name of the Father and of the Son and of the Holy Spirit, *teaching them to observe all that I have commanded you*. And behold, I am with you always, to the end of the age" (ESV). Notice the disciples weren't just called to baptize people into an experience but also to train others so that they could be salvation bearers to others.

Jesus was saying the same thing in the Great Commission as he said during his ministry. In life, he wanted his disciples to be with him and to be sent by him. In the Great Commission, Jesus sent them and reminded his disciples that he was still with them. This promise is true for us today. We are still sent, and he is still with us.

So those who are called are called to a task. Anyone can say they are called to

THOSE WHO ARE CALLED ARE CALLED TO A TASK.

do one task or another, but until the person's actions demonstrate their calling, the authenticity of the call will always be doubted. The disciples were called "disciples" because they did the work they were called to do. When Jesus exclaims, "Follow me," he's not asking us simply to experience salvation or repose in a state of grace; he's asking us to enact that grace and save others by pointing them to Jesus.

THE STAGES OF DISCIPLESHIP

JESUS OUTLINED THE CHURCH'S core mission in the Great Commission: to make disciples. Rather than a one-time event, disciple making is a process, and understanding the stages of that process can help us answer the Great Commission. Jesus modeled it for us, and Scripture records it. We just need to repeat it.

In my study of Scripture, I have discovered an astonishing pattern that led me to conclude that there are three stages of discipleship. The first stage is characterized by coming and seeing, which uses our *feet* and *eyes*. The second stage involves our *ears* and *mouths*, as we listen to Jesus and tell others about him. The third stage involves our *hands*, as we do what Jesus did. Each time I read a passage about discipleship, I simply ask, "What part of my body do I need to respond to Jesus' call to discipleship?" You can do the same.

It's important to know that these stages build on each other. There isn't a point where we stop using our feet and eyes because there is always an opportunity to see what Jesus is doing, and then follow him where he leads us. In the same way, there is always an opportunity to listen and tell. When we enter stage three, we are still coming, seeing, listening, and telling, but now we're also using our hands.

In the first chapter of John, a story is told about two disciples of John the Baptist that plainly shows this pattern of the three phases. They were standing together when they saw Jesus walk by. John proclaimed that Jesus was the Lamb of God. Both disciples began to follow Jesus as he left the area, in effect giving their loyalty to him. Jesus noticed them and asked what they sought. The two disciples asked where he was staying, and Jesus told them, "Come and you will see" (John 1:35–39, ESV). They responded to his invitation to use their feet and eyes to come and see. That's the first stage of discipleship.

The two disciples spent the day with Jesus; Andrew was one of them. After hearing Jesus, Andrew decided that he needed to invite someone else, so he went and found his brother, Simon, and invited him to come and see the Messiah. Andrew had already moved to stage two of discipleship because he started using his mouth to invite his brother. Simon began the first stage when he used his feet to come and see Jesus with his own eyes.

The invitation to "come and see" shows up now and again as an invitation to discipleship. In John 4, the Samaritan woman came to the well, although she had already seen Jesus there and knew it was culturally unacceptable for her to be there with a man. Then, she listened to him, which prompted her to invite her people to come and see Jesus (John 4:29). The people of her town responded and used their feet to come and see Jesus with their own eyes. Then, they too listened to Jesus and testified about their belief.

A stage three disciple is best characterized by the use of their hands. As discussed, the disciples were given authority to cast out spirits and heal people (Matthew 10:1). But the use of our hands is not limited to the miraculous. It can be something as simple as carrying a message (Matthew 11:2), getting a boat ready (Mark 3:9), or simply abiding in the words of Jesus (John 8:31). Sometimes it involves burying a mentor (Matthew 14:12) or investigating an empty tomb (John 20:3–9). The point is that a person in stage three discipleship has active hands.

There is a symbiotic relationship between salvation and discipleship. Authentic faith, as we have discussed, responds with loyalty to King Jesus and makes him famous. Salvation is not a state of mere being as much as it is a state of action. Put another way, if we placed a picture of a person in the dictionary next to the word "salvation," it would be best represented by a picture of someone *doing* something like caring for a person with special needs or serving the elderly, not someone sitting in a row at church. And since this is discipleship, the picture would not end there—but with others following the same example and doing the same acts that they have been shown.

For Jesus, salvation is not an event, but a lifelong relationship. Discipleship deepens that relationship by sustaining and expanding faith. Discipleship is not just a matter of coming and seeing, as we often do in a church building. It's also a call to go and do in a way that replicates the process.

4

WHAT IS FAITH WITHOUT WORKS?

Answer: Faith without works is like saying that you love your spouse but having no relationship with your spouse; it is like talking about helping someone but never doing it.

Not everyone who says to me, "Lord, Lord," will enter the kingdom of heaven, but only the one who does the will of my Father who is in heaven.
— Matthew 7:21

This question about faith and works is not new. In fact, Jesus' brother James addressed it in his little letter, now called James, one of the first books of the New Testament to be written. Since then, many have added their voice in the mix. I will add mine with a healthy dose of humility and hopefully some simplicity too.

As we have discussed previously, faith is not just intellectual assent or an emotive response. That type of faith, if it can be called faith, is the type which is held even by demons. Demons are fallen angels who betrayed their fidelity to God by rebelling against him. In James 2, the faith of demons is described as both an intellectual assent (in one God) and emotive response (fear), but this type does not include fidelity to King Jesus.

Authentic faith is characterized by fidelity and demonstrated by action.[8] For example, Jesus didn't call Peter to sit by the campfire and talk about, sing about, or study the act of fishing for men. He also didn't call Peter to be a spectator who watched as Jesus fished for men. Jesus called Peter with the understanding and

AUTHENTIC FAITH IS CHARACTERIZED BY FIDELITY AND DEMONSTRATED BY ACTION.

expectation that Peter would actually fish for men! And since Peter did fish for men, we don't question his faith today.

Matthew Bates—an author, a professor of theology, and a contributor to this series—puts it this way: "When referring to human activity, faith is generally relational and outward facing rather than psychological and emotional."[9] Faith (*pistis*) was described in the New Testament and first-century, extra-biblical literature as something people enacted. Typically, the faith described had *external performance* in view, not attitudes or feelings.[10] Cue the shocked gasps of many in our Christian world today.

Bates outlines several examples:

> A lawyer practices *pistis* (loyalty) toward a powerless client even when it is socially risky. A person who might be doubted gives *pistis* (evidence or security) as proof of their present or future reliability. You act to show *pistis* (fidelity) to your oath. A subject people shows their *pistis* (loyalty) to their overlords by supporting rather than undermining the regime. An evil leader practices bad *pistis* (faith) toward others by violating his treaty. An administrator is commended for displaying *pistis* (fidelity) to his king in the daily affairs of statecraft. Soldiers stand by their king in battle, showing him *pistis* (allegiance). All of these examples show that the actions that attend *pistis* are often outward facing and relational.[11]

But are we saying that works are required to earn salvation? Certainly not. Christianity stands alone from other religions because our works cannot earn salvation. We are saved by grace through faith (Ephesians 2:8). However, faith, when properly understood, is enacted.

AFFINITY VS. FAITH

JOHN 3 RECORDS A conversation between Jesus and a Pharisee named Nicodemus. Nicodemus came to Jesus at night, likely because he was a ruler of the Jews and was ruled by his desire to make a good impression (John 3:1). He couldn't be seen with certain types of people. In short, Nicodemus wasn't ready for his public persona to be associated with Jesus. At the time of their meeting, Nicodemus did not have faith in Jesus; he had affinity for him. This affinity could have been driven by political motivations, but he could have just as well been sincerely seeking whether or not Jesus was the Messiah.

The conversation began with an important statement by Nicodemus. He implicitly acknowledged that Jesus was sent by God and that God was with him (John 3:2). He even called Jesus "Rabbi," which means teacher. Some see this as a statement of faith, but it was far from complete. Nicodemus didn't quite elevate Jesus as others had. He called him "Rabbi" but not Lamb of God, Messiah, Son of God, or Savior of the world. Nicodemus was testing the water, not diving in. His words were closer to political banter than to a passionate belief.

In the following verses, it was the inward changes in Nicodemus, not his PR image, that Jesus addressed. He told Nicodemus that he had to be born again in order to see the kingdom of God (John 3:3). Nicodemus's response was literal: "How can a man be born when he is old? Can he enter a second time into his mother's womb and be born?" (John 3:4, ESV). This intellectual and literal response says much about his view of Jesus. His belief was like that of many Christians today: a mere intellectual assent. His heart was not open to spiritual teachings. As Jesus pointed out, if Nicodemus was unable or unwilling to understand earthly teachings about the kingdom of God, he certainly wouldn't be able to understand heavenly teaching (John 3:11).

The only record of Nicodemus's response indicates his incredulity. Although he acknowledged intellectually that Jesus was from God, he was not willing to follow him fully. Nicodemus is only mentioned two more times in the Bible. The first is when he stood up for the rule of law during a debate among the Pharisees about the arrest of Jesus (John 7:50–51). The last is when he came by night—again—to help a secret disciple, Joseph of Arimathea, bury Jesus (John 19:39–42). Nicodemus's brief appearance in Scripture portrays him as an ally of Jesus, but not as a true follower.

DO WORKS SAVE?

SOME USE MATTHEW 7:21–23 to argue against the necessity of works as evidence of faith. Here, Jesus said he will rebuke those who claim to have done things in his name and deny them access to the kingdom of God. The passage has two caveats that we need to address in order to understand it fully.

First, Jesus began the section by distinguishing between those who do the will of the Father and those who don't. He said, "Not everyone who says to me, 'Lord, Lord,' will enter the kingdom of heaven, but the one who does the will of my Father who is in heaven" (Matthew 7:21, ESV). In this passage, those who were *not doing* the will of the Father were calling on Jesus' name and boasting about their works. Their problem is they were doing their own will, not Jesus' commission. This means that their works were not focused on serving God, even though they used his name while doing them.

Second, Jesus will tell these people that he never knew them. If they were truly his disciples, they would have received his grace and followed him. Here we come back to faith and what it entails. Enacted faith displays good works as evidence of salvation. Good works, by definition, align with the will of God, not against it.

Nicodemus, like the people in this passage, was incredulous when Jesus questioned his understanding of what it means to be one of God's chosen people. Nicodemus and the people who claimed to be disciples had something in common: the prioritization of self over Jesus. The evildoers rebuked by Jesus were focused on their own will, not on Jesus' will. Nicodemus was interested in forming an alliance, not in following a king.

ENACTED FAITH

IN ANOTHER CLANDESTINE MEETING, Jesus encountered a Samaritan woman at a well (John 4:1–42). If the meeting at night between Jesus and a member of the Sanhedrin was unseemly, then this meeting was outright scandalous. The combination of ethnic tensions between the Jews and Samaritans and the cultural impropriety of a woman and man meeting together would have made headlines. It was the audacious beginning of a divine appointment.

Add to that the character of the woman herself. She *was a scandal.* She had five previous husbands and was currently living with another man. This explains why she arrived at the well in the sixth hour of the day, a time when no one else would have been there to bother her. But someone was there: Jesus, and she couldn't avoid him. Have you ever been in a moment that was so uncomfortable and awkward that you didn't have the right words? Or maybe it was a situation in which you thought words would just make it worse. This was one of those moments, but Jesus embraced the awkward as he started to speak to her.

He simply asked for drink. Her reply dripped with incredulity, just like Nicodemus's. "How is it that you, a Jew, ask for a drink from me, a woman of Samaria?" (John 4:9, ESV). The start of the conversation was like the unplugging of a water pipe. The yucky old stuff came out first—the hurt, assumptions, and defensiveness related to the ethnic tension. But the water eventually ran clean. Indeed, a change occurred as the conversation went on. She started to address him as "Sir" as her curiosity began to pique. Where Nicodemus couldn't get past intellectual incredulity, the woman showed openness to Jesus by asking for the living water that he offered (John 4:13–15).

At this point, Jesus called the woman out by asking her to go and get her husband. Her response, of course, was that she didn't have one. Jesus acknowledged this and revealed that he knew of her previous five husbands and of the man she currently lived with. The woman now began to experience more of the power and authority of Jesus. Her awareness of her own spiritual need likely drove her to ask her next question. It was one of the questions that had divided her people from the Jews: the proper location of the temple (John 4:19–20).

The Samaritan temple was destroyed by the Jews in 127 BC. Jesus and the woman could see the ruins on Mt. Gerizim in view from the well. The moment was pregnant with symbolism because at the foundation of the woman's question was her need to be right with God. Her life was in shambles, just like the temple where she believed her forgiveness was found.

Jesus' response placed hope in her heart. The location of the temple didn't matter anymore. Now, the woman was finally able to identify her core need: the Messiah. The woman said, "I know that Messiah is coming (he who is called Christ). When he comes, he will tell us all things" (John 4:25, ESV). The conversation ended with Jesus revealing his identity to her, showing her that he was the thing she needed all along.

But how did she respond? John tells us specifically. When Jesus' disciples returned, she abruptly left her water jar at the well and ran back to town, a place she was despised. Once there, she told everyone about Jesus, and her testimony was so compelling, the whole town went out to the well in the middle of the day (John 4:28–30)! Jesus saw the coming harvest of souls and remarked:

> Already the one who reaps is receiving wages and gathering fruit for eternal life, so that sower and reaper may rejoice together. For here the saying holds true, "One sows and another reaps." I sent you to reap that for which you did not labor. Others have labored, and you have entered into their labor. (John 4:36–38, ESV)

Who was it that sowed the seed for the harvest in this passage? It was Jesus, the prophets, and perhaps John the Baptist as well. But we can't forget the Samaritan woman. Her testimony impacted her entire town, and many came to believe for themselves (John 4:39–41).

The difference between Nicodemus and the Samaritan woman's faith is clear. The Samaritan woman enacted her faith publicly, which bore fruit immediately. Nicodemus kept his affinity a secret, and his legacy is that of a secret pallbearer. The Samaritan woman's faith got her involved in things of life: a harvest of souls and life change. Nicodemus's affinity got him involved in things of death: Jesus' trial and burial. Faith without works is indeed dead.

FAITH WITHOUT WORKS IS INDEED DEAD.

5

HOW DOES FAITH RESPOND TO THE ENTHRONEMENT OF KING JESUS?

Answer: Faith responds to Jesus' enthronement by faithfulness and by fulfilling the Great Commission with compassion, hope, and worship despite circumstances.

> Every day they continued to meet together in the temple courts. They broke bread in their homes and ate together with glad and sincere hearts, praising God and enjoying the favor of all the people. And the Lord added to their number daily those who were being saved.
> — Acts 2:46–47

In the past four chapters, we've talked about the definition of faith, why faith is a necessary response to grace, how Jesus calls us to salvation and discipleship, and what "faith" is without works. We have seen that faith understood as fidelity and allegiance is another way of describing discipleship, or what it means to follow Jesus. Our conversation has focused on interactions with Jesus in the Gospels before his death, burial, and resurrection. Yet how does faith respond to a risen king? It's time to take a deeper look at the response of faith to the enthronement of King Jesus. Since we are placing our faith not merely in events that happened in the past, but in a presently ruling king, faith presents urgent implications for each day. Let us take a look at how our faith responds each day to Jesus' kingship.

The book in the New Testament immediately following the four Gospels is the book of Acts. The title of the book of Acts is no coincidence. If we want to understand the appropriate faith response to Jesus' enthronement, we have to look at how the disciples and the church responded to his ascension to the throne. One of the last things Jesus corrected for his disciples was their persistent belief that an earthly kingdom seated in Jerusalem would immediately be restored to Israel. After Jesus' resurrection and forty days of instruction about the kingdom of God, the disciples were still clinging to this idea. Jesus' response to their inquiry was to expand their focus beyond their own culture, location, and ethnicity (Acts 1:1–8).

On Pentecost, the disciples were emboldened and empowered by the Holy Spirit to evangelize. Describing this, many people point to four practices that were normative in the early church: teaching, fellowship, breaking of bread, and prayers. But there were other normative practices of the early church, such as evangelism, public preaching, and miracles. Every day, the believers met in the temple, and every day the Lord added to their number (Acts 2:46–47). The faith of the early church did not compel them simply to focus inward but outward as well.

By the grace of God, today's church goes even further than the early church in outwardly focusing on society's down and outers. When compared to what we know about the church in Acts, today's church outperforms them in social justice and compassion to outsiders. Today, Christian organizations can be found working in the field of a wide array of issues, such as human trafficking, education, poverty alleviation, medical care, foster care, counseling services, and others. Most recently, major Christian organizations, such as HOPE International, Samaritan's Purse, and others, have allocated resources to help the world fight the COVID-19 pandemic.

When Jesus says, "Follow me," he is really saying, "Imitate me." So when the church reaches out to meet the needs of those who are helpless, derided, or overlooked, it truly represents the love of Christ. This kind of compassionate outreach brings vitality to the body of Christ. It is those who have experienced these sufferings—or have a God-given call on their life—that are heavily invested in these issues. This focus on outreach promotes the priesthood of believers and imbues believers with an outward-focused purpose.

HOW OUTWARD IS "OUTWARD"?

GOD'S COMMANDS TO THE nation of Israel in the Old Testament contained a reoccurring theme: to be different and set apart from the nations around them. Unfortunately, an ethnocentrism developed that was still present in the first century, as evidenced by the Jews' hatred for the Samaritans, whose lineage was mixed with the Assyrians. Jesus' own ministry did not focus on crossing cultural, ethnic, social, and political boundaries. There was the rare moment when he would heal a Gentile or allow a woman to follow him. And even though he mandated global ethnic evangelism, the early church was slow on the uptake. Diversity is hard. Any time different cultures, ethnicities, traditions, and backgrounds come together and try to find unity, they will experience challenges. Just the other day, I was speaking to a Christian brother who had grown up in Burkina Faso before moving to the United States for college. One of the most difficult cultural practices for him to overcome in the United States was the cultural norm of sustained eye contact during conversation. In Burkina Faso, extended eye contact is considered rude. After being here in the United States for over twenty years, he still finds our practice of this to be exceedingly strange!

ANY TIME DIFFERENT CULTURES COME TOGETHER, THEY WILL EXPERIENCE CHALLENGES.

If my friend from Burkina Faso is still disturbed by eye contact after twenty years of living among Americans, you can imagine how difficult it was for the first-century Jews to force themselves to undo centuries of tradition and religious dogma by engaging other cultures—cultures they had always believed to be unclean and an affront to their personal holiness. Just as it is for us in today's world, it was not natural or easy for those in Jesus' day to undo tradition. It is true that Peter's sermon on the day of Pentecost was proclaimed in different languages to Jewish people from numerous countries (Acts 2:7–11). Yet from there the church in Jerusalem simply had no outward geographical expansion—none! It took a combination of direct visions from the Spirit as well as persecution to cause the early church to expand its geographic borders. The journey from a Jewish-only Christian church to the first Gentile convert occurred in steps.

SIX STEPS TO SAVING THE WORLD

Step 1. Some Hellenistic Jewish widows needed extra care in Jerusalem. There was a complaint that the Hellenistic widows were being treated unequally. The solution of the apostles was to appoint seven Greek men to oversee the distribution of food. One of those appointed was Stephen (Acts 6:1–6).

Step 2. God had Stephen dispute the Jews from the sect of the Freedmen, as well as Jews from Cyrene, Alexandria, Cilicia, and Asia Minor. None of them could defeat Stephen with the wisdom he had been given by the Spirit. As a result, they bitterly brought false accusations against him in order to have him arrested. This led to Stephen's well-known speech to the Sanhedrin in Acts 7. What is less well-known is that Stephen focused his speech on Abraham, Moses, and Joseph. Abraham and Moses for sure belonged in the mix of Hebrew heroes. But the addition of Joseph? This was unusual for historical accounts of Israel's history. However, they all had one thing in common: these three heroes had their greatest impact *outside of Israel*. That truth might have been one of the factors that led to Stephen's stoning.

Step 3. After Stephen was stoned by the furious crowd, a persecution arose and the believers were scattered geographically. Philip, one of Stephen's Greek friends who helped with the Hellenistic widows, went to Samaria and broke boundaries just like the heroes of Stephen's speech. Philip was so successful in Samaria that Peter and John were sent to explore what was happening. Many people had believed the word of God—the gospel—and had been baptized, but none had received the Holy Spirit. When Peter and John came to Samaria, they prayed for the people to receive the Holy Spirit and witnessed the people's reception of it. This delay of the Spirit until the arrival of the apostles allowed them personally to witness the greater outward focus of Jesus' mission! In response, Peter and John stopped in many Samaritan villages on their way back to Jerusalem to preach the word of God (Acts 8:1–25).

Step 4. Next, the Spirit directly prompted Philip to go south on a road that went from Jerusalem to Gaza. Here, Philip encountered an Ethiopian eunuch reading Isaiah 53. Philip was able to explain the gospel to the eunuch and also baptize him. The Holy Spirit's prompting and Philip's obedience enabled the gospel to cross an even more significant ethnic boundary. They also enabled the eunuch to overcome his permanent ritual defilement from castration, which would have previously excluded the eunuch from the temple (Acts 8:26–40).

Step 5. Paul had his encounter on the Damascus Road and was called specifically to the Gentiles. Paul's radical transformation set the stage for massive outward expansion of the gospel. He was not only a Jew, but he was also a Roman citizen and a very educated man. His experience, education, and devotion to God made him the perfect man to be sent to the Gentiles.

Step 6. While traveling, Peter stopped in a place called Lydda, where he healed a bedridden man. While there, he learned that a disciple named Tabitha in nearby Joppa had died. Peter went to Joppa and prayed for Tabitha, raising her from the dead. This miracle opened the doors for the gospel in Joppa, and Peter stayed in the home of a tanner named Simon. It was here that Peter received his vision of the animals (unclean animals, which God in the vision announced were no longer unclean). This vision prepared Peter for his encounter with Cornelius, the first Gentile convert (Acts 9:32–10:48). When Peter later recounted the event to the apostles, they praised God because the Gentiles had been granted repentance (Acts 11:18). At this point, it seems like the disciples were finally getting a grasp of God's grand vision to save the world, not just the Jews.

From this, we can learn that it takes intentional and uncomfortable steps to spread the gospel. If we don't voluntarily become good at spreading the gospel geographically, we will become good at it involuntarily through persecution or the direct intervention of the Sprit. If we are going to do what God wants us to do, we need to accept people who are ethnically, economically, and culturally different from us. This acceptance is completely necessary, anything but easy, and absolutely worth it. Furthermore, it's how disciples respond to the enthronement of King Jesus.

NOW AND TO ETERNITY

THE NEW TESTAMENT BOOK that is most similar to the book of Acts is Revelation. Both books focus on God's sovereignty through persecution. They are also similar to each other because they both record a historical movement toward a culmination. The big difference, of course, is that Acts is a historical book and Revelation is an apocalyptic prophecy. Acts tells us what the church did, and Revelation tells us what the church will do. When we consider our faith response to the enthronement of King Jesus, both Acts and Revelation are extremely relevant. But because Revelation moves beyond history into eternity, it shows us two more important ways that believers respond to the enthronement of King Jesus: worship and hope.

REVELATION TELLS US WHAT THE CHURCH WILL DO.

Worship. People described in Revelation worship in two ways: perpetually and responsively. Perpetual worship means constant, and the reason that perpetual worship exists is that God is worthy of it because of *who he is.* Responsive worship, on the other hand, is a response to *what he has done.* The circumstances of God's acts do not change the response of worship. Again, this points to the fact that God is worthy of worship, and that worship is a positive response to God no matter our circumstances.

The author of Revelation clearly describes perpetual worship in Revelation 5. The four living creatures who surrounded the throne never ceased to praise God both night and day. In addition to these creatures were twenty-four elders who joined in the worship of God (Revelation 4:4–11). Examples of responsive worship are laced throughout the book of Revelation. When Jesus was found worthy to open the scroll with seven seals, the creatures and elders sang a worship song. Myriads of angels joined them, along with all the living creatures on earth (Revelation 5). After they blew the seventh trumpet, heaven responded with worship (Revelation 11:15–18). In Revelation 14:1–3, a group of people who were redeemed from the earth worshiped God with a song that only they could learn. In Revelation 19, God was praised after Babylon was destroyed. There are other examples, but both the continual and responsive worship described in Revelation tell us that God is worthy. Moreover, fidelity results in perpetual and responsive worship.

Hope. The other guiding principle for our faith response as presented in Revelation is hope. Revelation is the only book in the Bible that declares that anyone who reads it aloud or hears it will be blessed (Revelation 1:3). These days, we don't need an elder or church leader to procure a scroll and read Revelation aloud for us. Furthermore, most of us know how to read, and we can carry Revelation around with us wherever we go by simply downloading a Bible app on our cell phones.

But why will we be blessed by reading it? The simple yet profound answer is that it provides hope. As Christians, we know the end of the story. We know who the rider on the white horse is. We know that God wins and that every troubling thing in this world will pass away. In paradise, there will be cities of gold, music, harmony, peace, and the best thing of all: the presence of God himself, the author of our hope.

God hasn't forgotten us, and he is not distant. He is patiently waiting for the right time to swoop in and save the world—finally and fully. In the meantime, our faith response to the gospel should continually reach outward, especially when it is hard. It responds to the call of the king and does not fail to act, despite circumstances or difficulty. In the end, faith is characterized by hope and worship.

So how does faith respond to the enthronement of King Jesus? Simply put, it expands the borders of his kingdom to include the whole world. This is not merely a geographical expansion but a cultural and ethnic expansion. The book of Acts traces the arduous steps the Holy Spirit took to include all peoples into the kingdom. The book of Revelation shows the endgame of multicultural worship of our God and King Jesus. He is the reason for our hope and the focus of our worship. Anything less is a faltering fidelity, arrested allegiance, and truncated loyalty.

APPENDIX

BOOK RECOMMENDATIONS FOR FURTHER STUDY

Norman L. Geisler and Frank Turek, *I Don't Have Enough Faith to Be an Atheist* (Wheaton: Crossway, 2004).

Matthew W. Bates, *Salvation by Allegiance Alone: Rethinking Faith, Works, and the Gospel of Jesus the King* (Grand Rapids: Baker Academic, 2017).

Matthew W. Bates, *Gospel Allegiance: What Faith in Jesus Misses for Salvation in Christ* (Grand Rapids: Brazos, 2019).

David Platt, *Radical: Taking Back Your Faith from the American Dream* (Colorado Springs: Multnomah, 2010).

Dietrich Bonhoeffer, *The Cost of Discipleship* (New York: Touchstone, 1995).

Robert Picirilli, *Discipleship: The Expression of Saving Faith* (Nashville: Randall House, 2013).

NOTES

1. Teresa Morgan, *Roman Faith and Christian Faith: Pistis and Fides in the Early Roman Empire and Early Churches* (Oxford: Oxford University Press, 2015).

2. No translation has been found to contain "the faithfulness of Christ" before the eighteenth century. See George Brunk III, "Faith of Jesus Christ (in Galatians)," Anabaptistwiki, last modified April 3, 2017, https://anabaptistwiki.org/mediawiki/index.php?title=Faith_of_Jesus_Christ_(in_Galatians).

3. Paul G. Hiebert, *Transforming Worldviews* (Grand Rapids: Baker Academic, 2008), 142.

4. Hiebert, 154.

5. John H. Elliott, "Patronage and Clientism in Early Christian Society," *Foundations & Facets Forum* 3/4 (1987): 39–48.

6. Mark E. Moore, *Core 52* (Colorado Springs: Waterbrook, 2019), 190.

7. Biljana Bauer Petrovska, "Historical Review of Medicinal Plants' Usage," *Pharmacogn Rev* 6, no. 11 (2012): 1, doi:10.4103/0973-7847.95849. For example, see Jeremiah 8:22.

8. See Robert Picirilli, *Discipleship: The Expression of Saving Faith* (Nashville: Randall House, 2013).

9. Matthew W. Bates, *Gospel Allegiance: What Faith in Jesus Misses for Salvation in Christ* (Grand Rapids: BrazosPress, 2019), 153.

10. Bates, 154.

11. Bates, 154.

6

NEW BIRTH

CONVERSION
AND BAPTISM

MICHAEL STRICKLAND
AND ANESSA WESTBROOK

In memory of Jim Brinkerhoff, who discipled me and many others.
— Michael Strickland

To my husband, Tim, and our children, Alina, Anna, and Theo, for your unwavering support and love. To my parents, Ken and Ann Hobby, who believed, supported, and equipped me on my ministry journey.
— Anessa Westbrook

CONTENTS

General Editors' Note 283

Introduction 287

CHAPTER 1: Why Is the New Birth Necessary? 291

CHAPTER 2: What Does It Mean to Place Our Faith in Jesus? 295

CHAPTER 3: What Does It Mean to Repent? 301

CHAPTER 4: What Does It Mean to Confess Jesus as Lord? 307

CHAPTER 5: What Does It Mean to be Baptized for the
Forgiveness of Our Sins? 315

Conclusion 325

Appendix: Book Recommendations for Further Study 327

Notes 329

GENERAL EDITORS' NOTE

When Jesus Christ saves a person, they experience a new birth. As we disciple people, we must understand and teach people what Scripture teaches about this new birth. Conversion and its relationship to baptism can be difficult to understand. Churches and friendships have even divided over their understandings and practices regarding baptism. So knowing what the Bible says about these important issues and teaching it with clarity are crucial.

Michael Strickland and Anessa Westbrook are helpful guides into this investigation of what the Scriptures have to say about the new birth.

Michael Strickland is Director of Instruction and Associate Professor of Theology and Mathematics at Amridge University. He holds a Bachelor of Mathematics and a Master of Science in Mathematics from Auburn University, a Master of Arts in Biblical Studies from Lipscomb University, and a Doctor of Philosophy in Theology from the University of Birmingham, United Kingdom. He and his wife, Mary, live in Murfreesboro, Tennessee, with their three children: Helen, Lila Beth, and Charlie.

Anessa Westbrook is an Associate Professor of Bible and Ministry at Harding University. She holds a Master of Arts in Church Growth and a Master of Divinity from Harding School of Theology as well as a Doctor of Ministry from Fuller Theological Seminary. Her doctoral research focused on the spiritual development of women. She and her husband, Tim, live in Searcy, Arkansas, with their three adult children: Alina, Anna, and Theo.

This book expounds on the section from the Renew.org Leaders' Faith Statement called "New Birth":

> God so loved the world that he gave his one and only Son, that whoever believes in him shall not perish but have eternal life. To believe in Jesus means we trust and follow him as both Savior and Lord. When we commit

to trust and follow Jesus, we express this faith by repenting from sin, confessing his name, and receiving baptism by immersion in water. Baptism, as an expression of faith, is for the remission of sins. We uphold baptism as the normative means of entry into the life of discipleship. It marks our commitment to regularly die to ourselves and rise to live for Christ in the power of the Holy Spirit. We believe God sovereignly saves as he sees fit, but we are bound by Scripture to uphold this teaching about surrendering to Jesus in faith through repentance, confession, and baptism.

*See the full Network Faith Statements at the end of this book.

Support Scriptures: 1 Corinthians 8:6; John 3:1–9; 3:16–18; 3:19–21; Luke 13:3–5; 24:46–47; Acts 2:38; 3:19; 8:36–38; 16:31–33; 17:30; 20:21; 22:16; 26:20; Galatians 3:26–27; Romans 6:1–4; 10:9–10; 1 Peter 3:21; Romans 2:25–29; 2 Chronicles 30:17–19; Matthew 28:19–20; Galatians 2:20; Acts 18:24–26.

The following tips might help you use this book more effectively (and the other books in the *Real Life Theology* series):

1. *Five questions, answers, and Scriptures.* We framed this book around five key questions with five short answers and five notable Scriptures. This format provides clarity, making it easier to commit crucial information to memory. This format also enables the books in the *Real Life Theology* series to support our catechism. Our catechism is a series of fixed questions and answers for instruction in church or home. In all, the series has fifty-two questions, answers, and key Scriptures. This particular book focuses on the five that are most pertinent to the new birth.
2. *Summary videos.* You can find three to seven-minute video teachings that summarize the book, as well as each chapter, at Renew.org. These short videos can function as standalone teachings. But for groups or group leaders using the book, they can also be used to launch discussion of the reading.

May God use this book to fuel faithful and effective disciple making in your life and church.

For King Jesus,
Bobby Harrington and Daniel McCoy
General Editors, *Real Life Theology* Series

INTRODUCTION

The supreme adventure is being born.
— G. K. Chesterton, *Heretics*

The Bible uses several metaphors to describe the change that God brings about when we become disciples of Jesus. We were dead in our sins but raised with Christ (Ephesians 2:5–6). We were rescued from darkness and brought into the light (1 Peter 2:9). We were lost but now found (Luke 15:32). We were slaves to sin but set free by Jesus (Romans 6:1–3). All of these descriptions convey the drastic change that takes place when someone declares that Christ is Lord. It's not just a change in behavior, but a change in the way they view the world, the people around them, and themselves.

This book is about the meaning of this change that Jesus enables, empowers, and requires for his followers, centered around the biblical metaphor of "new birth." We strive to provide helpful teaching from the Scriptures, examples of fellow disciples, and wisdom from church history—all to better understand the new birth.

WHY IS IT CALLED THE NEW BIRTH?

THROUGHOUT HISTORY, HUMANS HAVE used the language of pregnancy and birth as a metaphor for great changes. Today, we speak of companies "giving birth" to new products, and in ancient Greece, Socrates described himself as a midwife helping new philosophers to be born. The Bible uses the concept of childbirth to describe important times of great change, such as new creation in Christ and Jesus' Second Coming (Romans 8:22; Matthew 24:8). However, the most common use of the birthing metaphor in the Bible Testament deals with the transformed life that Jesus brings when we are born again through faith in him.

Why do we use this term "new birth" to describe becoming a Christian? The phrase "born again" appears in two passages in the New Testament. In John 3, a Jewish teacher named Nicodemus came to Jesus, marveling at his miracles, and Jesus advised him, "No one can see the kingdom of God unless they are born again" (3:3). Though Nicodemus seemed puzzled, Jesus explained that to be born again was to be born of water and of Spirit (likely referring to our baptism in water when we also receive the Spirit). The other occurrence of this phrase occurs in

THE BIBLE USES THE CONCEPT OF THE NEW BIRTH AS A VIVID DESCRIPTOR OF THE LIFE-CHANGING MOMENT.

1 Peter 1:22–23, where Peter encourages believers that they have "purified [their] souls by [their] obedience to the truth" and that they are "born again, not of perishable seed but of imperishable" (ESV). Here, Peter is referring to the purification of baptism, when a person is born anew to live forever (of eternal "imperishable seed"). Thus, the Bible uses the concept of the new birth as a vivid descriptor of the life-changing moment when a person chooses to follow Jesus.

OUR CONVERSION STORIES

LIKE MANY AMERICANS, I (Michael) was raised in a nominally Christian home. I went to church on and off during childhood in my rural Alabama town. But by the time I was a teenager, I had stopped going. When I was sixteen years old, I started dating a girl who invited me to church. While the relationship with the girl fizzled, the newfound love of a church family did not. I had never experienced the kind of open, honest friendship or the mentorship that this church offered. On July 9, 1991, I was born again in the waters of baptism. The next year, I left for Auburn University, where I first participated in campus ministry and where I eventually trained for vocational ministry. Since then, it has been my privilege to introduce people young and old to the kingdom of God, and at times to baptize them. My new birth is the beginning of God's plan for me, and to introduce others to it is the greatest privilege in the world!

I (Anessa) was raised in an active Christian home by ministry-oriented parents and grandparents. My interest in baptism came naturally to me, and I entered the waters of baptism at the age of nine. Over the years, I have talked with many who were baptized at a young age like I was and have wondered if it was too early, if they really understood what they were doing. This ignorance about baptism is similar to the lack of understanding couples often have when they say "I do" on their wedding day. They generally understand what is required in marriage, but one can never fully grasp what the marriage commitment means at first. Our understanding about it deepens with the necessary changes and sacrifices involved in marriage.

That's how it is with the new birth: Jesus doesn't expect us to have all the answers at the beginning. He just expects us to step out in faith toward him, and baptism is one of the first steps on the journey. This journey is beautiful and bursting with grace-filled vistas and provision when we find ourselves in the forest. It involves experiencing the faithfulness of God, even in the most unexpected ways. I will say that helping others, especially my children, experience God and watching them grow as they embark on this journey has been one of the highlights of my life.

1

WHY IS THE NEW BIRTH NECESSARY?

Answer: Sin separates us from God, and the decision to trust and follow Jesus is a necessary part of restoring that relationship.

> For all have sinned and fall short of the glory of God.
> — Romans 3:23

Are you a perfect person? Without fail, every time I've asked a group of people to raise their hands if they are perfect, no one does. Even though we often say we feel pressure to appear perfect, we seem to know that we are not. To be flawed is to be human, and we respect the humility and authenticity of those who can accept their imperfections. However, when it comes to deciding if we need to be saved, which is to acknowledge our flawed nature, some people struggle to admit their imperfections as readily. We learn in 1 John 1:8, however, "If we claim to be without sin, we deceive ourselves." Romans 3:23 says, "All have sinned and fall short of the glory of God." Sin separates us from God, and in order to restore that relationship, we need intervention.

SIN SEPARATES US FROM GOD.

When God created humanity, he created us in his image. However, since the Garden of Eden, we as people have struggled with giving in to our own will and sinful desires. Humanity, who bears the image of God, has not reflected his image well. We have not lived up to the standards that God intended for us. Recognizing this human struggle, God assisted by giving the Israelites the law so they might maintain a holy relationship with him. The law was to provide justification, which means the removal of sin and guilt from our hearts plus the conveyance of righteousness to our lives. The people were told to be "consecrated," a term meaning to separate out people or things for holy service and dedicating them to God.[1] The priests were commanded to consecrate themselves (Exodus 19:22), the Levites were told to consecrate the temple (2 Chronicles 29:5), and Moses was told to consecrate the Israelites (Exodus 19:10). In the Old Testament, various avenues were used in consecration: animal sacrifices (Exodus 29:1), washing (Exodus 29:4), and anointing with oil (Exodus 29:7). This was all done in an effort to maintain holiness and relationship with God. If these things were not done, Israel was at risk of God turning away from them (Deuteronomy 23:14).

The reason God would turn away, however, was not that he was judgmental or angry, as we might be tempted to view him. Instead, it's because God is perfectly holy, and sin cannot be in his presence. In Leviticus 11:44, God says, "I am the LORD your God; consecrate yourselves and be holy, because I am holy." We should not approach him lightly. Coming into his presence involves preparation. Just as Moses was commanded to take off his sandals when approaching the burning bush, we too should be prepared to stand in the presence of God (Exodus 3:5). When we stand in his presence with our sin, the contrast highlights our shortcomings and the gap between us and God.

God allowed the people to atone for their sins through the laws and purification he commanded to Israel. However, the law was difficult to keep. It was imperfect and unable to completely bridge the gap between them and God. On its own, the law was powerless to save God's people. Romans 8:3 says, "For what the law was powerless to do because it was weakened by the flesh, God did by sending his own Son in the likeness of sinful flesh to be a sin offering." Mending the broken relationship with God caused by sin required special intervention.

MENDING THE BROKEN RELATIONSHIP WITH GOD CAUSED BY SIN REQUIRED SPECIAL INTERVENTION.

God looked forward to the time when he would have this new relationship with his people. In Jeremiah 31:31–34, God promised to make a new covenant with his people. While Israel broke their old, written covenant with God, a new covenant would be written on their hearts. He anticipated this day, saying in verse thirty-three, "I will be their God, and they will be my people." We see God's heart in his constant pursuit of Israel, as he looked forward to the day when he would remember their sins no more (Jeremiah 31:34). Hebrews 10:1 says the law was a shadow of what was to come because its repeated sacrifices could not make people perfect. Jesus also referred to the limitation of the law in Matthew 5:17, stating, "Do not think that I have come to abolish the Law or the Prophets; I have not come to abolish them but to fulfill them."

Although the recurring sacrifices could not truly cleanse people from their sin, Jesus sacrificed himself and made us holy through his sacrifice (Hebrews 10:10). Because we are made holy, we can enter into that relationship with God in which he is our God and we are his people.

After accepting our sinfulness and our need for a Savior, the next question is *how* we are saved. This question provides the backdrop of the rest of the book. In the chapters that follow, we will learn that the Bible teaches the new birth as a death-to-life matter of placing our faith in Jesus. We express this faith in Jesus by

- Repenting from sin
- Confessing his name
- Receiving baptism

Thanks for joining us on this journey of exploring how God makes us new!

2

WHAT DOES IT MEAN TO PLACE OUR FAITH IN JESUS?

Answer: Believing in Jesus means that we trust and follow him as Savior, Lord, and King in all things.

Whoever believes in the Son has eternal life, but whoever rejects the Son will not see life, for God's wrath remains on them.
— John 3:36

In the Gospel of John, we learn that belief is anything but passive. Its original readers were likely Jewish Christians who had been pushed out of their Jewish communities because they believed that Jesus was the Messiah. This created among the Jewish Christians discouragement, doubt, and fear. John hoped that retelling the good news of Jesus would reassure those who were suffering and prompt to action those who were wavering.

In John 9, Jesus healed a man who was blind from birth. He put mud on his eyes, and then told him to wash at the pool of Siloam. When the Jews asked the healed man what happened to him, the man simply told the story of what Jesus had done but said he did not know who Jesus was. When the Pharisees investigated the healing later, their concern rested on the fact that Jesus had healed on the Sabbath. They called Jesus a sinner. They questioned the ability of a sinner to do miracles, and they asked the healed man about Jesus. The man replied, "He is a prophet" (John 9:17).

His growing faith led to action. When the man persisted in defending Jesus to the religious leaders, they threw him out of the synagogue. When Jesus heard this, he immediately found him again. When Jesus explained his identity to the formerly blind man, Jesus asked, "Do you believe in the Son of Man?" (John 9:35). The man responded, "Lord, I believe," and worshiped him (John 9:38). Clearly, faith in Jesus is not a passive act of our mere thinking; it involves action. Interestingly, in John's Gospel, belief is never used as a noun, but it is used nearly one hundred times as a verb.[2]

After Jesus found the man in John 9, he used blindness as a spiritual metaphor: "For judgment I have come into this world, so that the blind will see and those who see will become blind" (John 9:39). Hearing him, the Pharisees asked if they too were blind. Jesus replied, "If you were blind, you would not be guilty of sin; but now that you claim you can see, your guilt remains" (John 9:41). This is the same position we find ourselves in when we are blind to our need for a new birth. Once we come to see our need clearly, we must decide to act.

When our eyes are opened to our need for salvation in Jesus, then we are ready to place our faith in him. What does it mean to place our faith in Jesus? Believing in Jesus means that we trust and follow him as Savior, Lord, and King in all things. Listen to the recurring language in the Gospel of John, as we're invited to place our faith in Jesus:

- "For God so loved the world that he gave his one and only Son, that whoever believes in him shall not perish but have eternal life" (John 3:16).
- "Whoever believes in the Son has eternal life, but whoever rejects the Son will not see life, for God's wrath remains on them" (John 3:36).
- "The work of God is this: to believe in the one he has sent" (John 6:29).
- "I am the bread of life. Whoever comes to me will never go hungry, and whoever believes in me will never by thirsty" (John 6:35).
- "For my Father's will is that everyone who looks to the Son and believes in him shall have eternal life, and I will raise them up at the last day" (John 6:40).
- "Whoever believes in me, as Scripture has said, rivers of living water will flow from within them" (John 7:38).
- "I am the resurrection and the life. The one who believes in me will live, even though they die" (John 11:25).

- "Whoever believes in me does not believe in me only, but in the one who sent me" (John 12:44).
- "I have come into the world as a light, so that no one who believes in me should stay in darkness" (John 12:46).
- "Do not let your hearts be troubled. You believe in God; believe also in me" (John 14:1).

When we place faith in Jesus, we show faith in the truth of his ministry and claims. Those who study the Bible for the first time often have questions about the miracles of Jesus. One of the earliest steps in coming to faith is accepting his miracles. Likewise, the teachings and claims of Jesus must be accepted, which may be difficult to understand from our limited human perspective. Jesus is God's Son (Mark 1:11; 9:7), and he is the Messiah, the one chosen to save the world (John 1:34). Jesus is part of the Trinity (or Godhead), which is made up of God the Father, God the Holy Spirit, and God the Son. He is an eternal being who came to earth to identify with us and create a way to save us from our sins (Hebrews 2:14–17). On earth, he obeyed the will of God the Father (John 6:38), and his miraculous ministry was done through the power of the Holy Spirit (Matthew 12:28).

Yet we should notice that "believing in" Jesus goes beyond simply believing that Jesus did miracles or spoke true teachings. It is a choice to accept Jesus, to actively entrust oneself to God for salvation and life. This involves wholehearted trust in Jesus and a shift in allegiance to him. In *Salvation by Allegiance Alone*, Matthew Bates suggests that in the first-century context faith could be understood as "allegiance or loyalty or faithfulness."[3] He points to Jesus as the universal king and how Christians would have displayed loyalty toward him as such. This allegiance could also manifest itself as obedient action, such as Christ giving up his life on the cross to bring about salvation for us.[4] Bates describes faith (*pistis*) as the framework into which the action of our ongoing allegiance is also part of our salvation.[5]

BELIEVING IN JESUS IS TO ACTIVELY ENTRUST ONESELF TO GOD.

The concept that Jesus is a member of the Godhead distinguishes the Christian understanding of God from other religions. In John 10:9, Jesus says, "I am the gate; whoever enters through me will be saved." If Jesus is the gate, this means that we receive salvation by acceptance of him. This means accepting him, his teachings, and his claims. It excludes our acceptance of gods from other religions and the belief that we ultimately worship the same god. When we show faith in Jesus, we show faith *in him* as both our Lord and Savior.

WHAT IS THE CONNECTION OF FAITH TO BAPTISM?

RECALL THAT WHEN THE Holy Spirit arrived on the day of Pentecost, after Jesus had ascended into heaven, Peter preached to the gathered crowd saying, "Repent and be baptized, every one of you, in the name of Jesus Christ for the forgiveness of your sins. And you will receive the gift of the Holy Spirit" (Acts 2:38). This verse shows us that the natural response to having faith is to declare that faith in baptism. This pattern was taught to the early church, and its relevance continues for us today.

BAPTISM IS A DECLARATION OF OUR FAITH IN JESUS CHRIST. Baptism is a declaration of our faith in Jesus Christ. Because of that faith, baptism is the avenue through which we receive forgiveness of our sins. While baptism is a visible way to demonstrate our faith in Jesus and accept the gift of God's grace, it does not earn our salvation. Owen Olbricht in his book on baptism writes:

> If baptism were a work of self-accomplishment, then it could be discounted from having anything to do with salvation and forgiveness of sins. The power to remove sins is not in the water, the action of the one doing the baptizing, or the submission of the one being baptized. Only the blood of Jesus has that power (Matthew 26:28; Hebrews 9:22).[6]

Rather salvation is given by the grace of God. Martin Luther is quoted as saying, "Your baptism is nothing less than grace clutching you by the throat: a gracefull throttling, by which your sin is submerged in order that ye may remain under grace."[7] When we are baptized, we are accepting the gift of grace and forgiveness by God. We are submitting ourselves, and our will, to God.

WHAT IS THE CONNECTION OF FAITH TO ACTION?

WHILE RECEIVING THE GIFT of salvation is an act of grace and mercy on God's part, faith is lived out in embodied action. It involves action-oriented allegiance and faithfulness to Jesus. James 2:17 says, "Faith by itself, if it is not accompanied by action, is dead." There is a connection in the Bible between belief and action, as the Renew.org book *Faithful Faith* (Book 5 in this Collection) shows us in more detail.[8]

In Matthew 12:34–35, Jesus said that the mouth speaks of what is in the heart, and the good or bad stored up in someone will come out. It is not enough merely to do the right things, but we must have the right heart. In Matthew 15, Jesus was questioned by the Pharisees and teachers of the law about why his disciples did not ceremonially wash their hands before eating. In response, Jesus told a parable. They asked him to explain it, and he replied:

> Don't you see that whatever enters the mouth goes into the stomach and then out of the body? But the things that come out of a person's mouth come from the heart, and these defile them. For out of the heart come evil thoughts—murder, adultery, sexual immorality, theft, false testimony, slander. These are what defile a person; but eating with unwashed hands does not defile them. (Matthew 15:17–20)

What defiles us are our thoughts and what is in our hearts. Owen Olbricht points out the words "faith" and "belief" can be defined as "trust and reliance" and stand in contrast to "disobey," "disobedient," and "disobedience."[9] Putting one's faith in Jesus involves trusting obedience. Just "doing the right things" without involving our inner selves is not enough.

Declaring our faith in Jesus is not a way to earn our salvation, but to acknowledge our need for God's help. As someone prepares to participate in the decision of declaring their faith in Jesus, it must be done from the heart. In John 15, we see the metaphor of the vine and the branches. In verse five Jesus said, "If you remain in me and I in you, you will bear much fruit; apart from me you can do nothing." We must never forget that our first priority is to remain connected to God, to grow in our relationship with him. Our actions should come out of the overflow of that relationship and heart-connection to God.

FAITH IS FOUNDATIONAL TO REPENTANCE, CONFESSION, AND BAPTISM

As mentioned earlier, baptism is a declaration of our faith in the work of God in the world. Colossians 2:12 says that when we are buried with Jesus in baptism, we are raised with him through our "faith in the working of God, who raised him from the dead." We acknowledge that the activity and power of God are at work in our lives, communities, and world. When we have faith in God, we look forward toward salvation at the end of time, without neglecting our role in the world until then.

When we are ready to put our faith in Jesus, we are ready to let the world know that our eyes have been opened. We repent of our sins (Chapter 3), confess Jesus as Lord (Chapter 4), and show our faith publicly through baptism (Chapter 5). As we declare our faith in Jesus, we are also showing faith in his work, his message, his miracles, and his divinity. It is Jesus and his Father's most earnest desire to save us to spend eternity with them. In fact, shortly before his death in John 17, Jesus spent a significant amount of time praying for his disciples then and today. While our faith begins on the inside, that relationship overflows into everyday life, and our faith in Jesus shines throughout the rest of our lives.

3

WHAT DOES IT MEAN TO REPENT?

Answer: Repentance means a change in heart and behavior, turning from living for ourselves to living like Jesus.

First to those in Damascus, then to those in Jerusalem and in all Judea, and then to the Gentiles, I preached that they should repent and turn to God and demonstrate their repentance by their deeds.
— Acts 26:20

In the first-century Jewish world, large numbers of people were drawn to the simple message of repentance. Both John the Baptist and Jesus preached, "Repent, for the kingdom of heaven has come near" (Matthew 3:2; 4:17). Mark 1:4 tells us that John "preached a baptism of repentance for the forgiveness of sins." We will focus on forgiveness in Chapter 5 of this book, but here we'll focus on repentance, pointing out the link between baptism, repentance, and forgiveness. All three of these assume humans share the same predicament: we are sinful (Romans 3:10). In fact, in order to receive forgiveness of sins, we need to confess our sins (1 John 1:9).

However, confessing one's personal sins—as distinguished from confessing Jesus as Lord—isn't the end of the journey of following Jesus. King Jesus calls us to a life of discipleship. Being a disciple means surrendering our own will and submitting to his. In biblical times, followers of Jesus were called to turn from their own sins and reject the worldliness of the predominant culture (Romans 12:2). Today we are also called to turn from our sin toward God. Repentance is this change of mind and change in action. The Greek noun used in the New Testament that we translate as "repentance" is *metanoia*. Both *metanoia* and its verb form, *metanoeō*, had been used by Greek philosophers for centuries to describe a change of mind, but by Jesus' day, the Jews also used it to refer to a change of behavior.[10] So when Peter told a crowd of onlookers to "repent and be baptized" (Acts 2:38), he was calling them to change their lives—a process that begins at baptism, yes, but continues for a lifetime (2 Corinthians 7:1). John Mark Hicks and Greg Taylor rightly describe the relationship between repentance and baptism like this:

> Baptism signals transformation, but God's work in us is far from complete. Though discipleship begins before baptism, the event of immersion marks a new identity, ethic, and world view that defines discipleship. . . . Baptism marks a lifetime process of dying to sin and renewing our appeal to God for a new life.[11]

WHAT DOES REPENTANCE LOOK LIKE?

AN EXAMPLE OF BIBLICAL repentance is found in Acts 19. The Holy Spirit had been working miracles through Paul, and after one particularly remarkable display of God's power (Acts 19:13–16), Luke describes the response of the people of Ephesus:

> When this became known to the Jews and Greeks living in Ephesus, they were all seized with fear, and the name of the Lord Jesus was held in high honor. Many of those who believed now came and openly confessed what they had done. A number who had practiced sorcery brought their scrolls together and burned them publicly. When they calculated the value of the scrolls, the total came to fifty thousand drachmas. In this way the word of the Lord spread widely and grew in power. (Acts 19:17–20)

Here we see that repentance followed belief in the Lord Jesus, and it involved an admission of sin and a dramatic turning away from that sin—a single act that cost the equivalent of fifty thousand days' wages! But those new disciples were not merely destroying their sinful instruments; they were signifying that they were turning away from their former lifestyles, never to return again.

Yet not all repentance is demonstrated in grandiose deeds of sacrifice. When people asked John the Baptist what repentance would look like for them, he gave practical advice:

And the crowds asked him, "What then shall we do?" And he answered them, "Whoever has two tunics is to share with him who has none, and whoever has food is to do likewise." Tax collectors also came to be baptized and said to him, "Teacher, what shall we do?" And he said to them, "Collect no more than you are authorized to do." Soldiers also asked him, "And we, what shall we do?" And he said to them, "Do not extort money from anyone by threats or by false accusation, and be content with your wages." (Luke 3:10–14, ESV)

These aren't grandiose demonstrations of religious devotion—sharing your food and clothing; not abusing your position—but they are the very kinds of "mundane" acts that reflect a changed life.

WHAT IS THE NEW LIFE?

THE APOSTLE PAUL REFLECTED on his own life in his letter to the Philippians. He had excelled above his contemporaries as a Jewish leader, yet he had more to say:

But whatever were gains to me I now consider loss for the sake of Christ. What is more, I consider everything a loss because of the surpassing worth of knowing Christ Jesus my Lord, for whose sake I have lost all things. I consider them garbage, that I may gain Christ and be found in him. (Philippians 3:7–9a)

This explains how Paul become consumed with sharing the same gospel he once despised. He still believed in the same God of Abraham, Isaac, and Jacob, but he no longer allowed his own ambitions to cloud his view of Jesus. He was convinced that losing all things was worth it, just as the man who found the pearl of great price sold all he had in order to get it (Matthew 13:46). He was truly born anew into a new existence—from persecutor to persecuted.

HE WAS TRULY BORN ANEW INTO A NEW EXISTENCE.

Here we come to a major barrier for most people when they consider Christianity: the cost that must be paid in giving up sinful behavior.[12] A story important enough to be repeated in three Gospels is that of the rich young ruler who asked Jesus how to have eternal life (Matthew 19:16–22; Mark 10:17–27; Luke 18:18–23). Jesus responded by telling him to keep God's commands. The young man explained that he had spent his life doing just that. Notice Jesus' response:

> When Jesus heard this, he said to him, "You still lack one thing. Sell everything you have and give to the poor, and you will have treasure in heaven. Then come, follow me." When he heard this, he became very sad, because he was very wealthy." (Luke 18:22–23)

Why did he go away sad? It's because the word "give" echoed so loudly in his mind that he failed to hear the words "Follow me!" He might have heard the words, but he didn't believe that they would lead to eternal life. To put it plainly, repentance is hard.

As Christians grow in their faith, we will no doubt find new areas to devote to God, and thus continue to offer ourselves a living sacrifice (Romans 12:1). We are not, however, left to make these changes on our own. The Scriptures assure us that the Holy Spirit empowers all disciples of Jesus to live holy lives and to make the sometimes difficult sacrifices that repentance requires (Romans 8:11). Some people, both inside and outside the church, think that followers of Jesus are self-righteous, but the Bible expresses a very different idea. As New Testament scholar Scot McKnight notes:

> Repentance . . . cannot be manufactured by strenuous effort. Furthermore, as the rebellious son learned, it involves both the inner and outer dimensions of life (Luke 15:14–21; cf. 2 Corinthians 7:9–10). It is a work in the heart by the Spirit of God as one is awakened to the goodness, mercy, and holiness of God.[13]

God grants repentance and provides the strength and grace for us to pursue holy lives (2 Timothy 2:25). We are called to holiness in our private lives and in our relationships (Hebrews 12:14), but without the intervention of God, we would be powerless to achieve it. The church is, then, a fellowship of repenters. The Holy Spirit uses repentance to build a holy community of believers as we forgive and receive forgiveness. In fact, when true repentance takes place, a beautiful fellowship of grace is offered and received.[14] While it is not the purpose of this book to explore the fullness of God's eternal design for the church,

THE CHURCH IS, THEN, A FELLOWSHIP OF REPENTERS.

we must understand that a lifelong habit of repentance is impossible without a loving community of support.

Ancient Christians knew this, so they frequently pointed to repentance as an act of love. For example, one of the earliest ancient Christian documents records:

> Therefore let us love one another, so that we all may enter into the kingdom of God. While we still have time to be healed, let us place ourselves in the hands of God the physician, and pay him what is due. What is that? Sincere, heartfelt repentance.[15]

As you travel the path of repentance, God is calling you to show love to those whom you have wronged or neglected. Repentance can be demonstrated by a long talk, a gracious letter, or a humble act of service to a former enemy. We must demonstrate repentance in how we treat our friends and those most difficult to love.

One last word on repentance is appropriate. Many in the world think that repentance means turning to a dry, stale religious life. However, the Gospels say just the opposite. Luke records several stories of repentance involving feasts, which make clear that the best life comes from repentance. Levi, also known as Matthew, was the tax collector who left his profession and immediately threw a banquet for Jesus and his former associates. When the prodigal son repented, his father hosted a huge celebration. The son had left home to find joy, but instead wound up in a pig pen. His path to true happiness involved coming back to his father—and joining in on the celebration! The tagline of the previous parables in Luke 15 is, "In the same way, I tell you, there is rejoicing in the presence of the angels of God over one sinner who repents" (15:10; cf. Luke 15:7). Likewise, the story of Zacchaeus reminds us that when a sinner meets Jesus (and later feasts with him), they experience the joy of repentance: "Here and now I give half of my possessions to the poor, and if I have cheated anybody out of anything, I will pay back four times the amount" (Luke 19:8). When a person becomes a disciple of Jesus, they are born again. Their life begins again. From then on, their journey will be shaped by the Lord's and not their own will. This is biblical repentance.

4

WHAT DOES IT MEAN TO CONFESS JESUS AS LORD?

Answer: Confession of Jesus as Lord is a declaration of allegiance to Jesus as king and a rejection of all other claims of lordship.

> And now what are you waiting for? Get up, be baptized
> and wash your sins away, calling on his name.
> — Acts 22:16

When you read the book of Acts, you may notice that there is no simple list of steps for someone to become a disciple of Jesus. For example, as quoted earlier, Peter commanded the crowd in Jerusalem, "Repent and be baptized, every one of you, in the name of Jesus Christ for the forgiveness of your sins. And you will receive the gift of the Holy Spirit" (Acts 2:38). In Acts 8, some Samaritans "accepted the word of God" (8:14), were baptized, and then received the Holy Spirit (8:16–17). In that same chapter, the Ethiopian eunuch learned the gospel from Philip and was baptized (Acts 8:26–40). Paul's conversion is told three times in Acts—Acts 9; Acts 22; Acts 26—and in each story, he mentioned different elements of his salvation. According to Acts 9:18, after Paul's encounter with Jesus, he was baptized, and we find out later why. He was told, "Get up, be baptized and wash your sins away, calling on his name" (Acts 22:16). In Acts 26, Paul mentioned nothing of his baptism.

This brief survey of a few narratives in Acts demonstrates the common figure of speech known as metonymy, wherein one part of a concept embodies the entire thing. The New Testament uses metonymy to describe what it means to become a Christian. We see these truths in the New Testament:

- To be a follower of Jesus means that you believe in him.
- To be baptized means you are a believer.
- To be a believer means that you have confessed Jesus as your Lord.
- To have confessed Jesus as Lord means you have repented of your sins.
- To have repented of your sins means that you have received the Holy Spirit.

Any of these terms can be a metonymy describing the entire process, which begins at the new birth. So Paul can say in Romans 10:10, "For it is with your heart that you believe and are justified, and it is with your mouth that you profess your faith and are saved." Belief and confession are necessary parts of the process, but that doesn't mean repentance and baptism are excluded. Instead, the new birth begins when a person no longer claims their own lordship, but instead surrenders to King Jesus. Hearing, believing, repenting, confessing, being baptized, and receiving the Spirit are all crucial elements of the new birth.

WHAT IS THE "GOOD CONFESSION"?

UNFORTUNATELY, THROUGHOUT HISTORY THE church has tended to emphasize certain elements of the new birth and neglect others. When the church began baptizing infants in the third century, the role faith plays in discipleship was muddied. When penance—an outward demonstration of repentance such as saying a required number of prayers—was emphasized, the importance of the Holy Spirit was often ignored. When the Reformers attempted to correct these omissions by placing greater emphasis on faith (*sola fide*, "by faith alone") and grace (*sola gratia*, "by grace alone"), they offered a helpful corrective, but they also tended to neglect the important role that repentance and baptism play in the new birth. As the renowned Reformed theologian Karl Barth remarked:

> It is a strange gap in the baptismal teaching, of all Confessions—the Reformed included—that the meaning and work of baptism have never been understood in principle as a glorifying of God, that is as a moment in his self-revelation.[16]

Protestants have unfortunately tended to de-emphasize baptism because they feared the focus on what humans do, not on the God-glorifying moment when Jesus shines through the newly baptized person.

Following this idea, confessing Jesus is not a mere religious rite. It is a moment of cognitive and verbal affirmation, publicly proclaiming that Jesus is Lord and Christ, and it is the beginning of the process of a lifelong commitment.[17] Paul admonished Timothy, "Take hold of the eternal life to which you were called when you made your *good confession* in the presence of many witnesses" (1 Timothy 6:12b). In fact, Jesus also made the good confession (Matthew 27:11; Mark 15:2; Luke 23:3), as did Peter (Matthew 16:16; Mark 8:29; Luke 9:20). In addition, Jesus emphasized that his disciples needed to be willing to make the good confession in the face of a hostile world at any time:

> Therefore, everyone who confesses Me before people, I will also confess him before My Father who is in heaven. But whoever denies Me before people, I will also deny him before My Father who is in heaven. (Matthew 10:32–33, NASB)

Jesus knew that his first followers would face pressure from family and friends to shy away from their faith in him, and he directly challenged them to openly confess their devotion to him.

WHY DO WE CONFESS JESUS AS MESSIAH AND LORD?

WE CALL THE "GOOD confession" what Christians confess out loud when they convert to Christ. Early Christian formulations of the good confession point to two important ideas. First, confessing that Jesus is the "Christ" is saying that he is the promised Messiah of Israel. The Old Testament contains promises, titles, prophecies, and sufferings regarding the Messiah, and Jesus fulfilled them all. Second, confessing Jesus is Lord acknowledges him as God and king of the universe—and, therefore, king over our lives. That's why Peter preached in his first gospel sermon, "Therefore let all Israel be assured of this: God has made this Jesus, whom you crucified, both *Lord* and *Messiah*" (Acts 2:36).

One of the earliest formulations of the good confession is found in Acts 8:37, where an Ethiopian official heard and believed the gospel. The story describes his baptism and belief. But what did he believe? The earliest Greek manuscripts do not tell us, but later manuscripts do. The King James Version documents the eunuch's statement: "I believe that Jesus Christ is the Son of God" (Acts 8:37). Whether this reflects the actual statement made by the eunuch on that day, or it is an insertion made by an early Christian scribe, it nevertheless reflects an early Christian version of the good confession. In the Roman world, to say Jesus was the "Son of God" was to say that he was Lord and King.[18]

Just how significant was it at the time to confess Jesus as Lord, especially when "lord" had more than one meaning at the time? Today, most modern English-speaking countries don't regularly use the word "lord." Mostly, it is used in Britain and its commonwealth countries to refer to someone with a political role, or it is used as a religious word. We can see this broader usage of the word "lord" (*kurios* in Greek) in England's 1611 King James Version of the Bible. For example, in Matthew 10:24, while the NIV says, "The student is not above the teacher, nor a servant above his master," the KJV has, "The disciple is not above his master, nor the servant above his lord." In Greek, terms such as *kurios* reflected a difference in social or religious status.[19] A Greek-speaking Jew in the first-century Roman world could gladly say that Jehovah God is the Lord and still refer to his social superior (master, government official, royalty) as lord.[20]

However, there were times when followers of God had to make it clear that they would worship Jehovah God alone. To understand the implications of confessing Jesus as Lord, we must place this confession against the backdrop of the Roman Empire. When Jesus was born, there was already a powerful king who called himself "Son of God." It was Augustus Caesar.[21] While he did not envision himself as the Jewish messiah, he did claim for himself the right to absolute obedience from his subjects. Augustus also began a tradition of Roman emperors who called themselves "Father of the fatherland." They envisioned their empire to be one big family of which they were head, appointed by the gods to offer blessings and discipline to their children.

The average pagan Roman of the time would have no problem recognizing his social superior as lord, as well as the emperor himself. This is why modern Christian historians such as N.T. Wright have pointed out that when believers claimed Jesus as Lord in the early church, they weren't simply making a personal religious commitment. They were rejecting all earthly claimants to ultimate allegiance—familial, political, and social—in favor of Jesus. To say Jesus was Lord was to say Caesar was not.[22] This does not mean that the early Christians saw themselves as revolutionaries seeking to overthrow the emperor. It does mean, however, that they had to make it clear where their allegiances lay. This is the point of making the good confession.

> TO SAY JESUS WAS LORD WAS TO SAY CAESAR WAS NOT.

An important early Christian document from the second century called *The Martyrdom of Polycarp* recounts the story of the aged Christian leader Polycarp. He was being led to his death for his Christian faith, when some attempted to get him to try and save himself by simply swearing allegiance to Caesar and the Roman gods. The author explains:

> They also, transferring him to their carriage, were trying to persuade him, sitting beside him and saying, "For what harm is it to say 'Caesar is Lord' and to offer incense," and so forth, and thus to be delivered. And he did not answer them at first. But, as they were persisting, he said, "I am not about to do what you are advising me."[23]

Why would this old man refuse to save his life with a simple statement that Caesar was *kurios*? As he was about to die, Polycarp explained, "For eighty-six years I have been serving him, and he has done me no wrong. How then can I blaspheme my King who has saved me?"[24]

DO WE CONFESS ALONE?

To CONFESS JESUS AS Lord means that we make a public proclamation that we are submitting our lives to him alone. Even if others refuse to join us, we realize we each must stand before the Lord to be judged as individuals. However, confession is not a solo endeavor. In fact, believers need to come together regularly to confess Jesus as Lord to encourage and remind each other of their king and his kingdom.

> BELIEVERS NEED TO REMIND EACH OTHER OF THEIR KING AND HIS KINGDOM.

Throughout the centuries, Jewish synagogues have collectively recited an important confession from Scripture they call the *Shema*, which means "to hear" in Hebrew. It is called by this name because of the first word of the proclamation, which is found in Deuteronomy 6:4, "Hear [*shema*], O Israel: The LORD our God, the LORD is one." Since the very first

Christians were all Jewish, they continued to share this firm belief in the one God of Israel, but they added an important element to the confession in the *Shema*. Paul wrote to the Corinthians:

> For us there is but one God, the Father, from whom all things came and for whom we live; and there is but one Lord, Jesus Christ, through whom all things came and through whom we live. (1 Corinthians 8:6)

Many biblical scholars believe that Paul was quoting one of the earliest Christian confessions, which added the lordship of Jesus to the oneness of God. In the context of 1 Corinthians 8, he used it to admonish Christians to look out for one another and refrain from causing another believer to sin. There are scores of these early Christian confessions embedded in the New Testament. For example, Paul wrote to Timothy, "For there is one God and one mediator between God and mankind, the man Christ Jesus, who gave himself as a ransom for all people" (1 Timothy 2:5–6a).

As Christianity spread throughout the Roman Empire and beyond, the gospel message left its original Jewish context and entered into a pagan matrix that accepted many competing gods. Christians continued to formulate confessions of Jesus' lordship to help explain who Jesus was in a polytheistic culture, and these confessions eventually came together to form the great creeds of Christianity.

The word "creed" comes from the Latin for *credo*, which means "I believe." Creeds are merely statements of belief, and in the first centuries of the Christian church, they helped bind believers in a unified confession of Jesus' lordship. One of the earliest creeds was recorded by the church father Justin Martyr in the middle of the second century. It states:

> We piously believe in the God of the Christians, whom we regard to be the only one of these things from the beginning, the Maker and Fashioner of the whole creation, what is visible and invisible; and the Lord Jesus Christ, Child of God, who was proclaimed beforehand by the prophets as one who was going to be present with the race of humanity, the herald of salvation and teacher of good doctrines.[25]

Perhaps you have heard of the famous creeds from later centuries, such as the Nicene Creed or the Apostles' Creed. While they are not Scripture and should not be considered divinely inspired, they demonstrate how important it has always been for Christians to be ready to confess Jesus as Lord, both to each other and to the world. In a culture noisy with competing calls for our allegiance, we believers in Jesus continue to confess that he is Lord. In this way, we encourage faithfulness in each other and reaffirm our reason for confidence.

5

WHAT DOES IT MEAN TO BE BAPTIZED FOR THE FORGIVENESS OF OUR SINS?

Answer: Baptism is the normative place where our faith connects with God's grace and we become new, with a clean slate and a restored relationship with God.

> Peter replied, "Repent and be baptized, every one of you,
> in the name of Jesus Christ for the forgiveness of your sins.
> And you will receive the gift of the Holy Spirit."
> — Acts 2:38

After God created the earth, he called it "good." But it didn't take long for Adam and Eve to sin. In fact, they sinned even before the second generation began. Genesis 3:8 tells us they heard God walking in the garden and hid themselves. The narrative implies that Adam and Eve were familiar with God through these sorts of walks. It appears that God enjoyed fellowship with Adam and Eve in the Garden of Eden. Imagine that: being able to converse with God, asking questions and receiving answers much like you would with a friend!

Sin entered the world and created an issue for all humanity because it destroyed our once close relationship with God by creating a separation between us and God.[26] We are called to be holy because God is holy. Leviticus 11:44 says, "I am the LORD your God; consecrate yourselves and be holy, because I am holy." We are to strive for holiness in order to be in God's presence, knowing that ultimately our humanity will get in the way despite our best efforts. Like Adam and Eve we have all sinned and fallen short of God's glory (Romans 3:23), and our sin separates us from God. Isaiah 59:1–2 addresses this issue:

> Surely the arm of the LORD is not too short to save,
>> nor his ear too dull to hear.
> But your iniquities have separated
>> you from your God;
> Your sins have hidden his face from you,
>> so that he will not hear.

While this passage from Isaiah notes the separation that sin creates between us and God, it also bears good news: the Lord can save us.

WHAT IS THE CONNECTION OF OUR BAPTISM TO JESUS' BAPTISM?

WHEN JESUS WENT TO John the Baptist to be baptized, John initially resisted, saying, "I need to be baptized by you, and do you come to me?" (Matthew 3:14). But Jesus replied, "Let it be so now; it is proper for us to do this to fulfill all righteousness" (Matthew 3:15). So John baptized Jesus. By being baptized, Jesus set an example for us to follow. By undergoing baptism, Christ identified with broken humanity. As Vander Zee says,

> Jesus, being the sinless one, did not have to repent of sin, but he nevertheless buried himself in the waters of repentance with sinners. In his baptism, Jesus identifies himself as our brother and there begins to assume our sin and guilt.[27]

While Jesus didn't need forgiveness, we do, and we claim that forgiveness at our baptism. When we are baptized, Colossians 2:12 says, we are "buried with him in baptism" and "raised with him through [our] faith." Our baptism symbolizes Jesus' ultimate sacrifice for our sins and his resurrection into newness of life. Romans 6:4–5 says this:

> We were therefore buried with him through baptism into death in order that, just as Christ was raised from the dead through the glory of the Father, we

too may live a new life. For if we have been united with him in a death like his, we will certainly also be united with him in a resurrection like his.

This promise of new life with Christ is a beautiful gift from God. A chance to start again, and to make things right with God. A chance to spend eternity with God forever.

WHY DO WE NEED TO HAVE OUR SINS "WASHED AWAY"?

IN THE WATER OF baptism, our sins are washed away. This teaching is made explicit in Acts 22:16 and the Nicene Creed, which ends with the expression, "We acknowledge one baptism unto remission of sins."[28] Another word for sin is "transgression." In Colossians 2:13, Paul says those who were once dead in their transgressions are now "alive together with Him, having forgiven us all our wrongdoings" (NASB). G. Walter Hansen says in his commentary on Galatians:

> A transgression is the violation of a standard. The law provides the objective standard by which the violations are measured. In order for sinners to know how sinful they really are, how far they deviate from God's standards, God gave the law. Before the law was given, there was sin (see Rom 5:13). But after the law was given, sin could be clearly specified and measured (see Rom 3:20; 4:15; 7:7).[29]

God's law provided a standard by which sin could be recognized. God's standards, as recorded in his Word, are the measurement by which we should base our lives. When we sin, we violate God's standard, causing a rift in our relationship with him. God's desire for relationship with his people was steadfast, even though the people fell short. He wanted to maintain the relationship and forgive their sins. In Jeremiah 33:8, God looked forward to forgiving Israel. He said, "I will cleanse them from all the sin they have committed against me and will forgive their sins of rebellion against me." We see this desire to have relationship with people from the Garden of Eden in Genesis to the Tree of Life in Revelation. In Scriptures such as Jeremiah 33:8, we can see God's desire to have a relationship with people. At times in wisdom literature and the prophets, he seems to ache for a renewed relationship with his people.

WHAT DOES JESUS PROVIDE THAT THE LAW CANNOT?

In the Old Testament, God provided a means to restore relationship through the giving of the law. The law's purpose was to train the Israelites about what was right and wrong. This was important because when they left Egypt, they were beaten down and struggled with their identity as the people of God. God had to train them how to be holy and follow his ways.

When I teach class, I (Anessa) compare the purpose of the law to bowling alley bumpers, which are used for children's birthday parties. The bumpers increase the chance of hitting the mark, and they help young bowlers develop some skills along the way. In the same way, the law helped the Israelites follow the law carefully, so they would have some success in holiness. At first, this required merely doing what they were told to do. But the real goal was for God's law to seep deeply into their character and change their heart. Deuteronomy 6:5 instructed Israel to love God with their heart and soul.

However, as mentioned earlier, the law was inadequate to bridge the rift completely. God promised a Messiah to save Israel, and then he sent his Son, Jesus, to fulfill the law and be the ultimate sacrifice (1 John 4:9; Hebrews 10:12). The purpose of these actions was to save us from our sins by forgiving us. The Greek word for "save" is *sōzō*. It also means to "deliver," "protect," "heal," "preserve," and "make whole."[30] Baptism plays a role in restoring our relationship with God by removing our sins and healing our relationship with him. This was something that the law was incapable of doing on its own, and it required Jesus to be the final sacrifice in order to restore our relationship with God.

WHAT IS THE CONNECTION OF BAPTISM TO FORGIVENESS?

The New Testament makes frequent connections between baptism and forgiveness. For example, Ananias—who would soon baptize Paul—told him, "Get up, be baptized and wash your sins away, calling on his name" (Acts 22:16). Peter told the crowd at Pentecost, "Repent and be baptized, every one of you, in the name of Jesus Christ for the forgiveness of your sins. And you will receive the gift of the Holy Spirit" (Acts 2:38). When we are raised from the water of baptism, we are new people with new, clean slates. The Greek verb "to forgive" is *aphiēmi*. It connotes "sending away," which is exactly what happens in the water of baptism: baptism sends our sins away from us.[31] God himself sanctifies us and gives us forgiveness of our sins (Acts 26:18).

Baptism is the normative time at which we are forgiven of our sins and are given the Holy Spirit (Acts 2:38). However, it is also worth noting that in Acts we see that God can sovereignly choose to give the Spirit before baptism (e.g., Cornelius in Acts 10:44–48) and after baptism (e.g., the Samaritans in Acts 8:12–18). We know that God looks at the heart in conversion (Acts 15:8–9), not just our actions. So we want to make sure we uphold this norm without limiting our understanding of God's sovereign role in granting salvation. The Roman Catholic Church has a saying, "God has bound salvation to the sacrament of Baptism, but he himself is not bound by his sacraments."[32]

HOW SHOULD WE BE BAPTIZED?

OVER THE PAST TWO thousand years, adopting human theology rather than Jesus' teachings created confusion about how one should be baptized. The baptisms of John the Baptist, Jesus, and the disciples all demonstrate baptism by immersion. In fact, the Greek word for "baptism" is *baptizō*, which means "to dip" or "to immerse."[33] During the second century, the practice of baptism developed consistency. The early church practiced immersion, except for one example in the *Didache* when enough water was not present. That was referred to as the act of "pouring" rather than baptism.[34] John Mark Hicks and Greg Taylor write about this adaptation, saying:

> This diversity, while minor at first, grew through the fifth century and by the end of the medieval period a consensus had been established that was the opposite of the practice of the second-century church. . . . However, one constant was a consensus understanding that baptism was for the remission of sins and that an unbaptized saved adult was a rare exception.[35]

By journeying back and reading baptism stories in the Scriptures and examining the original Greek word for "baptism," we discover immersion as the normative mode of baptism envisioned in the New Testament. By participating in this act, we are weaving our own story into the tapestry of Christ and of Christians throughout the world spanning across two millennia.

AFTER WE'RE FORGIVEN, WHAT'S NEXT?

FORGIVENESS GIVES US A clean slate, one that must be filled with God. While forgiveness happens at once, the lifelong process of pursuing holiness begins. Theologian Stanley Grenz writes:

> When seen from our vantage point, therefore, the experience of salvation occurs in three stages. "Conversion" marks the inauguration of personal salvation. The transformation the Spirit effects in us is a lifelong process which we label "sanctification." We anticipate at the end of the age our "glorification," the completion of the Spirit's work of renewal.[36]

In 2 Thessalonians 2:13, we learn that we are "saved through the sanctifying work of the Spirit and through belief in the truth." While it is God who sanctifies us, we are also expected to pursue purity. The good news is that God wants us to succeed in this. In fact, Jesus prayed for the sanctification of his present and future disciples before his crucifixion: "My prayer is not for them alone. I pray also for those who will believe in me through their message" (John 17:20). This is an important process because those who are sanctified are given an inheritance in him (Acts 20:32). The Holy Spirit was given to us to help us. God wants us to succeed!

GOD WANTS US TO SUCCEED IN THIS.

Our first step in joining God in the process is our baptism, as we've mentioned, where we are buried and resurrected *with Jesus*. Being baptized does not mean a life without temptation or struggle. As forgiven people whom Jesus is sanctifying, we must invest ourselves into the process of sanctification, not cheapening the incredible sacrifice of Christ in forgiving our sins by not pursuing holiness. Owen Olbricht explains the importance of our personal investment well:

> In order for baptism to be valid, the one submitting to the physical act must also be spiritually involved. He must understand that he is being forgiven of past sins. He must understand that his burial and resurrection ends an old life—that he is entering into a new relationship with Jesus and is accepting his lordship.[37]

When we remove sin from our lives, it leaves a void to be filled. If we do not intentionally fill that void with righteousness, sin creeps back in. We remember this ourselves, and when we disciple others, we need to be prepared to walk with them through spiritual struggles into holiness.

AM I READY TO GET BAPTIZED?

ONE QUESTION THAT OFTEN comes up when someone is studying to become a Christian is if a person is ready to take the step of baptism. The one considering baptism often feels pressure to have it all together and have all their questions answered before taking this step. However, if we look at the ministry of Jesus, we see examples of the apostles teaching, followed by people immediately responding in baptism (Acts 2:38–41; Acts 10:47–48; Acts 16:32–33; Acts 19:4–5). The urgency of their decision surely indicated that they did not have every question answered, but that they understood their need for a Savior. Part of growing a deeper faith is asking questions, and this is also a sign of our humanity. One example of a believer's questioning is John the Baptist in Luke 7:18–23. John the Baptist faithfully lived out his role as the forerunner to the Messiah and even baptized Jesus. However, while he was in prison, he began to question things in his life and if Jesus was truly the Messiah. John sent his followers to ask Jesus if he was the one they were expecting or if there would be another. This brings comfort, because if John the Baptist can ask tough questions, it is reasonable to expect that we may too. Any unrealistic expectation that all our questions must be answered before we get baptized could keep us from taking this step.

The gift of the Spirit helps us with our spiritual walk and can help us find answers to our questions. Even if we are stuck with a particular faith question for an extended period before baptism, but decide to move ahead with repentance and baptism, we can end up figuring out the answer to our questions post-baptism. This displays how the Spirit reveals Jesus' message and guides people to truth after immersion (John 16:12–15; Romans 8:1–17). He also helps us overcome sin once we've been born again (Romans 8:13–14; Galatians 5:24). The Holy Spirit is a powerful resource we are granted access to at baptism. Again, that God gives us this gift shows us that he wants us to succeed.

Part of having faith is taking the step and trusting God to provide what we need. I (Anessa) remember having a conversation about the Christian life with a woman I had great respect for in college. She was married to a prominent leader in the school and in the church, and she was nearing retirement age. She told me that someday she hoped to have "this Christianity thing all worked out." I felt immediately reassured that I did not have to have it all together, and then a little fear. Was it ever possible to "make it" in our Christian walk?

I have discovered that the Christian life is a journey. If we wait to act until we are perfect or have it all together, then we will be waiting forever. God accepts us as we are when we take the step of baptism, and he walks with us as we grow. We must take that step of faith in faith.

A COMMITMENT TO BE A DISCIPLE OF JESUS

BAPTISM IS NOT THE finish line, but the starting line. Baptism expresses our commitment to discipleship. A disciple is someone who is following Jesus, being changed by Jesus, and is committed to the mission of Jesus (Matthew 4:19). The focus of our lives is not just on eternity but also on life in God's kingdom, here and now. We want to live our lives as Jesus would if he were living our lives in our bodies.

The apostle Paul poignantly describes something similar, focusing on his post-conversion life as a disciple:

> I have been crucified with Christ and I no longer live, but Christ lives in me. The life I live in the body, I live by faith in the Son of God, who loved me and gave himself for me. (Galatians 2:20)

> I eagerly expect and hope that I will in no way be ashamed, but will have sufficient courage so that now as always Christ will be exalted in my body, whether by life or by death. For to me, to live is Christ and to die is gain. (Philippians 1:20–21)

> But whatever were gains to me I now consider loss for the sake of Christ. What is more, I consider everything a loss because of the surpassing worth of knowing Christ Jesus my Lord. . . . I want to know Christ—yes, to know the power of his resurrection and participation in his sufferings, becoming like him in his death. (Philippians 3:7–10)

Like Paul, we want Christ to live in us, to see him exalted in our bodies, and even to share in his sufferings, if needed. After baptism, as spiritual infants, we come up and out of the waters to live for Jesus. In the light of this vision for living like Jesus, Paul describes our post-baptism life as a brand-new life (Romans 6:4).

And just like spiritual infants need a parent to guide them and raise them, when we rise from the waters of baptism, we need mature disciples to teach us how to live as disciples of Jesus. In this way, we learn how to live our lives as disciples who recognize the incredible gift of forgiveness we have been granted and the vitally important life to which God has called us, both here and now in this world and then and there in the afterlife.

> WE NEED MATURE DISCIPLES TO TEACH US HOW TO LIVE AS DISCIPLES OF JESUS.

CONCLUSION

Our entire spiritual life is the activation of the seed planted in baptism.
— Mark the Ascetic (sixth century)[38]

In the five brief chapters of this book, we have attempted to demonstrate the importance of the new birth into Jesus Christ. While there's always more to say, we believe that the message of the new birth is actually simple: we all need to be born again into the kingdom of God. The emphasis is not on the good that we do in the flesh (though good deeds will surely follow), but on the work that God begins in us through the Spirit. Paul wrote that God "saved us, not because of righteous things we had done, but because of his mercy. He saved us through the washing of rebirth and renewal by the Holy Spirit" (Titus 3:5).

WE ALL NEED TO BE BORN AGAIN INTO THE KINGDOM OF GOD.

Just as it was good news in biblical times to hear that Jesus offers people a new life, so it is good news today. Rebirth. Renewal. Resurrection. God can take his creation, though seemingly dead, and make it new again. This is the divine miracle we were created for. Our individual stories join up with Jesus' story when he begins to breathe new life into them. C. S. Lewis observed, "Death and resurrection are what the story is about and had we but eyes to see it, this has been hinted on every page, met us, in some disguise, at every turn."[39]

John writes, "Unless a kernel of wheat falls to the ground and dies, it remains only a single seed. But if it dies, it produces many seeds" (John 12:24). The world says that we are born, we live, and we die. But Jesus says, *You can be born again into a life with meaning and hope.* We pray that you find life in Jesus and that you plant the seeds of new birth into the hearts of a dying world.

APPENDIX

BOOK RECOMMENDATIONS FOR FURTHER STUDY

Rees Bryant, *Baptism, Why Wait?: Faith's Response in Conversion* (Joplin: College Press, 1999).

Jack Cottrell, *Baptism: A Biblical Study* (Joplin: College Press, 2006).

Everett Ferguson, *Baptism in the Early Church: History, Theology, and Liturgy in the First Five Centuries* (Grand Rapids: Eerdmans, 2009).

John Mark Hicks and Greg Taylor, *Down in the River to Pray: Revisioning Baptism as God's Transforming Work* (Siloam Springs, AR: Leafwood Publishers, 2004).

Tony Twist, Bobby Harrington, and David Young, *Baptism: What the Bible Teaches* (Renew.org, 2019).

NOTES

1. E. A. Livingstone, *Oxford Concise Dictionary of the Christian Church* (New York: Oxford University Press, 2006), 143.

2. C. Marvin Pate, *The Writings of John* (Grand Rapids: Zondervan, 2011), 48.

3. Matthew W. Bates, *Salvation by Allegiance Alone: Rethinking Faith, Works, and the Gospel of Jesus the King* (Grand Rapids: Baker Academic, 2017), 83.

4. Bates, 83.

5. Bates, 109.

6. Owen Olbricht, *Baptism: A Response of Faith* (Delight, AR: Gospel Light Publishing Company, 200), 45–46.

7. Martin Luther, quoted by Karl Barth, *The Epistle to the Romans*, trans. Edwyn C. Hoskyns (London: Oxford, 1933), 96.

8. See Mark E. Moore, *Faithful Faith: Reclaiming Faith from Culture and Tradition* (Renew.org, 2021).

9. Olbricht, 42.

10. *Theological Dictionary of the New Testament*, ed. Gerhard Kittel and Gerhard Friedrich, trans. Geoffry W. Bromiley (Grand Rapids: Eerdmans, 1964–1976), 4:975–1003. The Jewish historian Josephus and the Jewish philosopher Philo of Alexandria both used *metanoia* in a sense of a change heart and behavior, as opposed to the pagan Greek idea that "never suggests an alteration in the total moral attitude, a profound change in life's direction, a conversion which affects the whole conduct." See *TDNT*, 4:979.

11. Hicks and Taylor, 168.

12. Michael J. Ovey bluntly states that the twenty-first century is "a time of repentanceless Christianity" in the Western world. See his *The Feasts of Repentance: From Luke–Acts to Systematic and Pastoral Theology*, New Studies in Biblical Theology (Downers Grove, IL: InterVarsity Press, 2009), 1.

13. Scot McKnight, *The Letter of James*, The New International Commentary on the New Testament (Grand Rapids: Eerdmans Publishing Company, 2011), 353.

14. For an in-depth look at how repentance and forgiveness build Christian community, see Miroslav Volf, *Free of Charge: Giving and Forgiving in a Culture Stripped of Grace* (Grand Rapids: Zondervan, 2009).

15. This quote comes from one of the earliest extant non-biblical Christian documents, 2 Clement 9:6–8. Some think it was written by the early church leader Clement of Rome, while others consider it an early Christian sermon. Either way, it was clearly written by a Christian in the late first or early second century. This translation comes from Michael W. Holmes, *The Apostolic Fathers: Greek Texts and English Translations*, 3rd ed. (Grand Rapids: Baker Academic, 2007), 149.

16. Karl Barth, *The Teaching of the Church Regarding Baptism*, trans. Ernest A. Payne (London: SCM, 1948), 31.

17. This is where the so-called "sinner's prayer" gets it right, in that it involves confessing sin and confessing to belief in Jesus. However, such a prayer is never found in the Bible. While the New Testament supports confession of Christ, baptism is the appropriate response connected with this confession, not prayer.

18. See D. A. Carson, *Jesus the Son of God: A Christological Title Often Overlooked, Sometimes Misunderstood, and Currently Disputed* (Wheaton, IL: Crossway, 2013). See also the confession of Jesus as king made by the repentant thief on the cross, who said to Jesus, "Jesus, remember me when you come into your kingdom" (Luke 23:42).

19. *TDNT*, 3:1056.

20. *Kurios* is used of God some six thousand times in the Greek version of the Old Testament. See also C. E. Cranfield, *A Critical and Exegetical Commentary on the Epistle to the Romans*, vol. 2 (Edinburgh: T&T Clark International), 529.

21. The Latin term Augustus used was *divi filius*.

22. See, for example, Wright's chapter "Paul's Gospel and Caesar's Empire," in *Paul and Politics, Ekklesia, Israel, Imperium, Interpretation: Essays in Honor of Krister Stendahl*, ed. Richard A. Horsley (Harrisburg: Trinity Press International, 2000), 160–183.

23. Paul Hartog, *Polycarp's Epistle to the Philippians and the Martyrdom of Polycarp: Introduction, Text, and Commentary* (Oxford: Oxford University Press, 2013), 251.

24. Hartog, 253.

25. Acts of Justin 2, recension B. As quoted in Everett Ferguson, *The Rule of Faith: A Guide* (Eugene: Cascade Books, 2015), 3.

26. See Chapter 1 for a fuller discussion of this.

27. Leonard J. Vander Zee, *Christ, Baptism and the Lord's Supper: Recovering the Sacraments for Evangelical Worship* (Downers Grove, IL: InterVarsity Press, 2004), 80.

28. "The Nicene Creed" in *Documents of the Christian Church*, ed. Henry Bettenson and Chris Maunder (Oxford: Oxford University Press, 1999), 29.

29. G. Walter Hansen, *Galatians* (Downers Grove, IL: IVP Academic, 2010), 101.

30. James Strong, *Strong's Expanded Exhaustive Concordance of the Bible,* (Nashville: Thomas Nelson, 2009), #4982.

31. *Strong's,* #863.

32. CCC #1257.

33. Walter Bauer, *A Greek-English Lexicon of the New Testament and Other Early Christian Literature*, 2nd ed. (Chicago: University of Chicago Press, 1958), 131.

34. John Mark Hicks and Greg Taylor, *Down in the River to Pray* (Siloam Springs, AR: Leafwood Publishers, 2004), 96.

35. Hicks and Taylor, 94.

36. Stanley Grenz, *Theology for the Community of God* (Grand Rapids: Eerdmans, 1994), 433.

37. Olbricht, 128.

38. As quoted in Eric E. Peterson, *Wade in the Water: Following the Sacred Stream of Baptism* (Eugene: Cascade Books, 2018), 79.

39. C. S. Lewis, *Miracles: A Preliminary Study* (London: The Centenary Press, 1947), 117.

7

HOLY SPIRIT

FILLED,
EMPOWERED,
AND LED

DAVID YOUNG

"Son of man, can these bones live?"

CONTENTS

General Editors' Note 339

Introduction 341

CHAPTER 1: What Is a Spirit? 345

CHAPTER 2: How Does the Holy Spirit Move Us
Toward Jesus? 351

CHAPTER 3: What Does It Mean for the Holy Spirit
to Live Within Us? 359

CHAPTER 4: How Does the Holy Spirit Make Us like Jesus? 365

CHAPTER 5: How Do We Seek the Holy Spirit's
Leadership in Our Lives? 375

Conclusion 379

Appendix: Book Recommendations for Further Study 381

Notes 383

GENERAL EDITORS' NOTE

The Bible teaches that we can know a person is saved or lost by the indwelling presence of the Holy Spirit in their life (Romans 8:9). At the heart of a disciple's life is walking in the Spirit. We are taught to be filled with the Spirit, led by the Spirit, and to keep in step with the Spirit. But what exactly is the Holy Spirit? How do we follow what the Bible teaches?

David Young is a trusted guide on the work of the Holy Spirit. He serves as the Lead Minister for the North Boulevard Church in Murfreesboro, Tennessee. He has worked for churches in Missouri, Kansas, and Tennessee, taught New Testament at several universities, and traveled widely as a teacher and preacher. He is the former host of the New Day Television Program, a board member for the Renew.org Network, and the author of several books, including *A New Day* (NB Press), *The Rhetoric of Jesus in the Gospel of Mark* (Fortress Press, coauthored with Michael Strickland), *A Grand Illusion* (Renew.org), and *King Jesus and the Beauty of Obedience-Based Discipleship* (Zondervan). He holds multiple degrees in religion, including a PhD in New Testament from Vanderbilt University. David and his wife, Julie, have two married children.

This book expounds on the section from the Renew.org Leaders' Faith Statement called "The Holy Spirit":

> We believe God's desire is for everyone to be saved and come to the knowledge of the truth. Many hear the gospel but do not believe it because they are blinded by Satan and resist the pull of the Holy Spirit. We encourage everyone to listen to the Word and let the Holy Spirit convict them of their sin and draw them into a relationship with God through Jesus. We believe that when we are born again and indwelt by the Holy Spirit, we are to live as people who are filled, empowered, and led by the Holy Spirit. This is how we

walk with God and discern his voice. A prayerful life, rich in the Holy Spirit, is fundamental to true discipleship and living in step with the kingdom reign of Jesus. We seek to be a prayerful, Spirit-led fellowship.

*See the full Network Faith Statements at the end of this book.

Support Scriptures: 1 Timothy 2:4; John 16:7–11; Acts 7:51; 1 John 2:20, 27; John 3:5; Ephesians 1:13–14; 5:18; Galatians 5:16–25; Romans 8:5–11; Acts 1:14; 2:42; 6:6; 9:40; 12:5; 13:3; 14:23; 20:36; 2 Corinthians 3:3.

The following tips might help you use this book more effectively (and the other books in the *Real Life Theology* series):

1. *Five questions, answers, and Scriptures.* We framed this book around five key questions with five short answers and five notable Scriptures. This format provides clarity, making it easier to commit crucial information to memory. This format also enables the books in the *Real Life Theology* series to support our catechism. Our catechism is a series of fixed questions and answers for instruction in church or home. In all, the series has fifty-two questions, answers, and key Scriptures. This particular book focuses on the five that are most pertinent to understanding the Holy Spirit.
2. *Summary videos.* You can find three to five-minute video teachings that summarize the book, as well as each chapter, at Renew.org. These short videos can function as standalone teachings. But for groups or group leaders using the book, they can also be used to launch discussion of the reading.

May God use this book to fuel faithful and effective disciple making in your life and church.

For King Jesus,
Bobby Harrington and Daniel McCoy
General Editors, *Real Life Theology* series

INTRODUCTION

The great human dogma, then, is that the wind moves the trees.
The great human heresy is that the trees move the wind.
— G. K. Chesterton

Years ago, I came to the unhappy conclusion that many of us don't understand the Holy Spirit because we really don't want to. He is too wild, unpredictable, untamed, full of power, risky, unsettling, disruptive, and challenging. We prefer a domesticated faith, where our comfort is never upended by his power.

So if your church had two classrooms in its hallway, one labeled "The Study of the Holy Spirit" and the other labeled "The Holy Spirit Is Here," many of us would choose the former. We'd rather *study* the Holy Spirit than *experience* him. We like having a theology of the Spirit, but we are hesitant to embrace the real thing.

This is the story of many in the Western church: literally equipped with the best resources the church has ever possessed, many of us fear the one resource that can actually change the world—the Holy Spirit.

The early church exploded in growth not because they had fancy mission statements and programs. The early church exploded in growth because they had the power of the Holy Spirit. Imagine a church whose strategic vision looked like this:

> I will pour out my Spirit on all people. . . . I will show wonders in the heavens above and signs on the earth below, blood and fire and billows of smoke. The sun will be turned to darkness and the moon to blood before the coming of the great and glorious day of the Lord. And everyone who calls on the name of the Lord will be saved. (Acts 2:17–21)

Blood and fire and billows of smoke. This is the vision God has planned for you. This is the power of the Holy Spirit. It's not merely a matter of having the right doctrine. It's rather a matter of experiencing the Spirit himself. If I could accomplish one thing in this book, it would be to convince you to stop quenching the Spirit's fire and start experiencing his power.

So who is the Holy Spirit and what does he want to do in me?

Questions about the Holy Spirit have been around ever since Paul was told by the disciples of John the Baptist that "we have not even heard that there is a Holy Spirit" (Acts 19:2). Our many questions about the Holy Spirit arise for three reasons. First, the Spirit is God, and because God is so much bigger than we are, there will always remain questions about what the powerful Spirit is doing.

Second, the church has often argued about the Spirit. We've argued over such things as the relationship of the Spirit to the Father and Son, how believers get the Spirit, and whether or not the gifts of the Spirit are still available. These conflicts have sometimes left the typical follower of Jesus so confused they just ignore the Spirit altogether.

Third, many questions about the Spirit arise because the secular worldview meticulously cultivated in the Western world over the last half-millennium has left many of us bereft of *any* real spiritual awareness at all. Unable to discern deeply the presence of *anything* spiritual leaves us ill-equipped to understand the work of the most powerful of spirits—the Holy Spirit.

With this book, I seek to answer five of the most fundamental questions believers bring to the subject of the Holy Spirit:

- What is a spirit?
- How does the Holy Spirit move us toward Jesus?
- What does it mean for the Holy Spirit to live within us?
- How does the Holy Spirit make us like Jesus?
- How do we seek the Holy Spirit's leadership in our lives?

These comprise the five chapters of this book.

Before beginning, however, let's point out that the picture of the Spirit in the Bible is an evolving picture, coming into clear focus only when seen through Jesus Christ, and even then, most clearly when explained in the works of John and Paul.

In the earliest portions of Scripture, the Spirit is a dynamic and, at times, unpredictable power who personifies God's movements within the creation. In the first half of the Bible, the Spirit hardly appears as a person at all, but rather as a powerful force—like a mighty wind. In the latter pages of the Old Testament, the

Spirit begins to function in a more rational role and is frequently assigned the very specific task of inspiring prophetic speech. And in these latter pages, many of the prophetic oracles tell us that the Spirit will be characteristic of Jesus' ministry and the new covenant in its entirety.

In the New Testament, the Spirit does indeed characterize the messianic ministry of Jesus, providing power and direction for his work. The Synoptic Gospels—Matthew, Mark, and Luke—show that Jesus was led by the Spirit, and the Spirit still appears more as a power than as a person in the Synoptic Gospels. In the book of Acts, the same power is offered to all believers, since all believers are now offered the Holy Spirit, who brings divine power to the church.

In John's Gospel, however, we see that the Spirit is more than just a power, but is actually a person—distinct from the Father and the Son, but one with them. His personhood has been true all along, but we see it more clearly in John. Though John still uses the neuter pronoun to describe the Spirit, he speaks of the Spirit as a person.[1] John continues to present the Spirit as providing power for the believers, but he goes further. For John, as we'll discover in what follows, the Spirit is a person who provides a new way of living. We are born of the Spirit, he explains. We worship in the Spirit. And the Spirit actually represents a new way of life, distinguished from that of mere flesh.

In the works of Paul, the fullest image of the Spirit in the Bible emerges. There we learn that the Spirit is the very air that Christians are to breathe—that we are to live in the Spirit, to be led by the Spirit, and to be sanctified by the Spirit. This last phrase sums up the work of the Spirit for the disciple. As the divine and personal presence of a powerful and holy God, the Spirit's main task in the Christian's life is to empower us to become like Jesus. The Spirit himself forms a new way of living for the believers. He is our new DNA in Christ, changing us into the likeness of Jesus at a core level.

> THE SPIRIT'S MAIN TASK IN THE CHRISTIAN'S LIFE IS TO EMPOWER US TO BECOME LIKE JESUS.

Let's take the five questions relevant to this work and seek their biblical answers. As you continue reading, however, please remember that our ultimate goal is not simply to develop a doctrine about the Holy Spirit. Our ultimate goal that extends out of a renewed understanding of the Spirit is to have an immersive experience of the Spirit. Don't settle for merely knowing *about* the Spirit. Seek instead to *know* the Spirit and to *live* in him.

1

WHAT IS A SPIRIT?

Answer: A spirit is a personal being, with rational, emotional, and volitional capacities, who transcends the known physical world but also acts within it.

God is spirit, and his worshipers must worship in the Spirit and in truth.
— John 4:24

We've all seen holograms: those images of dogs, doves, and people that seem to move as you turn the picture. Holograms are fascinating because they present what's called "parallax"—the quality that makes the foreground move differently from the background, changing the actual image as you turn the hologram and making the image appear to have life.

How does this work? Well, I'll leave the explanation to the laser physicists and simply point out that we are not attracted to holograms because of the physics behind them. Rather, we are attracted to holograms because they simulate real-life movement. We are drawn to life, not to mere explanations of life. So it is with the Spirit.

HOW AND WHY

SCIENCE CAN EXPLAIN THE *how* of life—how chemicals interact in nature, in the human body, and in the universe—but science cannot explain *why* they do: Why is there matter? Why is there a universe? Why is there life? Why do we do the things we do? These are spiritual questions—questions about *why* life springs out of matter to end up thinking, reasoning, imagining, loving, and hoping. The entire 500-year scientific enterprise of the West has mistakenly believed that if we can explain *how* something happens, we have also explained *why* it happens. But the two questions are completely different.

If you lost your keys in the garage, you don't look for them in the kitchen simply because the lighting is better there. In the same way, looking for *how* a mixture of warm and cold air can create a storm doesn't explain *why* warm and cold mix in the first place. Explaining how a woman remembers to bring her purse does not explain why she remembers. Explaining how a community seeks justice does not explain why it does. Explaining how the brain functions does not explain why it does. A chemical or electrical reaction in the brain can be measured in a machine. A thought cannot.

To answer *why* questions, we must think in spiritual categories, which in fact we all do, whether we realize it or not. Rationality is not a mere chemical question; it is primarily a spiritual one. Justice is not a question merely for biologists; it is a question for all humans. And God is not a matter of particle physics; he is spirit and from his Spirit comes every particle.

Spirit is the *why*-force behind every *how*-answer in the universe. Embedded in all of reality is a spiritual dimension distinct from physics but forming a sort of fabric in which all of physics operates. This spiritual fabric is the animating force that

keeps the universe orderly. It is the reason for gravity, for electromagnetism, for waves, particles, purposes, intentions, plans, aspirations, and personhood. So even if you could gather organic matter matching every single molecule found in a human body and piece it together in a lab, it still wouldn't be alive, for life is not just the sum of the chemicals in a person's body. Life is that which is behind the chemicals in the body—it is the force, the energy, the person, who makes the chemicals breathe, act, and reason. It is spirit that makes us live. Chemicals are necessary, but without spirit, they are dead. Without spirit, they wouldn't even exist at all.

THE SPIRITUAL BEHIND THE PHYSICAL

LET ME PUT IT another way. If you could pull back the curtains on the visible universe—that part of creation that scientists study—you would see a deeper, spiritual reality behind the physical. You would see a world of personal forces animating the universe, giving it its purpose: now creating, now resting, now wrestling, now luring, now calming. You would see angels and demons. You would see the meaning of the universe (its *why*) and not just the mechanics of the universe (its *how*). You would see everything that is spiritual.

The book of Revelation bears this out graphically. Behind every earthquake in Revelation is a spiritual decision made in heaven. Behind persecution are evil spirits. Behind the rise and collapse of empires are spirits in mortal combat. And behind every person's life is a spirit—an immaterial, rational, individual person-animating life. In this sense, one's spirit is almost like one's life itself: that mysterious force that makes the two plus two of mere matter equal the five of a living person. When used in the sense of "life," the Bible can occasionally speak of even animals as having "spirit"—that is, "life" (see Ecclesiastes 3:19).

Behind the curtain of the visible universe is an entire world of the spiritual. It is analogous to the way that a movie screen shows a mere projection of real actors filmed a year before it ever entered the theater. If the movie is good, even though it is composed only of pixels on a screen, it elicits real emotions. That's because behind the projection lie real people who actually generated the feelings, who live and breathe and themselves have feelings. In the same way, behind every single physical phenomenon is a spiritual force animating and empowering it.

This mystical dimension of the universe explains why the cluster of terms in the Bible typically translated "soul" and "spirit" are connected to ideas of wind, breath, and life. In the Hebrew Bible, the typical terms are *ruach* and *nephesh*. The former sometimes means "wind"—that unseen force that moves the trees and cools the skin. We cannot see the wind, but we can see that there is wind. The latter Hebrew term sometimes means life—the breath that makes matter think, plan, and create.[2] We cannot see life, but we can see that there is life, just as we can see the tragedy of the end of life.

This interpretation of reality is also presented in the New Testament, often using the words *pneuma* and *psyche*.[3] These terms derive their meaning from concepts of wind, breath, and one's rational, emotional, and volitional capacities. To see the spiritual is to see behind (or within) the physical—to perceive the ultimate and animating power that generates the physical.

If we want a rich experience of the Holy Spirit, it is imperative that we recover a sense of what a spirit is. Many of us fail to have a rich experience of the Holy Spirit because we are unaware that there are such things as spirits at all. But spirits are real. They are all around us, and we *already* follow one spirit or another.

THE SPIRIT AND THE BODY

SPIRITS ARE METAPHYSICAL PERSONS (that is, persons who transcend our experience of physics). They have individuality and volition. They think, feel, and act—both above and within creation. They include angels, spiritual beings who are charged with doing God's will both in heaven and on earth (see Hebrews 12:4). They also include the devil and his demons (Revelation 16:14). Spirits inhabit the ethereal realm (Ephesians 2:2) and constitute the powers of the unseen world (Ephesians 6:11–12; Colossians 2:20). Though they may appear in bodily form, they are essentially otherworldly in nature (Luke 24:39). Hence, both John and Paul frequently make contrasts between *flesh* and *spirit* (see John 3:6; 6:63; Romans 8:5; Philippians 3:3).

All humans possess a "spirit." The spirit is that inner part of a person that gives life and is inherently related to God. A person's spirit is their conscious essence—something like one's mind. In some ways, the spirit is what we mean when we say "I" or "me"—as opposed to "my." So we can say things like, "I (the spirit) *have* two legs (the body)." We instinctively know our spirits and bodies are not the same thing. We can *know* with our spirit (1 Corinthians 2:11), *rejoice* in our spirit (Luke 1:47), be *anguished* in our spirit (Job 7:11), be *refreshed* in our spirit (1 Corinthians 16:18), and *worship* with our spirit (John 4:24; 1 Corinthians 14:15). A person's spirit lives on after that person's body is dead (1 Samuel 28:13–14; 1 Corinthians 5:5; 14:16; Hebrews 12:23).

RECOVERING THE SPIRIT

IN ORDER TO UNDERSTAND and fully experience the Holy Spirit, we must recover a spiritual view of the creation. I say "recover" because there was once a time (and still is in much of the world) when humans naturally perceived spiritual realities. We knew that the world is, to borrow a concept from Canadian philosopher Charles Taylor's often-quoted *A Secular Age*, enchanted—that there is a "ghost in the machine" of creation animating and enlivening it.[4] That's why, Taylor explains, most of history's populations could not imagine a world without God and spirits. Rather than asking whether or not the Holy Spirit exists, most of the world would naturally ask, "Which spirit exists here?" But in the West, where we have settled for *how* questions instead of *why* questions, we have lost much of our sense of enchantment. So we are left asking the impoverished question, "Is there a spirit at all?"

To understand the Holy Spirit, we must first comprehend the spiritual realities behind, or beneath, or within our daily lives. Indeed, comprehending the meaning of "spirit" is half the game in understanding the Holy Spirit. The problem so many Western churches have with the Holy Spirit is not really theological; it is cultural. Our culture struggles to understand *anything* spiritual, so when we speak of "the Holy Spirit," we don't have a category for him. We are like a man writing a book on how it feels to have a baby. He can say anything he wants, of course, but we all know

THE PROBLEM . . . IS NOT REALLY THEOLOGICAL; IT IS CULTURAL.

that he really has no idea what he's talking about. In the same way, people who do not live aware of the spiritual dimension of life cannot understand the Holy Spirit. But when we awaken to God's Spirit in our spirit, we gain the necessary language for discerning his presence. We begin to have an experience of the Spirit that enriches our lives.

Since the Spirit is everywhere, in order to see his work, we don't have to look elsewhere. Rather, we have to look more deeply at what's already before us. Rather than seeing our lives as a set of random coincidences, we learn to see that there is a purpose and design to them. Rather than seeing loneliness as a mere state of mind, we learn to see it as the howl of our spirits against their separation from God. Rather than seeing the rise and fall of nations as the mere result of social and political changes, we learn to see the spiritual war behind physical war, with God directing all of history for the sake of his ultimate victory. Rather than seeing mere physics behind the growth of grass, the food on our table, and the loves in our lives, we learn to see the power of God behind each of these. We must learn to see that the spiritual is behind everything physical. *Everything.*

As we develop a biblical theology of the Holy Spirit, don't forget that the first step is to recognize the spiritual depths of creation. It's only then that we can understand this, the third member of the Holy Trinity. It's only then that we can experience the fullness of the power of the Holy Spirit.

2

HOW DOES THE HOLY SPIRIT MOVE US TOWARD JESUS?

Answer: The Holy Spirit moves us toward Jesus through the Word, through his power, and through deep conviction.

> For we know, brothers and sisters loved by God, that he has chosen you, because our gospel came to you not simply with words but also with power, with the Holy Spirit and deep conviction. You know how we lived among you for your sake.
> — 1 Thessalonians 1:4–5

The Spirit of God is the creative power and the life-giving essence of God.[5] The Holy Spirit is the personal force of God beneath, behind, and within the universe that holds it all together and gives it its purpose. God himself is a spirit (John 4:24), but he also *has* a Spirit—who is one person of the Trinity—distinct from the Father and the Son yet also completely one with them. The Spirit is above us, beneath us, around us, and if you are a believer in Jesus, within you. He is the presence of God hovering over creation. He animates the universe, motivates it, and shapes it. He is the life-giving and world-transforming presence of God, permeating every crevice of creation. As the psalmist writes, "Whither shall I go from thy spirit?" (Psalm 139:7, KJV).

But the Spirit does not point to himself. Rather, the Spirit's work is to point us to Jesus (John 15:26). He is very unselfish. And so our primary interest in the Holy Spirit should always be motivated by a desire to become like Jesus. It's worth remembering that the Holy Spirit has no name; he points to the one named Jesus.

So how does this Spirit draw us to Jesus? Even more deeply, why is it necessary for the Spirit to draw us to him? Couldn't we just choose Jesus on our own volition?

Paul's comment to the Thessalonian church gives us a short answer for how the Spirit draws us toward Jesus. Speaking of his experience with the Thessalonians, Paul says, "For we know, brothers and sisters loved by God, that he has chosen you, because our gospel came to you not simply with words but also with power, with the Holy Spirit and deep conviction" (1 Thessalonians 1:4–5). The Spirit works through the Word, through his power, and through deep conviction.

These works of the Spirit are necessary because none of us can come to Jesus on our own. Jesus plainly says it: "No one can come to me unless the Father has enabled them" (John 6:65). Paul puts it this way: "For who knows a person's thoughts except their own spirit within them? In the same way no one knows the thoughts of God except the Spirit of God" (1 Corinthians 2:11). In order to see the spiritual things of God, we require the Spirit of God. "As the heavens are higher than the earth, so are my ways higher than your ways and my thoughts than your thoughts," says the Lord (Isaiah 55:9). We need the Spirit to draw us to God because only the Spirit fully knows the will of God.

There is another reason, however, that we need the Spirit to draw us to God: we are hopelessly plunged in sin and are simply too broken by sin to come to God without his drawing power. Our purposes are selfish. Our desires are disordered. And worst of all, our will is broken. Blinded by our sin, we do not have sufficient power to draw ourselves to God. To quote Paul again, "The god of this age has blinded the minds of unbelievers, so that they cannot see the light of the gospel that displays the glory of Christ, who is the image of God" (2 Corinthians 4:4). We are like the GPS on our phones when the battery is dead. No matter how much we might think we can navigate our lives toward God, we don't have the power to do it.

So God uses his Spirit to draw us to him through Jesus.

How does the Spirit do this? Using 1 Thessalonians 1:4–5 as a key passage, let's explore three ways.

THE WORD

THE FIRST WAY THE Spirit draws us to God is through the Word of God. In the Old Testament, the Spirit gave physical strength, executive prowess, and engineering skills to various individuals. But he also gave them the very words of God. The

Spirit has a rational function—that of communicating the specifics of God's will to humans. In the prophetic works of the Old Testament, the Spirit is frequently described as revealing the details of God's will. He inspired the prophets to communicate the exact message of God. He inspired the writing of the Bible.

This is claimed by the Old Testament writers themselves.

- "But the Spirit of God came even on him, and he walked along prophesying" (1 Samuel 19:23).
- "Then the Spirit of God came on Zechariah son of Jehoiada the priest. He stood before the people and said, 'This is what God says'" (2 Chronicles 24:20).
- "My Spirit, who is on you, will not depart from you, and my words that I have put in your mouth will always be on your lips" (Isaiah 59:21).
- "Then the Spirit of the LORD came on me, and he told me to say" (Ezekiel 11:5).
- "They made their hearts as hard as flint and would not listen to the law or to the words that the LORD Almighty had sent by his Spirit through the earlier prophets" (Zechariah 7:12).

The Old Testament writers were inspired by the Spirit of God to record the things they wrote.

In the New Testament, the Spirit's inspiration of the Old Testament is explicitly maintained over and over again. Jesus affirmed the authority of the Old Testament saying, for example, that not a single dot or line of the Old Testament should be broken (Matthew 5:17–20). The book of Acts declares that the Old Testament came by the Holy Spirit (Acts 1:16; 4:25). Paul pronounces the law to be holy, righteous, and good (Romans 7:12).

In the same way, Jesus promised the apostles that the Spirit would guide them in the truth that's preserved for us in the New Testament (John 14:26; 15:26; 16:13; 16:15). Paul claims to have spoken the very words of God because, as he explains, he has the Spirit of God (1 Corinthians 14:37). Paul points out that God's Word has "now been revealed by the Spirit to God's holy apostles and prophets" (Ephesians 3:5). The Scriptures are fully trustworthy because they are "God-breathed," a term that literally means "Spirited-of-God" (2 Timothy 3:16–17). The

Word of God is described as the Spirit's sword (Ephesians 6:17). Peter says that the Scripture came to us by prophets who were moved by the Holy Spirit (2 Peter 1:21).

We do not come to God merely by looking deeply within our own selves. We require specific instruction in order to follow Jesus. Without the Word, we would not even know who Jesus is! This is why the functions of the Word of God and those of the Spirit are often described in the same language in Scripture. Here are a few examples:

Function	Spirit	Word
Creating	Genesis 1:2	Hebrews 1:3; 2 Peter 3:5
Giving new birth	John 3:8	1 Peter 1:23–25
Giving life	2 Corinthians 3:6	James 1:18
Purifying	Titus 3:5	James 1:21
Sanctifying	1 Corinthians 6:11	2 Thessalonians 2:13
Indwelling	Romans 8:11	Colossians 3:16
Bearing truth	1 John 5:7	John 17:17

When we read the Word of God, we are listening to the Spirit's voice. In this way, the Word is a primary way the Spirit draws us to God. The Spirit draws us to Jesus, in part, through the Word of God.

SIGNS, WONDERS, AND POWERS

SECOND, THE SPIRIT DRAWS us to God through what the Bible typically calls signs, wonders, and powers (see 1 Corinthians 2:4–5; Ephesians 3:16–29). Whereas the Word gives us very specific instructions for how to approach God, the Spirit often provides signs, wonders, and powers in order to confirm to us the Word of God. The Word constitutes a specific and rational form of revelation. Signs, wonders, and powers constitute a general form of revelation that can transcend rational knowledge.

THE SPIRIT OFTEN PROVIDES SIGNS, WONDERS, AND POWERS TO CONFIRM TO US THE WORD OF GOD.

Many Christians, including myself, grew up in churches that held cessationist views of miracles—that is, we were taught that God doesn't do miracles anymore. Defining miracles as "things contrary to the laws of nature," we came to believe that God ceased doing things contrary to the laws of nature after the first century (hence the term "cessationist"). But we should know that this definition of miracles is not biblical, but was rather bequeathed to us by the Enlightenment philosopher David Hume, who was an agnostic. Using Hume's Enlightenment definitions, many of us were taught that the most we could hope for was "providence," which we defined as God working *through* the laws of nature.

Beholden to Hume's definitions, many of us are left with the impoverished view that God does almost nothing in our daily lives—so we experience very little of the power that the Holy Spirit offers. We are left with mere doctrines about the Spirit. Where are the blood, the fire, and the billows of smoke? In the Bible, we do not find Hume's definition of miracles. Rather, we learn that the Spirit performs all kinds of signs, wonders, and powers all of the time (whether contrary to or through the so-called "laws of nature"). In the Bible we are invited to a better definition of miracles, namely, that God acts among us in significant, powerful, or wonderful ways.

For example, the Bible calls the rainbow a "sign." It is a physical phenomenon that springs from and points to a spiritual reality. The rainbow is a sign that God will never destroy the earth by flood again. When we see a rainbow, we see a "sign" from God demonstrating his faithfulness. And such signs have not ceased. God has been performing signs since the beginning of creation, in fact, and he will never stop performing them. To miss this spiritual reality is to miss the point of the rainbow, no matter how much you understand about photons, air mass wavelengths, and receptor cells.

The Spirit places all kinds of signs before us—people of influence and natural phenomena, such as mountain vistas and terrifying storms. He places intimate signs before us, such as joy or even sickness. In each case, the Spirit is using physical phenomena to point us to spiritual realities, thereby drawing us to God. The intense human desire to receive justice is, for example, a sign that God wants us to live in his image, since he is a just God.

The same can be said of wonders and powers. The Bible does not distinguish between things done "contrary to nature" and things done "through nature" as we do today. Rather, the Bible simply affirms that God has always done powerful and wonderful things. The Spirit still uses wonders and powers to draw us to God. This is not complicated: when God gives us a gift that makes our jaws drop, that's a "wonder," and when God provides us with the resources we need in order to do something he wants, that's a "power."

At times, God's powers and wonders are so big that they defy physical explanation—such as when Jesus walked on water (Matthew 14:23–33) or when Peter raised Dorcas from the dead (Acts 9:36–43). God has often performed such physics-defying feats, and the book of Revelation indicates that God has not stopped doing these. He still does, at his discretion, such physics-defying wonders and powers. He still heals the sick, enables people to walk across water, and raises the dead. Just because these are not common in our part of the world doesn't mean they don't happen. There are numerous testimonies from reliable people all over the world that God is still doing such things, and I have personally seen such powers and wonders.[6]

At other times, however, God does less extraordinary wonders and powers—such as offering us peace during the storms of life, supplying us with people who love us, encouraging us through his church, and much more. Remember, *everything* has a spiritual dimension, and *everything* truly good comes from God.

We've been conditioned by our modern world to say that it's only a miracle when two plus three equals six. But another form of miracle occurs when two plus three equals five, even though we had neither the two nor the three necessary to get the five. God does this all the time! He is always performing signs, wonders, and powers in this sense.

Such signs, wonders, and powers are meant to draw us to Jesus. Here's how John puts it: "Jesus performed many other signs in the presence of his disciples, which are not recorded in this book. But these are written that you may believe that Jesus is the Messiah, the Son of God, and that by believing you may have life in his name" (John 20:30–31). Mark says it this way: "Then the disciples went out and preached everywhere, and the Lord worked with them and confirmed his word by the signs that accompanied it" (Mark 16:20).

So the second way the Spirit draws us to God is through the constant use of signs, wonders, and powers. To experience the work of the Spirit is to open our eyes to his power among us. It is to see and give credit to the Spirit for what he is already doing in your life—works that your theology may have caused you to miss. It is to stop using the word "luck," and to start speaking of the power of the Spirit of God in everything good that happens in life.

CONVICTION

IT IS NOT ENOUGH to have a written text of the Bible, and signs, wonders, and powers alone won't convict sinners. The Jewish people in Jesus' day had a written text that was inspired by the Holy Spirit, and they witnessed many miracles. But that was not enough. "The letter kills," Paul explains, "but the Spirit gives life" (2 Corinthians 3:6). So the Holy Spirit does more than merely give us an inspired book or perform miracles. He personally convicts our hearts so we can believe and obey God.

This is what the prophet Ezekiel promised about the coming of Jesus: "And I will put my Spirit in you and move you to follow my decrees and be careful to keep my laws" (Ezekiel 36:27). Note that in this text the Spirit works consistently with the Word of God, but apart from it too. This was also the case for Lydia. When Paul preached the Word to her, "The Lord opened her heart to respond to Paul's message" (Acts 16:14). Note that there is a twofold work of the Spirit in this text: the proclamation of the Word *and* the opening of the heart.

God gives us the written Word, but we require the movement of the Spirit in order to obey it. We are simply too sinful to make fully good choices on our own, so the Spirit moves our hearts to say *yes*. The work of the Spirit includes knowledge, but it also *transcends knowledge*: "Out of his glorious riches he may strengthen you with power through his Spirit in your inner being . . . to know this love that *surpasses knowledge*" (Ephesians 3:16–19).

> GOD GIVES US THE WRITTEN WORD, BUT WE REQUIRE THE MOVEMENT OF THE SPIRIT IN ORDER TO OBEY IT.

Perhaps this convicting work of the Spirit is what is meant in other texts where we read of hearts being moved by God. God moved the heart of Cyrus and of Ezra (2 Chronicles 36:22; Ezra 1:5). God puts things on the hearts of David, Nehemiah, and Titus (1 Chronicles 28:12; Ezra 1:1; Nehemiah 2:12; 7:5; 2 Corinthians 8:16). The phrase "moving the heart" seems to describe the Spirit impressing truth in a new or persuasive way in the mind of the listener. When the phrase is used in Ezra and Nehemiah, the Lord is not revealing new truths but opening up the hearts of those who already have his truth to see its full implications.

So how does the Spirit convict our hearts? We sense the voice of God within our human spirit. It is a quiet, prompting voice by which God seeks to lead, guide, and fill us (Galatians 5:18; 5:25; Ephesians 5:18). It is resistible because Scripture describes people resisting the Spirit (Acts 7:51). But by his personal presence, the Spirit will lead us and guide us and impress on us things that only come from God. Paul's prayer about the convicting work of the Spirit is thrilling yet somewhat mystical: "that the eyes of your heart may be enlightened in order that you may know the hope to which he has called you" (Ephesians 1:18). Perhaps it is enough to say that when you feel convicted to obey the Word of God, that's the Holy Spirit.

One more word about how the Holy Spirit moves in us. We must be cautious about the convicting work of the Spirit, for there are other spirits who want to convict us as well (1 John 4:1). These false spirits encourage us to follow our own sentiments and to label them the work of the Spirit. We should always test our feelings by consulting other believers and the Scriptures themselves. There are few dangers greater than confusing our thoughts with the thoughts of the Spirit.[7]

However we are drawn to Jesus, we must affirm that we require the Spirit's movement in our hearts in order to be drawn.

3

WHAT DOES IT MEAN FOR THE HOLY SPIRIT TO LIVE WITHIN US?

Answer: The Spirit lives within us by immersing us in a relationship with God and by transforming us into the image of Christ.

And we all, who with unveiled faces contemplate the Lord's glory, are being transformed into his image with ever-increasing glory, which comes from the Lord, who is the Spirit.
— 2 Corinthians 3:18

The Holy Spirit is everywhere at all times because he is God. This is implied in the opening verses of the Bible, where the Spirit of God is described as hovering over creation (Genesis 1:2). In a special sense, however, the Holy Spirit lives within us as believers. The Old Testament prophets had promised that the Spirit would be widely available to the people of God in these last days (Isaiah 44:3–4; Joel 2:28–29; Ezekiel 37:1–14). John the Baptist preached that though his baptism was in water Jesus would baptize his followers in the Holy Spirit (Matthew 3:11). Jesus himself promised the disciples that they would receive the Spirit whom "the world cannot receive" (John 14:17, KJV). And Peter announced that the Spirit is given to all who obey Christ (Acts 5:32). The rest of the New Testament indicates that having the Spirit within us is a mark that we belong to Christ and are separate from the world (Romans 8:11; 1 Corinthians 6:19; Galatians 5:18; 2 Timothy 1:14). As Paul says, "Because you are his sons, God sent the Spirit of his Son into our hearts, the Spirit who calls out, 'Abba, Father'" (Galatians 4:6).

So what does it mean for the Spirit to live within those of us who believe?

THE SPIRIT PROVIDES US AN IMMERSIVE EXPERIENCE IN GOD

LET'S START BY DESCRIBING the normative way that believers receive the Holy Spirit: through faith in Christ.[8] Jesus promised that the Spirit would be given to those who believe: "'Whoever believes in me, as Scripture has said, rivers of living water will flow from within them.' By this he meant the Spirit, whom those who believed in him were later to receive" (John 7:38–39). This is also what Paul affirms in his rhetorical question to the Galatians: "Did you receive the Spirit by the works of the law, or by believing what you heard?" (Galatians 3:2). He goes on: "He redeemed us in order that the blessing given to Abraham might come to the Gentiles through Christ Jesus, so that *by faith* we might receive the promise of the Spirit" (Galatians 3:14).

In the same way that we receive the indwelling Father and Son upon our profession of faith, we also receive the Holy Spirit (see also Ephesians 3:17; John 14:23).

There are several important metaphors for our reception of the Spirit that are used in Scripture. One is that of new birth. Jesus puts it this way: "Very truly I tell you, no one can enter the kingdom of God unless they are born of water and the Spirit. Flesh gives birth to flesh, but the Spirit gives birth to spirit" (John 3:5–6). The idea Jesus presents here is that our conversion changes our very nature from that of what he calls "the flesh" to that of the Spirit. To receive the Spirit is to adopt a new mode of living that is different from that of the world—to live by spiritual means rather than by the bodily lusts. This is why the Bible can say that we are made alive *through* the Spirit (John 6:63; Romans 8:2). Real life is not the life of lusts and bodily pleasures. Real life is spiritual life in Christ. When we are born of the Spirit, we become God's children, and the Spirit himself testifies that we now belong to God (Romans 8:16; Galatians 4:6).

We should not neglect the reference to water in John 3, since baptism provides a second metaphor for our reception of the Holy Spirit. John the Baptist had promised that Jesus would baptize believers in the Holy Spirit. Just prior to his ascension, Jesus told the disciples to remain in Jerusalem until they received this promised Holy Spirit. Then in Acts 2, the disciples received the outpouring of the Spirit and used the occasion to preach the first sermon about the resurrected Jesus. They concluded the sermon by promising all who repented and were baptized that they too would receive the Holy Spirit: "The promise is for you and your children and for all who are far off—for all whom the Lord our God will call" (Acts 2:39).

The Bible links water baptism to an immersion in the Holy Spirit. Just as believers are baptized in water to wash away sins, so we are baptized in the Spirit to become new creatures, typically at the same time (Acts 22:16).[9]

This explains why Jesus' final words in Matthew 28:18–20 include the command for the disciples to baptize *into* the name of the Father, the Son, and the Holy Spirit (AT). The word "into" (*eis* in Greek) does not mean "by the authority of" but rather "into a relationship with." Jesus' command for us to baptize "into the name of the Spirit" implies that baptism is the point at which we enter a relationship with the Spirit. So when Paul is urging Christian unity, he refers to our Holy Spirit baptism: "For we were all baptized by one Spirit so as to form one body—whether Jews or Gentiles, slave or free—and we were all given the one Spirit to drink" (1 Corinthians 12:13). And when speaking of our salvation, Paul says, "He saved us through the washing of rebirth and renewal by the Holy Spirit, whom he poured out on us generously through Jesus Christ our Savior" (Titus 3:5–6).

To say that we are "baptized in the Spirit" is to say that at the moment of our justification, we are offered an immersive experience in the Spirit of God. No wonder he is called a gift (Acts 2:38–39)! Faith accompanied by water baptism constitutes the normative way that we receive the Holy Spirit.[10]

THE SPIRIT TRANSFORMS US INTO THE IMAGE OF CHRIST

So WE RECEIVE THE Spirit when we respond in faith to Jesus Christ—typically at the point of our water baptism. But what is the role of the Spirit in our lives? In the next chapter, we'll look at some ways that the Spirit equips us for the work of Jesus, but here, let's explore the most fundamental work of the Spirit: he transforms us into the image of Jesus. In fact, transformation is the real essence of the Spirit's work. Everywhere we read of him in the Bible, the Spirit is working to effect a transformation of God's creation or of God's people. This is true in the historical sections of the Old Testament, where the Spirit occasionally appears as an undefined power—at times even an event—who dynamically swept down upon persons to accomplish God's will. This is also true in the prophetic passages of the Old Testament, where the Spirit was more rational and functioned to give knowledge to the people of God. And it is true in the writings of Paul, where we learn that the Spirit's very substance provides the realm for

> TRANSFORMATION IS THE REAL ESSENCE OF THE SPIRIT'S WORK.

a new existence for disciples of Christ. In each case, the Spirit works to transform the creation according to God's will.

Paul describes the transformational role of the Spirit in beautiful language. Arguing that the Jews had an inspired book but needed more, Paul states that Christians get an inspired book plus the power of the Holy Spirit: "Now the Lord is the Spirit, and where the Spirit of the Lord is, there is freedom. And we all, who with unveiled faces contemplate the Lord's glory, are being transformed into his image with ever-increasing glory, which comes from the Lord, who is the Spirit" (2 Corinthians 3:17–18).

The Spirit works inside of us, transforming us into the image of Christ by joining with our own spirits. This is, at least in part, what is meant by the metaphor of a seal, which Paul uses a couple of times with regards to the Holy Spirit. In the Greco-Roman world, important documents were stamped with a seal that confirmed ownership and authenticity. The seal often had an image on it that reflected the name or character of the owner. Twice in the New Testament Paul says that the Holy Spirit is God's seal on believers, giving us a down payment for the life we'll enjoy after the resurrection (2 Corinthians 1:22; Ephesians 1:13). The Holy Spirit bears in us the image of God who is working to mature us spiritually.

If we were to use biological terms, we could say that the Holy Spirit is God's own DNA transplanted into our lives upon our baptism. Our physical DNA determines a great deal about our lives—what we will look like, what strengths we will possess, and how we will interact with the world. As we grow older, our DNA often makes us look more and more like one or both of our parents. For instance, the older I get, the more I look like my mother.

In the same way, our spiritual DNA is provided for us in the person of the Holy Spirit, God's image stamped on our hearts. When we faithfully obey, the Spirit responds by bringing out the Jesus in us until, one day, we mature fully into his image. In theological terminology, the Spirit "sanctifies us"—meaning the Spirit takes us after our justification and leads us to the power, the beauty, and the truthfulness of a fully spiritual life. We should never underestimate the power that comes from having God personally dwell in us through his Spirit. We are, quite literally, temples of the Spirit (1 Corinthians 6:19; 1 Corinthians 3:16). Having God dwell in us through his Spirit changes who we are; through the Spirit we literally participate in the divine nature of God (2 Peter 1:4).

This is what is meant by the phrase "filled with the Spirit." Though this term sometimes means in Scripture that a person is given some extraordinary power, it often only means that a person has become fully spiritual. For example, Barnabas is described in Acts 11:24 as "full of the Holy Spirit." Here the term seems to signify that he was a spiritually mature person.

It is in this sense that the Scriptures can actually *command* us to be filled with the Spirit (Ephesians 5:18). As we allow the Spirit to shape us into the image of Jesus, we become full of the Spirit. It is worth noting that Paul's command in Ephesians 5 to be "filled with the Spirit" is qualified by a participial phrase "*by* (or *while*) speaking to one another with psalms, hymns, and songs from the Spirit, singing and making music from your heart to the Lord always giving thanks to God . . . and submitting to one another" (Ephesians 5:19–21, AT). Singing, praising, giving thanks, and submitting to one another are a means given in this text for becoming spiritual. We fill ourselves with the Spirit when we sing, praise, give thanks, and love others.

Other phrases describe the transformational work of the Spirit in the Bible. Jesus promised to clothe the apostles with the power of the Spirit (Luke 24:49). We are taught to be led by the Spirit (Galatians 5:18). We should walk by the Spirit (Galatians 5:18). We are invited into a fellowship with the Spirit (1 Corinthians 12:13). And we can be strengthened inwardly through the power of the Spirit (Ephesians 3:16–17).

How does the Spirit sanctify us? We'll deal with this question in the next chapter, but here we must say at least one thing. The Spirit serves to draw attention to Jesus, who bears the fullness of the image of God. In Jesus' own words, the Spirit will "remind you of everything I [Jesus] have said to you"; will "testify about me"; and will "speak only what he hears" because "it is from me that he will receive what he will make known to you" (John 14:26; 15:26; 16:13–15). Discipleship is following Jesus in the power of the Spirit.

DISCIPLESHIP IS FOLLOWING JESUS IN THE POWER OF THE SPIRIT.

We cannot become like Jesus without divine help. So God gives us a new birth in the Spirit; Christ baptizes us in the Spirit; and we are invited to be full of the Spirit. And all of this is for one overarching reason: to transform us into the image of him whom we follow.

4

HOW DOES THE HOLY SPIRIT MAKE US LIKE JESUS?

Answer: The Holy Spirit makes us like Jesus by uniting us with other believers, by interceding with the Father on our behalf, by producing the goodness of Jesus in our lives, and by equipping us for the mission of Jesus.

But the fruit of the Spirit is love, joy, peace, forbearance, kindness, goodness, faithfulness, gentleness and self-control. Against such things there is no law.
— Galatians 5:22–23

So the Holy Spirit transforms us into the image of Jesus. This is *his work*, not ours. But how does he work? Can we say exactly what the Spirit does to transform us into Christ's image? A full answer to this question would require volumes of material, but for our purposes, I'll summarize the methods of the Spirit's work under four headings. Each heading is a biblical category from which we'll draw out implications for how the Spirit transforms our lives.

THE SPIRIT UNITES US WITH OTHER BELIEVERS

First, we should note that following Jesus is not a solitary endeavor. When we become a believer, we join a worldwide communion of believers, and our relationship with them is critical to our becoming like Jesus. Just as God lives in the communion of a Holy Trinity, so we live in a holy communion—of the church.

Not only are our individual bodies temples of the Spirit; the collective body of the church is a temple of the Holy Spirit (1 Corinthians 3:16–17). We are united to one another through the same Spirit (1 Corinthians 12:13), and it is through the church that we unite to serve as priests to the world, offering up to God our sacrifice, worship, praise, and intercession. We are united together through him. It's worth noting that 1 Corinthians and Ephesians—two books that mention the Spirit as much as any in the Bible—mention him often in connection with the unity and fellowship of the community of believers.

Nothing compares to the beauty of a united fellowship whose members know that they all share in the same Spirit. We love each other in the same Spirit (Philippians 2:2); we unite with one another through the power of the Spirit (Ephesians 4:3); and we refuse to divide with one another because of the work of the Spirit (1 Corinthians 3:16ff). In fact, every "one another" command in the New Testament is possible for the believer only because we are bound together by the Spirit.

The result? The unity of the Spirit in the church allows us to present ourselves to the world as the mature body of Christ, unwavering in our faith (Ephesians 4:9–16).

THE SPIRIT INTERCEDES WITH THE FATHER ON OUR BEHALF

The Holy Spirit also intercedes with the Father on our behalf. Jesus had promised that he would give the apostles the Holy Spirit, whom he called "the Counselor"—a term that could well be translated as "the Attorney" (John 14:16, AT). By using this term, Jesus envisioned the Spirit working as an intermediary. Paul goes further on this, explaining that "he who searches our hearts knows the mind of the Spirit, because the Spirit intercedes for God's people in accordance with the will of God" (Romans 8:27). Throughout Romans 8 Paul indicates how the Spirit does this: he sets us free from the bondage of our broken will, which chains us to our sin. He does this by dwelling within us, replacing our broken will by the power of God. And this power breaks our chains. The more we are filled with the Spirit, the less we want to sin, and the freer we become. The Spirit sets us free, and in that sense, he can be said to intercede for us.

Perhaps another way to envision the intercessory work of the Spirit is to imagine him witnessing to the Father about our struggles, our efforts, our fruit, and our mission—all of which he can do because he lives within us and knows us well. In any case, the intercessory work of the Spirit is what enables us to cry out "Abba" to God in our time of need (Romans 8:15).

He joins us to God just as our physical DNA joins us to our parents. He presents our case to God. When we struggle, suffer, experience despair, or face loneliness, the Holy Spirit appeals to the Father on our behalf. He offers us a pathway to God's healing grace.

THE SPIRIT PRODUCES THE GOODNESS OF JESUS IN OUR LIVES

IN GALATIANS 5, PAUL contrasts the works of the flesh with the virtues of the Spirit. "But the fruit of the Spirit is love, joy, peace, forbearance, kindness, goodness, faithfulness, gentleness and self-control" (Galatians 5:22–23). Having the Spirit's fruit in our lives, he explains, is to "live by the Spirit" and "keep in step with the Spirit" (v. 25). The Spirit makes us like Jesus by producing the goodness of Jesus in our lives.

It is important to note Paul's use of the term "fruit" in this text. Paul does not call the nine virtues of Galatians 5 "works," even though we must put forth effort to attain them. Rather, he terms these virtues "fruit." "Fruit" suggests that these moral traits will naturally flow out of those who live in the Spirit. In other words, if we permit the Spirit to have his way in our lives, a virtuous, Christlike life will emerge. Even though they must be cultivated, apple trees don't have to work at producing apples—it is in their DNA. And though Christian virtues must be cultivated in the life of the believer, Spirit-filled people naturally produce the virtues of Christ. It's in their DNA.

> SPIRIT-FILLED PEOPLE NATURALLY PRODUCE THE VIRTUES OF CHRIST.

Indeed, without the Spirit, we simply cannot produce the fruit of a Jesus-styled life, for without the Spirit we are forever stuck in the weakness of the flesh. We face a spiritual battle, and flesh alone cannot defeat the spiritual forces of evil (Ephesians 6:12). Victory requires the power of God's Spirit. Jesus is said to have cast out evil spirits through the power of God's Holy Spirit (Matthew 12:28). In the same way, to overcome the sinful desires of the body, we need the power of the Spirit of God.

At this point, it is important to note several texts that give us a warning about the work of the Spirit: Ephesians 4:30, which warns us not to grieve the Spirit; 1 Thessalonians 5:19, which teaches us not to put out the Spirit's fire; and

Mark 3:28–30, where Jesus warns us about speaking against the Holy Spirit.[11] These warnings reveal an important truth: we cannot *force* the Spirit to work in us, no more than one can force an apple tree to produce apples. But we can *hinder* the work of the Spirit, just as we can hinder the growth of apples through neglecting the tree. We are taught to seek God according to the Spirit, so that we will set our minds on what the Spirit desires (Romans 8: 5–6). If we do not pursue God this way but live by our flesh, we will thwart the work of the Spirit and hinder the fruit he wants to produce in us. This is why we have an obligation to put to death the misdeeds of the body so that the Spirit can produce the fruit of rightness in our lives (Romans 8:12–13). We are encouraged to keep alive our "spiritual fervor" (Romans 12:11). The Spirit does not override our free will, as 1 Corinthians 14 makes clear (see, for example, 14:32). Rather, the Spirit acts in concert with our will, empowering us to choose that which is holy, while leaving us free to choose—at our peril—to be unholy.

If we cultivate the Spirit in our lives, he will produce in us the goodness of Jesus—from one degree of glory to another.

THE SPIRIT EQUIPS US FOR THE MISSION OF JESUS

IN ADDITION TO JOINING us to the people of God, interceding for us, and producing fruit in our lives, the Holy Spirit distributes gifts to equip us for the mission of Jesus. In the Old Testament, the Spirit equipped certain people to perform the tasks to which God had called them. He gave Samson his strength (Judges 15:14); he supplied the seventy elders with their judicial abilities (Numbers 11:17); he gave David leadership powers (1 Samuel 16:13); and he even gave technical skill to Bezalel, who made designs for the tabernacle (Exodus 31:2–3).

Three passages in the New Testament list the main spiritual gifts the Spirit gives to Christians: Romans 12, 1 Corinthians 12, and Ephesians 4. In these texts, the gifts sometimes appear to describe a limited office of some sort. At other times, however, these gifts appear to be general in nature—referring to any power, talent, or opportunity given by God for the purpose of fulfilling the mission of Jesus.

Before we look at some specific gifts, it is important we remember that all the gifts are given for the purpose of building up the body. They are not given for personal gratification: "Now to each one the manifestation of the Spirit is given for the common good" (1 Corinthians 12:7). This point matters greatly because we might be tempted to seek the gifts for our own gratification, but that's not why the Spirit gives his gifts. He gives them so we can carry out the mission of Jesus (Romans 12:4ff; Ephesians 4:12ff).

So what about the gifts? The more general gifts of the Spirit include such things as generosity, encouragement, leadership, discernment, and the like. It is fairly obvious how these gifts can be used to build up the body of Christ. If you have the gift of generosity, you should actively seek ways to fund good works for Jesus. If you have the gift of leadership, you should offer it to help others mature in faith. If you are an encourager, you should seek ways to lift up others. If you are a teacher, you should help others come to know the truth of Christ.

In addition to what appear to be these more ordinary gifts, however, there are other gifts mentioned in the New Testament that seem specialized—even comparable to an office. Let's take a brief look at three of these.

Apostleship. Though occasionally the Greek term for "apostle" may mean "missionary" in the Bible (e.g., Romans 16:7), there is a specialized use of the term "apostle" that refers to the twelve inspired disciples called during the earthly ministry of Jesus (as well as their designated successors—Matthias and Paul). The apostles were endowed with the authority to reveal the Word on behalf of Jesus (Matthew 16:16–18; John 14–16). They were expected to have been with Jesus personally (Acts 1:21–22). They demonstrated their authority as apostles through their ability to perform signs, wonders, and powers (2 Corinthians 12:12; Hebrews 2:2–4). Apostles were chosen directly by the Lord (see Mark 3:13–19; Galatians 1:1). They were given the keys to the kingdom of God (Matthew 16:16–19). They had the ability to confer gifts on others (Acts 8:17–18). The apostles have a unique place in heaven: their names are inscribed forever in the foundations of heaven's wall (Revelation 21:14). Peter says that we are to embrace the command of the Lord as it was given through the apostles (2 Peter 3:2). Believers today participate in the work of the apostles when we accept their writings, the Scriptures. Though we still have "missionaries" in the contemporary church, we should not claim the title "apostle" today—at least not in the sense of the Twelve—since the office of the apostle was restricted to the Twelve plus Paul and perhaps a few others, and these were not replaced in subsequent generations with others who held their unique status.[12]

Prophet. In the Old Testament, the gift of prophecy was given to ensure that the people of God received the reliable and infallible Word of God. It appears that the New Testament may sometimes use the term "prophet" in a more general way—simply as one who proclaims the Word of God based on the works of the inspired authors of Scripture.[13] This seems to be the case in 1 Corinthians 14, where it seems that a number of church members were taking turns "prophesying." In a stricter sense, however, the default New Testament use of "prophet" meant someone who held a similar office as did an "apostle," and the gift of prophecy was limited primarily to those who worked alongside the apostles. This is why Ephesians 2:18–19 says that the church is built upon the foundation of the apostles and prophets. It also explains why Peter can affirm that the writings of the prophets did not have their origins in the minds of the prophets, but were delivered by the Spirit himself (2 Peter 1:20–21). The work of these prophets is preserved for us in the Scriptures, alongside the work of the apostles.

As we think of prophecy, we should be mindful that the Bible repeatedly warns against false prophets and false prophecies, as it also warns against false apostles.[14] Not everyone who claims to be speaking the very words of God should be believed. Rather, we are to test people's claims against the truth of Scripture. Those who fabricate utterances in the name of God are guilty of a serious sin.

Miracle worker and healer. Paul does not define these gifts when he mentions them in 1 Corinthians 12, but they seem to mean someone who can perform, by the power of the Spirit, powerful deeds such as healing the sick. The New Testament rarely gives examples of anyone working miracles or healing others except for Jesus and the apostles, so we should not assume that receiving the Spirit automatically gives us the ability to perform these powers. After all, none other than John the Baptist was filled with the Spirit, but he never performed a miracle (Luke 1:15; John 10:41). Whether or not we can receive the gift of powers today, we must, however, always gratefully accept that *God* still performs powers. Healings still occur, regardless of whether or not the Spirit gives *us* that particular gift.

Speaking in tongues. In addition to these three "offices," the Bible also mentions the phenomenon of tongue-speaking. What is tongue-speaking? The question has been much debated in Christian history, especially in the last one hundred years. We should note that the subject is only occasionally mentioned in the Bible; only a handful of texts bring it up (Mark 16:17; Acts 2; 19:6; and 1 Corinthians 12–14). In technical language, the phenomenon is called "glossolalia" in English, which is a combination of the Greek terms for "tongues" and "speaking." There appear to be two kinds of glossolalia in the New Testament, although the New Testament doesn't distinguish these. The first is when a speaker appears to speak in a real human language that the speaker doesn't actually know. We might call this "xenolalia" (although the term is not used in the New Testament). Xenolalia appears to be what happened in Acts 2, where the early church preached in numerous languages that are even called "dialects" by Luke (Acts 2:8, AT). The second use of "tongues" appears to be private utterances—not words of an actual human language. We might call this "idiolalia" (although, again, the term is not used in the New Testament). Idiolalia can range from private groans all the way to the rhythmic utterance of syllables using tones and inflections and sounding a lot like a real human language.

Xenolalia is likely rare based on its rarity in the New Testament, although we have examples of missionaries using this gift, even in the twenty-first century.

If idiolalia includes "groaning with words we cannot utter," as mentioned in Romans 8:26 (AT), the phenomenon appears to be widespread among believers. Who hasn't groaned in times of distress with sighs and moans that are not actual language? If by "idiolalia" we mean the full expression of syllables spoken like a real language (although not any known language), the phenomenon is generally practiced only by those who identify as charismatics.[15] In either case, such idiolalia shouldn't pretend to be authoritative, as though it possesses apostolic or prophetic authority. Rather, it is simply the soul bypassing ordinary language in response to the ups and downs of the Christian life—not unlike humming, self-talk, or even a person singing unaware. It is like the soothing baby talk a child uses to calm themselves down.[16]

We should note that Paul limits the use of *tongues*: it should not be done in a congregational gathering unless it can be interpreted (1 Corinthians 14:19, 26, 28), and it should be used in public only if it builds up the body of believers.

What are we to make of the gifts of prophecy, healing, and tongues today? Though claims to these gifts are very common in today's global church, for centuries such claims were rare. In fact, for most of the history of the church, the foundation of the Scriptures, the service of the pastor, and the teaching ministry of the church were understood to have made prophecy, healing, and tongues unnecessary. But perspectives changed in the opening years of the 1900s, when the Pentecostal movement broke out in America. Though Pentecostalism started with only a few thousand members, various charismatic practices born out of Pentecostalism are now embraced by as many as half of the world's Christians.[17]

The leaders at the Renew.org Network have different understandings on specifics with regard to the gifts of the Spirit, even though all our leaders agree to seek all that God has for us through his Spirit. The Renew.org Network is a movement that relies on God's Spirit, especially through the classic spiritual habits of regular fasting and prayer. Some of our leaders do not see God fully activating the special gifts of tongues, prophecy, or healing today, while others do witness and uphold those activations.

I personally believe that, rightly understood, God still gives these gifts. God still gives some the ability to speak truth to current circumstances (prophecy). He still gives some a special calling to pray for healing, prayers to which he often says yes (healing). And he still gives, on occasion, xenolalia, and, much more commonly, idiolalia (tongue-speaking).

Even so, I do not believe these gifts are inspired in the same way as were the prophets and apostles of the Bible. Indeed, no gift we might receive today should be viewed as possessing the same authority as Scripture. Scripture was written under the unique inspiration of the apostles, and so Scripture possesses final authority. Scripture is infallible. We are not apostles, nor do we live in the apostolic age.

SCRIPTURE POSSESSES FINAL AUTHORITY. SCRIPTURE IS INFALLIBLE.

So none of our gifts should claim such inspiration, infallibility, or apostolic authority. Rather, our gifts are designed to encourage us to go back to the authority of the inspired and infallible Bible. Nothing can stand in the place of the Scriptures.

Further, we should exercise caution with respect to these spiritual gifts. Not every claim of prophecy, healing, and tongues represents authentic works of the Holy Spirit. There are well-documented examples of frauds who have claimed to possess such gifts—one only need think of the myriad of television evangelists whose deceit has been exposed. Such individuals and their thousands of supporters are an embarrassment to the church. They insult the Spirit. Further, some prominent charismatic leaders have been associated with heretical teachings—such as denying the deity of Christ or preaching the health-and-wealth gospel. The association of claims of prophecy and tongues with such heresies is a caution against accepting every claim to such gifts. The church should not discourage the gifts of God when rightly understood. But the church also should not accept every claim that is made. Discernment and wisdom should guide us in exercising the gifts the Spirit gives.

Those who seek the empowerment and use of these special gifts in a public manner should seek to use them in step with the leadership of their local church and with what is fitting and orderly (1 Corinthians 14:40).

To conclude, then, the Spirit distributes gifts for the building up of the body, and in this way, he helps transform us into the image of Jesus. While we can describe the ways the Spirit does this, we should not be surprised that his gifting will remain something of a mystery. As Jesus says, the Spirit moves like the wind—we see its effects, but cannot really tell how it works (John 3:8). Regardless of how the Spirit does it, because we have him in our lives, we can become like our Lord. So we should seek the gifts of the Lord, and in so doing, we can experience his power in our lives (1 Corinthians 14:1).

5

HOW DO WE SEEK THE HOLY SPIRIT'S LEADERSHIP IN OUR LIVES?

Answer: We open our lives to the Holy Spirit's leadership with spiritual practices such as prayer, fasting, and virtuous living.

And pray in the Spirit on all occasions with all kinds of prayers and requests. With this in mind, be alert and always keep on praying for all the Lord's people.
— Ephesians 6:18

Several Scripture passages mention being "led by the Spirit":

- "Teach me to do your will, for you are my God; may your good Spirit lead me on level ground" (Psalm 143:10).
- "Then Jesus was led by the Spirit into the wilderness to be tempted by the devil" (Matthew 4:1).
- "For those who are led by the Spirit of God are the children of God" (Romans 8:14).
- "He carried me away in the Spirit to a mountain great and high, and showed me the Holy City, Jerusalem, coming down out of heaven from God" (Revelation 21:10).

Though the term "led by the Spirit" sometimes appears simply to mean that a person is in deep communion with God, at other times the term appears to be closely connected to prayer, fasting, and even the feeling of being compelled to do something virtuous (e.g., Ezekiel 37:1; Mark 1:12; Acts 8:29; 15:28; 16:6–7; 20:22; Revelation 4:2). In light of these Scripture passages, how are we led by the Spirit today?

I have already stated that we cannot control or manipulate the Spirit. We can only submit to the divine work that he wants to do. But this does not mean that there is nothing we should do. On the contrary, in addition to repenting of our sin and focusing our life on Jesus, we must ask the Spirit to have his way in our lives. This is of critical importance. If we do not ask, we will not receive.

WE MUST ASK THE SPIRIT TO HAVE HIS WAY IN OUR LIVES.

So, at the simplest level, we are led by the Spirit when we ask God to show us the spiritual dimension of our lives and live out his response. For example, when struggling in your marriage, being led by the Spirit can mean looking at your struggle not as between flesh and blood, but between the Holy Spirit *in us* and the powers of evil working *against us*. It involves perceiving the lies the evil one uses to make you bitter, rageful, unfaithful, and the like. It involves asking the Spirit to use your struggles to create in you love, righteousness, faith, hope, and the like (Ephesians 6:10ff).

Consider how this is like running a race. I've run numerous charity races in my life, and at every one of them I've seen encouragers standing on the side of the road. They supply water, shout out encouragement, and remind me of how little distance I have to go. The race depends on my legs and lungs. But the commentary on the race is offered by the encouragers, who help me remember why I chose such a painful activity. In the same way, whenever we seek to live a godlike life, there are spiritual forces of evil shouting out lies to us: "You cannot do this," "It's not worth it," "You should cheat," and the like. But there is also the Holy Spirit cheering us on: "This will save lives," "You are doing the right thing," "You will finish strong." Being led by the Spirit involves refusing to listen to the lies of the evil one. Instead, we listen to the voice of the Spirit.

This is, at least in part, what it means to say that the Spirit tugs at our consciences, opens the eyes of our hearts, and gives us spiritual aspirations. This is promised in Acts 2, when Peter preached that the last days—in which we currently find ourselves—will be marked by dreams and visions from the Spirit. Peter concluded his sermon by saying that this same Spirit was available to anyone who repented and was baptized—"for all whom the Lord our God will call" (Acts 2:17–18, 38–39).

And as in biblical examples, being led by the Spirit today is closely connected to prayer and fasting. Indeed, it may be that the Spirit holds the deepest levels of guidance *only* for those who are fully devoted to prayer and fasting. And so we see a connection between prayer and the Holy Spirit in the Scriptures. Paul commands us to "pray in the Spirit" on all occasions, and he connects this with spiritual alertness (Ephesians 6:18–19). Jude says something similar, connecting prayer in the Spirit with actively waiting for the coming Jesus (Jude 20–21). Jesus said that the Father will give the Holy Spirit to those who ask (Luke 11:13).

So in order to be led by the Spirit, we must learn the disciplines, especially those focused on prayer and fasting. This makes sense for through intense prayer and fasting we empty ourselves of fleshly desires and worldly interests and become increasingly dependent on the power of God. It's worth remembering that the outpouring of the Holy Spirit in Acts 2:19—described with such awe-inspiring terms as "blood, fire, and billows of smoke"—came only after the church had constantly devoted itself to prayer in Acts 1:14. If we want Acts 2 results, we must practice Acts 1 prayer.

In fact, it's possible that one reason why many of us rarely experience signs, wonders, and powers in our lives is that we don't seriously pray, fast, or take great risks of faith for Christ. Powerful experiences are regular occurrences for those who take great risks, who fast intensely, who pray day and night—for those who are so deeply immersed in the Spirit that they become wholly unconcerned with what the world might think. If you live a spiritually boring life, you will get spiritually boring results. But when you stick out your neck for Christ, seasoned by prayer and fasting, you will see more and more signs, wonders, and powers. It just grows more for those who are increasingly led by the Spirit of God.

IF YOU LIVE A SPIRITUALLY BORING LIFE, YOU WILL GET SPIRITUALLY BORING RESULTS.

The Holy Spirit will not force you to follow his lead, and the world with its secular veil will make following the Spirit difficult. But if you want to be led by the Spirit and thereby experience the richness of life that God has intended for you, devote yourself to prayer and fasting. There the Spirit opens the eyes of our hearts and draws us to him. Devote yourself to prayer and fasting, and the Spirit will respond in one way or another. You will see him, and he will lead you where he wants you to go. You will experience the power, the fruit, and the transformation the Spirit provides.

There is a spiritual dimension to everything we do. Look for it, and live in that dimension. Refuse to follow the fleshly side of life. Follow the spiritual life instead.

CONCLUSION

The Holy Spirit is essential to the life of the believer. In fact, it is not possible to be a follower of Jesus without the Spirit of God: "If anyone does not have the Spirit of Christ, they do not belong to Christ" (Romans 8:9). But with the Holy Spirit in our lives, we celebrate our status as God's children (Romans 8:14–15) who receive the love of God poured into our hearts (Romans 5:5), liberating us from the bondage of sin and death (Romans 8:2–4), giving us life and peace (Romans 8:6), including us in Christ (Romans 8:9), sanctifying us (Romans 15:16), washing us (1 Corinthians 6:11), transforming us (2 Corinthians 3:17–18), producing fruit in us (Galatians 5:22–23), and giving us access to the Father (Ephesians 2:18).

With the Holy Spirit, we discover who God is, and we are empowered to become like him. Thank God for his Spirit!

I once read an imaginative story about a man who had a dream in which he visited heaven's mansion. While there, he was taken by the Lord into heaven's library, where he began to browse the amazing collection. Soon, he found a volume on a shelf that contained the complete biography of the man's life. Thrilled, he opened the book and read of all sorts of amazing things that the Spirit had accomplished in his life—people he had brought to the Lord, amazing powers and wonders he had experienced, boundless fruit God had developed in his life, a profound sense of peace and joy that permeated everything he did, and a whole lot more.

Looking at the Lord, he said, "Lord, this is a fantastic biography of my life, but there's a problem. I never experienced any of this. It's not accurate!" The Lord responded by reaching for a flimsy manila folder that had only a page or two of handwritten notes in it. "You're right," the Lord responded. Then, handing the manila folder to the man, the Lord explained: "This folder is your *actual* biography. The amazing biography in the big book is the life I wanted to give you. It's what you would have had if you had asked for my Spirit!"

The Holy Spirit is here! May God give us the insight and courage to ask for him—and act in faithful obedience to receive the life God wants to give us by his Spirit.

APPENDIX

BOOK RECOMMENDATIONS
FOR FURTHER STUDY

Leonard Allen, *Poured Out: The Spirit of God Empowering the Mission of God* (Abilene: ACU Press, 2018).

Francis Chan, *Forgotten God: Reversing Our Tragic Neglect of the Holy Spirit* (Colorado Springs: David C. Cook, 2009).

Gordon Fee, *God's Empowering Presence: The Holy Spirit in the Letters of Paul* (Peabody: Hendrickson Publishers, 1994).

Michael Green, *I Believe in the Holy Spirit* (Grand Rapids: Eerdmans, 1975).

David Roadcup, Michael Eagle, et al., *Prayer and Fasting: Moving with the Spirit to Renew Our Minds, Bodies, and Churches* (Renew.org, 2020).

M. James Sawyer and Daniel B. Wallace, eds., *Who's Afraid of the Holy Spirit?* (Dallas: Biblical Studies Press, 2005).

NOTES

1. The grammar surrounding the word "spirit" in the Bible is a bit complex. The Old Testament word for "spirit" is a feminine word. Grammatically, a feminine pronoun (she) can be used with the Hebrew word for "spirit," and feminine verbal forms are used with the phrase "Spirit of the Lord" in the Hebrew Old Testament (e.g., Judges 3:10; 1 Samuel 10:6). In the New Testament, the Greek word for "spirit" is neuter, being neither masculine nor feminine. Grammatically, the Greek word should take the pronoun "it." In biblical Hebrew and Greek, however, gender is usually a grammatical construct and not a gendered one. In other words, having a feminine noun for the word "spirit" does not necessarily imply that the Hebrews thought of the Spirit as feminine, and having a neuter noun in Greek does not imply that Greeks thought of the Spirit as non-personal. Since the Spirit is a person and a member of the Godhead, it is proper to refer to the Spirit as "he." To refer to the Spirit as "it" is not wrong, but this may create confusion about his personal nature. To refer to the Spirit as "she" in English would be misleading, since the English word "spirit" is not feminine (even though the Hebrew word is).

2. Michael Green, *I Believe in the Holy Spirit* (Grand Rapids: Eerdmans, 1975), 18ff. Green argues that *nephesh* generally means the life and consciousness of humans and generally belongs to *us*, while *ruach* denotes a God-like quality in humans that belongs to God and is only loaned to us. Even Green, however, understands that there is considerable overlap in Scripture between the two terms.

3. See Luke 12:55 and 2 Thessalonians 2:8 where verbal forms of *pneuma* are used; see also Jesus' pun on "spirit/wind" in John 3:3–8.

4. Charles Taylor, *A Secular Age* (Cambridge: Belknap Press, 2007).

5. The Bible uses several terms for "the Holy Spirit." The most common is simply "the Spirit" (see Numbers 11:25; 1 Peter 3:18). Also used are the terms "the Spirit of God" (see Genesis 1:2; Matthew 12:28) and "the Spirit of the Lord" (see Judges 3:10; Acts 8:39). The term "Holy Spirit" occurs nearly one hundred

times (see Psalm 51:11; Mark 1:8), and the term "Spirit of holiness" occurs once (Romans 1:4). The Spirit is referred to as "the Spirit of the Father" (Matthew 10:20) and "the Spirit of Christ" (Romans 8:9). Paul also declares "the Lord is the Spirit" (2 Corinthians 3:17). In John's Gospel, Jesus refers to the Spirit as a "Comforter" (Greek = *parakletos*) (John 14:26; 15:26).

6. Craig Keener's book *Miracles: The Credibility of the New Testament Accounts*, 2 vols. (Grand Rapids: Baker Academic, 2011) is helpful here. Keener, an evangelical scholar, documents numerous examples of God doing extraordinary miracles in recent years. See volume 1, pp. 264–358. Add to this the endless number of witnesses who have experienced such miracles, including me personally. One could perhaps easily dismiss a claim about miracles here or there, but when confronted with hundreds of examples, it becomes impossible to say that God is not doing such physics-defying wonders and powers. As G. K. Chesterton once quipped, "Believers in miracles accept them (rightly or wrongly) because they have evidence for them. The disbelievers in miracles deny them (rightly or wrongly) because they have a doctrine against them." *Orthodoxy* (New York: Cosimo Classics, 2007), 143.

7. The dangers of confusing our thoughts with those of the Spirit's has been pointed out by others, including those who insist that a primary work of the Spirit is to illuminate the Word in our hearts. The sixteenth-century reformer John Calvin explained that though we can hear the Spirit-inspired Word of God, the sinfulness of our minds prevents us from believing it without an inner testimony of God's Spirit. "For the Lord has so knit together the certainty of his word and his Spirit, that our minds are duly imbued with reverence for the word when the Spirit shining upon it enables us there to behold the face of God; and, on the other hand, we embrace the Spirit with no danger of delusion when we recognize him in his image, that is in his word" (John Calvin, *Institutes of the Christian Religion* [Albany: The Ages Digital Library, Version 1.0, 1996], 112). John Wesley speaks of this same work of the Spirit, explaining, "By the testimony of the Spirit, I mean, an inward impression on the soul whereby the Spirit of God immediately and directly witnesses to my spirit, that I am a child of God; that Jesus Christ hath loved me, and given himself for me; that all my sins are blotted out, and I, even I, am reconciled to God" (John Wesley, Sermon Ten: "The Witness of the Spirit," in *The Works of John Wesley*, vol. 5 [Albany: The Ages Digital Library, Version 1.0, 1996], 188). Both Calvin and Wesley were, however, concerned that the doctrine of illumination would one day degenerate into a cheapened concept of intuition or sentiment.

Both explicitly warned against following an "inner voice" or one's "inner visions." Calvin chastises those who would "fasten upon any dreaming notion which may have casually sprung up in their minds" as though these notions were from the Spirit (Ibid., 112). And realizing the possible abuses some would make of the doctrine of illumination, Wesley sympathizes with those who might deny any illumination at all. "How many have mistaken the voice of their own imagination for this witness of the Spirit of God, and thence idly presumed they were children of God while they were doing the works of the devil!" (Ibid., 175).

8. For more on what it means to have a biblical faith, see Mark E. Moore, *Faithful Faith: Reclaiming Faith from Culture and Tradition* (Renew.org, 2021).

9. We should not downplay the role of water baptism in the convert's response of faith because water baptism is a normative part of faith in the New Testament. Indeed, the very New Testament that states that we receive the Spirit through faith also says that we receive it through obedience (Acts 5:32). This is not a contradiction, for biblical faith is faithful and obedient. See Tony Twist, Bobby Harrington, and David Young, *Baptism: What the Bible Teaches* (Renew.org, 2019) and David Young, *King Jesus and the Beauty of Obedience Based-Discipleship* (Grand Rapids: Zondervan, 2020).

10. I say "normative" because there are examples in the Bible where the Spirit worked in close connection with a believer's baptism but not at the actual point of baptism. In Acts 8, the Samaritans were baptized in water by Philip but did not receive the Spirit until the arrival of Peter and John. In Acts 10, Cornelius received the Spirit before Peter had even completed his sermon and shortly before Cornelius's baptism. Both cases appear to be exceptional. In the first, the gospel had made its first crossover from Jews to Samaritans and therefore required an act of the apostles before the Spirit could be received. In the second, the gospel made its first crossover to the Gentiles, and God himself had to pour out the Spirit in order to demonstrate that he wanted Peter to accept Gentile conversions. In fact, it is possible that neither exception refers to receiving the indwelling of the Spirit at all. Rather, it is possible that these exceptions refer to receiving a momentary ecstatic act of the Spirit—such as that which overtook Samson (Judges 13:5) or Saul (1 Samuel 10:11)—neither of whom had the indwelling of the Spirit.

11. In all three Synoptic Gospels, Jesus warned against "blaspheming the Holy Spirit" (Matthew 12:31–37; Mark 3:28–30; Luke 12:10). He stated that such a sin is an "eternal sin" that cannot be forgiven "either in this age or in the age to come."

What is the sin against the Holy Spirit, and how does one commit it? In all three Gospels, Jesus' warning was issued in response to the Jewish leaders' accusation that Jesus was driving out demons by the power of Satan. This accusation goes way beyond a rejection of the Savior. Instead, the sin involves accusing the Spirit of being Satan. It strikes at the very root of good and evil and the very nature of the righteousness of God. Jesus' response severely warned that those who commit this sin will not be forgiven. One should remember, though, that 1 John 1:5–2:4 promises us that the blood of Jesus cleanses "all sin" from those who "walk in the light." In Acts 6:7 and 15:5, Luke even indicates that many Jewish leaders (perhaps even those who earlier had blasphemed) were later converted to Christ. For this reason, we should not understand the sin against the Spirit to be something God refuses to forgive, but rather, we should understand the sin against the Holy Spirit to be any sin so egregious that people refuse to come back to God afterward. These persons leave themselves without any possible application of the redemptive blood of Christ. Living in such a condition leaves one in an unforgivable state. When sinners come to Christ, however, even from such a cut-off position, they can be forgiven. It is only those who will not return who are guilty of the "eternal sin."

12. For an analysis of some of the dangers of claiming the authority of the Twelve, see Douglas Geivett and Holly Pivec, *A New Apostolic Reformation?: A Biblical Response to a Worldwide Movement*, 2nd ed. (Bellington: Lexham Press, 2014).

13. There is considerable disagreement over what the New Testament considers to be prophecy. The typical evangelical view is reflected in the work of C. C. Ryrie, *The Holy Spirit* (Chicago: Moody, 1965). Ryrie believes that all references to prophecy in the New Testament involve inspired, infallible speech. For Ryrie, this gift is limited only to the first century. Charismatic scholars such as Wayne Grudem distinguish between the kind of prophecy given to the apostles, which was fully inspired and never wrong, from that of ordinary prophets, which carries much less authority and is more analogous to preaching. See Grudem, *The Gift of Prophecy* (Wheaton: Crossway, 1988, 2000). A comprehensive study of the question can be found in Max Turner, *The Holy Spirit and Spiritual Gifts* (Peabody: Hendrickson, 1996).

14. Deuteronomy 13:1–5; 18:22; Isaiah 9:14–15; Jeremiah 6:13; Ezekiel 22:28; Micah 2:11; 3:11; Matthew 7:15; 24:11, 24; Acts 13:6; 1 Corinthians 12:3; Galatians 1:6–9; 2 Peter 2:1; 1 John 4:6.

15. John Kildahl was a clinical psychologist who devoted ten years to the study of idiolalia. He concluded that it is not any known language, even though it has fluidity, rhythm, and feeling. Idiolalia, he explains, has no fixed or shared meaning, which explains why interpreters of idiolalia typically don't agree on what any given idiolalia act means. Kildahl describes idiolalia as "psychological regression," by which he means "a reversion to an earlier level of maturity, during which the rational, common-sense, ego-controlled way of relating to life is somehow diminished. It is perhaps more childlike, less critical, and generally more free-floating in its nature" (*The Psychology of Speaking in Tongues* (New York: Harper and Row, 1972), 59. The phenomenon occurs in other religions as well (Tibetan Buddhist monks, Muslims, animists, Eskimos, even early Hellenistic religions). Idiolalia even occurs outside of religious circles. For example, the fascinating music of Australian artist Lisa Gerrard often employs idiolalia, which, Gerrard explains, she invented in her teen years to express the inexpressible.

16. Christopher Dana Lynn; Jason Paris; Cheryl Anne Frye; and Lawrence Schell, "Salivary Alpha-Amylase and Cortisol Among Pentecostals on a Worship and Nonworship Day," *American Journal of Human Biology*, vol. 22 (2010: 6): 819–822.

17. Frederick Dale Bruner published a comprehensive study of whether the Pentecostal movement's claims about the miraculous gifts of the Spirit could be justified by the Scriptures, generally concluding that they could not. See *A Theology of the Holy Spirit: The Pentecostal Experience and the New Testament Witness* (Grand Rapids: Eerdmans, 1970). One of Bruner's primary objections to the Pentecostal movement was its belief that such gifts were necessary to validate one's salvation, which clearly goes beyond the text of the Scriptures, dangerously adding to the process of salvation articulated in the New Testament. Contrary to Bruner's thesis, however, a wrongly understood claim to miracles doesn't mean that the Holy Spirit has ceased to give gifts to believers. It only means that contemporary churches can grossly misunderstand these gifts. More recent teachings by charismatic churches have largely corrected the concerns that Bruner raises.

8

DISCIPLE MAKING

THE CORE MISSION
OF THE CHURCH

BOBBY HARRINGTON
& W. SCOTT SAGER

CONTENTS

General Editor's Note 393

Introduction 397

CHAPTER 1: Why Are the Life and Teachings of
Jesus Important for Disciple Making? 401

CHAPTER 2: What Is a Disciple of Jesus? 409

CHAPTER 3: Why Is Disciple Making the Core Mission
of the Church? 415

CHAPTER 4: What Is the Result of Disciple Making? 421

CHAPTER 5: How Do Disciples Live in This World? 427

Postscript: A Parable of Urgency 439

Appendix: Key Disciple Making Resources 441

Notes 443

GENERAL EDITOR'S NOTE

God desires disciple making to be a key focus for the local church because he wants more than just "Christians": he wants disciples of Jesus. At the Renew.org Network, we like to say God wants disciples who make disciples and who plant disciple making churches. This fulfills the vision of heaven in Revelation 7:9:

> I looked, and there before me was a great multitude that no one could count, from every nation, tribe, people and language, standing before the throne and before the Lamb.

The purpose of this short book is to make the scriptural case that disciple making is the core mission of the local church.

Bobby Harrington and Scott Sager both currently serve as lead ministers/pastors of local churches. They are engaged daily in the practical implications and nuts-and-bolts reality to which they point in this book.

Bobby is the founding and lead pastor of Harpeth Christian Church (Franklin, Tennessee). He is the CEO of both Renew.org and Discipleship.org, national disciple making networks. He has degrees from Harding University and a Doctor of Ministry from The Southern Baptist Theological Seminary. He is the author or co-author of more than a dozen books on disciple making.

Scott is the lead minister at The Green Hills Church in Nashville, Tennessee, and a vice president of Lipscomb University, teaching for its College of Bible and Ministry. Scott recently published *Jesus in Isolation: Lazarus, Viruses, and Us*. He founded Christ's Family Ministries and serves with several charities. He earned degrees from Abilene Christian University and a Doctor of Ministry from Southern Methodist University.

This book expounds on the section from the Renew.org Leaders' Faith Statement called "Disciple Making":

We believe the core mission of the local church is making disciples of Jesus Christ—it is God's plan "A" to redeem the world and manifest the reign of his kingdom. We want to be disciples who make disciples because of our love for God and others. We personally seek to become more and more like Jesus through his Spirit so that Jesus would live through us. To help us focus on Jesus, his sacrifice on the cross, our unity in him, and his coming return, we typically share communion in our weekly gatherings. We desire the fruits of biblical disciple making, which are disciples who live and love like Jesus and "go" into every corner of society and to the ends of the earth. Disciple making is the engine that drives our missional service to those outside the church. We seek to be known where we live for the good that we do in our communities. We love and serve all people, as Jesus did, no strings attached. At the same time, as we do good for others, we also seek to form relational bridges that we prayerfully hope will open doors for teaching people the gospel of the kingdom and the way of salvation.

*See the full Network Faith Statements at the end of this book.

Support Scriptures: Matthew 28:19–20;
Galatians 4:19; Acts 2:41; Philippians 1:20–21; Colossians 1:27–29;
2 Corinthians 3:3; 1 Thessalonians 2:19–20; John 13:34–35; 1 John 3:16;
1 Corinthians 13:1–13; Luke 22:14–23; 1 Corinthians 11:17–24; Acts 20:7.

The following tips might help you use this book more effectively (and the other books in the *Real Life Theology* series):

1. *Five questions, answers, and Scriptures.* We framed this book around five key questions with five short answers and five notable Scriptures. This format provides clarity, making it easier to commit crucial information to memory. This format also enables the books in the *Real Life Theology* series to support our catechism. Our catechism is a series of fixed questions and answers for instruction in church or home. In all, the series has fifty-two questions, answers, and key Scriptures. This particular book focuses on the five that are most pertinent to disciple making.

2. *Summary videos.* You can find three to seven-minute video teachings that summarize the book, as well as each chapter, at Renew.org. These short videos can function as standalone teachings. But for groups or group leaders using the book, they can also be used to launch discussion of the reading.

May God use this book to fuel faithful and effective disciple making in your life and church.

For King Jesus,
Daniel McCoy
Co-General Editor, *Real Life Theology* series

INTRODUCTION

> The Church exists for nothing else but to draw men into Christ,
> to make them little Christs. If they are not doing that, all the
> cathedrals, clergy, missions, sermons, even the Bible itself, are
> simply a waste of time. God became Man for no other purpose.
> — C. S. Lewis

In this book, we teach you the basics of disciple making and encourage you to make it a core focus of your life. We believe disciple making is the core mission of the church and that C. S. Lewis got it right when he said, "The Church exists for nothing else but to draw men into Christ, to make them little Christs."[1] Making "little Christs" is another way of saying "disciple making."

Being clear with definitions is important, so let's begin with our definition of disciple making:

> *Disciple making is entering into relationships to intentionally help people follow Jesus, be changed by Jesus, and join the mission of Jesus.*[2]

Although Jesus officially comes onto the scene in the New Testament, disciple making is a common theme throughout the whole Bible. Disciple making was God's preferred method long before it became the church's core mission. Let's start with an important Old Testament passage, where God taught disciple making to parents when he formed the nation of Israel.

THE MASTER PLAN FOR DISCIPLE MAKING IN THE OLD TESTAMENT

WHILE THE OLD TESTAMENT contains many examples of disciple making, one key section in Deuteronomy captures it best. We must not overlook this passage because it is the central passage of Judaism even to this day. When God (through Moses and his disciple, Joshua) led the people of Israel out of Egypt and into the Promised Land, he established a core method for disciple making for families. By this method, the Israelites would learn to love God, know his ways through Scripture, and obey him.

The key verses are from Deuteronomy 6:4–9, and the Israelites deemed them so important that they incorporated the verses into a prayer called the *Shema*,[3] which they later required to be recited *daily* and in the synagogue as formative to living a life that both pursues and pleases God. You can think of this passage as the Great Commission *before* the Great Commission of Jesus in Matthew 28:18–20 (a passage we will explain in greater detail in Chapter 1). This earlier Great Commission offers the core method by which the Old Testament people of Israel made disciples and also offered the relational framework of disciple making that Jesus himself would utilize centuries later when he chose his first disciples. This method is intentional, relational transformation (more on this description below). Notice how the *Shema* begins:

> Hear, O Israel: The LORD our God, the LORD is one. Love the LORD your God with all your heart and with all your soul and with all your strength. (Deuteronomy 6:4–5)

Moses first announced God as the unifying force behind all of creation and all of human existence—he is *one*. Allegiance to this one God requires all a person has to offer: we are to love him with our heart, soul, and strength. It is a full-bodied and relentless pursuit to know and love God. It is the core mission of God's people, Israel, so much so that the nation of Israel derives its name "Israel" from being the people "who strive and wrestle with God" (see Genesis 32:28). God wanted to create for himself a people who would struggle mightily to love him, and through loving him they would disciple their children to know and love him as well.

Passing on the faith to the next generation was so critical to Israel's budding future that Moses called parents to intentionally and sacrificially spend time relationally discipling and helping their children to know, love, and follow God. Moses then gave specific instructions to parents as the disciple makers of their children:

> These commandments that I give you today are to be on your hearts. Impress them on your children. Talk about them when you sit at home and when you walk along the road, when you lie down and when you get up. Tie them as symbols on your hands and bind them on your foreheads. Write them on the doorframes of your houses and on your gates. (Deuteronomy 6:6–9)

As we see, the one passing on faith must have a relentless and transformative pursuit of God (what we call a "God-life") as the focus of their living. That person is then to "impress" the God-life upon their children through purposively living out the faith and faith-filled instruction. These instructions show us the pursuit of God was to be *the* topic of conversation around the house for God's people as they sat together and along the road as they traveled together. Devotion to God was to be the last thing inputted into a child's "hard drive" at night and the first thing coming out of their parent's mouth when the family rebooted again the next morning. A pursuit of God was to be evident at the entrance to the home, through the home's decor, as well as how they adorned their bodies. Parents were to be intentional, courageous, and conspicuous in their pursuit to know God.

The disciple making commission from Deuteronomy 6 begins with God first calling parents to be disciples themselves—by fully loving him with all of their heart, soul, and strength—and then it calls parents to disciple their children so they too will love God with their heart, soul, and strength.

Notice three key elements God prescribes that apply to parents both then and now:

Intentional. Parents are to be purposeful and goal-oriented. Their mission is to *impress* the teachings of God on their children so they too will love God. In God's estimation, "impressive parents" are not the ones who raise the most accomplished kids, but the ones who impress their own God-life into the moldable clay of their children's lives. It is a thorough and all-encompassing mission, from the time they "get up," until the time they "lie down" each day. This intentionality expresses itself by the use of Scripture everywhere—on arms, foreheads, and even the doorframes of their houses. Yes, that is a lot of intentional focus! And, yes, that kind of diligence is necessary to disciple children both then and now.[4]

Relational. Parents should disciple their children in a relational way and in the normal stuff of life. The text envisions many natural conversations, for example, at home, during walks, in the mornings, and at bedtime. With their minds focused upon the discipling of children, parents constantly use the relational conversations and discussions that come up in life to integrate the teachings of God into their children's lives.

Transformation. The end goal of disciple making is to make true disciples. When children grow up with the Deuteronomy 6 disciple making model, they are very likely to grow up as those who love God with all their heart, soul, and strength. They become disciples who leave their homes to establish families of their own, where—following the example of their parents and the teaching of the *Shema*—they too are equipped to disciple their children, repeating the model generation after generation.

A careful examination of Jesus' life shows how Jesus used this same model when he made disciples as a spiritual parent. He formed his disciples through this intentional, relational process in the normal, everyday course of Jewish life in the first century. Then he commissioned his disciples to go and repeat the process by making disciples of others, doing for others what he had done for them.

> Therefore, go and make disciples of all nations, baptizing them in the name of the Father and of the Son and of the Holy Spirit, and teaching them to obey everything I have commanded you. And surely I am with you always, to the very end of the age. (Matthew 28:19–20)

Let's now turn to the teachings and life of Jesus to understand better what he meant when he commissioned his disciples to make disciples.

1

WHY ARE THE LIFE AND TEACHINGS OF JESUS IMPORTANT FOR DISCIPLE MAKING?

Answer: Jesus shows us by his life and teachings how we should live as his disciples.

> Therefore go and make disciples of all nations, baptizing them
> in the name of the Father and of the Son and of the Holy Spirit,
> and teaching them to obey everything I have commanded you.
> And surely I am with you always, to the very end of the age.
> — Matthew 28:19–20

The Christian world emphasizes Christmas and Easter, the two most prominent holidays on the Christian calendar. These two days focus on the incarnation (how God became flesh in baby Jesus) and the death, burial, and resurrection (how God forgives our sins). Along with the emphasis on these two days, a lot of theology focuses on these two points about Jesus too. Preachers regularly emphasize how Jesus was 100 percent human and divine and that he died and rose from the dead to forgive us of our sins (and provide us with heaven). These two focal points are good and true, but isolated from the rest of the Gospels, they do not provide enough emphasis on what happened between Jesus' birth and resurrection.

To follow the Bible truly, we must also focus on the teachings and life of Jesus.

If we exclude this middle focus, we can inadvertently create a *transactional gospel*, in which the call is simply to place our faith in Jesus' identity and cross (the human part of "the deal"), and then God will forgive our sins (God's part of the deal). That gospel—if we are not careful—simply becomes a transaction. By excluding what it means to follow Jesus' teachings and imitate his life, we share a gospel not taught in the Word of God.

God calls us to more than a transaction.

God calls us to become disciples of Jesus.

GOD CALLS US TO BECOME DISCIPLES OF JESUS. This is why we need to know Jesus and his teachings. This focus was made clear at the end of Jesus' time on earth when he gave the Great Commission to his disciples.

> All authority in heaven and on earth has been given to me. Therefore go and make disciples of all nations, baptizing them in the name of the Father and of the Son and of the Holy Spirit, and teaching them to obey everything I have commanded you. And surely I am with you always, to the very end of the age. (Matthew 28:18b–20)

These are Jesus' final words—and that fact alone makes them important. But they are more than just final words: they are Jesus' final mission to his disciples and the expression of God's heart for everyone on earth.

Jesus wants disciples.

And Jesus wants his disciples to make more disciples.

Many people mistakenly think that the Great Commission is about conversions. But that is not what the text says. It is about conversation and living as disciples. The text says that disciple making includes baptizing people and teaching them to obey all Jesus' teachings and trust his presence until the end. Jesus' master plan for his disciples was to reach the whole world by making other disciples.

It is that simple.

Notice two crucial descriptions of how we are to teach as we disciple people. First, Jesus did not tell his disciples just to baptize and share information. He instructed them to teach *obedience* to his commands ("teaching them to obey"). Second, Jesus taught his disciples to teach obedience to *everything he commanded* ("to obey everything I have commanded you"). As David Young points out in his wonderful book on this topic, Jesus commanded *obedience-based disciple making.* That is the type of disciple making God wants us to uphold today.[5] We are to obey everything Jesus commanded.

This short book is a part of the *Real Life Theology* series that focuses on how we can know and obey everything that Jesus commands as disciples.[6] Our main goal is to show that disciple making—which involves helping people in every nation come to Jesus for both salvation and transformation—is the core mission of the church. Before we focus directly on how and why we make disciples, let's see why the teachings and life of Jesus form the core curriculum in disciple making.

> **JESUS' TEACHINGS ARE OUR CURRICULUM FOR DISCIPLE MAKING.**

JESUS' TEACHINGS

JESUS CLAIMED THAT FOLLOWING his teachings was foundational for living life as it was intended: "I am the light of the world. Whoever follows me will never walk in darkness, but will have the light of life" (John 8:12). Jesus described himself and his teachings this way:

> I have come into the world as a light, so that no one who believes in me should stay in darkness. If anyone hears my words but does not keep them, I do not judge that person. For I did not come to judge the world, but to save the world. *There is a judge for the one who rejects me and does not accept my words; the very words I have spoken will condemn them at the last day.* For I did not speak on my own, but the Father who sent me commanded me to say all that I have spoken. I know that his command leads to eternal life. So whatever I say is just what the Father has told me to say. (John 12:46–50)

Elsewhere Jesus compared his words and teachings to the foundation of a house. Merely claiming to follow him and doing great things in his name will not be enough on the day of judgment. Rather, only those who truly build their lives on his teachings will enter the kingdom of heaven.

> Not everyone who says to me, "Lord, Lord," will enter the kingdom of heaven, but only the one who does the will of my Father who is in heaven. Many will say to me on that day, "Lord, Lord, did we not prophesy in your name and in your name drive out demons and in your name perform many miracles?" Then I will tell them plainly, "I never knew you. Away from me, you evildoers!" *Therefore everyone who hears these words of mine*

and puts them into practice is like a wise man who built his house on the rock.
(Matthew 7:21–24)

Jesus makes it clear: our adherence to his teachings will be the basis by which God will evaluate our lives.

Just before his ascension back to heaven, Jesus committed his words and teachings to his apostles (Matthew 28:18–20). Jesus also promised that God would guide the apostles, ensuring they accurately recalled everything through the Holy Spirit. Notice the following promise.

These words you hear are not my own; they belong to the Father who sent me. All this I have spoken while still with you. *But the Advocate, the Holy Spirit, whom the Father will send in my name, will teach you all things and will remind you of everything I have said to you.* (John 14:24b–26)

According to Jesus, the Holy Spirit would ensure that the disciples be properly taught and remember everything he had told them. God did not just rely on the impressive memory practices of the ancient people. He guided them and protected the accuracy of Jesus' teachings by his Holy Spirit.

This is why the first Christians devoted themselves to the apostles' teachings: these teachings were not just inspirational thoughts but the inspired teachings of Jesus himself!

They devoted themselves to the apostles' teaching and to fellowship, to the breaking of bread and to prayer. (Acts 2:42)

Jesus Christ's words were God's *final* message for the human race.

In the past God spoke to our ancestors through the prophets at many times and in various ways, but in these last days he has spoken to us by his Son, whom he appointed heir of all things, and through whom he made the universe. (Hebrews 1:1–2)

As mentioned earlier, at a basic level, a disciple is a student, apprentice, learner. So, yes, at a basic level we look to Jesus as a teacher. Yet Jesus calls us to a much higher level of devotion than we typically give the teachings we study. He calls us to *live out* the teachings of his kingdom. These teachings are our curriculum for disciple making. Thankfully, however, Jesus gives us more than just teachings and an expectation to live according to them. He also gives us *himself* as the model to follow.

JESUS' LIFE

THE GOSPEL OF MARK describes how Jesus began his ministry by calling people into God's kingdom reign (Mark 1:14–18). A prominent focus of Jesus' teachings was describing what this kingdom was like. Take, for example, Jesus' kingdom parables in Matthew 13. Jesus also spent much of his time describing how to live life as citizens of God's kingdom. For example, the countercultural ethics of the Sermon on the Mount confront every reader with the radical righteousness that characterizes kingdom life.

Yet as the Gospel of Mark describes, Jesus did more than just invite people to follow his teachings about the kingdom. His invitation into the kingdom involved following *him*. He used words that described a total lifestyle renovation, such as "repent" (turning from evil and turning back to God) and "believe" (from the Greek word *pistis,* which entails more than mental assent to an idea; in royal contexts, it often denotes allegiance to a king).[7]

> Jesus went into Galilee, proclaiming the good news of God. "The time has come," he said. "The *kingdom of God* has come near. *Repent* and *believe* the good news!" As Jesus walked beside the Sea of Galilee, he saw Simon and his brother Andrew casting a net into the lake, for they were fishermen. "Come, *follow me*," Jesus said, "and I will send you out to fish for people." At once they left their nets and followed him. (Mark 1:14–18)

Notice how the explicit invitation came to two brothers, Peter and Andrew, casting their nets on the Sea of Galilee, "for they were fishermen" (Mark 1:16). Jesus offered them a front row seat to his life and teachings if they would follow him. These two career fishermen made their livelihoods from the sea. But now Jesus was asking them to drop their nets and set off with him into his kingdom waters to cast spiritual nets that would capture the hearts of men and women everywhere.

This invitation to leave a familiar source of income was a lot for Jesus to ask. But we learn an important focus: don't focus on what you are walking away from, but on whom you are walking toward. The text tells us "at once" they dropped their nets and entered into the greatest adventure anyone has ever known (Mark 1:18). They had found more than a body of information worth learning; they had discovered a life worth following.

Jesus gave us a life to imitate. Whether we are male or female, Jew or Greek, rich or poor—the more we look like Jesus, the more we become our truest self, the self for which God created us. Jesus is the model for what it looks like to live as God intends. Because of this, we are to follow after Jesus by walking in his steps. John described it poignantly: "Whoever claims to live in him must live as Jesus did" (1 John 2:6).

This is why the expression "Follow me" was one of Jesus' favorite invitations (Matthew 4:19; 8:22; 9:9; 10:38; 16:24; 19:21). He explained to his disciples, "The student is not above the teacher, but everyone who is fully trained will be like their teacher" (Luke 6:40). For example, notice how Jesus pointed to his own example when teaching about love.

> A new command I give you: Love one another. As I have loved you, so you must love one another. By this everyone will know that you are my disciples, if you love one another. (John 13:34–35)

Jesus demonstrated what it meant to love sacrificially, and then held up his example to define love in his teaching.

Jesus' life is our example, model, and the one we imitate. For example, suffering is a common challenge that we face when we are disciples. How do we handle something like that? Peter explains our need to have Jesus as our model in suffering in 1 Peter 2:21–23.

> To this you were called, because Christ suffered for you, leaving you an example, that you should follow in his steps. "He committed no sin, and no deceit was found in his mouth." When they hurled their insults at him, he did not retaliate; when he suffered, he made no threats. Instead, he entrusted himself to him who judges justly.

There are so many situations in life and God wants us to respond to each of them as disciples of Jesus. Yet the Word of God does not tell—nor could it tell us—how to handle each situation. Instead, Scripture focuses on the underlying principles. As God inspires Paul, he urges Christians to *imitate the mindset of Jesus*.

> Have the same mindset as Christ Jesus: Who, being in very nature God, did not consider equality with God something to be used to his own advantage; rather, he made himself nothing by taking the very nature of a servant, being made in human likeness. (Philippians 2:5–7)

TEACHINGS AND MODEL

BETWEEN THE INCARNATION OF Jesus and his death and resurrection, we find crucial curriculum for disciple making. For in Jesus' teachings and life we learn how to live as disciples of Jesus. As pivotal as the cross and resurrection are to our salvation, we must not skip over the bulk of the Gospels and the teachings of the apostles in defining what it means to be a disciple of Jesus. His disciples hold up his teachings and life as central to their calling as Christians.

Yet the point can be stated even more strongly. Jesus' teachings and life provide us with more than just important content in our disciple making curriculum. They also demonstrate the best way to *communicate* that content. Put another way, Jesus gives us both our teaching *and model* for disciple making. For when we study how Jesus taught and lived, we see a life-on-life method for making disciples far more transformational than mere instruction in a classroom.[8]

Just as the Israelites discipled their children to grow up and disciple their children in turn, so Jesus discipled a group of twelve men who matured and then went out to repeat the process. Jesus' intentional, relational transformation is a disciple making process, and it is the ideal plan by which people from every nation, language, and tribe will come to be disciples (Revelation 7:9) and fulfill the Great Commission. Our next step is to focus on Jesus' teachings more precisely with the aim to define what exactly it means to be a disciple of Jesus.

2

WHAT IS A DISCIPLE OF JESUS?

Answer: A disciple of Jesus is someone who is following Jesus, being changed by Jesus, and is committed to the mission of Jesus.

And Jesus said to them, "Follow me, and I will
make you become fishers of men."
— Mark 1:17, ESV

(Bobby) became friends with Larry as we watched our sons play hockey together. Larry happily accepted my invitation to join a Bible discussion group. Through this discussion group, it became clear Larry knew nothing about the Bible. Growing up in a rough New York community, he had experienced trauma at the early age of twelve, when he saw a member of the mafia kill his father. It so traumatized him that he spent the next thirty-plus years of his life keeping himself far from conversations about death—and ultimately about God. Yet because of this new friendship, he was getting into the Bible—and learning a lot too.

One day, Larry described to a co-worker what he was learning about the Bible. In response, the man questioned and challenged Larry's new realizations about God, Jesus, and the Bible. Returning to our Bible study confused and seeking clarity, Larry wanted to be sure this new path would be worth it.

"Bottom line," he asked me, "what is it all about?" He wanted to know the point of life and how Jesus fit in. People have always asked questions like this in various ways: *Why am I here? What is God's purpose for my life? Where is my life going? How does it all end?* These were probably the same questions Adam and Eve had asked God during their daily visits in the Garden of Eden, and people are still seeking answers to them in our day.

I gave Larry a quick answer: "God wants a relationship with you, in which you become a disciple of Jesus." This bottom-line, one-sentence response didn't include a warning about hell (although I was concerned about that for him), or the reality of life after death in general (even though that is important), or that he would need to follow the teachings of the Bible (which developing a relationship with God requires). There was time for those things. He needed to know, bottom line, what it was all about, and I told him it's all about *being a disciple of Jesus.* It included receiving both salvation in Jesus and transformation into the image of Jesus. That is what God wants for all of us. He wants everyone in the world—of "every nation, tribe, people and language" (Revelation 7:9)—to become a disciple of Jesus Christ.

So what exactly *is* a disciple?

A BIBLICAL DEFINITION OF A DISCIPLE

LINGUISTICALLY, THE WORD FOR "disciple" in the Greek is *mathētēs*, and, although we translate it "disciple," it also means learner, student, or follower. This word is most akin to the environment of an internship where an expert apprentices a student toward competency in a trade or skill. This relationship involves knowledge but focuses upon applying that knowledge to everyday situations of life to equip the learner with wisdom. The hope is that the apprentice in a trade will be the master-teacher of others in the years to come.

In addition to the linguistic route, we could also answer the question, "What is a disciple?" by looking at the descriptions of disciples of Jesus found in the New Testament. Taking our cue from various Bible passages (e.g., John 13:13; Galatians 4:19; 1 John 2:6), we discover a disciple is someone who:

- Trusts Jesus so much they pledge their full allegiance (called "faith") in him,
- Imitates Jesus' life completely as both their teacher and Lord,
- Looks to Jesus' teachings as the basis of moral decision-making,
- Loves Jesus so much that love spills over into every other relationship as well, and
- Forms their life around Jesus Christ.

Does that feel overwhelming? Don't lose heart. Instead, slow down and return to the simple-yet-radical call of Jesus to follow him. Those of us who regularly help churches learn to focus on disciple making have learned that people need a practical, specific, and memorable definition of a disciple.

We offer here a definition of a disciple that makes sense of (and room for) all the important descriptions of kingdom living we just listed. It's based on Jesus' invitation to Peter and Andrew that we discussed in the last chapter.

> And Jesus said to them, "Follow me, and I will make you become fishers of men." (Mark 1:17, ESV)

In this single verse, we find three elements of what it means to be a disciple.

- Following Jesus ("Follow me"),
- Being changed by Jesus ("and I will make you become"), and
- Joining Jesus' mission ("fishers of men").

This framework is the basis by which thousands of church leaders working with the Renew.org Network have adopted the following definition of a disciple.

> A disciple is someone who is following Jesus, being changed by Jesus, and is committed to the mission of Jesus.[9]

Mark did not include Mark 1:17 for the purpose of defining a disciple, but it serves as a helpful framework for understanding what it means to be a disciple. Everything the New Testament teaches about being a disciple can be categorized under these three elements.[10] Let's look at the three parts.

Following Jesus. Read through the New Testament and you will find the word "Christian" used only 3 times. Look for the word "disciple," though, and it shows up 296 times in the NIV. This means the English word "disciple" shows up 99 times more often than the word "Christian." While some people today might read Jesus' command to follow him in Mark 1:17 and Matthew 28:18–20 and assume it to be only for the Twelve and not for modern-day believers, that is simply a false narrative. Jesus calls us to salvation with a desire to "obey everything" Jesus commanded.

That obedience, by the way, includes the command to make disciples (Matthew 28:19–20). In this way, Jesus' original call extends to everyone to follow Jesus as a lifelong learner—to the very end of the age—and also to help make disciples and become disciple makers.

Being Changed by Jesus. Second, as we follow Jesus, we change. The New Testament promises that, as we pursue God's glory, the Holy Spirit transforms us into his image (2 Corinthians 3:18). When Jesus told Peter and Andrew, "I will make you become" (Mark 1:17, ESV), he was promising core transformation. And as we read the disciples' stories, that's precisely what we see.

AS WE FOLLOW JESUS, WE CHANGE.

For example, take James and John who left their father, the nets, and the hired hands to follow Jesus. What kind of character did these men have when Jesus called them? Mark's Gospel tells us Jesus gave them a nickname "Sons of Thunder" (Mark 3:17). This means that their father, Zebedee, was a hothead or that they were hotheads, or both. We discover that James and John had a dark streak inside them that wanted to destroy their enemies.

Their anger and rage boiled to the surface one day in a region called Samaria, a region of half-Jews who hated the Jews as much as the Jews hated them. When the Samaritans snubbed Jesus and his band of apostles, James and John's anger boiled over, and they asked Jesus, "Do you want us to call fire down from heaven to destroy them?" (Luke 9:54). Jesus rebuked them for their suggestion, but did not exclude them from the group. In today's "cancel culture," James and John would have been shamed, shunned, and shuttled out the door for their inbuilt dislike of Samaritans. But instead of canceling them, Jesus saw that the two brothers needed more training from him and pulled them closer and strove even more to impress on them his God-life. Amazingly, by the end of his life, the elderly John was known not as a "Son of Thunder," but as the Apostle of Love, having referenced love in his Gospel and first letter (1 John) more than any other New Testament writer. Our world tells us, "People don't change," and although that may be true, when people follow Jesus, *Jesus* changes them.

WHEN PEOPLE FOLLOW JESUS, *JESUS* CHANGES THEM.

Joining Jesus' Mission. Third, the change Jesus works into our lives leads us to model our entire lives after Jesus, which includes our commitment to join him and "fish for people." In this, we learn to make disciples as Jesus made disciples. After all, if we obey everything Jesus commanded, that means we too will learn to replicate the process by which we became his disciples. To be a mature disciple of Jesus is to become a disciple maker like Jesus as well. It is a natural process: we follow Jesus, we are changed by Jesus, and—as we follow the one who spent 65–90 percent of his time making disciples—we too commit to make disciples as he did.[11] Loving people as Jesus loved people through service means that we want to see people come to faith in Jesus and embrace God's kingdom rule in their lives (John 13:34). Because we love people and want God's best for them, we want to help them become disciples and grow as disciples.

With our definition of a disciple in mind, with its three elements, a follow-up question is in order. Every one of us should ponder the question, *Am I a disciple of Jesus?* Answering this question calls for more deliberation than, *Where do I go to church?* Or, *When did I get saved?* Whether or not you are a disciple of Jesus has strong implications for how you live *today*, not just for a decision made years ago.

IS BEING A DISCIPLE OPTIONAL?

IN SCRIPTURE, THE CONCEPT of being a disciple is not an add-on to conversion; it is part of conversion. An adage says, "What you win them with is what you win them to," and if people are won over only to the obvious benefits of salvation—say, forgiveness of sins and an eternity in heaven—then we cannot expect them to become the kind of disciples who "deny themselves and take up their cross daily and follow [Jesus]" (Luke 9:23). We must, therefore, be clear and upfront about the call to become a disciple: the Word of God teaches that the decision to receive Christ's salvation is also a decision to follow the path of discipleship found in the Bible.

Consider the following analogy: Whenever a newborn enters this world, immediately upon arrival, a nurse administers a simple health test called the "Apgar"— assessing the new baby's health with five basic criteria. A nurse will check the newborn's color, heart rate, reflexes, muscle tone, and respiration. They conduct this test not because a healthy birth is the end goal of every child or parent but because a healthy birth is only the beginning of their life—and they need to ensure the baby begins well. A healthy birth is the best indicator of a healthy life to follow.

A spiritual birth is the same: When a person makes the decision to embrace Jesus fully as both Savior and King, they enter into a spiritual new birth best seen as the coming together of five elements: faith, repentance, baptism, the reception of the Holy Spirit, and the forgiveness of sins. When these five elements come together into one single decision, together they become a fierce commitment to live for Jesus.

Just as with the Apgar test at physical birth, having all five elements fully functioning in a new spiritual birth makes for the healthiest outcome.

The apostle Paul describes our new birth with a focus on water baptism this way:

> Or don't you know that all of us who were baptized into Christ Jesus were baptized into his death? We were therefore buried with him through baptism into death in order that, just as Christ was raised from the dead through the glory of the Father, we too may live a new life . . . . In the same way, count yourselves dead to sin but alive to God in Christ Jesus. (Romans 6:3–4, 11)

Baptism imitates the death, burial, and resurrection of Jesus: the person's old self dies and is buried, and the person rises up from the waters committed to a "new life." In that new life, they learn what it means to be dead to sin and "alive to God in Christ Jesus."

But here's our main point: baptism no more serves as the ultimate moment of the Christian life than the Apgar test serves as the ultimate moment of a person's human existence—it is only the start of a new life! A healthy spiritual birth launches the follower of Jesus fully and freely into the life of a disciple. Faith gives them wings to fly, repentance removes the hindrances of flight, baptism is the moment of leaving the nest, the Holy Spirit allows the believer to spread wings, and with the commitment to soar into the life intended for them—the rich life of a disciple of Jesus.

As each person remembers the day of their physical birth, spiritual followers also remember their baptism—but not as the day they checked a box, completed a transaction, or completed an exam. Rather, spiritual followers see baptism as the launching pad where they stepped out of the nest of this fallen world and soared into the great adventure of being a disciple, the life God created for them.

Now that we have looked at the definition of a disciple, we would like to explain why we are convinced that making disciples is the core mission of the church.

3

WHY IS DISCIPLE MAKING THE CORE MISSION OF THE CHURCH?

Answer: The church is God's plan to help everyone come to faith in Jesus and become more like Jesus to the glory of the Father in the power of the Spirit.

He is the one we proclaim, admonishing and teaching everyone with
all wisdom, so that we may present everyone fully mature in Christ.
— Colossians 1:28

The Word of God nowhere states the mission of the church in a single verse that everyone easily agrees serves as a modern-day "mission statement." There are so many crucial tasks to which a local church in the New Testament is called that it can be difficult to bring it all down to one core mission. As an example, Rick Warren's *The Purpose Driven Church* proposes five ways to reach the ultimate purposes of the church—worship, fellowship, discipleship, ministry, and mission.[12] He connects these purposes to both the Great Commandment (Matthew 22:37–40) and the Great Commission (Matthew 28:19–20). Yet we are convinced that the five purposes Warren articulates are all expressions of one core mission that undergirds them all. We believe the underlying core mission of the church is disciple making.[13]

Consider an analogy from the sport of golf to bring together the core mission in light of the other purposes. The purpose in golf is to get a ball into a hole in the fewest strokes possible. That is how golfers keep score, and they use golf clubs to accomplish the goal of golf. The clubs are not the ultimate purpose of golf; they merely help golfers get the ball in the hole in as few strokes as possible. Similarly, the goal of disciple making is to help disciples imitate Jesus: to follow Jesus, be changed by Jesus, and to live life in order to please Jesus. The activities of worship, fellowship, discipleship, ministry, and mission are the tools a disciple uses to realize the goal of becoming more like Jesus, and helping others do the same.

THE GOAL OF DISCIPLE MAKING IS TO HELP DISCIPLES IMITATE JESUS.

We explained in the previous chapter that disciple making includes bringing people to both salvation (into God's kingdom) and transformation (into the image of Jesus). Stated differently, God wants everyone on planet earth to be saved by Jesus and to become more and more like Jesus. In this way, becoming a disciple of Jesus—one who follows Jesus, is being changed by Jesus, and is committed to the mission of Jesus—is what life is all about. Once we are saved, growth into Christlikeness is the best way we as Jesus-followers should score ourselves.

For those in full-time ministry, there is an incredible joy and a rush of excitement that comes with beginning in a ministry role inside a local church. New leaders get excited about their roles and want to lead well, please God, and bless the people. Yet the problem most new ministers soon discover is this: their role is poorly defined. A church leader can be asked—and even expected—to play an impossible number of roles for people. Some members will think church leaders should focus on personally pastoring each member. Others will see the leaders' primary responsibility as making church run smoothly and attractively so that people keep coming. Still others will expect church leaders to be the prophetic mouthpiece for their own cultural pet peeves. It can be hard to define one's role clearly as a church leader.

So let's get specific: What exactly should happen in a local church? If we look to the Word of God, we will see that church leaders (and indeed the whole church) are tasked with this one core disciple making mission.

The apostle Paul clearly described it in his letter to the ancient church in Colossae. He reminded them that Christ is his message, and then he pointed to the goal of every church leader.

> Christ in you [is] the hope of glory. He is the one we proclaim, admonishing and teaching everyone with all wisdom, so that we may present everyone fully mature in Christ. To this end I strenuously contend with all the energy Christ so powerfully works in me. (Colossians 1:27b–29)

Paul's goal was not just proclaiming and teaching everyone about Christ. His goal—and he gave it every ounce of energy he had—was to present everyone in the church as fully mature in Christ. His goal was fully formed disciples.

The New Testament repeatedly teaches us that growth means to fundamentally focus on being formed into the image of Jesus. Paul described his own life with these words: "I have been crucified with Christ and I no longer live, but Christ lives in me" (Galatians 2:20).

Notice the following passages from the New Testament which flesh out the disciple making ministry of the church using the language of formation and transformation.

> You show that *you are a letter from Christ, the result of our ministry*, written not with ink but with the Spirit of the living God, not on tablets of stone but on tablets of human hearts. (2 Corinthians 3:3)

> And we all, who with unveiled faces contemplate the Lord's glory, are being *transformed into his image* with ever-increasing glory, which comes from the Lord, who is the Spirit. (2 Corinthians 3:18)

> My dear children, for whom I am again in the pains of childbirth *until Christ is formed in you,* how I wish I could be with you now and change my tone, because I am perplexed about you! (Galatians 4:19–20)

> Those God foreknew he also predestined *to be conformed to the likeness of his Son,* that he might be the firstborn among many brothers and sisters. (Romans 8:29)

The heart of being a disciple boils down to this one thing: God wants us to come to salvation in Jesus and then become more like Jesus to the glory of the Father in the power of the Spirit. For those who want to engage in a deeper dive on the emphasis in these verses and more, we recommend an article by Bobby's colleague Curtis Erskine called "Conversion, Theology, and Discipleship" at Discipleship.org.[14]

Let us explain our core mission from another angle. During our study of the Bible, both of us as authors have sought to understand the underlying teaching of every book in the New Testament on a detailed level. Here is our conclusion: although the circumstances of every book in the New Testament vary for each of the recipients, each book was ultimately written to help people come to faith in Jesus and become more and more like Jesus. If we go back to our definition of a disciple, we can frame it this way: everything was written to help us follow Jesus, be changed by Jesus, and join the mission of Jesus.

Similarly, New Testament scholar Richard Longenecker's book, *Patterns of Discipleship in the New Testament*, shows that the New Testament, in all of its diversity, makes discipleship the major, fundamental, and underlying theme of the entire New Testament.[15] N. T. Wright's *Following Jesus: Biblical Reflections on Discipleship* guides us down a similar path. He puts it this way: "Each writer talks about the life, death, and resurrection of Jesus in order to encourage his readers to follow this Jesus wherever he leads."[16]

Once people orient their hearts to Jesus' way of discipleship, all the weighty questions of life are reframed to include "imitating Jesus" as the core focus. Notice a few examples of the ways in which New Testament writers teach people to follow the ways of Jesus as disciples.

- How do we love people, in the way of Jesus? (John 13:34)
- How do we worship God, in the way of Jesus? (John 4:24)
- How do husbands treat their wives and wives treat their husbands, in the way of Jesus? (Ephesians 5:22–33)
- How do children treat their parents, in the way of Jesus? (Ephesians 6:1–3)

These examples show the numerous challenging situations and difficult circumstances that confront a disciple. But the answer to every situation comes from asking ourselves the same question: How can we follow Jesus and do what Jesus would do in our situation?

The mindset of being a disciple helps us with secondary but vital aspects of the mission of the church community.

Here are four church examples:

- Why does the local church care about the poor? Because we follow Jesus and he cared about the poor.
- Why do we help with our local community? Because Jesus teaches us to love and do good to our neighbors.

- Why do we care about the environment? Because Jesus created the world and put humans over it as stewards.
- Why do we care about racial justice? Because Jesus gives us a new identity and we see everyone through his eyes.

Why were Jesus and the apostles activists for disciple making? If we follow Jesus above all, then we will live like he lived and do what he did in his life, both individually and corporately. But if we overemphasize important causes and neglect our fundamental call to follow Jesus, we will make those secondary things primary. We will not end up with a Jesus-centered life.

Everything written in the New Testament guides us, ultimately, to put on the mind of Christ (1 Corinthians 2:16). In fact, the apostle Paul explained that our formation and obedience to Christ should extend to *each and every thought.*

> We demolish arguments and every pretension that sets itself up against the knowledge of God, *and we take captive every thought to make it obedient to Christ.* (2 Corinthians 10:5)

DeYoung and Gilbert's comprehensive study *What Is the Mission of the Church?* deals with many of the complicated questions about the mission or purpose of the church that thoughtful people ask. These authors thoroughly discuss the role of the kingdom of God, service to the poor, and the place for peace in the church. This is an important book for church leaders to read, especially for young leaders. The two authors sum up their findings in a simple statement: "The mission of the church—your church, my church, the church in Appalachia, the church in Azerbaijan, the church anywhere—is to make disciples of Jesus Christ in the power of the Spirit to the glory of God the Father."[17]

Please take a moment to note an important and practical implication from this chapter. Because disciple making is the core mission of the church, it should invoke a key question for every activity in the church: How does this activity help us to be disciples and make disciples? In this way, church leaders make sure that everything in the church has a clear focus related to the church's core mission.

A disciple making focus keeps the church from less crucial ministries and activities that detract from its mission. It also stops the church from trying to be "everything to everybody." Devoting herself to too many unnecessary activities can distract the local church from her core mission. We must keep coming back to Jesus and disciple making.

Let's make it practical: we must work hard to make disciple making our true core mission. We have both worked extensively with churches and church leaders, and as we've worked with these leaders, we've landed on definitions that many leaders have found helpful. A team of national disciple making leaders developed them to help the local church find greater effectiveness as disciple makers. As you read these definitions, ask yourself, *What would it take for my home church to understand these definitions and fully function according to them?*

a. Disciple: someone who is following Jesus, being changed by Jesus, and is committed to the mission of Jesus (Matthew 4:19).

b. Disciple making: entering into relationships to intentionally help people follow Jesus, be changed by Jesus, and join the mission of Jesus (Matthew 28:18–20).

c. Disciple maker: a disciple of Jesus who enters into relationships with people to intentionally help them follow Jesus, be changed by Jesus, and join the mission of Jesus.

d. Disciple making church: a church whose beliefs, habits, and narrative focus on disciple making to such an in-depth level that it quickly becomes clear to everyone, including newcomers, that disciple making is the mission of this church.

We invite you to join us by using these definitions (see Appendix A for additional help). A disciple making focus will energize and give life to every group and church which adopts it. This invitation leads us to our next question: With a church *committed* to this kind of disciple making, what kind of results are possible?

4

WHAT IS THE RESULT OF DISCIPLE MAKING?

Answer: Disciple making results in a church that grows fruitfully and loves generously.

> After this I looked, and there before me was a great multitude that no one could count, from every nation, tribe, people and language, standing before the throne and before the Lamb. They were wearing white robes and were holding palm branches in their hands.
> — Revelation 7:9

Jesus told a parable in Matthew 25:14–30 about a master who went on a trip. Before going away, the master entrusted three of his servants with money to invest and grow while he was in a far country (interestingly, the specific currency was called a "talent"). Upon his return, the master asked each of his servants to give an account of what they had produced by using what he had entrusted to them. Two of the servants approached the master with great joy and showed him how they had doubled their money by investing, but the third hid his entrusted money by burying it in the ground. When this third servant showed the master his unearthed and uninvested "talent," the master went berserk, saying, "You wicked, lazy servant!" (Matthew 25:26). He cast that servant out of his house and distributed his talents to the servants who had produced results.

GOD CARES ABOUT RESULTS.

This story reveals a simple truth: God cares about results.

Yet when it comes to disciple making, defining results can be a mixed bag. Jesus warned disciple makers of this challenge when he told the first of a string of parables in Matthew 13 often called the "kingdom parables." This string of parables could just as well be called the "Parables of Disciple Making," for they string together the major issues and questions facing serious disciple makers of any age. Take, for example, the first parable, which involves a farmer scattering seed.

> A farmer went out to sow his seed. As he was scattering the seed, some fell along the path, and the birds came and ate it up. Some fell on rocky places, where it did not have much soil. It sprang up quickly, because the soil was shallow. But when the sun came up, the plants were scorched, and they withered because they had no root. Other seed fell among thorns, which grew up and choked the plants. Still other seed fell on good soil, where it produced a crop—a hundred, sixty or thirty times what was sown. Whoever has ears, let them hear. (Matthew 13:3–9)

Jesus' parable reveals how our disciple making efforts will always lead to mixed results. As we see in this parable, disciple makers sometimes scatter seed in places not ready to receive it, not ready to embrace it fully, and not ready to make room for it to thrive. Many will choose to enjoy the seed as a snack a few Sundays a month when they happen to be staying in town on the weekends, but they never embrace the message of discipleship. Others we invite into a discipling relationship might start off with great fanfare and amazing spiritual growth, but for them, their journey ends up being a short-lived fad with no roots. Still others make a serious and heartfelt commitment to following Jesus—but their decision is just one among *many* priorities in their busy and overscheduled lives. Over time, the thorns and thistles of material endeavors in life begin to choke out the nutrients and block out the sunlight needed for fully devoted followers of Jesus to thrive. With all these scenarios, Jesus reminds disciple makers they will always encounter apparent setbacks: people merely wanting a snack on a drive-thru Sunday visit, people who start strong but treat discipleship like a fad, and people too busy chasing anything and everything other than the disciple's life.

Yet disciple makers need not get too discouraged! Jesus closes with a description that makes our disciple making efforts worth it: "Still other seed fell on good soil, where it produced a crop—a hundred, sixty or thirty times what was sown"

(Matthew 13:8). Disciples fully trained become "like their teacher" (Luke 6:40). And "like their teacher," they also make disciples, who, when fully trained, then make disciples. Paul explained it to Timothy this way: "And the things you have heard me say in the presence of many witnesses entrust to reliable people who will also be qualified to teach others" (2 Timothy 2:2). A single life fully devoted to Jesus as a disciple maker wins, by the Spirit's power, thirty, sixty, maybe even a hundred more disciple makers. The method of the Master multiplies and multiplies—and the results are staggering.

This parable is important for leaders in the church. As Jesus focused his time and energy raising up "fourth-soil" people—those who produce great fruit—wise leaders similarly seek to raise up "fourth-soil" disciple makers.[18] Leaders in healthy disciple making churches learn to follow Jesus and focus their efforts on raising up these type of disciple makers.

GROWING FRUITFULLY

IN ANOTHER FARMING PARABLE found in Mark's Gospel, Jesus describes the multiplication process in a way that credits the unseen power of God.

> This is what the kingdom of God is like. A man scatters seed on the ground. Night and day, whether he sleeps or gets up, the seed sprouts and grows, though he does not know how. All by itself the soil produces grain—first the stalk, then the head, then the full kernel in the head. As soon as the grain is ripe, he puts the sickle to it, because the harvest has come. (Mark 4:26–29)

By the unseen, miraculous working of God, the seed planted by disciple makers sprouts, grows, multiplies, and produces a harvest. A bumper crop of disciples in one location produces a harvest of disciple makers larger than any storehouse or church can hold. So instead of building a bigger barn, those disciple makers venture out to cast the seeds of discipleship on fresh soil in both local church plants and internationally through missions.[19]

This multiplication is not merely theoretical; multiplying disciples produces a multiplication of disciple making and church planting. It is exciting to hear about these movements springing up around the globe.[20] The results are amazing. Imagine the results of one disciple maker.

- One disciple maker wins 30 disciple makers to the Lord Jesus in a lifetime . . .
- And those 30 disciple makers each win 30 to the Lord Jesus in a lifetime . . .
- And those 900 disciple makers each win 30 to the Lord Jesus in a lifetime . . .
- And those 27,000 disciple makers each win 30 to the Lord Jesus in a lifetime . . .
- And those 810,000 disciple makers each win 30 to the Lord Jesus in a lifetime . . .
- And those 24.3 million disciple makers each win 30 to the Lord Jesus in a lifetime . . .
- And those 729 million disciple makers each win 30 to the Lord Jesus in a lifetime . . .
- And those 2.187 billion disciple makers each win 30 to the Lord Jesus in a lifetime . . .

If this happened, the entire planet would have the opportunity to become fully devoted followers of Jesus in about eighty years. While the parable of the sower teaches us that the math will break down because not everyone will positively respond, there is great encouragement to be found in the reality of what happens when disciples make disciples. This kind of multiplication, in the power of the Holy Spirit, gives us a vision of how to win many in the world for Christ in our lifetime. But exponential growth is just a small portion of the actual results that would follow.

LOVING GENEROUSLY

JESUS TAUGHT US ANOTHER clear result of being a disciple: "By this everyone will know that you are my disciples, if you love one another" (John 13:35). What kind of love sets Jesus' disciples apart? Jesus described it as loving one another "as I have loved you" (John 13:34). This went beyond politeness and niceness to being the kind of profuse, generous love Jesus kept showing until it culminated in his sacrificial death on the cross. Generous love is the signature card of a true disciple. In Book 9, Kelvin Teamer provides a good definition of Christlike love: "Love is a cross-shaped action that glorifies God and benefits someone else."[21]

GENEROUS LOVE IS THE SIGNATURE CARD OF A TRUE DISCIPLE.

The New Testament repeatedly emphasizes the centrality of love for how we treat people (e.g., Mark 12:31; Colossians 3:14; 1 John 3:23). The apostle Paul explained that the three greatest attributes of a disciple are faith, hope, and love—yet the greatest is love (1 Corinthians 13:13). In everything a disciple does, love should be the driving force. And put in the context of a local body of believers, a disciple making church loves like Jesus.

Jesus spoke another parable in Matthew 25 about sheep and goats. The sheep represent the fully devoted followers (the same idea as those who come from the "good soil"). The life of each sheep has a multiplying impact for good in the world. Disciples that are trained as "kingdom-first" people actually do more good for state and nation than anyone else. Jesus implied that the results of disciple making would be seen in changed lives, reshaped communities, compassionate ministries for those at the margins, and a heightened awareness of the value of every person as the image of God or even as the hidden image of Jesus himself.

Look at Jesus' words:

> Then the King will say to those on his right, "Come, you who are blessed by my Father; take your inheritance, the kingdom prepared for you since the creation of the world. For I was hungry and you gave me something to eat, I was thirsty and you gave me something to drink, I was a stranger and you invited me in, I needed clothes and you clothed me, I was sick and you looked after me, I was in prison and you came to visit me."

> Then the righteous will answer him, "Lord, when did we see you hungry and feed you, or thirsty and give you something to drink? When did we see you a stranger and invite you in, or needing clothes and clothe you? When did we see you sick or in prison and go to visit you?"

> The King will reply, "Truly I tell you, whatever you did for one of the least of these brothers and sisters of mine, you did for me." (Matthew 25:34–40)

Disciple making produces nothing less than world change. This result is the ultimate answer to praying the Lord's Prayer, "Your kingdom come, your will be done, on earth as it is in heaven" (Matthew 6:10). As C. S. Lewis explained, "If you read history you will find that the Christians who did most for the present world were just those who thought most of the next."[22]

But even that is still not the end of the story for disciple makers who make other disciple makers. Imagine if the prayers of the saints on earth were multiplied thirty, sixty, or a hundred-fold. What would that do to the unfolding will of our Almighty God? Prayer is far more powerful than we typically assume from our earthly vantage point. We read in Revelation 8 that in response to the prayers of God's people came "peals of thunder, rumblings, flashes of lightning and an earthquake" (v. 5).

The church on earth is made up of disciple makers who pray and change the world. In cooperation with their efforts, God holds back evil, lifts oppression, thwarts violence, and eliminates famines and plagues. Angels gather up the prayers of the saints with the incense of God's holiness and take them up to heaven where they are heard—and then hurl them back to earth as "reversed thunder." These prayers "reenter history with incalculable effects. Our earth is shaken daily by it."[23]

Do you long to see generous love and fruitful growth inside the church which changes the world outside the church? Are you willing to spend time on your knees asking God to make it so? Are you willing to arrange your schedule to become a disciple maker whom God uses to answer your prayer?

God uses serious disciple makers to alter history and shape eternities, all by his grace and power. Disciple making churches love generously and experience fruitful growth. Now, practically speaking, what does this look like in a fallen world?

5

HOW DO DISCIPLES LIVE IN THIS WORLD?

Answer: Disciples of Jesus live in the world but are not of it. They are distinctive even as they permeate a dark world with light.

The kingdom of heaven is like treasure hidden in a field.
When a man found it, he hid it again, and then in his joy
went and sold all he had and bought that field.
— Matthew 13:44

The poster child for counter-cultural living in almost every way was John the Baptist. He dressed strangely, wearing camel skins and a broad belt, ate an odd diet—devouring locusts and wild honey—and lived without concern for political correctness—denouncing the religious leaders of his time and confronting the immoral marriage arrangement of the king. John also called his disciples to live countercultural lives as well—not calling them to adopt his style of clothing or diet, but to live counterculturally.[24] John explained to the crowds that their heritage as Jews could not save them. Instead, each person must produce the fruit of a repentant life committed to being a fully devoted God-follower. When asked what this type of repentance looked like, he got specific. He said, "Anyone who has two shirts should share with the one who has none, and anyone who has food should do the same." To tax collectors he said, "Don't collect any more than you are required to." Then, to soldiers he said, "Don't extort money and don't accuse people falsely—be content with your pay" (Luke 3:11–14).

John's model of discipleship instructs disciples to give sacrificially as needs arise and be willing to share half of their wardrobe to help another find dignity. He directed those with food to share their table, their pantry, and their smokehouse in order to provide for those going without. Behind these actions, his disciples were to maintain an attitude of contentment, being satisfied with enough and not harboring an insatiable desire to acquire more. Fairness in the treatment of others was to mark those who held power, and honesty and integrity were to be displayed in every human interaction. John the Baptist called his followers into a countercultural life of service to others as they strove to be fully devoted God-followers. When John the Baptist transferred some of his followers over to Jesus (John 1:29–31), they found in their new disciple making leader one who not only lived counterculturally but also one who stood against the culture to transform it.[25]

DON'T BE AFRAID OF DIFFERENT

IN JESUS' GREATEST MESSAGE, the Sermon on the Mount, the tone remains countercultural from the beginning and throughout. He opens his message describing what it means to live the "blessed life," with language that opposed the values their culture would suggest—spiritual poverty, mourning, meekness, purity, peacemaking, mercy-giving, and joy in accepting persecution. Upon completion of these countercultural "Beatitudes" (Matthew 5:3–12), Jesus then laid out his vision for how a disciple should live in the world.

> You are the salt of the earth. But if the salt loses its saltiness, how can it be made salty again? It is no longer good for anything, except to be thrown out and trampled underfoot. You are the light of the world. A town built on a hill cannot be hidden. Neither do people light a lamp and put it under a bowl. Instead, they put it on its stand, and it gives light to everyone in the house. In the same way, let your light shine before others, that they may see your good deeds and glorify your Father in heaven. (Matthew 5:13–16)

Simply put, Jesus' disciples should live so dynamically, so boldly, and so brightly that their lives elevate and illuminate everything in the world around them.

Salt does that. Just as salt adds flavor to a bland meal, disciples add the spice of life to real living—showing a confused world where to turn for the meaning of life. As salt preserves food from decay and putrefaction, disciples keep the world from falling further into chaos and destruction. By living counterculturally to everyone around them, disciples renew the world by renewing the teachings of Jesus.

We live in a time where it can be easy to lose our saltiness. In fact, the Laodicean church in Revelation showed what happens when "salt" loses its saltiness. The Lord described the church this way:

> DISCIPLES RENEW THE WORLD BY RENEWING THE TEACHINGS OF JESUS.

> I know your deeds, that you are neither cold nor hot. I wish you were either one or the other! So, because you are lukewarm—neither hot nor cold—I am about to spit you out of my mouth. You say, "I am rich; I have acquired wealth and do not need a thing." But you do not realize that you are wretched, pitiful, poor, blind and naked. (Revelation 3:15–17)

There was nothing countercultural, nothing salty, about them. They were rich, proud, self-assured, and confident, but Jesus saw them only as completely pitiable. There were no distinguishing markers of kingdom life. The salt had lost its saltiness. The church had become indistinguishable from her surroundings. Using disciple making language, it appears that the church was filled with converts but not disciples. The Laodicean Christians were followers lacking in the substance of authentic discipleship.

If a Christian is being discipled into a lifestyle that looks indistinguishable from the world, something is fundamentally wrong. "Different" is to be expected. In fact, the meaning of the word "holy"—which describes God *and* his people—means "set apart." True disciples live as salt and light. We keep our distinctive differences (our "saltiness") even as we permeate darkness with light. When we lose our distinctive "saltiness," we lose our effectiveness as "light." Both are necessary for disciples of Jesus. We cannot reach people of the world by living lives indistinguishable from them. Therefore, Jesus tells us that true disciples arrange their lives around countercultural priorities.

> TRUE DISCIPLES LIVE AS SALT AND LIGHT.

- True disciples abide in the Word of God (John 8:31).
- True disciples love one another sacrificially (John 13:34–35).
- True disciples bear fruit—such as love, joy, and peace—which the world craves but cannot produce (John 15:7–8).

Wholehearted followers of Jesus live differently from the world but are respected by many in the world simply because followers of Jesus know what they believe, they know how to love, and the character of their lives is compelling enough to win the respect of outsiders.

START WITH PRAYER

THERE IS SOMETHING ELSE important to note about Jesus' disciple making. He uniquely relied on the power of God through prayer and fasting. Jesus started his ministry by first spending forty days fasting and praying (Matthew 4:1–11). Then during his ministry, he regularly withdrew to pray privately (Mark 1:35). And when he had a monumental decision to make that would determine the success of his entire ministry, it was so critical he spent the entire night in fervent prayer discussing the matter repeatedly with his Father (Luke 6:12).

The life of prayer that marked Jesus' life and preceded his invitation to disciple making became the foundation stone of the earliest disciple making practices as well. As early as the first chapter of Acts, the church "joined constantly in prayer" (Acts 1:14), and prayer both preceded and empowered important decisions. In Jesus' own ministry, notice that it was after a night of prayer that he selected the Twelve.

> When morning came, he called his disciples to him and chose twelve of them, whom he also designated apostles: Simon (whom he named Peter), his brother Andrew, James, John, Philip, Bartholomew, Matthew, Thomas, James son of Alphaeus, Simon who was called the Zealot, Judas son of James, and Judas Iscariot, who became a traitor. (Luke 6:13–16)

From this motley crew of twelve—less a traitor—Jesus would influence the entire world. His vision was to reconcile fallen humanity to God through himself and restore them to their original image and glory.

FOCUS ON A FEW

HOW WOULD JESUS FULFILL this magnificent vision to redeem the world? Surprisingly, his process entailed raising up a handful of followers and molding them into disciples who make disciples, who then make disciples. His values centered around relationship, imitation, practical experience, service, and multiplication. He gave three years of his life to invest in relationships with the Twelve; he gave special attention to the Three (Peter, James, and John); and he found in the young apostle John a confidant and close friend for his own journey. Look at the math; it's all small numbers: three years and twelve disciples. Yet it worked.

Jesus focused his time and energy upon a few concentric circles, which allowed him to invest himself fully into the lives of a few, allowing them to become imitators of himself. John's Gospel tells us, "God so loved the world that he gave his one and only Son" (John 3:16). But each Gospel also shows that Jesus so loved the world that he invested his greatest energy and largest amount of time impressing his life upon a few close followers whom he believed could then disciple others. Notice this is exactly the opposite of the focus of most contemporary churches. Let us explain what we mean.

Imagine a bullseye target. Then, think of each concentric circle working out from the bullseye as a level of relationship Jesus had with people. One could say Jesus had great relationships at every level of the target.

- Level One: one-to-one with John (John 19:26).
- Level Two: one-to-three with Peter, James, and John (Matthew 17:1).
- Level Three: one-to-twelve with the apostles (Matthew 10:2–4).
- Level Four: one-to-seventy-two with the disciples on the "Limited Commission" (Luke 10:1).
- Level Five: one-to-five hundred to whom Jesus appeared after the resurrection (1 Corinthians 15:6).
- Level Six: one-to-thousands (or multitudes) in settings such as the Sermon on the Mount (Matthew 5:1).[26]

Jesus focused *most* of his attention upon Levels One to Three, while most modern churches focus their primary focus upon Levels Four to Six. The problem with this overemphasis on Levels Four to Six is that converts are typically made at Levels Four to Six but disciples are typically formed at Levels One to Three.

The following diagram contrasts the two models.

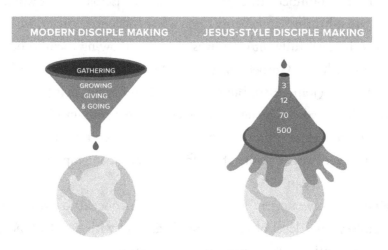

MODERN DISCIPLE MAKING   JESUS-STYLE DISCIPLE MAKING

GATHERING

GROWING
GIVING
& GOING

3
12
70
500

Source: Emotionally Healthy Discipleship

Jesus so loved the whole world that he wanted to save it—which required him to focus on just a few.

In my book *Discipleship that Fits*, I (Bobby) and my co-author, Alex Absalom, note a slightly different model based on social spaces in which Jesus formed his disciples.[27] There is the public context (e.g., Jesus and the crowds); social context (e.g., Jesus and the Seventy-Two); personal context (e.g., Jesus and the Twelve); transparent context (e.g., Jesus and the Three); and the divine context (e.g., Jesus and the Father). Each context is important, and none should be neglected. Yet it is important to remember that Jesus spent most of his focused attention on the smaller contexts. In other words, he focused on just a few, and it paid off.

In Jesus' disciple making parables of Matthew 13, two of them explain his strategy of focusing on smaller things in order to produce maximum results.[28] It is counterintuitive to think small, but there is a hidden truth in small things Jesus probably learned from helping around the house or in the yard. Jesus revealed the truth this way:

> The kingdom of heaven is like a mustard seed, which a man took and planted in his field. Though it is the smallest of all seeds, yet when it grows, it is the largest of garden plants and becomes a tree, so that the birds come and perch in its branches." He told them still another parable: "The kingdom of heaven

is like yeast that a woman took and mixed into about sixty pounds of flour until it worked all through the dough. (Matthew 13:31–33)

Jesus knew that the secret to "impressive" results was multiplication. Multiplication required Jesus to focus on a different formula for lasting results rather than his "massive gatherings" that often stemmed from one of his miracles that gathered a crowd. Make no mistake, Jesus could and would draw, entertain, and engage a crowd—and leave everyone spellbound. Jesus sometimes did massive feats. But to change the world, he regularly and intentionally kept his focus on the small size of gatherings—the best for disciple making. We recommend church leaders follow Jesus' lead here by implementing the same focus for their ministry. In Appendix A, we provide some key resources that will help you focus on a few.

WHY SMALLER THINGS?

THE MIDDLE EASTERN MUSTARD seeds of Jesus' day, which still exist today, were about the size of a poppy seed—almost impossible to hold between two fingers because they were so small. But when planted in the ground, the smallest of all garden seeds produced a bush large enough—some thirty feet high with a twenty-foot spread—that it is more often called a tree. The North American bush with similar results is the crepe myrtle that grows so large that at some point, once again, a bush must then be called a tree.

Jesus' parable of the mustard seed is incredibly encouraging. This small seed is potent and powerful enough to make a huge impact. After all, the potency of a small seed does not lie in the gardener's skill but in the Creator's genius. In the same way, the potency of disciple making is unlocked by God's Spirit. The gardener plants the potent seed into the ground, yielding massive results that would be unimaginable from such a tiny beginning. The power of this small seed is that it grows to such heights and stability—then becomes the gathering place for others.

When churches are intentional about making disciples who make disciples, the increase can create a hundred-fold movement of the Spirit, bringing a fresh harvest that can sweep through a nation. Jesus believed that investing in a few was the secret to exponential growth, but will churches follow his lead? Will church leaders want the results badly enough to think and strategize differently? Return once again to the disciple making parables of Matthew 13 and notice the courageous acts of bold people who carry this kind of entrepreneurial spirit in their approach to the kingdom.

> The kingdom of heaven is like treasure hidden in a field. When a man found it, he hid it again, and then in his joy went and sold all he had and bought that field. Again, the kingdom of heaven is like a merchant looking for fine pearls. When he found one of great value, he went away and sold everything he had and bought it. (Matthew 13:44–46)

Churches that make disciples who make disciples value the disciple making mission of Jesus above all other practices. When the leadership of a church returns to disciple making as its core mission, it values making disciples who make disciples over every program that might exist in their church. The disciple making, exponentially multiplying kingdom is the treasure hidden in a field that must be purchased and the pearl of greatest price that must be obtained.

Disciple making church leaders shepherd with the goal in mind, knowing that one day, they will give an answer for their congregation as to why it was filled with converts but so few disciples making disciples. Jesus closes the disciple making parables with a reminder of how each life, each kingdom believer, will be judged.

> Once again, the kingdom of heaven is like a net that was let down into the lake and caught all kinds of fish. When it was full, the fishermen pulled it up on the shore. Then they sat down and collected the good fish in baskets, but threw the bad away. This is how it will be at the end of the age. The angels will come and separate the wicked from the righteous and throw them into the blazing furnace, where there will be weeping and gnashing of teeth. (Matthew 13:47–50)

One day Jesus will likely ask churches why they gathered so many crowds, yet produced so few disciples. Jesus concluded his parables with a reminder that the stakes are high, and that the one casting the net is looking for good fish to gather and keep.

WHAT PRICE ARE WE WILLING TO PAY?

WE WANT TO END this chapter by describing the legacy left by the apostle John.[29] It comes to us from the writings of church father Clement of Alexandria, who lived AD 150–215. This ancient tradition tells us that John left his exile on the Island of Patmos after the death of a tyrant emperor named Domitian and returned to Ephesus to serve the churches of Asia. John, now an old man, lived in the surrounding cities, where he helped appoint elders and set churches in order. In one city not too far away, John saw a young man, "powerful in body, handsome in appearance and ardent in faith." John entrusted the young man to the leaders of the church and said, "This youth I commit to you in all earnestness, in the presence of the Church and with Christ as a witness." One of the church leaders in particular accepted the charge from John to disciple this young man and took personal responsibility for his growth. Taking the young man into his home, this elder reared, kept, and finally baptized him. The young man grew as a disciple under the guiding influence of the elder, but after some time the elder relaxed his disciple making posture, assuming the seal of the Lord would keep the boy in secure protection.

Eventually, he began hanging around youths who led him into moral laziness, wild parties, and even crime. Before long, he was joining these friends at night in highway robberies. The young man soon gave up on his walk with God. He seemed to be once again lost, and he lived as a rebel. Forming a band of robbers, the talented young man became the captain of the bandits—even becoming the fiercest, bloodiest, and cruelest of them all.

Time passed, and the apostle John returned to the province to check up on the churches. While there, he inquired of the elder entrusted with the responsibility to disciple the young man: "Restore to us the deposit which Jesus and I committed to you in the presence of the Church."

The church leader was at first confused, thinking that it was a false charge about stolen money. But when John explained that he was referring to the young man, the church leader, groaning deeply and bursting into tears, said, "He is dead."

"How and what kind of death?" John replied.

"He is dead," he said, "to God. For he turned wicked and abandoned the faith, and is now a robber. He and his band of robbers have taken possession of the mountain in front of the church."

John tore his clothes in lament and then called for a horse. John rode away, just as he was, straight from the church. When John arrived at the foot of the mountain, the robbers' outpost, they arrested him. The apostle neither fled nor complained, but cried out, "It was for this I came. Take me to your captain."

When the young bandit leader recognized John, he turned, ashamed, and tried to run. The old man followed with all his might, forgetting his age, and cried out:

> Why, my son, do you flee from me, your spiritual father? Fear not; there is still hope for you. I will give account to Christ for you. If need be, I will willingly endure death, as the Lord did die for us. For your sake, I will surrender my life. Stand and believe, for Christ has sent me.

The young man threw down his arms, trembled, and began to weep bitterly. The old man approached, embraced him, and baptized him again. The man then reengaged in the life of a disciple with the apostle John as his teacher. Through a life of copious prayers, continual fasting, and the renewal of his mind with the Word of God, the young man was restored to the church. His life became a model of true repentance, a token of regeneration, and a trophy of the hope all have in the resurrection of Jesus.

Even in his old age, John was a disciple maker to the very end. His core mission was the mission of Jesus: making disciples. This hard and costly work combined the Great Commandment *and* the Great Commission. The Apostle of Love knew that a life that loves both God and people will make disciples. Then, that disciple likewise disciples yet others, who in turn disciple others. Each disciple maker stands in a holy line of world-changers. Looking toward the front of that long line, we see such heroes as Moses, Elijah, and Hannah, not to mention Peter, Paul, Priscilla—and many others. And at the very front of the line is the Lamb whom they are all following.

> They follow the Lamb wherever he goes. They were purchased from among mankind and offered as firstfruits to God and the Lamb. (Revelation 14:4)

May God grant you a legacy of joining the long line of disciple makers. The line of disciples-who-make-disciples curves its way through every culture and every age, connecting us to the great reformers, church fathers, apostles, and even to Jesus himself. Our desire for you—when you close your eyes at the end of your life and reflect upon what your life has been all about—is that you will think of the people you have discipled to become Jesus-followers. You will feel the same way Paul felt about those he discipled.

> For what is our hope, our joy, or the crown in which we will glory in the presence of our Lord Jesus when he comes? Is it not you? Indeed, you are our glory and joy. (1 Thessalonians 2:19–20)

Are you convinced that disciple making is the core mission of the church? Are you ready to make it *your* core mission? We urge you to make a specific and concrete decision right now, by taking these four actions steps:

1. Determine if making disciples will be a core personal mission for your life.
2. Make a commitment to God about this new priority in your life through prayer, as you ask for his help in order to make the commitment a reality.
3. Review the recommended resources in Appendix A.
4. Meet with a leader(s) from your church to enlist their help explicitly so that, with their support, you make your commitment a reality. If the leaders from your church cannot help you, find someone outside your church who will help you.

POSTSCRIPT

A PARABLE OF URGENCY

King Hezekiah, king of the Jews in the seventh century BC, feared the Assyrians would lay siege to the royal city of Jerusalem over which he ruled. He also feared a season of starvation and slow death would be brought upon Jerusalem's inhabitants. Hezekiah knew the primary water source for the city, the Gihon Spring, was located outside the city walls and was protected only by a guard tower. The spring lay vulnerable to attack by Sennacherib, the cruel dictator of Assyria, and its water could be easily diverted by Sennacherib's soldiers to supply the enemy. Hezekiah acted quickly.

> It was Hezekiah who blocked the upper outlet of the Gihon Spring and channeled the water down to the west side of the City of David. He succeeded in everything he undertook. (2 Chronicles 32:30; see also 2 Kings 20:20; 2 Chronicles 32:2–4; Isaiah 22:11)

Hezekiah accomplished his mission by designing an aqueduct that would channel all the water of the Gihon into a tunnel, known today as "Hezekiah's Tunnel," and from there into the Pool of Siloam.[30] His mission-critical decision brought life-giving sustenance to the people of God.

But how did he accomplish this great feat? According to the Siloam Inscription,[31] found at the halfway mark inside the 583-yards-long ancient tunnel, we learn about the method he employed (for reference, a cubit is approximately 20 inches):

> And this is the story of the tunnel while . . . the axes were against each other and while 3 cubits were left to cut . . . and on the day of the tunnel being finished the stonecutters struck each man towards his counterpart, axe

against axe and flowed water from the source to the pool for 1,200 cubits. And 100 cubits was the height over the head of the stonecutters.[32]

The mission was vital to the life of the community, and the people gave it the highest priority. The project was carried out in teams working from different directions toward the same goal. Each team involved skilled stonecutters, trained by earlier generations in the use of an axe and chisel. And each stonecutter had others working alongside him, assisting and also carrying out the rock and debris. The teams used the best math and technology of their day, but also trusted in their own wisdom and intuition. At the most critical point of the venture, they had to listen to one another, come together, and work toward a common cause that would save them all. When the last strike of the axe landed its blow, water came rushing forth. The tunnel has been a steady supply of water for the city now for more than 2,800 years.

Many people were saved by Hezekiah's focus on the mission. He did not give in to fate, nor did he shirk back from a big challenge. He led and his people followed. They overcame the enemy's siege.

Satan has laid siege to our civilization. To survive and thrive, we must act quickly; for us in the West, this is a mission-critical moment as the culture continues its slide into post-Christian secularism. Jesus, as our king, has given us the mission of bringing living water to our culture, our communities, and our congregations. To do so, we must employ Jesus' strategy for Jesus' mission. This moment in Western history will call us to work in teams, learn from our craftsman, use the latest research, engage the latest technology, employ age-old wisdom, and listen to the voice of him calling us to come together.

King Jesus is calling us to make disciples—his core mission for the church—and join him in this exciting journey. Unless Jesus' core mission becomes again our core mission, the siege-works of the enemy will overwhelm the faithful and the civilization will be led off into spiritual captivity. The King is calling his disciple-makers to pick up their axes, rally their followers, and usher in a season when living water flows upon the land.

APPENDIX

KEY DISCIPLE MAKING RESOURCES

Ten Key Books on Disciple Making for Church Leaders

1. David Young, *King Jesus and the Beauty of Obedience-Based Discipleship* (Grand Rapids: Zondervan, 2020).
2. Jim Putman, Bobby Harrington, and Robert Coleman, *DiscipleShift: Five Shifts That Help Your Church to Make Disciples Who Make Disciples* (Grand Rapids: Zondervan, 2013).
3. Robert Coleman, *The Master Plan of Evangelism*, 2nd ed. (Grand Rapids: Revell, 2006).
4. Bobby Harrington and Alex Absalom, *Discipleship that Fits: The Five Kinds of Relationships God Uses to Help Us Grow* (Grand Rapids: Zondervan, 2016).
5. Brandon Guindon, *Disciple Making Culture: Cultivate Thriving Disciple-Makers Throughout Your Church* (Nashville: HIM Publications, 2020).
6. Will Mancini and Cory Hartman, *Future Church: Seven Laws of Real Church Growth* (Grand Rapids: Baker Books, 2020).
7. Bill Hull, *The Disciple-Making Pastor: Leading Others on the Journey of Faith*, rev. ed. (Grand Rapids: Baker Books, 2007).
8. Bobby Harrington and Josh Patrick, *The Disciple Maker's Handbook: Seven Elements of a Discipleship Lifestyle* (Grand Rapids: Zondervan, 2017).
9. Peter Scazzero, *Emotionally Healthy Discipleship: Moving from Shallow Christianity to Deep Transformation* (Grand Rapids: Zondervan, 2021).
10. Jim Putman and Chad Harrington, *The Revolutionary Disciple: Walking Humbly with Jesus in Every Area of Life* (Nashville: HIM Publications, 2021).

Six Content Resources to Use in Disciple Making

1. Bobby Harrington, *Trust and Follow Jesus: Discipleship Conversations* (Renew.org, 2019).
2. Bobby Harrington, *Trust and Follow Jesus: Discipleship Conversations: The Leader's Guide* (Renew.org, 2020).
3. Bobby Harrington, *Starting a Transparency Group Using the Teachings of Jesus*, renew.org/ebook/starting-a-discipleship-group.
4. Discovery Bible Study: dbsguide.org.
5. Jim Putman, Bill Kraus, Avery Willis, Brandon Guindon, *Real-Life Discipleship Training Manual*, Teacher's Guide ed. (Colorado Springs: NavPress, 2010).
6. James Bryan Smith and Richard Foster, *A Spiritual Formation Workbook: Small Group Resources for Nurturing Christian Growth*, rev. ed. (San Francisco: HarperOne, 2010).

Church Coaching

The Relational Discipleship Network specializes in helping churches make the shift toward a disciple making focus. See rdn1.com for more information.

NOTES

1. C. S. Lewis, *Mere Christianity* (San Francisco: Harper Collins, 2001), 199.

2. Renew.org Network and Discipleship.org are both national and international disciple making ministries. Bobby serves as the co-founder and point leader of both ministries. Renew.org's mission is to "renew the teachings of Jesus to fuel disciple making" and discipleship.org's mission is to "champion Jesus-style disciple making." Renew.org upholds specific teachings whereas discipleship.org is a broader evangelical network. Both organizations feature some of the same leaders. Both share the same conviction that disciple making is the core mission of the church. Where possible, like this instance, we will use definitions that all the many ministry leaders, scholars, and practitioners involved with Discipleship.org vetted out. See https://discipleship.org/about-discipleship-org/.

3. The word *Shema* is the Hebrew word for "hear," which is also the first word of Deuteronomy 6:4. Hearing and passing along these truths were crucial to the future faithfulness of succeeding generations in Israel. These verses from Deuteronomy are the most recited and formative verses in Judaism even to this day.

4. For more on the Deuteronomy 6 model of disciple making, see Jason Houser, Bobby Harrington, and Chad Harrington, *Dedicated: Training Your Children to Trust and Follow Jesus* (Grand Rapids: Zondervan, 2015).

5. David Young, *King Jesus and the Beauty of Obedience-Based Discipleship* (Grand Rapids: Zondervan, 2020).

6. The commands of Jesus are the commands of the whole Bible. *Real Life Theology: Fuel for Faithful and Effective Disciple Making* (Renew.org, 2021) emphasizes this concept.

7. For more on this idea, see Matthew Bates, *The Gospel Precisely* (Renew.org, 2021) and Matthew Bates, *Gospel Allegiance* (Grand Rapids: Brazos, 2019).

8. For the gold-standard description of Jesus' disciple making model, see Robert Coleman, *The Master Plan of Evangelism*, 2nd ed. (Grand Rapids: Revell, 2006).

9. For more information on this definition and how to use it, see Jim Putman, Bobby Harrington, and Robert Coleman's book, *DiscipleShift: Five Steps That Help Your Church to Make Disciples Who Make Disciples* (Grand Rapids: Zondervan, 2013).

10. For more information, see Bobby Harrington and Josh Patrick, *The Disciple Maker's Handbook: Seven Elements of a Discipleship Lifestyle* (Grand Rapids: Zondervan, 2017).

11. The exact percentage of time that Jesus spent focused on discipling the Twelve is hard to peg, but this is commonly quoted. Dave Ferguson quotes 73 percent as a good number, see https://churchleaders.com/pastors/pastor-articles/320680-essential-practices-leaders-multiply-leaders-carey-nieuwhof-dave-ferguson.html, accessed March 3, 2021.

12. Rick Warren, *The Purpose Driven Church: Growth Without Compromising Your Message and Mission*, rev. ed. (Grand Rapids: Zondervan, 2010).

13. For further development on how disciple making encompasses all the major functions of church, see Jim Putman, Bobby Harrington, and Robert Coleman, *DiscipleShift: Five Steps That Help Your Church to Make Disciples Who Make Disciples* (Grand Rapids: Zondervan, 2013).

14. Curtis Erskine, "Conversion, Theology, and Discipleship," Discipleship.org, accessed March 18, 2021, https://discipleship.org/bobbys-blog/conversion-theology-discipleship/.

15. See Richard Longenecker, *Patterns of Discipleship in the New Testament* (Grand Rapids: Wm. B. Eerdmans, 1996).

16. N. T. Wright, *Following Jesus: Biblical Reflections on Discipleship*, rev. ed. (Grand Rapids: Wm. B. Eerdmans, 2014).

17. Kevin DeYoung and Greg Gilbert, *What Is the Mission of the Church? Making Sense of Social Justice, Shalom, and the Great Commission* (Wheaton: Crossway, 2011), 265.

18. For more information on Jesus' method, see Robert Coleman, *The Master Plan of Evangelism*, 2nd ed. (Grand Rapids: Revell, 2006).

19. On the topic of building "bigger barns," see Jesus' parable about the rich fool who kept building more and more properties but gave no thought to eternity (Luke 12:16–21).

20. For a summary description of disciple making in the USA and disciple making movements, see "National Study on Disciple Making in USA Churches:

High Aspirations Amidst Disappointing Results, 2020" by Discipleship.org and Exponential.org, prepared by Grey Matter Research & Consulting: https://discipleship.org/national-study-on-disciple-making-in-usa-churches/.

21. See the volume in this series called *Kingdom Life: Experiencing God's Reign Through Love and Holiness* by Kelvin Teamer (Renew.org, 2021).

22. C. S. Lewis, *Mere Christianity* (San Francisco: Harper San Francisco, 2001), 134–135.

23. Eugene Peterson, *Reversed Thunder: The Revelation of John and the Praying Imagination* (San Francisco: Harper San Francisco, 1988), 88. The phrase "reversed thunder" is a phrase that originates with the poet George Herbert.

24. See Carol Swain, *Counter-Cultural Living: What Jesus Has to Say About Life, Marriage, Race, Gender Identity, and Materialism* (Renew.org, 2021).

25. For a classic understanding of this issue, see H. Richard Niebuhr, *Christ & Culture* (New York: Harper & Row, 1951). The author has a helpful discussion of Jesus' five responses to the challenges of culture by the church.

26. See Milton Jones, *Discipling: The Multiplying Ministry* (Ft. Worth: Star Bible, 1982), 80–84, for the best treatment of this concept. Jones credits Gary Collins, *How To Be a People Helper* (Santa Ana: Vision House, 1976) for these categories.

27. Bobby Harrington and Alex Absalom, *Discipleship that Fits: The Five Kinds of Relationships God Uses to Help Us Grow* (Grand Rapids: Zondervan, 2016).

28. Churches that have added a small group strategy to their church have experienced a growth built around community, relationship, and full-member participation. However, the next step for a church that wishes to multiply is to think smaller by investing in a few. Often, this means that the idea is to focus on discipleship groups of three or four where everyone fits around a table at a local restaurant or park.

29. Clement of Alexandria, "Who Is the Rich Man Who Can Be Saved?" (Section *XLII*, trans. William Wilson) in Vol. 2 of *Ante-Nicene Fathers,* eds. Alexander Roberts, James Donaldson, and A. Cleveland Coxe (Buffalo: Christian Literature Publishing Co., 1885). Some of the quotes have been modernized in language.

30. Jesus would later send the blind man of John 9 to this pool to wash and be healed.

31. Interestingly, it was while snorkeling in the tunnel that a young boy named Jacob Eliahu Spafford found the inscription. He was the adopted son of Horatio Spafford who wrote, "It Is Well With My Soul."

32. Gary Rendsburg and William Schniedewind, "The Siloam Tunnel Inscription: Historical and Linguistic Perspectives," *Israel Exploration Journal*, 60, no. 2 (2010): 188–203. *Research with Rutgers.*

9

KINGDOM LIFE

EXPERIENCING GOD'S
REIGN THROUGH
LOVE AND HOLINESS

KELVIN TEAMER

To Kim . . . you are my love and my inspiration.
To Joshua and Jordan . . . "Whatever it takes!"

CONTENTS

General Editors' Note 453

Introduction 455

CHAPTER 1: What Is the Kingdom of God? 457

CHAPTER 2: What Does the Kingdom of God Look Like
Through the Church? 469

CHAPTER 3: What Is Holiness and Why Is It Important? 475

CHAPTER 4: What Is Love and Why Is It Important? 479

CHAPTER 5: How Does the Church Express Love to
the World? 485

Appendix: Book Recommendations for Further Study 491

Notes 493

GENERAL EDITORS' NOTE

Jesus talked more about the kingdom of God than any other topic. After his resurrection, and before he ascended to heaven, the kingdom was the focus of what Jesus taught his disciples (Acts 1:3). It is important for disciples of Jesus to understand the kingdom.

Kelvin Teamer is uniquely suited to teach us about the kingdom. Kelvin serves as the evangelist of the Church of Christ at Bouldercrest in Atlanta, Georgia. Kelvin has earned degrees from Southern Illinois University, Georgia School of Preaching and Biblical Studies, and Amridge University (MDiv and DMin). He also serves as Adjunct Professor of Theology at Amridge University. Kelvin has been married to Kim for the past twenty-three years, and they have two children, Joshua and Jordan.

This book expounds on the section from the Renew.org Leaders' Faith Statement called "Kingdom Life":

> We believe in the present kingdom reign of God, the power of the Holy Spirit to transform people, and the priority of the local church. God's holiness should lead our churches to reject lifestyles characterized by pride, sexual immorality, homosexuality, easy divorce, idolatry, greed, materialism, gossip, slander, racism, violence, and the like. God's love should lead our churches to emphasize love as the distinguishing sign of a true disciple. Love for one another should make the church like an extended family—a fellowship of married people, singles, elderly, and children who are all brothers and sisters to one another. The love of the extended church family to one another is vitally important. Love should be expressed in both service to the church and to the surrounding community. It leads to the breaking down of walls (racial, social, political), evangelism, acts of mercy, compassion, forgiveness, and the

like. By demonstrating the ways of Jesus, the church reveals God's kingdom reign to the watching world.

*See the full Network Faith Statements at the end of this book.

Support Scriptures: 1 Corinthians 1:2; Galatians 5:19–21; Ephesians 5:3–7; Colossians 3:5–9; Matthew 19:3–12; Romans 1:26–32; 14:17–18; 1 Peter 1:15–16; Matthew 25:31–46; John 13:34–35; Colossians 3:12–13; 1 John 3:16; 1 Corinthians 13:1–13; 2 Corinthians 5:16–21.

The following tips might help you use this book more effectively (and the other books in the *Real Life Theology* series):

1. *Five questions, answers, and Scriptures.* We framed this book around five key questions with five short answers and five notable Scriptures. This format provides clarity, making it easier to commit crucial information to memory. This format also enables the books in the *Real Life Theology* series to support our catechism. Our catechism is a series of fixed questions and answers for instruction in church or home. In all, the series has fifty-two questions, answers, and key Scriptures. This particular book focuses on the five that are most pertinent to kingdom living.
2. *Summary videos.* You can find three to seven-minute video teachings that summarize the book, as well as each chapter, at Renew.org. These short videos can function as standalone teachings. But for groups or group leaders using the book, they can also be used to launch discussion of the reading.

May God use this book to fuel faithful and effective disciple making in your life and church.

For King Jesus,
Bobby Harrington and Daniel McCoy
General Editors, *Real Life Theology* Series

INTRODUCTION

On May 19, 2018, numerous people in the United States awakened from their slumber to witness what many believed to be the "wedding of the year." Such is usually the moniker given to any would-be "royal wedding." Although the US has no official ties to the British monarchy, Americans (whether or not they admit it) seem to be fascinated with the activities of the royal family of Queen Elizabeth, Prince Charles, and the late Princess Diana. On this day in 2018, Prince Harry, the youngest of the Charles and Diana brood, was set to wed American actress Meghan Markle.

Meghan Markle to Americans is no ordinary bride. She is one of ours and at the time was going to become part of the British royal family. She would emerge a *princess* (a duchess to be exact), and the intrigue of that to those bearing witness was palpable.

In the weeks leading up to the wedding, many British traditionalists resisted the marriage, taking issue with Harry marrying an American, not to mention one who had African-American genes. Little did anyone know at the time that this resistance (which the couple would later allege was racially based) would eventually become a factor in why they left the very realm that intrigues so many of us.

Being in the British royal family brings great scrutiny and attention, not to mention its strict traditions, guidelines, rules, and responsibilities that come with the kingdom life. For Meghan to move from a career in acting into the family of a ruling monarch involved a sacrifice and surrender of all that she was used to in order for her to "take" to a new kingdom. To do this, she would have to move from a do-it-yourself, American self-rule, to being ruled by the guidelines of another kingdom. The Duke and Duchess of Sussex felt the pressure to break away from that kingdom.

Less than two years following their celebrated wedding, Harry and Meghan announced that they were opting out of their duties as senior royals to live a more independent life. One could not blame them. And it isn't my goal to take a stance on this or disparage this couple, nor any other parties involved, including the Queen of England. My goal is to highlight the fact that not everyone "takes" to the kingdom life. Many, if given the choice, would choose something else for their lives: something more independent, something freer.

We all want freedom. People have sacrificed their lives for the thought and hope of freedom, whether that freedom was from foreign oppressors or from the Jim Crow despotism in America. Freedom is a treasured value. Surrendering to the life of a kingdom rarely brings the freedom that people crave.

But what if you could have both? What if freedom and surrender could be simultaneously experienced? What if freedom could be enjoyed underneath the rule of another? What if there were a way to have that type of heaven here on earth?

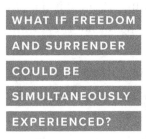

I want to propose a way to have that and a lot more. There is an existing kingdom that offers freedom, joy, peace, love, and hope. It is ruled by a king who is just and honorable and even perfect.

To experience this kingdom, however, we must surrender our own kingdom, our own freedom, and our own rule. The result? We get to enjoy a freedom that is so much greater than anything a kingdom of self-rule could possibly bring us. This kingdom is the kingdom of God. The king whom I am speaking about is King Jesus. The life I want to reveal in this book is kingdom life.

This life will ask everything of you, but it promises to replace everything you have given up with something better, more precious, and more valuable. This is available to all people. Now, when we leave, our old kingdom offers resistance to the new rule. Like a foreign kidney struggles in an unnatural host, your body will seek to reject it, but if it "takes," your future will be much better than your past. And, truthfully, it is vital that it "takes." It is God's fervent hope that we surrender to this new rule.

I believe our life within God's kingdom begins by understanding what the kingdom life is all about. If you are keenly interested in living this way, I invite you to read on. Each of us has a life to lose, but everything to gain. When we join it, we do it all for King Jesus! So to Harry, Meghan, and anyone else seeking freedom, I introduce you to the great kingdom of God. I present to you *Kingdom Life*.

1

WHAT IS THE KINGDOM OF GOD?

Answer: The kingdom of God is the realm where God's will is being done on earth as it is in heaven through the reign of King Jesus.

> But seek first his kingdom and his righteousness, and
> all these things will be given to you as well.
> — Matthew 6:33

For me, high school was tough. I had been a "big man on campus" during my junior high years, but then, all of a sudden, I was thrust into a new environment with so many more new people and a boatload of new classes. Socially and academically, I felt like everyone was moving at a different speed than I was. High school . . . I just didn't get it.

A microcosm of my high school experience was Algebra 1. For years, before this class began, I had been taught real-life numbers, but then I was transported into a world of integers, x's, y's, and square roots. Everyone around me seemed to understand this mathematical foreign language except for me. I just didn't get it.

My *not* understanding it was problematic because I was told that I would need to learn this form of math to "get through life." So, I tried to buckle down. I stayed after class, came to school early, got tutors, and hoped that I would finally understand. My efforts didn't work. I still just didn't get it.

Now before this point, my default excuse when I struggled in school had been to blame the teacher. It *had to* be their fault that I didn't understand what they were teaching, but this time I realized it wasn't because of them. It was all on me. I didn't get it because it was hard for me to see a world through anything other than what I had been used to.

I didn't adjust well to high school in general because I had been too used to elementary and middle school. And I didn't get Algebra 1 because I was too used to "regular math." Things finally began to change for me, however, when I allowed myself to put down my expectations and move away from what I had been used to. Once I approached Algebra with a sense of discovery, things began to click, and my grades began to improve—all because I opened myself up to something new!

SOMETHING NEW

SOMETHING NEW WAS WHAT the kingdom of God would have represented to those of Jesus' day, and it represents the same for us today. As such, I find that people often approach any talk of the kingdom in the same way I approached Algebra 1 early on—they have trouble understanding it.

While many of today's biblical scholars commonly hold that Jesus spoke about the kingdom of God more than anything else, as the editors of this series mentioned in the introduction, I don't think the church at large realizes it. More than love, heaven, or the church, Jesus spoke about the kingdom of God. Jesus came to earth because of the kingdom of God (John 18:37). Since this is the case, how did this deficiency in the church's teaching happen?

MORE THAN LOVE, HEAVEN, OR THE CHURCH, JESUS SPOKE ABOUT THE KINGDOM OF GOD.

Now, I was raised in the church. My dad was an evangelist who helped plant two churches in Illinois. Yet throughout my childhood and into my adulthood, I never heard anything besides a passing remark about the kingdom of God. When I heard about it, people used the term "synonymously" with the "church," not some grand kingdom of the God of heaven and earth! For me, the kingdom of God was a muted reference, at best. I believe for many people, it still is, and because of such, the kingdom of God is often viewed as a complicated concept.

But think about it: Would Jesus spend more than three years on this earth preaching about something that was too complicated to understand? I think not. Why are we missing the importance of Jesus' message of the kingdom? Maybe we're missing the significance of the kingdom because we are not used to seeing it as anything beyond the functions of the church. And if we don't understand the kingdom of God, how can we expect for the kingdom life to "take" within the lives we've already built?

So let's try to understand the kingdom by defining it. To do so will require us to immerse ourselves in Scripture, for there we find the kingdom of God described and the kingdom life exemplified. The kingdom of God is a supremely biblical concept, and Scripture unveils its nature through the unfolding of the biblical record. The kingdom spans the Old and New Testaments. It is found in the stories of Adam, Abraham, David, Jesus, Peter, and Paul. It is seen in Israel and the church. The kingdom is here and yet it is coming. It is complex yet surprisingly simple.

WHAT IS THE KINGDOM?

THE COMMON HEBREW WORD used in the Old Testament for kingdom is *mamlāḵâ*, meaning "dominion" or "sovereignty." The Greek word for "kingdom" used in the New Testament is *basileia*, which is typically defined as "reign" or "rule." The kingdom of God in both these biblical languages, in its most basic sense, means *the reign and rule of God*. It is the space in which God has dominion. It is where God rules as king. Knowing this basic definition, however, only takes us so far. One must *see* it in practice in order *to* practice it.

THE GENESIS OF THE KINGDOM

THE KINGDOM OF GOD is birthed in the creation story. The picture of Adam, Eve, and the garden are a microcosmic foreshadowing of the kingdom. As we imaginatively venture into the majestic garden, planted by God himself, we see everything that is good—a wonderful image of the kingdom.

We know from Genesis that man and woman were formed and shaped by God and given the task to work, tend, and rule creation for God. While they were to rule over the garden *for* him, it was God who truly ruled. Everything was the way he designed it to be. *His will had been done on earth as it was in heaven.* I want you to breathe in that last statement and its context. *God's will being done on earth as it is in heaven* is a key point in understanding (and even witnessing) what the kingdom looks like, for it is what the very reign of God produces.

> HIS WILL HAD BEEN DONE ON EARTH AS IT WAS IN HEAVEN.

THE KINGDOM OF GOD IN THE OLD TESTAMENT

AUTHOR AND MINISTER DAVID Young wrote, "The Old Testament was written so that we could understand what the kingdom of God is."[1] I agree. From Eden to Abraham, from Moses to David, from Isaiah to Malachi, we come face-to-face with the kingdom of God.

Scholar Scot McKnight professes that the biblical idea of the kingdom is deeply rooted in the Old Testament Scriptures and is grounded in the confidence that there is one eternal, living God who has revealed himself to us and who has a purpose for the human race, which he chose to accomplish through Israel.[2] After Eden, it is to the ancient people of Abraham, Isaac, and Jacob that we will look to understand the kingdom of God.

> Now the LORD said to Abram, "Go from your country and your kindred and your father's house to the land that I will show you. And I will make of you a great nation, and I will bless you and make your name great, so that you will be a blessing. I will bless those who bless you, and him who dishonors you I will curse, and in you all the families of the earth shall be blessed." (Genesis 12:1–3, ESV)

This great, blessed nation that God would make would ultimately become the people of his kingdom reign. Through this nation, all families of the earth would indeed be blessed. From Abram a great, blessed kingdom people would be born—the nation known as Israel. The nation of Israel was God's chosen people. He ruled over them as king on earth, in a way that mirrored his rule in heaven.

> For you are a people holy to the LORD your God. The LORD your God has chosen you to be a people for his treasured possession, out of all the peoples who are on the face of the earth. (Deuteronomy 7:6, ESV)

God ruled Israel and they represented that rule on earth.

> Now therefore, if you will indeed obey my voice and keep my covenant, you shall be my treasured possession among all peoples, for all the earth is mine; and you shall be to me a kingdom of priests and a holy nation. (Exodus 19:5–6, ESV)

With these words, God established a symbiotic relationship between the people and himself. The relationship rooted in God's reign over his people put on display to the earth what the kingdom life looked like.

Of course, the story continues. Israel enjoyed kingdom life—until they didn't. Their chosen status would eventually meet human resistance. Instead of being ruled *by* God, Israel sought to rule *like* God. Their desire to rule like God was never clearer than when the nation of Israel asked for a human king to judge them, just as kings ruled all the other nations. God clearly understood what was taking place and told Samuel the prophet, "They have not rejected you, but they have rejected me from being *king* over them" (1 Samuel 8:7, ESV). This choice, however, did not come without consequences, for it began a cycle of separation and sin for Israel as the people of God.

We can see a few bright spots on the timeline of the kingdom of Israel, noted by monarchs who did what was right in the sight of God. The most notable was King David. Of course, David was not without major flaws, but he was a king who had a heart that was likened to God's. And it was to David that God promised to establish a kingdom forever (2 Samuel 7:13–16). Ironically, this promise—combined with the continued rebellion of the people, their allegiance to their own rule, and the subsequent penalty for their actions—brought about the hope of a figure who would ultimately deliver them from the oppression and separation that the sin of self-rule had brought upon them.

The prophet Isaiah spoke of the grim reality facing ancient Israel when he wrote, "But your iniquities have made a separation between you and your God, and your sins have hidden his face from you so that he does not hear" (Isaiah 59:2, ESV). Though the separation was prophesied, Isaiah also spoke bountifully about the coming of the One who would deal with their sin and rescue the people from captivity and separation to begin a new era of the kingdom.

Consider a few more prophecies of this coming figure:

> For to us a child is born, to us a son is given; and the government shall be upon his shoulder, and his name shall be called Wonderful Counselor, Mighty God, Everlasting Father, Prince of Peace. Of the increase of his government and of peace there will be no end, on the throne of David and over his kingdom, to establish it and to uphold it with justice and with righteousness from this time forth and forevermore. (Isaiah 9:6–7, ESV)

Behold, a king will reign in righteousness, and princes will rule in justice. (Isaiah 32:1, ESV)

Biblical scholar N. T. Wright detects in the Psalms and in Ezekiel further descriptions of this great Deliverer. He sees that the Rescuer would be the manifestation of God himself. Wright contends that Psalm 145 reveals that this redeemer would come as a king.[3]

I will extol you, my God and King, and bless your name forever and ever. . . . All your works shall give thanks to you, O LORD, and all your saints shall bless you! They shall speak of the glory of your kingdom and tell of your power, to make known to the children of man your mighty deeds, and the glorious splendor of your kingdom. Your kingdom is an everlasting kingdom, and your dominion endures throughout all generations. The LORD is faithful in all his words and kind in all his works. (Psalm 145:1, 10–13, ESV)

And Ezekiel describes the shepherding role of this king.

I will rescue my flock; they shall no longer be a prey. And I will judge between sheep and sheep. And I will set up over them one shepherd, my servant David, and he shall feed them: he shall feed them and be their shepherd. And I, the LORD, will be their God, and my servant David shall be prince among them. I am the LORD; I have spoken. (Ezekiel 34:22–24, ESV)

What Wright gathers from Psalms and Ezekiel isn't just a keen observation; rather, it serves to cement a critical point for understanding the kingdom of God beyond the bounds of the Old Testament. It serves to point us to perceiving what the kingdom of God would look like within the realm of the New Testament age and beyond. But before we venture there, let's review the ground we've already covered.

From our look into Eden, we learned that the kingdom of God can indeed exist on earth as it does in heaven. Then we saw that there was a period of time in which God's rule over Israel displayed the kingdom, until the people's desire to rule like God consumed them. This decision, along with the sin that came with it, separated them from their true king. In the context of this separation, the prophets spoke of the hope that one day God would again actively rule his people. What we see in the New Testament is that God would rule and his kingdom would again be established by the Davidic line through Jesus.

THE KINGDOM OF GOD IN THE NEW TESTAMENT

IF WE SEE THE concept of the kingdom of God introduced in the Old Testament Scriptures through the story of Israel, then we see it fulfilled in the life of Jesus of Nazareth in the New Testament. As we look at Jesus, it should be noted that in order to understand and define the kingdom of God, we can't divorce ourselves from the story of ancient Israel. Jesus is the grand connector of both Israel and the kingdom, for he is the fulfillment of the story of ancient Israel and the true king in the kingdom of God.

Jesus not only spoke often about the kingdom, as I mentioned, but his entire ministry focused on the kingdom. From the preparatory ministry of John the Baptist, who announced that the kingdom of heaven (synonymous with the "kingdom of God") was at hand in Matthew 3:2, to the Great Commission of Matthew 28:18–20, we see vivid examples of the divine monarchy breaking through on earth through the life of Jesus.

The Gospel of Matthew details the beginning of Jesus' earthly ministry: "From that time Jesus began to preach, saying, 'Repent, for the kingdom of heaven is at hand'" (Matthew 4:17, ESV). Then, in Matthew 4:23, we read that after Jesus called his first disciples, "he went throughout all Galilee, teaching in their synagogues and proclaiming the gospel of the kingdom, and healing every disease and every affliction among the people" (ESV). If Jesus' typical synagogue experience was similar to the one Luke narrated in Luke 4:16–19, then Matthew was describing the ways Jesus demonstrated in word and deed what the kingdom of God was all about.

Jesus' words help us to gain clarity on the mystery of the kingdom. They will allow us to define the kingdom of God by enabling us to connect it to something observable. He helps us transport something that might be viewed as theoretical into something tangible. In other words, Jesus helps us take something from the pages of the Bible and see how it could be lived out in everyday life. He takes something that was two-dimensional for us and makes it four-dimensional.

Jesus said:

> Pray then like this: "Our Father in heaven, hallowed be your name. Your kingdom come, your will be done, on earth as it is in heaven. (Matthew 6:9–10, ESV)

> But seek first the kingdom of God and his righteousness, and all these things will be added to you. (Matthew 6:33, ESV)

> Not everyone who says to me, 'Lord, Lord,' will enter the kingdom of heaven, but the one who does the will of my Father who is in heaven. (Matthew 7:21, ESV)

To illustrate this movement from "theoretical to tangible," allow me to diagram two of these texts. Matthew 6:10a says, "Your kingdom come, your will be done." This phrase does a lot to define what the kingdom of God meant to Jesus. The word *kingdom* in these texts is the Greek word *basileia*, which means "realm" or "rule." For Jesus, the kingdom was the realm where God's will would be done.

Your Kingdom Come   Your Will Be Done

Where would this take place?

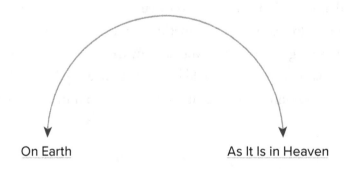

On Earth   As It Is in Heaven

Now, let's look at Matthew 6:33 again. Here, Jesus says to "seek first the kingdom of God and his righteousness" (ESV). Within this imperative, we find a way to see the kingdom of God on earth. The righteousness of God that mankind is to seek comes through obedient and faithful behavior, which ultimately models the life of Jesus.

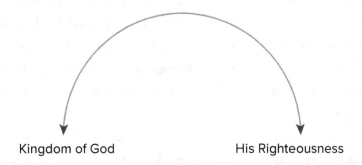

Kingdom of God   His Righteousness

When we look at all these Scriptures combined, we see that the kingdom is the realm where the righteous will of God is being done on earth as it is in heaven.

As Matthew 4:23 indicates, whenever Jesus came into a town, he brought the message and manifestation that God's righteous will was being done on earth as it was in heaven. Not just through words but also through actions. We see the emphatic stamp of this rule over brokenness on Calvary. Jesus overcame all demonic powers, and the fate of the ruler of this world—Satan— was finally sealed at his hands (and feet) when he was crucified.

Jesus' death brought forgiveness and deliverance, not just from a salvation perspective, but from an end times perspective. It symbolized deliverance from Israel's exile and from the separation of a nation from its God. The cross extended beyond the borders of Israel and brought fulfillment to something uttered to Abraham centuries before—that in Abraham (through his seed) all families of the earth would be blessed (Genesis 12:1–3). Through the life of Jesus, promises were coming true. Righteousness was reigning. Jesus was ruling.

Jesus said in Matthew 28:18, "All authority in heaven and on earth has been given to me" (ESV). In the realm where God's will was being done, Jesus had all authority. In other words, Jesus is the king of the kingdom!

PUTTING THE PIECES TOGETHER

We can begin finding the answer to the question, "What is the kingdom of God?" by putting together the pieces of Jesus' ministry and proclamations we've covered so far. In summary, the kingdom of God is the reign of God over the brokenness of humanity, through Jesus. It is God's will being done on earth as it is in heaven, through Jesus. It is the righteousness of God poured out over the world that he created, taking place through Jesus. Karl Barth said, "The kingdom of God was more or less God ruling."[4] I would agree with Barth; however, I think it is important to add that it is God ruling *through Jesus* and that the kingdom brings the joy, peace, righteousness, and deliverance that would come through such a Messianic reign.

God's kingdom exists on the earth, but at the same time, his kingdom won't be fully consummated until eternity dawns. It is a present and eternal kingdom at the same time. In either case, Jesus is on the throne.

As George Eldon Ladd states,

Fundamentally, as we have seen, the Kingdom of God is God's sovereign reign; but God's reign expresses itself in different stages throughout redemptive history. Therefore, men may enter into the realm of God's reign in several stages of manifestation and experience the blessings of His reign in differing degrees. God's Kingdom is the realm of the Age to Come, popularly called heaven; then we shall realize the blessings of His Kingdom (reign) in the perfection of their fullness. But the Kingdom is here now. There is a realm of spiritual blessing into which we may enter today and enjoy in part in reality the blessings of God's Kingdom (reign).[5]

This reign affects our lives when our hearts are surrendered to the kingship of Jesus. This surrender brings peace, righteousness, and deliverance into the life of the believer. When this happens, the old way of existence is buried, and a new life is born. This kingdom reign begins when we surrender to God in baptism (see Acts 2:14–41).

This reign is at the heart of what it means to be disciples of Jesus. We seek God's kingdom reign as we trust and follow Jesus as king. When we make disciples, we are gathering people into the kingdom reign of the One who has all authority, who sends us to make other disciples, and who tells us that as disciples we are to obey all of his teachings (Matthew 28:18–20). This is actually the core mission of the church on earth—to which we turn our attention to next. Specifically, the next question the book will explore is: What does the kingdom of God look like through the church?

2

WHAT DOES THE KINGDOM OF GOD LOOK LIKE THROUGH THE CHURCH?

Answer: The church is an assembly of kingdom people who display the reign of God through King Jesus.

> For the kingdom of God is not a matter of eating and drinking,
> but of righteousness, peace and joy in the Holy Spirit.
> — Romans 14:17

Now that we have established a firm foundation of the nature of the kingdom of God in Chapter 1, we will move more quickly through the remaining chapters of this work, starting with the connection between kingdom and church. As we have discovered, the kingdom of God is a central tenet of both the Old and New Testament Scriptures, but many theologians view our next subject, the church, as a focus of the New Testament Scriptures only. Partly, as a result of this perceived reality, they view the church in lesser standing than the dynamic kingdom of God.

I contend that the church is more than we tend to make her out to be. As a matter of fact, we see God's righteous will being done on earth as it is in heaven *through the church*. The church is just as biblically meaningful as the kingdom and should be held in as high esteem.

We live in an age in which it seems popular to criticize and even disparage the church. A tremendous amount of literature has been written in recent years that speaks to what the church *isn't* doing right or how irrelevant the church is in danger of becoming. Because of such thinking, movements have sprung up in the world seeking to fulfill the role of the church, without actually being the church. Such is the case with some parachurch organizations around the world who devote themselves to doing "kingdom work."

While a case can be made for groups and organizations like these coming alongside the church—which is what the "para" in "parachurch" refers to—sometimes these organizations venture into a territory of seeking to fulfill the role of the pillar and buttress of truth (1 Timothy 3:15). Yet even with its shortcomings, the grand purpose of the church is to *reveal the kingdom*. No other grouping of people or even parachurch organization is meant to reveal God's kingdom like the church.

THE LOCAL CHURCH IS GOD'S PLAN A FOR KINGDOM AND DISCIPLE MAKING. Disciple making—entering into relationships to help people follow Jesus, be changed by Jesus, and join the mission of Jesus—is the core work of the local church. True disciples reveal the kingdom. The local church is God's Plan A when it comes to both the kingdom and disciple making.

THE CALL TO A DIFFERENT PERSPECTIVE

TRUTHFULLY, I USED TO see things a lot differently. I would speak of "kingdom work" and associate it with many acts of service being done by people and organizations around the world. From building schools in Africa, feeding homeless people in Atlanta, or homeschooling one's kids, to me it was all "kingdom work." The idea behind my broad use of the phrase was that doing good works was clearly showing that God was reigning over an area, a city, a home, or an entire culture. Surely, it was God's will that a school be brought to an underprivileged area, right? Surely, it was God's will that the homeless were able to eat and find shelter. Surely, it was God's will that parents take a more active role in teaching their kids.

But when you consider the definition that we uncovered about the kingdom in the last chapter, simply applying the phrase "kingdom work" to a good deed doesn't quite fit. Remember, the kingdom of God is seen through God's will being done on earth as it is in heaven, *through the reign of King Jesus,* in such a way that brings peace, righteousness, and deliverance—now and in the age to come.

Good works might indeed display God's will being done, but it isn't always necessarily done through the reign of King Jesus. And though it might bring some peace, it isn't bringing the peace that King Jesus brings nor his righteousness, let alone his deliverance. Since the kingdom of God is a biblical idea, we must look to the Bible to see how this was carried out. When we do, we discover that there is only one grouping of people who ever truly lived this out through the reign of King Jesus—the church!

There are many scholars who have gone through great pains to elaborate on the idea that the kingdom and the church are different. Indeed, they are different, but they are closer than many might make them out to be. On the other hand, others seem to insinuate that the kingdom and church are synonymous. They are close, but not *that* close.

KINGDOM AND CHURCH

THE KINGDOM OF GOD speaks of the reign and rule of God. As I mentioned, "kingdom" is the Greek word *basileia*. The word "church" that we read in the New Testament is the word *ekklēsia* (Greek), which is connected to the Hebrew word *qahal*. These words speak of the idea of a public gathering or assembly. In the Greco-Roman world, the word went beyond just a public gathering and into the area of politics. "The *ekklēsia* was a governing council that established policies, legislated, conferred or denied citizenship, and elected officials. The *ekklēsia* had ruling powers. Don't let this fact escape you. It is the very basis of Jesus using this word."[6] The idea of a governing or ruling council is not only important for the sake of etymology, but for us understanding the purpose of the *ekklēsia*.

Jesus spoke of the *ekklēsia* in Matthew 16:15–19, where he connected it with his kingdom. In the mind of Jesus, there was no church (*ekklēsia*) without the kingdom, and there wouldn't be a visible demonstration of the kingdom without the church. Here is what he says:

> "But who do you say that I am?" Simon Peter replied, "You are the Christ, the Son of the living God." And Jesus answered him, "Blessed are you, Simon Bar-Jonah! For flesh and blood has not revealed this to you, but my Father who is in heaven. And I tell you, you are Peter, and on this rock I will build my *church* [*ekklēsia*], and the gates of hell shall not prevail against it. I will give you the keys of the *kingdom* [*basileia*] of heaven, and whatever you bind on earth shall be bound in heaven, and whatever you loose on earth shall be loosed in heaven." (Matthew 16:15–19, ESV)

Peter's confession was "You are the Christ"—that Jesus was king! Upon hearing this, Jesus declared that Peter was blessed, for such knowledge didn't come from human teaching but from God himself. This led to another declaration by Jesus that the reality of such a rock-solid statement—that Jesus was king—would be the foundation of the church he was building. Let's make sure we grasp Peter's confession. Upon the conviction that he was king, Jesus was going to establish his people, the church. The church would be the people of King Jesus. The *people* of a king are the human representation of his kingdom rule.

Then Jesus said that he would give Peter the keys to the kingdom of heaven. On the foundation of his kingship—the truth which Peter spoke—Jesus would build his church. That is, Jesus' kingdom would be the bedrock of the church's growth and expansion. Because Jesus said he would give the keys to Peter—the rest of the apostles and every disciple from every generation— would have the authority to open the doors of the kingdom. This would be the role of the assembly of Christ followers: to speak and live out that Jesus is king, and in so doing, open the door for men and women of any age to be ruled by him as well.

The words of the apostles, particularly Peter, opened the majestic doors of his rule in a fresh way on the day of Pentecost in Acts 2. The gospel-saturated message, combined with a powerful and visible manifestation of the Holy Spirit, enabled about three thousand souls to accept an invitation to enter into the kingdom of God. This acceptance happened through their faith expressed by repentance and baptism. Through these acts of surrender, they became the very people about whom Jesus spoke to Peter in Matthew 16—the church.

Those who heard Peter that Pentecost day were engaged in a full and complete transference from one kingdom to another. The apostle Paul explains this transference to the church in Colossae, "He has delivered us from the domain of darkness and transferred us to the kingdom of his beloved Son, in whom we have redemption, the forgiveness of sins (Colossians 1:13–14, ESV). The church is composed of those who have made the transition into the kingdom of God.

A FOREVER PEOPLE

To further understand this kingdom-church dynamic, let's look now at the message in Matthew 16 between where Jesus announced the building of his church and his declaration about the giving of the keys of the kingdom. At the end of Matthew 16:18, Jesus said the "gates of hell shall not prevail against it" (ESV)—"it" being the people of the kingdom, or the church. The word for "prevail" here means to overcome or become the dominant force over another. By saying that the gates of hell or "hades" wouldn't prevail, Jesus was saying that the powers of death and darkness wouldn't dominate the kingdom. In other words, the powers of satanic opposition would not be enough to destroy this kingdom or cause its demise. The church, then, would be a forever people of a forever kingdom of light.

The church puts on display the liberating effects of the kingdom of God for the world to see. Ancient Israel once held this role, as detailed in the previous chapter. The church is the fulfillment of the vision of God's people in Isaiah 61:1 ("freedom for the captives and release from darkness for the prisoners"), whom the king has liberated, beyond the boundaries of ancient Israel. As Scot McKnight explains, "The church is Israel expanded."[7]

By the faith expressed in repentance and baptism, the church has gained not only the forgiveness of sins but also a return from the spiritual exile that came because of such rebellion. Ancient Israel had truly been in exile and were suffering from their plight, even until the day of Pentecost in Acts 2. Yet when the three thousand converts heard the words of the gospel of the kingdom, repented, and were baptized, they were forgiven of their sins and released from the bondage that had begun with their ancestors. This return wasn't physical, for they still remained under Roman rule, but it was spiritual and real, nonetheless. How? They were delivered from the domain of darkness of sin and death, which is the deepest liberation a human can experience.

The nation of Israel that we read about in Acts 2 and every subsequent people group after them would be invited to experience the blessings of the Great Jubilee. The Great Jubilee (or year of jubilation) was first described in Leviticus 25:8–12 as a joyous year of canceled debt and returned property.

> You shall count seven weeks of years, seven times seven years, so that the time of the seven weeks of years shall give you forty-nine years. Then you shall sound the loud trumpet on the tenth day of the seventh month. On the Day of Atonement you shall sound the trumpet throughout all your land. And you shall consecrate the fiftieth year, and proclaim liberty throughout the land to all its inhabitants. It shall be a jubilee for you, when each of you shall return to his property and each of you shall return to his clan. That fiftieth year shall be a jubilee for you; in it you shall neither sow nor reap what grows

of itself nor gather the grapes from the undressed vines. For it is a jubilee. It shall be holy to you. You may eat the produce of the field. (ESV)

When Jesus described the liberation that his ministry would bring in Luke 14:18–19, King Jesus was announcing that the Great Jubilee had come again. We see the fulfillment of that jubilee in Acts 2. The church is—in a sense—the "Jubileed people!"

Since then, those of us in the church have issued an invitation to the world to enjoy the great freedom and deliverance they experience in the kingdom of God. We are ambassadors of freedom. We show the universe what the reign of God through King Jesus looks like. We invite them to be transferred from the kingdom of self-rule into the kingdom of light.

This is Peter's point when he writes,

> But you are a chosen race, a royal priesthood, a holy nation, a people for his own possession, that you may proclaim the excellencies of him who called you out of darkness into his marvelous light. Once you were not a people, but now you are God's people; once you had not received mercy, but now you have received mercy. (1 Peter 2:9–10, ESV)

Christians are a priesthood of the kingdom who seek to announce the excellencies of the kingdom and the king. Such Christians make up the church.

The church manifests the kingdom of God through true disciples. It is vitally important to form our understanding of disciples as those people who demonstrate the kingdom reign of Jesus. Disciples advance this kingdom reign in the church by carrying out God's mission in the world.

THE CHURCH MANIFESTS THE KINGDOM OF GOD THROUGH TRUE DISCIPLES.

While Peter puts a bow on the question of how the kingdom is seen through the church, by showing us the purpose of the church, he also brings up something that we must not miss: the holiness of God's people. Holiness is a paramount subject when it comes to kingdom living, and it begs further exploration.

3

WHAT IS HOLINESS AND WHY IS IT IMPORTANT?

Answer: Holiness is a lifestyle of separation from self-rule to kingdom-rule. It is important because holiness reveals a people dedicated to God. Holiness is a marker of kingdom life.

> But just as he who called you is holy, so be holy in all you
> do; for it is written: "Be holy, because I am holy."
> — 1 Peter 1:15–16

To the first-century church, the apostle Peter wrote a series of letters of instruction and exhortation. We know them as 1 Peter and 2 Peter. In the first of these letters, Peter taught the scattered and persecuted Christians in his audience about the importance of holiness. For them and for us, holiness is part of the kingdom lifestyle.

Peter sets the thematic tone early in this epistle when he instructs these pilgrims not to be conformed to the passions of their former ignorance, but "as he who called you is holy, you also be holy in all your conduct, since it is written, 'You shall be holy, for I am holy'" (1 Peter 1:15, ESV). As I mentioned already, their former ignorance came from the former kingdom under which they once lived—the kingdom of darkness. Now, however, they were to demonstrate behavior befitting the kingdom of light.

Statements such as "you shall be holy, for I am holy" are often quoted within the realm of the church, but they sometimes seem to lack the real power of expectation, which is nonetheless placed upon anyone who hears such words. This statement feels so quotable to us, but when Peter wrote it, he did it with the expectation that the church would regard it under the full weight of divine inspiration.

Yet it is difficult for us *to be holy*, largely because we don't have a sense of what it takes to accomplish this state of being. Thankfully, the New Testament writers go into much detail in order to give believers a sense of what it takes to live out our holiness in the world (e.g., 1 Peter 1:13–25; Romans 12; Hebrews 12). They took the time, not just to inform readers that God desires holiness, but also to explain what holiness looks like and how to live it out. We will delve into this, but before we listen to Peter explain the *how* of holiness, let's hear him explain the *why* behind his call to holiness. Since Peter was one of those Spirit-inspired authors and the one who revealed the issue, we can lean on him to show us the way of holiness.

HOLINESS AS SEPARATION

THE WORD "HOLY" COMES from the Greek word *hagios*, which expresses the idea of being uniquely separate. There was no God like Yahweh, no kingdom like his kingdom, and no people like his people. As God is separate, so his people are called to be separate. For both God and humanity, behavior and conduct reflect separateness. Holiness is a lifestyle of separation from self-rule to kingdom-rule. This is important because our lifestyle of holiness displays that the kingdom has invaded our lives.

Let's face it: life can be challenging. It often throws us circumstances and situations that tempt us to be anything but holy. Peter intimates that we as kingdom people will constantly feel a pull back into the darkness from which we came in 1 Peter 1:14: "Do not be conformed to the passions of your former ignorance" (ESV). Since that is the case, Christ-followers must distance themselves from the way they lived before they surrendered to Jesus. We must intentionally choose the holy life over our old life, distinguishing between the light and the dark. In 1 Peter 2:11–16, Peter delves into the importance of a distinctly holy life and how to live it.

WE MUST INTENTIONALLY CHOOSE THE HOLY LIFE OVER OUR OLD LIFE.

> Beloved, I urge you as sojourners and exiles to abstain from the passions of the flesh, which wage war against your soul. Keep your conduct among the Gentiles honorable, so that when they speak against you as evildoers,

they may see your good deeds and glorify God on the day of visitation. (1 Peter 2:11–12, ESV)

Peter begins this instructive list by urging Christians to distance themselves from the passions and cravings of the flesh that war against their souls. When we read a phrase like "passions of the flesh," it is easy to think of it as resting solely in the realm of the sexual appetite. However, Peter is referring to *any* fleshly or worldly behavior. He urges us against any hedonistic, self-seeking tendency that characterizes the pre-Christian, pre-church, pre-kingdom lifestyle.

As Peter explains in 1 Peter 4:2, Christians should not "live the rest of their earthly lives for evil human desires, but rather for the will of God." In other words, once we surrender to Christ, we must live not for our own will, but for the kingdom.

Such a radical approach is necessary because the kingdom life is often a life of resistance. Notice how Peter describes his audience in 1 Peter 2:11: "foreigners" and "exiles." In other words, kingdom people really aren't from "around these parts," as it were. We are citizens of heaven (Philippians 3:20). We are foreigners on enemy soil, and although we strive to love everyone genuinely and sacrificially, we stand in contradiction to the culture of the land.

After Peter tells Christ-followers about the importance of our separation from our old lives, he speaks about the seriousness of living out our holiness in front of those who are still stuck in the old way of life from which we were delivered. This "live-out-loud" quality was supposed to be seen as honorable among the unbelievers of the day, whom Peter calls "pagans." When the pagans speak evil against them (notice I said *when* not *if*), Peter says their conduct is to be such that pagans might see their good deeds and glorify God as a result: "Keep your conduct among the Gentiles honorable, so that when they speak against you as evildoers, they may see your good deeds and glorify God on the day of visitation" (1 Peter 2:12, ESV).

Peter believed that a holy lifestyle characterized by good works would counteract the slanderous words of the ancient society. The good deeds the church would do would invite others to see God. The same principle applies to the church and the world today: keep doing good and invite others to see God through those actions. After all, the church was created for good works (Ephesians 2:10) and to represent the kingdom of God to the world.

Peter writes that God would be glorified from these good deeds on the "day of visitation (1 Peter 2:12)." The "day of visitation" is either the day Jesus returns or a future conversion of some sort. I believe the latter, for we do the works of a holy priesthood so that mankind might know and obey Jesus before he returns.

Peter continues with his explanation of how to live this holy life by stating that Christians are to be subject to every human institution, whether governors or Caesar himself, as he wrote: "Be subject for the Lord's sake to every human institution, whether it be to the emperor as supreme, or to governors as sent by him to punish those who do evil and to praise those who do good (1 Peter 2:13–14, ESV)." This would have been a difficult command because the church was being persecuted in large part by the very government he told them to subject themselves to.

It is important to note that the church isn't a collection of anarchists. The church comprises citizens of a different kingdom. They don't seek to overthrow the current government; instead, they seek to win people over to a better one. They don't do that by rabble rousing; they do it only by serving. They do it by persistently serving King Jesus.

THE IRONY OF HOLINESS

SEEKING TO LIVE THIS type of holy lifestyle pleases our king but seeking to do so on one's own power leads only to our failure, disappointment, and discouragement. It isn't possible to live a holy existence *unless* we lean on King Jesus. As a matter of fact, allow me to say it more emphatically: we cannot live a holy life without Jesus.

WE CANNOT LIVE A HOLY LIFE WITHOUT JESUS. He is our model of holiness, and he is our advocate when we fail. His life shows us how to succeed in living the holy life, while his sacrificial death testifies to our failings and desperate need for him. The "Holy One of God" (John 6:69) is also the "Lamb of God, who takes away the sin of the world" (John 1:29).

Because of Jesus, we can live a holy, abundant life (John 10:10). Anyone can have that if they are willing to leave the kingdom of darkness for where God wants them to be—his kingdom of light. As a result, making difficult lifestyle choices becomes easier, and those choices that seem impossible become possible when we follow the pattern already set in place by King Jesus.

The life of Christ is our pattern for holiness, and our holiness is lived out each day through love.

4

WHAT IS LOVE AND WHY IS IT IMPORTANT?

Answer: Love is a cross-shaped action that glorifies God and benefits someone else. It is important because it is the action that best models King Jesus.

> A new command I give you: Love one another. As I have loved you, so you must love one another. By this everyone will know that you are my disciples, if you love one another.
> — John 13:34–35

What is love? As tempted as I am to begin singing a song by musical artist Haddaway, I will refrain. Music like that can be a wonderful window into the difficulty of answering a question like this, even as pop culture will give us mixed and even false messages about love. What is love? We *must* answer this question well if we are to live bountifully in the kingdom.

I did a recent Google search: "How many songs are about love?" The inquiry brought up a number of websites and articles, but the first one was an article by Martin Chilton called "Deconstructing the Love Song: How and Why Love Songs Work."[8] Chilton's article estimates more than 100 million love songs have been recorded in music history. I'll let that sink in a minute: *100 million!* The interesting thing, however, is that even though the same subject has been covered over and over in music, much of the music continues to struggle with what Leonard Cohen described as "the search for the exactly right language to describe the interior landscape."[9] Chilton also quotes author and Grammy Award winner Jimmy Webb, who said, "Love is an overused word, which coincidently doesn't rhyme well with anything else."[10]

So according to Chilton and others, love is difficult to universally define, yet we use it all the time as if everyone has a shared understanding of its meaning. In our society, two people can say, "I love you," to one another and mean totally different things. What on the outside sounds like beautiful words can end up being confusing and even destructive due to our failure to accurately settle on the language that would cement its definition.

With a myriad of definitions to choose from, how do we as disciples of Jesus settle on one that befits the lifestyle of our king? First, we must detach our definition from the world that seems to hold this word hostage to its relativistic and self-centered thinking. Then, we must look at how our king defines it. Jesus is our example, and the Bible is our source for this definition.

A KINGDOM-CENTERED DEFINITION OF LOVE

THE FIRST TIME JESUS used the word "love" in the Gospels was during his Sermon on the Mount.

> You have heard that it was said, "You shall love your neighbor and hate your enemy." But I say to you, love your enemies and pray for those who persecute you, so that you may be sons of your Father who is in heaven. For he makes his sun rise on the evil and on the good, and sends rain on the just and on the unjust. For if you love those who love you, what reward do you have? Do not even the tax collectors do the same? And if you greet only your brothers, what more are you doing than others? Do not even the Gentiles do the same? You therefore must be perfect, as your heavenly Father is perfect. (Matthew 5:43–48, ESV)

The word Jesus used for "love" is the Greek word *agapaō*, which is the verb form of the noun, *agapē*. These words suggest the unconditional love with which God himself loves. This is the highest level of love possible. The verb connotes the act of demonstrating, rather than being simply a feeling. When Jesus spoke of love, he wasn't referring to a fuzzy and warm feeling that someone has for their neighbor; he spoke of an action that is demonstrated toward them. But what type of action?

Jesus began to answer this question in John 3:16 when he said that love was displayed through the action of the Father's sending his only Son. This process would deliver eternal life to those who believed in him. It was ultimately this action of sacrifice that Jesus called his disciples to as he commanded them to love their enemies and pray for those who persecuted them. To follow through on these commands, his disciples would have to absorb pain, while someone else received the immediate benefit. By loving in this way, they would be in alignment with how God loves, for love mimics God. Love is an action that benefits another, even when it might cause our pain.

LOVE BENEFITS ANOTHER, EVEN WHEN IT MIGHT CAUSE OUR PAIN.

We again see a focus on this *agapaō* love in what is often called the Greatest Commandment passage. A scribe asked Jesus which was the greatest commandment. To which, Jesus answered:

> The most important is, "Hear, O Israel: The Lord our God, the Lord is one. And you shall love the Lord your God with all your heart and with all your soul and with all your mind and with all your strength." The second is this: "You shall love your neighbor as yourself." There is no other commandment greater than these. (Mark 12:29–31, ESV)

Jesus quoted a Hebrew prayer here, often known as the *Shema*. He illustrated the prioritization of loving God with everything that makes you *you*. It is an "all of me" type of love that extends upward to God and outward to the neighbor. It kindles worship and obedience; it cultivates consideration and care; and it ignites praise of God that fuels affection for others.

Love moves up and out. If I gave you a pen and paper and asked you to draw a line upward and a line outward with both lines intersecting one another, the shape you would end up creating would be a cross! And that is the picture of love. *Love is cross-shaped.*

LOVE MOVES UP AND OUT.

Jesus' death on a Roman cross was the full demonstration of love. It was upward—in that it was in full obedience to the Father's will—and it was outward—in that it was for the salvation of all mankind. It was a self-denying sacrifice that pleased the Father and helped others. What he did on that old, rugged cross was for God's glory and for our benefit. It brought us gain, while it brought him pain. "Greater love has no one than this, that someone lay down his life for his friends" (John 15:13, ESV).

So, with all of this being said, we can define love like this:

> *Love is a cross-shaped action that glorifies God and benefits someone else.*

This cross-shaped action must influence the life of those seeking to be his disciples. As a matter of fact, this type of love is the hallmark of one who walks as a disciple of Jesus.

> A new command I give you: Love one another. As I have loved you, so you must love one another. By this everyone will know that you are my disciples, if you love one another. (John 13:34–35)

Everyone will recognize the disciple of Jesus by the way they show love. Disciples commit to loving this way because they have committed themselves to Jesus. It is partly what makes the disciple and this cross-shaped level of love uncommon.

I DON'T SEE IT

WE DO NOT COMMONLY see love like this in the world today. We see the love of country, the love of a political party, and the love of freedom touted on political ads and evening news programs. But these forms of love-defining advertisements usually all come with boundaries or limitations. If I love my country and my political party, then that often means I must vehemently and negatively oppose those on the other side of the aisle, who—of course—want to "ruin" the country. The kingdom of darkness says if I love one group of people, then there is another group I must hate. The kingdom of God, however, says true love knows no bounds.

This non-cross-shaped "love" that characterizes the world's love too often attaches itself to the church under the radar. And when it does, it is destructive. Always. *HuffPost* contributor Hillary Adler penned a tragic plea to Christians from her now ex-Christian perspective. She writes in her article "The Ugly in Christianity":

> I proudly called myself a Christian. Now I shy away from the term. I avoid discussions about it because I have family members I love so much who are still part of the Church. But, I will never again be one of them. And I'll tell

you why: when I was 18, a freshman in college, on the cusp of adulthood, already questioning my faith and whether or not I even believed in organized religion, a woman stood up in a Wednesday Bible class and said, "Praise the Lord! Ted Kennedy is dead!" I sat there slack-jawed, shocked, and disgusted, and the dimming light to my already fragile faith flickered out as everybody in the room—even an elder—laughed.

You get the idea that she's dismayed by this experience. Then, she continues and ties her experience to love (or lack thereof).

They laughed and laughed, and the woman said, "If I could, I'd go dance on his grave." She did a little jig and turned around with her hands in the air and again, once again, there was more laughter. Louder laughter. I wish I could say that was an isolated event. But things like that happened often. They happened and nobody stopped them, and judging by Facebook comments, I'm pretty sure they probably continue today.

The truth is, that kind of attitude cannot coexist with God in any form. I loved that church dearly, I truly did. But at some point, I learned that the love of the Church only extended to the end of its borders, to the end of the doors. Outside those doors, there was very little love to give.[11]

Our hearts break for Hillary—and not only for her but for everyone she represents.[12] Hillary represents those who expected the supernatural love of the New Testament in the church but were left feeling bitterly disappointed.

Remember, the church is an assembly of kingdom people, who are set apart to live holy lives for our king. This is a loving kind of life—a life spent showing the love that points to God and blesses others. While stories like Hillary's are much too common, this can change. And since stories like this happen, we know that the church isn't always fulfilling its mandate to be kingdom people upon this earth. This needs to change—this must change. In the next chapter, I explore how we can change, beginning today.

5

HOW DOES THE CHURCH EXPRESS LOVE TO THE WORLD?

Answer: By letting love rule over all she does.

> Therefore, as we have opportunity, let us do good to all people,
> especially to those who belong to the family of believers.
> — Galatians 6:10

When I first got started in ministry, I was blessed to serve as a youth minister. I thoroughly enjoyed helping shape the spiritual lives of young people. We ran a children's worship program during the main gathering of the congregation that I served, in which we assembled children ages four to eleven in a separate part of the church building. We enjoyed a time of worship, praise, and instruction in a way all the kids could understand.

As part of the program, we had several rules, one of them being that parents had to check their kids into the kids' area by 10:30 a.m. This gave a few minutes of late-arriving "grace," since our main assembly started at 10:15 a.m. We established this check-in time because the space we used was extremely small and could only accommodate a certain number of kids. We also didn't want this time of worship to serve as a babysitting service for overactive children who had begun distracting their parents in the adult service. We really sought to point these kids to God during that time. With that being the case, I thought this rule was reasonable and figured everyone else felt the same way—until one Sunday morning.

A father brought his daughter around 10:45 a.m. and wanted me to admit her into our program. I informed him that we were unable to accommodate her, as we had passed the period of admittance. He was indignant: "What do you mean she can't come?"

Not wanting to cause a scene in the middle of the hallway at church, I said, "I'm sorry, that's our rule." Then I went on to explain the rationale behind it. I thought that would be good enough, but it wasn't.

He responded, "Rules?! What do you mean *rules*?"

What alarmed me wasn't so much *what* he said or even *how* he said it; it was the look on his face when he did. He seriously looked as if he were ready to punch me in the mouth and admit his daughter himself, so he could go back into the main assembly and resume praising God! I am glad to say that he didn't do any of that. Instead, he stormed off with his daughter, shaking his head, and uttering something about "rules" under his breath.

WE DON'T LIKE RULES: NO MATTER WHO MAKES THEM

People naturally resist rules. They confine us with boundaries, and people don't like feeling confined. Rules tell us what to do, but we don't like being told what to do—by anyone! People start wars over rules. We respond in rebellion because of rules. And youth ministers almost get punched in the face because of rules. People do not like rules!

Without rules, however, people experience chaos. Just as people start wars because of rules, wars also begin *in the absence of rules*. Even the person who hates rules will be forced to admit eventually that we need them. They help us make sense of things and get things done. In a sense, universal rules . . . rule.

For the church, love is the rule of life. It is *the* rule, and it rules over everything we do. For the church, love is a noun and a verb, and it must be treated as such at all times. It guides behavior, conversations, and attitudes. It governs how we operate, even when people are "breaking the rule" and not showing love toward us.

LOVE IS THE RULE OF LIFE.

LOVE RULES

Jesus firmly established "the rule" of love in a conversation with his disciples, in the sense of how he expected them to love one another: "A new command I give you: Love one another. As I have loved you, so you must love one another. By this everyone will know that you are my disciples, if you love one another" (John 13:34–35). Again, the command to love wasn't a new commandment, for we see love demonstrated throughout the Old Testament. The disciples were already familiar with love. What Jesus put forward here is not the introduction of what love is, but rather a new standard of how to love that is to characterize his disciples.

He charged them to love one another, the way in which he himself loved them. Jesus' love, as seen through laying down his life for his friends, displayed his allegiance to God and was done for the benefit of others. This type of love would be the billboard of their identity as disciples. This was his *rule* of love.

The church is full of disciples of Jesus and, as such, we are all held to his standard of loving. The rule we must live by is this: Love each other the way Jesus loves us. That love asks us to lift others up even if we might suffer in the process. This expression of sacrificial love surprises the world around us and allows them to see who we are truly.

LOVE *ACTUALLY*

We see the principles of love written by a variety of biblical writers, but I am going to focus on what many call the "love chapter," also known as 1 Corinthians 13. I have seen that whether someone is "churched" or "unchurched," this section of Scripture is referred to in many weddings as a rule of how people should love one another. Paul writes:

> Love is patient, love is kind. It does not envy, it does not boast, it is not proud. It does not dishonor others, it is not self-seeking, it is not easily angered, it keeps no record of wrongs. Love does not delight in evil but rejoices with the truth. It always protects, always trusts, always hopes, always perseveres. (1 Corinthians 13:4–7)

These verses reveal Paul's vision of how the church must display love to one another, and even to the world. Love must be even-tempered and gentle. It propels us to rejoice in the good that someone else has. Love causes us to humble ourselves and elevate someone else's needs or wants ahead of our own. It doesn't fly off the handle or keep score of someone's mistakes. If I truly love someone, I don't rejoice in their wrongdoing; instead, I find my delight in the truth. With love, I endure whatever comes up. I strive to think the best of someone, and I work to see the brighter side.

Cross-shaped love is the fuel that drives disciple making. It is the passion behind the church's highest priority. It is the key foundational motivation for all who want to love people and make disciples the way Jesus made disciples.

CROSS-SHAPED LOVE IS THE FUEL THAT DRIVES DISCIPLE MAKING.

We all want this type of love too. Men, women, boys, and girls—we all crave this love. Truth be told, our lives rarely feel complete unless we experience some semblance of God's love. And the church is the Christ-centered community where everyone who needs it can find it—all because the church is living under the rule of love.

This love should stand out because people in the world typically live angry, reactive, and self-centered lives. One might say that the world has always been this way, but I think we can agree that the advent of social media has taken things to a whole new level. If we post something someone doesn't like, that person can let the world know in real time about their anger. When they disagree, instead of simply voicing their opinion, they cancel the other, unfriend them, or rant against them.

All of this angry, self-centered reactivity reminds us all the more that the world needs God's love. When political rivals brutally attack one another, I know that what we need is more love. When the divorce rate stays on the rise instead of decreasing, I know that we need more love. When kids and others are still being abused, kidnapped, and sold into sex slavery, I know that we need more love. When the racism of the past is still with us in the present, I know that we need more love. When injustice reigns over justice, I know that we need more love.

King Jesus knows we need more love too. Thus, he left his church here with the command: to let love rule. We have countless Scriptures that tell us this, all of which come from Jesus' command for us to love.

> Love your neighbor as yourself. (Mark 12:31, ESV)

> Therefore, as we have opportunity, let us do good to all people, especially to those who belong to the family of believers. (Galatians 6:10)

Anyone who loves their brother and sister lives in the light, and there is nothing in them to make them stumble. (1 John 2:10)

When the church lets Jesus' love rule, we become a haven for the broken-hearted, a sanctuary for the oppressed, and a refuge for the weary. Why? Because everyone, truly everyone, is searching for the love that the church has to share. We display love when we let love rule our lives.

APPENDIX

BOOK RECOMMENDATIONS
FOR FURTHER STUDY

Francis Chan, *Letters to the Church* (Colorado Springs: David C. Cook, 2019).

Tony Evans, *The Kingdom Agenda* (Chicago: Moody Publishers, 2013).

David Young, *King Jesus and the Beauty of Obedience-Based Discipleship* (Grand Rapids: Zondervan Reflective, 2020).

David Platt, *Radical Together: Unleashing the People of God for the Purpose of God* (Colorado Springs: Multnomah Books, 2011).

N. T. Wright, *How God Became King: The Forgotten Story of the Gospels* (New York: HarperOne, 2016).

NOTES

1. David Young, *King Jesus and the Beauty of Obedience-Based Discipleship* (Grand Rapids: Zondervan, 2020), 18.

2. Scot McKnight, *Kingdom Conspiracy: Returning to the Radical Mission of the Local Church* (Grand Rapids: Brazos Baker, 2016), 66–73.

3. N. T. Wright, *Simply Jesus: A New Vision of Who He Was, What He Did, and Why He Matters* (New York: HarperOne, 2018), 43–56.

4. Karl Barth, *The Christian Life* (Grand Rapids: Eerdmans, 1981), 233–260.

5. George Eldon Ladd, *The Gospel of the Kingdom: Scriptural Studies in the Kingdom of God* (Grand Rapids: Eerdmans, 2011), 22.

6. Tim Kurtz, *Leaving Church Becoming Ekklesia: Because Jesus Never Said He Would Build a Church* (Alison, MI: Kingdom Word Publications, 2017), 58, Kindle.

7. Scot McKnight, *Kingdom Conspiracy: Returning to the Radical Mission of the Local Church* (Grand Rapids: Brazos Baker, 2016), 89.

8. Martin Chilton, "Deconstructing the Love Song: How and Why Love Songs Work," uDiscover Music, accessed September 10, 2020, https://www.udiscovermusic.com/in-depth-features/deconstructing-the-love-song-how-they-work/.

9. Ibid.

10. Ibid.

11. Hillary Adler, "The Ugly in Christianity," *HuffPost*, June 8, 2016, https://www.huffpost.com/entry/the-ugly-in-christianity_b_57588f08e4b053e219786f6b.

12. This response to Hillary Adler's plea to the church is well-expressed by Don McLaughlin in *Love First: Ending Hate Before It's Too Late* (Abilene: Leafwood Publishers, 2017), 28–29.

COUNTER CULTURAL LIVING

WHAT JESUS HAS TO SAY ABOUT LIFE, MARRIAGE, RACE, GENDER, AND MATERIALISM

CAROL M. SWAIN

To truth seekers and Christ followers around the world. Let us celebrate "him who is able to do immeasurably more than all we ask or imagine, according to his power that is at work within us" (Ephesians 3:20).

CONTENTS

General Editors' Note 501

Introduction 505

CHAPTER 1: How Should We View Human Life? 509

CHAPTER 2: How Should We View Marriage? 517

CHAPTER 3: How Should We View Race and Ethnicity? 525

CHAPTER 4: How Should We View Male and Female Roles? 535

CHAPTER 5: How Should We View Materialism? 543

Appendix: Book Recommendations for Further Study 549

Notes 551

GENERAL EDITORS' NOTE

There are some difficult teachings in Scripture for disciples of Jesus living in the modern world, especially in our Western secular culture. Our culture has adopted values and beliefs that differ from Scripture in ways sometimes subtle and sometimes blatant. Yet disciples of Jesus commit themselves to the way of Jesus. To be true to his teachings, we need clear guidance and courage.

Carol M. Swain is a strong role model and guide for us in this quest. As you read this book, you will find that she has personal experiences with many of the crucial countercultural challenges she describes in this book. She is an award-winning political scientist and a former tenured professor at Princeton, who left Princeton to become a political science and law professor at Vanderbilt University. She is an author or editor of nine books, one of which—*Black Faces: Black Interests*—has won three national awards. Dr. Swain has appeared on Fox News, ABC News, CNN, BBC Radio, and NPR, among other outlets. Her opinion pieces have been published in major newspapers, including the *New York Times*, *USA Today*, *CNN Online*, the *Epoch Times*, the *Washington Post*, and the *Wall Street Journal*. She has been a devout Christian since 1999.

This book expounds on the section from the Renew.org Leaders' Faith Statement called "Countercultural Living":

> We believe Jesus' lordship through Scripture will lead us to be a distinct light in the world. We follow the first and second great commandments where love and loyalty to God comes first and love for others comes second. So we prioritize the gospel and one's relationship with God, with a strong commitment to love people in their secondary points of need too. The gospel is God's light for us. It teaches us grace, mercy, and love. It also teaches us God's holiness, justice, and the reality of hell, which led to Jesus' sacrifice of atonement for us. God's light is grace and truth, mercy and righteousness,

love and holiness. God's light among us should be reflected in distinctive ways like the following:

1. We believe that human life begins at conception and ends upon natural death, and that all human life is priceless in the eyes of God. All humans should be treated as image-bearers of God. For this reason, we stand for the sanctity of life both at its beginning and its end. We oppose elective abortions and euthanasia as immoral and sinful. We understand that there are very rare circumstances that may lead to difficult choices when a mother or child's life is at stake, and we prayerfully surrender and defer to God's wisdom, grace, and mercy in those circumstances.

2. We believe God created marriage as the context for the expression and enjoyment of sexual relations. Jesus defines marriage as a covenant between one man and one woman. We believe that all sexual activity outside the bounds of marriage, including same-sex unions and same-sex marriage, are immoral and must not be condoned by disciples of Jesus.

3. We believe that Jesus invites all races and ethnicities into the kingdom of God. Because humanity has exhibited grave racial injustices throughout history, we believe that everyone, especially disciples, must be proactive in securing justice for people of all races and that racial reconciliation must be a priority for the church.

4. We believe that both men and women were created by God to equally reflect, in gendered ways, the nature and character of God in the world. In marriage, husbands and wives are to submit to one another, yet there are gender specific expressions: husbands model themselves in relationship with their wives after Jesus' sacrificial love for the church, and wives model themselves in relationship with their husbands after the church's willingness to follow Jesus. In the church, men and women serve as partners in the use of their gifts in ministry, while seeking to uphold New Testament norms that teach that the lead teacher/preacher role in the gathered church and the elder/overseer role are for qualified men. The vision of the Bible is an equal partnership of men and women in creation, in marriage, in salvation, in the gifts of the Spirit, and in the ministries of the church but exercised in ways that honor gender as described in the Bible.

5. We believe that we must resist the forces of culture that focus on materialism and greed. The Bible teaches that the love of money is the root of all sorts of evil and that greed is idolatry. Disciples of Jesus should joyfully give liberally and work sacrificially for the poor, the marginalized, and the oppressed.

*See the full Network Faith Statements at the end of this book.

Support Scriptures: Romans 12:3–8; Matthew 22:36–40; 1 Corinthians 12:4–7; Ephesians 2:10; 4:11–13; 1 Peter 4:10–11; Matthew 20:24–27; Philippians 1:1; Acts 20:28; 1 Timothy 2:11–15; 3:1–7; Titus 1:5–9; 1 Corinthians 11:2–9; 14:33–36; Ephesians 5:21–33; Colossians 3:18–19; 1 Corinthians 7:32–35.

The following tips might help you use this book more effectively (and the other books in the *Real Life Theology* series):

1. *Five questions, answers, and Scriptures.* We framed this book around five key questions with five short answers and five notable Scriptures. This format provides clarity, making it easier to commit crucial information to memory. This format also enables the books in the *Real Life Theology* series to support our catechism. Our catechism is a series of fixed questions and answers for instruction in church or home. In all, the series has fifty-two questions, answers, and key Scriptures. This particular book focuses on the five that are most pertinent to countercultural living.

2. *Summary videos.* You can find three to seven-minute video teachings that summarize the book, as well as each chapter, at Renew.org. These short videos can function as standalone teachings. But for groups or group leaders using the book, they can also be used to launch discussion of the reading.

May God use this book to fuel faithful and effective disciple making in your life and church.

For King Jesus,
Bobby Harrington and Daniel McCoy
General Editors, *Real Life Theology* Series

INTRODUCTION

Build houses and settle down; plant gardens and eat what they produce.
Marry and have sons and daughters; find wives for your sons and
give your daughters in marriage, so that they, too, may have sons and
daughters. Increase in number there; do not decrease. Also, seek the
peace and prosperity of the city to which I have carried you into exile.
Pray to the LORD for it, because if it prospers, you, too, will prosper.
— Jeremiah 29:5–7

Sometimes it seems as if we as Christ followers are living in a modern-day version of ancient Babylon. If we follow the teachings of Jesus in societies where everyone does what is right in their own eyes, we find ourselves living outside the mainstream culture. Countercultural living for disciples of Jesus means living our lives in secular societies, where our biblical values and principles are often mocked, disdained, or misunderstood. When our societies change and we find ourselves on the outside looking in, we can find comfort and guidance in the words God gave to the prophet Jeremiah (quoted above). God advised the exiles, through Jeremiah, to participate in the life of their communities and that as the nation prospered, they would prosper too.

Throughout history, God's people have periodically found themselves living in hostile territories among nonbelievers. Such is the case in the present-day United States of America, as our country follows the trend of much of the globe, including many Western nations. This is new territory for Americans. For more than two centuries an overwhelming majority of American citizens identified themselves as Christians. In recent years, however, the percentage of Christians has slipped and continues to decline.[1] In the coming days, no matter where in the world we were born and raised, our Christian values will be tested and tried. If we are to survive as Christ followers and if we are to engage in the kind of kingdom living that supports our being salt and light to a lost and dying world—we must know what we believe and why.

OUR CHRISTIAN VALUES WILL BE TESTED AND TRIED.

ABOUT MY STORY

I CAME TO KNOW Christ in my mid-forties, after having lived a life that had elements of spirituality but was more consistent with and acceptable to the dominant culture. When I look back at my childhood and teenage interests, I see in myself a spiritual person who knew that something much larger than me was guiding and directing my life. Although I was familiar with Christianity and had some exposure to it in my childhood, I was not raised in a practicing Christian home. My curiosity about all things spiritual took me into many different directions. Eventually, I rejected Christianity and traditional religions for the more acceptable embrace of the "one God, many paths" philosophy, which promotes endless exploration of New Age, Eastern spiritual practice, and other religions. The Christianity I witnessed around me was weak and ineffectual. That's because the Christians I knew lived dreadful lives and engaged in behaviors that were unacceptable, based on what I knew the Bible had to say about lifestyles. As I explored other religions, I came to condemn Christians as hypocrites and to believe that Christianity lacked the power it professed to change people and lives.

After achieving success as a tenured professor at Princeton University, I still struggled with depression and became disillusioned with the world of success. None of my academic achievements satisfied me, nor did the fact I was earning more money than I had ever imagined. Following a spiritual journey in which I was always a sincere traveler, God's providence allowed a series of events to take place in my life. These events culminated in my becoming a devout Christian. After I came to understand the gospel in an intellectual sense, I had a dramatic Paul-on-the-road-to-Damascus encounter. That was followed by a period of growth that culminated with my spiritual embrace of the gospel message and what it meant to follow Christ.

While earlier in my life I had been baptized without having an understanding or appreciation of the life-saving message of the gospel—I had been soaked but not saved—finally, I committed my life fully to Christ. As a result, for the first time in my life I grasped the gospel message and the admonition that Christ gives us to die to self. God removed a crippling shyness that had handicapped me for decades. I understood for the first time that my life did not belong to me. My life now belonged to Christ, and I saw now that everything I had was given to me to help glorify him. My journey has had its ups and downs as I have progressed from a new believer to a more mature one, and my growth in Christ continues today. There was certainly a personal cost to pay for following Christ, but the pleasure and excitement of being a Christ follower has enriched my life in ways I had never imagined possible.

When we are open to the direction of the Holy Spirit and are submitted to godly leadership and direction, we can grow in our ability to practice the first and second greatest commandments with joy: to love God with our whole heart, mind, and soul, and to love our neighbors as we love ourselves. Our ability to practice countercultural living like this originates from the strength we get from studying the Word of God, meditating on Scriptures, spending time in God's presence, and regularly fellowshipping with other believers who can serve as our accountability partners. The community of Jesus is especially important. Hebrews 10:25 encourages us to assemble together with fellow believers. It is also essential that we relate with pastors and elders from whom we can seek advice when the world seeks to blindside us. We are to have confidence in our leaders and submit to their authority because God has charged them with watching out for our souls (Hebrews 13:17). To flourish now and in every age, we must have enough humility to take correction from our leaders even when we respectfully disagree.

AN OVERVIEW OF THE CHAPTERS

IN THIS SHORT BOOK, I grapple with some of the issues facing Christ followers, whose biblically based worldviews place them outside the mainstream culture. This is an ongoing incongruity at the center of countercultural living.

In Chapter 1, I examine how Christians should view human life. Are practices like abortion, euthanasia, or physician-assisted suicide ever acceptable for Christians? The chapter covers murder versus capital punishment, plus the scientific creation and destruction of human-animal embryos.

Chapter 2 raises the question of how we should view marriage. After discussing God's ordination of the first marriage, the chapter covers the factors that play into marriage longevity, biblical grounds for divorce, and contemporary sexuality and same-sex marriage. We learn the difference between marriage viewed as a civil arrangement, with its state and federal laws, and marriage as a holy sacrament ordained by God. I also examine Scriptures that help us understand how we should view gay marriage, especially in places it is legalized and rapidly growing.

Chapter 3 explores how we should view race and ethnicity. Did God create differences that justify "supremacy" thinking and practices among different groups? I discuss slavery in America and how blacks and whites can move beyond the current stalemate toward true healing and reconciliation. I also examine God's view of individuals and nations and what he has to say about slavery and race. In addition, I look at critical race theory, what it is, and how it has impacted the church.

Chapter 4 explores God's creation of males and females, starting with Adam and Eve. I look into the origination of the concept of gender and how different views about gender roles impact the church. We delve into secular debates about the philosophical concepts of complementarianism versus egalitarianism that are part of the theological debates concerning the roles of men and women in the home and church. In addition, I discuss Scriptures that apply to biblical teachings about male and female leadership positions in the church.

Chapter 5 examines materialism and how we as believers should view the pursuit and acquisition of wealth, fame, and fortune. This chapter discusses the pitfalls associated with greed and the love of money. In addition, it addresses the stewardship of wealth and our obligations to support the church and the poor among us, which gets complicated in nations like ours whose governments distribute generous welfare benefits.

I have written this book drawing on my knowledge of Scripture and my life experiences as a believer who came to Christ later in life. As you shall see in these chapters, I have made many mistakes over the years, and given my human imperfections, I am sure to make more. The mistakes I make going forward, however, will be those that come largely because of those parts of human nature that make countercultural living feel challenging but certainly not impossible. My prayer for you is that you will find value in what I have written and that the Holy Spirit will anoint the chapters of this book and the other books in this series so that every reader, such as you, will be strengthened and empowered to walk in the light of Christ. We have an opportunity to shine and glow as we go out as ambassadors for our Lord and Savior.

1

HOW SHOULD WE VIEW HUMAN LIFE?

Answer: We should view human life as sacred because, unlike other beings, humans were created in the image of God.

So God created mankind in his own image, in the image of God
he created them; male and female he created them.
— Genesis 1:27

*W*ho am I? Where did I come from? And who are these people who make up my family? As a child I grappled with questions like these about life and my place in the world around me. I was born in 1954 and grew up feeling like a misplaced alien in a family of twelve. My situation was complicated by being black and poor in the rural South just when the civil rights movement was hitting new strides. At some point in our lives, most of us have questions about life and our place in the universe. Fortunately for us, the Bible provides answers. We can find meaning and understanding to help us understand our place in the world and the range of life's possibilities in whatever nation in which any one of us happens to be born.

From the moment of their conception to their last breath, every human being possesses a godlikeness that distinguishes us from all of God's other creatures. Our knowledge and understanding of human origins is found in the Old Testament, where God spoke his intentions of creating a unique being that would stand above every other creation.

Then God said, "Let us make man in our image, after our likeness. And let them have dominion over the fish of the sea and over the birds of the heavens and over the livestock and over all the earth and over every creeping thing that creeps on the earth." So God created man in his own image, in the image of God he created him; male and female he created them." (Genesis 1:26–27, ESV)

There is a lot of information in these two verses that answers the questions I grew up asking myself. The first detail we notice is the word "us" used to describe God. Many theologians recognize the "us" here as the Godhead of the Trinity: Father, Son, and Holy Spirit. God gave mankind authority and stewardship over the earth and all its inhabitants. We also learn about the biological difference between men and women, which is of growing significance in today's gender-confused world. Western culture increasingly claims that gender is fluid and that men can be women and women can be men. But God's Word refers to males and females from the beginning. As we shall see in a later chapter, our biological differences correspond to the unique roles men and women play in life.

This passage also answers the question of where we came from. Human beings did not evolve out of nothingness, nor are we God's afterthought. Each human life has purpose, potential, and meaning. This includes children born with severe birth defects such as Down's syndrome, spina bifida, and anencephaly, as well as adults who suffer from debilitating conditions such as Alzheimer's disease. We know from John 3:16 the heart of our faith: "For God so loved the world that he gave his one and only Son, that whoever believes in him shall not perish but have eternal life." God is love (1 John 4:7–21). This extends to *all people*, whoever believes. Therefore, he has compassion and love for the physically and mentally impaired.

EACH HUMAN LIFE HAS PURPOSE, POTENTIAL, AND MEANING.

As Christians, we categorically reject the reasoning of moral philosophers, such as Peter Singer, who argue that parents should be allowed to kill "defective" babies with severe disabilities. Our God values human life at every stage of development. Not even a sparrow falls to the ground without his knowledge (Matthew 10:29). We know from the prophet Isaiah that we are not in the same league as God:

"For my thoughts are not your thoughts, neither are your ways my ways," declares the LORD. "As the heavens are higher than the earth, so are my ways higher than your ways and my thoughts than your thoughts." (Isaiah 55:8–9)

Not even the great Albert Einstein can boast of the divine wisdom and understanding of the creator God—the God who made a universe that causes all people to ponder the meaning of life and where they fit.

"YOU SHALL NOT MURDER!"

STARTING WITH THE DEATH of Abel, God distinguishes between those who are killed by others and deaths that occur in situations such as wars, accidental deaths, and government-mandated capital punishment. Exodus 20:3–17 lists the Ten Commandments God gave the Israelites. The sixth commandment states, "You shall not murder" (v. 13). Honor killings, abortion, euthanasia, and suicide are forms of murder that God prohibits here because they involve the taking of an innocent life. According to Genesis 4:10, innocent blood cries out from the grave: "The LORD said, 'What have you done? Listen! Your brother's blood cries out to me from the ground.'"

Murder because of jealousy, to preserve family honor, or for any other reason is condemned by God: Proverbs 6:17 tells us that God hates "haughty eyes, a lying tongue, hands that shed innocent blood." In Leviticus 18:21, the Israelites are told, "Do not give any of your children to be sacrificed to Molek, for you must not profane the name of your God. I am the LORD." Likewise, we read in Psalm 106:37–38 (NKJV): "They even sacrificed their sons and their daughters to demons, and shed innocent blood, the blood of their sons and daughters, whom they sacrificed to the idols of Canaan, and the land was polluted with blood." These latter Scriptures should inform our awareness of nations, such as the United States, where courts and governmental entities have legalized abortion.

There are always consequences for great evil. As we know from the Old Testament, ancient Israel and its surrounding pagan nations suffered the wrath of God because of their detestable actions. As a young woman, I learned the hard way that just because an action is legal does not make it morally right. Like millions of other women around the world, I decided to abort an unplanned baby because of the burden I feared it would impose on my family. I reasoned that if the medical procedure was legal, it must also be moral. I now know governments legalize many actions that are harmful to people as well as condemned in Scripture either directly or indirectly. I suffered some of the many adverse medical and psychological effects discussed in Erika Bachiochi's path-breaking book *The Cost of Choice: Women Evaluate the Impact of Abortion*.[2] Bachiochi's book examines links between abortion and culture, women's health, law, regulation of abortion clinics, and abortion alternatives.

Doctors and medical journals refer to unborn babies as *fetuses*, which can imply by some that they see unborn babies as a lesser form of humanity. This is not biblical. References to *fetuses* rather than *unborn babies* often dehumanize for the world the life growing inside the mother's womb. Pregnant women throughout the Bible are always described as being "with child." Unborn babies are recognized as sons and daughters. Each unborn child has a unique identity and destiny. God told the prophet Jeremiah, "Before I formed you in the womb I knew you, before you were born I set you apart; I appointed you as a prophet to the nations." (Jeremiah 1:5). Similarly, David writes in Psalm 139:13, "For you formed my inward parts; you knitted me together in my mother's womb" (ESV). In the cases of Jesus and John the Baptist, an angel named each child before he was born, giving names connected with some aspect of the child's personality or destiny (Matthew 1:21; Luke 1:13).

In the modern world we continue to use language and concepts to obscure what is taking place. In America, for example, we face the concept of "reproductive rights," which has been disseminated around the world as a positive goal. Yet we know that these "rights" are nothing more than a euphemism for *abortion*. No matter how one attempts to justify their actions, abortion is the violent interruption of a pregnancy that results in the death of the unborn child and an end to the child's destiny and potential in the world. An abortion is nothing to celebrate or shout about with pride, as some women have done in recent years.[3]

Those who choose abortion cannot escape the consequences of their actions. I know this firsthand. Men and women worldwide who have participated in abortion decisions are often racked with guilt, walking around deeply grieved and wounded. Yet Jesus Christ offers hope for people who confess their sins and ask for his forgiveness through his shed blood on the cross. God forgave David of his cold-blooded murder of Uriah, husband to Bathsheba, for example (2 Samuel 11:14–18). That brings enhanced meaning to David's testimony to God's goodness, when he writes, "Blessed is the one whose transgressions are forgiven; whose sins are covered" (Psalm 32:1). Colossians 1:14 reminds us that "we have redemption, the forgiveness of sins." If you are struggling with guilt associated with these issues, then it is important to seek help from mature Christians and spiritual advisers who can walk with you through the process of healing.

There are rare occasions in which doctors recommend an abortion to save the life of the mother. In those special cases, each person needs to seek God's wisdom in the knowledge that he has enough grace and mercy to cover us in every situation we find ourselves. 1 Corinthians 10:13 reminds us, "No temptation has overtaken you except what is common to mankind. And God is faithful; he will not let you be tempted beyond what you can bear. But when you are tempted, he will also provide a way out so that you can endure it."

EUTHANASIA AND PHYSICIAN-ASSISTED SUICIDE

Euthanasia is the deliberate ending of a human life by another person who is attempting to relieve another person's purportedly incurable suffering. It is murder dressed up with a fancy name. Then there is *voluntary* euthanasia (sometimes called physician-assisted suicide), which occurs with the patient's consent. It is tantamount to suicide because it involves the taking of an innocent life. No matter the physical or mental condition of a person's life, every life belongs to God, not to oneself. Job 14:5 states, "A person's days are determined; you have decreed the number of his months and have set limits he cannot exceed." Romans 5:3–5 reminds us how we should respond to suffering: "We also glory in our sufferings, because we know that suffering produces perseverance; perseverance, character; and character, hope. And hope does not put us to shame, because God's love has been poured out into our hearts through the Holy Spirit, who has been given to us."

We have a hope the nonbelieving world lacks. Many of us have witnessed healing miracles for persons diagnosed as terminally ill, which produces its own hope. Plus, we have the comfort of the knowledge of Jesus Christ and his finished work on the cross. While the world might view euthanasia and physician-assisted suicide as viable options to end suffering, countercultural  Christians who live and die by the dictates of the Word of God believe otherwise. When it comes to suffering, we are told:

> Count it all joy, my brothers, when you meet trials of various kinds, for you know that the testing of your faith produces steadfastness. And let steadfastness have its full effect, that you may be perfect and complete, lacking in nothing. (James 1:2–4, ESV)

Among God's promises is one to end human suffering, as we read in Revelation 21:4–5:

> He will wipe away every tear from their eyes. There will be no more death or mourning or crying or pain, for the old order of things has passed away. He who was seated on the throne said, "I am making everything new."

No evidence in Scripture suggests that God condones or encourages us to take things into our hands when it comes to end-of-life decisions for ourselves or for those placed in our care. This has particular significance for those who care for elderly people and the unborn who are more vulnerable to government policies and healthcare decision-making that sometimes make ending their lives easier than the lives of able-bodied persons.

Modern science and technology are at the point where mankind has moved closer than ever to the rebellious builders of the ancient Tower of Babel. For decades now, scientists have had the ability to clone animals to create direct replicas that carry the exact same DNA as their original. Although there are laws specifically banning the cloning of human beings,[4] it is not clear how long these will stand and whether they have been violated in certain nations. In America, the National Institutes of Health allows experimentation with animal-human fusions that create entities called "chimeras." Chimeras are created by fertilizing non-human eggs (e.g., monkeys, mice, etc.) with human sperm. An article in *Live Science* discusses the ethical and moral dilemmas of creating new life forms: "Human-animal *chimeras* serve as a useful living test environment to help scientists better understand the underpinnings of human biology and the mechanisms of human disease."[5] The ethical issues that make it dangerous and unbiblical have to do with humanity's arrogant attempt to mimic God by creating new creatures imbued with human characteristics. The blending of human and animal DNA is a violation of the sacredness of human life.

It is our being created in the image of God that makes us human and invests us with the unique characteristics that distinguish us from other created beings. As theologian Gary Sutanto writes, "Freedom of the will, self-consciousness, rationality, and the capacity to have religious fellowship with God"[6] are characteristics of being created in the image of God.

As I have matured over the years, found God, and grown in my faith, the questions that troubled me as a child no longer hold sway. Although I don't know all the answers and I have much to learn, I do know Jesus loves me and he loves you.

2

HOW SHOULD WE VIEW MARRIAGE?

Answer: Marriage is a sacred covenant ordained by God for the permanent union of one man and one woman for purposes of mutual support, companionship, and propagation of humanity.

> For this reason a man will leave his father and mother and be united to his wife, and the two will become one flesh.
> — Matthew 19:5

My aunt and uncle recently celebrated their sixty-seventh wedding anniversary. Over the years, the couple, who were parents to six children, suffered many tragedies, sicknesses, financial hardships, and a brief period of separation. This octogenarian couple is now inseparable. Their marriage is an encouragement to many couples who expect to be together "until death do us part." Other members of my family, including my parents, were not successful with marriage longevity. I believe there's a secret to marital success, so let us explore this from a biblical perspective.

MARRIAGE IN THE BEGINNING

GOD IS THE ORIGINATOR of marriage since he officiated over the first one in human history. The spiritual basis of marriage takes us back to the Garden of Eden, the birthplace of sin and rebellion. The word "genesis" means the beginning or origin of something. In Genesis 1 and 2, we learn about the creation of earth and all

GOD IS THE ORIGINATOR OF MARRIAGE.

its inhabitants. When it comes to the creation of human beings, God had a particular order in mind.

God created Adam first and gave him authority and stewardship over the garden. He also gave him an explicit warning with an implied responsibility to share the God-given responsibility with anyone else who had a need to know. Genesis 2:15–17 states:

> The LORD God took the man and put him in the Garden of Eden to work it and take care of it. And the LORD God commanded the man, "You are free to eat from any tree in the garden; but you must not eat from the tree of the knowledge of good and evil, for when you eat from it you will certainly die."

After giving Adam the warning about the tree, God said, "It is not good for the man to be alone. I will make a helper suitable for him" (Genesis 2:18). God knew that no animal in the garden had the intelligence, rationality, and sensitivities Adam possessed as one created in the image and likeness of God.

According to the creation narrative, God placed Adam into a deep sleep; and while he was unconscious, God performed the first human surgery. It consisted of fashioning one of Adam's ribs into the body of the first woman. Adam was so fascinated by the woman God presented to him that he waxed poetically as he named her: "This is now bone of my bones and flesh of my flesh; she shall be called 'woman,' for she was taken out of man" (Genesis 2:23). The Hebrew writer explains, "That is why a man leaves his father and mother and is united to his wife, and they become one flesh" (Genesis 2:24). Not only did Adam name the animals, he named Eve "woman" after noticing biological and physical differences between them. The woman possessed unique characteristics and attributes that Adam did not have.

We know Adam obediently passed God's instructions to his wife, Eve, who later allowed her curiosity to get the better of her, not to mention her desire to be like God. Love, perhaps, enticed Adam to join her, rather than lose her to "death," whatever he thought that meant when God warned him of this fate (Genesis 2:17). We see how each part of this duo trespassed in 1 Timothy 2:14, where Paul states, "And Adam was not the one deceived; it was the woman who was deceived and became a sinner." Eve sinned and when Adam knowingly transgressed, he became a sinner as well.

Companionship and procreation were important to God's plan for men and women. Ecclesiastes 4:9–12 states:

> Two are better than one, because they have a good return for their labor: If either of them falls down, one can help the other up. But pity anyone who falls and has no one to help them up. Also, if two lie down together, they will keep warm. But how can one keep warm alone? Though one may be overpowered, two can defend themselves. A cord of three strands is not quickly broken.

In the book *Male and Female He Created Them: On Marriage and the Family,* Cardinal Medina Estévez summarizes the Old Testament teachings about God's divine plan for the sexes.

- "that man is an image of God and one of his works;
- that the difference between the sexes is God's work;
- that the reason for this difference is the propagation of the human race and mutual assistance;
- that woman has the same dignity as man;
- that the union between man and woman is so deep that it surpasses even the union between parent and child; and finally
- that before sin there was no sexual disorder."[7]

This understanding about God's plan for the sexes is biblical, even though it is sometimes contested by those who view marriage as merely an affirmation of love without thinking about the original purposes of the unions. God's design included making us drawn to the physical attractiveness of the opposite sex for reasons other than mere sexual gratification.

THE MARRIAGE COVENANT

"Holy matrimony" is a description Christians use when describing marriages done by a clergyman or rabbi as opposed to a justice of the peace or some other state official. It signifies the intention of a male and female couple to form a permanent bond in the presence of God and onlookers. It is much like the ceremony surrounding a baptism, where one is baptized publicly before a congregation. Members of Judeo-Christian religions recognize marriage as an institution ordained by God that carries with it certain obligations with regard to sexual monogamy and submission to the headship of the male, who is supposed to be the head of the family and its protector. The apostle Paul writes about male leadership in Ephesians 5:23–24, "For the husband is the head of the wife even as Christ is the head of the church, his body, and is himself its Savior. Now as the church submits to Christ, so also wives should submit in everything to their husbands" (ESV).

In *Mere Christianity*, C. S. Lewis writes:

> The need for some [headship] follows from the idea that marriage is permanent. Of course, as long as the husband and wife are agreed, no question of [headship] should arise. . . . But when there is disagreement, what is to happen? Talk it over, of course; but I am assuming they have done that and failed to reach agreement. What do they do next? They cannot decide by majority vote, for in a council of two there can be no majority.[8]

Because marriage is intended to be permanent, one individual in the relationship must make final decisions for the relationship to endure.[9]

God expects marriages to take place between individuals who share religious beliefs essential to maintaining their faith and raising any children born into the arrangement. In the New Testament, the apostle Paul warns,

> Do not be yoked together with unbelievers. For what do righteousness and wickedness have in common? Or what fellowship can light have with darkness? What harmony is there between Christ and Belial? Or what does a believer have in common with an unbeliever? (2 Corinthians 6:14–16)

Those who marry nonbelievers in hopes of converting them later are on shaky ground.

CHURCH ATTENDANCE AND STRONG MARRIAGES

BRAD WILCOX, DIRECTOR OF the National Marriage Project at the University of Virginia, and Steven Nock, former professor at the University of Virginia, found that a couple's commitment to marriage and their church attendance are associated with higher levels of female marital happiness. They also report that declines in church attendance and liberalized attitudes about sex and divorce have weakened the supports for marital longevity.[10] Cultures and laws matter. Maggie Gallagher, president of the Institute for Marriage and Public Policy, has argued, "Marriage, like a corporation or private property, is an institution that must be supported by law and culture; if it is to exist at all [it] has to be carved from nature by law, faith, custom, and society."[11] Since the 1960s, we have seen a weakening of the societal supports for marriage in Western nations such as the United States.

In *Soft Patriarchs, New Men: How Christianity Shapes Fathers and Husbands*, Wilcox shows that theologically conservative churches produce men who positively impact their families and societies. These men believe it is better for them as the husband to earn a living and for the wife to take care of the children and the home.[12] These attitudes are reinforced by their church's activities and social networks.[13] The impact of religion and the church is significant among young urban couples who attend church. Wilcox argues that the rate of single-parent households would be even higher if not for urban religious institutions that "depict marriage as a sacred institution that is the best context in which to have sex, raise children, and enjoy divine favor for an intimate relationship."[14]

BIBLICAL GROUNDS FOR DIVORCE

SOME PEOPLE WHO MARRY today and say "I do" are already planning their escape through divorce and elaborate prenuptial agreements. These agreements are meant to minimize the impact of a marriage dissolution. Jesus made his disapproval of divorce clear. In Mark 10:1–9 we read:

> Jesus then left that place and went into the region of Judea and across the Jordan. Again crowds of people came to him, and as was his custom, he taught them. Some Pharisees came and tested him by asking, "Is it lawful for a man to divorce his wife?" "What did Moses command you?" he replied. They said, "Moses permitted a man to write a certificate of divorce and send her away." "It was because your hearts were hard that Moses wrote you this law," Jesus replied. "But at the beginning of creation God 'made them male and female.' For this reason a man will leave his father and mother and be united to his wife, and the two will become one flesh.' So they are no longer two, but one flesh. Therefore what God has joined together, let no one separate."

Here Jesus quoted familiar Jewish Scriptures to his audience, which express God's original intent for marriage to be a sacred union between one man and one woman committed exclusively to each other. But are there exceptions to this?

In Matthew 5:32, Jesus said, "But I say to you that everyone who divorces his wife, except on the ground of sexual immorality, makes her commit adultery, and whoever marries a divorced woman commits adultery" (ESV). The Greek word translated as "sexual immorality" in this passage is *porneia*. Many scholars say that in today's language, the term would include homosexuality, bestiality, pornography, phone sex and cybersex, and other sexual perversions.

In 1 Corinthians 7:10–11, the apostle Paul emphasizes the importance of staying with your spouse if they're unbelieving.

> To the married I give this charge (not I, but the Lord): the wife should not separate from her husband (but if she does, she should remain unmarried or else be reconciled to her husband), and the husband should not divorce his wife. (ESV)

This passage shows that being married to a nonbelieving spouse is not a legitimate reason for a Christian to divorce their spouse. The apostle Paul continues,

> To the rest I say (I, not the Lord) that if any brother has a wife who is an unbeliever, and she consents to live with him, he should not divorce her. If any woman has a husband who is an unbeliever, and he consents to live with her, she should not divorce him. For the unbelieving husband is made holy because of his wife, and the unbelieving wife is made holy because of her husband. Otherwise your children would be unclean, but as it is, they are holy. But if the unbelieving partner separates, let it be so. (1 Corinthians 7:12–15a, ESV)

SAME-SEX MARRIAGE AND CONTEMPORARY SEXUALITY

ALTHOUGH NATIONS LIKE AMERICA recognize same-sex marriages, as do some progressive churches, this recognition and acceptance in Christian churches run counter to the biblical position on homosexuality. Direct Scriptures in the Old Testament give a clue as to God's thinking about same-sex relationships. Leviticus 18:22 states, "You shall not lie with a male as with a woman: it is an abomination." Leviticus 20:13 prescribes death for violating this command, providing a portion of the scriptural basis for rejection of homosexuality.

In the New Testament, Romans 1:24, 26–27 speaks to the issue:

> Therefore God gave them up in the lusts of their hearts to impurity, to the dishonoring of their bodies among themselves. . . . For their women exchanged natural relations for those that are contrary to nature; and the men likewise gave up natural relations with women and were consumed with passion for one another, men committing shameless acts with men and receiving in themselves the due penalty for their error. (ESV)

While Bible-believing Christians cannot affirm same-sex marriages and homosexual behavior, they can show love and compassion for those who find themselves caught up in sexual unions that are not God's best for their lives or the perpetuation of humans.[15]

The world's rules are often arbitrary. Unlike rules in the secular culture, rules governing biblical institutions are not arbitrary. God's view of the family does not change based on circumstances or the whims of a culture. Fornication (sex between unmarried people), adultery (sex with another person's spouse), and homosexual sex (sex between two people of the same sex) are all condemned in the Bible (e.g., 1 Corinthians 7:2; Exodus 20:14). The Bible does not teach that God changes his mind about sin. The Bible teaches that issues of sexual morality are life-and-death sin issues and that our attitudes about sin cannot change regardless of who engages in the behavior. Whether the sinner is a political leader, church leader, or our own son or daughter, we must speak the truth in love to them. Truth does not change based on who is caught up in the transgression.

GOD'S VIEW OF THE FAMILY DOES NOT CHANGE BASED ON THE WHIMS OF A CULTURE.

PERSONAL REFLECTIONS

I STARTED THIS CHAPTER with the discussion of the longevity of my aunt and uncle's marriage. My life story includes two marriages and divorces. The first marriage took place when I was sixteen and I decided to escape from my family of twelve. At the time of my first marriage, I was not pregnant, and I had such a low self-esteem that I was thrilled any man would want to be with me. So I married a man who was four years older than I. We had three children together. Our marriage started without a ceremony. My mother signed the papers and told me I was making a mistake. By the time I was twenty, the marriage had ended and I followed in my mother's footsteps and got a divorce. My mother was a pioneer and a radical. She had divorced my father in the 1950s, which is remarkable for a low-income person with limited education. She divorced twice, just as I would. Neither my mother nor I had a church wedding with family and friends, in which we pledged ourselves to love our husbands until "death do us part." Although many marriages end in divorce, I believe vows made in the presence of friends and family can make a difference in level of commitment and marital longevity.

Although my mother was raised in the church, I was not. My conversion experience came later in life. While I will probably never marry again, now in my sixties, my knowledge of God and his divine plan for each life and for the wife's role in relationship to her husband makes any such decision weightier for me. I know the responsibilities God has placed on the man and on the woman. Longevity of marriage is possible for believers and others who are willing to submit when necessary and work as a team, becoming the one that was envisioned when God brought men and women together for permanent unions.

3

HOW SHOULD WE VIEW RACE AND ETHNICITY?

Answer: God created one human race bearing his divine image from which emerged all the world's ethnicities and nationalities.

> From one man he made all the nations, that they should inhabit the whole earth; and he marked out their appointed times in history and the boundaries of their lands.
> — Acts 17:26

My views about race and ethnicity are filtered through the lens of having been born and raised in the rural South during the era of legalized segregation, as I mentioned. Everyone's story is different, including the life experiences of many black Americans. I am a descendant of slaves from Virginia, the state where the first Africans landed in 1619 and served as indentured servants until slavery for blacks was made permanent. You might be surprised to know that "permanent slavery became the law in 1662, but any slave who converted to Christianity and was baptized was set free."[16] This type of emancipation by Christian conversion, however, ended in 1667 when the Virginia General Assembly repealed the automatic emancipation for fellow Christians. It was not until January 1, 1863, that slaves again had a chance for emancipation, when President Abraham Lincoln signed the Emancipation Proclamation.

Virginia has been home to prosperous descendants of free blacks whose ancestors learned trades and became wealthy after their indentureship. Then there are others like my family's ancestors, whose slavery and lack of opportunities contributed to generational poverty and hopelessness. One plus for me was having a grandmother who was the daughter of a Methodist pastor, who descended from a line of freed blacks who had served as missionaries in Barbados.

I was not raised in a home of regular churchgoers, yet I understood I was a Christian and that there was a God, although my knowledge of him was limited. Racial disadvantage because of skin color was not a frequent topic in my home. Despite our oppressive poverty, my mother expected us to work hard; she held what I describe as a Protestant work ethic that discouraged the acceptance of handouts. She would later relent on the latter part of that as our family grew to include seven boys and five girls and we needed more help.

CIVIL RIGHTS AND RACISM

ALL I REMEMBER ABOUT race and civil rights at a young age was the injustice side of it. Over the years, though, racial and ethnic barriers gave way in America as opportunities opened for minorities like me. Despite dropping out of school and becoming a teen wife and mother, I eventually made my way to college and graduate school and earned five degrees. I also became a notable university professor, earning tenure at Princeton University and Vanderbilt University, before God put into motion the circumstances that led to my conversion. I now attend a predominantly white church in Nashville after having attended predominantly black and mixed-race churches most of my life. My background of varied worship experiences has given me the necessary foundation and confidence to discuss thorny contemporary church issues most people avoid.

I begin with the definition of "racism." People today are called "racist" and get silenced for reasons that have nothing to do with the traditional understanding of how racism impacts the world. Sociologists Joe and Clairece Feagin define "racism" accurately as:

> An ideology that considers a group's unchangeable physical characteristics to be linked in a direct, causal way to psychological or intellectual characteristics and that, on this basis, distinguishes between superior and inferior racial groups.[17]

Racism is prejudice that occurs when assumptions are made based on a person's membership in a particular racial, ethnic, or social group. Such racism might judge all white people as privileged beneficiaries because of their skin color just as blacks might be regarded as lazy individuals who commit crimes and prefer welfare to work. Such assumptions cause us to treat people differently and unfairly. Within the church and the human heart, racism is a sin problem that can only be addressed and absolved by practicing the teachings of Jesus and understanding what the Bible and gospel say about race.

GOD'S VIEW OF INDIVIDUALS AND NATIONS

THE BIBLE STATES THAT God created one human race imbued with his divine image (Genesis 1:27). Consequently, human distinction of racial superiority based on skin color, physical appearance, or perceived intellectual abilities are inconsistent with his Word and divine nature. From one man, Adam, God created all the nations of the earth, and he chose their national boundaries and their appointed times in history (Acts 17:26). God is intimately involved in the life and birth of every human being. In the Christian religion, we do not get to choose our parents, nationalities, race, ethnicity, or gender. Yet we know that God knows us before we are born. God told the prophet Jeremiah, "Before I formed you in the womb I knew you, before you were born I set you apart; I appointed you as a prophet to the nations" (Jeremiah 1:5). God chose the virgin Mary and her fiancé, Joseph, to become the birth parents of our Lord and Savior, Jesus Christ. Throughout the Bible we see God working in and through the parents of Samuel, John the Baptist, Samson, and others whom he used mightily. God's criteria for kingdom work are not based on demographic information such as race, ethnicity, nationality, or biological gender.

God displays his love for diversity as manifested throughout all creation. One trip to the zoo of any major city reveals the diversity in nature among birds, mammals, fish, reptiles, and other creatures. Why should anyone be surprised that human beings, likewise, share differences in skin color, physical characteristics, cultural traits, and more? Within the Christian church there is a basis for unity that brings together people from different social classes, races, ethnicities, and tribal backgrounds and clans. The love of Christ gives us a secret weapon that should empower us to serve as a light to the rest of the world. Jesus told his disciples: "A new command I give you: Love one another. As I have loved you,

THE LOVE OF CHRIST GIVES US A SECRET WEAPON.

so you must love one another. By this everyone will know that you are my disciples, if you love one another" (John 13:34–35).

Loving those who differ from us is preparation for heaven. In Revelation 7:9, the apostle John describes a scene of racial harmony and reconciliation:

> After this I looked, and there before me was a great multitude that no one could count, from every nation, tribe, people and language, standing before the throne and before the Lamb. They were wearing white robes and were holding palm branches in their hands.

The redeemed worship together in diversity as they proclaim the goodness of the Lord.

On earth we have tribulation with every nation of the world suffering from some form of racial, ethnic, or tribal differences that can lead to genocidal behavior. In 1991, historian Arthur Schlesinger, Jr. wrote:

> Within nation-states, nationalism takes the form of ethnicity or tribalism. In country after country across the third world—India, Burma, Sri Lanka, Indonesia, Iraq, Ethiopia, Nigeria, Angola, Trinidad, Guyana—ethnic groups struggle for power and, in desperate cases, for survival. The ethnic upsurge in America, far from being unique, partakes of the global fever. . . . The cult of ethnicity exaggerates differences, intensifies resentments and antagonisms, and drives awful wedges between races and nationalities.[18]

Believers in Christ who understand the kingdom message of Jesus and his call to make disciples from among all the nations of the world should demonstrate racial harmony to a divided world.

God offers salvation to individuals who willingly choose to receive Jesus as Lord and Savior, but he also deals with nations and their leaders. Deuteronomy 32:8 reminds us that when God "gave the nations their inheritance, when he divided all mankind, he set up boundaries for the peoples." He is involved with the rise and fall of leaders, and he judges nations. According to Daniel 2:21, "He changes times and seasons; he deposes kings and raises up others. He gives wisdom to the wise and knowledge to the discerning."

RACE, SLAVERY, AND SCRIPTURE

Slavery has been around since time immemorial, and unfortunately, it is still legal in parts of the world. During biblical times, it took different forms, including situations involving debt, persons captured in war, and indentured servitude, where people were released after serving a fixed number of years. Slavery in the United States was especially incompatible with American ideals as exemplified in the Declaration of Independence's promise that "all men are created equal . . . [and] are endowed by their Creator with certain unalienable Rights."

It was biblical principles that led British politician William Wilberforce to pioneer a successful campaign to abolish the slave trade in Britain. Yet the issue of slavery has divided Christians throughout history because of the Bible's nuances on the subject. It can be frustrating to contemporary Christians that the Bible never comes right out and condemns slavery. In fact, there have been Scriptures that slavery-friendly Christians throughout history have used to condone it. For example, Scriptures detailing curses against the sons of Ham and the Gibeonites have been quoted as a religious justification for keeping slaves in lifetime bondage. Genesis 9:22–27 says that Noah, after a drunken night, cursed the descendants of his son Ham because of an implied sexual transgression committed while he was asleep: "Noah awoke from his wine, and knew what his younger son had done unto him. And he said, Cursed be Canaan [Ham's son]; a servant among servants shall he be unto his brethren" (KJV). [19] A similar passage concerns Joshua's curse of the Gibeonites for tricking the Israelites into sparing their lives:

> Then Joshua called for them, and he spoke to them, saying, "Why have you deceived us, saying, 'We are very far from you,' when you dwell near us? Now therefore, you are cursed, and none of you shall be freed from being slaves— woodcutters and water carriers for the house of my God." (Joshua 9:22–23, NKJV)

Although the Old Testament permitted slavery, it was never a commandment of God. Instead, we find the Bible setting boundaries on how slaves should be treated. For example, Exodus 21: 26–27 states, "When a man strikes the eye of his slave, male or female, and destroys it, he shall let the slave go free because of his eye. If he knocks out the tooth of his slave, male or female, he shall let the slave go free because of his tooth" (ESV).

New Testament passages have been used to justify slavery up through modern times. For example, Colossians 4:1 has been quoted as offering approval for slavery: "Masters, give unto your servants that which is just and equal; knowing that ye also have a Master in heaven" (KJV). Ephesians 6:5 urges servants to be obedient "to your earthly masters."

However, using such passages to justify slavery in the modern world misses some important facts: first, slavery in the ancient world was not based on race (slaves could be of any race). Second, the Bible does not necessarily condone what it describes. It is true that the Old Testament law permitted slavery in keeping with the economic system of the time, but the Old Testament law brought more humane boundaries into an already existing system. For example, Israelite slaves were to be set free after six years (Exodus 21:2) and sent out with plenty of possessions (Deuteronomy 15:13–14). Exodus 21:16 states, "And he that stealeth a man, and selleth him, or if he be found in his hand, he shall surely be put to death" (KJV). Likewise, in the New Testament, we see slavery still as the economic situation for many people.

Clearly, the writers of the New Testament who deal with the issue were not revolutionaries seeking to upend the political order immediately. Yet it is also true that, as the New Testament teachings became disciples' cultural convictions, they would eventually go on to undermine and upend the political order.

Galatians 3:28 states, "There is neither Jew nor Greek, there is neither slave nor free, there is neither male nor female, for you are all one in Christ Jesus" (ESV). The apostle Paul told his fellow believers to receive former slave Onesimus as a brother in Christ:

> Perhaps the reason he was separated from you for a little while was that you might have him back forever—no longer as a slave, but better than a slave, as a dear brother. He is very dear to me but even dearer to you, both as a fellow man and as a brother in the Lord. (Philemon 1:15–16)

The New Testament makes clear that the kingdom of God encompasses people from every race, ethnicity, tribe, and nation of the world. All this to say that in the Bible discrimination based on racial prejudice, wealth, or ethnicity is sin.

In a sharply divided world, we as Christian believers have all the tools we need to model Christlikeness and heal a hurting world being torn asunder by racial and ethnic hatred and turmoil. Consider the following tools that Jesus gives us to fight racial and ethnic division, which I've included here from an article by Daniel McCoy:

> **WE AS CHRISTIAN BELIEVERS HAVE ALL THE TOOLS WE NEED TO MODEL CHRISTLIKENESS.**

1. He teaches us how to have compassion for those who are hurting: "But a Samaritan, as he traveled, came where the man was; and when he saw him, he took pity on him." (Luke 10:33)
2. He teaches us how to lament: "As he approached Jerusalem and saw the city, he wept over it." (Luke 19:41)
3. He teaches us how to repent: "From that time on Jesus began to preach, 'Repent, for the kingdom of heaven has come near.'" (Matthew 4:17)
4. He teaches us how to reconcile with people whom we have hurt: "First go and be reconciled to them." (Matthew 5:24)
5. He teaches us to seek justice for the oppressed: "He has sent me . . . to set the oppressed free." (Luke 4:18)
6. He teaches us how to bring people together who would naturally hate each other: for example, Jesus brought into his band of twelve both Simon the Zealot (who hated Roman oppression) and Matthew the tax collector (who benefited from Roman oppression).
7. He teaches us how to view each other this side of the cross: "Here there is no Gentile or Jew, circumcised or uncircumcised, barbarian, Scythian, slave or free, but Christ is all, and is in all." (Colossians 3:11)[20]

Unfortunately, many churches that mean well have abandoned the solid meat of the gospel and now find themselves embracing strange doctrines based on secular philosophies such as critical race theory, which is the subject of my final section in this chapter.

PROGRESSIVE CHRISTIANITY'S EMBRACE OF SOCIAL JUSTICE AND CRITICAL RACE THEORY

It has been said that a divided church cannot help a divided nation.[21] Churches across the world are dividing increasingly on issues such as race, homosexuality, and gender. Much of the division is being driven by a secular philosophy that has rapidly taken over the institutions of our culture. It's called critical theory.

The shorthand description of someone who endorses certain trends in our culture and in progressive churches is calling them "woke." Theologians Neil Shenvi[22] and Gerry McDermott[23] have spoken and written extensively about the incompatibility of critical race theory and Christianity. Shenvi and Pat Sawyer argue:

> Modern critical theory views reality through the lens of power. Each individual is seen either as oppressed or as an oppressor, depending on their race, class, gender, sexuality, and a number of other categories. Oppressed groups are subjugated not by physical force or even overt discrimination, but through the exercise of hegemonic power—the ability of dominant groups to impose their norms, values, and expectations on society as a whole, relegating other groups to subordinate positions.[24]

As a worldview, critical theory—along with all of its offshoots like critical race theory (CRT)—is at odds with the biblical message of Jesus Christ's finished work on the cross. Christians believe that human beings are created in God's divine image and that we are all sinners in need of the redeeming power of Jesus' shed blood on the cross. The critical theory worldview speaks of oppressive dominant groups and marginalized minority groups needing liberation. Such deliverance, according to critical theory, can only be granted by the dominant groups, who are expected to divest themselves of their privilege, power, and wealth. In these narratives, ethnic and racial minorities fall into the category of the oppressed. Whites and Western civilization, in particular, fall into the category of oppressors who must continually make amends for societal racism.

It is no wonder traditional churches often find themselves wading into controversies, where they are woefully unprepared for the rhetoric and strategies of social justice warriors steeped in philosophies such as CRT that emerged from cultural Marxism. Books like Robin De Angelo's *White Fragility*[25] have found their way into churches, and a new generation of racially sensitive leaders have begun to embrace ideas that take them away from the gospel of Jesus Christ and toward this new approach. It's a works-based approach too because supposed oppressors must repeatedly denounce their own racism (and the racism of long-dead ancestors deemed guilty of oppression) regardless of whether the accused was a descendant of abolitionists or someone who recently immigrated to the United States. CRT identifies white people as oppressors based on their skin color.

Within the church even, some people make other church members into oppressors or marginalized victims based on skin color, which are race-based and ethnic-based divisions. Whites are deemed as privileged oppressors of marginalized people; blacks are often deemed oppressed. Whites are expected to confess their racism and become explicitly anti-racist by confronting forms of injustice or anything that could be interpreted as such.

As McDermott and others point out, CRT redefines the Christian gospel, the meaning and pursuit of truth, the moral life, and the meaning of sin.[26] It is clearly incompatible with Christianity, and church leaders and laymen must acquaint themselves with this philosophy if they are to be able to disciple and make cogent arguments for truth in our times.

Some have noted how CRT and its relativism enter the church on the coattails of progressive Christianity, which can be seen as a rewriting of the script of Christianity to fit Western cultural values.[27] We must understand the subtle ways that dangerous ideas like CRT enter and take root in the church. Alisa Childers's eye-opening autobiographical account of her journey into and through progressive Christianity describes the slippery slope that led her from traditional Christianity along a path that almost destroyed her faith. She ended up finding hope and renewal through the core doctrinal teachings of Christianity.[28] If we are to be salt and light in the world, it is essential that we equip ourselves so we are not easily swayed by clever manipulations that often play on our heartstrings.

4

HOW SHOULD WE VIEW MALE AND FEMALE ROLES?

Answer: God created males and females to have complementary physical bodies and strengths, equal spiritual gifts and worth, and he placed them in relationships where partnerships and mutual respect contribute to human flourishing.

> Husbands, love your wives, just as Christ loved
> the church and gave himself up for her.
> — Ephesians 5:25

My entry into the church world naturally came later in life with my conversion. This happened after I was a university professor at secular elite institutions for almost thirty years. Within those academic structures, my views of male-female relationships were influenced by the women's liberation movement, which burst onto the scene during my childhood. By the time I entered college in the late 1970s, feminist theory and critical gender theories were dominant. We were encouraged to confront the patriarchal system by which fathers, brothers, and husbands held women in bondage through stereotypes and cultural traditions. Despite my exposure to these ideas, I never became a radical feminist, although I did notice that men held the most powerful positions in society and that some used their positions to abuse women.

Coming into the church and reading Bible stories such as the cowardice expressed by Abraham in his failure to protect his wife, Sarah—twice—were difficult to process. Women in the Bible clearly had fewer rights and protections than men. What is heartening, however, is the New Testament's treatment of women as well as God's fairness in the Old Testament, where he allowed the daughters of Zelophehad, for example, to inherit a portion of their father's estate (Numbers 27:7). It is good, too, that although the Israelites of the Old Testament lived under the stringent laws of the Old Testament, New Testament grace entered the world through Jesus Christ's sacrificial death on the cross.

Jesus Christ modeled love and caring for women at a time when they had a lower status than men.

- Jesus healed the woman with the issue of blood (Luke 8:43–48).
- Jesus chatted with the Samaritan woman (John 4:1–42).
- Jesus saved the life of the woman caught in adultery (John 8: 3–11).
- Jesus allowed women to be among his disciples (Luke 8:1–3).
- Women were the first to see Jesus after his resurrection (John 20:18).

Then, we know that God lovingly selected Joseph to be the father of Jesus, a decent man who respected his fiancée even though he did not initially understand the circumstances of her pregnancy (Matthew 1:18–25).

As we examine the modern-day roles of women in the church and home, we must keep in mind how God has repeatedly shown care and compassion for women and their more vulnerable positioning in society dating as far back as the Old Testament story of Hagar (Genesis 21:14–20). In recent years, there has been a revolution in the church sparked, in part, by the emergence of the MeToo movement.[29] In turn, that has spawned what many call a "ChurchToo" movement of "woke" women who are accusing pastors and ministerial staff of decades-long sexual and mental abuses that parallel what is happening in secular society.

The mostly male leaders in many evangelical churches face a changing environment that requires the exercise of extreme prudence when it comes to meeting with members of the opposite sex and those struggling with same-sex attractions. Now, every church needs clear lines of authority, accountability, and safe systems through which women and men can seek help before situations explode. And the inclusion of female ministers in churches can be helpful in situations where male elders and lead minister/pastors are the governing authorities, as required by Scripture (expounded on later in this chapter). We in the church world live and operate as a microcosm of the larger secular world, so I will begin by defining secular concepts that have entered theological discussions about relationships between males and females. Then, I will turn to Scripture for direction and answers about how to govern our lives in accordance with the Word of God.

GENDER AND THE CHURCH

People often use biological sex and gender as if the concepts are interchangeable. Those who want to discuss the appropriate roles for males and females in family relationships and in the church refer to "gender roles." Yet gender as defined in our culture is not a biblical concept. Male and female biological sexes are biblical, but the concept of male and female "gender" is not. Let me explain.

GENDER AS DEFINED IN OUR CULTURE IS NOT A BIBLICAL CONCEPT.

The phrase "gender roles" was first coined in 1955 by John Money, a New Zealand psychologist and sexologist who also developed the concepts of sexual identity and sexual orientation.[30] According to Money, gender roles refer to what a person does to "disclose himself or herself as having the status of boy or man, girl or woman." "Gender" has been expanded to include non-binary and third-binary genders.[31] Third-binary genders—where individuals reject male and female classifications—are now legally recognized in many nations and a growing number of US states. The concept of gender allows unlimited possibilities that go beyond male and female self-identifications.

This concept of gender was developed as a social construct to accommodate a range of behaviors that conflict with what is considered traditional male and female attributes.[32] A biblical view drives no wedge between gender and sexuality and ties sexuality to God's created order.[33] However, some in the church world have welcomed and now promote secular concepts of gender through critical gender studies, state and federal laws, and misguided efforts to be more inclusive by using the language and reasoning of the secular world. The church, I believe, should stick to the biblical understanding of males and females.

We recognize that God created two sexes and because of sin and cultural factors there exist people who suffer from gender dysphoria, believing that they were born into the wrong body, or same-sex attraction, which is actively encouraged by our society. If church leaders are unclear about their terminology, real problems can occur when legally recognized new forms of gender create situations that conflict with biblical teachings concerning the roles of men and women in church leadership positions. Transgenderism and legal protections for people who identify differently from their biological sex create new and difficult situations for Bible-believing churches. Each church leader needs to be prepared to take a stance and suffer whatever consequences might come.

Problems arise when Bible-believing churches begin to accept secular arguments that people can be born into the wrong bodies or that same-sex sexuality is separate from sin. Scripture calls us to affirm God's biological design, as we are made to be male or female (Genesis 1:26–28). We uphold God's design, while acknowledging the pain and struggles that some experience upholding these standards today (Deuteronomy 22:5).[34] We strive for obedience to Jesus, and we help each other carry our cross of obedience. We believe God's ways are ultimately best for human flourishing, even when the road is hard for some.

COMPLEMENTARIANISM VS. EGALITARIANISM

ADDITIONAL SECULAR CONCEPTS, SUCH as gender, have entered theological circles and become the latest buzzwords, and this includes the debate over complementarianism versus egalitarianism. These philosophical theories provide a more sophisticated language for debates about the roles of women in the family and in the church. *Theopedia* defines "complementarianism" as a theological view that men and women "are created equal in their being and personhood, (and) they are created to complement each other via different roles and responsibilities as manifested in marriage, family life, religious leadership, and elsewhere."[35] Author Alyssa Roat explains that men and women "complement" each other "like complementary colors work well together to create beauty, or one aspect of a dish complements another."[36] Therefore, masculinity and femininity are God-created attributes corresponding to the different roles men and women have in life. This makes possible the unity and oneness that occurs when the two become one in the marriage union.

The Renew.org Network upholds complementarianism because it is taught in Scriptures such as 1 Corinthians 11:3–16, 1 Corinthians 14:33–36, and 1 Timothy 2:11–3:16. These passages show us that the starting place for this discussion is the creation account of Genesis 1–2, especially the created order God intends.[37] We believe these passages offer God's normative and transcultural guidance for distinctive roles for godly male leaders in the church and respectful and strong wives.[38] Male leaders in the church have two roles: the authoritative teaching role (lead minister/pastor) and the elders of a church (the words "elder" and "pastor" are synonyms). The contrary view of complementarianism is egalitarianism, which is the theological view that there are no gender-based limitations on the roles that males and females can perform in the home, the church, and society. According to this view, Jesus and New Testament principles of equality erased all gender-specific distinctions. The Scripture most frequently cited by secularists to support this view is Galatians 3:28: "There is neither Jew nor Gentile, neither slave nor free, nor is there male and female, for you are all one in Christ Jesus."

In the church, men and women serve as partners in the use of their gifts in ministry. The vision of the Bible is an equal partnership of men and women in creation, in marriage, in salvation, in the gifts of the Spirit, and in the ministries of the church but exercised in ways that honor the biological sexes as described in the Bible.

In the Bible we see women serving as deacons, co-laborers, and in all other aspects of the ministry of the church besides the two roles outlined above. This would include women in positions leading teams, serving as chairs of committees, etc., because of their specialized knowledge and professional and spiritual experience and expertise. There are also roles men cannot have in the church and family life, such as leading women's ministry and nursing babies. God's view is equal value, different roles.

Yet the male headship role in the gathered church reflects God's created order. And this role is to be filled by qualified men only.[39] The headship role also reflects God's created order in the home as well. We find the scriptural basis for men only to fill the teaching-authority role and elder/pastor role in the New Testament.

- *On church-wide teaching and authority*, 1 Timothy 2:12–14 states, "I do not permit a woman to teach or to assume authority over a man; she must be quiet. For Adam was formed first, then Eve. And Adam was not the one deceived; it was the woman who was deceived and became a sinner."
- *On the elder/pastor role*, Titus 1:6–9 teaches us to appoint qualified men: "An elder must be blameless, faithful to his wife, a man whose children believe and are not open to the charge of being wild and disobedient. Since an overseer manages God's household, he must be blameless—not overbearing, not quick-tempered, not given to drunkenness, not violent, not pursuing dishonest gain. Rather, he must be hospitable, one who loves what is good, who is self-controlled, upright, holy, and disciplined. He must

hold firmly to the trustworthy message as it has been taught so that he can encourage others by sound doctrine and refute those who oppose it" (see also 1 Timothy 3:1–6).

Now, it's worth noting that Scripture doesn't just limit roles based on biological sex but also various other qualifications. These other qualifications make for what is indeed a high standard for leadership, often waived by churches seeking to fill elder and pastor positions with men who fall short on one or more of these criteria. But God wants us to uphold his standards because his standards are best for our flourishing.

GOD'S STANDARDS ARE BEST FOR OUR FLOURISHING.

The Bible makes it clear that husbands should be submitted to Christ and wives to the headship of their husbands. This basic principle is found in 1 Corinthians 11:3, which states, "But I want you to understand that the head of every man is Christ, the head of a wife is her husband, and the head of Christ is God" (ESV). Husbands and men in headship positions in the church are expected to be a covering over their wives and the members of the church as Christ is the covering over the church. Men are not to be overbearing or abusive to their wives or to the people in their churches—physically or verbally or in any other way. Husbands and these church leaders are admonished to love those they guide "as Christ loved the church and gave himself up for her" (Ephesians 5:25; see also Ephesians 5:33 and Matthew 20:25–28). Marriages and church relationships thrive when husbands and wives and church leaders and members commit to mutual respect and admiration for each other's unique contribution to the whole, which leads to loving relationships in which each half of the whole can flourish.

Supporters of the more biblically consistent complementarianism view are increasingly finding themselves attacked by those who throw out terms such as "misogyny," which is the hatred of women. Much of contemporary egalitarianism emerges from a secular worldview that not only pits men against women but is opposed to hierarchical relationships that are part of God's created order. In God's world order, Adam came first, and from his flesh, God created Eve (1 Corinthians 11:8–11).[40]

Embodied in this understanding of the created order is "primogeniture," the concept that attaches significance to being born first. This pertains to Adam being formed first, with the rights of the firstborn when it comes to inheritance and rights of succession. Primogeniture is a difficult concept in our society today, but it is important for us to maintain a scriptural understanding of men and women. This goes back to 1 Timothy 2:13, where Paul states, "Adam was formed first, then Eve." Adam's position as first-created person places him in a more senior role in the creation order and lends credence to the arguments of his headship.

An honest reading of the Bible finds this view of male headship and authority reflected by the authors of the Bible throughout the canon of Scripture. Even so, these concepts are focused on the home and the church. While the Bible speaks a lot about husbands and wives and the place of women in church leadership, I do not believe this supports the view that men have authority over every woman they encounter in workplace or church settings.

CONCLUDING OBSERVATIONS

WHEN WE LOOK IN the Bible, we find men and women being used of God in accordance with their spiritual gifts and according to complementarity. Even in the Old Testament, an era in which women had fewer rights than they did during the time of Jesus, we find women in leadership roles according to their positioning and callings. Let us be careful to note that God used Deborah as a judge and a prophetess who led an army when none of the men were brave enough to lead (Judges 4–5). And in the New Testament, Phoebe is believed to have been a deaconess; Lydia was a wealthy business owner and church leader who opened her home to others; and Priscilla and her husband, Aquila, were a ministry team. We should not place limits on God when it comes to how he might want to use women in the church.

This means women can be used equally with men in areas where their professional training and spiritual gifts give them special knowledge and insights. Elders and lead ministers submitted to the Holy Spirit should seek the Lord on a regular basis to identify those placed in the body to further the kingdom of God regardless of whether they are male or female.

One last observation: church leaders need to recognize that single women in their congregation might experience the church differently than married couples or even single men. Single women might find fewer opportunities to socialize or participate in events designed to accommodate married couples. Single women may also find themselves more vulnerable to unwanted sexual advances. Church leaders seeking to avoid problems must exercise wisdom and prudence. Every church needs to have clear lines of communication and safe channels where abuses of authority and dangerous practices can be detected and addressed. This must be done *before* churches find themselves in situations of an accusation, which can lead to the breakdown of trust and the disintegration of the church body.

5

HOW SHOULD WE VIEW MATERIALISM?

Answer: Materialism is sin because it causes us to focus on the acquisition of earthly treasures and rewards that detract from spiritual blessings and riches that come from being in a right relationship with Jesus.

> Do not love the world or anything in the world. If anyone loves the world, love for the Father is not in them.
> — 1 John 2:15

Malcolm Forbes, one of the world's wealthiest men at the time of his death, is said to have coined the phrase, "He who dies with the most toys wins."[41] Although Forbes's wealth allowed him to travel and amass many toys and luxuries, his mindset about life and enjoying the pleasures that money could buy contradicts the teaching found in Matthew 6:19–21, where Jesus tells us:

> Do not store up for yourselves treasures on earth, where moths and vermin destroy, and where thieves break in and steal. But store up for yourselves treasures in heaven, where moths and vermin do not destroy, and where thieves do not break in and steal. For where your treasure is, there your heart will be also.

Forbes lived through the Great Depression and was a member of the Greatest Generation, a demographic comprising people born between 1901 and 1927. This generation also endured the New Deal, two World Wars, and the turmoil of the 1960s. When Forbes died in 1990, he was remembered for his extravagant lifestyle and his interests in capitalism and free markets, but what about his treasures in the kingdom?

Proverbs 22:1 tells us, "A good name is more desirable than great riches; to be esteemed is better than silver or gold." What we learn from this Scripture is that the value of having a good name while on earth is worth more than acquiring wealth on earth. In other words, Forbes's priorities weren't straight, and he didn't win at the most important aspects of life, according to the Bible.

A PERSON'S CHARACTER IS THE TRUE MEASURE OF WEALTH. A person's character is the true measure of wealth, and it largely determines the impact they have on others who watch them walk through life, whether they be family members or others God places in their paths. A poor man with integrity is richer than a deceiver or a corrupt man (Proverbs 19:1; 28:6).

CHOOSING BETWEEN GRATITUDE AND GREED

While previous chapters in this book have dealt with our relationships with our fellow humans, it is important to recognize that our calling to countercultural living also extends to our relationship with the material world. A greedy disposition toward the material world has led to many significant problems, such as theft, warfare, betrayal, and waste. When we are on our death beds, we can minimize our regrets by learning from God what is truly important while we have an opportunity to make lasting differences in the lives of those who look to us for leadership and guidance.

The *Cambridge Dictionary* defines materialism as "the belief that having money, possessions, and comfort are the most important things in life."[42] We can become preoccupied with money to the point of greed. And greed manifests itself as an insatiable desire for more of whatever we lust after, whether it be money, possessions, or rewards. A greedy person never has enough. They are reluctant to share, and such behavior can lead to hoarding. The Old and New Testaments have a lot to teach us about the subject of money, greed, and hoarding. 1 Timothy 6:10 warns that "the love of money is a root of all kinds of evil. Some people, eager for money, have wandered from the faith and pierced themselves with many griefs." Continuing this theme, Paul states in 1 Timothy 6:17–19:

> Command those who are rich in this present world not to be arrogant nor to
> put their hope in wealth, which is so uncertain, but to put their hope in God,

who richly provides us with everything for our enjoyment. Command them to do good, to be rich in good deeds, and to be generous and willing to share. In this way they will lay up treasure for themselves as a firm foundation for the coming age, so that they may take hold of the life that is truly life.

Showing us how greed operates, Ecclesiastes 5:10 warns, "Whoever loves money never has enough; whoever loves wealth is never satisfied with their income. This too is meaningless."

One of the most sobering examples of greed and short-sightedness is found in Jesus' interactions with a man that ended with the parable of the rich fool (Luke 12:13–21). A man approached Jesus to complain about his brother's failure to divide the family inheritance with him. In the ancient world, it was not unusual for the firstborn son to inherit a double portion of the inheritance. How and whether he shared with others might have been a personal choice. Before Jesus told the parable, he pointed out to the man that he was not appointed as judge to this family matter. He warned the brother to watch out for greed because life is about much more than possessions.

To illustrate his point, Jesus delivered a parable about a rich man who had been blessed with an abundance of crops (Luke 12:16–21). Noticing that he had no place to store the harvest, he decided, "This is what I'll do. I will tear down my barns and build bigger ones, and there I will store my surplus grain. And I'll say to myself, 'You have plenty of grain laid up for many years. Take life easy; eat, drink and be merry'" (vv. 18–19). The story continues: "But God said to him, 'You fool! This very night your life will be demanded from you. Then who will get what you have prepared for yourself?' This is how it will be with whoever stores up things for themselves but is not rich toward God" (vv. 20–21).

Certainly, Jesus' parable was not the interaction this man was expecting, but it offered to him and to us a valuable reminder about what is enormously important in life, and just how little we fragile human beings can control. We cannot control the length of our days or the manner of our deaths unless we foolishly take our own lives. We can amass riches and possessions, but when we leave this earth, we also leave behind our possessions for someone else to enjoy or to squander. Estate planning is all we can really control. As 1 Peter 1:24 reminds us, "All flesh is like grass and all its glory like the flower of grass. The grass withers, and the flower falls" (ESV). And in Hebrews 13:5 God offers himself to us and tells us to be content with what we have because he will never leave us nor forsake us.

FAME AND FORTUNE

We all have our favorite sins. I do not think of myself as a greedy person, obsessed with the desire to acquire material possessions or to amass wealth just for the sake of getting wealthy. But one sin and temptation I *have* wrestled with has to do with seeking recognition for my work and accomplishments. Still, I often experience disappointment when I feel that I have been slighted or passed over for an award that I felt certain I deserved. And we're all tempted to make excuses for ourselves. My excuse for wanting recognition and credit for accomplishments could be connected with my status as a racial minority or the poverty that shaped my early life. I experienced much rejection in my life. But by the grace of God, I worked hard and became a tenured professor at Princeton and later Vanderbilt. It was there that I first earned national awards and recognition, often while experiencing a palpable depression and sense of emptiness that persisted even after I received the early tenure that I had made an obsession. Tenure, national awards, and accolades did not bring me the satisfaction and happiness I thought would ensue.

In fact, the accomplishment of my goals is what threw me into a deep depression. What followed was a spiritual journey that culminated with my Christian conversion experience, where for the first time in my life I understood the gospel message and received the freedom that comes from a relationship with Christ. Only through Christ did I find my peace and a sense of well-being that comes from understanding who I am in Christ and how he is working in my life. God saved me and freed me from a crippling shyness that had limited my ability to communicate in front of audiences. By his grace, I now have opportunities to speak in forums that reach millions.

Like anyone else, I sometimes fall into a dangerous trap when I get too focused on myself and the accolades people shower upon me. Perhaps this is one reason why success can lead to a person's downfall. That is, if they begin to take themselves too seriously and forget the role God played in choosing and blessing them. According to John 12:43, we can find ourselves in a fallen state, where we value the praise of men more than our love of God. This passage puts everything in good perspective.

Do not love the world or the things in the world. If anyone loves the world, the love of the Father is not in him. For all that is in the world—the desires of the flesh and the desires of the eyes and pride of life—is not from the Father but is from the world. (1 John 2:15–16, ESV)

Our protection from the traps of materialism, greed, and the quest for fame and fortune come from our relationship with Christ. God wants us to walk under the guidance of the Holy Spirit and not to succumb to the desires of the flesh that will always be nearby to tempt us. If we stay rightly connected with Christ, his people, and his Word, we have supernatural strength to resist the works of the flesh that inevitably lead to our downfall if we do not resist them (Galatians 5:16–26).

MONEY AND STEWARDSHIP

So what is the alternative to materialism? Stewardship. God expects us to be good stewards of the money and wealth and prosperity that he pours out on his people. Much wisdom about wealth is found in Proverbs where saving money and hard work are associated with wisdom (Proverbs 21:20; 14:23). We are warned about get-rich schemes and about boasting about our riches (Proverbs 28:20, 22; Jeremiah 9:23–24). As Christians, we are to be generous with our wealth (2 Corinthians 9:6; Luke 6:38; Acts 20:35), cheerful when we give (2 Corinthians 9:7), content with what we have (Philippians 4:11), and generous when it comes to meeting the needs of others (Matthew 25:35–40). We are also called to support the work of the church and to do so cheerfully.

In the various ways our Christian values are tested and tried, let us always remember that we are Jesus' disciples and discipleship has a cost (Luke 14:28–33).

APPENDIX

BOOK RECOMMENDATIONS
FOR FURTHER STUDY

Bobby Harrington, Renee Sproles, Daniel McCoy, Rick Oster, et al., "On Gender and the Bible," a twelve-part series at Renew.org, https://renew.org/on-gender-and-the-bible-a-summary-part-12/.

Carol M. Swain and Christopher J. Schorr, *Black Eye for America: How Critical Race Theory Is Burning Down the House* (Nashville: Be the People Publications, 2021).

Carol M. Swain, *Be the People: A Call to Reclaim America's Faith and Promise* (Nashville: Thomas Nelson, 2011).

Helen Pluckrose and James Lindsay, *Cynical Theories: How Activist Scholarship Made Everything About Race* (Durham: Pitchstone Publishing, 2020).

Steve Feazel and Carol M. Swain, *Abduction: How Liberalism Steals Our Children's Hearts and Minds* (Meadville: Christian Faith Publishing, 2016).

Thaddeus J. Williams, *Confronting Injustice Without Compromising Truth* (Grand Rapids: Zondervan, 2020).

NOTES

1. "In U.S. Decline of Christianity Continues at a Rapid Pace," Pew-Forum, October 17, 2019, https://www.pewforum.org/2019/10/17/in-u-s-decline-of-christianity-continues-at-rapid-pace/.

2. (San Francisco: Encounter Books, 2004).

3. "Shout Your Abortion," accessed May 24, 2021, https://shoutyourabortion.com/.

4. Henry T. Greely, "Human Reproductive Cloning: The Curious Incident of the Dog in the Night-Time," February 21, 2020, https://www.statnews.com/2020/02/21/human-reproductive-cloning-curious-incident-of-the-dog-in-the-night-time/.

5. Aparna Vidyasagar, "Human-Animal Chimeras: Biological Research & Ethical Issues," September 29, 2016, https://www.livescience.com/56309-human-animal-chimeras.html.

6. Gary Sutanto, "Herman Bavinck and the Image of God," September 1, 2020, accessed May 24, 20201, https://www.pastortheologians.com/articles/2020/9/1/humanity-in-its-entirety-herman-bavinck-and-the-image-of-god.

7. Medina Estévez, *Male and Female He Created Them: On Marriage and the Family* (San Francisco: Ignatius, 2003), 19–20.

8. C. S. Lewis, *Mere Christianity* (New York: Macmillan, 1952), 102.

9. For more information, see Renee Sproles and Rick Oster, "On Gender and the Bible: What About Husbands and Wives?" Renew.org, May 24, 2021, https://renew.org/on-gender-and-the-bible-what-about-husbands-and-wives-part-6/.

10. W. Bradford Wilcox and Steven L. Nock, "What's Love Got to Do with It? Equality, Equity, Commitment, and Women's Marital Quality," *Social Forces* vol. 84, no. 3 (March 2006): 1339.

11. Maggie Gallagher, *The Abolition of Marriage* (Washington, DC: Regnery, 1996), 9.

12. W. Bradford Wilcox, *Soft Patriarchs, New Men: How Christianity Shapes Fathers and Husbands* (Chicago: University of Chicago Press, 2004).

13. W. Bradford Wilcox, "Religion and the Domestication of Men," *Contexts* (Fall 2006): 42.

14. Ibid., 44. See also W. Bradford Wilcox and Nicholas Wolfinger, "Living and Loving 'Decent': Religion and Relationship Quality Among Urban Parents," *Social Science Research* 37 (2008): 828–843. For a contrary view, Joe Carter, "Why Complementarian Men Do More Housework," January 11, 2021, https://www.thegospelcoalition.org/article/why-complementarian-men-do-more-housework/.

15. For more information, see Kevin DeYoung, *What Does the Bible Really Teach About Homosexuality?* (Crossway, 2015).

16. Philip S. Foner, *History of Black Americans: From Africa to the Emergence of the Cotton Kingdom* (Westport: Greenwood, 1975), 191.

17. Joe R. Feagin and Clairece Feagin, *Racial and Ethnic Relations*, 6th ed. (Upper Saddle River, NJ: Prentice Hall, 1999), 6.

18. Arthur Schlesinger, Jr., *The Disuniting of America* (Knoxville: Whittle Direct Books, 1991), 48.

19. David Goldenberg, "The Curse of Ham, Race and Slavery in Early Judaism," (Princeton, NJ: Princeton University, 2003), https://www.researchgate.net/publication/263161577_The_Curse_of_Ham_Race_and_Slavery_in_Early_Judaism_Christianity_and_Islam.

20. This list is quoted from Daniel McCoy, "Corrupted or Co-opted: 2 Non-Options as Christians Fight Racism," Renew.org, https://renew.org/corrupted-or-co-opted-2-non-options-as-christians-fight-racism/.

21. For example, see Pastor Ronnie Floyd, as quoted in Abigail Robertson, "'A Divided Church Cannot Call a Divided Nation to Unity': Hundreds Pray in US Capitol on National Day of Prayer," CBS News, May 4, 2018, https://www1.cbn.com/cbnnews/politics/2018/may/a-divided-church-cannot-call-a-divided-nation-to-unity-hundreds-pray-in-us-capitol-on-national-day-of-prayer.

22. Neil Shenvi, "Social Justice, Critical Theory, and Christianity: Are They Compatible?" Southeastern Baptist Theological Seminary, April 29, 2020, YouTube video, 57:14, https://www.youtube.com/watch?v=E33aunwGQQ4.

23. Gerry McDermott, "Critical Race Theory: Is It Compatible with the Christian Faith?" February 10, 2020, https://www.patheos.com/blogs/northamptonseminar/2020/02/10/critical-race-theory-iii-is-it-compatible-with-christian-faith/; Gerry

McDermott, ed., *Race and Covenant: Recovering the Religious Roots for American Reconciliation* (Grand Rapids: Acton Institute, 2020).

24. Neil Shenvi and Pat Sawyer, "The Incompatibility of Critical Theory and Christianity," *The Gospel Coalition*, May 15, 2019, https://www.thegospelcoalition. org/article/incompatibility-critical-theory-christianity/.

25. Robin DeAngelo, *White Fragility: Why It's So Hard for White People to Talk About Racism* (Boston: Beacon Press, 2018).

26. Gerry McDermott, and Thaddeus J. Williams, *Confronting Injustice Without Compromising Truth* (Grand Rapids: Zondervan, 2020).

27. David W. Swanson, *Rediscipling the White Church: From Cheap Diversity to True Solidarity* (Downers Grove, IL: InterVarsity Press, 2020); Daniel Hill, *White Awake: An Honest Look at What It Means to Be White* (Downers Grove, IL: Inter-varsity Press, 2017).

28. Alisa Childers, *Another Gospel: A Lifelong Christian Seeks Truth in Response to Progressive Christianity* (Carol Stream, IL: Tyndale Momentum, 2020).

29. See "The #MeToo Movement and the Law," *FindLaw*, November 13, 2018, accessed January 22, 2021, https://www.findlaw.com/employment/employ-ment-discrimination/the--metoo-movement-and-the-law.html, and "Sexual Abuse Cases in Churches," *Newsome/Melton*, October 23, 2020, accessed January 22, 2021, https://www.newsomelaw.com/blog/sexual-abuse-cases-in-churches/.

30. John Money, J. J. Hampson and Hampson J. L., "An Examination of Some Basic Sexual Concepts: The Evidence of Human Hermaphroditism," *Bull Johns Hopkins Hospital* 97, no. 4 (October 1955): 301–19.

31. Carol Chetkovich, "How Non-Binary Gender Definitions Confound (Already Complex) Thinking About Gender and Public Policy," *Journal of Public Affairs Education* vol. 25, no. 2 (2019): 226–252, https://www.tandfonline.com/doi/full/10.1080/15236803.2018.1565050.

32. *Open Education Sociology Dictionary*, accessed January 22, 2021, https://sociologydictionary.org/gender/#definition_of_gender.

33. See Darren Williamson and Ellen Radcliff, "On Gender and the Bible: Thoughts of a Theologian and a Therapist on the Transgender Debate," Renew.org, accessed June 23, 2021, https://renew.org/on-gender-and-the-bible-thoughts-of-a-theologian-and-a-therapist-on-the-transgender-debate-part-11/.

34. See helpful guidelines promoted by the Assemblies of God, http://religiousin-stitute.org/denom_statements/transgenderism-transsexuality-gender-identity/.

35. "Complementarianism," *Theopedia*, accessed January 24, 2021, https://www.theopedia.com/complementarianism.

36. Alyssa Roat, "What Are Complementarianism and Egalitarianism? What's the Difference?" accessed January 20, 2021, https://www.christianity.com/wiki/christian-terms/what-are-complementarianism-and-egalitarianism-what-s-the-difference.html.

37. See the summary article by Bobby Harrington and Renee Sproles, "On Gender and the Bible: A Summary (Part 12)" https://renew.org/on-gender-and-the-bible-a-summary-part-12/.

38. Robert W. Yarbrough, *The Letters to Timothy and Titus* (Grand Rapids: Eerdmans, 2018), 140–182; ed. Andreas Kostenberger, Thomas Schreiner, and Denny Burk, *Women in the Church: An Interpretation and Application of 1 Timothy 2:1–15* (CrossWay Books, 2016).

39. For more on this topic, see the twelve-part series titled, "On Gender and the Bible" led by Bobby Harrington, Renee Sproles, and Daniel McCoy at Renew.org, https://renew.org/on-gender-and-the-bible-a-summary-part-12/.

40. Bobby Harrington and Renee Sproles, "On Gender and the Bible: Where Does Egalitarianism Lead? (Part 9)," Renew.org, accessed May 24, 2021, https://renew.org/on-gender-and-the-bible-where-does-egalitarianism-lead-part-9/.

41. Robert Forbes, "My Father, Malcolm Forbes: a Never-Ending Adventure," *Forbes*, August 19, 2021, https://www.forbes.com/sites/forbesdigitalcovers/2019/08/19/my-father-malcolm-forbes-a-never-ending-adventure/?sh=65a10f119fbb.

42. *Cambridge Dictionary*, s.v. "materialism," accessed June 18, 2021, https://dictionary.cambridge.org/us/dictionary/english/materialism.

11

THE END

THE RETURN OF KING JESUS AND THE RENEWAL OF ALL THINGS

GARY L. JOHNSON

To my grandmother, Mary B. Johnson,
who made certain I knew about heaven.

CONTENTS

General Editors' Note 561

Introduction 563

CHAPTER 1: Why Is the Second Coming of Jesus
So Important? 567

CHAPTER 2: What Is the Final Judgment? 573

CHAPTER 3: What Future Awaits the Unrepentant? 579

CHAPTER 4: What Is the Promise of the New Heaven
and the New Earth? 585

CHAPTER 5: How Can I Help Others Prepare for the
End of Time? 593

Appendix: Book Recommendations for Further Study 599

Notes 601

GENERAL EDITORS' NOTE

Scripture teaches that we are waiting for "the blessed hope—the appearing of the glory of our great God and Savior, Jesus Christ" (Titus 2:13). The expression "the blessed hope" demonstrates how the apostle Paul taught the earliest disciples to think about Jesus' return. It is to be a bright source of joy.

But what happens when Jesus returns? When will we face judgment? And what should we believe about hell and heaven? Most importantly, how can we help everyone who does not know Jesus and who is not waiting in anticipation of his return to get ready for that day?

Gary L. Johnson (DMin, Grace Theological Seminary) is Executive Director of e2: Effective Elders and author of *LeaderShift*. He has served in pastoral ministry for four decades. In addition to his Doctor of Ministry, he holds a Master of Arts in Church History (Lincoln Christian Seminary) and a Master of Ministry and a Master of Divinity (Cincinnati Bible Seminary). He and his wife, Leah, have two sons serving in the ministry, and one of his greatest joys in life is being called Grandpa by his six children.

This book expounds on the section from the Renew.org Leaders' Faith Statement called "The End":

> We believe that Jesus is coming back to earth in order to bring this age
> to an end. Jesus will reward the saved and punish the wicked, and finally
> destroy God's last enemy, death. He will put all things under the Father,
> so that God may be all in all forever. That is why we have urgency for the
> Great Commission—to make disciples of all nations. We like to look at the
> Great Commission as an inherent part of God's original command to "be
> fruitful and multiply." We want to be disciples of Jesus who love people and
> help them to be disciples of Jesus. We are a movement of disciples who make
> disciples who help renew existing churches and who start new churches that

make more disciples. We want to reach as many as possible—until Jesus returns and God restores all creation to himself in the new heaven and new earth.

*See the full Network Faith Statements at the end of this book.

Support Scriptures: Matthew 25:31–32; Acts 17:31; Revelation 20:11–15; 2 Thessalonians 1:6–10; Mark 9:43–49; Luke 12:4–7; Acts 4:12; John 14:6; Luke 24:46–48; Matthew 28:19–20; Genesis 12:1–3; Galatians 2:20; 4:19; Luke 6:40; Luke 19:10; Revelation 21:1ff.

The following tips might help you use this book more effectively (and the other books in the *Real Life Theology* series):

1. *Five questions, answers, and Scriptures.* We framed this book around five key questions with five short answers and five notable Scriptures. This format provides clarity, making it easier to commit crucial information to memory. This format also enables the books in the *Real Life Theology* series to support our catechism. Our catechism is a series of fixed questions and answers for instruction in church or home. In all, the series has fifty-two questions, answers, and key Scriptures. This particular book focuses on the five that are most pertinent to the end.
2. *Summary videos.* You can find three to seven-minute video teachings that summarize the book, as well as each chapter, at Renew.org. These short videos can function as standalone teachings. But for groups or group leaders using the book, they can also be used to launch discussion of the reading.

May God use this book to fuel faithful and effective disciple making in your life and church.

For King Jesus,
Bobby Harrington and Daniel McCoy
General Editors, *Real Life Theology* Series

INTRODUCTION

Have you ever taken the trip of a lifetime? Maybe when you were younger you took a trip of a lifetime to Disney or to a developing nation on a short-term mission trip. Perhaps you went to Hawaii or Alaska to celebrate a wedding anniversary, or you toured the Holy Land or the land of your ancestors. No matter the nature or destination of a trip of a lifetime, travelers can recall three common experiences associated with this kind of journey, and they are as simple as A-B-C.

Anticipation. Excitement builds within us as the day for our departure draws near. We count the days—whether crossing them off the calendar or watching them pass on a countdown app on our phone. We tell young children, "Just five more 'sleeps' until we leave for Disney World!" Anticipation builds with each enthusiastic conversation we have and with every suitcase we pack.

Brochure. Before deciding to make this once-in-a-lifetime trip, we research the destination. Glossy travel brochures and cutting-edge websites entice would-be travelers to sign up for a voyage or a land tour. Before departing, travelers study the details surrounding their destination: lodging, meals, activities, surroundings, and more.

Companions. We experience deep satisfaction when we go on a trip like this with others. We make memories, hear laughter, see smiles—various experiences are had with those whom we love. Who travels alone to Israel, Disney, or Europe? Who drives across the country or cruises around the world alone? Companions make this kind of trip special.

OUR TRIP OF A LIFETIME

EVERY PERSON WILL EVENTUALLY take a trip of a lifetime: when we pass from this life into the next. This is a once-in-a-lifetime experience like no other. And like all trips of a lifetime, we will want to incorporate the three common experiences: anticipation, brochure, and companions.

Christians should experience growing excitement about heaven and what awaits us there. Particularly when we grow older or battle a life-threatening illness, we should experience joyful anticipation as we prepare to depart from this life to be home with the Lord. If we have little knowledge or understanding of what is beyond death's door, we will have less excitement and anticipation for what awaits us. Yet we have a travel brochure—the Bible—that provides a myriad of details about heaven, and even of hell, affording us much insight into the nature of life after death.

People widely assume everyone goes to heaven—even claiming dogs go there. But do they? Most people assume heaven is up in the sky. But is it? Many individuals think that when a child dies, God needed another angel. But is that what babies become when they die? Much of our thinking about heaven and hell is just plain wrong, yet we do not have to remain blissfully ignorant about life after death. When we study the Scriptures—our travel brochure—we can know what awaits us beyond death's door and how to get to the right destination! Moreover, this indescribable journey is free to us. By God's outrageous generosity and grace, we have been saved through the death and resurrection of King Jesus.

WE HAVE BEEN SAVED THROUGH THE DEATH AND RESURRECTION OF JESUS CHRIST.

One more piece of advice: do not make this trip of a lifetime alone. Take as many traveling companions with you as possible, especially those you know and love. Just think, some people we know have already arrived in heaven and await our arrival. Once there, we will experience an indescribable celebration. For eternity, we will savor God's presence while serving, worshiping, and knowing him in ways we could never experience while on earth. If you're reading this, someone likely already told you about heaven and how to get there, so pay it forward: tell others this good news!

My sons are grown, married, and have children of their own. Yet one of my most joy-filled moments is when they are both home at mealtime. The table holds an abundant feast, and around the table sit my wife, sons, daughters-in-law, and six grandchildren. As I pray before the meal, I am overwhelmed with joy for they are all home with their feet under my table. Since I was made in God's image, I believe my joy reflects his overwhelming joy when we—and those we love—make it to our heavenly home someday with our feet under God's table.

My aim with this book is to help guide your thinking and understanding about what I believe are the most important aspects of this trip of a lifetime we all will take someday. I do not cover every aspect of this topic but focus upon the five core, orthodox elements of what the Bible teaches about the End.

- The Second Coming
- The resurrection of the dead
- The final judgment
- Eternal punishment
- The new heaven and new earth

These elements form a major part of the foundation of biblical orthodoxy. They are the focus of what Scripture teaches about end times and should help form the foundation of our beliefs. These are some of the key beliefs upon which the earliest Christians focused the earliest faith statements of the historic church: the Apostles' Creed and the Nicene Creed.[1]

The End does not focus on the other important elements about the End that are not essential beliefs.[2] Godly leaders often debate these nonessential beliefs in the church. These beliefs include the following:

- The rapture before the tribulation
- Cosmic disruptions on earth
- The Antichrist
- The conversion of Israel
- The 1,000-year reign

I join with the Renew.org Network as we champion a theological paradigm that upholds with vigor what is essential. Yet at the same time, we promote respect on secondary but important and personal beliefs.

Curious about what is beyond death's door? Do you have lingering questions about the next life? Join us as we discover what awaits us as we make the trip of a lifetime.

1

WHY IS THE SECOND COMING OF JESUS SO IMPORTANT?

Answer: It is the final battle that ends the war with evil, brings the resurrection of the dead, and leads to victorious, eternal life.

> Men of Galilee . . . why do you stand here looking into the sky? This same Jesus, who has been taken from you into heaven, will come back in the same way you have seen him go into heaven.
> — Acts 1:11

The day of June 6, 1944, will long be remembered as D-Day. For five years leading up to this point, World War II had raged throughout Europe and the Far East, claiming the lives of tens of millions of people. All of that would soon end. With steeled determination, the Allied Forces launched an invasion on the beaches of Normandy, France, that signaled the beginning of the war's eventual end. Imagine the sight and sound of more than 800,000 soldiers fighting on land, accompanied by more than 13,000 aircraft overhead and 6,000 boats afloat. Hitler and the Nazi war machine had to be stopped. Once the smoke of battle cleared, the war was decided.

On D-Day, it was decided that the Allies would eventually win World War II. Yet for eleven more months, the war in Europe continued, and casualties mounted. Then on May 8, 1945, the Allies celebrated "V-E Day" (Victory in Europe), followed three months later by "V-J Day" (Victory in Japan) on August 14. The war had officially ended—and the Allies had won.[3]

THINK D-DAY AND V-DAY

IMAGINE THE SIGHT AND sound when the people cried "Crucify him!" (John 19:15) accompanied by the sound on Calvary of nails pounding into his flesh. From his bruised and bloodied body came the declaration: "It is finished" (John 19:30). For the warrior Jesus, this moment marked victory as "mission accomplished." The price of our sin had been paid in full by the sinless Son of God. Moreover, his resurrection from the dead sealed our fate and the fate of Satan. Calvary is our D-Day, decided by the death and resurrection of King Jesus who would eventually win the war against the evil one and his kingdom. Moreover, Victory Day will happen the moment Jesus splits the clouds and all eyes behold the return of Jesus Christ, the King of kings and Lord of lords (Revelation 1:7).

CALVARY IS OUR D-DAY.

From our D-Day—Calvary—until our V-Day—the Second Coming—there will be untold numbers of *spiritual casualties*: people who reject Jesus Christ as their Savior and Lord. The evil one is "filled with fury, because he knows that his time is short" (Revelation 12:12), and he is doing all he can to "steal and kill and destroy" (John 10:10). So then, we believers must not only remain faithful to Jesus and receive the "crown of life" (Revelation 2:10b, NKJV) but also do all we can to reach people with the good news of King Jesus. Why? At his Second Coming, people can no longer be added to those who are saved. Every person must decide to surrender to Christ *before* that day. Once he returns, it will be too late to come to Christ.

The apostle Paul describes the suddenness of the Second Coming in 1 Thessalonians 5:1–4.

> Now, brothers and sisters, about times and dates we do not need to write to you, for you know very well that the day of the Lord will come like a thief in the night. While people are saying, "Peace and safety," destruction will come on them suddenly, as labor pains on a pregnant woman, and they will not escape. But you, brothers and sisters, are not in darkness so that this day should surprise you like a thief.

The return of Jesus will be sudden and without warning, which is all the more reason to be ready.

THE RESURRECTION OF THE DEAD

The Second Coming will also bring forth the resurrection from the dead of all who have lived. The Bible teaches that when a follower of Jesus dies prior to the End, they go instantaneously to be at "home with the Lord" (2 Corinthians 5:8). Similarly, when a non-believer dies, they instantaneously go to a place of punishment, separated from God (Luke 16:23). So at death, both the saved and the unsaved are in the intermediate state. Everyone remains in this temporary state prior to the Second Coming of Christ.

On that day, we will celebrate the resurrection of the dead. At that very moment, both the saved and the condemned will be resurrected and brought before the judgment of God to receive their eternal rewards or punishment. The saved will receive glorified bodies and enjoy eternal life in the new heaven and new earth. But sadly, those who die without Christ as their Savior will be condemned to an eternal punishment (Matthew 25:46).

For the disciple of Jesus, the resurrection of the dead will be an exciting reality. Our new bodies will not be made of perishable flesh and blood as we know it; rather, they will be imperishable, glorious, and powerful bodies. The apostle Paul describes it this way:

> So will it be with the resurrection of the dead. The body that is sown is perishable, it is raised imperishable; it is sown in dishonor, it is raised in glory; it is sown in weakness, it is raised in power; it is sown in a natural body, it is raised a spiritual body. If there is a natural body, there is also a spiritual body. (1 Corinthians 15:42–44)

Paul goes on to describe how it will happen:

> I declare to you, brothers and sisters, that flesh and blood cannot inherit the kingdom of God, nor does the perishable inherit the imperishable. Listen, I tell you a mystery: We will not all sleep, but we will all be changed—in a flash, in the twinkling of an eye, at the last trumpet. For the trumpet will sound, the dead will be raised imperishable, and we will be changed. For the perishable must clothe itself with the imperishable, and the mortal with immortality. (1 Corinthians 15:50–53)

Our new bodies will be fitted for the new heaven and new earth. But most importantly, our new bodies will be ideally suited for an everlasting life of intimate communion with God.

THINK TRIGGER

THE WORD "TRIGGER" IS most often associated with a gun. Yet the word can have far more applications. In the world of war, a trigger releases a missile from a fighter jet and a torpedo from a submarine. Just as a trigger releases a bullet, missile, or torpedo, God will send Jesus back and his return will initiate a series of vital events that will mark the beginning of everlasting life—whether in heaven or hell. The Second Coming is important to Jesus because it will trigger significant events.

First, many Christians interpret the Bible as teaching there will be tribulations and trials at the End, tied in with Jesus' return. For example, some expect a great and final battle known as Armageddon (Revelation 16:16). This battle will rage between all the forces of good and evil. Then even those individuals who have already died and are in heaven will return with Jesus as a part of his victorious army (Revelation 19:7–8, 14). Like a mighty army the "dead in Christ will rise first" (1 Thessalonians 4:16) when the last trumpet blows at his Second Coming. King Jesus will conquer Satan and his demons, casting them into the lake of fire (Matthew 25:41; Revelation 19:19–20). Victory will be more than sweet as Satan is vanquished forever. We will be free from temptation and sin forevermore.

After Jesus returns, we will all experience the final judgment (Revelation 20:11–15). God, the Righteous Judge, will take his seat and every person ever to have lived will be summoned before him to stand trial. Before anyone is condemned to hell or welcomed into heaven, everyone will clearly understand God's verdict for his or her eternity.

Third, God will destroy this earth and will create new heavens and a new earth. This moment will result in truly a "new and improved" earth, where there will be no sin, as God originally intended. Those individuals who have been declared not guilty of their sin by the blood of King Jesus will live everlasting with God on the new earth.

THE SECOND COMING IS IMPORTANT TO JESUS AND SHOULD BE TO US.

The Second Coming is important to Jesus and should be to us for it will trigger indescribable events: "'What no eye has seen, what no ear has heard, and what no human mind has conceived'—the things God has prepared for those who love him" (1 Corinthians 2:9). The majestic event to which we turn next is the final judgment.

2

WHAT IS THE FINAL JUDGMENT?

Answer: It is the time when God, the Righteous Judge, declares each person saved or condemned.

> So then, each of us will give an account of ourselves to God.
> — Romans 14:12

M any Americans have never been in a courtroom. Only a select few have had to appear in court, whether as a plaintiff, defendant, witness, jurist, or court official. Yet most Americans are familiar with the courtroom setting thanks to television productions. Whether fictional dramas or reality shows, television shows depict how a courtroom works. But the final judgment is neither fiction nor reality television. The final judgment is absolute. Familiar court images help us understand more clearly the proceedings of the great and final judgment. Court cases always involve a summons, the evidence, the verdict, and the exit.

THE SUMMONS

EVERY PERSON WHO HAS ever lived will be summoned to the final judgment, and not as a witness but as a defendant. Each of us will stand before the great Judge. Paul declares "all have sinned and fall short of the glory of God" (Romans 3:23). Because every person is a sinner, we will all stand before God's judgment seat where each of us will give an account of ourselves to God (Romans 14:11–12). In his book *Heaven*, Randy Alcorn reminds us that believers will face a final judgment of works—works that do not determine our salvation, but our eternal reward. Unbelievers too face such a final judgment.[4]

The apostle John received a vision of this future moment while on the island of Patmos:

> Then I saw a great white throne and him who was seated on it. The earth and the heavens fled from his presence, and there was no place for them. And I saw the dead, great and small, standing before the throne.
> (Revelation 20:11–12a)

NO ONE WILL BE EXEMPT FROM THE FINAL JUDGMENT. No one, no matter their rank in life, will be exempt from the final judgment. At the Second Coming, the earth and heavens will be destroyed, and God will judge all people. Imagine the sight as countless individuals "all rise" as our Judge takes his throne.

THE EVIDENCE

DESCRIBING THE FINAL JUDGMENT, John writes:

> And I saw the dead, great and small, standing before the throne, and books were opened. Another book was opened, which is the book of life. The dead were judged according to what they had done as recorded in the books. . . . Each person was judged according to what they had done.
> (Revelation 20:12–13)

According to John, the accused will be judged according to what they did. While this sounds like a works-based salvation, how does John's declaration harmonize with other New Testament writers? Take the apostle Paul's statement, for example: "For it is by grace you have been saved, through faith—and this is not from yourselves, it is the gift of God—not by works, so that no one can boast" (Ephesians 2:8–9). Clearly, according to this passage, we are saved by what Jesus did and not by what we do. The crucifixion of King Jesus was the atonement of our sin. So how does this comport with John's statement? And how are we to understand being judged "according to what [we] had done as recorded in the books"?

Think of *evidence*. During a trial, evidence is used by the judge or jury to reach a verdict. From witness testimony to exhibits, evidence is essential in a trial.

Similarly, God will look for evidence that individuals were sincere followers of King Jesus—or not. We are saved to serve Jesus with our lives.

James, the brother of Jesus, describes the evidence of a faithful life, bringing together the tandem relationship between faith and works:

> What good is it, my brothers and sisters, if someone claims to have faith but has no deeds? Can such faith save them? Suppose a brother or sister is without clothes and daily food. If one of you says to them, "Go in peace; keep warm and well fed," but does nothing about their physical needs, what good is it? In the same way, faith by itself, if it is not accompanied by action, is dead. (James 2:14–17)

The objective evidence of our lives will serve as proof that we were authentic Jesus-followers. Spiritually, we are saved by grace through faith in King Jesus, and such faith is accompanied by works.[5]

THE VERDICT

FROM THE OPENING PAGES of Scripture, God explained why he punished people. Consider how God did this at major moments of indictment throughout biblical history. When Adam and Eve were cursed and banished from the Garden of Eden, God explained why. God even explained why the serpent was cursed (Genesis 3:14–19). God clearly explained to the Israelites why they were condemned to wander in the wilderness for forty years (Numbers 14:26–35). God plainly described to Moses and Aaron why they would not set foot into the promised land (Numbers 20:12). When David committed adultery with Bathsheba and arranged for her husband to be killed, God succinctly stated why and how David would be punished (2 Samuel 12:9–12).

Just days before his death on a cross, Jesus explained to a crowd why some people will be saved and some condemned by using the metaphor of the sheep and the goats. Jesus started by warning people of the coming judgment upon his return:

> All the nations will be gathered before him, and he will separate the people one from another as a shepherd separates the sheep from the goats. He will put the sheep on his right and the goats on his left. (Matthew 25:32–33)

Then, Jesus clearly explained what evidence will be used to reach a verdict. To the saved, Jesus will say:

> For I was hungry and you gave me something to eat, I was thirsty and you gave me something to drink, I was a stranger and you invited me in, I needed clothes and you clothed me, I was sick and you looked after me, I was in prison and you came to visit me. (Matthew 25:35–36)

Conversely, Jesus cited the same evidence (or lack thereof) in condemning the lost (vv. 42–43). Both the saved and the lost will be surprised at the verdict and the mention of evidence, asking, "Lord, when did we see you hungry and feed you, or thirsty and give you something to drink? When did we see you a stranger and invite you in, or needing clothes and clothe you? When did we see you sick or in prison and go to visit you?" (vv. 37–39, see also v. 44). Both groups will be startled at Jesus' verdict. Which evidence will he cite regarding your life?

THE EXIT

WHEN THE TRIAL ENDS with a judge's verdict, the one on trial exits the courtroom, having been found innocent or guilty. They are either released or led to prison. One verdict brings great relief and joy, whereas another verdict brings defeat and misery. Similarly, when God, the Righteous Judge, declares everyone's verdict, we exit from the final judgment into an eternal existence—either condemnation (Revelation 20:15) or welcomed "home with the Lord" forever (2 Corinthians 5:8).[6]

WE EXIT FROM THE FINAL JUDGMENT INTO AN ETERNAL EXISTENCE.

A trial produces great stress that crescendos toward the declaration of the verdict. For a Christian, the final judgment does not need to produce worry or fear because we have a good and just Ruler. Just as a president can pardon those convicted of crime, God will pardon those who are in Christ: "Therefore, there is now no condemnation for those who are in Christ Jesus" (Romans 8:1). The prophet declared that Jesus "was pierced for our transgressions, he was crushed for our iniquities; the punishment that brought us peace was on him" (Isaiah 53:5). Every person stands accused for having sinned, yet those who have surrendered their lives to King Jesus are declared "not guilty," having been saved by the blood of the Lamb! We can rejoice, for Jesus is "able to keep you from stumbling and to present you before his glorious presence without fault and with great joy" (Jude v. 24).

There is, however, great reason to fear for the unrepentant. We turn to this sober subject in the next chapter.

3

WHAT FUTURE AWAITS THE UNREPENTANT?

Answer: The unrepentant will painfully suffer eternal separation from God.

Enter through the narrow gate. For wide is the gate and broad is the road that leads to destruction, and many enter through it. But small is the gate and narrow the road that leads to life, and only a few find it.
— Matthew 7:13–14

afety announcements are commonplace. From those sitting on a commercial flight to those boarding a cruise ship, federal law requires safety announcements to be made prior to a ship sailing or a jet liner climbing into the air. From the proper way to don a life vest to clicking a seat belt, necessary warnings are given to people cruising on the high seas or soaring in the sky.

The Scriptures issue a warning to the same effect. They warn people of potential danger before they embark on life's final journey beyond death's door. The difference is that whereas the vast majority of passengers on a plane make it safely to landing, not everyone will go to heaven. King Jesus himself, more than anyone else in Scripture, warned people of this truth. Yet many people today fail to heed his warnings. We need help grappling with them from Scripture. Interrogatives of speech—who, what, and why—can help frame this discussion and make space for Scripture to correct any absent, wrong, or misleading assumptions we might have about the reality of hell.

WHO GOES TO HEAVEN?

IN WESTERN CULTURE, PEOPLE commonly believe everyone goes to heaven for one reason or another. Many don't connect this with Jesus and think of God as a benevolent grandfather, who wants to make sure all his grandchildren make it safely home. This teaching is called universalism, and its popularity continues to grow among Christians today. Universalism teaches that everyone—sooner or later—goes to heaven, which is universal salvation. Universalists often vilify those who believe in a literal hell as a place of torment. They see these believers as being judgmental, irrelevant, and lacking in compassion with regard to life after death. However as Alcorn writes, "By denying the endlessness of hell, we minimize Christ's work on the cross."[7] According to the Scriptures, hell is real and *people really do go to hell.*

The final two chapters of Revelation speak not only of heaven's reality, as we often emphasize when quoting them, but also of the reality of hell.

> But the cowardly, the unbelieving, the vile, the murderers, the sexually immoral, those who practice magic arts, the idolaters and all liars—they will be consigned to the fiery lake of burning sulfur. This is the second death. (Revelation 21:8)

The apostle John clearly observes that some individuals will not enter heaven. The phrase "the second death" refers to the spiritual death of an individual when they are condemned to hell. Everyone experiences the first death when we cease living physically, while those who are condemned to hell experience the second death.[8] Again, Jesus had much to say about hell, and he taught that many people will spend eternity there. A pointed example comes from the Sermon on the Mount:

> Not everyone who says to me, "Lord, Lord," will enter the kingdom of heaven, but only the one who does the will of my Father who is in heaven. Many will say to me on that day, "Lord, Lord, did we not prophesy in your name and in your name drive out demons and in your name perform many miracles?" Then I will tell them plainly, "I never knew you. Away from me, you evildoers!" (Matthew 7:21–23)

Beyond doubt, hell is real after we pass through death's door. Again, Jesus warns of this reality: "Whoever believes in him is not condemned, but whoever does not believe stands condemned already because they have not believed in the name of God's one and only Son" (John 3:18). When people reject Jesus Christ as Lord and Savior of their lives, their decision comes at an enormous cost.

> WHEN PEOPLE REJECT JESUS, THEIR DECISION COMES AT AN ENORMOUS COST.

WHAT IS HELL?

WE LIVE IN A culture of comfort. From central heating and air to plush furniture and the latest and greatest technology, we enjoy being comfortable. Whether riding in a car, truck, or jet, we want to be comfortable. The thought of suffering, particularly in hell, is repulsive to our thinking. Westerners often shape their beliefs about hell to fit their desires. Many people no longer believe that hell actually exists, let alone define it as a place of eternal suffering.

The New Testament often associates hell with fire. For example, in Jesus' Sermon on the Mount, Jesus spoke of some people being "in danger of the fire of hell" (Matthew 5:22). The word Jesus commonly used for hell was "Gehenna" (also known as the "Valley of Hinnom"), which was a perpetual burn heap outside Jerusalem previously desecrated by child sacrifices (Jeremiah 7:30–33; 19:2–7). This location became a point of reference for his Jewish listeners as he described the future that awaits the wicked. The apostle John says the unsaved "will be consigned to the fiery lake of burning sulfur" (Revelation 21:8). Other terms used to describe the afterlife destination of the wicked—including terms for the intermediate state—include "outer darkness" (Matthew 22:11–14; 25:30, NKJV), "Hades" (Luke 16:23), and even "Tartarus" (2 Peter 2:4), a place regarded by the ancient Greeks as the destiny of the wicked dead—and thus a point of reference for a Greek audience just as "Gehenna" was for a Jewish audience.[9]

Going back to Jesus' warning in Matthew 25, we see how long hell's fire will burn. He said, "Then they will go away to eternal punishment, but the righteous to eternal life" (Matthew 25:46). "Eternal punishment" here means constant, never-ending suffering. Those saved and in Christ experience eternal paradise, while those without Christ experience everlasting misery.

Jesus further emphasized hell's long-lasting nature in Mark 9:47–48:

> And if your eye causes you to stumble, pluck it out. It is better for you to enter the kingdom of God with one eye than to have two eyes and be thrown into hell, where "the worms that eat them do not die, and the fire is not quenched."

Jesus cited Isaiah 66:24 here, stating that hell's fire is never extinguished. The reference to worms not dying emphasizes the eternal nature of hell and its unending torment. If we question how a fire can burn and never go out, we should remember that Moses saw a burning bush that was not consumed by the fire (Exodus 3:1–3). God created such a fire then, and it is not too difficult for him to be doing so now.

In light of the difficulty many people have with the concept of everlasting punishment, a belief in "annihilationism" is growing in popularity. This is the case although most church leaders throughout church history have believed that annihilationism is not taught in Scripture while the teaching of everlasting suffering is. One version of annihilationism holds that God is too compassionate to make the unsaved suffer in hell for eternity.[10] Some annihilationists believe that God annihilates an individual immediately at death while others believe that, after the resurrection of the dead and the final judgment, the lost will experience suffering in direct proportion to the evil that was committed by that person in their life, before then going out of existence.[11]

The doctrine of hell, where God punishes the unredeemed after the Second Coming, the resurrection of the dead, and the final judgment, is a part of the essential doctrines at Renew.org, but when it comes to the exact nature of hell—how much of the language is symbolic or metaphorical or the exact nature of the punishment in hell—these questions are up for open, honest discussion. What is not up for debate is the reality of hell as a place of punishment in eternity.

Though we may struggle with the concept of everlasting punishment, as Christ followers we must submit to the authority of God's unchanging and authoritative Word. Though we may prefer a benevolent, ever-gentle God, we must understand God is just (2 Thessalonians 1:6) and he alone will have vengeance (Romans 12:19). We do not have authority to describe hell according to our own likes or dislikes. Sadly, the unrepentant will be far removed from God, with their painful eternity marked by God's conspicuous absence.[12]

WHY DOES IT HAPPEN?

In keeping with his nature, God explains the "why" behind punishment. The unrepentant will clearly understand why they are condemned to hell. Jesus was explicit, saying a person will go to hell for rejecting him (John 3:18; Matthew 25:41–46). The apostle Paul succinctly states why people are condemned to hell.

> God is just: He will pay back trouble to those who trouble you and give relief to you who are troubled, and to us as well. This will happen when the Lord Jesus is revealed from heaven in blazing fire with his powerful angels. He will punish those who do not know God and do not obey the gospel of our Lord Jesus. (2 Thessalonians 1:6–8)

Why are people condemned? When individuals do not repent and reconcile with God through Jesus Christ, they are condemned to hell. And choices have consequences.

At the same time, there are strong scriptural indicators that judgment for the unrepentant is not a one-size-fits-all indictment. "God will repay each person according to what they have done" (Romans 2:6). It appears that the willful rejection of Jesus by people who should have known better will call for a stricter judgment. Jesus made the following warning to towns in which he had performed many miracles yet persisted in their unbelief:

> Woe to you, Chorazin! Woe to you, Bethsaida! For if the miracles that were performed in you had been performed in Tyre and Sidon, they would have repented long ago in sackcloth and ashes. But I tell you, it will be more bearable for Tyre and Sidon on the day of judgment than for you. And you, Capernaum, will you be lifted to the heavens? No, you will go down to Hades. For if the miracles that were performed in you had been performed in Sodom, it would have remained to this day. But I tell you that it will be more bearable for Sodom on the day of judgment than for you. (Matthew 11:21–24)

The reality of hell is indeed a frightening biblical promise. But it need not make us mistrust the rightness of God's judgment. As Abraham said, "Will not the Judge of all the earth do right?" (Genesis 18:25). We can heartily agree with Abraham here, for we have met this Judge and have completely entrusted ourselves to him. For Jesus himself said, "Moreover, the Father judges no one, but has entrusted all judgment to the Son" (John 5:22). From our observations of the time he spent loving, teaching, dying, and rising for us, we know we can fully trust the character of Jesus—as not only our Savior and Lord but also as our righteous Judge.[13]

REAL LOVE

In *Honest Evangelism*, British evangelist Rico Tice shares examples of how to share the good news, particularly with those we love.[14] Tice believes that if we truly love others, we will warn them. He tells of a time when he was in Australia visiting a friend. While on the beach at Botany Bay, Tice decided to go for a swim in the ocean. His friend stopped him, pointing out several posted warning signs declaring that sharks were present. People were to swim at their own risk. An important question to ponder is this: Do the warning signs help to save people's lives or ruin their fun?

The Scriptures contain warnings of hell's reality. Do these warnings serve to ruin our fun or to save us? Will we listen to Jesus' warnings or not? Each person must decide for themselves and for those they influence. The implications are real, as Jesus reminded us.

> I tell you, my friends, do not be afraid of those who kill the body and after that can do no more. But I will show you whom you should fear: Fear him who, after your body has been killed, has authority to throw you into hell. Yes, I tell you, fear him. (Luke 12:4–5)

Jesus spoke candidly about hell because he loves all people and wants no one to experience hell's torment. After all, Jesus suffered indescribable torment on a cross, saving people from the torments of hell. He knows what it's like to suffer, and his suffering can take the place of ours—if only we entrust ourselves to him. Those who do will experience the glory of the new heaven and new earth. We will witness what we have longed for all our lives: the coming of God's kingdom of love and holiness in all its fullness.

JESUS SPOKE CANDIDLY ABOUT HELL BECAUSE HE LOVES ALL PEOPLE.

4

WHAT IS THE PROMISE OF THE NEW HEAVEN AND THE NEW EARTH?

Answer: The saved will live eternally with God in the new creation, a home of righteousness.

> But in keeping with his promise we are looking forward to a new heaven and a new earth, where righteousness dwells.
> — 2 Peter 3:13

Too often, people make assumptions about heaven based on hearsay and not on what the Scriptures say. For example, assuming people become angels when they die is popular. Confusion also abounds concerning the whereabouts of our deceased loved ones. For the truth about questions regarding the afterlife, disciples of Jesus go to the Word of God. In 2 Corinthians 5:8, for example, the apostle Paul clearly states "to be absent from the body [is] to be present with the Lord" (NKJV). So we know that if we die prior to Christ's return, our last breath here becomes our first breath there in God's presence. The dead in Christ are not asleep in the grave as some people assume. Rather, they are home with the Lord in the abode of God—the "third heaven" or "paradise" that Paul describes experiencing in 2 Corinthians 12:1–4. The "first heaven" provides rain (Psalm 68:8); the "second heaven" is arrayed with the sun, moon, stars, and planets (Psalm 8:3; 19:1; 33:6); and Paul's "third heaven" is the abode of God, where Christians are "home with the Lord" prior to Christ's return.

THE CONCEPT OF CONTINUANCE

A POPULAR MISCONCEPTION OF heaven is that people stay "up there" throughout all eternity. This could not be further from the truth. The Bible explains that at Christ's Second Coming, God will make new heavens and a new earth. The first earth, on which we live, was perfect and without sin, as described in Genesis 1–2. At Christ's return, though, God will destroy this earth and create a new earth, one without sin. The first two chapters of the Bible (Genesis 1–2) describe life on a sin-free earth. Regretfully, Genesis 3 describes the first sin committed and the horrific consequences that followed. From Genesis 3 through Revelation 20, we read of sinful life in a broken world. But in the final two chapters of the Bible (Revelation 21–22), we read of life on a new sin-free earth. Like a pair of bookends holding many books together, the first two and last two chapters of the Bible have between them the story of humankind's rebellion against God. Yet in the end, King Jesus returns and God picks up where he left off. His initial plan to enjoy life with his image bearers on earth will become reality at the return of Jesus and the creation of a new earth. He will continue with his original plan for Christ-followers to reign with him throughout eternity (i.e., the concept of continuity).[15] Seven hundred years before Christ's birth, God spoke through the prophet Isaiah:

> See, I will create *new heavens* and a *new earth*. The former things will not be remembered, nor will they come to mind. (Isaiah 65:17)

> The *new heavens* and the *new earth* that I make will endure before me. (Isaiah 66:22)

"I WILL CREATE *NEW* HEAVENS AND A *NEW* EARTH."

At Christ's return, God will destroy our current earth and the heavens (i.e., the atmosphere and space; see 2 Peter 3:10). Peter uses a word for heavens that denotes the vaulted expanse of the sky and all that we can see within it, from low-lying clouds to lofty stars. The apostle Peter describes the unique details of this often-overlooked happening in the End.

> But the day of the Lord will come like a thief. The heavens will disappear with a roar; the elements will be destroyed by fire, and the earth and everything done in it will be laid bare. Since everything will be destroyed in this way, what kind of people ought you to be? You ought to live holy

and godly lives as you look forward to the day of God and speed its coming. That day will bring about the destruction of the heavens by fire, and the elements will melt in the heat. But in keeping with his promise we are looking forward to a *new heaven* and a *new earth*, where righteousness dwells. (2 Peter 3:10–13)

This sin-ravaged earth will be destroyed at the Second Coming of Jesus Christ, who himself said while on earth, "Heaven and earth will pass away" (Matthew 24:35). Moreover, when Jesus returns, God will create new heavens (i.e., the celestial heavens) and a new earth, which will be our home of righteousness (2 Peter 3:13). Finally, the new earth will be free of sin and temptation! The kingdom will be restored in its fullness! The apostle John repeats similar language from Isaiah's prophecy, writing of this future reality while exiled on the island of Patmos:

Then I saw "a *new heaven* and a *new earth*," for the first heaven and the first earth had passed away. (Revelation 21:1)

So then, from Isaiah to Peter to John to Jesus we learn that the abode of God will be *here*—on a new earth. When Christ returns, the current heavens (i.e., sun, moon, stars, planets, etc.) and this earth (on which we currently live) will be destroyed, and God will create new heavens and a new earth. God's kingdom will finally come in its complete glory, and we will resume our intended purpose of ruling creation and reigning with King Jesus (Revelation 22:5).

In Genesis 1–2, God spoke the earth and universe into existence by order of his command (Psalm 33:6–9). When finished with his first creation, God reflected on his handiwork and declared it was "very good" (Genesis 1:31), meaning it was not merely good, but it was excellent. Then, in Genesis 3 through Revelation 19, we read of a sin-saturated earth, which then gives way to new heavens and a sin-free new earth, "where righteousness dwells" (2 Peter 3:13).

Although we pray for and experience the inbreaking of God's kingdom on earth (Matthew 6:10), the proverbial saying "heaven on earth" will finally become full reality at Christ's return. The saved will dwell eternally with God (Revelation 21:1–4). Imagine a dwelling free from every form of evil and absolute peace with every individual, a home with our ever-present God providing for and protecting us. As Revelation 11:5 describes, "The kingdom of the world has become the kingdom of our Lord and of his Messiah, and he will reign for ever and ever."

THE LANDMARKS

WHEN WE TRAVEL TO a new destination, its landmarks might stand out to us. Think of how easily we can recognize Seattle's Space Needle, St. Louis's Gateway Arch, and San Francisco's Golden Gate Bridge. Cities in this life have landmarks, and the same will be true of places in the next life. In Revelation 21–22, the apostle John describes the New Jerusalem (i.e., new earth) as a city with certain landmarks. In ancient cultures, the reputation of a city was based on its size and features. High, thick walls and strong gates offered a sense of security for residents of the city. Similarly, an abundant fresh water supply and ample food offered people the hope of survival as they worked to live from day to day.

Revelation is apocalyptic literature such as we also find in Ezekiel, Daniel, and Zechariah. These books of the Bible include images, numbers, and colors that symbolize places, people, and things. Through study (often of the context of a passage), we can understand the meanings of many of these symbols. For example, the number seven means full and complete. In Revelation, the seven seals, seven trumpets, and seven bowls describe a full and complete amount of judgment on earth. The color white represents purity in Revelation, the color gold represents splendor, and the color red represents bloodshed and violence. As well, John saw a "new Jerusalem, coming down out of heaven from God" (Revelation 21:2). Think of the rich symbolism in such a sight. The landmarks that John described gave hope to readers in his day as well as to believers throughout the centuries.

In Revelation 21–22, John describes vivid landmarks in the New Jerusalem that provide insight as to what eternal life will be like on the new earth.[16] These landmarks fall into three categories: security, intimacy, and mercy.

1. Landmarks of Security. The first set of landmarks in the New Jerusalem is its walls, gates, and foundations, all of which speak to a strong sense of security (Revelation 21:12–14; 17–21). We have known some notable walls throughout history: notably the Berlin Wall, the Wailing Wall, and the Great Wall of China. These walls and others like them will amount to nothing compared to the walls of the New Jerusalem.

John's description of the wall denotes indescribable strength. The symbolic wall is both high and thick (Revelation 21:12, 17), describing how the saved will be safe from any harm, enjoying eternal life on the new earth in complete safety and security. The wall's thickness measures 144 cubits (twelve multiplied by twelve). Like the number seven, the number twelve is another number that represents fullness and completeness in apocalyptic literature. Moreover, there are twelve foundations made of priceless gemstones. Everlasting life on the new earth will be immovable and unshakable, an everlasting stability and security that is beyond priceless.[17]

The twelve gates represent full and complete access to life on the new earth. In another context, Jesus said that he is the gate (John 10:7, 9), and we will enjoy eternal life on the new earth only by entering through the atoning death of Jesus Christ. Moreover, city gates in biblical times provided protection and were a gathering place. Gates were closed at sundown for protection and opened at sunrise when people would come and go (e.g., Joshua 6:1; Nehemiah 7:3), with people often gathering at the gates to transact business (e.g., Ruth 4:1–12).

Yet in the New Jerusalem, "On no day will its gates ever be shut, for there will be no night there" (Revelation 21:25). The imagery of continually open gates with no night further emphasizes absolute security. On our current earth and in this life, bad things happen in the darkness of night. Instability is ever present in our lives financially, physically, politically, and more—but not so on the new earth, our new home where righteousness dwells.

2. Landmarks of Intimacy. Across the country and around the world, some cities are known for their population size, not so much for their landmarks. Many cities today, such as Mexico City, Beijing, Johannesburg, Paris, and New York City, teem with millions of people. These cities and others are crowded. People live in close quarters, but the intimacy on the new earth will be the closeness of another kind. John describes it this way:

> And I heard a loud voice from the throne saying, "Look! God's dwelling place is now among the people, and he will dwell with them. They will be his people, and God himself will be with them and be their God. 'He will wipe every tear from their eyes. There will be no more death' or mourning or crying or pain, for the old order of things has passed away." (Revelation 21:3–4)

The words "dwelling" and "dwell" here are significant because they connote a tabernacle or a tent (in Greek). God commanded Moses to build the tabernacle ("tent of meeting"), and God dwelled among his people, as represented by the ark of the covenant in the Most Holy Place (e.g., Exodus 25:8; Numbers 7:89). As God "tented" among his people then, God will "tent" intimately among his people in the new creation. People who camp in tents live in close, intimate quarters. Similarly, God will closely dwell with and among us.

This picture of intimacy is further expressed by the phrase, God "will wipe every tear from their eyes" (Revelation 21:4). A mother may wipe tears from a little child's face, but such an action is much too intimate for adults, unless the individuals have a close, intimate, and personal relationship. Yet on the new earth, God will intimately and compassionately live with us. Moreover, we will see him face-to-face (Revelation 22:4).

GOD WILL CLOSELY DWELL WITH AND AMONG US.

The New Jerusalem's dimensions emphasize God's intimate presence with us. The city will have a cube shape (Revelation 21:15–16) with all sides measuring "12,000 stadia," which is not a literal distance but a symbol of fullness and completion (i.e., the number twelve multiplied by ten by ten by ten). Like the numbers seven and twelve, the number ten also represents completeness. The new earth will enjoy a perfect completeness.[18]

Jerusalem, sometimes called the "city of God" (Psalm 87:2–3), was home to Solomon's temple, which included the Most Holy Place (i.e., the Holy of Holies). The Most Holy Place housed the ark of the covenant. The ark represented God's presence among his people, and only the high priest could enter the Most Holy Place on one day of the year, the Day of Atonement (Leviticus 16:1–34). The dimensions of the Most Holy Place measured "twenty cubits long, twenty wide and twenty high" (1 Kings 6:16, 20). It too was a cube. This place—which represented God's presence among his people on our current earth—was shaped in the same way as the New Jerusalem is described on the new earth. At Christ's return, God will create a new earth, where he will personally dwell with us. No matter where we are on the new earth, every person will feel and know the close, intimate presence of our omnipresent and ubiquitous God.

Moreover, not only will we enjoy everlasting close relationship with God, but we will also enjoy the same with one another. When Jesus returns, there will be "no more curse" (Revelation 22:3, NKJV). The curse of death will be conquered as "there will be no more death" (Revelation 21:4). Death is the great separator, and once it is destroyed when Jesus returns, we will no longer be separated from one another in grief. John emphasizes this with yet another statement: "And there was no longer any sea" (Revelation 21:1). This statement shouts great hope. The apostle John wrote Revelation in exile on the island of Patmos, and more than fifty miles of open water separated him from his loved ones on the mainland. When Jesus returns, we will live everlastingly on a new earth, never to be separated by death from one another.

3. Landmarks of Mercy. Travel advisors advise tourists to purchase their tickets in advance for visiting popular sites. This type of pre-payment guarantees admission into the attraction. Entry into the new creation has been pre-paid through the suffering of Jesus Christ. What Jesus did, not what we do, pays the penalty of our sin, which is God's mercy at work. While living everlastingly on the new earth, we will never forget the undeserved mercy we received from our loving God.

Jesus made our pre-payment for entering the New Jerusalem, the entryway of which is symbolized by the language of twelve gates, each made by a single pearl (Revelation 21:21). This landmark represents God's great mercy and symbolizes our admission into the new earth.

The twelve gates emphasize that this is the full and complete manner by which we enter everlasting life in the kingdom of God. Moreover, the twelve names of Israel's tribes are on the gates, while the twelve names of the apostles are on the foundations (Revelation 21:12, 14). In writing of the gates bearing the names of the twelve tribes of Israel and the foundation bearing the names of the twelve apostles, New Testament scholar Grant Osborne writes,

> The presence of the distinct groups, the twelve tribes as the gates and the twelve apostles as the foundation stones, makes it more likely that these do indeed signify Israel and the church. Thus, the message of 21:12–14 is that entry into the celestial city comes through the whole people of God, Israel and the church.[19]

Consider the significance that each of the heavenly gates is made by a single pearl. Pearls are produced by oysters. When an irritant, like that of a grain of sand, enters an oyster, the oyster secretes nacre, a mineral substance also known as mother of pearl, that coats the irritant, and after many such layers of nacre, a pearl is created. Thus, what was once an irritant can actually produce something of great value.

The pearl image of the heavenly gate in Revelation might help us to remember a couple of important insights about the Christian life (though not necessarily intended by John). First, through Christ's suffering on the cross something supremely valuable was created: our entryway into everlasting life with God. Jesus said, "I am the way and the truth and the life. No one comes to the Father except through me" (John 14:6). By his suffering we are saved. Second, Christians too experience suffering (e.g., John 16:33; James 1:2; 2 Timothy 3:1; 1 Peter 1:6–7; 4:12–19), and when we remain "faithful to the point of death," we receive "the crown of life" from Jesus (Revelation 2:10, NKJV). Our entrance into everlasting life is through the suffering of King Jesus on the cross, and as his followers, we must remain faithful to him, particularly when we suffer.

LONGING FOR THIS NEW LAND

WHEN PAUL WAS IN prison on "death row," awaiting his eventual execution in Rome, he wrote of his heart's longing for the Second Coming of Christ—which should be our longing too.

> I have fought the good fight, I have finished the race, I have kept the faith. Now there is in store for me the crown of righteousness, which the Lord, the righteous Judge, will award to me on that day—and not only to me, but also to all who have longed for his appearing. (2 Timothy 4:7–8)

Like Paul, do we long for the "appearing" of King Jesus upon his return? Or are we more enamored with this world and all it offers? Is our faith in God's kingdom that will reign forever or in earthly kingdoms that will pass away? Those who truly understand the next life will long for Christ's return and for the new earth on which we'll enjoy everlasting life with God. Very importantly, they will also help others prepare for the End, which is the subject of our final chapter.

5

HOW CAN I HELP OTHERS PREPARE FOR THE END OF TIME?

Answer: If we truly love others, we will show them King Jesus and tell them about him and heaven to come.

> We are therefore Christ's ambassadors, as though God were making his appeal through us. We implore you on Christ's behalf: Be reconciled to God.
> — 2 Corinthians 5:20

When we plan and save for a trip of a lifetime, we typically involve someone else in our planning. We can go on a fun trip solo, but a trip of a lifetime? Most likely, that will involve others from among our family and friends. It's more fun going together.

That's why God intends for us to enjoy the most important trip of a lifetime—going to the new creation—with those we love. One of the reasons we "do not grieve like the rest of mankind, who have no hope" is due to our belief that we will be with one another in God's kingdom of love and holiness throughout eternity (1 Thessalonians 4:13). If we say we love someone, how could we not tell them about everlasting life through Jesus Christ?

Nationally known magician Penn Jillette is an outspoken atheist. He tells of a Christian who gave him a New Testament. Jillette spoke well of the encounter, though it did not change his atheistic beliefs. I find it striking what Jillette said in conclusion: "How much do you have to hate somebody to believe everlasting life is possible and not tell them that?"[20] Do we truly love those in our immediate and extended families if we have not shared with them the saving hope of Jesus Christ? Can we honestly say we love our neighbors, coworkers, fellow students, and others in our spheres of influence if we have not told them how King Jesus alone can save them from their sin and give them everlasting life?

Both the male and female octopus die after mating and giving birth the first time. God created this creature with the passion to reproduce once before dying.[21] We have been made by God, and what if each of us had a passion to reproduce *spiritually*—at least once—before we died? What if each Christian made a disciple of at least one other individual prior to passing from this life? The world would be a different place! Even more, imagine if each of us internalized Jesus' calling to be disciple makers, so that disciple making became the core mission of our lives? Such a focused mission would transform generations.

An individual's final words are important words. Some of the final words of Jesus were these:

> Then Jesus came to them and said, "All authority in heaven and on earth has been given to me. Therefore go and make disciples of all nations, baptizing them in the name of the Father and of the Son and of the Holy Spirit, and teaching them to obey everything I have commanded you. And surely I am with you always, to the very end of the age." (Matthew 28:18–20)

God has an urgency for the Great Commission—to make disciples of all nations. We want to be disciples of Jesus who love people and help them to be disciples of Jesus. His vision in Revelation 7:9 describes those who will enjoy everlasting life with God and one another as, "There before me was a great multitude that no one could count, from every nation, tribe, people and language, standing before the throne and before the Lamb."

How, then, can we help others prepare for life after death? By making disciples who make disciples—the way Jesus did. When he saw crowds of broken people, he had compassion for them (Matthew 9:36). The Greek word for "compassion" literally refers to one's bowels. Jesus had feelings of empathy welling up from deep with him when he encountered broken, hurting, lost people. Do we? To prepare people for the End requires that we show them the depth of God's love, and we can only do so by building relationships with them.

Disciple making requires a "show-and-tell" approach. When we were in kindergarten or grade school, "show and tell" meant showing our young classmates an object and telling them about it. In the same way, since we love our family and friends, we must first show them the love, compassion, and kindness of Christ. We must invest in a sincere relationship with those who are spiritually lost around us, thereby earning the privilege of then telling them the good news of King Jesus. Hence, there is a show-and-tell approach to reaching those we love with the saving hope of Jesus.

In school, we learned various math skills, even those skills that involved the use of letters alongside numbers in mathematical equations. So let me offer you a spiritual math equation with letters and numbers. If we spiritually reproduce, particularly among our family and friends whom we say we love, we can use this equation to think about that pursuit:

$$I + C + C + C = C$$

These letters remind us of this fact:

I am called to share the good news of King Jesus

+

I must have a *concern* for those who are spiritually lost

+

I must have frequent *contact* with them to
show God's love

+

I earn the privilege over time of *communicating* the
good news of King Jesus

=

Individuals surrendering their lives to King Jesus and
becoming his disciples.

This is a fundamental—and winning—equation in evangelism.

I MUST HAVE CONCERN

WE WILL NEVER SPIRITUALLY reproduce unless we have an honest concern about the eternal suffering of the unrepentant. Do we truly love our family and friends to warn them of hell? The unrepentant will be forever separated from God. Are we— or are we not—concerned for those we say we love?

How can we fully grasp everlasting life, whether in heaven or hell? Picture a mountain of solid granite, a thousand miles high and a thousand miles wide at its base (Mount Everest is only five and a half miles high from sea level, for reference). Once every one million years, a bird flies to the top of the granite mountain and is allowed to peck at it for only ten seconds. Once the entire thousand-mile-high mountain is completely worn away from the bird pecking at it for a mere ten seconds once every one million years, that is but one day to everlasting life. It's beyond our comprehension. Similarly, eternal punishment is beyond our understanding. Just how concerned are we for those who are spiritually lost? We will never help people prepare for the end of time until we begin to have genuine concern for them.

I MUST HAVE CONTACT

WE CAN NEVER EFFECTIVELY and intentionally lead someone to become a disciple of Jesus unless we have contact with them—and the more frequent and personal our contact with them, the better. In his Great Commission, Jesus commanded us to reach others for him. To many people, the Great Commission is both overwhelming and intimidating. Yet it comes with a Great Companion: "And surely *I am with you always*, to the very end of the age" (Matthew 28:20). We are never alone in trying to reach family and friends with the saving hope of Jesus. Pastor, author, and contributor to this series Mark Moore affirms that our mission is "merely to be available to go where God needs us to go and to be who we already are, influencing those whom we already have a relationship with."[22]

Having contact with spiritually lost people compassionately is vital. Romans 2:4 says, "God's kindness is intended to lead you to repentance." Each of us is made in the image of God (Genesis 1:26–27), so we must show the same God-honoring kindness, forgiveness, and compassionate understanding toward unsaved family and friends if we hope to share the good news of King Jesus with them. We cannot, and must not, be quick to judge unbelievers. When people do not believe in God, we should not expect them to live, think, and speak as disciples of Jesus. Since Jesus went around doing good (Acts 10:38), as his followers we should do the same. We must "show" the unsaved the compassion of Christ before we can "tell" them the good news of King Jesus.

When we read of love in the Scriptures, we must remember that the biblical authors thought of love more as an action than as an emotion. For example, "For God so loved the world that he gave his one and only Son" (John 3:16). Love is an action and not merely a warm, fuzzy feeling. Jay Pathak and Dave Runyon wrote an exceptional and practical book called *The Art of Neighboring: Building Genuine Relationships Right Outside Your Door.*[23] In it, the authors provide relevant, biblically based guidance for establishing and developing authentic relationships with the unsaved nearest us.

Typically, when driving, we come upon a bridge we must cross. As we approach the bridge, we often see a sign declaring the weight limit of the span. In the same way, before we can speak truth to unbelievers, we must build bridges of trust that can bear the weight of truth. Such trust is built over time with one act of kindness followed by another as we invest in relationship that is genuine and intentional. But at some point, we must "[speak] the truth in love" (Ephesians 4:15). Compassionate contact results in communication.

COMPASSIONATE CONTACT RESULTS IN COMMUNICATION.

I MUST COMMUNICATE

TENS OF MILLIONS OF Americans earn their living in the sales industry. Whether selling cars, homes, or time-shares, salespeople must close the deal. A salesperson might offer a vehicle for a test drive or a condo for a stay, but at some point, they must have a conversation to close the deal. Likewise, there comes a time when we must verbally share the good news of King Jesus with the spiritually lost. Performing never-ending acts of kindness without conversation does not result in salvation. After all, "faith comes by hearing, and hearing by the word of God" (Romans 10:17, NKJV).

KINDNESS WITHOUT CONVERSATION DOES NOT RESULT IN SALVATION.

Pastor and author Garry Poole equips people to open their lives and their homes to those seeking God. He advocates for small groups composed of people yet to be saved, and he urges us to engage seekers in communication, a vital part of which is "active listening and empathic evangelism."[24] And one much-needed group with whom to have more effective communication is the next generation. Far too many people want little to nothing to do with the Christian faith because those who are older have not communicated well with them. We have simply and often replied with the standard, "Because the Bible says so" response, instead of answering their questions in helpful and substantive ways. Sean McDowell and J. Warner Wallace remind us, "Young people want to know *why* we believe what we believe. If we want them to get excited, we need to help them see that the Christian worldview is reasonable and evidentially true."[25]

The Holy Spirit not only empowers us to share the good news of King Jesus, but he also impacts the listener as we speak. When the apostle Paul shared the good news with Lydia, "The Lord opened her heart to receive Paul's message" (Acts 16:14). As we deliberately speak the truth in love of salvation to others, pray and believe that God can still open minds of unbelievers to receive our message. This is especially true if we have faithfully tilled the soil of their souls so the seed of our message can take root in their minds.

Before we pass from this life into the next, let us make every effort to invite those we love to make this everlasting trip of a lifetime with us. After all, who would ever want to make such a trip alone? Let us be a movement of disciples who make disciples. And let us take it even further. Let's help renew existing churches and help start new churches that make more disciples. We want to reach as many as possible—until King Jesus returns and God restores all creation to himself in the new heaven and new earth.

APPENDIX

BOOK RECOMMENDATIONS FOR FURTHER STUDY

Randy Alcorn, *Heaven: A Comprehensive Guide to Everything the Bible Says About Our Eternal Home* (Wheaton: Tyndale House Publishers, 2004).

C. S. Lewis, *The Great Divorce* (New York: HarperCollins, 2015).

Erwin Lutzer, *One Minute After You Die* (Chicago: Moody Publishers, 1997).

John MacArthur, *The Glory of Heaven: The Truth About Heaven, Angels, and Eternal Life* (Wheaton: Crossway, 2013).

David Roadcup and Michael Eagle, *Prayer and Fasting* (Renew.org, 2020).

N. T. Wright, *Surprised by Hope: Rethinking Heaven, the Resurrection, and the Mission of the Church* (San Francisco: HarperOne, 2008).

NOTES

1. Dayton Hartman does a good job showing how these five elements are key. He demonstrates their connection to the early creeds as a key benchmark of what Christians believe in *Jesus Wins: The Good News of the End Times* (Bellingham, WA: Lexham Press, 2019).

2. For more information about the different levels of biblical teachings—essential, important, and personal—see Chad Ragsdale's *Christian Convictions: Discerning the Essential, Important, and Personal Elements* (Renew.org, 2021).

3. "Breakout, August 1944," *Britannica*, accessed May 14, 2021, https://www.britannica.com/event/Normandy-Invasion/Breakout-August-1944.

4. Randy Alcorn, *Heaven* (Carol Stream: Tyndale House Publishers, 2004), 47.

5. For more on what biblical faith entails, see Mark E. Moore, *Faithful Faith: Reclaiming Faith from Culture and Tradition* (Renew.org, 2021).

6. For more on condemnation, see Grant R. Osborne, *Revelation: Baker Exegetical Commentary on the New Testament* (Grand Rapids: Baker Academic, 2002), 690–91, 723. For more on the welcoming into glory, see John MacArthur, *The Glory of Heaven: The Truth About Heaven, Angels, and Eternal Life* (Wheaton: Crossway Books), 69, 71, 77.

7. Alcorn, *Heaven*, 25.

8. Osborne, *Revelation*, 722–724.

9. Rick Oster, "Thoughts About Hell from Jesus Himself," *Renew.org*, https://renew.org/thoughts-about-hell-from-jesus-himself/.

10. Gavin Ortlund, "J. I. Packer on Why Annihilationism Is Wrong," *The Gospel Coalition*, October 7, 2015, accessed May 14, 2021, https://www.thegospelcoalition.org/article/j-i-packer-on-why-annihilationism-is-wrong/.

11. Ed Fudge, *The Fire That Consumes: A Biblical and Historical Study of the Doctrine of Final Punishment*, 3rd ed. (Wipf and Stock Publishers, 2013).

12. Alcorn, *Heaven*, 63.

13. For more on how the goodness of God does not contradict the doctrine of hell, we recommend Francis Chan and Preston Sprinkle, *Erasing Hell: What God Said About Eternity, and the Things We've Made Up* (Colorado Springs: David C. Cook, 2011).

14. Rico Tice and Carl Laferton, *Honest Evangelism: How to Talk About Jesus Even When It's Tough* (London: The Good Book Company, 2015).

15. Alcorn, *Heaven,* 111–13, 131, 149, 158, 237–39.

16. I'm borrowing these from Robert A. Lowery's *Revelation's Rhapsody: Listening to the Lyrics of the Lamb* (Joplin: College Press Publishing, 2006), 199–203.

17. Lewis Foster, *Revelation* (Cincinnati: Standard Publishing, 1991), 312–314.

18. Ibid., 308.

19. Grant R. Osborne, *Revelation* (Grand Rapids: Baker Academic, 2002), 751–752.

20. "What Atheist Penn Jillette Taught Me About Evangelism," *Radically Christian*, March 24, 2013, accessed May 14, 2021, https://radicallychristian.com/what-atheist-penn-jillette-taught-me-about-evangelism.

21. Michelle Starr, "This Is Why Mother Octopuses Grimly Starve Themselves to Death," accessed May 14, 2021, https://www.sciencealert.com/mother-octopus-senescence-death-after-mating-eggs-reproduction-rna-sequence-optic-gland.

22. Mark E. Moore, *Core 52* (New York: Waterbrook, 2019), 174.

23. Jay Pathak and Dave Runyon, *The Art of Neighboring: Building Genuine Relationships Right Outside Your Door* (Grand Rapids: Baker Books, 2012).

24. Garry Poole, *Seeker Small Groups: Engaging Spiritual Seekers in Life-Changing Discussions* (Grand Rapids: Zondervan, 2003), 148–161.

25. Sean McDowell and J. Warner Wallace, *So the Next Generation Will Know: Preparing Young Christians for a Challenging World* (Colorado Springs: David C. Cook, 2019), 104.

12

TRUTH ABOUT GOD

WHAT CAN WE KNOW
AND HOW CAN
WE KNOW IT?

RICHARD A. KNOPP

In gratitude for my treasured wife, Paula, and our faith-filled children:

Nicki Green, Katie Young, and Andy Knopp

Proverbs 31:28–31

CONTENTS

General Editors' Note 609

Introduction 611

CHAPTER 1: The Biblical Emphasis on Truth and
Its Defense... 615

CHAPTER 2: Challenges to Knowing Truth About God 619

CHAPTER 3: How Can We Know Truth About God? 623

CHAPTER 4: What Truth Can We Know About God?................. 633

Conclusion 655

Appendix: Recommendations for Further Study............................ 657

Notes 659

GENERAL EDITORS' NOTE

W e all need a thoughtful foundation for our beliefs. What makes our trust in Jesus and in the Bible sufficiently grounded? How do we know if Christianity is true? What can we know with confidence?

From the earliest days, thoughtful followers of Jesus have pointed to evidence that convinced them Jesus was who he said he was. The Gospel of Luke, for example, begins with a statement that Luke investigated the evidence and then wanted to share what he found (Luke 1:1–4). What evidence has God provided that makes faith compelling?

Richard A. Knopp is uniquely gifted to guide us in our questions. He is Professor of Philosophy and Christian Apologetics at Lincoln Christian University, where he has taught since 1983. He is the Director of Room For Doubt (www.roomfordoubt. com), a grant-funded program that seeks to encourage questions, address doubts, and strengthen Christian faith. Since 2000, he has also served as the Director of WorldView Eyes (www.worldvieweyes.org), a project that received over one million dollars from the Lilly Endowment to help high school youth understand and embrace a Christian worldview. He holds a Doctor of Philosophy in Philosophy (University of Illinois), a Master of Divinity in Theology and Philosophy (Lincoln Christian Seminary), and a Master of Arts in Philosophy (Southern Illinois University). Prior to full-time teaching, he served in two youth ministries and in a five-year preaching ministry. "Rich" and his wife, Paula, have been married since 1971, and they have three children (two daughters and a son) and seven grandchildren.

This book lays a foundation for how we can have confidence embracing Christian beliefs, such as we have listed in the Renew.org Leader's Faith Statements (see Appendix B). The book seeks to help everyday disciples live out 1 Peter 3:15: "But in your hearts revere Christ as Lord. Always be prepared to give an answer to everyone who asks you to give the reason for the hope that you have. But do this with gentleness and respect." To this end, Knopp prepares us to make a defense of our faith in well-informed and practical ways.

The following tips might help you use this book more effectively (and the other books in the *Real Life Theology* series):

1. *Questions, answers, and Scriptures.* We framed this book around two key questions. This format provides clarity, making it easier to commit crucial information to memory. This format also enables the books in the *Real Life Theology* series to support our catechism. Our catechism is a series of fixed questions and answers for instruction in church or home. In all, the series has fifty-two questions, answers, and key Scriptures. This particular book focuses on two questions that are most pertinent to knowing truth about God: "What can we know?" and "How can we know it?"

2. *Summary videos.* You can find three- to seven-minute videos that summarize the book, as well as each chapter, at Renew.org. These short videos can function as standalone teachings. But for groups or group leaders using the book, they can also be used to launch discussion of the reading.

May God use this book to fuel faithful and effective disciple making in your life and church.

For King Jesus,
Bobby Harrington and Daniel McCoy
General Editors, *Real Life Theology* series

INTRODUCTION

> We continually ask God to fill you with the knowledge of his will
> through all the wisdom and understanding that the Spirit gives, so that
> you may live a life worthy of the Lord and please him in every way:
> bearing fruit in every good work, growing in the knowledge of God.
> — Colossians 1:9b–10

This book is for followers of Jesus who want to grow in their knowledge of God and who want to help others do the same. While this will require some mental effort, it is much more than an intellectual matter. According to Paul's prayer in Colossians 1 (quoted above), it is directly connected to who we are and how we live. I pray this book will help you grow in the knowledge of God, have greater confidence in your own faith, and have more boldness to share your faith with others.

This short volume features material I've presented in classrooms and in hundreds of conferences, conventions, camps, and churches for over forty years. It's designed to enable you to teach yourself, but it's also designed to help you teach others. In seminary, after my major professor, James D. Strauss, explained some awesome point, he often added, "And that'll preach." He helped me see the necessity of sharing the amazing truths of God with the person in the seat at church or, in his typical words, "with the truck driver on Route 10." In that sense, I hope the material in this book "will preach"—to you and to others.

The book will stretch you, but that's what growing involves. The main text covers a lot of ground, and the extensive endnotes will prompt you to go even deeper, though they might be most helpful for preachers, teachers, and other Christian leaders who could especially benefit from additional commentary and other resources to consult.

THE BOOK WILL STRETCH YOU, BUT THAT'S WHAT GROWING INVOLVES.

The book focuses a lot on "why" questions. We started asking such questions when we were very young. Now that we are older, we know what it's like to be hammered with provoking, sometimes even exasperating, "why" questions from little ones. Apparently, everyone has a deep desire to know—and to know *why*. In that sense, everyone is a philosopher.

The book also addresses another notable philosophical question: "*How* do you know that?" I'm amazed at the sophistication of young children who ask me that question. With no formal knowledge of philosophy, they are asking a gigantic question about epistemology, which is a major branch of philosophy that studies the nature of knowledge.

Christians make all kinds of claims—claims like God created the universe; Jesus is God's unique Son who was raised from the dead; the Bible is God's Word; and the Holy Spirit guides them. But as a Christian, *how* do you know these things? This work offers some guidance on where to start with that question.

The book is divided into four chapters. Chapter 1 discusses the biblical emphasis on truth and our obligation and privilege to defend it. Chapter 2 describes some challenges to knowing truth about God that come from modernism and postmodernism. Chapter 3 explains *how* we can know truth about God. It offers important considerations about doubt and some clarifications about what it means—and doesn't mean—to know something is true. Chapter 4 attempts to demonstrate *what* truth we can know about God. It addresses the existence of God, the character of God, the acts of God, the word of God, and the power of God.

Let's face it. If we cannot have confidence that what we say about God is true, then there's no basis or motivation for talking about the gospel (the good news) of Jesus, making disciples, the need for holiness, the importance of the church, or Jesus' return. However, by the book's end, I hope you will develop a deeper conviction that Christianity's basic claims about God are really true.

Making a case for knowing truth about God will not be easy in the days ahead. Increasingly, our culture and even our church members are skeptical. Consider these alarming statistics:

- The percentage of Americans who believe in a "biblical view of God" fell from 73 percent in 1990 to 51 percent in 2020. Among younger Americans (ages 18–29), it fell from 64 percent to 38 percent during that 30-year period.[1]

- The percentage of atheists and agnostics in America grew from 11 percent in 2003 to 21 percent in 2018.[2]
- The youngest generation, Gen Z (ages 13–18), has twice the percentage of "atheists" (12.8 percent) compared to all previous generations (6 percent).[3]

Clearly, we have our work cut out for us! Unfortunately, Christian leaders and parents are often not adequately prepared to answer tough questions about the Christian faith, so they either give unhelpful responses or simply keep silent.[4] But for us to act effectively, we dare not be unprepared or willing to remain silent.[5]

Pursue with me Peter's appeal: "Grow in the grace and knowledge of our Lord and Savior Jesus Christ" (2 Peter 3:18). In doing so, you will, by the grace of God and the power of His Spirit, become a more mature disciple and a more effective Christian witness.

1

THE BIBLICAL EMPHASIS ON TRUTH AND ITS DEFENSE

I n his 1993 classic work *No Place for Truth*, David Wells argued that truth had become marginalized in the church.[6] And Douglas Groothuis characterized the loss of truth more generally in the title of his book *Truth Decay.*[7] Their claims are even more pertinent today, but they're not really saying anything new. Isaiah said that "truth has stumbled in the streets, honesty cannot enter. Truth is nowhere to be found" (Isaiah 59:14–15). Jeremiah declared, "This is the nation that has not obeyed the Lord its God or responded to correction. Truth has perished; it has vanished from their lips" (Jeremiah 7:28). The prophets' words are eerily applicable to our modern world.

THE IMPORTANCE OF TRUTH

THE BIBLE PLACES CONSIDERABLE emphasis on *truth*. The words "true" or "truth" appear 260 times in the New International Version. The Old Testament primarily conveys the idea of truth by the Hebrew word *emet*, which has two interrelated emphases: (1) faithfulness and (2) truth in contrast to deceit or falsehood.[8] Sometimes, especially in the Psalms, *emet* is used as the faithful quality of a *person*. God is "abounding in love and faithfulness" (Psalm 86:15), and "his faithfulness will be your shield and rampart" (Psalm 91:4c; 146:6b).

But *emet* is also used as the quality of a *statement* and its connection to reality. Joseph, when interrogating his brothers in Egypt, kept them in prison so their "words may be tested to see if [they were] telling the truth" (Genesis 42:16b).[9] The general point is that truth in the Old Testament is not just an abstract, theoretical concept; it refers to the daily witness of one's character, and it identifies statements that accurately describe reality. There is a correspondence between one's words and one's deeds, and there is a correspondence between one's words and the way the world is.[10]

The New Testament primarily refers to "truth" or to what is "true" with the Greek word *alētheia*.[11] What becomes more prominent with *alētheia* is the idea of "truth as conformity to reality in opposition to lies or errors."[12] For example, Luke records the disciples' testimony, "It is true! The Lord has risen and has appeared to Simon" (Luke 24:34). John says, "This is the disciple who testifies to these things and who wrote them down. We know that his testimony is true" (John 21:24; cf. John 19:35). Paul says in his defense, "I am not insane, most excellent Festus . . . . What I am saying is true and reasonable" (Acts 26:25).[13] And Paul affirms that God desires "all people to be saved and to come to the knowledge of the truth" (1 Timothy 2:4).

The apostle John highlights the point that truth is not merely a quality of a *proposition*; it refers ultimately to a *person*: Jesus. Jesus said, "I am the way and the truth and the life" (John 14:6). It is Jesus who is "full of grace and truth" (John 1:14; cf. 1:17). In addition, John contends that truth is not just something we *have*, it is something we *do* as well. He writes, "If we claim to have fellowship with him and yet walk in the darkness, we lie and do not live out the truth" (1 John 1:6).[14] Truth, according to John, is a way of life.

The primary point here is that the Bible says a lot about *truth*. Truth, or what is true, can apply to persons; it can apply to propositions; and it can even apply to one's path in life.

THE IMPORTANCE OF DEFENDING TRUTH

THE BIBLE NOT ONLY speaks a lot about truth, but the Bible also provides considerable emphasis on the importance of *defending* it. The Old Testament describes numerous "champions" who fought for God's truth as opposed to a false alternative. Prominent ones include Moses opposing Pharaoh (Exodus 5–13), David facing Goliath (1 Samuel 17), Elijah challenging the false prophets of Baal (1 Kings 18), Shadrach, Meshach, and Abednego standing against Nebuchadnezzar (Daniel 3), and Daniel refusing to obey King Darius's decree (Daniel 6). The New Testament also offers notable examples of those who boldly presented and ably defended God's truth, often to their peril. Examples include John the Baptist, Jesus, Peter, Stephen, and Paul.[15]

The New Testament describes "defending" the faith with the Greek words *apologia* (a noun) and *apologeomai* (a verb). The English word "apologetics" is simply a transliteration of the Greek word, which etymologically means "reasoning from" (*apo* means "from" and *logia* refers to "reason/logic"). This reveals that the core nature of the Christian defense of truth is based on *reason*, not on emotion. It also shows that the use of reason in defending God's truth is a *biblical* practice and imperative, not just a modern concept.[16]

New Testament examples illustrate this. Peter says, "Always be prepared to give an answer [*apologia*] to everyone who asks you to give the reason [*logos*] for the hope that you have" (1 Peter 3:15). And Paul repeatedly makes his "defense" to charges against him.[17] He even claims that he was "put here for the defense [*apologia*] of the gospel" (Philippians 1:16). Another verb form of the idea is *dialegomai*, which is frequently used to describe Paul's reasoning with non-Christians.[18]

A primary takeaway here is that the Bible, and more specifically the New Testament, notably stresses that the *truth* about God stands in contrast to false alternatives; this truth was, and should be, *defended*; and it can be, and should be, defended with *reason*. It is no wonder, then, that New Testament preaching underscores that the resurrection of Jesus was accompanied by "many convincing proofs" (Acts 1:3); all Israel can be "assured" that God made Jesus both Lord and Messiah"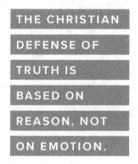
(Acts 2:36); and God has "given proof" of his coming judgment by raising Jesus from the dead (Acts 17:31).

Given the condition of our culture and many churches, I am convinced that Christian apologetics—defending God's truth—is needed now more than ever before. But we need to be adequately prepared. So let's see what we can learn about knowing truth about God and being better able to defend it.

2

CHALLENGES TO KNOWING TRUTH ABOUT GOD

Why do so many people deny we can know truth about God? There are many reasons, but a main one is that our Western culture is permeated with the consequences of several hundred years of philosophy that have created this skepticism. Philosophically, two major rivers flow into the cultural ocean in which we now swim: *modernism* and *postmodernism*. The bottom line is that modernism and postmodernism, while they exhibit notable disagreements with each other, actually *join forces to repudiate the possibility of knowing truth about God*. It's a kind of double whammy for the Christian.

This chapter will focus on the *philosophy* of modernism and the *philosophy* of postmodernism. However, there is a *cultural* sense according to which we can think of a modern culture and a postmodern culture. This *cultural* sense pertains more to social values, economic systems, and communication techniques.[19] One reason why it's important to distinguish between the cultural and philosophical senses is that some Christians unknowingly advocate postmodernism—the philosophy—when they are really thinking about postmodern *culture*. I contend that most people undeniably live in a postmodern *culture*, but this does not mean that we should endorse postmodernism as a *philosophy*.[20] As this chapter indicates, both philosophical modernism and philosophical postmodernism pose a serious threat to the truth claims of Christianity.

THE CHALLENGE OF MODERNISM

THE PHILOSOPHY OF MODERNISM received its impetus during the Enlightenment—a period that includes René Descartes (1596–1650), David Hume (1711–1776), and Immanuel Kant (1724–1804). In general, the Enlightenment stressed that humans should be freed from the superstitions and authority of religion and construct a society based on reason, empirical evidence, and scientific discovery.[21] Even though Descartes and Kant believed in God, all three of these philosophers helped dismantle our capacity to know truth about God.

René Descartes coined a famous phrase: "I think; therefore I am."[22] He used reason and turned inward to the self. He was trying to give an absolutely certain foundation for knowledge, and he believed his own existence provided that certainty. After all, it seemed impossible to doubt his own existence. However, since Descartes based knowledge within himself, it seemed he could only be certain of the ideas *in his own mind*. For many critics of Descartes, it wasn't clear that he could really know anything outside his own mind. So, ironically, Descartes's pursuit of certainty ended up laying the groundwork for skepticism. Though Descartes gave an argument for God's existence, his method actually diminished, if not destroyed, knowing truth about God.[23]

David Hume was a strong empiricist. He believed that everything we know, or can know, must come only from sense experience—from the physical senses. In his view, this excludes the possibility that we can know anything in the realm of metaphysics (what is beyond the world of sense experience). Any metaphysical claims—including claims about God—deserve only to be burned, because they are unknowable folly.[24] Hume's skepticism denies we can know *anything* about God. And Hume continues to have enormous influence in university classrooms and in our culture today.

Immanuel Kant believed in God, but like Hume he also denied we can have any *metaphysical* knowledge, which means we cannot know anything about God. Kant was actually trying to salvage belief in God, but he limited all of our knowledge and put God beyond its range. He summarized it this way: "I therefore found it necessary to deny *knowledge* [of metaphysics and God] in order to make room for *faith*."[25] He believed that many attacks against God were due to philosophers using their reason to speculate about metaphysical notions. By showing that reason cannot legitimately extend into the realm of metaphysics, he could undermine their baseless, atheistic attacks. But this had a disastrous consequence: we can believe in

God; we just cannot know anything about him. As theologian Kirk MacGregor puts it, "From Kant's perspective . . . there may be a God, but there is nothing we can really say about him as to his being an object of our knowledge."[26]

THE CHALLENGE OF POSTMODERNISM

Postmodernism as a philosophy denies that anyone can objectively know the world around us as it really is. We only see the world with different lenses (e.g., with different languages, races, genders, ages, personal experiences), and we project these cultural or personal notions onto the world.[27] As a result, there is no single reality for everyone; there are only multiple realities constructed by different groups or individuals, often fighting for power to dominate others.

In one sense, the philosophy of postmodernism is a *rejection* of key principles of modernism (see Table 1: Modernism vs. Postmodernism).[28] In another sense, postmodernism is an *extension* of modernism by playing out the consistent implications of modernism. Modernism uses reason to be skeptical of religious authority and metaphysical knowledge, but postmodernism applies skepticism to *everything*, including to reason itself.[29]

MODERNISM	POSTMODERNISM
Absolute truth is discoverable.	There is no universal or absolute truth.
We can have certainty based on a solid foundation of facts.	We have only skepticism.
All humans have the same rationality.	Different individuals and groups have different rationalities.
We know things objectively.	Objective knowledge is not possible, because we always see with the bias of our own perspective.
Reason and science reign and are often used to reject religion.	We should be skeptical of everything, including reason and even science.

Table 1

THE LOSS OF TRUTH ABOUT GOD

While both modernism and postmodernism offer something valuable to the Christian faith,[30] in their stronger and more secular forms, they pose a serious challenge to our knowledge of God and to biblical Christianity. Both deny we can have knowledge of God.[31] And this is the sentiment of many in our communities (if not also our churches), even if they don't know much, if anything, about Descartes, Hume, Kant, or later philosophers.

One form of modernism today is illustrated by secular humanism and by the so-called "new atheists," such as Richard Dawkins, Sam Harris, and Lawrence Krause, who have enormous influence through their popular books and online presence. They use science to attack religion—and Christianity in particular.[32] A notable postmodernist example is Jean-Francois Lyotard who emphasizes we must have an "incredulity toward metanarratives."[33] This means there is no story that is true for *everyone*. There is no metanarrative that rises above all other stories or narratives. As a consequence, it is not possible to have a gospel that can rightly claim to be true for the whole world. The Great Commission of Jesus (Matthew 28:18–20) is completely undermined. So whether it's from modernism or postmodernism, truth about God is threatened.

One point to keep in mind is that many deny knowledge of a God *constructed by philosophers*, but not necessarily the God *portrayed in Scripture*. As Alasdair MacIntyre explains, "The God in whom the nineteenth and twentieth centuries came to disbelieve had been invented only in the seventeenth century."[34] We might put it this way: The God that many *reject* is often the unbiblical God they *project*. A practical application of this would be to ask someone about the God they reject. Wait for the response. Then you can likely say, "I don't believe in that God either."

> THE GOD THAT MANY REJECT IS OFTEN THE UNBIBLICAL GOD THEY PROJECT.

The God presented in the Bible is not a philosopher's abstract God; he is a personal God who creates, reveals himself, and comes to us. The philosopher's God is illustrated by Thomas Paine, a notable eighteenth-century deist who claimed God is knowable by reason in creation, but only in creation. Reason alone can determine that God is a "first cause," the cause of all things.[35] But Paine's God is merely a distant God. His God is not a miracle-working God. His God has not come in the flesh to save us. His God is not the God of the Bible.

As we proceed to think about knowing truth about God, we want to make sure the God we can know from sources *outside of* Scripture (like from nature and reason) is the God who is also revealed *within* Scripture.

3

HOW CAN WE KNOW TRUTH ABOUT GOD?

Answer: We can know truth about God through God's general revelation in creation and special revelation in Scripture, in Jesus the Savior, and in the impact of the Holy Spirit.

For since the creation of the world God's invisible qualities—his eternal power and divine nature—have been clearly seen, being understood from what has been made, so that people are without excuse.
— Romans 1:20

Claiming to know truth about God forces us to consider two giant philosophical questions: *What is truth?* and *What is knowledge?* These are questions about "epistemology," a major area of philosophy that means a "study of knowledge."[36] In this chapter, I will offer some highlights on the nature of truth and knowledge, and then draw some applications to knowing truth about God that include practical considerations about doubt.

WHAT IS TRUTH?

PILATE POSED THIS QUESTION to Jesus in John 18: *What is truth?* Jesus offered no philosophical answer. However, he did say he came into the world "to testify to the truth" and that "everyone on the side of truth listens to me" (John 18:37c). When we address this question from a philosophical perspective, three main theories are offered on the nature of truth: (1) the correspondence theory, (2) the coherence theory, and (3) the pragmatic theory. According to the correspondence theory, a statement is true if it *corresponds* to the way the world is.[37] According to the coherence theory, a statement is true if it *coheres* with—or fits with—other statements we take to be true. According to the pragmatic theory, a statement is true if it *works*.[38] Each of these philosophical theories provides legitimate insights into the nature of truth, and the Bible incorporates some facet of each one.

Some version of the *correspondence* theory is foundational to the biblical notion of truth.[39] When the disciples said, "It is true! The Lord has risen" (Luke 24:34), they were claiming that the statement "the Lord has risen" corresponds to reality.[40] It was an *objective* truth claim. In other words, the truth of the statement is not determined by how we feel about it or whether we agree with it, but by whether it describes what actually occurred.

The *coherence* theory rightly emphasizes that what we regard as true often depends on other truths we accept. One application is that underlying worldview beliefs can heavily influence what one will accept as true. For example, if one's worldview rejects God's existence, then the statement "God has raised this Jesus to life" (Acts 2:32) will likely be rejected. On the other hand, if one's worldview accepts God's existence, then the truth of other statements (for example, about Jesus' resurrection or God's revelation) will likely be accepted as true—because they cohere or consistently fit with one another.

The *pragmatic* theory highlights a prominent sentiment in our "post-truth" culture:[41] Truth is not so much about objective facts but about what accomplishes our agenda.[42] We just want what works. *That* is what is true. We see it in politics, in social media, in family and church communication, and even in "scientific" claims. The valued commodity is *power*, not principle.[43] In response to this idea, while the Bible talks about how the Christian faith "works" (for example, it should produce good fruit),[44] this is very different from adopting a pragmatic theory of truth, which claims that something is true simply because it works. Against this view, we should see that the Christian faith works *because it is true;* it is not to be considered true simply *because it works.*

Even with these qualifications, I suggest that knowing truth about God includes insights from all three of these perspectives on truth. What we accept as true should *correspond* to reality; it should *cohere* with the vast array of rational, empirical, and existential considerations we regard as true; and it should generate valuable *pragmatic benefits* that are intellectual, social, psychological, emotional, and spiritual.

WHAT IS KNOWLEDGE?

To CLAIM WE KNOW truth about God requires some understanding of what we mean by "knowledge." What is knowledge? Everyone claims to know all kinds of things. I know I'm typing right now. I know I was born in Corinth, Kentucky. I know 9 times 9 equals 81. I know how to edit videos in Final Cut Pro. I know my wife, Paula. I know I have a headache. Clearly, we use the word "know" in many different ways, and we have different means by which we think we know something. Some of these knowledge claims are supported by personal experience, some by historical records, some by memory, and some more directly by our mind or reason.

While philosophers vigorously debate various views, the basic formula to describe knowledge was classically characterized by Plato as "justified true belief."[45] If we genuinely know something, it seems necessary that we also believe it. (It's hard to see how one can rightly claim to know cows give milk but not believe it.) But it's possible to believe something that is false. So to know something seems to require that it also be *true*.[46]

But how do we know anything is true? The basic answer is that we must have some *justification* or warrant for thinking it is true. It's not enough just to have true belief in order to have genuine knowledge. For example, I might have a true belief that I have ten coins in my pocket, but it might just be a lucky guess. Plato would say this is just "true opinion," not knowledge.[47] I think you would agree.

GUIDING PRINCIPLES ON KNOWLEDGE AND DOUBT: CERTAINTY VS. CERTITUDE

How CERTAIN CAN WE be in what we claim to "know"? I know for certain that I'm drinking coffee now. But what about the premise of the movie *The Matrix*—that everything is just an illusion?[48] While this seems pretty ridiculous, I'm forced to admit I cannot know *with absolute certainty* that it's not some illusion. This prompts a couple of important points: (1) If "knowing truth" requires that I be absolutely certain about it without any possibility of being mistaken, then I do not know the truth about much of anything! (2) If I can't be absolutely intellectually certain, then some level of doubt seems inevitable.

These two points are especially relevant to Christians. First, many Christians think having any doubts about God is dangerous and should be disapproved.[49]

Second, some Christians, especially younger ones, rightly understand that having at least periodic doubts about God is inescapable, because they cannot be absolutely certain about God. One unfortunate consequence is that those with doubts might simply not express those doubts to anyone who might be able to help. And when they do express their doubts, they too often receive only "trite and unhelpful answers."[50]

Given this problematic situation, here are some guiding principles we should understand and clearly communicate to Christians and non-Christians—to adults and to youth alike.

1. *Having genuine knowledge about something does not require that we be absolutely certain it's true.*[51]
2. *We cannot be absolutely certain in an intellectual sense that our truth claims about God are true.* We cannot provide "proof" in the sense that it's inconceivable for a reasonable person to doubt it.[52] However, it is still possible for us to have genuine knowledge about God if we can have sufficient justification for our truth claims about God.
3. *Lacking absolute certainty or proof, especially about metaphysical claims, is not a unique condition for Christians.* No one has that kind of certainty or proof. If we mean by "proof" something that is "beyond any possible doubt," then God's existence cannot be proven. But as Christian philosopher Stephen Evans contends, "Proof in this sense is an unrealistic ideal for both the theist and the atheist."[53]
4. *Having some doubts about God may be intellectually inevitable and therefore understandable.* So we should not categorically condemn those who experience some doubts about God. And Christians should also avoid making claims about having a level of certainty that is not attainable.[54] Austin Fischer poignantly observes,

> I've always found that unbelievers are much less offended by the hypocrisy of our morality than they are the hypocrisy of our certainty. . . . What unbelievers fail to understand is how we [Christians] can pretend to be certain of things we obviously cannot be certain of.[55]

In other words, we need to be more humble and avoid any appearance of arrogance.

5. *Doubt is not the same as disbelief.* I believe a strong case can be made that the apparent condemnations of doubt in the New Testament (for example, Matthew 14:31; 21:21; James 1:6), are referring to doubt *as disbelief,* not to doubt *as lacking absolute intellectual certainty.*[56] The father of the possessed boy illustrates the difference. He exclaimed to Jesus, "I do believe; help me overcome my unbelief" (Mark 9:24b). This exemplifies how it's possible to believe something strongly yet still have doubts about it. He strongly believed, but he did not have absolute certainty. In that sense, he had *doubt* but not *disbelief.*[57]

> IT'S POSSIBLE TO BELIEVE SOMETHING STRONGLY YET STILL HAVE DOUBTS ABOUT IT.

6. *It is helpful to distinguish between having intellectual certainty and having a comprehensive certitude.*
While we cannot have absolute intellectual certainty in knowing truth about God (for example, using arguments and evidence from nature or history), I propose we can have "certitude" (a sufficiently justified conviction) in knowing truth about God. This consists of an *inner assurance* that uses, but goes beyond, mere intellectual argument or external evidence. (In the next chapter, I will discuss how this certitude incorporates the internal witness of the Holy Spirit.)

The New Testament talks about "proof" and "certainty." For instance, Luke says Jesus "gave many *convincing proofs* that he was alive" after his crucifixion (Acts 1:3).[58] However, such passages should not be taken in the sense of providing *absolute intellectual certainty.* Matthew even acknowledges that some of those who saw the resurrected Jesus still "doubted" (Matthew 28:17). Instead, the *certitude* (or justified conviction) we can possess about God is consistent with the nature of Christian faith. Faith is the "confidence" (NIV) or the "assurance" (NASB) in what is hoped for; yet it is still "about what we do not see" (Hebrews 11:1).

These six guiding principles should greatly encourage those who face instances of doubt. Some doubts may be inevitable because we do not have absolute intellectual certainty. As a result, we should not only allow doubts; we should encourage their expression.[59] The good news is that our doubts can be adequately addressed.

So how can we know truth about God in the sense of having *certitude*—a justified inner conviction that includes many different considerations? How can we attain genuine knowledge of anything, but more specifically, of God?

THE SOURCES OF TRUTH AND KNOWLEDGE

GENERALLY SPEAKING, WE CAN identify four sources for knowledge of anything: (1) reason, (2) sense experience, (3) inner experience, and (4) information from others. These four sources significantly overlap and interact, but together they offer a common-sense way to distinguish how we can know truth about anything. More specifically, I propose we can know truth *about God* from these same four sources.

1. *Using Reason to Know Truth About God.* Our minds have amazing power, and God has endowed us with the capacity, and the responsibility, of utilizing reason in proper and effective ways. We are to "reason together, says the LORD" (Isaiah 1:18, ESV) and provide a reasoned answer (*apologia*) for the hope we have in Christ (1 Peter 3:15).

However, an important qualification needs to be registered about reason. Human reason can be used improperly, as though it is an *autonomous, purely human* instrument that is completely separated from God. Paul talks about how the thinking of those who do not acknowledge God can become "futile" (Romans 1:21) because they exchange "the truth about God for a lie" (Romans 1:25). Those who are "separated from the life of God" live "in the futility of their thinking" and "are darkened in their understanding" (Ephesians 4:17–18).

However, using reason to know truth about God does not mean we are necessarily using reason *autonomously*; nor does it mean we are "rationalists."[60] Reason is not autonomous.[61] It cannot, and should not, replace faith. Instead, reason should be seen as having an *adequate but limited capacity* to discover truth about God.

2. *Using Empirical Experience to Know Truth About God.* Another way we can know truth, including truth about God, is from empirical experience—experience that comes through our physical senses. We see, hear, touch, taste, and smell. Empirical experience gives us knowledge of physical reality.[62]

Initially, it might seem no one can have any empirical knowledge of God, because God is "spirit" (John 4:24).[63] While this seems true for religions like Hinduism, Buddhism, and some approaches to Christian theology, it is not true for the biblical characterization of God.[64] Biblical Christianity offers a God who is not merely some indetectable Spirit. Scripture stresses that God acts in nature and in history. So we can know some things about the non-empirical Spirit-God by observing the empirical *effects* of God's acts.[65]

Empirical knowledge of God can be inferred through *natural revelation*—"from what has been made" (Romans 1:20). Indeed, "The heavens declare the glory of

God; the skies proclaim the work of his hands" (Psalm 19:1). This means some knowledge of God can be gleaned from nature itself—from the macro-world of cosmology to the micro-world of cells and DNA.

In addition, the ultimate empirical expression of God is Jesus Christ. He was the "Word" who was "with God" and who "was God" (John 1:1) and who "became flesh and made his dwelling among us" (John 1:14). As a result, many in first-century Palestine saw, heard, and touched him (1 John 1:1–3).[66] This was one way they learned truth about God. By extension, we can too.

3. *Using Inner Experience to Know Truth About God.* Of course, empirical experience (using our five senses) generates an *inner* awareness. When we see an oak tree, the sense experience of an "outer" world becomes an "inner" experience. And using our reason is also an "inner" experience. So with these considerations, there is not a sharp distinction between reason, empirical experience, and inner experience. However, what I mean here by "inner experience" points more to our deepest feelings as well as to our conscience. It highlights our "existential" awareness: Who am I? What value, if any, do I have? Is there any ultimate meaning to my life? Such questions are not just a matter of what we *think* about ourselves; they focus on how we *feel* deeply within ourselves.

Inner experience is typically regarded as a *subjective* experience—an experience that arises *from within oneself.* As such, it can be greatly unreliable. Your inner experience may conflict with my inner experience. And your emotions, feelings, and even your conscience can change from day to day. If all we have is our personal, subjective experience, we would have no basis for rationally resolving our notable disagreements: "I feel this way; you feel that way. Let's fight about it!"

As a result, it's important to emphasize *objective* truth rather than *subjective* truth. *Objective truth* is true regardless of how one feels about it or even whether one accepts it.[67] The basic claims of Christianity are *objective* truth claims, and we should not exclusively or even primarily rely on inner experience to give truth about God. However, it's still important to note that Scripture itself affirms the value of inner experience.[68] In what follows, we'll consider two sources of truth about God from inner experience: the conscience and our deepest desires or needs.

- *Our Conscience.* One of the elements of inner experience is the conscience. The conscience certainly involves the use of reason, but conscience cuts deeper than mere rational contemplation. Conscience impacts the will and interacts with our emotions. All humans seem to possess the faculty of conscience that points toward moral truth, which is ultimately justified by God as the source of moral law.

However, while the conscience *can be* a source of truth, it can also be "corrupted" (Titus 1:15) and "seared as with a hot iron" (1 Timothy 4:2). That is, it can be desensitized. Even so, the conscience connects everyone with

SCRIPTURE ITSELF AFFIRMS THE VALUE OF INNER EXPERIENCE.

core principles about what is most fundamentally morally right or wrong. Paul affirms that even the Gentiles—those "who do not have the law"—still "do by nature things required by the law"; they "show that the requirements of the law are written on their hearts, their consciences also bearing witness" (Romans 2:14–15a). The conscience may not speak with specific words, but as John Frame describes it, "What it lacks in verbal precision, it gains in intimacy."[69] The conscience can be a powerful source that offers an internal witness to truth that is grounded in God. Jesus also seems to suggest the Holy Spirit works in conjunction with our conscience to bring moral and spiritual conviction.[70]

- *Our Deepest Desires or Needs.* A second source of truth that comes from inner experience is *our deepest desires or needs* for such things as meaning, love, and forgiveness.[71] At one level, everyone experiences meaning, love, and forgiveness. They find meaning from jobs, achievements, hobbies, etc., and they have relationships of love and forgiveness. But I am referring to an *ultimate* kind of meaning, love, and forgiveness—a kind that is not merely "constructed" but one that is "discovered."[72] This kind of meaning points to something (or someone) *beyond* us that is not fully explainable as merely arising *within* us. They are desires and needs that, as C. S. Lewis notes, are never fully satisfied in *this* life.[73]

In some ways, these deep existential desires or needs may actually point to divine truth more powerfully than mere intellectual contentions. The psalmist laments, "How long must I wrestle with my thoughts and day after day have sorrow in my heart?" (Psalm 13:2a); yet he rejoices in God's salvation (Psalm 13:5). Jesus exhorts the "weary and burdened" to come to him, so he can give "rest" to their "souls" (Matthew 11:28–29). Paul confesses how "wretched" he is (Romans 7:24); yet he rejoices because his need for deliverance is satisfied through Christ, and he now has "no condemnation"

(Romans 7:25; 8:1). These are examples that go beyond objective evidence; they spotlight deep human needs that demand a truth—a truth about God—that adequately satisfies them.

4. *Using Information from Others to Know Truth About God.* Much of what we know is not personally and directly acquired—by reason, by physical sense, or by inner experience. Instead, we learn from others: we read, we watch, and we listen. As a result, a primary source of much of what we know comes from others. In this section, I highlight two sources of knowledge that come from persons outside ourselves: *special revelation* and *tradition*.

- *Special Revelation as a Source of Truth About God.* Whereas *natural revelation* is a source of truth available to everyone, *special revelation* comes from God and is given to specific people in specific times and circumstances. God "speaks." The writer of Hebrews summarizes it: "In the past God spoke to our ancestors through the prophets at many times and in various ways, but in these last days he has spoken to us by his Son" (Hebrews 1:1–2a).[74] Special revelation has been communicated in various ways (e.g., dreams, visions, a burning bush). But as this verse in Hebrews says, God's special revelation eventually and ultimately came to us "by his Son."

  In addition, some of what was revealed was *written* and was incorporated in Christian Scripture, which provides a source of truth about God. It reveals what would otherwise be a "mystery."[75] Of course, other religions have their own scriptures, and the Bible itself explicitly warns against "false prophets."[76] So any specific claims to truth will need to be critically examined and compared. But if the Christian Scriptures can be sufficiently validated, especially when compared with its religious rivals, then we can be confident that it offers an indispensable source for knowing truth about God.

- *Tradition as a Source of Truth About God.* Compared to many Protestant groups, tradition has not typically been valued as much by the Restoration Movement, with which I have been closely affiliated. Alexander Campbell, one of the Restoration Movement's pioneers, and the movement in general have strongly resisted church tradition as authoritative, especially as expressed in various creeds.[77] Our movement has been known as "non-creedal": "No creed but Christ!" has been one motto.

In response, I want to stress that we should never elevate church tradition or creeds to the same level of authority as Scripture.[78] Jesus himself condemned the Pharisees because they "nullify the word of God for the sake of [their] tradition" (Matthew 15:6). And unfortunately, I suspect some denominations and local churches have occasionally wielded tradition with near-biblical authority. However, *I suggest that the insights of Christian leaders throughout history can be an important and informative source of truth about God.* As preeminent as Scripture should be, we can also learn truth about God from others throughout Christian history who were deeply devoted to Christ.[79]

In this chapter, I addressed the basic question, "How can we know truth about God?" In response, I identified four basic sources of knowing truth about anything, including God: reason, empirical experience, inner experience, and information from others.[80] Properly understood and applied, these four sources offer a valuable framework for knowing truth about God. The next chapter considers another critical question, "What truth can we know about God?"

4

WHAT TRUTH CAN WE KNOW ABOUT GOD?

Answer: We can know truth about God's existence, character, actions, word, and power.

Praise him for his acts of power; praise him for his surpassing greatness.
— Psalm 150:2

In the previous chapters I emphasized the prominence of truth and its defense in the Bible; I presented some challenges to knowing truth about God; and I laid some philosophical and theological foundations for knowing truth about God, including the point that knowing truth about God does not require that we have intellectual certainty. Instead, I proposed we can have *certitude*, a justified conviction based on a wide variety of considerations. In this chapter, I examine some of those considerations and contend we can know truth about the *existence* of God, the *character* of God, the *actions* of God, the *word* of God, and the *power* of God.

THE EXISTENCE OF GOD

MANY IN OUR WORLD do not accept the existence of any God (atheists), and many do not think we can know whether or not God exists (agnostics).[81] For atheists and agnostics, being able to know God exists is not possible. In spite of their sentiment, I'm convinced a strong case can be made for knowing God exists—the kind of God portrayed in Scripture.

Various arguments for God's existence have been offered that are based on *natural* revelation—what is given in nature. Some see these as "proofs," but I have explained that "proving" God in the sense of producing absolute intellectual certainty without any possibility of doubt is unreasonable, because it's unachievable. As a result, it's better to construe such arguments as "pointers" rather than "proofs."[82] Pointers in nature are powerful, but they are not adequate in themselves to reveal the God of the Bible. We also need *special* revelation.[83] However, these pointers from natural revelation can provide a compelling case that justifies our claim to know of God's existence. In this section, I highlight two pointers to God's existence: the existence of the universe and the design of the universe.

1. *The Existence of the Universe Points to God.* One approach, called the *cosmological* argument, examines the very existence of the universe as a pointer to God.[84] The big question is this: How can we explain the existence of the universe? Two logical options exist: (1) the universe has *always* existed or (2) the universe *came into* existence. Both Aristotle the philosopher (385–322 BC) and Thomas Aquinas the Christian theologian (1225–1274) argued that, even if the universe is *eternal*, God's existence is still necessary.[85] However, in the twentieth century, science provided a strong case that the universe is *not eternal*—that it had a beginning.

The scientific case that the universe came into existence prompted the Christian philosopher William Lane Craig to highlight a particular version of the cosmological argument called the *Kalam* argument.[86] The structure of the argument is quite simple:

> Premise 1: Whatever begins to exist has a cause.
> Premise 2: The universe began to exist.
> Therefore, the universe has a cause.[87]

The truth of premise one is rooted in a deep intuition as well as universal experience that things that come into existence cannot cause their own existence. In other words, something cannot come from nothing. The adage, "You can't get blood from a turnip," makes a similar point, but in this case, there is at least *something*: the turnip! On the other hand, if the physical universe *came into* existence, then there was a prior condition in which there was truly *nothing*. And something—whether it's the universe or any physical reality—cannot come from nothing.

The truth of premise two, scientifically speaking, is largely based on the reluctant but eventual wide acceptance of "Big Bang" cosmology. Some Christians think the idea of a Big Bang is incompatible with the biblical idea of divine creation. Certainly, if one takes a "young earth" view that the Bible *requires* the creation "days" in Genesis to be 24-hour solar days and the universe is no older than about 10,000 years, then a Big Bang over 13 billion years ago is a threat to be thwarted.[88] However, even if one holds to a young earth view, I submit that Big Bang cosmology can still appropriately be used to make a couple of crucial points on which all Christians should agree: (a) the universe is not eternal and (b) the universe cannot explain itself.

One irony is that while some Christians think the Big Bang is *incompatible with* biblical creation, some scientists resist the Big Bang because it sounds *too much like* creation! Fred Hoyle (1915–2001), an atheist British astronomer who disparagingly coined the term "Big Bang," strongly rejected a Big Bang, in part because "the big bang [*sic*] theory requires a recent origin of the universe that openly invites the concept of creation."[89] It seems that 13-plus billion years ago is "recent" when compared to an eternal universe. John Maddox, a former editor of the prestigious journal *Nature*, said the idea of a Big Bang is "thoroughly unacceptable" because it implies an "ultimate origin of our world" and gives creationists "ample justification" for their beliefs.[90]

The scientific notion of a Big Bang has a fascinating history. Coming into the twentieth century, the dominant view among scientists was that the universe was eternal. However, repeated observations increasingly supported the view that the universe actually *began*. Edwin Hubble's shocking telescope discoveries in the 1920s revealed the universe is rapidly expanding—ultimately from some "singularity."[91] In 1965, Arno Penzias and Robert Wilson gave a significant boost to the acceptance of a Big Bang. They unexpectedly detected background radiation throughout the universe—a kind of cosmic residue that would have been produced by a Big Bang. Subsequent and more precise satellite observations gave further confirmation of a Big Bang. All of this points to a *beginning* to the universe.

George Smoot, head of the Cosmic Background Explorer project, said they had "found evidence of the birth of the universe. . . . It's really like looking back at creation and seeing the creation of space and time and the universe and everything in it."[92] And Alexander Vilenkin, a notable cosmologist, summarizes it this way: "There are no models at this time that provide a satisfactory model for a universe without a beginning."[93]

The universe *began*. That is not only the affirmation of Genesis 1:1, but it is also the consensus of current cosmologists. I like to put it like this: the Big Bang is an attempt to describe *scientifically* what Genesis declares *theologically*. What could have caused the universe to begin to exist? Arguably, whatever it is—or whoever it is—would have to be outside of time (eternal), outside of space (immaterial), and unimaginably powerful. This, as Aquinas repeatedly asserted, is what everybody means by "God."[94]

So what are the alternatives to a divine creator? Surprisingly, a primary alternative is that the universe was *not caused by anything* and it came *from nothing*! Vilenkin claims that "there is nothing to prevent such a universe from being *spontaneously created out of nothing*."[95] Stephen Hawking, the late famous Cambridge physicist, argues that because there is a law like gravity, "the universe can and will *create itself from nothing*."[96] And Alex Rosenberg, an atheist philosopher, exclaims, "Why is there a universe at all? *No reason at all.* Why is there a multiverse in which universes *pop into existence for no reason at all? No reason at all!*"[97]

The irony is that atheists often condemn Christians for not being scientific and for not being rational. But here we find atheists who propose hypotheses that have little, if any, prospect of ever being scientifically confirmed.[98] When I consider what needs to be explained—the existence of the universe—and I compare a Christian view of creation with the alternatives, I come away with a justified conviction—*a certitude*—about knowing God exists.

2. *The Design of the Universe Points to God.* The cosmological argument points to God's existence based upon the fact *that* the universe exists. Another kind of argument, called the *teleological* argument, addresses *how* the universe is.[99] When I refer to "how" the universe is, I mean it more in the sense of asking a teenager, "How is your bedroom today?" I want to know: Is it a chaotic mess or is it orderly enough that, if you look at it, you would conclude someone had put it in order? As applied to the universe (and countless things within it), the teleological argument contends the universe possesses the kind of order or design that is far better accounted for by some vast intelligence (arguably God) rather than by mere accident or natural process.

A teleological argument was famously presented by William Paley (1743–1805) called the "watchmaker argument."[100] He argued if we found a functioning watch, we would rightly infer some watchmaker was responsible for it. In a similar way, the functioning design of the universe is best explained by a designer: God. Since the 1980s, another form of the argument (referred to as the "anthropic principle") has had enormous impact both on God-believers and those who are not. The anthropic principle focuses on the necessary conditions of the universe that allowed life to start *in the first place* and on how the universe can allow advanced forms of life, like humans, to exist.[101]

The "Goldilocks Principle" would be a simple way to think of it. Goldilocks experienced porridge that was too hot and too cold; chairs that were too big and too small; and beds that were too hard and too soft. But she also experienced porridge, a chair, and a bed that were "just right." In the children's story, the worst problem Goldilocks had was some discomfort and the bears. But as applied to the universe, if *everything necessary* for life were not precisely just right, Goldilocks would never exist!

One way to express a version of the anthropic principle is as follows: *The universe had to possess in its initial conditions (and in conditions since) precisely the right physical constants in order for life, and particularly for human life, to exist.* A quick illustration might help explain: If the universe began with a Big Bang, the expansion rate of the universe had to be "just right" for life to exist. If this rate were too much, the universe would just fly apart and never form galaxies, star and sun systems, etc. If it were too little, the universe would have collapsed in on itself because of gravity. In either case, Goldilocks is in deep trouble!

Just how precise would the expansion rate have to be to make it possible for Goldilocks (and us) to live in this universe? The answer is that the expansion rate would have to be "just right" to the level of 1 part in 10 to the 55th power.[102] That means that if it's off by just 1 in 10 followed by 54 zeros, the universe would not have allowed any of us to exist!

The amazing thing is there are several dozen such physical constants that have to be mind-blowingly precise for advanced forms of life to exist. These include the strength of gravity, the electromagnetic force, the density of mass in the universe, and many more.[103] The physicist Stephen Hawking summarized the point: "The remarkable fact is that the values of these numbers seem to have been very finely adjusted to make possible the development of life."[104] Roger Penrose, a Nobel Laureate in physics, described it in phenomenal fashion. He said if we tried to represent the improbability of producing "a universe compatible . . . with what we now observe," it would involve writing the number 1 followed by 10 to the 123rd power. To illustrate, if we wrote a zero on every particle in the entire universe, we would run out of particles before we could write the number![105]

It's easy to get lost—and perhaps confused—with all the numbers. The big point is this: both theists and atheists are absolutely amazed at these stunning and amazingly precise characteristics of our universe that made the existence of life possible. The atheist Fred Hoyle said, "A common sense interpretation of the facts suggests that a superintellect has monkeyed with physics, as well as with chemistry and biology."[106] The atheist Francis Crick, a co-discoverer of the DNA structure, conceded, "An honest man, armed with all the knowledge available to us now, could only state that in some sense, the origin of life appears at the moment to be almost a miracle, so many are the conditions which would have had to have been satisfied to get it going."[107]

Speaking of DNA, it shouts of intelligent design! DNA uses a phenomenally complex language to provide the specific instructions for twenty different amino acids to form long chains that become three-dimensional functioning proteins. Francis Collins, former director of the Human Genome Project, calls DNA "the language of God."[108] Stephen Meyer describes DNA as a "signature in the cell" that can only be produced by intelligence.[109]

The complexity of DNA is mind-blowing. A typical human adult has about 30 trillion cells with a DNA molecule. If one DNA molecule were uncoiled and stretched out, it would be about six feet long. That means that if the DNA molecules in one adult were all placed end-to-end, they would stretch out over 34 billion miles—enough to make 183 round trips from the earth to the sun!

However, the most amazing point of DNA is its *information capacity*. According to a 2017 study, one gram of DNA can hold 215 petabytes of information. With that capacity, DNA could physically store *all* of the information ever recorded by humans in one room![110] How did DNA acquire this capacity, and even more importantly, how did it acquire the information it possesses in order for life to exist and replicate?

How do we account for this spectacular "fine-tuning" of the universe and the existence of life? We could claim our universe is just one among an infinite number of universes, and we just happen to be in the one that's just right for life. But there are major problems with this view.[111] Or we could be compelled to acknowledge that a marvelously intelligent God "fashioned and made the earth"; "he did not create it to be empty, but formed it to be inhabited" (Isaiah 45:18b).[112] We could recognize the wonder of the psalmist who says, "The heavens declare the glory of God" and "day after day they pour forth speech; night after night they reveal knowledge" (Psalm 19:1–2).

When I consider what needs to be explained—the nature of the universe and life—and I compare a Christian view of creation with the alternatives, I come away with a justified conviction—a certitude—about knowing God exists.[113]

THE CHARACTER OF GOD

We can also know truth about the *character* of God. Much of this truth is revealed in Scripture, but the nature of the universe, including our own deep sense of morality, also reveals truth about God's character. God's characteristics are sometimes described in terms of "incommunicable" and "communicable" attributes.[114] *Incommunicable* attributes emphasize characteristics that only God possesses. *Communicable* attributes are those that are shared with humans. God (and humans to some extent) are (or can be) personal, loving, faithful, holy, and wise. In this section, we'll just consider some characteristics that are unique to God.

Romans 1–2 offers a valuable backdrop for our knowledge of the unique attributes of God. Paul claims everyone, even those who do not honor God, has some knowledge of God's attributes from nature. He says:

> What may be *known* about God is plain to them, because God has made it plain to them. For since the creation of the world *God's invisible qualities—his eternal power and divine nature*—have been clearly seen, being understood from what has been made, so that people are without excuse. (Romans 1:19–20)[115]

While many Christians have heard about these attributes of God, they sometimes have a simplistic understanding of them that can harm their witness to others. So it is important to look a little deeper at what some of these qualities mean (and don't mean). The qualities discussed below are among the most prominent qualities of God that also tend to be misunderstood and theologically challenging.

1. *God Is Eternal, Immortal, and Self-Existent.* Scripture describes God as eternal. He is "from everlasting to everlasting" (Psalm 90:2c). He is "the King eternal, immortal, invisible, the only God" (1 Timothy 1:17a).[116] In other words, God is infinite with respect to time. He, unlike humans, is immortal.[117] He has no beginning and no end. He is *self-existent*, which means that God's existence does not, and cannot, depend on anything else or anyone else.[118]

Properly understanding this helps us see why it is a mistake to ask, "If God made the universe, then who made God?" Initially, the question might make sense. We expect everything that exists in this universe must have a cause. But once we start the chain—"a" is caused by "b"; "b" is caused by "c"; "c" is caused by "d," and so on—we inevitably see the process cannot literally go back forever. There has to be something that was just there, or else the process never would have gotten started. Aristotle rightly acknowledged this by concluding there has to be some "unmoved mover" (God).[119] For Christian believers, the ultimate stopping point is the self-existent God, who is the only reality that requires no further cause or explanation.

Some critics might object and say to the Christian, "Well, isn't that convenient. You require an explanation for the universe and everything in it, but now you're just saying God doesn't need any explanation." The basic response is this: "You're correct. God needs no explanation. He alone is self-existent." However, the response should also include the following point: "There has to be some ultimate stopping point. One might claim that it's the universe itself. But that merely asserts the universe is self-sufficient instead of God." In other words, neither the Christian nor the critic avoids having an ultimate explanation. So when I compare a self-sufficient *God* to the prospects of a self-sufficient *universe* (which we know had a beginning), I have a justified conviction—a certitude—about which of the two makes more sense.[120]

2. *God Is Omnibenevolent (All-Good).* Scripture is filled with references to God's holiness, righteousness, and goodness: "There is no one holy like the LORD" (1 Samuel 2:2a); and this becomes the basis for God directing us to "be holy" because he is holy (e.g., Leviticus 11:44–45; 20:7; 1 Peter 1:15–16). The psalmist says that God's "right hand is filled with righteousness" (Psalm 48:10b) and that even "the heavens proclaim his righteousness, for he is a God of justice" (Psalm 50:6). Indeed, it is the *all-goodness* of God that makes the *grace* of God necessary for us.[121]

In addition, it is the all-goodness of God that makes the universal standards of morality and justice possible. In our world, we are overwhelmed by the cries for justice, human rights, and human equality—and rightly so. And these demands are seemingly made just as strongly by those who profess no belief in God as by those who believe in God. Why is that? I contend it's because there is a deep moral sense that some things are *objectively right or wrong*. That is, some things are right or wrong, independently of how we individually or culturally *feel* about them. The big question is: What is the *foundation* for our demands for justice, human rights, and human equality?

What are the alternatives? What entitles us to bring moral condemnation on acts of racism or any kind of injustice? Personal preference is inadequate; social custom is not sufficient; legislative dictates are inevitably deficient. What we need in order to justify our moral demands and criticisms is a moral foundation that is *universal*; one that *transcends* any human individual and any social or national group; one that is *unchanging*—even *eternal*; and one that is *all-good*. But those characteristics uniquely describe the God of Scripture!

When it comes to morality, it is the all-goodness of God that provides an argument for the necessity of God.[122] All other options to ground our universal sense of morality are destined to fail. But there is one superior option: "He is the Rock" (Deuteronomy 32:4a). *This* truth about God is proclaimed in Scripture, and it is also attested to in the deepest moral intuitions of humanity.

3. God Is Omnipotent (All-Powerful). We can know from Scripture and from nature that God is *all-powerful*. Paul mentions that God's "eternal power and divine nature . . . have been clearly seen, being understood from what has been made" (Romans 1:20b).[123] Being "all-powerful" is often taken to mean that God can literally do *anything* and *everything*. And various passages seem to support this. Job claimed that God "can do all things" (Job 42:2). When Mary heard she would bear a son, she affirmed that "nothing will be impossible with God" (Luke 1:37, NASB, ESV). Even Jesus said that "with God all things are possible" (Matthew 19:26b).

Such passages sometimes prompt critics to pose questions like this: "If God can do *anything*, can he create a rock so big that he can't move it? Can God create a square circle?" If Christians are not careful (or not prepared), they can be taken aback by such questions. I recommend the following response, though it may take some Christians by surprise: *God's omnipotence does not mean that God can do absolutely anything and everything.* He cannot make square circles, for example. As Christian philosopher Paul Copan explains, "No being, great or not, can do something *self-contradictory* or *nonsensical*."[124] C. S. Lewis put it this way: "His [God's] Omnipotence means power to do all that is intrinsically possible, not to do the intrinsically impossible. . . . It remains true that all *things* are possible with God: the intrinsic impossibilities are not things but nonentities."[125]

If this bothers you—that God cannot make square circles—it might help to think of other biblical passages that indicate that God cannot do some actions. Paul asserts God "cannot disown himself" (2 Timothy 2:13). The Hebrew writer says, "It is impossible for God to lie" (Hebrews 6:18). And James says, "God cannot be tempted by evil" (James 1:13).

The primary point about omnipotence is that *God can do anything he desires that is consistent with his nature.* He can do anything he wills to do, but God will never will to do anything contrary to his nature. This should be of great encouragement! God is good; God is faithful; and he will deliver what he has promised—because God has the omnipotence to make it happen. As expressed through Isaiah, God says, "My purpose will stand, and I will do all that I please" (Isaiah 46:10b).

> **GOD CAN DO ANYTHING HE DESIRES THAT IS CONSISTENT WITH HIS NATURE.**

4. *God Is Omniscient (All-Knowing).* Scripture proclaims that God is *all-knowing.* The apostle John succinctly says it: "He [God] knows everything" (1 John 3:20b). Throughout Psalm 139, David emphasizes God's intimate knowledge of who we are: "Before a word is on my tongue you, LORD, know it completely" (Psalm 139:4). God knows the count of the number of hairs on one's head and when a sparrow is sold or falls to the ground (Matthew 10:29–30). He not only knows what *does* happen, God knows what *will* happen. Through Isaiah, God says, "I make known the end from the beginning, from ancient times, what is still to come" (Isaiah 46:10a). God knows everything in advance.[126]

One way to construe God's omniscience is simply to say: "God knows everything—period." However, while the sentiment may be a commendable expression of faith, Christians should avoid being simplistic about what omniscience means. For example, if God knows everything—period, then does he know what it's like to *experience* sin—to *be* a sinner?[127] Does God know what it's like to be a woman or to be Richard Knopp with a headache? I suggest that God does *not* "know" such things in the same experiential sense as individual humans do.[128] However, this does not deny God's genuine omniscience. He knows all truths, and he intimately knows us as persons; but this does not require that God has *experiential* knowledge of sin or of one's individual identity.

God's omniscience generates significant questions regarding the problem of evil, human freedom, and individual salvation. If God knew that humans would sin and would initiate rampant suffering and pain, why did he create us in the first place? If God knows what I am going to do, am I really free in what I do? If God knows *now* whether I will experience heaven or hell, what choice do I really have in the matter?

These are challenging questions that elicit varied answers by devoted Christians. Let's focus just on the matter of salvation. Many Calvinists contend that God's sovereignty and human sinful depravity require that God alone determines who is saved and who is lost. He "predestines" them. If someone comes to saving faith, it is only because God has "elected" them to salvation and given that faith.[129] According to this view, a primary claim is that God's election is *unconditional*; one's salvation does not depend on anything other than God's own eternal decree.[130]

Non-Calvinists, on the other hand, generally stress that God's election is *conditional*: "God predestines those who meet the gracious conditions which he has set forth";[131] and God's election of those who are saved (or lost) is based on his *foreknowledge*, not his eternal, unconditional decree. Romans 8:29 says, "For those God foreknew he also predestined." And 1 Peter 1 addresses "God's elect . . . who have been chosen according to the foreknowledge of God the Father" (1 Peter 1:1–2a).[132] One important point is that *foreknowledge* by itself does not have any *causal* effect. Merely knowing something in advance does not, by itself, cause anything to occur. Just because God knows something *in advance* does not mean God *causes* it.

In sum, we can know much about God's character from Scripture as well as from God's creation. These qualities not only describe an amazing God, but they also offer marvelous benefits to us. God's eternality and self-existence provide ultimate stability. God's complete goodness justifies and sustains our deepest moral intuitions. And God's omniscience in conjunction with God's omnipotence provide enormous reassurance that God is providentially in control of our world.[133]

THE ACTIONS OF GOD

IT'S QUITE POSSIBLE THAT God can exist and have all of the unique divine attributes we've explored, yet choose *not to do anything within human history*. This is the view of *deism*, which says God exists as a powerful Creator but does not involve himself in this world. According to deism, God is only transcendent (above us) but not immanent (with us).[134] But the deistic god is not the biblical God. The God of Scripture has been patiently and persistently involved throughout human history. He has chosen to come to us. He is not merely *transcendent*; he is also *immanent*. He "became flesh and made his dwelling among us" (John 1:14). He appeared as "Immanuel," which means "God with us" (Matthew 1:23; cf. Isaiah 7:14).

This biblical view of God is also very different from *pantheism*, which says everything is God.[135] But if everything is God, then God does not exist as a transcendent being who is distinct from the physical universe. God *is* the universe; the universe *is* God.[136] In a sense, therefore, God is only immanent. For the Christian, however, God is both transcendent *and* immanent. Yet God's immanence does not mean, as in pantheism, that God just mystically permeates all space and time. It means God has acted in specific ways at particular times within human history. This is the uniqueness of the Christian message. It is a truth we can know with certitude because God has chosen to act *within* the universe he created.

Scripture uses various terms for God's acts—including "signs," "wonders," "works," and "miracles."[137] While the four terms carry different connotations, they generally designate what I will classify as *miracles*. Defining a "miracle" is not as simple as some may believe. Many may think a miracle is a "violation of the laws of nature."[138] But the Bible itself poses problems with this view. For example, the plague of locust (Exodus 10:12–15) and the big catches of fish (Luke 5:1–11; John 21:4–6) do not necessarily violate any law of nature; yet we properly think of them as miracles. Some may also think of miracles as supernatural events that are *exclusively caused by God*. But this is also problematic biblically because Scripture also attributes deceiving signs and wonders to Satan and to false prophets.[139]

To make some sense out of all this, it's helpful to (a) distinguish *different types* of miracles and (b) emphasize *various purposes* of miracles. Approaching it this way can enable us to understand why it is so difficult, if not impossible, to give a single definition of "miracle" that is adequate.[140] It can also help us be more effective in our presentation and defense of Christian truth when we talk to others about miracles.

1. *Different Types of Miracles*. Not all miracles are alike.[141] So what are the different types? I think it's useful to distinguish *five types of miracles*: (1) creational miracles; (2) sustaining miracles; (3) providential miracles; (4) predictive miracles; and (5) suspension miracles. The first type, *creational miracles*, are divine acts that bring things into existence—like God's creation of the physical universe.[142] God's creation of matter cannot be construed as suspending, much less violating, laws of nature because there were no laws of nature prior to the existence of the physical universe. Yet in a sense, the very existence of the universe and its natural laws is a miracle. As the psalmist says, "The heavens praise your wonders, LORD" (Psalm 89:5).

Second, *sustaining miracles* point to the ongoing operation of nature that especially allows humans to exist and flourish. God not only brings the universe into existence; he *sustains* it. Hebrews describes God's Son as "sustaining all things by his powerful word" (Hebrews 1:3b). And Paul refers to the Son as "the image of the invisible God" in whom "all things *hold together*" (Colossians 1:15, 17).[143] The Creator's sustaining miracles are ultimately responsible for the conditions and provisions that make ongoing life possible. In that sense, the birth of every baby is a "miracle," but I doubt any atheist would regard this as evidence of God. Even so, as a God-believer, I have a kind of certitude that God miraculously sustains the world around me and, more personally, sustains *me* (Psalms 3:5; 54:4).

Third, *providential miracles* do not appear to go against the normal operation of nature, but the *timing* of related events seems miraculous. Let's say I fervently pray for a new job, and three minutes after the "amen" I receive an email with an exciting job offer. Is it a "miracle"? It *could* be, but we should be cautious against claiming too much about coincidences. Even so, consider an incident with Jesus. Accused of not paying the temple tax, Jesus told Peter to go fishing: "Take the first fish you catch; open its mouth and you will find a four-drachma coin" (Matthew 17:27b). This was certainly a miracle *because of the timing* between what Jesus said and what then occurred. In a sense, it was a coincidence, but it was not just a coincidence. God acted.[144]

Fourth, *predictive miracles* arise from making accurate predictions that are not adequately explainable by mere luck. Catching the fish with the coin (Matthew 17) was both a providential miracle and a predictive miracle. Jesus foretold what Peter would find in the fish's mouth. Predictive miracles were critically important in biblical history. A predictive miracle was a fundamental Old Testament criterion to distinguish between true and false prophets.[145] And the New Testament highlights the fulfillment of predictive miracles.[146] Indeed, the NIV New Testament uses the word "fulfill" fifty-four times, at least thirty-four of which are presented as expressing a fulfillment of an Old Testament prophecy.[147]

Predictive miracles notably contribute to our knowing truth about God. God's power, his omniscience, and his faithfulness are manifested in the entire narrative of Scripture. Miracles are not merely extraordinary, isolated events; many are fulfillments of predictive prophecy. This fabric, which is woven throughout biblical history, helps us have certitude about God's actions.

Fifth, *suspension miracles* may appear to be "violations" of some natural law, but it's better to think of such miracles as "suspending" a natural principle.[148] Biblical examples include Jesus' healings and his nature miracles.[149] One important point about suspension miracles is that they were astonishing, *observable* events that offered truth about God and often authenticated a messenger of God. For instance, when Jesus healed the paralyzed man, he performed an *observable* physical healing to authenticate his authority to forgive sin—which otherwise would have been an unobservable act. It's also significant that Jesus wanted the miracle to grant *knowledge* of his authority. He said, "'*I want you to know* that the Son of Man has authority on earth to forgive sins.' So he said to the man, 'I tell you, get up, take your mat and go home'" (Mark 2:10–11; emphasis added).[150]

The most significant suspension miracle is *the bodily resurrection of Jesus*. In fact, the truth of Christianity depends on this historical event. Paul says, "If Christ has not been raised, our preaching is useless and so is your faith" (1 Corinthians 15:14). Without the resurrection of Jesus, Paul indicates that "only for this life we have hope," and in this case, "we are of all people most to be pitied" (1 Corinthians 15:19). It is therefore imperative that we examine the resurrection of Jesus. Was it really true? How can we have justified confidence in knowing this truth about God?

A comprehensive case for the resurrection of Jesus would require a sizable book, and many excellent works are available that provide impressive historical evidences and respond to various objections and alternative explanations.[151] For our purposes, I want to focus on a couple of considerations that especially help us have a justified conviction about the truth of Jesus' resurrection and the Christian faith as a whole.

First, the resurrection of Jesus was an *observable* event. At least ten different post-mortem appearances of Jesus are presented in the New Testament.[152] In addition, the resurrection of Jesus was publicly proclaimed, in Jerusalem where the event occurred, within fifty days of the event (Acts 2). And the disciples continued preaching the resurrection in spite of severe persecution and even death for doing so. (For instance, see Acts 4:1–22; 5:17–41; 7:1–59; 8:1–3).

Second, the resurrection of Jesus was an *unanticipated* event. The Greco-Roman and Jewish worlds offered no clearly understood theological, philosophical, or psychological basis for it. Pagan philosophies had dismissed the notion of an actual physical resurrection from the dead.[153] The Jewish doctrine about the resurrection only projected (a) a resurrection *at the end of the world* and (b) a resurrection that involved *everyone* rather than a single individual.[154] The Jewish view is illustrated by the conversation between Jesus and Martha at the death of her brother, Lazarus. Jesus told her that Lazarus "will rise again" to which Martha replied, "I know he will rise again in the resurrection *at the last day*" (John 11:23b–24). But Jesus transformed her thinking of resurrection only at the end of the world to a resurrection *in the middle of* human history: "I am the resurrection and the life" (John 11:25).

The Gospels offer no indication that the disciples of Jesus expected Jesus' bodily resurrection. Even though Old Testament prophecies foretold the resurrection, and Jesus taught his disciples about his impending death and resurrection (Matthew 16:21; 17:23; 20:19), John later wrote that at the time of the resurrection, "They still did not understand the Scripture that Jesus had to rise from the dead" (John 20:9). After the crucifixion, the disciples cowered in fear.[155] And it was only *after* Jesus' resurrection and their eyewitness experiences that they "recalled what he had said. Then they believed the scripture and the words that Jesus had spoken" (John 2:22).

All of this addresses a popular objection to the resurrection of Jesus—that it was fabricated by his followers. To put it bluntly: they made it up. But the basic point here is that the disciples did not have an adequate theological, philosophical, or psychological context to concoct the bodily resurrection of Jesus from the dead. They did not possess a sufficient framework to create what would amount to a "conspiracy" theory about Jesus' resurrection, and there was little basis to prompt a wished-for set of psychological hallucinations. Even so, hallucinations cannot account for the widely acknowledged fact that many disciples truly believed they saw a resurrected body on multiple occasions in different settings.[156]

2. *Different Purposes of Miracles.* In general, the Bible affirms that miracles are greatly intended to convey truth about God. And this can be more clearly recognized by understanding various purposes of miracles. How do miracles teach truth about God?

First, miracles *demonstrate* the lordship of the only true God. The Old Testament repeatedly reveals that a fundamental objective of God's miraculous acts was so we may *know* he alone is God.[157]

Second, many miracles *substantiate* the specific truth that Jesus is the Messiah (Christ), the Son of God. Jesus himself expressed that his "works" testify of him. He said, "Do not believe me unless I do the works of my Father. But if I do them, even though you do not believe me, believe the works, *that you may know and understand* that the Father is in me, and I in the Father" (John 10:37–38).[158] These substantiation miracles give us a strong case for knowing this truth about God and his incarnation in the flesh.[159]

Third, miracles *authenticate* Jesus' apostles and preachers in the early church, which gives us a foundation for having certitude about what they proclaimed. Miracles attended the preaching of Peter on Pentecost (Acts 2:43), of Peter and John (Acts 4:29–31), of the apostles (Acts 5:12), of Stephen (Acts 6:8), of Philip (Acts 8:6–7), and of Paul and Barnabas (Acts 14:3). Specifically, Acts 14 says the Lord "confirmed the message of his grace by enabling them [Paul and Barnabas] to perform signs and wonders" (14:3b).[160]

As we reflect on the actions of God, we see the various *types* of miracles were designed, in great part, for us to know truth about God. They exhibit truth about God's acts in the Old Testament, truth about Jesus, and truth about the message of Jesus as it was preached in the early church. We also see that God's *purposes* for miracles convey a confidence in their historicity. We can justifiably believe them to be true because they attest to God's appointed prophets and to the authority of the biblical narrative. As a result, knowing about God's actions should stimulate us to have greater courage in our witness.[161] In particular, the miracle of Jesus' resurrection is the primary incentive for boldly sharing the gospel with the entire world: "You are witnesses of these things" (Luke 24:48).

THE WORD OF GOD

IN ADDITION TO KNOWING truth about the existence of God, the character of God, and the acts of God, we can also know truth about the word of God. Biblically speaking, "word of God" refers to a message revealed by God, the Scriptures inspired by God, and the Son given by God.

1. *The Message Revealed by God.* While some truth can be known about God through God's *general* revelation in nature, much truth can be known about God through his *special* revelation: God has spoken in a variety of ways. The Hebrew writer says, "In the past God spoke to our ancestors through the prophets at many times and in various ways" (Hebrews 1:1). Sometimes God used *physical things* as a medium for his message. He spoke through a burning bush to Moses (Exodus 3),[162] through the Urim and Thummim to the high priest (Exodus 28:29–30),[163] and even through a donkey (Numbers 22:21–38). Also, sometimes God used *visions or dreams* to convey his message. This included dreams or visions to those who were

believers in God and even to those who were not.[164] At other times, God used *angels* to communicate his message.[165]

In most cases in Scripture, the phrase "word(s) of God" refers to the *content* of a message from God, not a set of existing writings.[166] Paul clearly distinguishes it from *human* words: "When you received the word of God, which you heard from us, you accepted it not as a human word, but as it actually is, the word of God, which is indeed at work in you who believe" (1 Thessalonians 2:13). This word is "alive and active" (Hebrews 4:12). It is the "sword of the Spirit" (Ephesians 6:17) that enables us to be born again (1 Peter 1:23). This word is the message that Paul charges Timothy (and us) to "preach" (2 Timothy 4:2).[167]

2. The Scripture Inspired by God. Although the "word of God" often refers to the *content* of God's message, it is also expressed in *written* form that possesses divine authority.[168] Jesus directly connected "the word of God" and "Scripture" when he cited what was written in Psalm 82:6. He said, "If he called them 'gods,' to whom the word of God came—and Scripture cannot be set aside" (John 10:35). Jesus notably acknowledged the authority of what was *written*.[169]

Various New Testament authors also stress the authority of what was *written*. According to Luke, Peter said "the Scripture had to be fulfilled in which the Holy Spirit spoke long ago through David concerning Judas" (Acts 1:16b). Paul says, "All Scripture is God-breathed" (2 Timothy 3:16).[170] And Peter contends, "No prophecy of Scripture came about by the prophet's own interpretation of things. For prophecy never had its origin in the human will, but prophets, though human, spoke from God as they were carried along by the Holy Spirit" (2 Peter 1:20–21).[171] These passages connect the word of God to Scripture, which derives its authority from God, whose Spirit animates and works in conjunction with human authors.[172]

Let's draw two important applications from this discussion on Scripture. First, we can know truth *about* the written word of God. We can study it, and it communicates truth about God. But second, we can know truth *from* the written word of God when we allow it to communicate truth *about us* and *for us*.[173] It describes our wretched human sinfulness and God's patient and persistent plan of salvation. And Scripture provides truth for how we *should* live, because it is "useful for teaching, rebuking, correcting and training in righteousness, so that the servant of God may be thoroughly equipped for every good work" (2 Timothy 3:16b–17).[174]

3. The Son Given by God. While it is important to see Scripture as the "word of God," it's also critical to understand that the ultimate word of God is a *person*, not a book.[175] John clearly makes this point when he speaks of the *logos*: "In the begin-

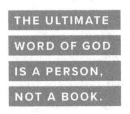

ning was the Word [*logos*], and the Word [*logos*] was with God, and the Word [*logos*] was God. . . . The Word [*logos*] became flesh and made his dwelling among us. We have seen his glory, the glory of the one and only Son, who came from the Father, full of grace and truth" (John 1:1, 14).[176] John emphasizes that the *logos* is not just *a* word; he is *the* word, who is eternal (1:2), who is God (1:1), who is Creator (1:3), and who becomes flesh (1:14). This *logos* is not an abstract mysterious force that pervades the universe; he is *personal*. This *logos* is not a distant, disinterested deity; he is "the one and only Son" of God (1:14b), who came to earth to make the Father "known" to us (1:18).[177] He is the one who came "to save the world" (John 3:17b).

Various New Testament passages provide truth about the Son who was given by God. Paul describes the Son as "the image of the invisible God" (Colossians 1:15; see also 2 Corinthians 4:4). The Greek word translated as "image" in these vers-es is *eikōn*. To illustrate the meaning of this word, every time you click on an icon on your mobile device or computer, you are clicking on an image that will open up some software application. I like to put it this way: "Click on the Jesus icon, and it will open up to God."[178] According to John, "The one and only Son, who is himself God and is in closest relationship with the Father, has *made him known*" (John 1:18b). Jesus is the "exegesis" or the explanation of God.[179]

The writer of Hebrews describes the Son as "the radiance of God's glory and the *exact representation* of his being" (Hebrews 1:3a). The Greek word translated as "exact representation" is *charaktēr*, which is an "exact reproduction of a particular form or structure."[180] One illustration of this is the typebars on old typewriters. Each typebar is a movable metal arm that has a small, molded character embed-ded in it. When a keyboard key is pushed, it causes the typebar to strike an inked ribbon and impress the character on the paper. Jesus is like that. If you push the "Jesus key," it will print "God."

No wonder Paul describes Christ Jesus as the Son whom God has exalted with a "name that is above every name, that at the name of Jesus every knee should bow, in heaven and on earth and under the earth, and every tongue acknowledge that Jesus Christ is Lord, to the glory of God the Father" (Philippians 2:9–11). *This* is the word of God who is the Son given by God!

THE POWER OF GOD

TO REVIEW, WE CAN know truth about the existence of God, the character of God, the actions of God, and the word of God. But we can also know truth about God in an even more direct way: *we can personally know the power of God in our own life.* A prime biblical illustration is presented in John 9 with the man who was blind from birth. After Jesus healed him, a major theological debate ensued about sin, the Sabbath, and Jesus' identity.[181] Basically, the blind man said, "I don't know" about all that theological stuff, but "one thing I do know. I was blind but now I see!" (John 9:25).

This is direct knowledge, this is personal knowledge, and this is a kind of knowledge that cannot be effectively refuted nor easily dismissed. "I was blind but now I see!"—that should be the courageous confession of *every disciple* of Jesus. Even if we are not familiar with the theological, philosophical, historical, or scientific issues pertaining to knowing truth about God, we can know what God has done *for us.* Our "new life" is a life of immeasurable joy, knowing we have been completely forgiven of our sin by God's grace. It is a life of hope rather than despair. It is a life of ultimate purpose rather than pointless existence. It is a life made possible by the power of God through the indwelling presence of God.

Christians can know this "new life" by personal experience.[182] However, this is not merely some *subjective* sentiment like, "I feel refreshed today." It is not based on how we *feel* at any particular moment. It is a stable existence of newness based on knowing two *objective truths*: we are *in Christ* and God's Spirit is *in us.*

1. *Knowing We Are "in Christ."* First, we can know we are in Christ. The phrase "in Christ" appears over eighty times in the NIV New Testament epistles. Many instances make the point that because we are "in Christ," we have this new life. For example, "If anyone is *in Christ*, the new creation has come: The old has gone, the new is here!" (2 Corinthians 5:17). God reconciled "the world to himself *in Christ*, not counting people's sins against them" (2 Corinthians 5:19). "There is now no condemnation for those who are *in Christ* Jesus" (Romans 8:1).[183] We have "new life" *in Christ*! This is knowing the power of God. And this is worth sharing. As the angel said—the one who miraculously opened the jail doors and let the imprisoned apostles out—"Go, stand in the temple courts . . . and tell the people all about this new life" (Acts 5:20).

2. *Knowing the Holy Spirit Is in Us.* Second, we can know God's Spirit is *in us*. Jesus promised this just before his death. He said that the "Spirit of truth . . .

lives with you and will be in you" (John 14:17). He said his Father "will send" the Holy Spirit "in my name" (John 14:26a; cf. John 15:26). And on Pentecost about fifty days later, the apostles were miraculously "filled with the Holy Spirit" (see Acts 2:1–4). They preached the first post-resurrection sermon, which concluded with the command to "repent and be baptized . . . in the name of Jesus Christ for the forgiveness of your sins. And you will receive the gift of the Holy Spirit" (Acts 2:38). This "gift of the Holy Spirit" should be seen as God's indwelling presence that seals us with a divine guarantee that we are God's possession and that we have assurance of our inheritance in Christ.[184]

Paul talks about how we are "marked in him [in Christ] with a *seal*, the promised Holy Spirit, who is a *deposit guaranteeing* our inheritance until the redemption of those who are God's possession" (Ephesians 1:13–14). The Holy Spirit is a "seal"[185] that "guarantees"[186] our inheritance. The picture is that the gift of the Holy Spirit is God's *guaranteeing deposit* that everything promised is coming!

The gift of the Holy Spirit provides an *internal witness* for us (2 Timothy 1:14; Romans 8:11a). This indwelling Spirit produces a variety of marvelous benefits for the Christian believer.

1. He offers God's guarantee of our inheritance (Ephesians 1:13–14; 2 Corinthians 1:22; 5:5).
2. He provides God's promise of our own bodily resurrection (Romans 8:11).
3. He confirms our identity as God's children (Romans 8:16).
4. He creates a special intimacy with God that allows us to call him "Abba, Father" and makes us "sons," not "slaves" (Galatians 4:6; Romans 8:15).[187]
5. He empowers us to live a new life with hope and conviction (Romans 15:13; 1 Thessalonians 1:5).
6. He "does not make us timid, but gives us power, love and self-discipline" (2 Timothy 1:7).
7. He enables us to "walk by the Spirit" and to bear "the fruit of the Spirit" (Galatians 5:16, 22–25).

From these points, we can see how the indwelling Holy Spirit significantly contributes to our *knowledge*. Through him, we can know, in a more direct experiential way, our identity as God's children and our intimacy with God. We can have greater confidence in everything God's message of hope provides. And we can live a new life with the conviction that God's power is present.

How can we know all of this? The apostle John summarizes it this way: "This is how we know that he lives in us: We know it by the Spirit he gave us" (1 John 3:24b; cf. 4:13). By his Spirit, we can know truth about the power of God!

CONCLUSION

In this book, I began by discussing the Bible's perspective on the nature of truth and the importance of defending it, especially in response to various philosophical and cultural challenges. Then I addressed two basic questions: "How can we know truth about God?" and "What truth can we know about God?" I ended by proposing we can know truth about the existence of God, the character of God, the actions of God, the word of God, and the power of God.

Atheists and agnostics reject the possibility of knowing any truth about God. Atheists simply deny God exists, and agnostics claim we cannot know enough to decide whether or not God exists. I emphasized that knowing truth about God does not require us to have absolute intellectual certainty. Instead, we can have *certitude* (or justified conviction) based on a wide variety of considerations that our core Christian beliefs about God are true. And I indicated that the God-less answers to the big questions of human existence are, by comparison, less adequate evidentially and less appealing existentially.

Even so, knowing truth *about* God is not nearly enough; we are called to *know God*. Jesus put it well in his prayer to the Father, "Now this is eternal life: that they know you, the only true God, and Jesus Christ, whom you have sent" (John 17:3). It's not a mere matter of knowing truths or facts about God; it's not a mere matter of mentally accepting truths about who Jesus was or is (Matthew 16:16) or about repentance or faith or the resurrection of the dead or eternal judgment (Hebrews 6:1–2). Knowing truth *about* God must drive us to *know God*.

> KNOWING TRUTH ABOUT GOD MUST DRIVE US TO KNOW GOD.

J. I. Packer elucidates how we can do this in his classic work *Knowing God*. He writes, "How can we turn our knowledge *about God* into knowledge *of* God? The rule for doing this is demanding, but simple. It is that we turn each truth that we learn *about* God into matter for meditation *before* God, leading to prayer and praise *to* God."[188] Knowing God calls us to a personal relationship. It calls us to a life of loving God and loving others. It calls us to faithful obedience. It calls us to sacrificial service. It calls us to devoted discipleship.

APPENDIX

BOOK RECOMMENDATIONS
FOR FURTHER STUDY

Paul Copan, *Loving Wisdom: A Guide to Philosophy and Christian Faith*, 2nd ed. (Grand Rapids: Eerdmans, 2020).

Timothy Keller, *Making Sense of God: An Invitation to the Skeptical* (New York: Viking, 2016). Book review by Richard Knopp at https://christianstandard.com/2017/02/helping-the-skeptical-see-god/.

Alister McGrath, *Mere Apologetics: How to Help Seekers and Skeptics Find Faith* (Grand Rapids: Baker, 2012).

J. P. Moreland, *Love Your God with All Your Mind: The Role of Reason in the Life of the Soul*, rev. ed. (Colorado Springs: NavPress, 2012).

Doug Powell, *Holman QuickSource Guide to Christian Apologetics* (Nashville: B&H Academic, 2006).

Room For Doubt, "Why Do You Still Believe?" Animated video at https://vimeo.com/327406232 and other resources at https://www.roomfordoubt.com/recommended-resources/.

NOTES

1. Cultural Research Center, "American Worldview Inventory 2020–at a Glance," April 21, 2020, https://www.arizonachristian.edu/wp-content/uploads/2020/04/CRC-AWVI-2020-Release-03_Perceptions-of-God.pdf. Data from a 2018 Pew Research study indicated that while 89 percent of US adults believe in "some kind" of God, only 56 percent believe in God "as described in the Bible," which refers to "an all-powerful, all-knowing, loving deity who determines most or all of what happens in their lives." Pew Research Center, "When Americans Say They Believe in God, What Do They Mean?" April 25, 2018, https://www.pewforum.org/2018/04/25/when-americans-say-they-believe-in-god-what-do-they-mean/.

2. Barna Research Group, "Tracking the Growth and Decline of Religious Segments: The Rise of Atheism," January 14, 2020, https://www.barna.com/rise-of-atheism/.

3. Barna Research Group, "Atheism Doubles Among Generation Z," January 24, 2018, https://www.barna.com/research/atheism-doubles-among-generation-z/.

4. See Kara Powell and Steven Argue, "The Biggest Hindrance to Your Kids' Faith Isn't Doubt. It's Silence," February 21, 2019, https://www.christianitytoday.com/ct/2019/february-web-only/doubt-parenting-biggest-hindrance-kids-faith-is-silence.html.

5. The Room For Doubt program attempts to address the growing presence of skepticism and doubt in our churches and in our culture, especially among churched youth. See roomfordoubt.com.

6. David F. Wells, *No Place for Truth: Whatever Happened to Evangelical Theology?* (Grand Rapids: Eerdmans, 1993). Wells says, "The disappearance of theology from the life of the Church, and the orchestration of that disappearance by some of its leaders, is hard to miss today but, oddly enough, not easy to prove. It is hard to miss in the evangelical world—in the vacuous worship that is so prevalent, for example, in the shift from God to the self as the central focus of faith, in

the psychologized preaching that follows this shift, in the erosion of its conviction, and its strident pragmatism, in its inability to think incisively about the culture, in its reveling in the irrational" (95).

7. Douglas Groothuis, *Truth Decay: Defending Christianity Against the Challenges of Postmodernism* (Grand Rapids: InterVarsity, 2000).

8. See A. C. Thiselton, "Truth," in *Dictionary of New Testament Theology* (Grand Rapids: Zondervan, 1978), 3:877–882.

9. Moses offered these instructions to Israel: "You must inquire, probe and investigate it thoroughly. And if it is true [*emet*] and it has been proved that this detestable thing has been done among you, you must certainly put to the sword all who live in that town" (Deuteronomy 13:14–15a; see also 1 Kings 17:24).

10. Thiselton, "Truth," in *Dictionary of New Testament Theology*, 3:881–882.

11. The Hebrew word *emet* is typically translated as *alētheia* in the Septuagint, the Greek translation of the Hebrew Scriptures. The notion of "faithfulness," which is embedded in the Hebrew word *emet*, is communicated in the New Testament more by the *pistos* family of terms that denote what is faithful, trustworthy, or genuine (e.g., Luke 16:10–11; 1 Corinthians 4:2; 2 Thessalonians 3:3; Acts 11:23). See Roger Nicole, "The Biblical Concept of Truth," in *Scripture and Truth*, ed. D. A. Carson and John D. Woodbridge (Grand Rapids: Zondervan, 1983), 292.

12. Nicole, "The Biblical Concept of Truth," in *Scripture and Truth*, 293. Nicole also states in the same source, "The primary New Testament emphasis is clearly on truth as conformity to reality and opposition to lies and errors" (293).

13. Other sample passages that emphasize truth include the following: Paul reflects on the people of Israel and states, "I speak the truth in Christ—I am not lying, my conscience confirms it through the Holy Spirit" (Romans 9:1); Paul says he and his fellow teachers "do not use deception," nor do they "distort the word of God." On the contrary, Paul says, "By setting forth the truth plainly we commend ourselves to everyone's conscience in the sight of God" (2 Corinthians 4:2). Paul challenges Timothy to be a worker who "correctly handles the word of truth" (2 Timothy 2:15b), and he charges the Ephesians to "stand firm . . . with the belt of truth buckled around your waist" (Ephesians 6:14a).

14. More literally, the Greek text says, "We are lying and are not doing the truth" (1 John 1:6, AT).

15. John the Baptist "testified to the truth" (John 5:33), even though it literally cost him his head (Matthew 14; Mark 6). Jesus "told . . . the truth" that he had

heard from God, which is why others sought to kill him (John 8:40). Peter and others preached the truth and were threatened and imprisoned for it (Acts 4:1–20; 5:17–33). Stephen, the first church deacon, craftily integrated the narrative of Hebrew history with the unjustified crucifixion of the promised Righteous One, even though it led to his immediate execution (Acts 7).

16. Some suggest that using reason to defend God's truth is a *modern* concept tied to the eighteenth-century Enlightenment. This claim is unjustified and ignores the clear biblical emphasis on giving a reasonable defense.

17. See Acts 22:1; 24:10; 25:8; 26:1–2; 1 Corinthians 9:3; and 2 Timothy 4:16.

18. The emphasis placed on Paul's persistent *reasoning* with Jews and Gentiles is remarkable. See Acts 17:2, 17; 18:4, 19; 19:8–9. In Acts 19:9, the NIV only says that Paul "had discussions daily in the lecture hall of Tyrannus," but this diminishes the point that the ESV properly conveys: Paul was "reasoning daily." (The Greek word, *dialegomai*, is used here.)

19. For example, modern *culture* is characterized by a Western-dominated industrial economy (England and America); the social value of conformity; and a word-based, linear system of communication (e.g., a typewriter). Postmodern *culture* is expressed more by a global economy that is service-oriented; the social value of diversity; and a digital system of communication with images, videos, and emojis. The shift to a postmodern *culture* underlies the church's "worship wars" in recent decades. A search for "worship wars" in *Christianity Today* generates sixty-six items from 1996 to late 2020. For instance, note Megan Fowler, "Turning Up the Volume: Joyful Noise or Noise Ordinance Violation?" *Christianity Today*, March 2, 2020, https://www.christianitytoday.com/news/2020/march/church-worship-too-loud-noise-ordinance-violation.html.

20. I discuss this further in Richard A. Knopp, "Understanding and Engaging the 'Nones,'" *Stone-Campbell Journal* 21 (Fall 2018): especially pages 234–236. I propose that we use the terms "modern" and "postmodern" to refer to the respective *cultural* characteristics, and the terms "modernism" and "postmodernism" to refer to the respective *philosophical* ideas. One reason this is important is because I too frequently read or hear a Christian leader who contends that the church should embrace "postmodernism." But they are often just referring to how the church should change its methods to be more appealing to a postmodern culture. However, their terminology unfortunately implies an endorsement of the philosophy of postmodernism. Some go further and advocate that the church should adopt

postmodernism as a philosophy. Examples of this latter approach are Carl Raschke, *The Next Reformation: Why Evangelicals Must Embrace Postmodernity* (Grand Rapids: Baker, 2004); James K. A. Smith, *Who's Afraid of Postmodernism? Taking Derrida, Lyotard, and Foucault to Church* (Grand Rapids: Baker, 2006); and Myron Penner, *The End of Apologetics: Christian Witness in a Postmodern Context* (Grand Rapids: Baker, 2013). While I believe philosophical postmodernism offers beneficial insights and valuable criticisms of modernism, in its stronger forms it is problematic for the proclamation and defense of Christian truth. In Penner's case, for example, he calls for an end to "apologetics," which he construes as "roughly the Enlightenment project of attempting to establish rational foundations for Christian belief" (ibid., 7). He claims, "Not only can apologetics curse; it actually *is* a curse" (ibid., 9; emphasis in original). I think Penner is mistaken to characterize apologetics as an "Enlightenment project." As Chapter 1 indicated, apologetics, properly understood, is a biblical practice and imperative, not a concoction of modern philosophy.

21. See Groothuis, *Truth Decay*, 35–38.

22. This famous phrase is presented in 1637 in Descartes's *Discourse on the Method of Rightly Conducting the Reason and Seeking for Truth in the Sciences*, part IV.

23. For Descartes, a good God would not allow us to be so deluded as to have a clear idea of a tree in front of us if that tree did not actually exist outside our mind. This is why Descartes's argument for God's existence was so important for his philosophy. However, many critics were not convinced by Descartes's argument for God's existence. And without an adequate argument for God's existence, our knowledge of external objects is therefore threatened. If all we know are our own ideas (which was Descartes's view), how can we know that our ideas correspond to anything outside our mind, including God? As Kelly and Dew express it, "It is far from clear how we can get from this starting point [our own thoughts] to beliefs about the external world." Stewart Kelly and James Dew, *Understanding Postmodernism: A Christian Perspective* (Grand Rapids: IVP Academic, 2017), 244. On Descartes's "idea theory of perception," see J. P. Moreland and William Lane Craig, *Philosophical Foundations for a Christian Worldview* (Grand Rapids: InterVarsity Press, 2003), 148.

24. In a well-known passage, Hume said, "If we take in our hand any volume—of divinity or school metaphysics, for instance—let us ask, *Does it contain*

any abstract reasoning concerning quantity or number? No. *Does it contain any experimental reasoning concerning matter of fact and existence?* No. Commit it then to the flames, for it can contain nothing but sophistry and illusion." See David Hume, *An Inquiry Concerning Human Understanding* (1748), ed. Charles W. Hendel (Indianapolis: Bobbs-Merrill, 1955), 173; emphasis in original. The passage is from section 12, part 3.

25. Immanuel Kant, *Critique of Pure Reason*, 2nd ed., trans. Norman Kemp Smith (New York: St. Martin's Press, 1965), 29; emphasis in original. The quotation is in the preface to the second edition (1787).

26. Kirk R. MacGregor, *Contemporary Theology: An Introduction: Classical, Evangelical, Philosophical, and Global Perspectives* (Grand Rapids: Zondervan, 2019), 21.

27. See J. P. Moreland, "Four Degrees of Postmodernism," in *Come Let Us Reason: New Essays in Christian Apologetics,* ed. Paul Copan and William Lane Craig, 17–34 (Nashville: B&H Academic, 2012).

28. For some helpful Christian orientations to postmodernism, see James Sire, *The Universe Next Door*, 5th ed. (Grand Rapids: IVP Academic, 2009), chap. 9; and Kelly and Dew, *Understanding Postmodernism: A Christian Perspective*, chap. 1.

29. Groothuis speaks of postmodernism as "modernism gone to seed" because it carries modernism to its logical conclusion and inevitable demise. See *Truth Decay*, 40–42.

30. Modernism correctly speaks of truth that can be true for everyone. Jesus and the Christian gospel make this claim. Postmodernism rightly reminds us of our finitude and the role of our cultural and personal perspectives in how we interpret the world—and even the Bible.

31. The Christian philosopher, J. P. Moreland, poignantly describes this: "The secularized perspective is constituted by two worldviews—naturalism (fueled by scientism) and postmodernism—that agree with each other . . . about one important point: *there is no non-empirical knowledge, especially no theological or ethical knowledge.*" J. P. Moreland, "How Christian Philosophers Can Serve Systematic Theologians and Biblical Scholars," *Journal of the Evangelical Theological Society* 63 (June 2020): 298–299; emphasis in original.

32. For examples, see Richard Dawkins, *The God Delusion* (Boston: Houghton-Mifflin, 2006); Sam Harris, *The End of Faith: Religion, Terror, and the Future*

of Reason (New York: W.W. Norton, 2005); and Lawrence Krause, *A Universe from Nothing: Why There Is Something Rather Than Nothing* (New York: Atria, 2012).

33. Jean-Francois Lyotard, *The Postmodern Condition: A Report on Knowledge*, trans. Geoff Bennington and Brian Massumi (Minneapolis: University of Minnesota Press, 1984), 24.

34. Alasdair MacIntyre, *The Religious Significance of Atheism*, ed. A. MacIntyre and Paul Ricoeur, 14; cited in Alister McGrath, *Intellectuals Don't Need God: And Other Modern Myths* (Grand Rapids: Zondervan, 1993), 101.

35. Paine says, "The word of God is the creation we behold and it is in *this* word . . . that God speaketh universally to man. . . . The only idea man can affix to the name of God is that of a *first cause*, the cause of all things." Thomas Paine, *The Age of Reason: The Definitive Edition*, part 1 (Grand Rapids: Michigan Legal Publishing, 2014), 24, 26.

36. "Epistemology" is linked to the Greek word *epistamai*. A form of the word is used about thirty times in the Septuagint, the Greek translation of the Old Testament, and also in the Greek New Testament (e.g., Acts 15:7; 19:15; 1 Timothy 6:4).

37. The *correspondence theory* was classically expressed by Aristotle: "To say of what is that it is not, or of what is not that it is, is false, while to say of what is that it is, and of what is not that it is not, is true." Aristotle, *Metaphysics* 1011b25; cited in "The Correspondence Theory of Truth," in *Stanford Encyclopedia of Philosophy*, https://plato.stanford.edu/entries/truth-correspondence/.

38. The "pragmatic" theory derives its name from the Greek root *pragma*, which is used eleven times in the New Testament to signify the notion of "events" or "happenings." Luke uses the word to describe "the things [or the events] that have been fulfilled among us" (Luke 1:1). It is closely related to the word *praxis*, which pertains to action, practices, or deeds (e.g., Matthew 16:27; Acts 19:18; Colossians 3:9). See Christian Maurer, "Pragma," in *Theological Dictionary of the New Testament* (Grand Rapids: Eerdmans, 1964), 6:638–639.

39. Chapter 1 affirmed that truth in the Bible includes the idea of "conformity to reality in opposition to lies or errors." However, remember that truth is more than propositions. Truth is personal, and it even refers to a path or way of life. Jesus claims to be "the way and the truth and the life" (John 14:6).

40. Of course, we must clarify who "the Lord" is and what "risen" means, but it is clear from the biblical record that the reference is to Jesus who experienced an actual bodily resurrection after his crucifixion.

41. In 2016, the word of the year for the *Oxford Dictionary* was "post-truth." The adjective was defined as "relating to or denoting circumstances in which objective facts are less influential in shaping public opinion than appeals to emotion and personal belief." See https://languages.oup.com/word-of-the-year/2016/.

42. For an informative and eye-opening discussion of how "post-truth" has affected our culture, see Abdu Murray, *Saving Truth: Finding Meaning and Clarity in a Post-Truth World* (Grand Rapids: Zondervan, 2018), 11–25.

43. Postmodernism raises a legitimate and perceptive point: truth is often little more than a power play. As James Sire says about postmodernism, "All narratives mask a play for power. Any one narrative used as a metanarrative is oppressive. . . . There is no purely objective knowledge, no truth of correspondence. Instead there are only stories, stories that, when they are believed, give the storyteller power over others." James Sire, *The Universe Next Door*, 225–226.

44. See James 2:26; Colossians 1:10; Matthew 7:16–20.

45. Plato presents his notion of knowledge as "justified true belief" (JTB) in his dialogues *Theaetetus* (202c) and *Meno* (98a). This conception of knowledge was nearly universally accepted by philosophers until 1963 when a philosopher named Edmund Gettier published a short article in which he described several somewhat odd but legitimate examples that showed it's possible for someone to have "justified true belief" without having genuine knowledge. Trying to resolve the "Gettier Problem" is still important to philosophers. Even so, Plato's notion of knowledge as "justified true belief" still rightly presents what is *necessary* for knowledge and, aside from some conjectured odd examples, it still poses a practical and acceptable understanding of what is *sufficient* for knowledge. For an excellent discussion of this by two Christian philosophers, see James K. Dew and Mark W. Foreman, "What Is Knowledge?" in *How Do We Know? An Introduction to Epistemology* (Grand Rapids: IVP Academic, 2014), 19–30.

46. This does not mean we only know things that are true. That would be ridiculous. Clearly, I *know* "2 plus 2 equals 5" is *false*.

47. In Plato's *Meno* (98a), Plato distinguishes genuine knowledge from true opinion. True opinions are certainly useful, but to have knowledge, one must "tether them *by working out the reason*" (emphasis added). In order words, one's opinion might accidentally be correct, but it's not real knowledge unless it has some justification or basis.

48. The scenario in *The Matrix* was raised over 350 years ago by René Descartes as he contemplated what an evil genius might do.

49. Those who disdain doubt typically point to various Bible passages. Jesus said to Peter when he slipped into the water: "You of little faith . . . why did you doubt?" (Matthew 14:31). He told his disciples, "If you have faith and do not doubt," you can command a mountain to fall into the sea (Matthew 21:21). And James says, "You must believe and not doubt" (James 1:6b).

50. This quoted phrase comes from Drew Dyck, who says of one study: "'The most frequently mentioned role of Christians in de-conversion was in amplifying existing doubt.' De-converts reported 'sharing their burgeoning doubts with a Christian friend or family member only to receive trite, unhelpful answers.'" Drew Dyck, "The Leavers: Young Doubters Exit the Church," *Christianity Today*, November 19, 2010, http://www.christianitytoday.com/ct/2010/november/27.40.html.

51. Two notable Christian philosophers say, "If someone knows something, it does not necessarily mean that the person has complete certainty about that thing." Moreland and Craig, *Philosophical Foundations for a Christian Worldview*, 84.

52. As Christian philosopher J. P. Moreland explains: "When we seek knowledge of God, . . . we should not assume that our search requires reaching a state with no doubt, no plausible counterarguments, no possibility of being mistaken. When people believe that knowledge *requires* certainty, they will fail to take themselves to have knowledge if they lack certainty. In turn, this will lead to a lack of confidence and courage regarding one's ability to count on the things one knows. I am not suggesting that certainty is a bad thing—not for a second. I'm merely noting that it is not required." J. P. Moreland, *Kingdom Triangle: Recover the Christian Mind, Renovate the Soul, Restore the Spirit's Power* (Grand Rapids: Zondervan, 2007), 121.

53. Evans, *Why Christian Faith Still Makes Sense* (Grand Rapids: Baker Academic, 2015), 23–24.

54. Kinnaman points out that over 35 percent of young adults with a Christian background say, "Christians are too confident they know all the answers." David Kinnaman, *You Lost Me: Why Young Christians Are Leaving Church . . . and Rethinking Faith* (Grand Rapids: Baker Books, 2011), loc. 2120, Kindle.

55. Austin Fischer, *Faith in the Shadows: Finding Christ in the Midst of Doubt* (Grand Rapids: IVP Books, 2018), loc. 304–307, Kindle.

56. For example, when Jesus chided Thomas, the NIV translates Jesus as saying, "Stop doubting and believe" (John 20:27). But the context clearly suggests Thomas had *disbelief* in Christ's resurrection; he was not merely expressing some intellectual uncertainty. For this reason, the New American Standard better translates this verse, "Do not continue in disbelief [*apistos*], but be a believer [*pistos*]" (John 20:27, NASB). The Greek for "disbelief" in this verse is present tense, and it simply adds a negation to the word *pistos*.

57. This distinction also helps make sense out of Jesus' reaction to John the Baptist, who went from confidently declaring, "Look, the Lamb of God, who takes away the sin of the world!" (John 1:29) to the question, "Are you the one who is to come, or should we expect someone else?" (Matthew 11:3). John's circumstances had changed. He was now in prison. He was no longer *absolutely certain* of his claim; he had doubt. But he had not reached a point of *disbelief.* As a result, Jesus did not condemn John's question or doubt. After giving John further evidence to address his doubt, Jesus went on to say that "among those born of women there has not risen anyone greater than John the Baptist" (Matthew 11:11a).

58. Peter concluded his great Pentecost sermon by saying, "Therefore let all Israel be *assured* of this" (Acts 2:36). The NASB says Israel can "know *for certain*." The Message translation even puts it this way: "All Israel, then, know this: There's *no longer room for doubt*" (Acts 2:36). And Paul says God has "given *proof* of this [coming judgment] to everyone by raising him [Jesus] from the dead" (Acts 17:31).

59. Kinnaman insightfully suggests that the most dangerous doubt is "unexpressed doubt." Kinnaman, *You Lost Me*, loc. 3088, Kindle. This is the motivational thrust behind the name of the "Room For Doubt" apologetics program. Let's provide room for doubt. See http://www.roomfordoubt.com.

60. Christians sometimes use the words "rationalist" or "rationalism" in a negative way—as though these terms necessarily mean that reason is used to attack religion or Christianity. While this is appropriate in some contexts, as a specific method of epistemology (knowledge), "rationalism" means reason can know some truth *without having to use sense experience.* If you believe that humans have a "built in" or "innate" knowledge of God, then you are a "rationalist" in this sense.

61. One of the major problems with a worldview without any God is how to explain the capacity of reason itself as a means to yield truth. If our minds are the evolutionary product of mere chance and purposeless order, why should we think that our minds give us *truth*? Darwin himself acknowledged this problem: "With

me the horrid doubt always arises whether the convictions of man's mind, which has been developed from the mind of lower animals, are of any value or at all trustworthy. Would anyone trust in the convictions of a monkey's mind, if there are any convictions in such a mind?" See *The Life and Letters of Charles Darwin*, ed. Francis Darwin (1897; repr., Boston: Elibron, 2005), 1:285; cited in Groothuis, *Christian Apologetics* (Grand Rapids: IVP Academic, 2011), 414. For more cited references on this point, see Groothuis's discussion (ibid., 410–415) and C. S. Lewis, "The Self-Contradiction of the Naturalist," chap. 3 in *Miracles* (New York: Macmillan, 1948).

62. Using empirical experience to acquire knowledge should not be equated with the more specific philosophical view of "empiricism." Empiricism emphasizes that we have knowledge *only through sense experience*. The mind is like a "blank tablet" that has no innate knowledge; we have knowledge only when we receive sense experience. John Locke and David Hume are classic examples of this view. For Christians, it is important to understand that one can know many things from sense experience without going further to claim, like the empiricists, that knowledge *only comes* from sense experience.

63. The biblical references to God having hands, eyes, a face, and a mouth are "anthropomorphic" (e.g., Deuteronomy 11:12; 31:18; Job 33:26; 1 Kings 8:15; Job 15:30; Matthew 4:4). God is described as having a human form, even though Scripture is clear elsewhere that God does not have such physical characteristics (e.g., Exodus 33:20; Acts 17:29).

64. I contend that biblical Christianity offers "empirical content" that vastly differs from other world religions and from some prominent theological perspectives within Christianity, such as existentialism and liberalism. See Richard A. Knopp, "On the Conceptual Relationship Between Religion and Science," in *Theology in the Present Age*, ed. Christopher Ben Simpson and Steven Cone (Eugene: Pickwick, 2013), especially pages 76–82.

65. This kind of inference even occurs in science. Physicists infer the existence of things like black holes and subatomic particles like quarks and mesons—not because they can directly see them, but because of their measurable effects.

66. Even though the apostle John acknowledges that "no one has ever seen God," two verses later he says that "we have seen and testify that the Father has sent his Son to be the Savior of the world" (1 John 4:12, 14). John uses the same Greek word for "seen" in both 1 John 4:12 and 14 (*theomai*).

67. This is a primary consideration that prompted Alexander Campbell, an early leader in the Restoration Movement, to devalue religious emotionalism that was rampant in nineteenth-century America. He stressed "facts" and he pursued an "evidentialist" apologetic that begins with objective facts of history and the facts presented in Scripture. Campbell said, "All revealed religion is based upon facts. Testimony has respect to facts only; and [in order] that testimony may be credible, it must be confirmed. . . . All true and useful knowledge is an acquaintance with facts. And all true science is acquired from the observation and comparison of facts." Alexander Campbell, "The Confirmation of the Testimony," *Millennial Harbinger,* 1st ser., 1, no. 1 (January 1830): 8–9. For more on Campbell's view, see Richard A. Knopp, "Lessons from the Philosophy of Science for the Restoration Movement Heritage (and Others)," in *Restoration and Philosophy: New Philosophical Engagements with the Stone-Campbell Tradition,* 121–151, ed. J. Caleb Clanton (Nashville: University of Tennessee Press, 2019).

68. What I discuss here about inner experience should not be identified as "subjective truth." Subjective truth, especially as it's popularly perceived, highlights the idea that a person *creates* truth or somehow determines what is true. I acknowledge that some truths may be thought of as "subjective." For instance, it may be true for me, but not for you, that chocolate ice cream is the best. However, my point is that some of our inner experiences (like our conscience and our deepest desires or needs) *can point to what is objectively true.* In this case, our inner experiences do not create these truths; they are used to *discover* these truths.

69. John Frame, *Nature's Case for God: A Brief Biblical Argument* (Bellingham, WA: Lexham Press, 2019), 48.

70. Jesus alludes to the conscience as a primary function of the "advocate" or "helper" (which is properly understood as the Holy Spirit): "And He, when he comes, will convict the world regarding sin, righteousness, and judgment" (John 16:8, NASB). The NIV translates the verse as follows: "When he comes, he will prove the world *to be in the wrong* about sin and righteousness and judgment" (John 16:8). But this translation is problematic. It might imply, falsely, that the world is *incorrect* in its notions of sin, righteousness, and judgment. But the more proper emphasis is that the Spirit of truth will "expose" or "convict" the world (or the unbelieving person) of sin, righteousness, and judgment. In John, the Greek word, *elencho,* means "to reveal and convict of sin," which is also a key function of the conscience. See H.-G. Link, "Guilt, Cause, Convict, Blame," *The*

New International Dictionary of New Testament Theology (Grand Rapids: Zondervan, 1976), 2:140–142.

71. The general point here is that there are *existential* reasons (as well as *intellectual* reasons) that point us to the truth of God. For a helpful analysis, see Clifford Williams, *Existential Reasons for Believing in God: A Defense of Desires and Emotions for Faith* (Grand Rapids: IVP Academic, 2011).

72. See the incisive assessment by Timothy Keller, *Making Sense of God: An Invitation to the Skeptical* (New York: Viking, 2016), especially pages 63–65.

73. C. S. Lewis uses the deep desire for an "unattainable ecstasy" in his case for the reality of heaven. See *The Problem of Pain* (New York: Macmillan, 1962), 144–154.

74. God spoke, for instance, to Abraham (Genesis 24:7; cf. Acts 7:2–6); to Moses (Exodus 19:19; cf. John 9:29); to David (2 Samuel 23:2–3); to Isaiah (Isaiah 21:16–17); to Jeremiah (Jeremiah 5:14); and to Ezekiel (Ezekiel 34:24). God spoke at the baptism of Jesus (Matthew 3; Mark 1; Luke 3) and at the Mount of Transfiguration (Matthew 17; Mark 9; Luke 9).

75. The New Testament uses the Greek word *mystērion* twenty-seven times. Paul especially emphasizes that "mystery" does not mean something that is *concealed*; instead, it is something that has been concealed but is *now revealed*. Christ is "the mystery of God" (Colossians 2:2b) who "appeared in the flesh" (1 Timothy 3:16) and who is proclaimed (Colossians 4:3). Paul and others "declare God's wisdom, a mystery that has been hidden" (1 Corinthians 2:7; cf. Ephesians 3:9). The gospel is "the message I proclaim about Jesus Christ, in keeping with the revelation of the mystery hidden for long ages past" (Romans 16:25). This "mystery" has been "made known" (Ephesians 1:9; 3:3; 6:19; Colossians 1:26–27). Paul wants everyone to "understand" his insight "into the mystery of Christ" (Ephesians 3:4). See G. Finkenrath, "Secret, Mystery," in *Dictionary of New Testament Theology*, 3:504.

76. See Deuteronomy 13:1–5; Jeremiah 23:25–30; Matthew 7:15; 24:11; 1 Timothy 1:3–4; 2 Peter 2:1; 1 John 4:1; and Revelation 2:2.

77. As Campbell put it, such creeds are devastatingly divisive because they create "colored glasses" that prompt people to be "divided in their general views of Scripture." He continues, "One professor reads the Bible with John Calvin on his nose, another with John Wesley on his nose." Alexander Campbell, "The Bible," *Millennial Harbinger* 3, no. 4 (August 6, 1832; repr. Joplin, MO: College Press, n.d.), 343–344.

78. The theologian Alister McGrath explains a helpful distinction between "creeds" and "confessions." A "confession" (like the Lutheran *Augsburg Confession* or the Reformed *Westminster Confession of Faith*) pertains to a denomination and includes its specific beliefs and emphases; whereas a "creed" (like the Apostles' Creed or the Nicene Creed) pertains to the entire Christian church and offers "a statement of beliefs which every Christian ought to accept and be bound by." See McGrath, *Christian Theology*, 14. For an interesting orientation from the perspective of the Churches of Christ, see Bobby Ross, "No Creed but Christ, No Book but the Bible," *The Christian Chronicle*, December 7, 2018, https://christianchronicle.org/no-creed-but-christ-no-book-but-the-bible/.

79. Many in the Restoration Movement have little interest in church history. Somewhat ironically, many in Restoration Movement churches now exhibit a growing disinterest in the Restoration Movement itself. My plea is that we reconsider "why church history matters," as my teaching colleague puts it. See Robert F. Rea, *Why Church History Matters: An Invitation to Love and Learn from Our Past* (Grand Rapids: IVP Academic, 2014).

80. These four sources roughly correlate with a prominent emphasis in the Wesleyan heritage: the "Quadrilateral." According to McGrath, John Wesley (1703–1791) held that "the living core of the Christian faith was revealed in Scripture, illuminated by tradition, brought to life in personal experience, and confirmed by reason." McGrath, *Christian Theology*, 104.

81. In America, the percentage of atheists and agnostics grew from 11 percent in 2003 to 21 percent in 2018. Barna Research Group, "Tracking the Growth and Decline of Religious Segments: The Rise of Atheism," January 14, 2020, https://www.barna.com/rise-of-atheism/.

82. For a good discussion, see Paul Copan, *Loving Wisdom: A Guide to Philosophy and Christian Faith*, 2nd ed. (Grand Rapids: Eerdmans, 2020), 157–158, Kindle; and Alister McGrath, *Mere Apologetics: How to Help Seekers & Skeptics Find Faith* (Grand Rapids: Baker Books, 2012), 93–125. A valuable book by Stephen Meyer characterizes this as the God "hypothesis." Stephen C. Meyer, *Return of the God Hypothesis: Three Scientific Discoveries That Reveal the Mind Behind the Universe* (New York: HarperCollins, 2021).

83. Copan suggests these pointers from nature produce, at best, a "thin theism" rather than "thick theism." Copan, *Loving Wisdom*, 158–160, Kindle. However,

these pointers "at least present a reasonable basis for believing in the existence of a transcendent being" (ibid., 164).

84. The term "cosmos" is derived from the Greek word *kosmos*, which is used in 151 verses in the Greek New Testament. It is almost always translated as "world" (e.g., John 3:16, "For God so loved the world").

85. Aquinas personally believed the universe was not eternal, because God revealed in Scripture that the universe was created. But he did not think the *beginning* of the universe could be scientifically or philosophically demonstrated. So he constructed his cosmological argument on the assumption that the universe was eternal. See Aquinas's "five ways" to demonstrate God's existence in his *Summa Theologica*, 1, q. 2, a. 3 (available at https://www.newadvent.org/summa/1002.htm).

86. See William Lane Craig, *Reasonable Faith: Christian Truth and Apologetics*, 3rd ed. (Wheaton, IL: Crossway, 2008) and his website at https://www.reasonablefaith.org/.

87. Ibid., 96–97.

88. The issue about the age of the universe is contentious among Christians. One point to stress is that many devoted Christians who strongly advocate the truth and authority of Scripture see no problem with accepting the universe as being over 13 billion years old. Of course, this does not make this view true, but it does suggest we should be extremely careful about forcing others to think a "young earth" view is the only acceptable option for a Christian disciple. Personally, I fear this is the dilemma some young Christians face: accept science and reject the Bible (which purportedly requires a young earth) or accept the Bible and reject science. See John Lennox, *Seven Days That Divide the World: The Beginning According to Genesis and Science* (Grand Rapids: Zondervan, 2011); and Hugh Ross, *The Creator and the Cosmos: How the Latest Scientific Discoveries Reveal God*, 4th ed. (Covina, CA: Reasons to Believe, 2018) along with his website at https://www.reasons.org.

89. Fred Hoyle, *The Intelligent Universe* (New York: Holt, Rinehart, and Winton, 1988), 237.

90. John Lennox, *God's Undertaker: Has Science Buried God?* Updated ed. (Oxford: Lion, 2009), 68; citing John Maddox in *Nature* 340 (1989): 425.

91. Most cosmologists believe they can use the laws of physics to calculate backward to this singularity to when the universe was just 10^{-43} seconds old. Beyond that, the laws of physics break down. Among many resources on this, one helpful

description is Fred Heeren, *Show Me God: What the Message from Space Is Telling Us About God* (Wheeling, IL: Searchlight Publications, 1995), 114–126.

92. Cited in Heeren, *Show Me God*, 141–142.

93. Alexander Vilenkin, "Did the Universe Have a Beginning?" YouTube video, 39:32, http://www.youtube.com/watch?v=NXCQelhKJ7A. Cf. Alexander Vilenkin, "The Beginning of the Universe," *Inference* 1, 4 (October 2015), https://inference-review.com/article/the-beginning-of-the-universe.

94. See Craig, *Reasonable Faith*, 154. Cf. Aquinas, *Summa Theologica*, 1, q. 2, a. 3, https://www.newadvent.org/summa/1002.htm.

95. Vilenkin, "The Beginning of the Universe," https://inference-review.com/article/the-beginning-of-the-universe; emphasis added.

96. Stephen Hawking and Leonard Mlodinow, *The Grand Design* (New York: Random House, 2010), 180; emphasis added.

97. Alex Rosenberg, *The Atheist's Guide to Reality: Enjoying Life Without Illusions* (New York: W.W. Norton, 2011), 38–39; emphasis added. The "multiverse" idea is that there are many different universes, not just one.

98. For more on this, see Richard A. Knopp, "Where Will We Go Without God?" *Christian Standard* 149 (June 2014): 38–40; accessible at https://christian-standard.com/2014/06/where-will-we-go-without-god/.

99. The word "teleology" is derived from the Greek words *telos* ("goal") and *teleios* ("complete; perfect"). These words were widely used by the Greek philosophers. Plato and Aristotle used the terms to communicate the idea of a goal or completeness or perfection. For Aristotle, an acorn's goal (*telos*) is to become an oak tree (its *teleios*). See R. Shippers, "Goal," in *Dictionary of New Testament Theology* (Grand Rapids: Zondervan, 1978), 2:59–60. These words are also frequently used in the Old Testament Septuagint (246 times) and the New Testament (117 times). For example, we are to "become *mature*" (Ephesians 4:13); Paul wants to "present everyone *fully mature* in Christ" (Colossians 1:28); "solid food is for the *mature*" (Hebrews 5:14); and we should "let perseverance *finish* its work" so we "may be *mature* and complete, not lacking anything" (James 1:4). The NIV translates each emphasized word from a form of the word *telos*. The idea is that every Christian disciple has a *goal*—to become *mature*.

100. William Paley, *Natural Theology or Evidences of the Existence and Attributes of the Deity* (1802).

101. Many Christians rightly oppose Darwinism—evolution by *purely natural* processes. While responses to Darwinism are important, I believe Christians make a strategic error by not focusing more on an even stronger case: how life began *in the first place.* Darwinian natural selection cannot explain anything *unless life already exists,* so it's more important to press the point about the *origin* of the universe and the *origin* of life, especially to those who have no belief in any God.

102. Lennox, *God's Undertaker,* 71. On this point, Lennox, an Oxford mathematician, cites Alan Guth, a notable theoretical physicist at MIT.

103. For lists and a discussion, see Hugh Ross, "Astronomical Evidences for a Personal, Transcendent God," in *The Creation Hypothesis,* ed. J. P. Moreland (Downers Grove, IL: InterVarsity Press, 1994), 160–169.

104. Stephen Hawking, *A Brief History of Time* (New York: Bantam Books, 1998), 129–130.

105. See Roger Penrose, *The Emperor's New Mind* (Oxford: Oxford University Press, 1989), 445–446. The Christian astronomer Hugh Ross describes another astounding example: the *number of electrons* in relation to the *number of protons* must be accurate to 1 in 10 to the 37th power or better; otherwise, life would not exist. He graphically illustrates what this number means. He says to (1) cover North America with dimes stacked to the moon; (2) do the same with a million other similar-sized continents; (3) paint one dime red and hide it among all these dimes; (4) ask a blindfolded friend to select one dime. Now the question is: What is the mere chance that the friend would select the red dime? The answer is 1 in 10 to the 37th power! Hugh Ross, *The Creator and the Cosmos,* 4th ed., 196.

106. Cited in Lennox, *God's Undertaker,* 70.

107. Francis Crick, *Life Itself: Its Origin and Nature* (New York: Touchstone, 1982), 88.

108. Francis Collins, *The Language of God* (New York: Free Press, 2006).

109. Stephen Meyer, *Signature in the Cell: DNA and the Evidence for Intelligent Design* (New York: HarperOne, 2009).

110. Robert F. Service, "DNA Could Store All of the World's Data in One Room," March 2, 2017, https://www.sciencemag.org/news/2017/03/dna-could-store-all-worlds-data-one-room.

111. One of the many problems with the idea that there are many different universes is that such a view is complete mathematical speculation that can never be

confirmed by any scientific means. For a brief, relatively simple discussion, see Lee Strobel, *The Case for a Creator* (Grand Rapids: Zondervan, 2004), 138–140.

112. The physicist Freeman Dyson puts it this way, "As we look out into the Universe and identify the many accidents of physics and astronomy that have worked together to our benefit, it almost seems as if the Universe must in some sense have known that we were coming" (cited in Lennox, *God's Undertaker*, 59).

113. See the short video animation produced by Room For Doubt, "Why Do You Still Believe?" at https://vimeo.com/327406232.

114. See Michael F. Bird, *Evangelical Theology: A Biblical and Systematic Introduction* (Grand Rapids: Zondervan, 2013), 126–137.

115. Unfortunately, many people, while they possess this knowledge of God, "suppress the truth by their wickedness" (1:18), which includes "shameful lusts" (1:26) and "every kind of wickedness, evil, greed and depravity" (1:29). We might summarize Romans 1 as follows: (1) everyone has a *sense* of God, but (2) some *suppress* that knowledge and (3) *speculate* an alternative by exchanging "the truth about God for a lie" (1:25). In response, (4) God *severs* them by "[giving] them over" to their shameful lusts (1:24, 26), which results in (5) their *sinful* perversion.

116. Isaiah describes God as "he who lives forever" (Isaiah 57:15b). In John's revelation, God says, "I am the Alpha and the Omega" (Revelation 1:8; cf. 21:6; 22:13).

117. The issue of immortality as applied to *humans* is especially interesting. Plato thought the human soul is *inherently* immortal, and many Christians hold this belief as well. However, Scripture may not so clearly support this view. Paul refers to "God, the blessed and only Ruler, the King of kings and Lord of lords, who *alone is immortal*" (1 Timothy 6:15b–16a). For a discussion, see Tony Gray, "Destroyed For Ever: An Examination of the Debates Concerning Annihilation and Conditional Immortality," *Themelios* 21, 2 (January 1996), https://www.thegospelcoalition.org/themelios/article/destroyed-for-ever-an-examination-of-the-debates-concerning-annihilation-and-conditional-immortality/.

118. God's self-sufficiency is referred to as God's *aseity*, which means "God's all-sufficient greatness as himself without being tied to anything else." Bird, *Evangelical Theology*, 128–129. The very name of God delivered to Moses denotes this idea: "I am who I am" (Exodus 3:14a). As James Packer points out, "This 'name' is not a description of God, but simply a declaration of His self-existence, and His eternal changelessness; a reminder that He has life in Himself, and that what He is

now, He is eternally." J. I. Packer, *Knowing God* (Grand Rapids: InterVarsity Press, 1973), 69.

119. Aristotle discusses the "unmoved mover" in his *Metaphysics*, Book XII (especially 1072a–b and 1073a).

120. The section above on "The Existence of the Universe Points to God" explained that the *Kalam* cosmological argument only says that "whatever *begins to exist* must have a cause." It does not say that "whatever exists must have a cause." It properly excludes a self-sufficient and eternal God who can have no cause or explanation.

121. Paul says that "in the gospel the righteousness of God is revealed" (Romans 1:17). Indeed, this is the essence of Christian faith—that it is possible for us sinful humans to be declared righteous by a righteous God's grace on the basis of our faith in Christ and his death on our behalf (see Romans 3:20–25; 4:5, 24–25; 5:16–18; 2 Corinthians 5:21; Galatians 3:6; Philippians 3:9).

122. The "moral argument" for God's existence is powerful—for some, more potent than cosmological and teleological considerations. To illustrate, Francis Collins, who led the Human Genome Project, was once an atheist, but he claims that C. S. Lewis's use of the moral argument prompted his move from atheism to belief. See Collins, *The Language of God*, 21–22. Collins points to Book One in Lewis's *Mere Christianity*, "Right and Wrong as a Clue to the Meaning of the Universe." For more on the moral argument, see Room For Doubt's lesson on "Christianity: The Ultimate Basis for Justice and Equality," available at https://www.roomfor-doubt.com/syf-curriculum/.

123. In 2 Corinthians, Paul uses the Greek word *pantokrator* to refer to "the Lord *Almighty*," which literally means "all-powerful" (see 2 Corinthians 6:18). Paul is referring to 2 Samuel 7:8 where the Septuagint uses the same word—*pantokrator*. Accordingly, the NIV translates the verse with "Lord Almighty." (The NASB says "Lord of armies," and the ESV says "Lord of hosts"—which follow more closely the meaning of the Hebrew word *saba*.) "Almighty" [*pantokrator*] is also a core description of God in Revelation (e.g., "Holy, holy, holy is the Lord God Almighty, who was, and is, and is to come" (Revelation 4:8). For other uses of *pantokator* in Revelation, see 1:8; 11:17; 15:3; 16:7, 14; 19:6, 15; and 21:22.

124. Copan, *Loving Wisdom*, 117, Kindle.

125. C. S. Lewis, *The Problem of Pain* (New York: Macmillan, 1962), 28; emphasis in original.

126. God knew in advance the evil direction that the children of Israel would take (Deuteronomy 31:16–18). He knew in advance Jerusalem would be rebuilt and Cyrus would be used to accomplish it (Isaiah 44:24–28). He knew in advance Bethlehem would give rise to the "one who will be ruler over Israel, whose origins are from of old, from ancient times" (Micah 5:2b). It is clear that the first-century chief priests and teachers understood the Micah 5 prophecy to be about the birthplace of the Messiah (Matthew 2:3–7; cf. John 7:41–42). Micah 5:2 also implies the pre-existence of the Messiah, which John stressed (John 1:1, 14) and which Jesus affirmed (John 8:57–58).

127. 2 Corinthians 5:21 says God "made him [Christ] who had no sin to be sin for us." But God's imputing sin to Jesus does not mean that Jesus knew (*experienced*) sin in the same sense that humans do.

128. Paul Copan rightly says, "Insisting that 'God must know all things that humans know in the way that they know' is nonsensical—metaphysically absurd." Copan, *Loving Wisdom*, 105, Kindle.

129. There is no question that the concepts of election and predestination are biblical. The NIV uses "elect" or "election" fifteen times (e.g., Matthew 24:22; Romans 9:11; 11:7, 28; 2 Timothy 2:10; Titus 1:1; 1 Peter 1:1; 2 Peter 1:10). The NIV uses "predestine" four times (Romans 8:29, 30; Ephesians 1:5, 11), and the NASB adds Acts 4:28 and 1 Corinthians 2:7 to the list. The big issue is what these terms mean.

130. Classical Calvinism uses the TULIP acrostic: total depravity; unconditional election; limited atonement; irresistible grace, and perseverance of the saints. See McGrath, *Systematic Theology*, 346–348.

131. Jack Cottrell, *God the Ruler* (Joplin, MO: College Press, 1984), 338. Cottrell has several excellent sections that discuss sovereignty and free will (168–179); the views of "Christian Absolute Foreordination" held by Luther, Zwingli, Calvin, and Gordon Clark (71–83); and predestination (331–352).

132. Cottrell claims, "The Bible explicitly relates predestination to God's foreknowledge, and a correct understanding of this relationship is the key to the whole question of election to salvation." Cottrell, *God the Ruler*, 341.

133. God not only knows all truth about what *does* occur, he knows what *has* occurred, what *will* occur, what *could* occur, and what *would* occur (given the array of changing variables). As a result, he knows how and when to influence people and

circumstances to achieve his historical and redemptive purposes. Cf. Acts 17:26–27; Romans 8:28–29.

134. See the chapter on deism in Sire, *The Universe Next Door*, 47–65. Sire characterizes deism as a philosophy that has a transcendent God who created the universe "but then left it to operate on its own." As a result, God is "not immanent." He is "only a transcendent force or energy" (51).

135. See the chapter on Eastern Pantheism Monism in Sire, *The Universe Next Door*, 144–165.

136. As Sire puts it, "God is the cosmos. God is all that exists; nothing exists that is not God" (ibid., 149).

137. Signs, wonders, and miracles appear together in three NIV New Testament verses: Acts 2:22; 2 Corinthians 12:12; and Hebrews 2:4. Signs and wonders appear together in thirty-two NIV Bible verses, with sixteen each in the Old and New Testaments. For Old Testament examples of the use of "signs" and "wonders" together, see Exodus 7:3; Deuteronomy 6:22; Nehemiah 9:10; Jeremiah 32:20–21; and Daniel 4:2–3.

138. This was the view of the skeptic David Hume. See David Hume, "Of Miracles," *An Inquiry Concerning Human Understanding* (Indianapolis: Bobbs-Merrill, 1955), 122. Philosophically, one of Hume's problems with defining a miracle as "a violation of the laws of nature" is that Hume's theory of knowledge cannot even justify the existence of necessary universal laws of nature in the first place. See Richard Purtill, "Defining Miracles," in *In Defense of Miracles*, ed. R. Douglass Geivett and Gary Habermas (Downers Grove, IL: InterVarsity, 1997), 67–68.

139. See Matthew 7:21–23; 24:24; 2 Thessalonians 2:8–9; and Revelation 16:13–14. The Egyptian magicians were able to replicate the first two of the ten plagues—turning water into blood and adding to the glut of frogs (Exodus 7:17–22; 8:5–6). However, Moses's staff becoming a snake suggests that miracles caused by forces other than God cannot ultimately compete with genuine God-miracles. The Egyptian magicians were able to turn their staffs into snakes, but Moses's snake ate those of the Egyptians. See Exodus 7:8–12.

140. Win Corduan insightfully asserts that "any attempt to specify a convenient formula or absolute criterion for identifying a genuine miracle will only lead to disappointment." Winfried Corduan, "Recognizing a Miracle," in *In Defense of Miracles*, ed. R. Douglass Geivett and Gary Habermas (Downers Grove, IL: InterVarsity, 1997), 102.

141. Ibid., 103–106.

142. Creational miracles would also include God's creation of heavenly beings and realities, but here we will consider only creational miracles in the context of physical reality.

143. The Greek verb *synesteken* in Colossians 1:17 means "to bring together something in its proper or appropriate place or relationship." Johannes P. Louw and Eugene Albert Nida, *Greek-English Lexicon of the New Testament: Based on Semantic Domains* (New York: United Bible Societies, 1996), 613. This does not mean God holds things together in some physical sense, as though he were the strong nuclear force that binds protons and neutrons together. See "Strong Nuclear Force" at https://energyeducation.ca/encyclopedia/Strong_nuclear_force.

144. Ronald Nash refers to these as "coincidence-miracles." While he characterizes them as "apologetically inconclusive" (246), he says we can still cautiously construe them to support God's action in the world. See the excellent discussion in Ronald Nash, *Faith and Reason* (Grand Rapids: Academie Books, 1988), 244–247.

145. "'How can we know when a message has not been spoken by the Lord?' If what a prophet proclaims in the name of the Lord does not take place or come true, that is a message the Lord has not spoken" (Deuteronomy 18:21–22a). However, making a true prediction is not sufficient by itself as evidence of a true prophet. God's law to Moses also says if a prophet accurately foretells some sign or wonder but also attempts to entice others to "follow other gods . . . [and] worship them," those prophets must be ignored (see Deuteronomy 13:1–3).

146. The birth of Jesus "took place to fulfill what the Lord has said through the prophet" (Matthew 1:22; cf. Isaiah 7:14). Jesus began his ministry by reading Isaiah 61:1–2 and saying, "Today this scripture is fulfilled in your hearing" (Luke 4:21). Jesus said to the two confused disciples who were disheartened by Jesus' crucifixion and who had not yet recognized his resurrected body, "Everything must be fulfilled that is written about me in the Law of Moses, the Prophets and the Psalms" (Luke 24:44b).

147. Peter interpreted what happened to Judas as a predictive miracle: "The Scripture had to be fulfilled in which the Holy Spirit spoke long ago through David" (Acts 1:16a; cf. Acts 1:18–20; Psalm 69:25; 109:8). The miraculous signs on the day of Pentecost fulfilled "what was spoken by the prophet Joel" (Acts 2:16). And the crucifixion and resurrection of Jesus were prominent predictive miracles preached on Pentecost (Acts 2:30–35). Peter later described what happened to Jesus

as "how God fulfilled what he had foretold through all the prophets" (Acts 3:18; cf. 13:27, 33). Paul, in his defense of his conversion to Christ, explained to King Agrippa he was "saying nothing beyond what the prophets and Moses said would happen—that the Messiah would suffer and, as the first to rise from the dead, would bring the message of light to his own people and to the Gentiles" (Acts 26:22b–23).

148. For example, an airplane's flight does not violate the law of gravity; it uses principles of aerodynamics to suspend what gravity would otherwise do. Even the case of God raising Jesus from the dead can be construed as God suspending some natural processes through (a) other as yet unknown natural processes; (b) through God's more direct supernatural action in the physical world; (c) or both. One important point is that miracles, even if they are supernatural actions by God that intervene in natural processes, do not violate the principle of cause and effect. They merely acknowledge that God is a legitimate causal agent within time and space.

149. Jesus' healings include cleansing a leper (Matthew 8:2–3), healing a withered hand (Matthew 12:9–13), raising a widow's son (Luke 7:11–15), healing a blind man (Mark 8:22–25; John 9:1–7), restoring a cut-off ear (Luke 22:49–51), casting out demons (Matthew 8:28–32; 12:22), and many others. His miracles over nature turned water into wine (John 2:1–11), instantly stilled a storm (Matthew 8:23–27), and fed thousands (Matthew 14:15–21).

150. See Matthew 9:1–7; Mark 2:1–12; and Luke 5:17–26.

151. For an overview of sources on the resurrection, see Richard A. Knopp, "Resurrection Resources," *Christian Standard* (April 3, 2015), https://christianstandard.com/2015/04/resurrection-resources/. For a more current collection of relevant essays, see W. David Beck and Michael Licona, ed., *Raised on the Third Day: Defending the Historicity of the Resurrection of Jesus* (Bellingham, WA: Lexham Press, 2020).

152. These include post-mortem appearances to Mary Magdalene (John 20:11–18) and the women (Matthew 28:8–10); to Peter (Luke 24:34; 1 Corinthians 15:5); to the two on the way to Emmaus (Luke 24:13–32); to the Twelve, minus Thomas and Judas (Luke 24:36–48; John 20:19–22); to the Twelve, with Thomas and minus Judas (John 20:24–29); to those at the Sea of Galilee (John 21); to more than five hundred at once (1 Corinthians 15:6); to James, the brother of Jesus who once did not believe in Jesus as Messiah (John 7:3–5; Acts 15:12–13; 1 Corinthians 15:7; Galatians 1:19; 2:9); to those at Jesus' ascension (Acts 1:9–11); and to Saul (Acts 9:1–9).

153. Various ancient religions characterized gods or goddesses as disappearing, as being assumed into some netherworld, or as symbolizing seasonal crops; but they did not present any precedent for an individual literally returning to *this* world of human experience after physical death. See Craig, *Reasonable Faith*, 390–391.

154. Ibid., 392–393.

155. For example, the disciples' fear is presented in Matthew 26:56, 69–75; Mark 14:50; and John 20:19.

156. See Zach Breitenbach, "A New Argument That Collective Hallucinations Do Not Adequately Account for the Group Appearances of Jesus in the Gospels," *Journal of the Evangelical Society* 62 (June 2019), 341–351.

157. The Egyptians "will know that I am the Lord" (Exodus 7:5a); Pharaoh "may know that there is no one like the Lord our God" (Exodus 8:10b; cf. 9:14, 29); and the children and grandchildren of the Israelites "may know that I am the Lord" (Exodus 10:2b). Later, Solomon said that God's mighty hand responding to prayers will even help the foreigners "know that this house [temple] I have built bears your Name" (1 Kings 8:43). And Elijah prayed for, and received, God's miracle at Mount Carmel "so these people will know that you, Lord, are God" (1 Kings 18:37b).

158. The healing of the paralytic emphasizes the same point. Jesus physically healed the man because, "I *want you to know* that the Son of Man has authority on earth to forgive sins" (Mark 2:10a).

159. John informs us that Jesus performed "many other signs" that are "not recorded in this book" (John 20:30).

160. In addition, Paul uses his miracle-working to argue that he is "not in the least inferior to the 'super-apostles,'" because he "persevered in demonstrating . . . the marks of a true apostle, including signs, wonders and miracles" (2 Corinthians 12:11b–12). And the Hebrew writer argues that the salvation message, which was "first announced by the Lord, was confirmed to us by those who heard him. God also testified to it by signs, wonders and various miracles" (Hebrews 2:3b–4a).

161. That is what happened in the early church. See Acts 4:29–30; 9:26–28; and 14:3.

162. The instance of the burning bush is referred to by Jesus (Mark 12:26; Luke 20:37) and by Stephen (Acts 7:30).

163. While there are eight references to the Urim and Thummim in the Old Testament, we know little about them. They were apparently two or more small objects worn on the breastplate of the high priest that were used to signify God's response to specific yes-no questions. They may have been light and dark pebbles that were cast like lots. Though it appears to be a form of divination, which the law otherwise prohibited (Leviticus 19:26), it was sanctioned by God. See Allen C. Myers, "Urim and Thummim," in *The Eerdmans Bible Dictionary* (Grand Rapids: Eerdmans, 1987), 1032.

164. Notable examples include Abimelek (Genesis 20:3, 6), Jacob (Genesis 31:10–13), Joseph (Genesis 37:5–7), Pharaoh (Genesis 41:15–24), King Nebuchadnezzar of Babylon (Daniel 2:1–3), Daniel (Daniel 2:19), Joseph the husband of Mary (Matthew 1:20; 2:13, 19), and Peter (Acts 10:9–20).

165. The NIV uses the word "angel" 108 times in the Old Testament and 182 times in the New Testament. Both the Hebrew word *mal'āk* and the Greek word *angelos* mean "messenger." Those to whom God's message came by angels included Hagar (Genesis 16:7–12), Lot (Genesis 19:1, 15), Abraham (Genesis 22:11–12), Zechariah (Zechariah 1:9–21), the shepherds at Jesus' birth (Luke 2:8–15), Philip (Acts 8:26), Cornelius (Acts 10:3–6), Paul (Acts 27:22–24), and John (Revelation 1:1).

166. The phrase "word(s) of God" is used in the NIV five times in the Old Testament and forty times in the New Testament, including eleven times in the book of Acts where preaching is central. For example, the "word of God" was given to Saul through Samuel (1 Samuel 9:27), to Shemaiah the man of God (1 Kings 12:22), and to John the son of Zechariah (Luke 3:2). The people crowded Jesus, "listening to the word of God" (Luke 5:1b). The early Christian disciples "spoke the word of God boldly" (Acts 4:31) and it spread (Acts 6:7) and was accepted by the Samaritans (Acts 8:14) and the Gentiles (Acts 11:1).

167. The NIV properly translates 1 Corinthians 1:21 to say, "God was pleased through the foolishness *of what* was preached to save those who believe." The NASB is even clearer by referring to "the foolishness *of the message* preached" (emphases added). Somewhat misleadingly, the KJV talks about "the foolishness *of preaching*" as though the focus is on the style of speaking. Even so, Paul later emphasizes both his "message" and his "preaching" "were not with wise and persuasive words, but with a demonstration of the Spirit's power," so that their faith "might not rest on human wisdom, but on God's power" (1 Corinthians 2:4–5).

168. The word "written" appears 128 times in the Old Testament and 119 times in the New Testament (NIV). And the word "Scripture(s)" appears 53 times in the NIV New Testament. Almost all of these instances specifically undergird the *authority* and the *veracity* of the message. "It is written" (e.g., Matthew 4:4–10; 21:13; 26:24, 31; Mark 14:27; Luke 3:4; John 6:31, 45). The Scriptures "must be fulfilled" (e.g., Mark 14:49; cf. Matthew 26:54; John 17:12; 19:24, 28, 36; 20:9; Acts 1:20; 7:42; 13:29).

169. At least twenty-one times in the Gospels (NIV), "it is written" is specifically attributed to Jesus who uses it as an authority for his position. In Matthew, he used it in each reply to Satan's three temptations (Matthew 4:4, 6, 10). Interestingly in Luke, it is *Satan* who said, "It is written" in the third temptation, as though that would somehow prompt Jesus to yield (see Luke 4:10). Here, Jesus replied, "It is said" (Luke 4:12), which appeals to what is written in Deuteronomy 6:16. In another noteworthy verse, Jesus appealed to Scripture twice: "It is written: 'And he was numbered with the transgressors'; and I tell you that this must be fulfilled in me. Yes, what is written about me is reaching its fulfillment" (Luke 22:37).

170. The Greek word translated as "God-breathed" (NIV) or as "inspired by God" (NASB) is *theopneustos*. It is derived from the Greek words *theos* (God) and *pneuma* (breath or spirit).

171. Peter includes Paul's writings as authoritative "Scripture" when he says, "[Paul's] letters contain some things that are hard to understand, which ignorant and unstable people distort, *as they do the other Scriptures*, to their own destruction" (2 Peter 3:16b).

172. Explaining the precise relationship between God's "inspiration" and what (and how) humans contribute to Scripture is challenging. Minimally, however, we should not think the exact vocabulary and grammar of Scripture are simply "recitations" from God (like Muslims believe that the Qur'an consists of direct "recitations" from Allah). Scripture is simultaneously both divine and human. Remember that Jesus was also simultaneously divine and human. For a brief discussion of various theories of inspiration and some helpful qualifications, see Bird, *Evangelical Theology*, 638–642.

173. As Paul reflects on some of the Old Testament narrative, he says, "These things happened to them as examples and were written down as warnings for us" (1 Corinthians 10:11a).

174. Defending the authority and reliability of Scripture is critically important but beyond the purposes of this book. For helpful resources, see Craig Blomberg, *Can We Still Believe the Bible? An Evangelical Engagement with Contemporary Questions* (Grand Rapids: Brazos Press, 2014); and Steven Cowen and Terry Wilder, ed. *In Defense of the Bible: A Comprehensive Apologetic for the Authority of Scripture* (Nashville: B&H Academic, 2013).

175. The preeminence of the *person* of Jesus especially appears in John 5. In an encounter with Jewish leaders, Jesus said, "You study the Scriptures diligently because you think that in them you have eternal life. These are the very Scriptures that testify about me, yet you refuse to come to me to have life" (John 5:39–40). In a sense, they knew a lot about a *book*, but they missed the *person* the book was about!

176. The Greek word *logos* is employed 331 times in the New Testament with a wide range of meanings. The meanings refer to a word(s), an utterance, a report, a teaching, reason, etc. See Brown, "Word," in *Dictionary of New Testament Theology*, 3:1106. Revelation says Jesus' "name is the Word of God" (Revelation 19:13b).

177. The term *logos* had a rich philosophical heritage before the time of Jesus. Heraclitus (ca. 500 BC), who thought that everything is in constant flux, also believed the *logos* brought order or stability to the cosmos. The Stoics thought the *logos* structures matter according to its plan. The apostle John may well be incorporating such ideas, but the *logos* for John is not some philosophical principle or cosmic function. The *logos* is God who *came to us* in the *person* of Jesus. For some philosophical background, see John Frame, *A History of Western Philosophy and Theology* (Phillipsburg, NJ: P&R Publishing, 2015), 54–56, 77–78.

178. This is reminiscent of Jesus' conversation with Philip when Philip said, "Lord, show us the Father and that will be enough for us"—to which Jesus replied, "Don't you know me, Philip, even after I have been among you such a long time? Anyone who has seen me has seen the Father. How can you say, 'Show us the Father'?" (John 14:8–9).

179. The Greek word translated as "made him known" (John 1:18) is from *exegeomai*, from which we get the English word "exegesis." The Greek word means to offer an explanation or an interpretation. In a sense, Jesus, as the *logos*, is the *exegesis* of God. The Greek word is "a technical term in Judaism for making known interpretations of the law . . . *and* a term in Greek religion for making known divine truths. The incarnate Word brings from the heart of God a revelation both for Jew

and for Greek." A. C. Thiselton, "Explain," in *Dictionary of New Testament Theology*, 1:575.

180. Louw and Nida, *Greek-English Lexicon of the New Testament: Based on Semantic Domains* (New York: United Bible Societies, 1996), 591.

181. Jesus' disciples wanted to know if the man was born blind because of his sin or his parents' sin (John 9:2). The Pharisees accused Jesus of not being from God because he violated the Sabbath, and they denounced both Jesus and the healed man for being sinners (John 9:13–16, 24, 34).

182. Paul claims this new life is a consequence of our baptism. We were "buried with him [Christ Jesus] through baptism into death in order that, just as Christ was raised from the dead through the glory of the Father, we too may live a *new life*" (Romans 6:4).

183. Other notable NIV passages about being "in Christ" include the following (with emphasis given): God is thanked "because of his grace given you *in Christ* Jesus" (1 Corinthians 1:4). "For no matter how many promises God has made, they are 'Yes' *in Christ*" (2 Corinthians 1:20a). "So *in Christ* Jesus you are all children of God through faith" (Galatians 3:26). God "has blessed us in the heavenly realms with every spiritual blessing *in Christ*" (Ephesians 1:3). God's great love "made us alive with Christ . . . and God raised us up with Christ and seated us with him in the heavenly realms *in Christ* Jesus" (Ephesians 2:5a–6). "The dead *in Christ* will rise first" (1 Thessalonians 4:16).

184. Sometimes, the presence of the Holy Spirit produced miraculous signs (e.g., Acts 4:29–31; 10:44–47; cf. 11:15–17; 13:9–11; 19:6) or special visible spiritual gifts (1 Corinthians 12:1–11; 14:1–19). But the "gift of the Holy Spirit" referred to here is a miraculous *indwelling presence*.

185. The Greek word for "sealed" is a past-tense verb (from *sphragizō*). The same word is used to say the tomb of Jesus was made secure by the Roman guard and had a "seal" placed on the stone in front of it (see Matthew 27:66).

186. The Greek word is the noun *arrabōn*, which the NIV translates as a "deposit guaranteeing." The NASB translates it as "first installment." *Arrabōn* is an ancient business term that involves making a deposit on a debt or putting "earnest money" down for a legal contract. See Johannes Behm, *"Arrabōn,"* in *Theological Dictionary of the New Testament*, ed. Gerhard Kittel, Geoffrey W. Bromiley, and Gerhard Friedrich (Grand Rapids: Eerdmans, 1964–), 1:475. The word is used

only three times in the New Testament, and each time it refers to the Holy Spirit (Ephesians 1:14; 2 Corinthians 1:22; 5:5).

187. "Abba" is an Aramaic word that means "Father," and it denotes warm intimacy. It was never used in ancient Jewish devotional literature to address God because of the perceived great gap between God and humans. O. Hofius, "Father," in *The New International Dictionary of New Testament Theology*, 1:614. The great gap between God and humans is also stressed in Islam. The notions of God coming in flesh or God's indwelling us with his Spirit are impossible according to the Qur'an. See Winfried Corduan, "A View from the Middle East," in James Sire, *The Universe Next Door*, 249–250.

188. Packer, *Knowing God*, 18.

ETERNAL SECURITY

WALKING IN
FAITHFULNESS

BOBBY HARRINGTON

CONTENTS

General Editor's Note 691

CHAPTER 1: Are We Automatically Eternally Secure or
Must We Have Faithful Faith? 693

CHAPTER 2: Can a Christian Forfeit Their Salvation? 699

CHAPTER 3: Does Hebrews Teach the Reality of Apostasy? 707

CHAPTER 4: How Does a Person Forfeit Their Salvation? 713

CHAPTER 5: How Can I Be Forgiven When I Sin Again
and Again? 723

Conclusion 727

Appendix: Common but Misleading Affirmations About
Our Salvation 729

Notes 731

GENERAL EDITOR'S NOTE

Just how secure is our salvation as Christians? The topic of our secure status as God's children *ought* to give us reassurance. Yet the topic can cause a lot of anxiety. True, some Scriptures seem to indicate people can never lose their salvation. For example, Jesus promised in John 10:28, "I give them eternal life, and they shall never perish; no one will snatch them out of my hand." Yet some Scriptures also strongly indicate we *can* forfeit our salvation. According to 1 Timothy 4:1, "In later times some will abandon the faith." Hebrews promises "a fearful expectation of judgment and of raging fire" for those who "deliberately keep on sinning after we have received the knowledge of the truth" (Hebrews 10:26–27). So which is it?

There is no shortage of Bible teachers who go to great lengths to reassure Christians that once they are saved, it is literally impossible for them to lose their salvation. Yet this optimism seems to go far beyond what the Bible actually teaches. And such optimism contradicts our experiences of having people who once loved Jesus eventually leave him behind because they found him hard to follow or difficult to believe. Ironically, such entrenched optimism about our eternal security can actually backfire, as Christians aware of their own weaknesses find themselves second-guessing whether they are really part of the group whose salvation God has made bulletproof.

Yet there is a way of teaching this topic without succumbing to an excessive optimism on the one hand or a shoulder shrug on the other. It is by trying to set aside predetermined theological systems and walking step-by-step through what the New Testament teaches. As you will discover in *Eternal Security: Walking in Faithfulness*, the New Testament radiates a shining hopefulness for the person who trusts and follows Jesus, even as it remains realistic about the folly of leaving Jesus behind.

Many people know of Bobby Harrington as a disciple making author and as CEO of Renew.org and Discipleship.org. As co-general editor with Bobby

Harrington on this *Real Life Theology* series, I have gotten a front-row seat to see Bobby as a passionate and precise theologian. In *Eternal Security: Walking in Faithfulness*, Bobby combines his careful skills as a theologian with the practical concerns of a pastor. This book steers you through theological impasses and spiritual crises alike. Internalizing this book will help you fit together the theological puzzle pieces of your eternal security with your human responsibility. Even more importantly, the book will practically guide you into a more faithful life of trusting and following Jesus.

For King Jesus,
Daniel McCoy
Co-General Editor, *Real Life Theology* Series

1

ARE WE AUTOMATICALLY ETERNALLY SECURE OR MUST WE HAVE FAITHFUL FAITH?

One of Jesus' central teachings is God forgives our sins. In conversion, among the greatest joys is the realization that through the gospel, *all* of our sins are forgiven. It is a time of great happiness. Yet what happens when someone no longer possesses a repentant faith—when they live in a deliberately sinful lifestyle or turn their back on Jesus and the gospel? What kind of security before God does this person possess?

We want to explore this question: What does the Word of God teach about the security of a believer?

Ever since the Protestant Reformation in the 1500s, two major views about the security of a believer have existed among Protestant Christians. Yes, other views are out there, but two views dominate the history of Protestant and evangelical theology.

On the one hand, some Christians believe that once a person is truly saved, God makes them eternally secure: "once saved, always saved." God makes that person's security evident by giving them a transformed life by his power alone, which results in faithfulness to the end of their life.[1]

On the other hand, some Christians believe once a person is truly saved, God empowers that person to live a transformed life, but that person can still possibly resist the Holy Spirit, turn away from God, and become lost.[2] The Christian teachers in this second camp do not believe a person is saved one day and lost the next, contrary to what their detractors often say, but that over time a genuine Christian can reach the point where they turn away from Christ, abandon their true faith, and forfeit salvation. They become non-believers.

Good Christian leaders are on each side of these two positions, and both sides focus upon living a faithful life as emphasized in the Bible. Both groups also question the salvation of those without a transformed life—people who don't grow in their faith and who don't respond to temptation with sincere struggle. One side believes such people were never truly saved in the first place, whereas the other side believes they might have once been genuine believers who have now abandoned the faith.

The two positions regarding this in-house theological debate are called Calvinism and Arminianism. Here is a summary statement on the two positions:

- *Calvinists* believe the following: once saved, always saved, and *God makes sure* the saved persevere with faithful faith.
- *Arminians* believe the following: once saved, always saved, as long as the person *responds to God and chooses* to persevere with faithful faith.

They look similar, but there is a key difference: Calvinists believe *God alone* will ensure that once a person is saved, they will always have an active, true faith. Contrarily, Arminians believe that once a person is saved, they *must choose an active faith* in response to God and his Spirit. Arminians hold a person can resist God and give up on a true faith, while Calvinists believe God will not allow a Christian to make that choice.

Even though most Christians do not think of themselves as systematic Calvinists or systematic Arminians, Christian theologians tend to think, lead, and teach with one of the frameworks. Consequently, knowing the theological framework that influences our professors, teachers, and preachers is important. Here is a brief summary of the two positions:

CALVINISM AND ARMINIANISM

Calvinism	Arminianism
Founder: John Calvin (1509–1564)	**Founder:** Jacobus Arminius (1560–1609)
Denominations: Presbyterians, some Baptists, others	**Denominations:** Methodists, Christian Church, others
Total Depravity: People are trapped in sin and cannot choose God. God's will alone determines salvation (monergism).	**Total Depravity:** People are trapped in sin and need the Spirit's guidance to choose God by faith. Humans respond to God in salvation (synergism).
Unconditional Election: Salvation is given to those God alone picks/elects, with no basis in a human response. *God alone regenerates and God alone causes people to have faith.*	**Conditional Election:** Salvation is given to those who hear and willingly respond to the gospel and the Holy Spirit *by faith.*
Limited Atonement: Jesus died only for the sins of the elect (those *chosen for salvation by God*).	**Unlimited Atonement:** Jesus atoned for the sins of everyone if they will respond to the gospel and the Spirit *by faith.*
Irresistible Grace: God's calling and election to salvation of certain individuals is irresistible; if chosen, they cannot say no.	**Resistible Grace:** God by the Holy Spirit woos people, but God has given people the ability to resist and reject his Spirit or *respond by faith.*
Perseverance by God: People *elected by God* cannot be *separated from God.*	**Perseverance by Faith:** People cannot be snatched away from God, but they can develop hard hearts and turn from him and *give up their faith.*

Again, the average church member might not understand or spend time advocating for one of these two systems. Yet these two belief systems represent the two dominant ways of looking at salvation among Bible-following Christians. Thus, the majority of churches and Christian leaders will find themselves on a spectrum between these two—some strongly leaning one way, others strongly leading the other way, some finding themselves somewhere in the middle.

Yet let's not neglect a crucial area of agreement between both sides. Regardless of which of the two theological understandings are adopted, both of these two camps believe those who claim to be Christians but participate in lifestyles of disobedience are in eternal peril. This peril is the most pressing and practical biblical issue when it comes to the question of lost salvation, and it was never meant to be a matter of debate by Bible-believing Christians of either theological camp. And that concern raises grave concerns about the following types of behaviors (although the list is not exhaustive) by people who claim to be Christians:

- A person stops attending church altogether
- A person actively engages in a sexually immoral relationship
- A person enters an ongoing lifestyle of drunkenness or drugs
- A person turns to another religion or just gives up on Jesus
- A person turns from Jesus to a lifestyle focused on themselves—or to another faith or no faith at all

There is grave spiritual danger in lifestyles of disobedience because it's living in

THERE IS GRAVE SPIRITUAL DANGER IN LIFESTYLES OF DISOBEDIENCE.

rebellion to the teachings of Jesus. Calvinists and Arminians frame the same danger in two ways. They are either on a path demonstrating God never truly saved them in the first place (Calvinism), or they are on a path leading to apostasy (Arminian view).

Stated differently, those who hold both positions believe that saving faith is an allegiant, obedient, and faithful faith (Romans 1:5). Yes, we all stumble and fall (James 3:2). On a daily basis we confess our sins and ask for forgiveness through Jesus (1 John 1:8–9). But as we stumble and fall, our relationship with Jesus remains. This is what walking in God's light means (1 John 1:5–2:2). But the dominant truth about faithful Christians is that we *trust and follow Jesus as a lifestyle*.

A THIRD WAY: DANGEROUS FALSE TEACHING

AT THE SAME TIME, a relatively new view in the history of theology has arisen that is both biblically false and spiritually harmful. This view of faith isn't actually based on the Word of God. Thus, people who hold to historic Calvinism and Arminianism explicitly reject this teaching.

It is the view that:

- Once saved, always saved, no matter how you live.

This recent belief in mainstream Christian theology (especially since the early 1960s) has been made popular by certain preachers, especially those who want to comfort those with loved ones who no longer follow Jesus. Though popular, the belief is a false and dangerous one.

Think about what claiming a saving relationship with Jesus yet walking in a disobedient lifestyle entails. The apostle John gives us a succinct statement about these people's status with God:

> If we claim to have fellowship with him and yet walk in the darkness, we lie and do not live out the truth. (1 John 1:6)

The Bible teaches that in the absence of a transformed life, the claim to be a Christian is false. In Matthew 7:21–23, Jesus states the danger plainly.

> Not everyone who says to me, "Lord, Lord," will enter the kingdom of heaven, but only the one who does the will of my Father who is in heaven. Many will say to me on that day, "Lord, Lord, did we not prophesy in your name, and in your name drive out demons, and in your name perform many miracles?" Then I will tell them plainly, "I never knew you. Away from me, you evildoers!"

Note this important implication from the words of Jesus: some influential people appear to be saved by their claims about Jesus, but they are not.

Not only does the popular false belief of "once saved, always saved, no matter how you live" give false comfort, but it calls into question the moral influence of Christianity as a whole and harms the cause of Jesus by encouraging shallow faith and hypocrisy. The people Jesus described thought they had a saving relationship with him, but they did not. Even though they were religious and used his name, they did not *do the will* of God, and Jesus did not have a *genuine relationship* with them.

The root problem of this false belief is an emphasis on religion and grace not based on the Word of God. Salvation, as false teachers often present it, is granted totally by grace. No meaningful human response is required, or the human part of faith is reduced to just mental assent or a shallow trust—a simple affirmation that Jesus died on the cross for our sins. And that, we are told, is all one needs.

The problem is that this kind of faith *does not* include faithfulness, loyalty, allegiance, or obedience. But even the demons have that kind of faith as James 2:19 tells us:

You believe that there is one God. Good! Even the demons believe that—and shudder.

Numerous passages in Scripture, such as the following, contradict this false conception of faith:

If you keep my commands, you will remain in my love, just as I have kept my Father's commands and remain in his love. (John 15:10)

We know that we have come to know him if we keep his commands. Whoever says, "I know him," but does not do what he commands is a liar, and the truth is not in that person. (1 John 2:3–4)

Then he called the crowd to him along with his disciples and said: "Whoever wants to be my disciple must deny themselves and take up their cross and follow me." (Mark 8:34)

For of this you can be sure: No immoral, impure or greedy person—such a person is an idolater—has any inheritance in the kingdom of Christ and of God. (Ephesians 5:5)

As these passages and others show us, true faith is faithful and obedient to Jesus. Again, to have saving faith is both to *trust and follow* Jesus.

> **TO HAVE SAVING FAITH IS BOTH TO *TRUST AND FOLLOW* JESUS.**

False teachers will claim that faith is saving faith when it is not characterized by faithfulness and obedience, which distorts God's Word. Jude warns us about such teachers: "They are ungodly people, who pervert the grace of our God into a license for immorality and deny Jesus Christ our only Sovereign and Lord" (Jude 1:4). Grace was never meant to be received as a blank check for sin.

Such teaching is also a major distortion of the biblical teaching on grace. What the Bible actually teaches is that we are saved "by grace . . . through faith" (Ephesians 2:8). The biblical formula has two parts: *God's grace* and the *human response of faith*. A healthy understanding of both grace and faith is necessary to comprehend what the Bible actually teaches. Grace in the New Testament comes with the expectation of a certain kind of faith.[3] One of those expectations is that we will *persevere* in our faith, a subject to which we turn next.

2

CAN A CHRISTIAN FORFEIT THEIR SALVATION?

The question of eternal security can be an inflammatory one for many Bible believers. Some were raised by parents or pastors who taught unqualified security as an essential doctrine. "Never go to a church," they said, "where they do not teach eternal security." By that statement they meant, "Don't ever go to a church that teaches a Christian can turn their back on Christ."

There are three problems with that sentiment.

First, under that teaching, far too many wrongly assume the posture of "once saved, always saved, *no matter how you live*." As we have seen, in the history of Christianity, this is a recent teaching that is biblically false and spiritually harmful. By this doctrine, many have felt justified in being unfaithful to Jesus' commands. They make the conscious or unconscious decision that faithfulness to inconvenient teachings in the Word of God is an optional part of saving faith.

Second, the view that a completely unfaithful person is still a saved person puts oneself outside the mainstream of both classic Calvinism and Arminianism. When it comes to having a faithful faith, many do not realize, in the words of John Wesley, there is a "hair's breadth"[4] of difference between those who hold a classic Calvinist view of eternal security and the classic Arminian view of apostasy. Here is what I mean:

- *Classic Calvinists* believe we should take the warnings of apostasy seriously and by these warnings God helps us to stay faithful.
- *Classic Arminians* believe we should take the warnings of apostasy seriously and by these warnings God exhorts us to choose to stay faithful.

Notice the difference: one camp sees the warning passages as *only hypothetical warnings* that are part of God's sovereign guidance ensuring that people remain faithful, while the other camp believes *the warnings are real* and part of how people learn to stay faithful. At this important level, John Wesley was right: there is only a "hair's breadth" of difference in practical terms in how these teachings are lived out in a local church. Here is what I mean: we can hold to different theological systems yet still agree that we need to help each other to live faithfully. Both Calvinists and Arminians believe God uses the warnings in Scripture and the exhortations of God's people to help us stay faithful.

Third, most people who warn against Arminian beliefs do not actually understand them. They only know false representations of the view. They will say, for example, that non-Calvinists believe one is saved one day and lost the next. Or they will be warned to be careful of Arminians because they are really just "semi-pelagians." (Pelagianism was an ancient heresy that downplayed the sinful nature to such an extent that it became theoretically possible for people to achieve perfection without God's intervention.)

Strangely, few of the people who object to Arminian beliefs have actually read the one-page Arminian statement of faith. When people actually read it, the vast majority pause. To their surprise, a surprising number find themselves acknowledging that it describes something similar to what they actually believe. The statement is short; read it for yourself below.

THE ARMINIAN CREED, 1610[5]

Article 1 (Conditional Election)

That God, by an eternal and unchangeable purpose in Jesus Christ his Son before the foundation of the world, has determined that out of the fallen, sinful race of men, to save in Christ, for Christ's sake, and through Christ, those who through the grace of the Holy Spirit shall believe on this his son Jesus, and shall persevere in this faith and obedience of faith, through this grace, even to the end; and, on the other hand, to leave the incorrigible and unbelieving in sin and under wrath and to condemn them as alienated from Christ, according to the word of the Gospel in John 3:36: "He that believes on the Son has everlasting life: and he that does not believe the Son shall not see life; but the wrath of God abides on him," and according to other passages of Scripture also.

Article 2 (Unlimited Atonement)

That, accordingly, Jesus Christ the Savior of the world, died for all men and for every man, so that he has obtained for them all, by his death on the cross, redemption and the forgiveness of sins; yet that no one actually enjoys this forgiveness of sins except the believer, according to the word of the Gospel of John 3:16, "For God so loved the world, that he gave his only begotten Son, that whosoever believes in him should not perish, but have everlasting life." And in the First Epistle of John 2:2: "And he is the propitiation for our sins: and not for ours only, but also for the sins of the whole world."

Article 3 (Total Depravity)

That man does not possess saving grace of himself, nor of the energy of his free will, inasmuch as in his state of apostasy and sin he can of and by himself neither think, will, nor do anything that is truly good (such as saving Faith eminently is); but that it is necessary that he be born again of God in Christ, through his Holy Spirit, and renewed in understanding, inclination, and will, and all his faculties, in order that he may rightly understand, think, will, and effect what is truly good, according to the Word of Christ, John 15:5, "Without me you can do nothing."

Article 4 (Resistible Grace)

That this grace of God is the beginning, continuance, and accomplishment of all good, even to the extent that the regenerate man himself, without prevenient or assisting, awakening, following and cooperative grace, can neither think, will, nor do good, nor withstand any temptations to evil; so that all good deeds or movements that can be conceived must be ascribed to the grace of God in Christ. But with respect to the mode of the operation of this grace, it is not irresistible, since it is written concerning many, that they have resisted the Holy Spirit (Acts 7, and elsewhere in many places).

Article 5 (Perseverance)

That those who are incorporated into Christ by true faith, and have thereby become partakers of his life-giving Spirit, as a result have full power to strive against Satan, sin, the world, and their own flesh, and to win the victory; it being well understood that it is ever through the assisting grace of the Holy Spirit; and that Jesus Christ assists them through his Spirit in all temptations, extends to them his hand, and if only they are ready for the conflict, desire his help, and are not inactive, keeps them from falling, so that they, by no deceit or power of Satan, can be misled nor plucked out of Christ's hands, according to the Word of Christ, John 10:28: "Neither shall any man pluck them out of my hand." But whether they are capable, through negligence, of forsaking again the first beginning of their life in Christ, of again returning to this present evil world, of turning away from the holy doctrine which was delivered them, of losing a good conscience, of neglecting grace, that must be more particularly determined out of the Holy Scripture, before we ourselves can teach it with the full confidence of our mind.

What do you think? Many people who read and reflect on it say this creed is in step with a natural reading of the Bible.

MY VIEW ON APOSTASY

I AM A PART of church fellowships that include both Calvinists and Arminians—because where one lands on the Calvinism-Arminian debate does not affect a person's salvation and pursuit of a faithful faith. At the same time, most of the leaders in the Renew.org Network, but not all, agree that the Word of God, properly understood, affirms Arminian beliefs. Specifically, we believe a true Christian can leave their salvation through apostasy. New Testament scholar I. Howard Marshall states what I believe to be true when he writes, "If people wish to attain to final salvation, they must persevere in faith."[6] Perseverance and human choice are not exclusive to each other.

PERSEVERANCE AND HUMAN CHOICE ARE NOT EXCLUSIVE TO EACH OTHER.

Let me share a key difference when it comes to the Calvinist and Arminian views on apostasy. It begins with how we understand certain watershed passages, such as Romans 9. If a person believes that Romans 9 teaches God predetermines which individuals go to hell and which go to heaven—apart from any human response of faith—they are a Calvinist. Salvation to a Calvinist has no dependence on any human response; salvation is totally based on God's mystical choice of individuals predetermined to heaven or hell before the creation of the world. Thus, if God predetermines you are saved, then surely God also predetermines you can never lose that salvation.

Consequently, those who lean toward Calvinism will feel a great need to re-explain parts of the Bible, such as the warning passages in Hebrews (see Chapter 3). On the face of it, the warning passages in Hebrews clearly support an Arminian point of view. So Calvinist scholars, such as Thomas Schriener, R. C. Sproul, and Michael Horton, explain these passages away.[7] But their interpretations seem strained to me.

There are also other reasons I cannot embrace the Calvinist approach to these Scriptures (and others). First, I do not want to explain away any set of passages in the Bible under the pressure of a systematic theology that predetermines, in advance, how I must understand them. This is the case whether it be a Calvinist system or any other system. I want Scripture to be my primary and ultimate guide that forms and reforms my theology. Yes, that means I might end up with some loose ends when it comes to nonessential issues, but at the same time, Jesus and his gospel do not require certainty about every detail in the Christian faith.

Second, I *do not* believe the Calvinist interpretation of foundational passages such as Romans 9 or Ephesians 1 is the most accurate understanding. Let me recommend some easy-to-access resources for a better way to understand these passages that form the basis of a Calvinist view of salvation. These resources show what I believe to be a better way to understand these passages:

- Matt O'Reilly, "How Romans 9–11 (and Romans 8) Make Me an Arminian," https://www.theologyproject.online/post/how-romans-9-11-and-romans-8-make-me-arminian.
- James M. Rochford, "Romans 9: An Arminian Interpretation," https://www.evidenceunseen.com/bible-difficulties-2/nt-difficulties/romans-2/romans-9-an-arminian-interpretation/.
- Picirilli, Robert, *Grace, Faith, and Free Will: Contrasting Views of Salvation: Calvinism and Arminianism* (Nashville, TN: Randall House Publications, 2002).
- Matthew Pinson, *40 Questions About Arminianism* (Nashville, TN: Randall House Publications, 2022).

For those who appeal to other passages in the New Testament to bolster their Calvinist views, see the short statements in the appendix as well as Matthew

Pinson's exposition of passages on the security of the believer in his book *40 Questions About Arminianism*.

Third, I cannot personally reconcile the Calvinist portrait of God with the rest of Scripture's teaching on God's love and goodness. In Calvinism, God predetermined that the vast majority of individuals will go to hell before he ever created the world. In turn, God predetermined that he would only save a small number of specific individuals—before they were created. It is hard for some to admit it, but as theologian Jerry Walls says, *God does not truly love everyone* in Calvinism.[8] Furthermore, in the theology of people who apply their Calvinism consistently, God predestined specific evils such as the Holocaust and Mao's murders in China. For these reasons and others, I am sympathetic with those ex-Calvinists, described by Austin Fisher in his book *Young, Restless, and No Longer Reformed*, who have concluded that the God of Calvinism, at an in-depth level, is morally problematical.[9]

The view of God I find in the Bible is that God loves us *all* (e.g., John 3:16). As such, God wants to save as many as possible. Yet he saves only those who respond to him by faith in Jesus. God does not want anyone to go to hell, but he respects our individual and group choices to live without him. God does not desire the evils of the Holocaust and the like, but he chose a sovereignty that permits human and demonic choices and a cursed world, all while working toward a greater good in the end. In this age God uses free will and suffering as a means of clarifying our relationship with God, refining our character, and living in a world of choice. We live in this world in a refining process often called "soul making." In the world to come, evil will be eradicated because of the destruction of Satan and the demons and the renewal of all things.

God permits evil works in this world, but evil choices are not his preference. Calvinists, on the other hand, believe this is the world God predetermined—and that God predestined the majority of people to go to hell. To me, these logical implications of Calvinism are inconsistent with Scripture and with God's love.

Genesis 6:5–6 states concisely the posture that I believe reflects God's view of this world.

> The LORD saw how great the wickedness of the human race had become on the earth, and that every inclination of the thoughts of the human heart was only evil all the time. The LORD regretted that he had made human beings on the earth, and his heart was deeply troubled.

God's posture of love for the world is why he sent Jesus. He wants to save as many as possible.

> God our Savior, who wants all people to be saved and to come to a knowledge of the truth. (1 Timothy 2:3–4)

> The Lord is not slow in keeping his promise, as some understand slowness. Instead, he is patient with you, not wanting anyone to perish, but everyone to come to repentance. (2 Peter 3:9)

In short, since the fall of Adam and Eve, people have been free to make evil choices. God allows this to happen, but it breaks his heart. In this age, between God's creation of the heavens and the earth and his creation of a new heaven and new earth, God determined human faith, as a response to his love in Christ, while risky, is still worthwhile. God wants a genuine relationship with people who have the true freedom to respond—not the pre-programming found in robots and computers.

GOD DETERMINED HUMAN FAITH, WHILE RISKY, IS STILL WORTHWHILE.

Furthermore, I believe the overall teaching of the New Testament *assumes Christians will persevere* (because of God's help), but it also teaches a true Christian can resist God's empowering presence, turn from the faith, and thereby be lost. This ability to forfeit salvation is described in the New Testament's "warning passages," the subject to which we turn in the next chapter.

3

DOES HEBREWS TEACH THE REALITY OF APOSTASY?

believe if a person just carefully reads the book of Hebrews, with as few preconceptions as possible, they will conclude a person can turn from Christ, become a non-believer, and forfeit salvation. Other New Testament books also teach this sobering truth. The book of James provides key insights into the nature of saving faith. People sometimes question if this teaching is opposed to the doctrine of grace. As we will see, the warnings about forfeiting salvation present no contradiction with the Bible's teaching on salvation "by grace . . . through faith" (Ephesians 2:8). The key item is to gain clarity on what faith actually entails.

Let me start off with two clear sections from Hebrews that describe the reality of apostasy (forfeiting salvation).

> It is impossible for those who have once been enlightened, who have tasted the heavenly gift, who have shared in the Holy Spirit, who have tasted the goodness of the word of God and the powers of the coming age, and who have fallen away, to be brought back to repentance. To their loss they are crucifying the Son of God all over again and subjecting him to public disgrace. (Hebrews 6:4–6)

> If we deliberately keep on sinning after we have received the knowledge of the truth, no sacrifice for sins is left, but only a fearful expectation of judgment and of raging fire that will consume the enemies of God. Anyone who rejected the law of Moses died without mercy on the testimony of two or three witnesses. How much more severely do you think someone deserves to

be punished who has trampled the Son of God underfoot, who has treated as an unholy thing the blood of the covenant that sanctified them, and who has insulted the Spirit of grace? For we know him who said, "It is mine to avenge; I will repay," and again, "The Lord will judge his people." It is a dreadful thing to fall into the hands of the living God. (Hebrews 10:26–31)

It is hard to believe that these two passages in Hebrews describe anything other than genuine Christians who turn from Christ and forfeit salvation.[10]

Hebrews 6:4–5 states they have:
- Been enlightened
- Tasted the heavenly gift
- Shared in the Holy Spirit
- Tasted the goodness of the Word of God
- Tasted the powers of the coming age

Hebrews 10:26–30 states they have:
- Received knowledge of the truth
- Been sanctified by the blood of the covenant
- Deliberately and continually turned away from Jesus

The respected Hebrews scholar William Lane reviews these passages in detail and summarizes the reality that these people are Christians: "God's presence and salvation are the undoubted reality of their lives."[11] He goes on to show how these passages warn that if they abandon their faith in Christ, they will face the eternal punishment of unbelievers. Again, Lane puts it well when he writes these passages "affirm the magnitude of the sin of apostasy and of the impending judgment from which there is no escape."[12]

Apostasy is the sin of turning away from Christ. I do not see how these passages in Hebrews can be interpreted authentically (and in context) without affirming the possibility of turning from Christ and forfeiting one's salvation. To understand what it means to "become an apostate" and "fall away," we need a bigger perspective on what the New Testament as a whole teaches. Join with me by reading the material below as I hope it will help you see this teaching in the broader contours of the Bible.

THE "BY GRACE, THROUGH FAITH" FORMULA

THE BIBLE TEACHES WE can only get right with God if we place our faith in Christ and his gospel (1 Corinthians 15:1–8). The gospel does not save people in and of itself, but it does provide the basis upon which God, in full harmony with his holiness, can save those who have sinned against him. Christ died on the cross for our sins (2 Corinthians 5:19–21). That being said, what is required for us to establish our freedom and guiltlessness before God?

God offers salvation as a gift. We are saved by grace in that through Jesus, God offers us the gift of complete forgiveness and right standing with God, now and in eternity.

However, a condition is in place if we are to receive God's grace. This gift can only be received if we place our *faith* in Christ. The Bible clarifies this in Ephesians 2:8–10:

> For it is by grace you have been saved, through faith—and this is not from yourselves, it is the gift of God—not by works, so that no one can boast. For we are God's handiwork, created in Christ Jesus to do good works, which God prepared in advance for us to do.

Again, God provides the offer of his grace, but humans must accept it through faith. As Greek expert A. T. Robertson put it, "Grace is God's part, faith ours."[13] Faith springs from God and his Spirit's influence upon us, yet it is also our response. Faith is both to "trust and follow" God through Jesus. The word for "faith"—*pistis* in Greek—includes mental assent and trust, but it also includes allegiance, loyalty, and faithfulness.[14]

Faith should never be understood as earning salvation. Faith is the human response to God's free offer of salvation. Genuine faith is a living, active thing and leads to perseverance and good works. Stated differently, good works result from the kind of faith that brings salvation.

Good works reveal the presence of genuine faith and salvation. Likewise, when faith weakens, it manifests its condition in disobedience and ongoing sin. Evil deeds and sinful lifestyles reveal a problem with one's faith. Because of how crucial it is to understand faith, let's gain a deeper grasp on the nature of saving faith and persistent faithfulness.

GENUINE FAITH IS A LIVING, ACTIVE THING AND LEADS TO PERSEVERANCE AND GOOD WORKS.

FAITH AND FAITHFULNESS

As POINTED OUT ABOVE, "faith" is the key word in the human side of our relationship with God. "Faith," "belief," and "trust" are all similar words in the Bible. The entire Christian life is lived by faith:

> This Good News tells us how God makes us right in his sight. This is accomplished from start to finish by faith. As the Scriptures say, "It is through faith that a righteous person has life." (Romans 1:17, NLT)

Again, biblical faith includes trust, allegiance, loyalty, and faithfulness.[15] Faith is holistic; when present, faith transforms our lives. [16] The Bible says, "Without faith it is impossible to please God, because anyone who comes to him must believe that he exists and that he rewards those who earnestly seek him" (Hebrews 11:6). Faith is a living reality that transforms the mind, the heart, and the will.

Let's unpack some of the ways faith transforms the mind, heart, and will.

Faith transforms the mind by calling us to a rational assent to the facts of the Bible. It involves cognitively believing that Jesus Christ came to earth to show us the way and to save us. In our minds, we rationally believe what the Bible says about him. As thoughtful people, we base our eternal destiny upon the historical truth of Christ's life, death, and resurrection (1 Corinthians 15:1–8).

Faith also includes personal reliance on God through Christ. We rest our souls—in our personal, subjective selves—in Christ as our Savior (Philippians 3:7–10). We rely not just on Christ's work on the cross, but on the indwelling presence of his Holy Spirit (Philippians 2:12–13). Put another way, faith calls us not only to *believe that* Jesus is who he says he is but also to *believe in* him, in the sense of existentially relying upon him.

Just as importantly, faith is also a surrender of our will—a volitional commitment—to God. We give ourselves to God through Christ's leadership, committing **FAITH IS ALSO** ourselves to repentance and the determination to follow Christ **A SURRENDER** in all things (Acts 2:38; Mark 8:34–38). By faith, we commit **OF OUR WILL.** to be submissive to what God teaches. If we do not follow Christ's teachings, something crucial is missing in our faith. Consider these words from the book of James:

> What good is it, my brothers and sisters, if someone claims to have faith
> but has no deeds? Can such faith save them? Suppose a brother or a sister
> is without clothes and daily food. If one of you says to them, "Go in peace;
> keep warm and well fed," but does nothing about their physical needs, what
> good is it? In the same way, faith by itself, if it is not accompanied by action,
> is dead. . . . As the body without the spirit is dead, so faith without deeds is
> dead. (James 2:14–17, 26)

God shows us through the teaching of James that actions and deeds must accompany faith. As mentioned in Chapter 1, if mental assent were the only requirement, the demons would also be saved because they believe Jesus is real (James 2:19).

But as we have seen, saving faith is a substantive, holistic faith. This is why the Bible does not recognize faith apart from obedience. True faith leads to a life lived toward obedience and aimed away from sin. John MacArthur articulates the biblical balance well with these fitting words: "Faith obeys. Unbelief rebels. The fruit of one's life reveals whether that person is a believer or an unbeliever."[17] The Bible describes it this way: "We know that we have come to know him if we keep his commands. Whoever says, 'I know him,' but does not do what he commands is a liar, and the truth is not in that person" (1 John 2: 3–4). Faith is to "trust and follow Jesus." If someone claims to be right with God, yet lives without a trust that results in obedience, then that person is deceived.

William Booth, the Bible-believing founder of the Salvation Army, described it this way: "Faith and works should travel side by side, step answering to step, like the legs of men walking. First faith, and then works; and then faith again, and then works again—until they can scarcely distinguish which is the one and which is the other."[18]

Let's get specific. A lack of church involvement or a sexually immoral lifestyle or a lifestyle of drug usage does not, in and of itself, put us in eternal peril (as an external action). But something is wrong with the faith and the heart of the person engaging in these activities. The flickering light of true faith is being put out. Regardless of their words, the person living in ongoing and deliberate sin is not living with true and active faith in Jesus Christ.

We must not focus too much on actions alone (although they remain centrally important) but on the deeper heart issues and the nature of one's personal faith that results in such actions. A hardness of heart to God's teachings, with its lack of repentant faith, leads to the slow death of a saving relationship with God. Sinful actions that are repeatedly engaged in—especially those that consciously involve rejecting Jesus and his teachings—are inconsistent with faith and lead to spiritual death. This concern with saving faith is the message of James 2. The lack of true faith is what Hebrews refers to when it describes those who have "fallen away" (6:6) and a rejection of faith is what Hebrews refers to when it describes those who should anticipate "a fearful expectation of judgment and of raging fire that will consume the enemies of God" (10:27).

So what does this spiritual death look like practically? The next chapter describes three paths.

4

HOW DOES A PERSON FORFEIT THEIR SALVATION?

The Bible teaches that through the Holy Spirit, God leads us to place our faith in Christ (John 16:7–11; 1 John 2:20, 27). Yet we can still resist the Holy Spirit as people did in the Bible (Acts 7:51–53). When we choose to respond to the leading of the Holy Spirit, we will find confirmation of the truth of Christ within our inner beings (1 Corinthians 2:10). After we believe, God gives us his indwelling Spirit (Acts 2:28). The Holy Spirit acts as a deposit, a "down payment," for the eternal life we will share with God forever (Ephesians 1:13–14).

God continues to work, through the Holy Spirit and providence, to protect us and enable us to persevere. God promises to keep us safe, so that no force, no circumstance, not even Satan himself, can snatch us out of God's hand.

> My sheep listen to my voice; I know them, and they follow me. I give them eternal life, and they shall never perish; no one will snatch them out of my hand. My Father, who has given them to me, is greater than all; no one can snatch them out of my Father's hand. (John 10:27–29)

As Christians, we are the sheep who listen to Christ and follow him by faith. We cannot be snatched away. We are secure in God, for he is always doing his part to strengthen us, protect us from the evil one, and keep us safe.

But this passage (and others like it) does not eliminate our free will. The Bible teaches we can walk away from the protection God provides. Satan cannot snatch us, but we have the free will to turn away from God and reject God's sustaining power by turning away from Christ.

The Bible teaches we are responsible for our moral choices (Luke 17:1–3). If we were not responsible for them, then God would not be fair in punishing us for our disobedience. But God is fair (Romans 2:3–7). As people who possess free will, we are ultimately responsible for our choices. And just as we once said yes to the pull of God's Spirit and placed our faith in Jesus, can we not, with that same ability to choose, turn and say no? Furthermore, if we have genuine freedom, then we can also choose, over time, to turn away from the protection God provides and leave him. God's grace is something that can be "resisted" (Acts 7:51); the Spirit's fire can be "put out" (1 Thessalonians 5:19); and we can become "hardened" in rebellion and turn away from God (Hebrews 3:7–14).

Thus, by God's power we must be faithful, lest our names be blotted out from the "book of life" (Revelation 3:5; Psalm 69:28). In short, God provides protection and God influences us for good, but God does not take away our free will to choose.

THE DANGER OF FALLING AWAY

THE BIBLICAL TEACHING ON God's sustaining power in our lives is foundational for understanding what being saved means. We can rest assured that God is doing all he promised to help us remain faithful. But resting in him doesn't mean becoming idle when it comes to the faithfulness he calls us to. God's provision must also be balanced with our Christian responsibility.

Jesus shows how the two work together in the Gospel of John.

> I am the true vine, and my Father is the gardener. He cuts off every branch in me that bears no fruit, while every branch that does bear fruit he prunes so that it will be even more fruitful. You are already clean because of the word I have spoken to you. Remain in me, as I also remain in you. No branch can bear fruit by itself; it must remain in the vine. Neither can you bear fruit unless you remain in me. I am the vine; you are the branches. If you remain in me and I in you, you will bear much fruit; apart from me you can do nothing. If you do not remain in me, you are like a branch that is thrown away and withers; such branches are picked up, thrown into the fire and burned. (John 15:1–6)

Jesus is the vine; as such, he provides nurture and sustenance. By his power, we, his disciples, are branches that *will bear fruit* as we remain attached to the vine. The fruit Jesus talked about in this context is obedience to his commands, especially the command to love people. Yes, again, we must remain in him.

WE MUST REMAIN IN HIM.

But Jesus gave a warning. If there is no fruitfulness, God will cut people off. They will be thrown into the fire (John 15:2, 6), surely a reference to hell. How does this work out? The key to our security in Christ is that we continue to "remain in Christ." God provides all we need to be saved, but we must stay in relationship with God (remaining in the vine) to bear the fruit of a changed life. Consistently living without a transformed relationship that relies on God's power becomes very dangerous; we can enter a point where we no longer remain in Christ.

If we consistently refuse to respond to God's presence and power, evident by our disobedience, a hard-heartedness toward God can develop within us. Our rebellious actions show we are turning away or have turned away from faith. If this becomes a pattern in our lives, it can become entrenched in active unbelief, and faith can die. We are then in danger of hell, of being "thrown into the fire and burned" (John 15:6).

THE PATHS OF APOSTASY

APOSTASY DESCRIBES THE PROCESS by which someone turns away from "saving faith" and forfeits salvation because they have become apostate. It is not an instantaneous thing, but the result of ongoing choices made—typically in the face of challenges and ongoing temptations. And no outside person can know, for sure, when someone has crossed the line and forfeited their relationship with God. Only God truly knows.

It is sobering because such a person may still claim to believe, but they do not have true faith in Jesus. The biblical balance teaches that God gives his grace and protection so a Christian will remain with him. But Christians must continue to follow God by faith. We have a relationship with God through a faith that is obedient. Obedience does not bring salvation, but it is the inevitable fruit produced by genuine faith.

From the Bible itself, we can identify three general paths that lead to a termination of genuine faith and the forfeiture of salvation.[19] In what follows, we will examine paths that the Bible points to as warnings, describing those who turn away from the faith.

1. Turning from Jesus and His Gospel. The first path that leads to apostasy is when someone renounces the faith. These people give up on the gospel. Salvation is promised to anyone who places their faith in Jesus' gospel, but only *if,* according to Paul, "you hold firmly to the word I preached to you. Otherwise, you have believed in vain" (1 Corinthians 15:2). Carefully note the essence of the gospel, according to the apostle Paul:

> For what I received I passed on to you as of first importance: that Christ died for our sins according to the Scriptures, that he was buried, that he was raised on the third day according to the Scriptures, and that he appeared to Cephas, and then to the Twelve. After that, he appeared to more than five hundred of the brothers and sisters at the same time, most of whom are still living, though some have fallen asleep. 7 Then he appeared to James, then to all the apostles, and last of all he appeared to me also, as to one abnormally born. (1 Corinthians 15:3–8)

The gospel is that upon which we rely when we become Christians. To abandon and no longer firmly rest our faith on this foundation is to repudiate the whole basis of salvation. To renounce the gospel is to commit spiritual suicide.

This is *not* to say a person must be right on every biblical doctrine to be saved. True, Christians strive to hold correct beliefs on all biblical doctrines. For every part of God's truth is valuable. But there are different weights in God's truth. Some elements are essential, some elements are important, and some elements are personal.

We forfeit salvation when we turn from Jesus' gospel—for it is essential for salvation. Stating it properly, Jesus' gospel and our faith in his gospel are essential. Jesus and his gospel are both narrow and wide. We embrace Jesus' gospel by faith to become saved, and that makes it narrow. But we spend the rest of our lives learning to live out the implications of Jesus's gospel by faith, and that makes it wide.

But the centrality and essential nature of Jesus' gospel never changes.[20] Those who turn from Jesus and his gospel to other religions forfeit their salvation.[21] Paul addressed the book of Galatians to a group of Christians in spiritual danger of the suicide of faith because they were turning from Jesus and his gospel. Paul warns about abandoning the gospel and becoming apostates with these stark words:

> I am astonished that you are so quickly deserting the one who called you to live in the grace of Christ and are turning to a different gospel—which is really no gospel at all. Evidently some people are throwing you into confusion and are trying to pervert the gospel of Christ. But even if we or an angel from heaven should preach a gospel other than the one we preached to you, let them be under God's curse! As we have already said, so now I say again: If anybody is preaching to you a gospel other than what you accepted, let them be under God's curse! (Galatians 1:6–9)

Paul uses the strongest language possible to warn these Christians not to turn away and forfeit their salvation. Those who leave the gospel of Jesus will switch from being saved to being condemned (v. 9).

When we examine the entire book of Galatians, the real problem is clarified. False teachers were saying that faith in the gospel of Jesus Christ was *not enough*. They were advocating that Gentile Christians had to adopt the practices of ethnic Jews to be saved. In doing this, these false teachers had changed the *basis of salvation*.[22] The false teachers held that salvation was not by faith in Jesus and his gospel but by the practices of circumcision and Judaism. Paul's response and warning against apostasy is clear:

> Mark my words! I, Paul, tell you that if you let yourselves be circumcised, Christ will be of no value to you at all. . . . You who are trying to be justified by law have been alienated from Christ; you have fallen away from grace. (Galatians 5:2, 4)

Paul resorts to such strong words because souls were put in jeopardy by the teaching that faith in Christ and his cross was not enough. The New Testament also warns against this peril elsewhere:

> Watch out that you do not lose what we have worked for, but that you may be rewarded fully. Anyone who runs ahead and does not continue in the teaching of Christ does not have God. (2 John 1:8–9)

> Timothy, my son, I am giving you this . . . so that by recalling them you may fight the battle well, holding on to faith and a good conscience, which some

have rejected and so have suffered shipwreck with regard to the faith. Among them are Hymenaeus and Alexander. (1 Timothy 1:18–20)

As we see, Christians can leave their relationship with God if they turn from the essential elements of the faith.[23] Thus, such matters are of utmost seriousness. Turning from the faith is a danger for those who flirt with or actively embrace the general secularism of our culture and for those who live in practical disbelief even though they claim to be Christians. The danger is also very real for those who adopt a "progressive Christianity" that denies the exclusivity of Jesus and gives the ways of the culture priority.[24] It also happens to those who turn from Jesus to another religion (Islam, Buddhism, Hinduism, Judaism, etc.). We must remain diligent to defend and uphold the faith that God has entrusted to us (Jude 3).

2. Turning from Jesus Because of Testing and Hardships. A second path that can lead to apostasy is testing and hardships. Thus, a new Christian must become rooted and grounded in the faith. A person can have a weak faith for many reasons, including immaturity, lack of discipleship, and a lack of nurture and training in what it means to seek God. Like newborn children, such people are often in spiritual danger. Jesus made this danger clear in Luke 8:4–15 as he described seed sown by a farmer. The seed that fell among the rocks represents those who abandon Christ because they have no spiritual depth. Jesus described the soil with these words:

Those on the rocky ground are the ones who receive the word with joy when they hear it, but they have no root. *They believe for a while, but in the time of testing they fall away.* (Luke 8:13, emphasis added)

This passage describes Christians who believe, but they do not possess a deeply rooted, sustaining faith. During a time of testing, they fall away.[25] The source of "testing" can be many things. For some it might be struggles with family members or with lifestyle choices or even with general hardships that come from living in a fallen world; as a result, they falter and fall away. New Christians and even those who have been Christians for years without maturing are in particular danger at this point. Their faith is not rooted to withstand the hardships of life.

FAITH REQUIRES NURTURING AND ONGOING GROWTH.

Faith requires nurturing and ongoing growth. For this reason, discipleship is essential. To develop this kind of faith, we must learn to practice seeking God, studying the

Bible, remaining active in church, and receiving help through intentional discipling relationships. Helping each other grow in the faith, in this way, is essential. We must not only believe in God, but earnestly seek him (Hebrews 11:6). We must seek God through active efforts of faith if we are to make our salvation sure (2 Peter 1:3–10). Near the end of his life, even the apostle Paul describes the challenge this way: "I have fought the good fight, I have finished the race, I have kept the faith" (2 Timothy 4:7). If even Paul had to strive to "keep the faith," then surely we must train people and help them to learn to do the same.

3. Embracing Sinful Lifestyles Inconsistent with Repentant Faith. The third path that can lead to apostasy is the active, ongoing practice of sin. Every Christian engages in a lifelong struggle with sin, but the Bible warns that deliberate and ongoing sin, as a conscious choice that involves rejecting Jesus' leadership (i.e., his lordship), can lead to the death of faith and, consequently, to apostasy. This person's will is in rebellion against God's teaching.

Repentance is a key part of saving faith. The apostle Paul summarized his ministry with these words: "I have declared to both Jews and Greeks that they must turn to God in repentance and have faith in our Lord Jesus" (Acts 20:21). Repentance is the "no" side of faith, describing what we will turn from. Obedience is the "yes" side of faith, describing what we are turning to.

Turning back to what one repented from to engage in deliberate and ongoing sin again is a problem. The combination of deliberate choices that are ongoing (continuous) and involve a rejection of Jesus lead to a denial of faith and a bad ending.

The book of Hebrews describes the basic principles:

> If we deliberately keep on sinning after we have received the knowledge of the truth, no sacrifice for sins is left, but only a fearful expectation of judgment and of raging fire that will consume the enemies of God. (Hebrews 10:26–27)

According to this passage, the key characteristic of those in danger is they "deliberately keep on sinning" after obtaining "the knowledge of the truth."[26] This passage is not saying a Christian cannot sin. Every Christian struggles with sinful acts, giving in to its power in one area or another (James 3:2). But this passage teaches that giving in to a *lifestyle of deliberate and continual pattern of sin* is a different matter entirely. Such behavior rejects Jesus Christ and genuine faith in him as the next few verses show:

> Anyone who rejected the law of Moses died without mercy on the testimony of two or three witnesses. How much more severely do you think someone deserves to be punished who has trampled the Son of God underfoot, who has treated as an unholy thing the blood of the covenant that sanctified them, and who has insulted the Spirit of grace? For we know him who said, "It is mine to avenge; I will repay," and again, "The Lord will judge his people." It is a dreadful thing to fall into the hands of the living God. (Hebrews 10:28–31)

The deliberate and ongoing practice of a sinful lifestyle hardens a person's heart to the Holy Spirit and leads to repudiation of true, submissive faith. Why is this presented as either/or in Scripture? Well, something will be our master—sin leading to death or obedience leading to righteousness (Romans 6:16). We must either reject God or reject sin. Notice what this person is doing according to the passage from Hebrews 10:28–31 listed above:

- Trampling the Son of God underfoot
- Treating as an unholy thing the blood of the covenant that sanctified him
- Insulting the Spirit of grace

A faith that does not continue in a pursuit of faithfulness is not a saving faith. The problem described here is not giving into a small sin or even giving into a big one, because God provides ongoing forgiveness when we confess (1 John 1:7–9). The problem is a rebellious heart.

This rebelliousness often manifests in major sins, such as actively living in sexual immorality, hard-hearted divorce, a pattern of stealing or drug abuse, etc. These actions involve ongoing participation in sinful lifestyles. In reality, these are premeditated sins that reflect a heart problem. Hebrews 3:12–14 describes this state:

> See to it, brothers and sisters, that none of you has a sinful, unbelieving heart that turns away from the living God. But encourage one another daily, as long as it is called "Today," so that none of you may be hardened by sin's

deceitfulness. We have come to share in Christ, if indeed we hold our original conviction firmly to the very end.

Notice the progression: a sinful heart nurtures unbelief, and then it turns away. Sin hardens a person and creates a deceived heart. The person turns away from the living God because they cannot both actively seek a heart for God and justify (in their heart) an active lifestyle of sin.

One of the clearest sections of the New Testament that describes sinful lifestyles and what they practically do to a person is Galatians 5:19–21. In a warning to Christians, the apostle Paul explicitly lists lifestyles that characterize those living in ongoing rebellion.

> The acts of the flesh are obvious: sexual immorality, impurity and debauchery; idolatry and witchcraft; hatred, discord, jealousy, fits of rage, selfish ambition, dissensions, factions and envy; drunkenness, orgies, and the like. I warn you, as I did before, that those who live like this will not inherit the kingdom of God.

This passage lists for us the types of *lifestyles* ("those who live like this") that give evidence that a Christian is being hardened to God and not living with an active and submissive faith. This passage serves as a warning to Christians, ancient and modern. People who live this way turn their backs on Christ by their lifestyles. The key is a *sinful lifestyle* that denotes ongoing willful sin, as opposed to the occasional sinful acts with which every Christian struggles.

True faith follows the teachings of Jesus. Notice the following sobering warning. The Bible teaches it is better to have never become a Christian than to become one and turn your back on Christ.

> If they have escaped the corruption of the world by knowing our Lord and Savior Jesus Christ and are again entangled in it and are overcome, they are worse off at the end than they were at the beginning. It would have been better for them not to have known the way of righteousness, than to have known it and then to turn their backs on the sacred command that was passed on to them. (2 Peter 2:20–21)

This concern is why the book of James says, "My brothers and sisters, if one of you should wander from the truth and someone should bring that person back, remember this: Whoever turns a sinner from the error of their way will save them from death and cover over a multitude of sins" (James 5:19–20).

A person who embraces an actively sinful lifestyle is in danger of apostasy because their heart is hardening to God and no longer manifesting a submissive faith. If such a person claims to be a Christian, we must recognize the root faith problem. They are not trusting and following Jesus. They are living in active rebellion against what the Bible teaches and are not submitting to Jesus as Lord and King of their lives.

This attitude of internal rebellion can become entrenched. This rebellious heart was revealed in the lives of King Saul and King Solomon in the Old Testament. God is always willing to accept us back when we truly repent, no matter what we have done. But we must be careful that our heart does not get irreversibly hard in such a way that we do not want to come back and surrender again with submissive faith in Christ.

Again, this is a point of balance. All Christians struggle with intermittent sin, and sometimes in dangerous ways. Such times are perilous, and we should be fearful of the consequences. But if rebellious Christians come to their senses and truly repent, they can return to God. He is like the prodigal son's father, always willing and waiting to welcome back his children if they repent and turn back to him (Luke 15:11–32).

The problem with entrenched sin in our lives is the hardness that develops within our hearts when we continually reject Christ in favor of sin. Sin's strangulation is an especially big danger for new or immature Christians. This is why Jesus gave us a hyperbolic but sobering warning in Matthew 18:8: "If your hand or your foot causes you to stumble, cut it off and throw it away. It is better for you to enter life maimed or crippled than to have two hands or two feet and be thrown into eternal fire." Sometimes drastic measures need to be taken to turn from sinful lifestyles to submit to God and his will instead of submitting to our own deceptive hearts.

What about when we have zero desire to reject the faith and we are resolved to follow Jesus—yet we frustratingly find ourselves persisting in sin? How can we be forgiven when we want to follow Jesus yet sin again and again? That's the topic of the next chapter.

5

HOW CAN I BE FORGIVEN WHEN I SIN AGAIN AND AGAIN?

The Bible teaches that God loves to forgive our sins. All we have to do is to confess them and, where necessary, turn from them (Luke 15:18–22). The most common sins for those with genuine faith are sinful actions that are not premeditated. They involve moments of weakness. Other sins are more deeply rooted and, in some cases, so deeply rooted that we may not even consciously be aware they are sin patterns. But God will help us to see them and turn from them in time.

God forgives us as we walk in the light with a humble faith in him. The apostle John describes how those with genuine faith are to deal with sin:

> If we claim to have fellowship with him and yet walk in the darkness, we lie and do not live out the truth. But if we walk in the light, as he is in the light, we have fellowship with one another, and the blood of Jesus, his Son, purifies us from all sin. If we claim to be without sin, we deceive ourselves and the truth is not in us. If we confess our sins, he is faithful and just and will forgive us our sins and purify us from all unrighteousness. (1 John 1:6–9)

This passage shows that Jesus' blood continues to cleanse us as we walk with him, even when we are not conscious of our sin. And when we become conscious of our sin—from the teaching of God's Word or as the Holy Spirit reveals it inwardly—we are to confess it. As soon as we confess it with a genuine, repentant heart, God forgives us instantly!

There are four points to keep in mind to help us maintain a healthy and balanced perspective when it comes to the sin with which we all must handle. The first point comes cumulatively from other passages we looked at: If a person persists in living in an ongoing, deliberately sinful way, then this person is living without saving faith. As the text says, "If we claim to have fellowship with him and yet walk in the darkness, we lie and do not live out the truth" (1 John 1:6). Hebrews 10:26 gives us another vantage point on the same behavior: we are in danger with God "if we deliberately keep on sinning." The problem is both deliberate sin (rebellion) and staying in the sin (i.e., it is ongoing). These are people not walking in the light, but in darkness. They are deceiving themselves and others if they claim to have fellowship with God. But the opposite is also true: someone who is walking in God's direction and living a responsive, Christ-centered lifestyle while struggling with sin can still boldly have confidence of forgiveness.

This text leads us to the second insight: struggling with sin is part of a genuine faith in Christ. Our basic lifestyle testifies to our faith and our security because it demonstrates we are true believers (1 John 5:12–13). We still have the ongoing certainty of salvation.

> **STRUGGLING WITH SIN IS PART OF A GENUINE FAITH IN CHRIST.**

The Word of God is crystal clear: to walk in the light includes the continuing struggle with sin. Years ago I came across the writings of Chuck Jones, who points out what 1 John 1:7–9 teaches:

> "Walking in the light" does not mean, however, that you have rid yourself of every sinful act. The verse itself makes this clear—one of the two blessings we receive as a result of this walk is that Jesus' blood "cleanses us from every sin." That phrase is meaningless if a person is not walking in the light until he has conquered every sin. *Sinning, not as a lifestyle, but as an occasional act, is part of walking in the light.*[27]

This is an important clarification. As mentioned earlier, all Christians continue to struggle with sin throughout this life (James 3:2). But the difference is that faithful Christians resist rebellious and ongoing sin. We are to look at the basic direction of our lives and our relationship with God, by which we can know our faith is real and making a difference in our lives.

Third, when we become conscious of our sin, we stop and come to God with our transgression(s). We acknowledge it by being honest with ourselves and we confess it to God. The presupposition in 1 John 1 is that we are repentant after we sin because we strive to walk in the light of Jesus. We do not want to sin, yet we become weak, and then stumble and fall. It happens to every one of us.

Sometimes we stumble into sin regularly and it bothers our consciences. What do we do? We confess our sins directly to God and hold to full confidence that through Jesus, God forgives us.

> If we confess our sins, he is faithful and just and will forgive us our sins and purify us from all unrighteousness. (1 John 1:9)

Please note: God promises to forgive us immediately. We do not need to do anything more. There is no version of personally doing something good to overcome the sin we have committed; the Word of God requires no acts of penance. By faith, we acknowledge, confess, and trust the blood of Jesus. What a wonderful promise: our Savior purifies us from all unrighteous acts.

Fourth, while we walk in Christ's light, the cleansing from sin never stops. Again, consider an observation from Chuck Jones:

> Here lies the most liberating revelation in the highly liberating verse: the cleansing of Jesus never stops. . . . An occasional sin does not stop the cleansing power of Jesus. It is instead the very thing that calls the power into action. . . . I'm convinced that whether they know it or not, the majority of committed Christians live their entire lives from the moment of their baptism to the hour of their death without spending one day in danger of hellfire. The cleansing never stops. Only one thing can cause it to cease: my making the premeditated decision to abandon Jesus' lifestyle, leave all he stands for and rebel against his Lordship.[28]

A God-ward direction in our lives authenticates our faith and gives us great reassurance.

We know that when we sin, the blood of Christ will continually cleanse us. We are perpetually forgiven as long as we cling to him by faith. In this way the apostle John teaches us how to know we are on the path of authentic faith (1 John 5:13).

A GOD-WARD DIRECTION IN OUR LIVES AUTHENTICATES OUR FAITH.

CONCLUSION

We began this book with two questions: Are we eternally secure because we became a Christian and God forgave our sins through the gospel of Jesus—without the necessity of faithfulness? Or are we eternally secure as long as we maintain a saving relationship with God by faithful faith (sustained by God's empowering presence)? We now know the answer—we are eternally secure by faith in Jesus Christ. And true faith, though it includes struggling with sin, is *faithful faith*.

It is a grave theological error to accept the common understanding of "once saved, always saved" if it gives people false assurance they will be saved while living in ongoing, rebellious sin or believing in doctrinal error that denies the gospel. Those preachers, leaders, and individuals who teach "once saved, always saved, no matter how you live" are unwittingly being used by Satan to do great damage to the cause of Christ. They are harming people for eternity.

God provides everything we need for our security: he draws us to Christ, he builds us up in Christ, he leads us, he protects us, etc. (Philippians 2:12–13). Nothing, not even Satan, can snatch us from God's hand (John 10:28–29). But God also gives us true free will. And because human beings are free, we have freedom by which we can even choose, over time, to turn away from a saving relationship with God (Luke 8:13; Galatians 5: 4; 1 Timothy 1:19–20).

By faith, we must continuously strive for a continued faithful faith, which means to trust and follow Jesus. This is loyalty, allegiance, and faithfulness that is demonstrated through obedience. Even though we struggle with sin and faithfulness, as long as we remain in Jesus and walk in his light, we remain secure.

God looks at the heart. The heart's motives spur most of our actions (Matthew 15:18–19). And we need each other to encourage and help us to have hearts of faith (Hebrews 3:12–14; 10:23–25). This is why the Bible teaches us

(Galatians 6:1–2) to reach out to our brothers and sisters and warn them of ongoing sinfulness as well as situations such as the following:

- When a Christian starts attending a church that holds to progressive Christianity that undermines the biblical gospel and promotes a false gospel
- When a Christian becomes involved in a non-Christian religion
- When a Christian stops reading the Bible, becomes sporadic in church attendance, etc.
- When a Christian's life revolves around their work or other idols and not God
- When a Christian starts living as though God did not exist

We must love each other enough to lovingly point to the dangers of sin and turning from Jesus (Matthew 18:15–17). We enter into danger when we deliberately turn away from our faith in Jesus Christ and from the lifestyle he calls us to follow. Also, we cannot be passive about these teachings in the local church because unrepentant sin can spread throughout the church and bring shame upon it (1 Corinthians 5:1–13). Because slowly turning away from true faith and the lifestyle of a disciple is possible, we must watch ourselves, help others, and faithfully follow God.

We don't want to point fingers judgmentally; rather, we want to reach out in love and help everyone to live on the sure path of a faithful faith in Christ. Above all, we desire to be disciples who genuinely trust and follow Jesus and who disciple others to do the same.

APPENDIX

COMMON BUT MISLEADING
AFFIRMATIONS ABOUT OUR SALVATION

Here are some sentiments that are common and seem reassuring, but they can be misleading in light of what the Bible teaches about salvation:

Statement: Once you are a child (of God), you never cease to be a child. God would never disinherit his children.

Sorry, but this statement is not accurate. On the one hand, the Bible says we were once children of disobedience and wrath (Ephesians 2:1–3), but we switched families when we became children of God by faith. So switching families is possible. In the same way, the Bible also warns that by apostasy a Christian would be treated as the "[enemy] of God" (Hebrews 10:26–27). Parents sometimes must disinherit their children (for criminal, rebellious, terrible, and continuous acts). The same is true with God.

Statement: God doesn't erase names from the Book of Life.

This is a false belief because the Bible explicitly warns this is possible. See Psalm 69:28 and Revelation 3:5. God sees ahead in time and knows who will truly finish their lives with active faith in Christ; he has seen it from the creation of the world (Revelation 17:8). God gives us free will, or else we would not be accountable for our actions. God will not take someone to heaven who perpetually determines to reject him.

Statement: A child of God is safe, for "no one will snatch them out" of Christ's hand (John 10:28).

True, no one can snatch a child out of God's hand. And this gives us great peace. But this passage does not address our free will or the need for ongoing faith, both of which are addressed in other passages. According to these other passages, we can walk away from Christ's protective hand when we turn from him and reject him.

Statement: The eternal life we received is everlasting life.

Eternal life is indeed a quality of present life as well as a lasting promise for eternity. However, the apostate had this gift of everlasting life, and then turned their back on it. Would God save a non-believer who rejects Christ? Similarly, when a person no longer has faith, the promise is forfeited.

Statement: One who is born again cannot be unborn!

"Born again" is a helpful metaphor for salvation, but we would be taking the metaphor too far to try to force apostasy into the mold of the same metaphor (i.e., of becoming unborn). When a person rejects Jesus, the more accurate biblical metaphor is that of spiritual death (1 John 5:16–17). This is apostasy.

Statement: If I have been sealed by the Holy Spirit, how could I become unsealed?

King David prayed that God would not take the Holy Spirit away from him (Psalm 51:10–12). The New Testament also warns us not to put out the Spirit's fire (1 Thessalonians 5:19). The Spirit is a seal in our lives, but it is nowhere described as an "un-removable seal." We cannot say—one way or the other—that God would "unseal" someone, but we can say the Spirit of God can lose all influence in a person's life.

Statement: God does not take back his gifts!

This statement originates from Romans 11:29, which says, in the context of Israel's identity as God's chosen people, that "God's gifts and his call are irrevocable." Applying this verse about God's chosen nation to the situation of the apostate is questionable. Moreover, when apostasy happens, God does not take back his gift. Rather, the apostate turns away and rejects God's gift.

NOTES

1. These Christians identify with John Calvin and are referred to by scholars as Calvinists.

2. These Christians identify with Jacob Arminius and are referred to by scholars as Arminians.

3. The lifestyle implications of Christian faith are fleshed out in Chapter 1 of Mark E. Moore, *Faithful Faith: Reclaiming Faith from Culture and Tradition* (Renew.org, 2021). For the expectation that grace for Christians came with the implication of a "return gift," see Matthew W. Bates, *Gospel Allegiance: What Faith in Jesus Misses for Salvation in Christ* (Grand Rapids: Brazos Press, 2019), 146.

4. "Q&A: John Wesley," *Holiness Today*, accessed July 12, 2021, https://www. holinesstoday.org/QA-John-Wesley.

5. "The Articles of the Remonstrants" are adapted from Phillip Schaff, *The Creeds of Christendom,* vol. 3 (Grand Rapids: Baker Books, 1996), 545ff.

6. I. Howard Marshal, "The Problem of Apostasy in New Testament Theology," in *Jesus the Saviour* (London: SPCK, 1990), 306–324. See also I. Howard Marshall, *Kept by the Power of God: A Study of Perseverance and Falling Away* (Eugene: Wipf & Stock, 2008); Robert Picirilli, *Grace, Faith, and Free Will: Contrasting Views of Salvation: Calvinism & Arminianism* (Nashville: Randall House Publications, 2002); Leroy Forlines, *The Quest for Truth: Theology for Post Modern Times* (Nashville: Randall House Publications, 2001).

7. See Thomas Schreiner and Ardel Caneday, *The Race Set Before Us: A Biblical Theology of Perseverance & Assurance* (Downers Grove, IL: InterVarsity Press, 2001); Matthew Pinson, ed., *Four Views of Eternal Security* (Grand Rapids: Zondervan, 2002); and Herbert Bateman IV, ed., *Four Views of the Warning Passages in Hebrews* (Grand Rapids: Kregel Publishing, 2007).

8. Jerry L. Walls, "Does God Love Everyone? The Heart of What Is Wrong with Calvinism," *Denver Seminary*, accessed April 19, 2021, https://denverseminary.edu/article/does-god-love-everyone-the-heart-of-what-is-wrong-with-calvinism/.

9. See Austin Fisher, *Young, Restless, and No Longer Reformed: Black Holes, Love, and the Journey In and Out of Calvinism* (Cascade Books, 2014), 46, Kindle. Fisher puts it this way: "For those who might object that this is going too far, I can only disagree and confess that it seemed Calvinism forced me to call things 'good,' when they could only be considered the most morally repugnant atrocities imaginable, perpetrated by the Creator himself" (26).

10. See the work listed above for even more detail that backs up these points.

11. William Lane, *Hebrews 1–8*, Word Biblical Commentary, vol. 47 (Dallas: Word Publishing, 1991), 145.

12. Ibid., 296.

13. A. T. Robertson, *Word Pictures*, vol. 14 (Ada, MI: Baker Pub Group, 1982), 525.

14. See Matthew Bates, *Gospel Allegiance* (Grand Rapids: Brazos Press, 2019), 61–62.

15. The Greek word *pistis* (traditionally "faith") is better translated "faithfulness," "fidelity," "loyalty," or "allegiance" in Romans 1:17 (and also in 1:5; 1:8; 1:12; 3:3; 3:22; etc.). In Romans 1:17, "by *pistis*" likely refers to Jesus the King's faithful loyalty to God and "for *pistis*" likely refers to our faithful loyalty to Jesus as the King. For discussion, see Bates, *Gospel Allegiance*, 73–82.

16. For a thorough discussion of the biblical nature of faith, in addition to the work by John MacArthur, Jr. in *The Gospel According to Jesus* (Grand Rapids: Zondervan Publishing House, 1988) and *The Gospel According to the Apostles* (Nashville: Word Publishing, 2000), see Joseph Fitzmyer, *Paul and His Theology: A Brief Sketch* (Englewood Cliffs, NJ: Prentice Hall, 1987), 85ff, and especially Everett Ferguson, *The Church of Christ* (Grand Rapids: Eerdmans, 1996), 165ff.

17. John MacArthur, Jr., 178.

18. William Booth, "The Founder's Messages to Soldiers," *Christianity Today*, October 5, 1992, 48.

19. The following points are adapted from Jack Cottrell, *The Faith Once for All: Bible Doctrine for Today* (Joplin, MO: College Press, 2002).

20. For more on the gospel see Matthew Bates, *Gospel Allegiance* (Grand Rapids: Brazos Press, 2019) and *The Gospel Precisely: Surprisingly Good News About Jesus Christ the King* (Renew.org, 2021).

21. Bobby Harrington and Jason Henderson, *Conviction and Civility: Thinking and Communicating Clearly About What the Bible Teaches* (Renew.org, 2018). For a free copy of the e-book, see https://renew.org/ebook/conviction-and-civility/.

22. There is a great deal of scholarly discussion in recent times on just what these false teachers advocated. Thomas Schriener offers what I believe to be the most sensible perspective on this complicated issue. See "'Works of Law' in Paul," *Novum Testamentum* 33, 3 (1991): 217–144. See also F. F. Bruce, *Commentary on Galatians*, New International Greek Commentary (Grand Rapids: Eerdmans, 1982).

23. Robert Shank, *Life in the Son: A Study of the Doctrine of Perseverance* (Minneapolis: Bethany House Publishers, 1989), 264.

24. See Alisa Childers, *Another Gospel?: A Lifelong Christian Seeks Truth in Response to Progressive Christianity* (Carol Stream, IL: Tyndale Momentum, 2020) and David Young, *A Grand Illusion: How Progressive Christianity Undermines Biblical Faith* (Renew.org, 2019).

25. See Robert Stein, *The Gospel According to Luke,* The New American Commentary, vol. 24 (Nashville: Broadman Press, 1992), 246–248; see also, Joel B. Green, *The Gospel of Luke*, The New International Commentary on the New Testament (Grand Rapids: Eerdmans, 1997), 329.

26. It is helpful to know the exact Greek phraseology in this passage because the old KJV translation confused some people and made them wonder if the warning is over continuous sin or just one sin. Paul Ellingworth and Eugene Nida's scholarly work *A Translator's Handbook on the Letter to the Hebrews* (New York: United Bible Societies, 1983) helps. They write, "The key word of this passage is *purposely*, which is the first word in the Greek sentence. The 'sinning' is not only deliberate but repeated and continued, as *go on sinning* shows; similarly, NEB 'if we persist in sin.' *If we purposely go on sinning* may be rendered as 'if we decide we want to go on sinning,' or 'if we make our plans so that we can go on sinning,' or . . . 'continue in sin'" (530–532). See also Paul Ellingworth, *The Epistle to the Hebrews: A Commentary on the Greek Text* (Grand Rapids: Eerdmans, 1993).

27. Chuck Jones, "Walking in the Light," *Image* (September 1987): 24.

28. Ibid., 25.

CONCLUSION

WHAT YOU CAN DO RIGHT NOW

Finishing the final pages of some books can feel like quite an accomplishment. We hope that is not the feeling you get when you finish *Real Life Theology*. For the work of disciple making is only beginning. The real accomplishment is not getting through the book or even memorizing some of its contents. Any lasting accomplishment is what this book is meant to *fuel*. And what is that? The book's subtitle says it all: *Fuel for Effective and Faithful Disciple Making*.

This book will only function as the tool we wrote it to be if it spurs you toward action. So what are you, the reader, to do next? The answer is simple: Get what you have learned into the hands of everyday people. Disciple people in God's grand story. Disciple them in what the gospel is precisely. Disciple them in how to be born again. Disciple them in knowing the truth about God and following his Word. Disciple them in the essential elements of the faith. Disciple them in how to live a faithful, eternally secure faith. Disciple them in what it looks like to be filled, empowered, and led by the Holy Spirit. Disciple them in countercultural living for Jesus' kingdom life. Disciple them in preparing for the end. Disciple them to disciple others.

Why do we disciple people? Why can't we do theology in a way that merely inflates the intelligence of spiritual academics? It all goes back to the people Jesus chose to disciple—and how it changed the world.

THE GOSPEL FOR EVERYDAY PEOPLE

THE GOSPEL MESSAGE DELIVERS like a good joke. A good joke leads an audience down one path (the setup), but then jolts them with an unexpected turn at the end (the punchline). In the first chapter of Mark's Gospel, we may not read any jokes, but we experience an unexpected twist.

Mark 1:15 gets us going down one path. Jesus began his ministry with an epic invitation: "The time has come. . . . The kingdom of God has come near. Repent and believe the good news!" For a single verse, it packs some serious theological heft with words such as "kingdom," "repent," "faith" ("believe"), and "gospel" ("good news"). Obviously, Jesus was taking us down the path of theological substance and historic magnitude.

But that's verse fifteen. When we get to verse sixteen, it's as if the car swerves onto a side road—a bumpy gravel road—where we see a couple good ol' boys fishing. Here's verse sixteen: "As Jesus walked beside the Sea of Galilee, he saw Simon and his brother Andrew casting a net into the lake, for they were fishermen."

Those of us familiar with this story easily miss the strangeness of the twist.

After millennia of anticipation, Jesus the Messiah finally had arrived, and he began announcing the kingdom and preaching the gospel. It does not get more epic than this. Yet out of nowhere, he went from cloud-splitting pronouncements to hanging out with a couple of blue-collar fishermen nobody had ever heard of.

Shouldn't Jesus have eaten dinner with the governor? Shouldn't he have reclined with the high priest of the temple and explained the kingdom to him? Shouldn't Jesus have called a meeting with the most prominent teachers of the law, mesmerizing them with how their teachings were now fulfilled in him?

Instead, all of history built to his coming, his announcing the kingdom, and then his hanging out with a couple of fishermen—almost as if he decided to construct his messianic kingdom with construction workers. They weren't masters of theology. They weren't politically powerful. They weren't cultural influencers.

Why build his kingdom with fishermen?

The answer had everything to do with what Jesus said in that epic verse fifteen: "Repent and believe the good news!" Translation: Change your mind ("repent") and place your faith in the gospel ("good news")!

Jesus could have built his kingdom with the "really good" people in society—professional holy men such as Pharisees, for example. The problem, however, was they didn't believe in *Jesus'* good news. They had their own good news. For these religious leaders who studied comprehensively, tithed meticulously, and prayed impressively, the *real* gospel was good news for good people. Jesus' good news, which was good news for everybody—especially sinners—didn't feel as good as their good news.

Jesus could have spent most of his time with the rich and powerful—loaded, politically savvy insiders such as the Sadducees. Yet they had their own good news. Their version of the gospel was good news for the rich and powerful. When Jesus came with good news for everybody—especially for the poor—the Sadducees thought, *We've got way better news than that.*

Jesus could have allied himself with the Zealots. The Zealots hated the Romans who had occupied their nation and understandably conspired to drive them out. God hadn't promised the land to the Romans, after all. Jesus could have spent most of his time with Zealots, yet they too had their own gospel. Their good news was for *their* country, *their* people. But Jesus came with good news for everybody—even the Romans.

When Jesus said, "Repent and place your faith in *the* gospel," the people with all the righteousness responded, "We've got a better gospel than that." The people with all the money and power said, "Perhaps, but we've got an even better gospel still." The people sharpening their knives said, "We've got the best gospel of all."

That's why Jesus started his kingdom with a couple of fishermen.

It was a kingdom for *whosoever*. It was for fishermen. It was for filthy-rich tax collectors whom nobody liked. It was for poor people who had trouble paying their bills. It was for untouchables like lepers. It was for *everybody*.

And this kingdom of everyday people following King Jesus grew exponentially, just as he predicted with his parable of the mustard seed: "Though it is the smallest of all seeds, yet when it grows, it is the largest of garden plants and becomes a tree, so that the birds come and perch in its branches" (Matthew 13:32). Though treated as gods in their day, Roman emperors died and became footnotes in the story of Jesus and his kingdom (e.g., Luke 3:1). Meanwhile, Jesus' following of everyday disciples became an everlasting kingdom.

> THIS KINGDOM OF EVERYDAY PEOPLE FOLLOWING KING JESUS GREW EXPONENTIALLY.

TEN STEPS TO USING *REAL LIFE THEOLOGY* TO MAKE EVERYDAY DISCIPLES

WHY DO WE MAKE everyday disciples? Why can't we do theology in a way that merely inflates the intelligence of spiritual academics? As the Jesus movement showed us, the people with the spiritual clout, political power, or radical agenda didn't change the world. It was regular people whom Jesus discipled—fishermen, for example—who then discipled others, who discipled others, and so on.

The church in many areas of the world is currently stagnant and in decline, especially in the global West. There may be theological education in such places, but the churches are not effective at disciple making. Meanwhile, the church is growing exponentially in other areas in what are called "disciple making movements." In these movements, the emphasis is on everyday followers of Jesus making disciples, who then make disciples. As in the first century, these are everyday people doing eternally significant work.

We *all* have a role to play in the core mission of the church, which is to make disciples of King Jesus. In fact, one of the key elements of church renewal and disciple making is the mobilization of everyday people that leads to the expansion of the church. If you get excited about God's strategy for mobilizing everyday people into a movement of disciple makers, then how do you join in Renew.org's mission toward this end? We have put together a ten-part plan for how you can get started, beginning today. Here is a specific path you can follow to use this book or the series of individual books that make up the *Real Life Theology Collection* to disciple people.

1. Decide on the size of group that you will form.
Discipling people in a group context is best. That is how Jesus did it, and experience has shown us it is the best way. The group itself helps to disciple each other, as they discuss what they are learning as they journey together in the ways of God. This means ministry is shared by those who are in the group.

Your group size may range from three to four people (a "transparent-sized" group) to ten to twelve people (a small group or personal-sized group). Most churches in North America encourage or facilitate small groups, and *Real Life Theology* can be used effectively in that size group. Although small groups are popular, you might want to consider a transparent-sized group. At Discipleship.org and Renew.org, we have found that the transparent-sized group, with a leader and two to three people, is especially effective. The advantages of this size are the following:

- Finding a common meeting time amid busy schedules is easier.
- Engaging introverted people is easier.

- Becoming transparent with each other is easier.
- Creating opportunities for more life-on-life transformation is easier.

At Renew.org we have a guide for the various types of groups that you can form in discipling relationships.[1]

2. Pray about people to invite into the group, and ask God to guide you.
Prayer is the foundation of discipling relationships. Jesus started his public ministry with fasting and prayer. Jesus also spent the night in prayer before he chose his disciples in Luke 6:12–16. It is wise that we do the same. And remember, you are not going out of your way to look for Bible scholars who love talking theology. The ideal is finding everyday people willing to take a step toward following Jesus in the real world.

3. Select a book in the Real Life Theology series to utilize.
We recommend that you start with an individual book from the *Real Life Theology* series to use in your group.[2] Utilizing this one-volume Collection for discipling relationships is possible; however, we formatted each of the individual books to make it ideal for discipling groups. Each one comes with questions at the end of each chapter that are ideal for short journaling and for group discussion. Although the books have a logical sequence, someone can start a group with any of the individual books based on interest or need.

4. Recruit an apprentice leader before you start.
We believe each group should be formed with multiplication in mind. That means the leader starts the group with a vision of how the group will transition to the next phase. The formatting of the individual books makes it easy to lead a group. The individual books are ideal for multiplication, since each leader can simply convene the meeting and use the discussion questions at the end of each chapter.

5. Invite people to meet with you and discuss how the group will work.
We have found that it helpful when starting a group to ask people to join you for one meeting before you get officially started for a discussion about the group. You want the people you invite to know the purpose of the group, the time the group will meet, and the material you will utilize. This discussion will also help the people you and your apprentice leader have recruited to gain clarity on the exact nature

of the group before they make a commitment. You can pass out a copy of the individual books at that time.

6. Ask people for a specific commitment to the group.

The group will work best when everyone makes a commitment to the group. At its simplest, you might ask people to commit to five weeks as you work through one of the books in the *Real Life Theology* series. Or you may ask them to commit to more time. One of the keys to effective engagement in a group like the one you are starting is commitment. People will be much more faithful in attendance and engagement if they start with an explicit commitment. You can find examples of group agreements at Renew.org.[3]

7. Ask everyone to come to the first meeting prepared.

The first meeting, in most cases, will set the DNA of how the group will function. So you want to make sure you and everyone in the group is prepared. Here is a short checklist of things to remember for the first meeting.

- Make sure everyone has what they need in advance of the first meeting (e.g., a Bible and the *Real Life Theology* book).
- Start and end on time.
- Ask someone to start and close the group with a short prayer.
- Follow the questions at the end of the chapter.

Preparation will really help the group to start strong and establish the group on a solid foundation.

8. Set the example of transparency and vulnerability.

Effective discipling relationships involve people's holistic development: head, heart, and hands. It is especially important that the group not just focus on the head (information). As Tony Twist and Mihai Malancea reminded us in Book 1, good theology is "full-body engagement involving our head, heart, hands, and feet" (see page 56 of *Grand Metanarrative*). As the leader, people will follow you. This means you will want to be an example to the group in transparency and vulnerability, or else the group will stay surface-level. Here are some principles about transparency and vulnerability to help you.

- Be transparent about yourself. In your own way, let people see your heart.
- Be appropriately vulnerable about your fears, concerns, and shortcomings. This will make it safe for others to share at the same level. This vulnerability helps people to deal with the elements of their life that God wants to change.
- Be willing to go off topic during a particular meeting to focus on a person's individual needs if it is important for their growth and connection with the group (but it's best not to make this a regular practice).

The more the group relates to each other in a life-on-life and heart-to-heart manner, the more God will use it to change lives.

9. Connect relationally outside the group meetings.

Jesus showed us how disciple making includes all of life. Unlike how Jesus lived in the first century, however, most people will not spend time living or traveling with the one leading their disciple making group. But you will still want to engage each other as much as possible outside the group meeting itself. You can connect with each other by phone, text, and e-mail during the week. Find ways to reach out to each other and share your lives.

10. Make plans from the beginning to multiply the group.

This last point is crucial if disciple making is to be the end result. Too often disciple making is hindered within a church or ministry because people are inwardly focused. They enjoy their group and value the relationships and do not want what they are experiencing to end.

Yet discipling relationships, as Jesus showed us, need to lead to multiplication. There are lost people to reach and un-discipled Christians to help. After a set period, multiplication is both healthy and necessary.

Multiplication will most naturally be achieved when a group begins with an apprentice leader and a multiplication plan. We recommend that groups plan to meet for a set period of time and then multiply. Many groups will choose to meet for the school calendar year, starting in the late summer or early fall and ending just before summer break. That's just one example. In this general model, the group stays together for the calendar year and then multiplies.

Here is a brief plan that will help you multiply your group (with some points being repeated for emphasis).

- Recruit the apprentice leader before the group begins.
- Be explicit that the apprentice leader will lead a group when the group multiplies at the end.
- Make it clear to everyone at the first meeting that the goal is to multiply the group at a set period of time.
- Ask the apprentice leader to lead discussions regularly (so they learn how to lead a group throughout the group's existence, not just at the end).
- As you move into the last third of the group meeting cycle, remind everyone that the group will multiply, and ask people to pray about who will stay and who will go to start the new group.
- As the group meeting cycle comes to an end, the apprentice will either leave to start a new group (typically with one or more from the current group) or the original leader will go out to start a new group and leave those remaining in the hands of the apprentice leader. In this way, one group multiplies into two groups.

There are variations on this model for groups, but experience has shown us that these principles will be very helpful.

ONE FINAL QUESTION

WE ARE SO GRATEFUL to you for taking the time to walk through *Real Life Theology* and to learn how to use the material in discipling relationships. As mentioned above, this book will only be the tool we wrote it to be if it helps to fuel disciple making. When you have been taught how to do something and given the tools to make it happen, whether you follow through is at root a question of *value*. Do you value Jesus and people enough to take the time to connect them together in discipling relationships?

DO YOU VALUE
JESUS AND PEOPLE
ENOUGH TO
TAKE THE TIME
TO CONNECT
THEM TOGETHER
IN DISCIPLING
RELATIONSHIPS?

Another way of asking the same question is this: Do you really believe the gospel? Believing the gospel means seeing Jesus' kingship as the best news ever. It means enthusiastically inviting others into his kingdom ruled by love and holiness. So do you believe the gospel? The first-century church was discipled to believe the gospel by fishermen who had outshone everybody in their willingness to drop their nets and follow the King. The twenty-first-century church needs to be discipled by these fishermen again.

NOTES

1. For a free download with additional materials useful in leading a discipling group, see "A Guide for Leading Discipling Groups Based on *Real Life Theology* Books," at www.renew.org.

2. You can purchase these books individually, or for quantities of twenty or more you can contact info@renew.org.

3. These group agreements are included in the free download called "A Guide for Leading Discipling Groups Based on *Real Life Theology* Books," at www.renew.org.

APPENDIX A

RENEW.ORG NETWORK LEADERS' VALUES AND FAITH STATEMENTS

Mission: We Renew the Teachings of Jesus to Fuel Disciple Making

Vision: A collaborative network equipping millions of disciples, disciple makers, and church planters among all ethnicities.

SEVEN VALUES

RENEWAL IN THE BIBLE and in history follows a discernible outline that can be summarized by seven key elements. We champion these elements as our core values. They are listed in a sequential pattern that is typical of renewal, and it all starts with God.

1. *Renewing by God's Spirit.* We believe that God is the author of renewal and that he invites us to access and join him through prayer and fasting for the Holy Spirit's work of renewal.
2. *Following God's Word.* We learn the ways of God with lasting clarity and conviction by trusting God's Word and what it teaches as the objective foundation for renewal and life.
3. *Surrendering to Jesus' Lordship.* The gospel teaches us that Jesus is Messiah (King) and Lord. He calls everyone to salvation (in eternity) and discipleship

(in this life) through a faith commitment that is expressed in repentance, confession, and baptism. Repentance and surrender to Jesus as Lord is the never-ending cycle for life in Jesus' kingdom, and it is empowered by the Spirit.

4. *Championing disciple making.* Jesus personally gave us his model of disciple making, which he demonstrated with his disciples. Those same principles from the life of Jesus should be utilized as we make disciples today and champion discipleship as the core mission of the local church.

5. *Loving like Jesus.* Jesus showed us the true meaning of love and taught us that sacrificial love is the distinguishing character trait of true disciples (and true renewal). Sacrificial love is the foundation for our relationships both in the church and in the world.

6. *Living in holiness.* Just as Jesus lived differently from the world, the people in his church will learn to live differently than the world. Even when it is difficult, we show that God's kingdom is an alternative kingdom to the world.

7. *Leading courageously.* God always uses leaders in renewal who live by a prayerful, risk-taking faith. Renewal will be led by bold and courageous leaders—who make disciples, plant churches, and create disciple making movements.

TEN FAITH STATEMENTS

We believe that Jesus Christ is Lord. We are a group of church leaders inviting others to join the theological and disciple making journey described below. We want to trust and follow Jesus Christ to the glory of God the Father in the power of the Holy Spirit. We are committed to *restoring* the kingdom vision of Jesus and the apostles, especially the *message* of Jesus' gospel, the *method* of disciple making he showed us, and the *model* of what a community of his disciples, at their best, can become.

We live in a time when cultural pressures are forcing us to face numerous difficulties and complexities in following God. Many are losing their resolve. We trust that God is gracious and forgives the errors of those with genuine faith in his Son, but our desire is to be faithful in all things.

Our focus is disciple making, which is both reaching lost people (evangelism) and bringing people to maturity (sanctification). We seek to be a movement of disciple making leaders who make disciples and other disciple makers. We want to renew existing churches and help plant multiplying churches.

1. *God's Word.* We believe God gave us the sixty-six books of the Bible to be received as the inspired, authoritative, and infallible Word of God for salvation and life. The documents of Scripture come to us as diverse literary and historical writings. Despite their complexities, they can be understood, trusted, and followed. We want to do the hard work of wrestling to understand Scripture in order to obey God. We want to avoid the errors of interpreting Scripture through the sentimental lens of our feelings and opinions or through a complex re-interpretation of plain meanings so that the Bible says what our culture says. Ours is a time for both clear thinking and courage. Because the Holy Spirit inspired all sixty-six books, we honor Jesus' Lordship by submitting our lives to all that God has for us in them.

Psalm 1; 119; Deuteronomy 4:1–6; 6:1–9; 2 Chronicles 34; Nehemiah 8; Matthew 5:1–7:28; 15:6–9; John 12:44–50; Matthew 28:19; Acts 2:42; 17:10–11; 2 Timothy 3:16–4:4; 1 Peter 1:20–21.

2. *Christian convictions.* We believe the Scriptures reveal three distinct elements of the faith: *essential* elements which are necessary for salvation; *important* elements which are to be pursued so that we faithfully follow Christ; and *personal* elements or opinion. The gospel is *essential*. Every person who is indwelt and sealed by God's Holy Spirit because of their faith in the gospel is a brother or a sister in Christ. *Important* but secondary elements of the faith are vital. Our faithfulness to God requires us to seek and pursue them, even as we acknowledge that our salvation may not be dependent on getting them right. And thirdly, there are personal matters of opinion, disputable areas where God gives us personal freedom. But we are never at liberty to express our freedom in a way that causes others to stumble in sin. In all things, we want to show understanding, kindness, and love.

1 Corinthians 15:1–8; Romans 1:15–17; Galatians 1:6–9; 2 Timothy 2:8; Ephesians 1:13–14; 4:4–6; Romans 8:9; 1 Corinthians 12:13; 1 Timothy 4:16; 2 Timothy 3:16–4:4; Matthew 15:6–9; Acts 20:32; 1 Corinthians 11:1–2; 1 John 2:3–4; 2 Peter 3:14–16; Romans 14:1–23.

3. *The gospel.* We believe God created all things and made human beings in his image, so that we could enjoy a relationship with him and each other. But we lost our way, through Satan's influence. We are now spiritually dead, separated from God. Without his help, we gravitate toward sin and self-rule. The gospel is God's

good news of reconciliation. It was promised to Abraham and David and revealed in Jesus' life, ministry, teaching, and sacrificial death on the cross. The gospel is the saving action of the triune God. The Father sent the Son into the world to take on human flesh and redeem us. Jesus came as the promised Messiah of the Old Testament. He ushered in the kingdom of God, died for our sins according to Scripture, was buried, and was raised on the third day. He defeated sin and death and ascended to heaven. He is seated at the right hand of God as Lord and he is coming back for his disciples. Through the Spirit, we are transformed and sanctified. God will raise everyone for the final judgment. Those who trusted and followed Jesus by faith will not experience punishment for their sins and separation from God in hell. Instead, we will join together with God in the renewal of all things in the consummated kingdom. We will live together in the new heaven and new earth where we will glorify God and enjoy him forever.

> *Genesis 1–3; Romans 3:10–12; 7:8–25; Genesis 12:1–3; Galatians 3:6–9; Isaiah 11:1–4; 2 Samuel 7:1–16; Micah 5:2–4; Daniel 2:44–45; Luke 1:33; John 1:1–3; Matthew 4:17; 1 Corinthians 15:1–8; Acts 1:11; 2:36; 3:19–21; Colossians 3:1; Matthew 25:31–32; Revelation 21:1ff; Romans 3:21–26.*

4. *Faithful faith.* We believe that people are saved by grace through faith. The gospel of Jesus' kingdom calls people to both salvation and discipleship—no exceptions, no excuses. Faith is more than mere intellectual agreement or emotional warmth toward God. It is living and active; faith is surrendering our self-rule to the rule of God through Jesus in the power of the Spirit. We surrender by trusting and following Jesus as both Savior and Lord in all things. Faith includes allegiance, loyalty, and faithfulness to him.

> *Ephesians 2:8–9; Mark 8:34–38; Luke 14:25–35; Romans 1:3, 5; 16:25–26; Galatians 2:20; James 2:14–26; Matthew 7:21–23; Galatians 4:19; Matthew 28:19–20; 2 Corinthians 3:3, 17–18; Colossians 1:28.*

5. *New birth.* God so loved the world that he gave his one and only Son, that whoever believes in him shall not perish but have eternal life. To believe in Jesus means we trust and follow him as both Savior and Lord. When we commit to trust and follow Jesus, we express this faith by repenting from sin, confessing his name, and receiving baptism by immersion in water. Baptism, as an expression of faith, is

for the remission of sins. We uphold baptism as the normative means of entry into the life of discipleship. It marks our commitment to regularly die to ourselves and rise to live for Christ in the power of the Holy Spirit. We believe God sovereignly saves as he sees fit, but we are bound by Scripture to uphold this teaching about surrendering to Jesus in faith through repentance, confession, and baptism.

1 Corinthians 8:6; John 3:1–9; 3:16–18; 3:19–21; Luke 13:3–5; 24:46–47; Acts 2:38; 3:19; 8:36–38; 16:31–33; 17:30; 20:21; 22:16; 26:20; Galatians 3:26–27; Romans 6:1–4; 10:9–10; 1 Peter 3:21; Romans 2:25–29; 2 Chronicles 30:17–19; Matthew 28:19–20; Galatians 2:20; Acts 18:24–26.

6. *Holy Spirit.* We believe God's desire is for everyone to be saved and come to the knowledge of the truth. Many hear the gospel but do not believe it because they are blinded by Satan and resist the pull of the Holy Spirit. We encourage everyone to listen to the Word and let the Holy Spirit convict them of their sin and draw them into a relationship with God through Jesus. We believe that when we are born again and indwelt by the Holy Spirit, we are to live as people who are filled, empowered, and led by the Holy Spirit. This is how we walk with God and discern his voice. A prayerful life, rich in the Holy Spirit, is fundamental to true discipleship and living in step with the kingdom reign of Jesus. We seek to be a prayerful, Spirit-led fellowship.

1 Timothy 2:4; John 16:7–11; Acts 7:51; 1 John 2:20, 27; John 3:5; Ephesians 1:13–14; 5:18; Galatians 5:16–25; Romans 8:5–11; Acts 1:14; 2:42; 6:6; 9:40; 12:5; 13:3; 14:23; 20:36; 2 Corinthians 3:3.

7. *Disciple making.* We believe the core mission of the local church is making disciples of Jesus Christ—it is God's plan "A" to redeem the world and manifest the reign of his kingdom. We want to be disciples who make disciples because of our love for God and others. We personally seek to become more and more like Jesus through his Spirit so that Jesus would live through us. To help us focus on Jesus, his sacrifice on the cross, our unity in him, and his coming return, we typically share communion in our weekly gatherings. We desire the fruits of biblical disciple making which are disciples who live and love like Jesus and "go" into every corner of society and to the ends of the earth. Disciple making is the engine that drives our missional service to those outside the church. We seek to be known where we

live for the good that we do in our communities. We love and serve all people, as Jesus did, no strings attached. At the same time, as we do good for others, we also seek to form relational bridges that we prayerfully hope will open doors for teaching people the gospel of the kingdom and the way of salvation.

Matthew 28:19–20; Galatians 4:19; Acts 2:41; Philippians 1:20–21; Colossians 1:27–29; 2 Corinthians 3:3; 1 Thessalonians 2:19–20; John 13:34–35; 1 John 3:16; 1 Corinthians 13:1–13; Luke 22:14–23; 1 Corinthians 11:17–24; Acts 20:7.

8. *Kingdom life.* We believe in the present kingdom reign of God, the power of the Holy Spirit to transform people, and the priority of the local church. God's holiness should lead our churches to reject lifestyles characterized by pride, sexual immorality, homosexuality, easy divorce, idolatry, greed, materialism, gossip, slander, racism, violence, and the like. God's love should lead our churches to emphasize love as the distinguishing sign of a true disciple. Love for one another should make the church like an extended family—a fellowship of married people, singles, elderly, and children who are all brothers and sisters to one another. The love of the extended church family to one another is vitally important. Love should be expressed in both service to the church and to the surrounding community. It leads to the breaking down of walls (racial, social, political), evangelism, acts of mercy, compassion, forgiveness, and the like. By demonstrating the ways of Jesus, the church reveals God's kingdom reign to the watching world.

1 Corinthians 1:2; Galatians 5:19–21; Ephesians 5:3–7; Colossians 3:5–9; Matthew 19:3–12; Romans 1:26–32; 14:17–18; 1 Peter 1:15–16; Matthew 25:31–46; John 13:34–35; Colossians 3:12–13; 1 John 3:16; 1 Corinthians 13:1–13; 2 Corinthians 5:16–21.

9. *Counter-cultural living.* We believe Jesus' Lordship through Scripture will lead us to be a distinct light in the world. We follow the first and second Great Commandments where love and loyalty to God come first and love for others comes second. So we prioritize the gospel and one's relationship with God, with a strong commitment to love people in their secondary points of need too. The gospel is God's light for us. It teaches us grace, mercy, and love. It also teaches us God's holiness, justice, and the reality of hell which led to Jesus' sacrifice of atonement

for us. God's light is grace and truth, mercy and righteousness, love and holiness. God's light among us should be reflected in distinctive ways like the following:

A. We believe that human life begins at conception and ends upon natural death, and that all human life is priceless in the eyes of God. All humans should be treated as image-bearers of God. For this reason, we stand for the sanctity of life both at its beginning and its end. We oppose elective abortions and euthanasia as immoral and sinful. We understand that there are very rare circumstances that may lead to difficult choices when a mother or child's life is at stake, and we prayerfully surrender and defer to God's wisdom, grace, and mercy in those circumstances.

B. We believe God created marriage as the context for the expression and enjoyment of sexual relations. Jesus defines marriage as a covenant between one man and one woman. We believe that all sexual activity outside the bounds of marriage, including same-sex unions and same-sex marriage, are immoral and must not be condoned by disciples of Jesus.

C. We believe that Jesus invites all races and ethnicities into the kingdom of God. Because humanity has exhibited grave racial injustices throughout history, we believe that everyone, especially disciples, must be proactive in securing justice for people of all races and that racial reconciliation must be a priority for the church.

D. We believe that both men and women were created by God to equally reflect, in gendered ways, the nature and character of God in the world. In marriage, husbands and wives are to submit to one another, yet there are gender specific expressions: husbands model themselves in relationship with their wives after Jesus' sacrificial love for the church, and wives model themselves in relationship with their husbands after the church's willingness to follow Jesus. In the church, men and women serve as partners in the use of their gifts in ministry, while seeking to uphold New Testament norms which teach that the lead teacher/preacher role in the gathered church and the elder/overseer role are for qualified men. The vision of the Bible is an equal partnership of men and women in creation, in marriage, in salvation, in the gifts of the Spirit, and in the ministries of the church but exercised in ways that honor gender as described in the Bible.

E. We believe that we must resist the forces of culture that focus on materialism and greed. The Bible teaches that the love of money is the root of all sorts of evil and that greed is idolatry. Disciples of Jesus should joyfully give liberally and work sacrificially for the poor, the marginalized, and the oppressed.

Romans 12:3–8; Matthew 22:36–40; 1 Corinthians 12:4–7; Ephesians 2:10; 4:11–13; 1 Peter 4:10–11; Matthew 20:24–27; Philippians 1:1; Acts 20:28; 1 Timothy 2:11–15; 3:1–7; Titus 1:5–9; 1 Corinthians 11:2–9; 14:33–36; Ephesians 5:21–33; Colossians 3:18–19; 1 Corinthians 7:32–35.

10. *The end.* We believe that Jesus is coming back to earth in order to bring this age to an end. Jesus will reward the saved and punish the wicked, and finally destroy God's last enemy, death. He will put all things under the Father, so that God may be all in all forever. That is why we have urgency for the Great Commission—to make disciples of all nations. We like to look at the Great Commission as an inherent part of God's original command to "be fruitful and multiply." We want to be disciples of Jesus who love people and help them to be disciples of Jesus. We are a movement of disciples who make disciples who help renew existing churches and who start new churches that make more disciples. We want to reach as many as possible—until Jesus returns and God restores all creation to himself in the new heaven and new earth.

Matthew 25:31–32; Acts 17:31; Revelation 20:11–15; 2 Thessalonians 1:6–10; Mark 9:43–49; Luke 12:4–7; Acts 4:12; John 14:6; Luke 24:46–48; Matthew 28:19–20; Genesis 12:1–3; Galatians 2:20; 4:19; Luke 6:40; Luke 19:10; Revelation 21:1ff.

APPENDIX B

GLOSSARY OF 100 THEOLOGY WORDS

Agnosticism – the belief that we do not or cannot know whether or not God exists

Angels – spiritual beings who are charged with doing God's will both in heaven and on earth; there are various types of angels described in the Bible, such as seraphim, cherubim, and archangels

Apocalyptic Literature – a genre characterized by rich symbolism describing cataclysmic events; "apocalypse" means an "uncovering" or "revealing"; books using the apocalyptic genre include Revelation and Daniel

Apocrypha – over a dozen additional books included in Roman Catholic and Eastern Orthodox Bibles that were written between the testaments (during the "intertestamental" period), for example, 1 and 2 Maccabees, the Wisdom of Solomon, the Book of Tobit, and the Book of Judith; "apocrypha" means "hidden"

Apologetics – the discipline of defending your faith with good reasons

Apostasy – the desertion of the faith through engaging in ongoing lifestyles of rebellion toward God, rejecting essential Christian beliefs, or falling away because of hardship

Apostle – one of the twelve disciples Jesus called and sent out during his earthly ministry (including their designated successors—Matthias and Paul); this word means "one who is sent" and is occasionally used more generally to mean "missionary"

Arminianism – the theological camp that emphasizes that, while faith is prompted and inspired by God's Spirit, it is accepted or resisted through a person's own volition; although saved people cannot "lose" their salvation on accident, people can forfeit their salvation

Ascension – Jesus' return to heaven after his earthly ministry; this took place forty days after Jesus' resurrection

Atheism – the belief that there is no God; sometimes it is defined in a weaker form as a lack of belief in the existence of God

Atonement – the reparation made for our sins that was paid by Jesus on the cross in order to fulfill divine justice

Baptism – immersion in water, which is the normative place where our faith connects with God's grace and we become new, with a clean slate and a restored relationship with God

Calvinism – the theological camp that teaches that God's sovereignty and human sinful depravity require that God alone determines who is saved and who is lost; because God has preordained who will be saved, it is impossible to forfeit salvation once it is given

Canon – the books that are recognized by the people of God as sacred Scripture

Canonization – the process of recognizing which books were considered Scripture by the people of God

Christ – Greek word for "messiah" or "anointed one"; Jesus as Christ points to his royal, kingly identity

Christology – the branch of theology that studies Jesus Christ

Church – an assembly or gathering of kingdom-people who display the reign of God through King Jesus

Communion – the regular remembering of Jesus' sacrifice on the cross, our unity in him, and his coming return through a ritual of eating and drinking elements reminiscent of the body and blood of Jesus; Christians throughout history have had varying interpretations of the way in which Jesus is present at Communion; also called the Lord's Supper (because Jesus instituted it the night before he was crucified) and the Eucharist (from the Greek for "giving thanks")

Complementarianism – the theological view that men and women are created equals as co-image bearers of God and co-heirs of salvation, yet they complement each other as reflected in gender-based distinctions in the family and church

Confession – in the context of being born again, this is a declaration of allegiance to Jesus as King and a rejection of all other claims of lordship; also known as the "good confession," a public proclamation that Jesus is Lord

Cosmological Argument – a family of logical arguments showing how the existence or creation of the universe points to the existence of a Creator

Covenant – a sacred agreement made before God and sometimes *with* God; the Old Testament describes the old covenant (the "Old Testament") that God entered into with Israel, and the New Testament describes a new covenant ("New Testament") made with the people of God through Jesus Christ

Demons – fallen angels who followed their leader (the devil or Satan) in rebelling against God; although they bring destruction through oppression and even possession, they are consistently threatened and thwarted by the power and presence of Jesus

Disciple – a learner or an "apprentice"; a disciple of Jesus is someone who is following Jesus, being changed by Jesus, and is committed to the mission of Jesus

Disciple making – entering into relationships to intentionally help people follow Jesus, be changed by Jesus, and join the mission of Jesus

Disciple making church – a church whose beliefs, habits, and narrative focus on disciple making to such an in-depth level that it quickly becomes clear to everyone, including newcomers, that disciple making is the mission of this church

Doubt – a struggle to believe something; since absolute certainty isn't possible for most of what is true, some level of doubt seems inevitable; doubt is not the same as disbelief or unbelief, terms that suggest a persistent and even willful rejection of God's revelation

Ecclesiology – the branch of theology that studies the church

Egalitarianism – the theological view that there are no gender-based distinctions in the roles that males and females can perform in the home and church; like complementarianism, this also involves the view that men and women are created equals as co-image bearers of God and co-heirs of salvation

Eschatology – the branch of theology that studies the end things

Essential elements – elements of the faith that are necessary for salvation; the essential truths are that God exists, Jesus is Lord, Jesus is the risen Savior, and salvation is by grace and not by human effort; the essential markers of our salvation are the indwelling of the Holy Spirit and a faith that perseveres

Evangelism – process of sharing the good news of Jesus with people for the purpose of inviting them to trust and follow Jesus

Faith – trust in and faithfulness to Jesus; it is fidelity or allegiance to God and his promises

Fasting – the voluntary abstinence from food (or other things) for a season for the purpose of drawing closer to God; the Bible describes various types of fasts based on length and types of food being abstained from

Final Judgment – the time at the end of history when God, the righteous Judge, declares each person saved or condemned

Foreknowledge – knowledge of something beforehand; non-Calvinists teach that God's determination of who is saved (or lost) is based on his foreknowledge of their decisions, not based solely on his eternal unconditional decree

General Revelation – what God has revealed that has been made available to all people, not just to his chosen people (e.g., what God has revealed about himself through nature)

Genre – a general word for the various kinds of literature; the Bible includes numerous genres, such as historical narrative, epistles, poetry, and wisdom literature

Glory – a characteristic of God that radiates outward and involves weightiness, splendor, reputation, and honor; God created humans to reflect and spread God's glory across creation

Glossolalia – the supernatural phenomena of speaking in other languages; this can take the form of a real human language that the speaker doesn't actually know (xenolalia) or a private utterance that is not based on an actual human language (idiolalia)

Gospel – Jesus is the saving king; he preexisted with God the Father; in accordance with God's promises, he became human in the line of David, died for our sins, was buried, was resurrected on the third day, was seen, was installed as king at God's right hand, sent the Spirit, and will return to rule

Gospel (literature) – an ancient biography meant to teach about the life, ministry, death, and resurrection of Jesus; four Gospels were written in the first century and are part of the New Testament canon

Grace – God's unearned favor through which he offers us forgiveness and life in his kingdom; it is by God's grace we are saved through faith (Ephesians 2:8–9)

Hades – Greek term for place of the dead

Heaven – a general term for where the saved will live eternally with God in the new creation, a home of righteousness

Hell – the place where the unrepentant will painfully suffer eternal separation from God

Hermeneutics – the study of interpreting the Bible; includes interpretive tools such as studying the genre, culture, language, and history pertaining to a particular text

Holiness – a lifestyle of separation from self-rule to kingdom-rule; a marker of kingdom life that reveals a people dedicated to God

Holy Spirit – the third member of the Godhead; sent out by the Father and Son, he moves us toward Jesus through the Word, through power, and through deep conviction, and he lives within us by immersing us in God and transforming us into the image of Jesus

Imago Dei – the "image of God"; because humans were created in God's image, each life is sacred, from the unborn to the disabled to the elderly

Immanence – characteristic of God that describes how he is near to his creation; this is to be balanced with his transcendence (how God is above us and separate from us) and to be distinguished from pantheism (the non-Christian belief that God *is* his creation)

Important elements – secondary elements to the faith that faithfulness to God requires us to seek and pursue, even as we acknowledge that our salvation may not be dependent on getting them right

Incarnation – a term describing how the Son of God took on human flesh and entered history bodily at a particular time and place as narrated in Luke 2 and Matthew 1

Infallibility – the Bible's inability to fail in what God sets out to accomplish; in particular, God's Word cannot fail to communicate the truths we need about God, especially those truths related to salvation, godly living, and how to love God and love people; it is the reliability of God's truth for teaching, rebuking, correcting, and training in righteousness, and for transforming people into the image of Jesus

Inspiration – guidance by the Holy Spirit for a person to write down God's revelation

Justification – the process of gaining right standing before God so we are no longer under the penalty for sin; we are justified by his grace through our faith

Kingdom of God – the realm where God's will is being done on earth as it is in heaven through the reign of King Jesus

Love – a cross-shaped action that glorifies God and benefits someone else; it is the action that best models King Jesus

Major Prophets – five Old Testament prophetic books considered "major" because of their length; includes Isaiah, Jeremiah, Lamentations, Ezekiel, and Daniel

Marriage – a sacred covenant ordained by God for the permanent union of one man and one woman for the purposes of mutual support, companionship, and propagation of humanity

Messiah – Hebrew for "anointed one"; the anointed prophet, priest, and king who was prophesied to come as Israel's savior

Millennium – a thousand-year reign of Jesus described in Revelation 20; the main end-times theological frameworks are built around their interpretation of the thousand years, including premillennialism (the Second Coming comes before the millennium), postmillennialism (the Second Coming comes after the millennium), amillennialism (the millennium is a metaphor for the modern church age)

Minor Prophets – twelve Old Testament prophetic books considered "minor" because of their short length; these include Hosea, Joel, Amos, Obadiah, Jonah, Micah, Nahum, Habakkuk, Zephaniah, Haggai, Zechariah, and Malachi; collectively, they are known as the "Twelve"

Miracle – an event that happens whenever God acts among us in significant, powerful, or wonderful ways; others more narrowly define miracles as an act of God that could not be explained through the laws of nature

Moral Law Argument – a family of logical arguments showing how the moral law within points to the existence of a moral lawgiver who created us

New Birth – a metaphor for salvation that Jesus taught to the Pharisee Nicodemus when he said, "You must be born again" (John 3:7); the imagery is enacted at baptism as death, renewal, and resurrection to a new life

New Testament – the teachings of Jesus' apostles in twenty-seven books that reveal a new covenant through Jesus the Messiah and how the covenant was lived out in the early church

Old Testament – Thirty-nine books containing God's promises, covenant laws, and guidance for ancient Israel through its history; it served as a tutor to lead Israel to recognize their need for a coming messiah

Omnipotence – the all-powerfulness of God; means he can do anything that he desires that is consistent with his nature

Omniscience – the all-knowingness of God, according to which God knows what happens and what will happen

Pentateuch – the first five books of the Bible ("penta" means "five"), often referred to as the "law of Moses" or the "Torah"

Personal elements – elements of the faith that are not essential or important, but based on marginal, disputed convictions or preferences

Pneumatology – the branch of theology that studies the Holy Spirit

Postmodernism – a philosophy that emphasizes no one can objectively know reality as it is; it is a rejection of key principles of modernism (e.g., optimism about knowing truth) as well as an extension of modernism by playing out the implications of modernism (e.g., that we are in the dark about knowing reality beyond the physical)

Prayer – talking with God; among the many prayers recorded in Scripture, the book of Psalms records 150 songs that are prayers to God from various life situations (fear, joy, repentance, etc.)

Preexistence – word describing how the Son of God existed before appearing as a human on earth; as the divine Son of God, Jesus preexisted with God the Father and was part of the redemptive plan before his incarnation

Progressive Christianity – a rewriting of essential and important elements of biblical Christianity to fit Western secular values

Prophet – someone who received and spoke messages from God (e.g., Elijah, Isaiah, and Jeremiah in the Old Testament; Agabus, Anna, and the daughters of Philip in the New Testament); yet because not all prophecies were necessarily from God, they needed to be tested by church authorities; the term can also refer more generally to someone who proclaims the Word of God based on the works of the inspired authors of Scripture

Repentance – a change in mind and behavior, turning from living for ourselves to living like Jesus

Resurrection – the historical event in which Jesus rose from the dead on the third day, by God's power, thus proving himself to be God's Son and our Savior; without the resurrection, there is no salvation; because of his resurrection, his disciples too will be raised after death in an imperishable body; resurrection is also a general term to describe the raising of the dead at the end of time for the final judgment

Salvation – the state and process of being saved by God; God saves us from the penalty of sin (justification) as well as the power of sin (sanctification) and eventually from the very presence of sin (in the new heaven and new earth)

Sanctification – the process by which God brings disciples of Jesus to maturity through the work of the Holy Spirit, thereby decreasing sin's power over their lives and restoring God's glory in their lives

Satan – a Hebrew term that means "adversary" or "accuser"; the New Testament explicitly applies this term to the divine cosmic enemy of God (also called the "devil," once an angel called "Lucifer"); the book of Revelation links this cosmic enemy to the serpent who tempted Eve in Genesis

Second Coming – the event of Jesus' return to the earth; it is the final battle that ends the war with evil, brings the resurrection of the dead, then the final judgment, and leads to victorious, eternal life

Sheol – Hebrew term for place of the dead

Sin – acts and attitudes of rebellion against God's will; falling short of God's will, which derails his purposes for our lives and distorts his glory in our image-bearing; human sin has personally separated us from God and caused destructiveness on both a social and cosmic level

Soteriology – the branch of theology that studies salvation

Soul – the immaterial part of a person that lives on after physical death

Special Revelation – what God has revealed to specific people in specific times and circumstances (e.g., prophecies and miracles that God accomplished in ancient Israel's history)

Spirit – a personal being, with rational, emotional, and volitional capacities, who transcends the known physical world but who acts within it; more generally, "spirit" can refer to the immaterial part of a person that lives on after physical death

Teleological Argument – a family of logical arguments showing how the order and design in the universe point to the existence of a Creator

Theology – the study of God, reasoning about God

Torah – Hebrew for "instruction" or "law"; often used to refer to the first five books of the Bible and more generally to God's laws and commandments

Transcendence – characteristic of God that describes how he is above and separate from his creation; this is to be balanced with his immanence (how God is near to his creation) and to be distinguished from deism (the non-Christian belief that God exists as Creator but does not involve himself in this world)

Trinity – a term describing how God is three persons but one God; the Father sent his only Son and they sent forth the Spirit; thus, the people of God experienced God above (the Father), God beside (the Son), and God within (the Spirit)

Truth – conformity with reality; a statement is true when it corresponds with what actually is (i.e., with reality)

Wisdom Literature – writings that encourage the attaining of virtue for navigating various life situations, including books such as Job, Proverbs, Ecclesiastes, and the Song of Songs

Works – good deeds that should be seen as the outworking of our salvation, never its foundation; we are saved to do good works, and faith without works is dead

Worship – the act of declaring the supreme worth of something; this can be done through various means, such as artistic expression, heartfelt homage, and Godward service; in the Bible, this is to be directed at God alone (and thus, it is instructive that Jesus welcomed worship from his disciples)